The American Association for
Adult and Continuing Education (AAACE)

The American Association for Adult and Continuing Education (AAACE) is the national professional association for all individuals and institutions involved in adult and continuing education. The association has its roots in two pioneer organizations: the Adult Education Association and the National Association for Public Continuing and Adult Education. In 1982, these organizations merged to form AAACE.

AAACE's mission is to unify the profession; to provide advocacy for adult and continuing education to legislators and the public; to promote research; to provide professional development opportunities through conferences, seminars, and workshops on a national and local level; and to disseminate information through newsletters, books, pamphlets, and reports.

The 3,300 members served by AAACE work in a wide variety of settings in education, government, and business. Members include trainers of adults in business, in federal, state, and local government, and in community, voluntary, and religious organizations; adult educators who teach literacy skills; directors of adult and continuing education programs at community colleges, four-year colleges, and universities; business planners for those seeking to upgrade work skills; administrators of adult basic education programs; professors and students; and researchers.

AAACE has seven divisions with over forty program units organized around specialized programs and professional interests. The divisions are Theory, Research, and Evaluation; Special Populations and Issues; Occupational and Professional; State, Local, and Institutional; Providers of Service; Life Skills Programs; and Government Education and Training. AAACE is also affiliated with over sixty state and regional adult and continuing education associations throughout eight regions.

AAACE conducts a variety of conferences and seminars to meet members' needs. Each spring AAACE sponsors a legislative and leadership seminar in conjunction with National Adult and Continuing Education Week; each fall it holds its national convention and exposition; and throughout the year it offers several theme seminars on specialized professional topics.

AAACE publishes *Adult Learning* magazine eight times annually; the research journal *Adult Education Quarterly;* and the newsletter *Online,* which appears ten times annually. Other publications, sponsored cooperatively with major publishers and other organizations, are also available through AAACE. Other services include the AAACE Speakers Bureau, a program of international study/travel and educational tours, and an awards program that recognizes outstanding service to the field.

For additional information about AAACE and its services, write or call the American Association for Adult and Continuing Education, 1112 16th Street, N.W., Suite 420, Washington, D.C. 20036, (202) 463-6333.

Handbook of
Adult and Continuing
Education

Sharan B. Merriam
Phyllis M. Cunningham
Editors

Handbook of
Adult and Continuing
Education

Jossey-Bass Publishers

San Francisco • Oxford • 1990

HANDBOOK OF ADULT AND CONTINUING EDUCATION
by Sharan B. Merriam and Phyllis M. Cunningham, Editors

Copyright © 1989 by: American Association for
Adult and Continuing Education
1112 Sixteenth Street, N.W.
Washington, D.C. 20036

Jossey-Bass Inc., Publishers
350 Sansome Street
San Francisco, California 94104

**Jossey-Bass Limited
Headington Hill Hall
Oxford OX3 0BW**

Library of Congress Cataloging-in-Publication Data

Handbook of adult and continuing education / Sharan B. Merriam,
Phyllis M. Cunningham, editors. — 1st ed.
p. cm. — (The Jossey-Bass higher education series)
Includes bibliographies and index.
ISBN 1-55542-161-X (alk. paper)
1. Adult education. 2. Continuing education. I. Merriam, Sharan
B. II. Cunningham, Phyllis M. III. Series.
LC5215.H25 1989
374-dc20

89-45601
CIP

Manufactured in the United States of America

The paper in this book meets the guidelines for
permanence and durability of the Committee on
Production Guidelines for Book Longevity of the
Council on Library Resources.

JACKET DESIGN BY WILLI BAUM

FIRST EDITION
First printing: September 1989
Second printing: July 1990

Code 8935

The Jossey-Bass
Higher Education Series

Consulting Editor
Adult and Continuing Education

Alan B. Knox
University of Wisconsin, Madison

Contents

Contents

Preface

We have more information at our fingertips than we can comprehend. We are required to inform ourselves about complex international issues concerning everything from how much we pay for the gas we pump to the ultraviolet rays that seep through the ozone. Our jobs may disappear at the very time that a dozen new jobs appear in the occupational handbook. The only thing that is certain is that change requires us to attend to systematically recasting information, knowledge, and our views of the world.

These are the major reasons why adult continuing education has become a household word—why books, films, and television dramas depict plots in which the effect of an adult education experience is analyzed for its intended and unintended consequences and why the adult is the new-breed student causing industries to become schools and learning institutions to recast their bureaucratic structures to fit this new clientele.

At the end of the 1980s, the adult continuing education enterprise, in all its settings, is approaching the size of the more traditional formal education enterprise; training and development in United States business and industry alone is a $210-billion activity. This figure compares with a $238-billion budget for all United States elementary, high school, and postsecondary schools combined (as discussed by Watkins in Chapter Thirty-Two). This handbook is important because adult education has become big business.

This *Handbook of Adult and Continuing Education* is the seventh in a series of handbooks issued by the major North American professional association to provide an overview of an emerging and evolving field. The American Association for Adult Education (AAAE) brought out the first three editions in 1934, 1936, and 1948, respectively. The Adult Education Association of the U.S.A. (AEA), which grew out of AAAE, and the American Association for Adult and Continuing Education (AAACE), which replaced AEA, were responsible for the editions of 1960, 1970, and 1980.

The rationale for publishing decennial editions of a handbook of adult and continuing education is to provide a reference that both defines and interprets the field from the viewpoints of a cross section of leaders within the profession. Although each edition stands by itself as a kind of snapshot of the field and discipline every ten years, together the handbooks can—through analysis of their content, presentation of issues, and ideological perspectives—provide a sense of movement and suggest priorities for the sponsoring professional organization.

Audience

The *Handbook of Adult and Continuing Education* is intended for two primary audiences: professionals working in the field and those who are unfamiliar with the field. Included in the latter group are uninformed practitioners who have entered adult education through the "back door," practitioners who function as educators in other fields, policymakers, philanthropists, and the general public. The primary need of this audience is for an information-rich, holistic presentation, with a contextually grounded overview of the relevant issues and trends within the field.

Another group who will find the handbook useful are graduate students who may be relatively uninformed about the field. The book will help them, as well as practicing professionals involved in self-directed study, gain a definition of the field and an understanding of its diversity and its common themes. The handbook attempts to provide enough contextual description of a subject area to give readers a starting point for developing a critical analysis of issues and for satisfying the personal concerns that motivated their turning to the handbook in the first place.

Overview of the Contents

The content of this handbook is based on the principles of *inclusivity* and *utility*. Inclusivity, on the one hand, demands that differing ideological viewpoints in conjunction with a broad definition of adult education provide the framework for organizing content. This principle promoted substantive treatment of issues and encouraged an analytical framing of content, as well as careful description. On the other hand, utility is the pragmatic principle that sets reasonable limits for both number and length of chapters. Accordingly, the reader will find a straightforward style that minimizes jargon and provides a clear organization of subject areas.

This book is divided into five parts: "Adult Education as a Field of Professional Practice," "Adult Learners and the Educational Process,"

"Major Providers of Educational Programs for Adults," "Adult Education Program Areas and Special Clienteles," and "Adult Education in the Future."

The thirteen chapters in Part One lay out the social context, the conceptual foundations, and the shared terrain of both voluntary and professional areas of adult education. The social context refers not only to demographic, technological, social, and political factors but also to the ways in which we choose to frame our views. While the first chapter, on social context, offers North American social indicators, the succeeding chapters move beyond description to provide contrasting viewpoints of the field. Chapter Two demonstrates how different ways of defining context lead to different definitions of the field. This tension is further explored in the four foundation chapters that follow (Chapters Three through Six).

Chapter Three asks us to reflect on our definitions of historical knowledge: As we recount the past, whose past are we celebrating? Whose history is included and whose is excluded? How can we maximize the benefits from the contributions of those whose cultural histories have yet to be written (for example, the early settlers of our country, the Spanish, the French, the Russians, Native Americans, and African Americans)?

In Chapter Four, we are challenged to think about the purposes and philosophies of adult education. Is the purpose of our educational practice to promote the liberal tradition of Western thought, to increase human capital, to promote equality and justice, to reproduce the existing social relations, or to facilitate the self-actualization of individuals? Not only must we become aware of the possibility of multiple goals, but we also are challenged to become aware of our theoretical stance in choosing these goals.

Chapter Five invites the reader to reflect on theories of society. If we assume a consensus-oriented sociological position and believe in the importance of the individual, our adult education practice is framed quite differently than if we assume a conflict-oriented sociological position and embrace an ideology favoring communitarianism. These contrasting sociological viewpoints are used to examine adult education in North America.

Chapter Six discusses foundational concerns by examining comparative and international adult education. How can we in North America learn from other systems of adult education that are based on differing assumptions and that operate in different social contexts? What can we contribute to them, and what are the limitations of our contributions?

Related to social context and foundations is the ideology that organizes educational programs in a society, which is discussed in Chapters Seven and Eight. Adult education programs are organized by the voluntary and nongovernmental sectors, as well as by formal institutions employing professionals in the private and public sectors. Voluntary and nonformal provision of adult education do not exclude the professional's contributions, but the degree of voluntariness is an issue. Does professionalization of the field tend to squeeze out voluntary organizations and volunteers? What is the significance of the fact that the voluntary sector within North American adult education is shrinking? To what degree is adult education simply an extension of formal schooling? What can be learned from nonformal educational practices in other countries? These and other issues are addressed in Chapters Seven and Eight.

In contrast to voluntarism, the professionalization of North American adult education is described in Chapters Nine through Twelve. The evolution of professional associations, the formal preparation of adult educators, the literature and information sources of the field, and the issues and directions involved in knowledge production are discussed in these chapters. Part One closes with a chapter (Chapter Thirteen) on public policy and the financing of adult education.

Part Two examines adult learners and the educational process. It moves from basic conceptual questions to practical concerns by focusing on the individual adult learner, and then it probes the ways programs are organized, implemented, and evaluated.

Adulthood is characterized by psychological and biological changes. The conditions under which adults learn best and the role of the teacher or facilitator change as internal maturation proceeds. Chapters Fourteen and Fifteen analyze the interaction of the adult learner through his or her life span with the learning environments constructed to serve her or him.

How does adulthood affect educational processes? A universally accepted factor in making such an evaluation is the experience and knowledge the learner has gained as a result of taking on social responsibilities and roles. These responsibilities and roles keep learners very busy and at the same time continually and increasingly differentiate them as individuals. Thus a homogenous learner cohort located in one place that can learn through full-time instruction is more characteristic of children than of adults. Accordingly, Chapter Sixteen on assessing prior learning shows how we can legitimate experiential learning by assessing it in ways that can be recognized by formal schools. Chapter Seventeen on distance education describes how to conceptualize and provide an effective educational environment for those who, because of their responsibilities, cannot participate in face-to-face study.

What adult educators do constitutes a common core of practice that unites an otherwise diverse field. All practitioners work directly or indirectly with adult learners. It is thus important that all have some understanding of common components of practice. These common components are: planning (Chapter Eighteen), managing (Chapter Nineteen), and evaluating (Chapter Twenty) adult programs.

Part Three, "Major Providers of Educational Programs for Adults," and Part Four, "Adult Education Program Areas and Special Clienteles," examine the way we conceptualize, organize, and structure the adult education enterprise. Chapter Twenty-One categorizes providers of adult education according to their institutional sponsorship: (1) tax-supported agencies and institutions, (2) nonprofit, self-supporting agencies, (3) for-profit providers, and (4) nonorganized learning opportunities. Chapters Twenty-Two through Twenty-Nine examine the tax-supported adult education institutions in detail: public schools (Chapter Twenty-Two), four-year colleges and universities (Chapter Twenty-Three), community colleges (Chapter Twenty-Four), cooperative extension (Chapter Twenty-Five), the armed forces (Chapter Twenty-Six), correctional facilities (Chapter Twenty-Seven), libraries and museums (Chapter Twenty-Eight), and the federal and provincial agencies that administer the public funds that support these institutions (Chapter Twenty-Nine).

Publicly funded adult education promotes access, since financial support is at least in part a public responsibility; however, the fastest-growing sector in the provision of adult education is for-profit agencies. The sector that has declined the most in sponsorship of adult education is the nonprofit, self-supporting agencies. Thus issues of access, effects of technology, and quality control develop out of the highly competitive nature of these various sectors. Religious institutions, which exemplify nonprofit institutions, are described in Chapter Thirty, while Chapter Thirty-One on proprietary schools and Chapter Thirty-Two on business and industry document the increased activity in the for-profit sector.

Turning from institutional provision, Part Four discusses two other dimensions of the field of adult education: program areas and special clienteles. These dimensions cut across the different types of sponsorship. Depending on the historical moment, certain program areas become so ubiquitous that personnel in these areas base their professional identities on them. For example, twenty years ago basic education slumbered in a tiny ''literacy'' niche in the AEA called the Committee of 100. When significant federal funding for literacy became available in 1964, ''literacy'' was renamed *adult basic education* (ABE—after Abraham [Abe] Lincoln, who is said to have learned to read as a young adult), and it has grown to be one of the larger program areas in the field. Not restricted to any one institution, adult basic education is offered by, among others, churches, universities, labor unions, business and industry, and the military, as well as public schools and community colleges. Currently, ABE personnel have their own national conferences, journals, and professional associations.

Six program areas in adult and continuing education are examined in Part Four: community-based education (Chapter Thirty-Three), public affairs education (Chapter Thirty-Four), adult basic education (Chapter Thirty-Five), adult secondary education (Chapter Thirty-Six), English as a second language (Chapter Thirty-Seven), and health education (Chapter Thirty-Eight). Community-based education is defined as education in which control remains in the community; this type of education sometimes finds itself in direct conflict with the status quo as represented by more traditional institutions. Public affairs education underlines the importance of civic participation and democratic responsibilities and, like community-based education, champions popular participation. Literacy, basic education, and English-language concerns for the most part represent publicly financed, institutionally oriented programs developed in response to policymakers' perceptions of the direct positive relationship between literacy and employment as well as to the growth in limited-English speakers due to refugee and immigration programs. Health education is a new program area that has developed as more and more people have changed their thinking relative to conceptualizing their well being. The concepts of health promotion and disease prevention with decision-making power in the hands of the consumer, in contrast to our time-honored emphasis on the curing of diseases, where decision-making power is in the hands of the physician, have made large gains and thus have promoted health education as a program area.

Beyond organizational schemes based on institutional sponsorship and program area, adult education is also organized according to the special clienteles served. Educators working with these special populations tend to bond together in order to elaborate techniques or gain political leverage for their special clienteles. Seven chapters on special populations complete Part Four. These chapters examine: continuing education for the professions (Chapter Thirty-Nine), educating older adults (Chapter Forty), education for rural adults (Chapter Forty-One), continuing education for women (Chapter Forty-Two), workers' education (Chapter Forty-Three), adult education for racial and ethnic minorities (Chapter Forty-Four), and adult education and developmentally disabled adult learners (Chapter Forty-Five).

Several of these chapters are concerned with populations for which education has taken on new significance in recent decades. One notable special population is professionals, who cannot stay abreast of new technology and knowledge without systematic ongoing education. Practitioners in many professions are required by law to continually update their knowledge and skills. All of this activity has made continuing education in the professions one of the fastest-growing special populations.

Another group for which educational programs are growing exponentially is older adults. Lengthening life expectancy and the likelihood of an active retirement have triggered educational activity either sponsored by or offered through organized groups of older adults.

The remaining special populations covered in Part Four can be termed marginalized: "forgotten" rural people, women, workers, minorities, and disabled learners. Advocates for each of these groups have organized to solve or at least help alleviate problems that lend themselves to educational solutions. Of particular relevance to programmers that target special populations are questions of access and opportunity. It seems that those deemed most in need are least likely to take advantage of educational opportunities. The typical participant in adult education programs is middle class, white, educated, and relatively well-off financially. A challenge for adult educators is to design and offer programs that a broad range of adults will find relevant and accessible.

In Part Five, the future of adult education is projected. Chapter Forty-Six on new educational technologies for the future shows us that "the future is now," as the impact of the microchip on the practice of adult education is considered. The last two chapters project adult education into the year 2000: Chapter Forty-Seven uses imaging to look at how we might create alternative futures, while Chapter Forty-Eight uses trend extrapolation to view the future as an empirical extension of the past.

A final section (Resource A) lists the titles of the chapters in the series of handbooks from 1934 to 1981. The reader may wish to examine the changes that have occurred over the years in the way the field of adult education has been described by its leaders and theorists. The table of contents of each handbook reveals much about the way the field was then conceptualized and its ideological orientation, as well as who was to be educated, by whom, and for what purposes. Changes during this fifty-year period in the numbers of female and black authors provide insights into the politics of the field, as does the very language used to describe each chapter.

Acknowledgments

We would like to say a word about the people and the processes involved in producing this book. The chapter authors were selected because of their expertise; they include both theorists and practitioners, depending on the subject matter. Care was taken to select a broad spectrum of adult educators who were prepared to develop an original current assessment of their assigned topics. The authors worked as a group to integrate subject matter and avoid redundancy. Each chapter was critiqued by at least three AAACE members with expertise in the subject covered. When there were coauthors, a coin toss determined the order of name placement. The coeditors followed the same procedure.

We would also like to acknowledge the contributions of those who supported the chapter authors. We wish to thank James Parker and the handbook committee, as well as Beverly Cassara, Larry Martin, and Jane Tedder, for identifying knowledgeable persons to review the chapter drafts. Roger Boshier, David Deschler, and Jane Evanson provided helpful systematic review of all the chapters. Lan Jiang of Northern Illinois University contributed editorial and logistical assistance. Finally, we thank Lynn Luckow, executive editor at Jossey-Bass, and Alan Knox, Jossey-Bass consulting editor, for their support of the editors throughout the process.

July 1989

Phyllis M. Cunningham
DeKalb, Illinois

Sharan B. Merriam
Athens, Georgia

The Editors

Sharan B. Merriam is professor of adult and continuing education at the University of Georgia, where her responsibilities include developing a research program under a Kellogg Foundation grant in continuing education and lifelong learning. She received her B.A. degree (1965) in English literature from Drew University, her M.Ed. degree (1971) in English education from Ohio University, and her Ed.D. degree (1978) in adult education from Rutgers University. Before coming to the University of Georgia, she served on the faculties of Northern Illinois University and Virginia Polytechnic Institute and State University.

Merriam's main research and writing activities have focused on adult education, adult development and learning, and qualitative research methods. She has served on steering committees for the annual North American Adult Education Research Conference and the Commission of Professors of Adult Education, chaired the 1984 Midwest Research-to-Practice Conference, and is an active member of the American Association for Adult and Continuing Education (AAACE) and the Postsecondary Division of the American Educational Research Association. She has written or coauthored a number of books, including *Philosophical Foundations of Adult Education* (with J. Elias, 1980); *Coping with Male Mid-Life: A Systematic Analysis Using Literature as a Data Source* (1980); *Adult Education: Foundations of Practice* (with G. Darkenwald, 1982), winner of the 1985 Cyril O. Houle World Award for Literature in Adult Education; *Themes of Adulthood Through Literature* (1983); *A Guide to Research for Educators and Trainers of Adults* (with E. L. Simpson, 1984), winner of the 1984 Phillip E. Frandson Memorial Award for Literature in Continuing Education; *Selected Writings on Philosophy and Adult Education* (editor, 1984);

Adult Development: Implications for Adult Education (1985); and *Case Study Research in Education* (1988).

Phyllis M. Cunningham is professor of adult continuing education at Northern Illinois University. She received her A.B. degree (1947) from Elmira College in biology/chemistry, both an M.S. degree in nursing (1950) and an M.S. degree in administration (1960) from Western Reserve University, and her Ph.D. degree (1973) from the University of Chicago in adult education.

Cunningham's career has involved her in five years of nursing administration, eleven years of program development and administration in a voluntary organization, three years as dean of open learning in a community college, and twelve years as a professor of adult education. She served in a number of different administrative positions in the Illinois Adult and Continuing Education Association and the American Association for Adult and Continuing Education, including vice-president of programs in the latter. She served two years as editor of the *Yearbook of Adult and Continuing Education* and six years as coeditor of *Adult Education: A Journal of Theory and Research,* and she currently edits *Participatory Formation of Adult Educators,* a newsletter of the Participatory Formation Network of the International Council for Adult Education (ICAE).

Active in the ICAE, Cunningham has attended its world congress meetings in Paris and Buenos Aires, as well as the Shanghai International Seminar on Adult Education in China. She was instrumental in establishing an exchange program between Northern Illinois University and the Shanghai Second Institute of Adult Education; the Shanghai Institute awarded her an honorary professorship in 1988. Her major intellectual interests are community-based and popular education, the participatory formation of adult educators, and the applications of critical theory to problems in adult education.

Contributors

Jerold W. Apps is professor of continuing and vocational education, University of Wisconsin, Madison.

Paulette T. Beatty is associate professor of adult and extension education, Texas A&M University.

Hal Beder is associate professor of adult education, Rutgers University.

Marcie Boucouvalas is associate professor of adult education, Virginia Polytechnic Institute and State University.

Diane Buck Briscoe is assistant professor of adult and vocational education, University of South Florida.

Ralph G. Brockett is associate professor of technological and adult education, University of Tennessee.

Stephen D. Brookfield is professor of higher and adult education, Teachers College, Columbia University.

Rosemary S. Caffarella is associate professor of adult education, Virginia Commonwealth University.

Ronald M. Cervero is associate professor of adult education, University of Georgia.

Mary C. Chobot is president of Mary C. Chobot and Associates, Annandale, Virginia.

Michael Collins is associate professor of communications, continuing and vocational education, University of Saskatchewan.

Peter S. Cookson is associate professor of adult education, Pennsylvania State University.

Bradley C. Courtenay is associate professor and department head of adult education, University of Georgia.

Sean Courtney is assistant professor of adult education, National College of Education.

Paul F. DeLargy is director of The Center for Community Education, University of Georgia.

David Deshler is associate professor of extension, continuing, and adult education, Cornell University.

D. Merrill Ewert is director of extension and continuing education, Wheaton College.

James C. Fisher is associate professor of adult education, University of Wisconsin, Milwaukee.

LaVerne B. Forest is professor of continuing and vocational education, University of Wisconsin, Madison.

Pamela J. Fujita-Starck is director of professional and special programs, University of Hawaii, Manoa.

Michael W. Galbraith is associate professor of adult education, Temple University, Philadelphia.

D. Randy Garrison is associate professor and director of the distance education faculty of continuing education, University of Calgary.

William S. Griffith is professor of adult education, University of British Columbia.

Nancy Hagan is a graduate research associate in the Department of Education, Cornell University.

Edwin Hamilton is professor of adult education, Howard University.

Laird W. Hastay is instructor and tutor coordinator for the Evenstart Literacy Project, Whitman County, Washington.

Thomas M. Hatfield is dean of continuing education, University of Texas, Austin.

Matthew J. Hayes is director of religious education and coordinator of adult catechesis, Archdiocese of Indianapolis.

Mickey R. Hellyer is adjunct instructor, Department of Leadership and Educational Policy Studies, Northern Illinois University.

Paul J. Ilsley is associate professor of adult continuing education, Northern Illinois University.

Susan Imel is director of the ERIC Clearinghouse on Adult, Career, and Vocational Education, Ohio State University.

Ronald M. Jimmerson is associate professor of adult and youth education, Washington State University.

Patrick Keane is professor of education, Dalhousie University, Halifax, Nova Scotia.

Phyllis B. Klugerman is director of adult and continuing education, East Brunswick Public Schools, East Brunswick, New Jersey.

Judy-Arin Krupp is president of and consultant for Adult Development and Learning, Manchester, Connecticut.

Linda H. Lewis is associate professor of adult education, University of Connecticut.

Huey B. Long is Kellogg Professor of Continuing Professional and Higher Education and director of the Oklahoma Research Center for Continuing Professional and Higher Education, University of Oklahoma.

James S. Long is evaluation specialist of cooperative extension and professor of adult and continuing education, Washington State University.

Patricia McDivitt is project director, educational measurement, The Psychological Corporation, San Antonio, Texas.

Victoria J. Marsick is associate professor of adult education, Teachers College, Columbia University.

Larry G. Martin is associate professor of adult education, University of Wisconsin, Milwaukee.

Susan Meyer is assistant training manager, Office of Staff Development and Training, Human Resources Administration of New York City.

Donald W. Mocker is professor of education, University of Missouri, Kansas City.

Allen B. Moore is associate professor of adult education and on the staff of the Institute of Community and Area Development, University of Georgia.

Michael J. Offerman is director of continuing education, University of Wisconsin, Stevens Point.

John Ohliger is director of Basic Choices, Inc., Madison, Wisconsin.

Richard A. Orem is associate professor of adult continuing education, Northern Illinois University.

John R. Rachal is associate professor of adult education, University of Southern Mississippi.

Joy K. Rice is professor of educational policy studies and women's studies, University of Wisconsin, Madison.

Amy D. Rose is assistant professor of adult continuing education, Northern Illinois University.

Jovita Martin Ross is associate professor of adult education, Pennsylvania State University.

Kjell Rubenson is professor of adult education, University of British Columbia, and professor of adult education, Linkoping University, Linkoping, Sweden.

Beth Schulman is Midwest project director, Congress For a Working America (CFWA), DeKalb, Illinois.

Don F. Seaman is coordinator of interdisciplinary education, Texas A&M University.

Ronald W. Shearon is professor and associate department head of adult and community college education, North Carolina State University.

Henry Singer is with the Education Service Office, McConnell Air Force Base, Wichita, Kansas.

Robert R. Smedley is director of educational services and associate professor of medical education, Temple University School of Medicine.

Douglas H. Smith is associate professor of educational policy and human resource development, Florida International University.

Thomas J. Sork is associate professor of administrative, adult, and higher education, University of British Columbia.

George E. Spear is professor of education, University of Missouri, Kansas City.

Sara M. Steele is professor of continuing and vocational education, University of Wisconsin, Madison.

Harold W. Stubblefield is associate professor of adult education, Virginia Polytechnic Institute and State University.

Maurice C. Taylor is professor of adult education, Algonquin College, Ottawa, Ontario.

Terrence A. Tollefson is associate professor of adult and community college education, North Carolina State University.

Emmalou Van Tilburg is associate professor of agricultural education and leader evaluation, Ohio Cooperative Extension Service, Ohio State University.

Frank C. Veeman is director of adult/community education, Butler County Community College, El Dorado, Kansas.

Karen E. Watkins is associate professor of adult education and human resource development, University of Texas, Austin.

Bruce I. Wolford is director of The Training Resource Center, Eastern Kentucky University.

Bonnie S. Zelenak is associate professor of higher and adult education and foundations and director of the Learning Center, University of Missouri, Columbia.

Handbook of
Adult and Continuing
Education

Part 1

Adult Education as a Field of Professional Practice

Despite the enormous diversity characteristic of the field of adult education, numerous areas of common interest and concern provide a foundation for professional practice. The chapters in this section of the handbook explore the context of adult education and the development of adult education as a field of practice.

The context of adult education is defined by the social setting in which it occurs. Our aging population, the influx of women into the labor force, changing career patterns, advances in science and industry, increased numbers of racial and ethnic minorities, and more leisure time and discretionary income have all contributed to the changing character of education. Education is no longer viewed as preparation for productive adulthood; it is increasingly being seen as a lifelong necessity for personal and social well-being. Adult education's role in lifelong learning is becoming more prominent as the social context changes. Defining adult and continuing education within this shifting context, and in a manner comprehensive enough to include its various dimensions and characteristics, has been a continual challenge to adult educators. This topic—defining adult education—is explored in a chapter immediately following one on the social setting of adult education.

The history, philosophy, and sociological characteristics of adult education all help to define the nature of our field. We can learn much by reviewing the historical development of the field and by relating a particular sociohistorical period to the particular forms of adult education and the issues the period generated. Chapter Three presents a historical overview of the field.

Historically and philosophically, adult education has served many purposes, including increasing proficiency at work, at home, or in the community; maintaining a democratic society; and enhancing personal growth. The nature of adult education tends to be a function of sociological factors related to participation, organizational behavior, and societal structure. With this in mind, we can gain a perspective on our own practice in North America by comparing it with adult education in other countries. Thus, chapters on the philosophy and sociology of adult education are followed by chapters on international and comparative adult education, adult education and international development, and the voluntary sector and adult education.

Adult education as a field of professional practice is a relatively new phenomenon. Many date the beginning of the field with the formation of the Adult Education Association in 1926. As late as the 1950s, there were only a few graduate programs to prepare people for roles in adult education. Today there are over eighty graduate programs, and thousands of graduates are working as administrators, instructors, counselors, and policymakers. The literature related to practice, research, and theory has also grown considerably, as have the means of building and disseminating new knowledge. Chapters on professional associations in adult education, the education of adult and continuing education practitioners, literature and information sources, research and theory in adult education, and how adult education is financed serve to document the growth of adult education as a field of professional practice.

1

The Social Context
of Adult and
Continuing Education

John R. Rachal

As we approach the new millennium, the force and contemporary relevance of Heraclitus's maxim, "Everything flows and nothing abides; everything gives way and nothing stays fixed" (Wheelwright, 1981, p. 29), belies the fact that that tidbit of wisdom is twenty-five centuries old. But while change itself is constant, the rate of change is not. There have been periods of relative quiescence, such as the centuries following the fall of Rome, and periods of great flux, such as the period extending from the Industrial Revolution to the present. As Toffler (1970) has observed, the current pace of change seems to be ever-accelerating—a fact that has profound implications for the role adult education may serve in helping individuals adjust to such change. The fact that there are some 2.7 million living Americans who conceivably could have witnessed the Wright brothers' lift-off at Kitty Hawk, an event that might serve as the representative technological achievement of the beginning of the century, gives some perspective to both the magnitude of change and its increasing rate.*

Historically, adult and continuing education has arisen as a response to particular needs. For this reason, adult education, even more so than childhood and adolescent education, has a direct and symbiotic relationship with the environment in which it occurs. Adult education both responds

*For the sake of readability, citations are not provided for all statistics discussed. Except where citations are provided, all statistics included may be found in one of the following: *A Profile of Older Americans: 1986,* by the Administration on Aging and the American Association of Retired Persons; *Statistical Abstract of the United States: 1987* (107th ed.), by the U.S. Bureau of the Census; or *Trends in Adult Education 1969–1984,* by the Center for Education Statistics.

to societal change and tends to feed further change. Given this interrelationship, a discussion of the social setting of adult education can provide a useful preface to discussion of other common concerns—institutions and organizations, program areas, and the future of the field. In this chapter, the term *social setting* is being used in the broadest possible sense—the sociological, economic, demographic, and even political factors that impinge on adult education (see also Chapter Five, "The Sociology of Adult Education"). In short, this chapter attempts to place adult education in the context of the North American and, to some extent, the international scene in the last decade of this millennium. Like a still photograph of a horse race, it cannot reproduce the flow of change, nor can it capture the full swirl of surrounding events; perhaps, however, it can capture some of the factors that can affect and be affected by adult education at one moment in time. Unlike camera and film, however, this chapter, like adult education itself, will not merely reflect the current setting. Much of the chapter will be necessarily descriptive, and its basic theme will be *change*. But adult education can and should play an integral role in improving not only individuals' lives, but also in improving society; adult education can promote change as well as react to it. The meliorative role of adult education—its responsibility to make things better—is suggested throughout the chapter.

The Demographic Picture

Demographically, the United States and Canada are changing. The United States is, for example, getting older as a nation (in terms of median age) as well as living longer. Whereas only 4.1 percent of the American population was sixty-five or older in 1900, 12.0 percent were that age in 1985, and 13.0 percent are expected to be by the year 2000. As of 1985, there were 5,600 people reaching sixty-five years old every day. A male child born in 1983 could expect to live to age 71.7 and a female to age 78.7 (compared to a world mean for both sexes of about 59.5). If, however, a male reached age sixty-five in 1982, he could have expected to live another 14.6 years, whereas a woman reaching sixty-five could have expected another 18.6 years. Such actuarial trends are likely to affect adult education. Although the elderly are traditionally less likely to participate in adult education (the sixty-five and older population constituted only 3 percent of those enrolled in the nearly forty-one million courses reported taken in 1984), other variables such as higher educational level and higher income, which are correlated with higher levels of participation, may counteract the traditional noninvolvement of the elderly. From 1970 to 1985, the median educational level of the noninstitutionalized elderly increased from 8.7 to 11.7 years, and their high school completion rate increased from 28 percent to 48 percent. Additionally, in 1985, the poverty rate of 12.6 percent for this group was lower than that for those under sixty-five at 14.1 percent. As retirees generally become better educated and financially more secure, they are more likely to use their average 16.8 years remaining from age sixty-five in active pursuits that include adult educational activities (see also Chapter Forty-One, "Education for Older Adults").

An even more profound age-related factor is the existence of the baby boom cohort, those born between 1947 and 1961 (Barnhart, Steinmetz, and Barnhart, 1980). Representing roughly one-third of the total age sixteen and older population, this large group, though by no means as homogeneous as its name might suggest, inevitably commmands the respect of politicians, producers of consumer goods and services, and educators. And it will continue to do so as it moves, in the graphic phrasing of *The New Yorker,* as quoted by Barnhart, Steinmetz, and Barnhart, "like a rat moving through the body of a python" (1980, p. 48). Continuing a general American trend, the baby boomers are better educated than their parents. And educational level, as Cross (1981) has noted, is the best predictor of participation in adult education. The yuppie (young urban professional) phenomenon may not typify the baby boomer, but it is clearly a notable presence, consuming both BMW automobiles and education. The age twenty-five to thirty-four cohort is the largest consumer of adult education, and the age thirty-five to forty-four cohort is the second largest (taking 16 percent and 11 percent, respectively, of the total courses taken in 1984). The effects of this population bulge on colleges and universities are already being felt, and the flush times of the seventies, when traditional students were plentiful, have come to an end. The median age of students, like the median age of the American population at large (31.5 in 1985, over 34 in 1990), is rising, and institutions of higher education will have to respond for their own survival. Inevitably, nontraditional adult degree programs, pioneered by private liberal arts colleges, will proliferate, and postsecondary institutions must seek other ways to accommodate older students—not so much out of altruism as out of economic necessity. Even more dramatic from the adult education perspective is the role of private industry in the education and training of the baby boomers. This topic will be discussed below.

The United States is also changing ethnically—though more gradually than it is changing in age composition—and with more ambiguous implications for adult education. Clearly, however, there is increasing ethnic diversity. Blacks made up 11.1 percent of the American population in 1970, 11.8 percent in 1980, 12.1 percent in 1985, and a projected 12.6 percent in 1990. The Hispanic population grew from 6.4 percent of the total population in 1980 to 7.0 percent in 1985, and will grow to a projected 7.9 percent by 1990. A disturbing trend is that of all adult education participants, the percentage of black participants declined slightly from around 7 percent of the total in 1969 to 6.4 percent in 1984. In addition, the country has grown by 500,000 to 600,000 each year since the late seventies through legal immigration, mostly from the Caribbean, Mexico, and various parts of Asia. The interplay of cultures is a constant source of learning opportunity, but it can also breed a divisive and dangerous "them versus us" attitude. Adult education's greatest social responsibility may well be a fostering of social tolerance and interdependence.

A number of other demographic factors provide a background for adult and continuing education. For example, median household money income (exclusive of noncash benefits) in 1985 was about the same in constant 1985 dollars as it was in 1970. But the distribution of that income shows blacks to be losing ground: in 1970 black income was 61 percent that of whites, whereas by 1985 it had declined to under 58 percent. Black unemployment has risen to well over twice white unemployment (15 percent versus 6.6 percent in 1986 compared to 6.7 percent for blacks and 3.9 percent for whites in 1970). What is particularly disturbing is that the disparity has increased despite the fact that blacks have largely closed the educational gap during the same time frame (a gap of 2.3 years of schooling in 1970 narrowed to a gap of 0.4 years in 1985). The lesson is clear that education's role in promoting equality is necessary but not sufficient. More encouraging is that, in roughly the same time period, the bill for adult education was paid by the participant (or family) 57 percent of the time in 1969 compared to only 47 percent of the time in 1984, thus effectively offering more educational opportunity free of charge to the adult.

Another factor is the partial reversal of the rural to urban population shift. Whereas 27 percent of the population in 1980 lived in cities, only 23 percent will in 1990 (Aslanian and Brickell, 1980). Many of these, however, will be exurban or suburban, and current innovative delivery systems such as credit courses offered on commuter trains may well expand. Americans' mobility has appeared in other ways as well. Darkenwald and Merriam (1982) cite a study suggesting that the average American male makes seven career changes in his lifetime, changes often requiring new job skills. Additionally, four out of ten Americans moved between 1980 and 1985, almost 9 percent from one state to another. For the twenty-five to twenty-nine-year-old cohort, the numbers rise to seven out of ten and 16 percent, respectively. There is also greater movement toward the Sun Belt states. During the 1990–2000 decade, the Northeast and Midwest will lose population (by 4.2 percent and 0.9 percent respectively), while the South and West will gain (by 12.8 percent and 18.1 percent). The South in 1984 had more adult education participants (31 percent) than the North Central states (26 percent), the West (24 percent), or the Northeast (17 percent). This represents a reversal of the South's and West's relative positions from the 1969 data, with 33 percent in the West, 30 percent in the North Central region, 24 percent in the South, and 23 percent in the Northeast. And finally, the farmer, despite annual federal subsidies of over $20 billion, made up only 2.2 percent of the 1985 population, down from 8.7 percent in 1960. Movement, especially westerly movement, has always characterized North Americans seeking change for the better. Americans are in transition, as Aslanian and Brickell (1980) have noted, and these transitions, often precipitated by "trigger events," are significant motives for adult education and learning.

The Workplace

Without question, the workplace is the engine that is changing the nature of adult education, and technology is its fuel. If the airplane is the technological metaphor for the beginning of the century, the computer is the symbol of technology for its last quarter (unless, of course, it is the specter of the atomic bomb). The computer clearly represents a watershed in technological capability, analogous perhaps to the printing press of 500 years ago and the enormously expanded opportunities for literacy that it provided— literacy that is a necessary condition for technological expansion. The introduction of the personal computer in 1977 and the widespread adoption of computers in the work setting have made it more of an Everyman's tool. In fact, the increase in job-related adult education is at least partially attributable to computerization in the work setting.

Adult education is thus increasingly becoming a work-related phenomenon. When the obtaining or renewing of a license or certificate is added to the other job-related reasons for taking a course, a full 80 percent of American adult education was job-related in 1984. This is up from about half of adult education being job-related in 1969 (excluding licensure and certification, which constituted 15.7 percent of the 1984 total). Although comparable statistics are not available for the 1920s and 1930s, a look at the contents of the first few volumes of the *Journal of Adult Education* (American) reveals a distinct liberal adult education and self-help direction rather than a training orientation. Even the early articles that deal with workers' education often slant toward the cultural uplift of the worker ("What can adult education do to inculcate in the worker ideals of creative living?" asked Jacob Berg in the June 1931 issue [p. 280].) This increasing trend toward vocationalism in adult education (including continuing professional education) is inextricably tied to technological change.

One critical indicator of the importance of adult education is the investment the private sector—which more likely will call it training or human resource development—puts into it (see also Chapter Thirty-Two, "Business and Industry"). While the United States federal government's vocational and adult education outlays have discouragingly shrunk as a percentage of total federal outlays ($863 million of a $591 billion budget in 1980 compared to $914 million of a $946 billion budget in 1985), the private sector is spending $30 billion per year in formal training of its employees, according to the American Society for Training and Development (1986). Of course, the federal government, at $5 billion per year, and state and local governments are also deeply involved in employee training. Training, however, no longer is simply the on-the-job variety. There are at least 400 business sites that have a separate building labeled a college, institute, education center, or training center, and over 2,250 courses offered by at least 140 companies award academic credit (Watkins, 1983). At least thirty companies will offer entire college level degree programs on-site by 1990 (American Association for Adult and Continuing Education, 1987). Much of this training is not voluntary, however, and for that reason some question its appropriateness as true adult education. Mandated education is especially common in the professions for which the pace of change is presumed to alter or to add to the knowledge base from which professionals operate. The most common measure of participation in mandated education is the *continuing education unit,* based on ten hours of classroom or workshop activity per unit. The magnitude of mandated education can be inferred from the nearly 9 percent of the courses in the United States that were taken in 1984 to renew licenses or certificates. Perhaps the greatest challenge of mandated learning is in making a nonvoluntary and sometimes resented activity into a worthwhile learning experience.

Training is a vital component in an increasingly competitive world economy. The United States has seen its economic primacy erode over the last forty-five years. By 1945, American manufacturing output was nearly half of the world total, but as other countries have become more productive, the United States has become relatively less productive (Kennedy, 1987). During the 1980s, the United States became a net importer of goods rather than a net exporter, and another equivocal milestone was reached in the early 1980s when the majority of American jobs shifted from manufacturing to services, many of which are low-paying, low-skill jobs. In some countries, manufacturing wage earners such as textile workers make one-twentieth an American textile worker's pay (Kennedy, 1987), and that disparity is the main reason such industries are declining—not because there is no demand, but because the demand is being met more cheaply elsewhere.

The role of adult education, particularly work-related training, is an important one in the midst of this disquieting picture. Some recent union contracts have focused more on job security and job retraining than on wage increases. All job categories associated with computers (programmers, systems analysts, operators) as well as engineers, accountants, physicians, and teachers will experience some of the largest growth of all categories during the period 1984 to 1995, and such roles will create an increasing demand for training and other forms of continuing education. However, other fast-growing job categories, such as cashiers, waiters and waitresses, nursing aides and orderlies, fast-food workers, guards, and switchboard operators, require initial training, but far less continuing education. Clearly, a significant American challenge is the retraining of labor in declining industries for jobs in greater demand. Part of this challenge is being met by increased collaboration between industry and two-year and four-year colleges. Even so, there is an ominous knowledge gap between changing technological labor needs and the workers with lower-demand, specialized skills—or worse, workers with limited literacy and inadequate numerical skills. Further, retraining and entry level training can only expand as the end of the baby-boom cohort enters the job market. The private and public sectors must inevitably adjust to a contracting labor pool by offering attractive training opportunities.

The Social Dimension

Intertwined with demographic and workplace change is social change, all of which act and react with each other in such a way that the relationship of cause and effect is often a blur. For example, to what extent does the rising median age of women at their first marriage (from 20.6 in 1970 to 22.5 in 1983), or their deferring of childbearing to their late twenties, influence and result from demographic, work setting, or social forces? In sheer numbers of people directly affected, the shifting roles of women constitute perhaps the single most profound change in America's social, political, and economic dynamics (see also Chapter Forty-Two, "Continuing Education for Women").

Women are still underrepresented in most professions. For example, they made up less than 14 percent of American physicians in 1983 and only one-fourth of all scientists—including social scientists and psychologists—in 1984. Their average income is 70 percent of the average male's; yet they are joining the work force in increasing numbers. In 1985, 54.5 percent of women sixteen years old and older were employed, and that number will grow to 59 percent by 1995. The American work force was 44.2 percent female in 1985 (up from 33.4 percent in 1960 and 42.5 percent in 1980), and that figure also will rise. Women's roles have expanded beyond those of housewife, nurse, teacher, and secretary—partially as a result of society's becoming more egalitarian, the increasing need for a second income, the passage of affirmative action legislation, the feminist movement, and, generally, the growing recognition that gender is rarely a predictor of effectiveness on the vast majority of jobs. And, of course, adult education has played a large part in changing attitudes concerning gender roles.

This changing image of the American woman, particularly in the workplace, is a vital aspect of the contemporary setting for adult education. Women historically have been greater partakers of nonjob-related adult education; but beginning in 1981, women also surpassed men in the number of job-related courses taken. (Both sexes began a dramatic rise in job-related courses in 1978, interestingly, a year after the introduction of personal computers.) In all adult education courses, participation reversed from a 52 percent male majority in 1969 to a 55 percent female majority in 1984. By 1980, women for the first time constituted a majority (51 percent) of college freshmen, but 69.7 percent of all doctorates were still awarded to men in 1980 (down to 65.7 percent in 1985). Women apparently represent large majorities in the growing number of adult education graduate programs, though they only make up one-fourth of adult education professors.

As women's roles and influence have expanded, and as their participation in the educational system has increased, they have formed organizations that themselves assume an adult educational role. The most visible of these is the National Organization for Women, founded in 1966, which promotes women's issues through political action and education for its members and for the public at large. Numerous other common interest groups combine political advocacy with education: the Urban League, Common Cause, Mothers Against Drunk Driving, the Sierra Club, the American Association of Retired Persons, and Amnesty International. These organizations and countless others hold workshops, distribute literature, and often influence policy through the concerted influence of a more informed public.

The interplay of meritocratic and egalitarian forces in the political, social, and economic arenas has influenced adult education as well as attitudes about it. Egalitarian thrusts, such as affirmative action, have encouraged women and minorities to seek positions for which higher educational levels and continuing education or training are required. At the same time, the meritocratic ideal of getting ahead based on education and ability—Jefferson's aristocracy of talent and virtue—is an obvious and significant impetus affecting adult education. These two ideals, meritocratic and egalitarian, suggest contrast, but in fact they may be complementary. Americans are favorably disposed to the notion of advancing themselves through their own ability, initiative, and work—in effect, pulling themselves up by their bootstraps, in the best Horatio Alger tradition. This popular meritocratic ideal must, however, be founded on the equally popular egalitarian ideal of equal access and equal opportunity. Just as liberty without equality of opportunity is mere privilege, the ability to advance through merit is illusory where equality of opportunity is denied. The growth of two-year colleges and legislation barring discrimination have played significant roles in expanding postsecondary educational opportunity and employment opportunity. Despite unequivocal improvements in the last twenty years, "we can," as James Baldwin (1987) observed, "be better than we are."

Ironically, for many Americans and Canadians, educational opportunity is less an issue than are educational requirements in the form of mandated education. This increasing trend toward mandated education, primarily the result of occupational change, may also affect attitudes about lifelong learning broadly, though not necessarily positively. Still, the general acceptance of continuing education units (CEUs) and recertification activities is likely to help establish a general recognition of the need for lifelong learning, and possibly even a greater recognition of its pleasures. The term *lifelong learning* has been increasingly used in the media and has partially entered the popular consciousness. At the same time, the popularity of some books examining adult development has helped cement the notion that learning, whether experiential or formal, is a lifelong activity.

One other piece of the social mosaic is the ever-rising educational threshold of American society. Though a frightening one of four high school-age students does not graduate (Gorman, 1988), the mean level of education has inched upward from 12.1 years in 1970 to 12.5 years in 1980 to 12.6 years in 1985. As noted above, the overall gap between blacks and whites also has closed steadily, at least as measured by years in school. But as a high school education becomes the minimum educational standard, those who drop out are more likely to become members of an educational under-class, from which adult education (especially in the form of adult basic and secondary education) may be the only hope of escape. This clientele for adult education is potentially huge, though only in 1966 did the United States federal government attempt to address it (see also Chapter Thirty-Five, "Adult Basic Education," and Chapter Thirty-Six, "Adult Secondary Education"). At the other end of the educational spectrum are college graduates, who represented one-fifth of the age twenty-five and older population in 1985, and for whom continuing education is a persistent demand, both on and off the job. It is a rare metropolitan hospital, for example, that does not offer a range of community educational programs to an increasingly interested and sophisticated market. Among those who are better educated, adult education is, in effect, a consumer good for which supply and demand respond to each other in an ever-widening upward spiral. Among the educationally dispossessed, adult education is for some a sham, for others a beacon of hope.

Some Problem Areas

It is not easy to think of a contemporary social problem that could not be at least partially ameliorated through adult education. Crime, racism, AIDS, poverty, drug abuse, political chicanery, unemployment, and illiteracy all provide adult education a role. Few would argue, however, that adult education could eliminate such problems, inextricably tied as many of them are to economic forces. Some seem persistently intractable. Poverty, illiteracy, and crime are, individually, serious enough; but taken together they form a witches' brew of toxins. So many of our social problems seem to feed on themselves and on each other while so-called solutions tend to address only one dimension. Overcoming illiteracy, for example, is hardly a complete response to poverty in a depressed job market.

Given opportunity and motivation—the two necessary ingredients for adult education participation—the problems of illiteracy and educational disadvantage would seem particularly amenable to redress through adult education. Yet despite increasing legislative and media attention to the problem, Stedman and Kaestle (1987) reviewed several literacy studies and concluded that 30 percent of the adult population read below the eighth grade level, and 7 percent read below the fifth grade level. Equally unsettling, only about 5 percent of the eligible population participate in adult basic and secondary education programs (Rachal, Jackson, and Leonard, 1987). The Burger and Kennedy (1987) proposal for a corps of undergraduate tutors to expand opportunities for adult basic education on the job seems to be a positive development.

The relationship between adult learner and facilitator or teacher is usually portrayed as a collaborative one. Society has the responsibility to respond to real needs and to provide opportunity and encouragement, and the learner has the responsibility to bring motivation, however tentative.

For successful learning, both teacher and learner must have a sense of commitment. Among the urban poor, especially, such mutual commitment is rare. Though hardly the only setting for social problems, the inner city is a microcosm of American social ills—poverty, crime, drugs, unemployment, educational impoverishment, racism, violence, family disintegration, fear, and despair. In such environs, middle-class values about work and education are, at best, unfulfilled dreams; at worst, they are the objects of scorn. As one twenty-four-year-old drug peddler notes, "The minimum wage doesn't support my life style" (McCarroll, 1987, p. 20). And while education may be an escape for some, it is a ludicrous and pathetic fraud for others, like the twenty-three-year-old gang member who declares, "If I had a son, I would give him a choice: either he can go to school and be a goody-goody or hit the streets" (Hull, 1987, p. 22). Such attitudes reveal the impotence of facile solutions to complex problems, but they do not relieve society of its responsibility to help those willing to help themselves. Nor do they relieve adult education of its responsibility to address issues and engage in questions about the nature of public policy. For those in the American underclass, the social contract has disintegrated. Adult education must surely play a role in any effort to reestablish that covenant of mutual responsibility; indeed, for some, it may represent their last, best hope.

Conclusion

Like the society of which it is a part, adult education is of necessity changing, dynamic, responsive, and proactive. Historically, adult education has responded to need, and there is nothing to indicate that adaptability has diminished. As needs have changed, adult educational activities have risen to meet the new needs, and this has been especially true in the workplace. Both the socioeconomic and technological complexities of North American society pose considerable burdens on its educational system, requiring both ad hoc and ongoing educational responses as critical adjuncts to the established kindergarten through college system. The twentieth century has seen this adjunct role become institutionalized in the form of organizations such as the American Association for Adult and Continuing Education and the American Society for Training and Development. It remains to be seen whether such institutionalization will inhibit or foster the ability to respond to individual, organizational, and societal needs; thus far, the outlook seems positive. But even if our organizations were to become ossified, other elements, in the best necessity-is-the-mother-of-invention tradition, would develop to respond to new or persisting needs.

The reader should not infer, however, that adult education should limit itself to a merely reactive role. It must also, given the intransigence of so many of the world's problems, take a proactive role in promoting the change that will combat such problems. If John Donne's view that "no man is an island" was true in the seventeenth century, it is more true today, for now there is the human capability of doing harm to the world itself and to its inhabitants. We are all in the global community together. Of course our assumed common ground on some critical global issues—peace, protection of the ozone, stopping AIDS—is fragile, since even here there are conflicting interests. Adult education can be a powerful force in the marketplace of values to ensure that the narrowest interests do not prevail.

Over fifty years ago, Lyman Bryson made political education one of his five categories of adult education. By definition, political education implies not mere recognition or understanding of political concerns, but action and advocacy regarding them. He would not have argued that adult education and adult educators need to speak with one voice; rather, he would have argued that adult education can play a central role in enfranchising all adults in the political dialogue so that everyone has a voice. That vision, so universally appealing that even nondemocratic states pay lip service to it through sham elections, appalls many in power to the extent that they suppress what is probably the primary instrument of nonexperiential adult learning worldwide—a free press. Knowledge is indeed power—especially when some have it and others are intentionally deprived—and education is a potent force for either distributing or perpetuating power. Knowledge can be used to promote conformity, to protect the status quo, and to promulgate a particular societal view. (For example, a fear of educating the masses, except in their duties and responsibilities, has been a common theme of American and English education history.) Or knowledge can be used to promote, to enfranchise, even to liberate the individual through furthering individual self-interests—whether by improving job opportunities or by enhancing one's voice in matters of local or national policy. Often education does some of both, but adult education's emphasis clearly should be on the liberating rather than on the confining role. As Dewey (1916, p. 140) noted, "It is the aim of progressive education to take part in correcting unfair privilege and unfair deprivation, not to perpetuate them." And where adult education is not welcomed, it must play a subversive role.

Metaphors for society tend toward either the biological or the mechanical. Of the two, the biological is more attractive: society as a living organism, influenced by and influencing external events, and capable of growth. That idea of growth is fundamental to adult education as well; it is a means to growth both for individuals and for the society which they constitute. On a societal scale, adult education in its multiplicity of forms should be a central force in a democratic society for the planning and directing of desired change; on a personal scale, it should be a vital and available means for individuals to plan, direct, and improve their lives.

References

Administration on Aging and the American Association of Retired Persons. *A Profile of Older Americans: 1986.* Brochure No. PF3049 1086-D996. Washington, D.C.: Administration on Aging and the American Association of Retired Persons, 1986.

American Association for Adult and Continuing Education. "Workplace Learning Determines Our Earnings." *AAACE Newsletter,* Feb. 1987, p. 5.

American Society for Training and Development. *Serving the New Corporation.* Alexandria, Va.: American Society for Training and Development, 1986.

Aslanian, C. B., and Brickell, H. M. *Americans in Transition: Life Changes as Reasons for Adult Learning.* Princeton, N.J.: College Entrance Examination Board, 1980.

Baldwin, J. "A World I Never Made." Speech to the University Forum, University of Southern Mississippi, Hattiesburg, Miss., Feb. 3, 1987.

Barnhart, C. L., Steinmetz, S., and Barnhart, R. K. *The Second Barnhart Dictionary of New English.* Bronxville, N.Y.: Barnhart/Harper & Row, 1980.

Berg, J., "Educating Labor for Leisure." *Journal of Adult Education,* 1931, *3* (3), 278-282.

Burger, W., and Kennedy, E. "America Needs A Literacy Corps." *The New York Times,* July 2, 1987, p. A27.

Cross, K. P. *Adults as Learners.* San Francisco: Jossey-Bass, 1981.

Darkenwald, G. G., and Merriam, S. B. *Adult Education: Foundations of Practice.* New York: Harper & Row, 1982.

Dewey, J. *Democracy and Education.* New York: MacMillan, 1922. (Originally published 1916.)

Gorman, C. "The Literacy Gap." *Time,* Dec. 19, 1988, pp. 56-57.

Hull, J. D. "Life and Death with the Gangs." *Time,* Aug. 24, 1987, pp. 21-22.

Kennedy, P. "The (Relative) Decline of America." *The Atlantic,* Aug. 1987, pp. 29-38.

McCarroll, T. "Down and out and No Place to Go." *Time,* Aug. 24, 1987, pp. 20-21.

National Center for Education Statistics. *Trends in Adult Education 1969-1984.* NCES Publication No. CS 87-307. Washington, D.C.: U.S. Government Printing Office, 1987.

Rachal, J. R., Jackson, L., and Leonard, R. "Factors Affecting Persistence and Attrition of Students in Adult Basic and Secondary Education Programs." *Adult Literacy and Basic Education,* 1987, *11* (3), 129-138.

Stedman, L. C., and Kaestle, C. F. "Literacy and Reading Performance in the United States from 1880 to the Present." *Reading Research Quarterly,* 1987, *22* (1), 8-46.

Toffler, A. *Future Shock.* New York: Random House, 1970.

U.S. Bureau of the Census. *Statistical Abstract of the United States: 1987.* (107th ed.) Washington, D.C.: U.S. Government Printing Office, 1986.

Watkins, B. "Higher Education Now Big Business for Big Business." *Chronicle of Higher Education,* Apr. 13, 1983, pp. 1, 6.

Wheelwright, P. E. *Heraclitus.* Westport, Conn.: Greenwood Press, 1981. (Originally published 1959.)

2

Defining Adult and Continuing Education

Sean Courtney

Asked to define adult and continuing education, the man or woman in the street might conjure up senior citizens learning financial planning, immigrants studying English, middle-class housewives discussing the great books, and the like. The term might also suggest the idea of leisure time spent reading or attending classes. It might cover the phenomenon of illiteracy and its irradication. It might mean the older woman entering a university to achieve a degree. In summary, adult education might be seen to embrace a variety of prominent, visible, social activities lying somewhere between schooling and recreation. Indeed, often the intention among those who wish to promote it in the general population is precisely to obscure the boundaries between formal learning and leisure—to convey to the potential consumer the novel idea that study need not be the pain it was in school and that learning was always meant to be fun.

Terminology abounds: adult education, continuing education, lifelong learning, independent learning projects, community education, community development, adult learning, andragogy, adult basic education, animation, facilitation, conscientization. These terms all have been used at one time or another to mean more or less the same thing. As some have noted with particular frustration, "The field of adult education has evolved a vocabulary possibly unparalleled in its confusion" (Peterson, 1979, p. 13).

It is rare to come upon a single sentence that will do justice to the full range of this phenomenon or that will satisfy the many different kinds of practitioners who call themselves adult educators; but this need not be considered a problem. There are probably few single-sentence definitions of sociology, psychology, or economics, for example, that would do these disciplines sufficient justice. In such cases, as in adult education, the issue is less one of providing a formal definition, per se, than of being able to make some sense of what kinds of things psychologists, economists, and adult educators do, study, write about, wax hot and cold about, prove or disprove, discover, and so forth.

The purpose of this chapter is to bring some order into this world of multiple definitions and terminologies and to determine where the field stands on a current definition. In the remainder of the discussion, the term *adult education* will be used in place of the more cumbersome *adult and continuing education*.

Historical Perspective

What may well be the first systematic effort at defining adult education in the modern era came with the founding of the American Association for Adult Education (AAAE) in 1926. Ozanne (1934, p. 6), a researcher with that organization, observed, ''When the phrase 'adult education' first came into general usage in 1924 as a generic term to describe a group of previously unrelated activities, there was a natural attempt made to see how broad a meaning could be given to this definition.''

In this context, adult education became the total array of community facilities available to meet the needs of the adult learner. Ozanne's list included disparate groups such as lyceums, theater and art groups, libraries, museums, clubs, and voluntary associations, along with the more typical kind of organization such as the school or college.

There lately has been a revival of interest in the ideas of Eduard Lindeman concerning the nature of adult education (Stewart, 1987; Brookfield, 1987). Lindeman (1926, p. 6) never provided a formal definition, though his writings offer clues as to what is basically a Deweyan perspective on the field: ''Education is life—not a mere preparation for an unknown kind of future living. . . . The whole of life is learning, therefore education can have no ending. This new venture is called *adult education*—not because it is confined to adults but because adulthood, maturity defines its limits.''

In 1928, noted historian Charles Beard, a one-time president of the AAAE, explained what the term adult education meant for him. Life could be seen as brute survival, according to Beard, where ''men keep to the ancient profession of arms alone, [and] women merely grind corn in hollow stones and serve raw meat on a straw mat.'' Adult education represented for him the attempt to transcend such conditions and to establish what we call civilization. ''It is,'' argued Beard, ''a multitude of ideas, interests, and activities added to the bare routine of living that makes a complex and colorful civilization in which rich and many-sided personalities can be developed and thrive'' (Ely, 1936, p. vii).

In 1955, nine well-known adult educators accepted an invitation from the journal *Adult Education* to provide a ''working definition of adult education that indicates its differences from, and its relation to, other levels of education and other forms of social action'' (''What is Adult Education?'' 1955, p. 131). While the results varied with the author, certain consistencies emerged. Contributors singled out the voluntariness of learning, the commitment to growth, and the deliberate structuring of activities as essential features of any enterprise called adult education.

Nearer to the present time, the 1980 AEA Handbook series gave Boyd and Apps an opportunity to devote a whole book to the business of definition, which they associated philosophically with the concepts of *development* and *growth,* the latter meaning the ''progressive movement towards the solution of problems and the development of abilities to encounter similar future problems with greater competencies'' (Boyd, Apps, and Associates, 1980, pp. 10–11). Two years later, Darkenwald and Merriam (1982, p. 9) added their contribution when they defined adult education as ''a process whereby persons whose major social roles are characteristic of adult status undertake systematic and sustained learning activities for the purpose of bringing about changes in knowledge, attitudes, values or skills.''

Finally, it may be useful to invoke what is probably one of the most carefully crafted definitions in the literature, one which has enjoyed popularity, emerging as it did from one of the more neglected events in our history, the Exeter Conference of 1969: ''a process whereby persons who no longer attend school on a regular full-time basis . . . undertake sequential and organized activities with the conscious intention of bringing about changes in information, knowledge, understanding, or skill, appreciation and attitudes; or for the purpose of identifying or solving personal or community problems'' (Liveright and Haygood, 1969, p. 8).

In this chapter, we follow these historical categories of definitions. Adult education has been looked at from five basic, if overlapping, perspectives. First, it has been seen as the work of institutions and organizations. Second, it has been described as a special kind of relationship, as in the concept of andragogy or as in the distinction between adult education and the education of adults. Third, it has been considered a profession or a scientific discipline. Fourth, it has been seen as stemming from a historical identification with spontaneous social movements. Finally, it has been distinguished from other kinds of education by its goals and functions. Each of these perspectives contributes its own piece to the overall picture of adult education in the United States.

Adult Education as the Work of Institutions

Of all the ways of defining adult education, its identification with the growth and evolution of single and multipurpose institutions has been the most influential. It pervades the standard histories of Grattan (1971) and Knowles (1983). Griffith (1970, p. 172) captured the essence of this definition when he wrote, ''The history of adult education may be written as an account of the founding, growth, development, and demise of institutions which have served special interests.''

The institutional dimension is important, according to Darkenwald and Merriam (1982), because we cannot understand the field without considering the organizations that have helped shape it over the years. Furthermore, what organizations do, they argue, has implications for the roles played by adult educators in society. Adult and continuing education, from this perspective, is what organizations do. And what organizations do finds expression in the tasks that adult educators perform.

To date, however, few successful attempts have been made to classify organizations in terms of their adult education function or to draw out the implications of this relationship. One exception is the Schroeder typology. This scheme, developed for a chapter on definition in the 1970 AEA Handbook, has proved, despite evident shortcomings, remarkably resilient. According to Schroeder (1970), all adult education organizations can be grouped into four basic types. Type I consists of agencies for which adult education is a central function—for example, proprietary schools, alternative adult high schools, and the free university network. Type II consists of educational agencies for which adult education is a secondary function—that is, schools, colleges, and universities. Type III is made up of agencies for which adult education is an allied function employed to fill some of the needs that agencies recognize as their responsibility. Under this heading we find libraries, museums, health and welfare agencies. Type IV consists of agencies for which adult education is a subordinate function employed primarily to further the special interests of the agency itself. Here we find business, government, labor unions, churches, prisons, television, and newspapers.

Adult Education and the Education of Adults

The distinction between adult education and the education of adults (Grattan, 1971) has been around for some time and is perhaps the principal grounds for claiming adult education as a profession. Verner gave the fullest expression to this distinction. All adults, he felt, learned naturally in ordinary, everyday societal settings. They did so by reading, watching television, and the like. But this type of learning is both accidental and inefficient. In contrast, there is adult learning in the "formal, instructional setting in which the element of chance is minimized. This setting comes into being when an educational agent designs a sequence of tasks using specific learning procedures to help an adult achieve a mutually agreeable learning objective. This is adult education. . . . Whatever the form, content, duration, physical planning, or sponsorship, an activity is identified as adult education when it is part of a *systematic, planned, instructional program for adults*" (Verner and Booth, 1964, pp. 1–2; emphasis added).

Others have made a separate distinction among three types of adult learning—formal, informal, and nonformal. The term *informal* means the "truly lifelong process" (P. Coombs, quoted in Lowe, 1975, p. 24) by which adults inform themselves about life and its possibilities. This is what Verner refers to as natural or accidental learning. The term *nonformal* means organized adult education outside the established formal system. Clearly, what is intended here is a recognition that much of what we might legitimately call adult education takes place outside the purview of schools and universities—the mainstream, official sites of learning—and yet may be quite as organized, efficient, and under its own standards of control. (For further clarification of this distinction, see Chapter Seven.)

Currently, there are two trends within the field that reinforce the importance of the less formalized modes of learning. First, the concept of the self-directed learner has come to the fore, championed in the writings of Knowles (1980) and Tough (1971). Second, there has been a recent tendency, in the United States particularly, to substitute the term *adult learning* for *adult education,* as if to reflect the growing interest of the field in learning, however unorganized, episodic, or experiential, beyond the classroom. The implications these trends will ultimately have for the development of adult education as a profession or for the broader articulation of social policy toward the independent adult learner are currently hard to gauge.

Adult Education as a Profession or Scientific Discipline

Adult educators have long argued about whether adult education is a true profession or discipline. This argument was prominent in the so-called Black Book (Jensen, Liveright, and Hallenbeck, 1964); it was a feature of Houle's (1980) influential analysis of the concept of professionalization; and it was the propelling theme of the attempt by Boyd and Apps (1980) to redefine the field from within.

The concept of profession has been defined in many ways. The idealized model forming the basis for such definitions has often been medicine or the law. Accordingly, most professions are seen to share one or more of the following characteristics: satisfying a social need, requiring a period of intensive training, possessing a body of specialized knowledge, shared group norms, and public accountability. Two of these attributes are important in the present context—the emphasis on training or preparation and the notion of a specialized body of knowledge underpinning that training and preparation.

According to Plecas and Sork (1986, pp. 58–59), "the primary phenomenon under study would be organized learning, with the goal of the discipline being to develop a body of disciplined knowledge relating to how learning can best be facilitated . . . It follows that adult education would be considered a sociopsychological process, neither subject- or student-centered, but interaction centered." Building up this core body of scientifically based knowledge would lead eventually to the recognition of adult education as a university discipline through a process that would also include other conditions important to this end—the existence of broad, persuasive theories and a cadre of researchers collectively investigating the same set of theoretical problems. (See Courtney, 1986, for an elaboration of these points.)

According to this view, the way in which adults are encouraged to learn and aided in that learning is the single most significant ingredient of adult education as a profession. Indeed, Plecas and Sork's natural choice of the word *facilitate* in place of *teach* signals perhaps the accomplishment of the paradigmatic shift that Knowles urged on the field almost thirty years ago, and which he sought to capture in the term *andragogy*. Indeed, if there has been a single dominant theme to the field's claim to professional status since the 1950s, it has rested on the concept of andragogy, the etiology of which is philosophically traceable to modern humanism (see also Chapter Four).

Many writers have attempted to depict the kinds of knowledge or competencies an ideal adult educator might have. In this regard, Campbell's (1977) insightful monograph on Canadian adult education has important implications for the United States. Campbell isolated three "competencies marking the ideal in the adult educator which can be taken as generalized goals for training" (p. 58). First, there is a belief in the individual learner's ability to grow. Second, there is proficiency in a core of related skills, for example, leading groups effectively, directing complex administrative tasks, and developing innovative programs. Finally, a properly trained adult educator must understand the conditions, personal and societal, under which adults learn. Most academic departments of adult education in this country probably would subscribe to this core set of competencies, whether or not they felt they were achievable within their own institutional milieu.

For a different perspective on this issue see Brookfield (1986) and Chapters Thirteen and Fifteen.

Adult Education and Spontaneous Social Movements

One can often see what practitioners of a field think their subject is about—how they define it—by reading the histories they write and noting what they emphasize and what they leave out (Hellyer, n.d.). In the case of American adult education, that task is not hard, as the standard histories of Knowles (1983) and Grattan (1971) leave out a great deal. There is indeed no comprehensive history of American adult education (a claim also made for Canada by Welton, 1986) to compare with Cremin's three-volume history of American education (1970, 1980, 1988). (For recent attempts to close this gap, however, see Stubblefield, 1988 and Chapter Three.)

The histories of Knowles and Grattan are wonderful celebrations of the American spirit in all its various guises. There is Franklin and his passion for self-improvement, an idea captured in the Junto—a discussion group of like-minded friends, which he formed in 1727 and which has become the vivid symbol for adult education at its truest and most informal. There is the Lyceum movement, founded by Josiah Holbrook in 1826, which spread like wildfire over a thinly populated nation, with its passion for diffusion of useful knowledge. Similarly, there is Chautauqua, which, like the Lyceum movement, had humble origins as a Sunday school assembly but ended up reaching far beyond the shores of the lake that gave it its name. The Chautauqua brought higher learning to the culture-starved Protestants who lived on the frontier in the late 1800s. Then there is Americanization, university extension, and the cooperative extension movement. There are also the links between technology and the world of work, between religion and the rise of the college system, and between libraries and the mass media. In other words, adult educators celebrate an entity that is to be found in almost every institutional facet of American civilization and in every walk of life—from the most humble to the most proud and from the frankly serious to the frankly trivial. Adult education, from this perspective, echoes Beard and is truly "the entire process by which a culture transmits itself across the generations" (Bailyn, 1962, p. 14).

What is absent in this history? Quite a lot, when one looks more closely. First, there is the absence of conflict, as between groups and cultures and between competing ideologies (see for example, Rockhill's contribution to Taylor, Rockhill, and Fieldhouse, 1986). Second, there is the absence of the "big picture," that which links adult education, in its various historical guises, to society at large and to society's dominant social, political, and economic manifestations.

Our standard histories have little to say about the struggle of blacks for literacy in English (Rachal, 1986) or about the struggle of Native Americans to avoid it (Carlson, 1987). History has had little to say about the struggle by women for the vote—a struggle that began as a demand for equal education (Deckard, 1975). Similarly, history has given less than adequate attention to the decline and fall of utopian colonies in the early 1800s or to the emergence of socialism in the early 1900s, a phenomenon that led to the establishment of educational bureaus within existing trade unions and the founding of labor colleges. These labor colleges (for example, Brookwood Labor College in New York) had the linking of workers' education to radical social action as their guiding spirit.

While not at first apparent, these omissions have important practical consequences for the field's view of itself and of its moral imperative. History is thought to be an academic subject, important perhaps in the context of university-based training programs but hardly important for an activity that deals with contemporary problems and interventions. If we want to know how, as adult educators, we ought to intervene in a particular situation, we do not expect history to help us assess needs or select the right combination of learning activities for the occasion. Nevertheless, we ignore history at our peril, for by doing so we are unable to look at contemporary American society and to ask, Where do adult educators play a role? And do they contribute to changing or maintaining the status quo?

To take just one example, Rachal, in Chapter One, has addressed the social contexts that create a need for learning in the adult years. He mentions the current crisis around AIDS. The medical profession doubts they will discover a medical solution within the foreseeable future. So they have turned to education as one of the most important tools in the fight to stop the spread of this deadly disease. Surely AIDS presents a strong case for major interventions by adult educators, armed with the latest theories of how adults learn, how and why they change their habits, how to get information across to them, and so on. And yet, as a profession, we are not involved in this struggle, in this national crisis. Why not?

The answer is not obvious. It undoubtedly has something to do with the traditional role adult education has played in American society—where it is thought important and where not. By not examining this role, we are unable to understand why adult education has been confined rather than expanded in its potential for significant interventions in American life and culture. Moreover, failure to deal adequately with our history tends to reinforce the exclusive emphasis on the adult learner bereft of social context and leads to a de-emphasis on leadership and policy studies in the training of adult educators.

Adult Education in Terms of Functions and Goals

Finally, the definition of adult education in terms of goals and functions is probably the most common way to demarcate adult education from other forms of education and to distinguish it as a unique human service. Since the beginning of the modern era, leaders in the field have attempted to capture the essentials of the concept through a delineation of its major goals or purposes. Bryson (1936) spoke in terms of remedial, occupational, relational, political, and liberal goals for adult education. Grattan (1971) reduced these to vocational, recreational, informational, and liberal. Both agreed that adult education exists to provide education and training with respect to the world of work. They likewise agreed that adult education has a broad liberal function, which Grattan defined in relation to what we normally understand to be a liberal curriculum: humanities, the natural sciences, music, and so on.

In our discussion of goals and functions, we encounter for the first time, if it has not been hinted at already, a crucial dimension of all definitions that have to do with education, adult or otherwise: while we often couch our language in terms of what is, we cannot avoid an overture in the direction of what ought to be. As others have noted, our definition of education is almost always normative. It is not based simply on current scientific knowledge and a manipulation of technologies; just as significantly (some might argue more significantly), it has to do with moral choices about ways to intervene in people's lives.

Crucial to this normative element is the concept of need. Adult education exists to fulfill needs—those of the individual, those of the group or organization, and those of society (Knowles, 1980). Which are more important is a question to which answers have seesawed down the years. Should adult education really serve individual needs, leaving the purpose and consequences of that learning to individual choice? Or ought the emphasis be on education and on a recognition that society's needs may be more important? Currently, the popularity of andragogy as an American master concept suggests that the answer to the first question is yes and the answer to the second is a guarded maybe. Nevertheless, at a time when adult education, as a profession, appears to be moving into an era replete with new technologies and scientific theories, it is important to realize that programmatic and institutional decisions about educational provision are often not simply matters for strategic and technical planning, but are also decisions about people's lives—decisions that are as much moral as they are technical, and in which the people affected ought to have a say.

Conclusions

The value of a definition lies in its precision or ability to illuminate. These qualities often depend on how well we already know the concept the definition makes explicit. Definitions are rules for the correct use of terms; they are quasi-legalistic. At the same time, the workability of these definitions will depend on the extent to which the phenomena they describe are clearly bounded, standardized, or codified. That being the case, if the time is ever reached when it becomes easy to define adult education precisely, this may well be a case for worry rather than for rejoicing. A facile definition may tell us, not that we have become more skilled at the practice of definition, but that we have socially, politically, and philosophically so confined what adult education is allowed to be that definition is made easy.

It is clear that, for the forseeable future, adult education will remain an ambiguous term, sometimes being used to refer to the state of a society and its educational systems, sometimes being used to mean specific processes affecting individuals and their learning. What matters is how it is defined in a particular context and for a particular purpose.

All definitions, regardless of how abstract and wide-ranging they may appear, are crafted within a specific ideology of practice. The elements of that ideology consist of the ways men and women are socialized into the field, how they construct their professional worlds, and what they think about adults as learners. When adult educators define their occupation (for many it is truly a vocation), they are not simply telling us what they do in the day-to-day world; they are also saying something about what they like to think they are doing, what they hope to achieve as a member of a group of like-minded others, and what they believe education ought to be about in the world as they find it.

The business of defining adult education has been, in other words, an ideological more than a conceptual activity—more a reflection of what ought to be than what is the case. By invoking the notion of ideology (Kaestle, 1982), it is possible to argue that while the many definitions of adult education often appear as if from nowhere, and bereft of personal, historical, and cultural contexts, they are essentially products of these contexts, these value systems, each of which embodies its own ideological tension and compromise.

This discussion is taking place within the context of a handbook designed principally to be used by practitioners, by those preparing to enter the profession, and by curious others who have connections with the field. A definition for such a context might run as follows: Adult education is an intervention into the ordinary business of life—an intervention whose immediate goal is change, in knowledge or in competence. An adult educator is one, essentially, who is skilled at making such interventions.

References

Bailyn, B. *Education in the Forming of American Society.* New York: Norton, 1962.

Boyd, R. D., Apps, J. W., and Associates. *Redefining the Discipline of Adult Education.* San Francisco: Jossey-Bass, 1980.

Brookfield, S. *Understanding and Facilitating Adult Learning.* San Francisco: Jossey-Bass, 1986.

Brookfield, S. *Learning Democracy: Eduard Lindeman on Education and Social Change.* Dover, N.H.: Croom-Helm, 1987.

Bryson, L. *Adult Education.* New York: American Book, 1936.

Campbell, D. *Adult Education as a Field of Study and Practice.* Vancouver: The Centre for Continuing Education, University of British Columbia, 1977.

Carlson, R. *The Americanization Syndrome: A Quest for Conformity.* New York: St. Martin's Press, 1987.

Courtney, S. "On Derivation of the Research Question." *Adult Education Quarterly,* 1986, *36,* 160–165.

Cremin, L. *American Education: The Colonial Experience, 1607–1783.* New York: Harper & Row, 1970.

Cremin, L. *American Education: The National Experience, 1783–1876.* New York: Harper & Row, 1980.

Cremin, L. *American Education: The Metropolitan Experience, 1876–1980.* New York: Harper & Row, 1988.

Darkenwald, G. G., and Merriam, S. B. *Adult Education: Foundations of Practice.* New York: Harper & Row, 1982.

Deckard, B. S. *The Women's Movement: Political, Socioeconomic, and Psychological Issues.* New York: Harper & Row, 1975.

Ely, M. L. *Adult Education in Action.* New York: American Association for Adult Education, 1936.

Grattan, C. H. *In Quest of Knowledge: A Historical Perspective on Adult Education.* New York: Arno Press and *New York Times,* 1971.

Griffith, W. S. "Adult Education Institutions." In R. M. Smith, G. F. Aker, and J. R. Kidd (eds.), *Handbook of Adult Education.* New York: Macmillan, 1970.

Hellyer, M. "Uncovering the Untold Story of the History of Adult Education in the United States." Unpublished paper, Northern Illinois University, n.d.

Houle, C. *Continuing Learning in the Professions.* San Francisco: Jossey-Bass, 1980.

Jensen, G., Liveright, A. A., and Hallenbeck, W. (eds.). *Adult Education: Outlines of an Emerging Field of University Study.* Washington, D.C.: Adult Education Association of the U.S.A., 1964.

Kaestle, C. "Ideology and American Educational History." *History of Education Quarterly,* 1982, *22,* 123–137.

Knowles, M. S. *The Modern Practice of Adult Education.* (Rev. ed.) New York: Cambridge University Press, 1980.

Knowles, M. S. *The Adult Education Movement in the U.S.* (Rev. ed.) Melbourne, Fla.: Krieger, 1983.

Lindeman, E. *The Meaning of Adult Education.* New York: New Republic, 1926.

Liveright, A. A., and Haygood, N. (eds.). *The Exeter Papers.* Chicago: Center for the Study of Liberal Education for Adults, 1969.

Lowe, J. *The Education of Adults: A World Perspective.* (2nd ed.) Toronto: Ontario Institute for Studies in Education, 1975.

Ozanne, J. *Regional Surveys of Adult Education.* New York: American Association for Adult Education, 1934.

Peterson, R. E., and Associates. *Lifelong Learning in America.* San Francisco: Jossey-Bass, 1979.

Plecas, D. B., and Sork, T. J. "Adult Education: Curing the Ills of an Undisciplined Discipline." *Adult Education Quarterly,* 1986, *37,* 48–62.

Rachal, J. "Freedom's Crucible: William T. Richardson and the Schooling of the Freedmen." *Adult Education Quarterly,* 1986, *37,* 14–22.

Schroeder, W. L. "Adult Education Defined and Described." In R. M. Smith, G. F. Aker, and J. R. Kidd (eds.), *Handbook of Adult Education.* New York: Macmillan, 1970.

Stewart, D. *Adult Learning in America: Eduard Lindeman and His Agenda for Lifelong Education.* Melbourne, Fla.: Krieger, 1987.

Stubblefield, H. *Towards a History of Adult Education in America: The Search for a Unifying Principle.* Dover, N.H.: Croom-Helm, 1988.

Taylor, R., Rockhill, K., and Fieldhouse, R. *University Adult Education in England and the U.S.A.* Dover, N.H.: Croom-Helm, 1985.

Tough, A. *The Adult's Learning Projects.* Toronto: Ontario Institute for Studies in Education, 1971.

Verner, C., and Booth, A. *Adult Education.* Washington, D.C.: The Center for Applied Research in Education, 1964.

Welton, M. "In Search of a Usable Past for Canadian Adult Education." Unpublished Proceedings of the First International Conference on the History of Adult Education, Oxford, Eng., July, 1986.

"What is Adult Education? Nine 'Working Definitions.'" *Adult Education,* 1955, *V,* 131–145.

3

The History of Adult and Continuing Education

Harold W. Stubblefield
Patrick Keane

Practitioners and researchers in socially oriented fields such as adult education often turn a blind eye toward their history. When they do look at their history, the purpose often is to find examples to justify societal support or to seek inspiration through the lives of the great pioneers. As a social practice matures and gains greater acceptance, however, a history that remains only institutional, inspirational, and celebratory will prove to be inadequate to the demands of the future.

Beyond institutional development, other questions must be addressed— questions of ideas and purposes, questions of the relationship between segments of society, and questions of the social conditions that adult educators seek to redress through various programs of adult education. Within the scope of this chapter, only selected aspects of this story in the United States can be told. The history of adult education in the United States covers over three centuries, beginning with the colonial period and extending through the Reagan presidency in the 1980s.

Transition from Received Tradition

From the sixteenth and seventeenth centuries, members of divergent and competing cultures began to settle in North America, seeking to establish familiar patterns of life and to experiment with new forms. Little has been written about the education of adults in the Southwest as Junipero Serra established missions up and down the California coast. Little is known, generally, about the French efforts at education as they colonized the South or about the Russians' program of adult education in Alaska. However, according to Dauenhauer's (1980, pp. 24–25) Alaskan history, "there was a thriving language and flourishing literature in Aleut, complete with gospel translations, essays, journals, diaries, the result of a multilingual, multiethnic ideal established by Father Venaiaminon and the educational policies of the Russian Orthodox Church." Whatever was going on in the rest of the country, our recorded history is dominated by the English activities.

The Dominant Culture. In studying the colonial period on the East Coast, one is soon conscious of the degree to which English culture prevailed. In England, education seems to have developed further than in many countries as an instrument of public policy, although private endowment remained the norm. Perceived national interests in social stability, in religious conformity, in defense, and in skill training were furthered by legislative means as early as the Elizabethan period. A prosperous merchant class, benefiting from a state-encouraged export trade, endowed numerous education foundations. And it was this tradition they brought to the American colonies.

The Place of Literacy. By the seventeenth century, English settlements stretched along the entire eastern seaboard of America. The settlers sought to establish a new society, a utopia, conserving the best of their heritage yet exploring opportunities previously denied them. Improvement in all its forms, from intellectual to political and from social to economic, was implicit in their perceptions of the New World. The question thus arose as to whether adults could redress their inequalities and enhance their opportunities. This was a critical question particularly for the many indentured servants who received a free passage and maintenance in return for a fixed period of labor. They have been estimated to have made up between one-half and two-thirds of all post-1630s white immigrants to the thirteen colonies (Galeson, 1981). Tentative conclusions suggest skilled male workers came with a high literacy rate (80 to 81 percent), and even the less skilled and less literate male and female workers had typically undergone some informal education which improved their literacy in adulthood. Although restricted initially, after completing their years of servitude, these settlers were free to participate in the individualism, optimism, and enterprise ascribed to colonial society.

However, despite the much eulogized Puritan concern with schooling and literacy, one may question the degree to which it redressed inequalities or enhanced opportunities. Certainly, there was a healthy development of colonial printing, publishing, libraries, public lecturing, and there was a start on establishing the mutual improvement societies popularized by Cotton Mather and Benjamin Franklin. Yet, there were some major limitations, even in the educational transformation credited to New England. Research suggests (Lockridge, 1974) that between the mid-seventeenth century and the end of the eighteenth century, society here changed from being about half literate to being nearly universally (males) literate. The already literate merchants, storekeepers, and urban artisans were joined by rural artisans, farmers, and laborers. Impressive as this was, the literacy stemming from Puritan ideals appears to have left New Englanders with attitudes as traditional as those of their illiterate neighbors. It also left female illiteracy quite high. Elsewhere, as in colonial Pennsylvania or Virginia, even male literacy does not seem to have gone above the two-thirds level of contemporary England. Thus, despite the limitations of research into early literacy, it seems that as many as one-third of the males and the majority of the females were excluded from effective participation in a culture beyond their oral traditions. This applied with even greater force to others whose traditions were barely recognized—the blacks and Native Americans.

The true promise of adult education was apparent in the rich variety of learning resources, including the variety of formal and informal instruction, that existed on the eve of the Revolution. From the information and attitudes shared in churches, taverns, coffee houses, and clubs, to the independent study of printed works and enrollment in formal and evening courses, a seemingly endless variety of adult learning opportunities existed. Nevertheless, the scope of such opportunities did not differ markedly from those available in England. The question for the immediate future was less one of broadening the scope of opportunities than of broadening access to them.

Independence and Expansion. With independence came a public ideology of improvement, professing to harness such opportunities for the common good. Yet the signatories of the Declaration of Independence exemplified traditional political and economic power, and the early presidents (George Washington, John Adams, Thomas Jefferson, James Madison, James Monroe, and John Quincy Adams) continued an elite tradition. Indeed, the Articles of the Confederation interpreted the term *the people* to mean the free, white, male citizens (excluding vagrants and paupers)—leaving unclear the potential status of women, Native Americans, and most blacks. However, the image transcended the reality, and hopes were entertained of a classless, egalitarian society in which all would have ready access to a useful education enabling them to function in a democracy.

Hopes for an early emancipation of the slaves proved misplaced, and slave codes continued to prohibit teaching blacks to read. Nevertheless, some adult education did develop in response to conflicting objectives. Moral and religious instruction and basic skill training were provided in support of the status quo, while learning in abolitionist cells and in secret religious meetings developed in opposition to the status quo.

The federal government worked with missionary groups to assimilate the Native Americans by promoting agriculture, stock raising, and conversion to Christianity. Relatively few outside the Cherokees failed to resist the assimilation process, preferring their own skill training and education based on oral tradition and ceremony.

White women were constrained by a cult of true womanhood which idealized their attributes along with traditional domestic roles. A limited escape was provided for women who entered the labor market from the 1820s, particularly in the Lowell and Waltham textile mills in Massachusetts. In the latter, access to a factory library was supplemented by availability of circulating libraries, study groups, and night classes. The women were able to teach Sunday school and to launch their own weekly periodical—the *Lowell Offering*. For a minority who became skilled weavers, or for others who progressed to teach in the common schools, the economic opportunities were certainly enhanced. However, for the many unskilled spindle workers, the growing reality of paternalism and an eleven- or twelve-hour working day suggested the need for social and economic reform before the proclaimed benefits of education could be attained. Education was thus to become part of a broader movement for women's rights which developed from the 1840s.

A group traditionally imbued with the potentialities of adult education was the free male skilled workers and their apprentices. To their frequent membership in charitable and friendly societies (sometimes including a library) was often added membership in community lyceums and mechanics' institutes with a fundamentally educational aim. Indeed, the early nineteenth century witnessed a parallel development in the United States and Britain (as well as a continuing interaction) of innumerable voluntary societies for adult education. The scope of the education they provided expanded from a utilitarian useful knowledge to a more general exploration of often controversial social and economic issues on the eve of the Civil War. The participants likewise expanded until they constituted a more representative group of both men and women.

To the classic apprentice studying drawing in a mechanics' institute, the farmer studying new crop rotations in a farmers' institute, or the clerk studying bookkeeping in a mercantile library association were added new venues for communities to be entertained, enlightened, or provoked by often spellbinding presentations on foreign travel, literature, or slavery. But various utopian experiments and radicals of deistical and workingmen's societies challenged the pervasive advocacy of consonance and coherence, as in early Americanization or literacy programs. And while a golden age of publishing facilitated the self-culture advocated by William Ellery Channing, it still required extraordinary commitment to reach the degree of self-actualization achieved by such as Elihu Burritt, the so-called learned blacksmith. So the temptation was to accept the pervasive middle-class views on the nature of truth and reality, which were taught as much in prisons, poorhouses, and places of work as in evening classes.

As abolitionists, feminists, and socialists detected an underlying social control in the expanded educational facilities, an educated middle class perceived rich opportunities for the expression of cultural nationalism. An evolution from debating societies to subscription libraries to the early learned societies was paralleled by a growing interest in the sciences. The research of rising stars such as Louis Agassiz and James Dana, or of eminent visitors such as Charles Lyell, attracted increasing lecture attendance by ''political and civil leaders, academicians, physicians, lawyers, clergymen, artisans, merchants, and 'gentlemen scientists'" (Oleson, 1976, p. xx). Thus, on the eve of the Civil War, adult education was a vibrant, if fragmented, undertaking whose potential was perceived even by some denied equal access or alienated by its prevailing orthodoxies.

The Emergence of an Interdependent Society

Impulses toward self-culture and useful knowledge continued, in the adult education institutions organized after the Civil War, to diffuse popular culture and thought. The Chautauqua Institution combined residential education and leisure, and it extended into remote communities through the Chautauqua Literary and Scientific Circles. Women's clubs, local Chautauquas, traveling tent Chautauquas, and lyceum lecture bureaus formed a national network, bringing Americans in both urban and isolated rural areas into contact with scientific, cultural, international, and political ideas. And the philanthropy of Andrew Carnegie greatly expanded library facilities for the working and middle class.

An Alternative America. Other impulses were also at work among women, laborers, and farmers who envisioned an alternative America in which their grievances would be redressed. In the 1860s, 1870s, and 1880s, these movements took specific organizational form in the National American Woman Suffrage Association (a merger in 1890 of two earlier organizations), the Woman's Christian Temperance Union, the Knights of Labor, the National Grange of the Patrons of Husbandry, and the Farmer's Alliance. Through these voluntary forms of associations, they mobilized resources, became aware of the extent of their own subordinate status, acquired a vision of their power, and took action. Evans and Boyte (1986) called this process in democratic movements *movement education.* These democratic movements combined both education and political action. An example of movement education occurred in the Farmer's Alliance that led to the formation of the Populist political party in the 1890s. In their local, state, and regional meetings, farmers discussed political and economic questions that concerned them. They organized local newspapers, farmers' clubs, and circulating libraries that made reform literature available to members. Through these interpersonal and communication networks they created an ideology of reform.

Progressive Reform. In the 1890s, many Americans recognized that profound social changes had occurred. Expanded networks of communication and transportation had created national markets; industrialization had created a new work culture; and urbanization had created new patterns of community life. Persons were entangled in a web of influences over which they had little direct control. American society had become interdependent (Haskell, 1977).

One response was the search for more adequate explanations of this interdependency in the form of new academic disciplines—sociology, economics, political science, psychology, and history—and the modern research university. From the research universities—the University of Wisconsin is the best example—came the uniquely American form of university extension: applying research-produced knowledge to various domains of human life.

Agricultural education followed a similar course. The 1862 Morrill Act authorized land-grant universities for the states. But not until the 1914 Smith-Lever Act, creating the Cooperative Extension Service, did a formal system of adult education for the agricultural community appear. Several events made the Smith-Lever Act possible: aggressive promotion by special interest groups, the development of the agricultural sciences, and the creation of a method for knowledge dissemination.

A second response to the profound social changes centered upon the city. Some progressive reformers sought to make cities manageable through application of scientific administration. Still others turned to social reform, and their efforts included adult education, social welfare, and legislative reform. Reformers were particularly concerned about the plight of the new immigrants from southern and eastern Europe, who began in the 1880s and 1890s to come in great numbers to the United States and to settle principally in the cities. The new urban institutional forms of settlement houses, community school centers, people's institutes, and the institutional church attempted to meliorate the condition of the immigrants.

Jane Addams of Hull House is representative of those social reformers who, on the whole, respected immigrant traditions. The response of another faction of the so-called Americanizers was, however, less benign. Fearful of alien ideas, these Americanizers attempted to indoctrinate immigrants in the American way through educational programs in evening schools, factories, churches, and private organizations (Carlson, 1975). However, the immigrant institutions—churches, lodges, clubs, newspapers, lectures—had more success in influencing immigrant adjustment than did the Americanization efforts.

Though slavery was abolished with the Civil War, the education of Afro-American adults remained essentially a black enterprise. An alternative system grew up alongside the dominant system including black churches, Freedman's bureaus, black colleges, vocational schools, fraternities, and the largest black adult educational movement in America, Marcus Garvey's Universal Negro Improvement Association (McGee and Neufeldt, 1985).

The Idea of Adult Education in
Repression, Normalcy, and Depression

World War I brought a halt to progressive reform. The federal government, through massive propaganda efforts, mobilized public support for the war and repressed opposition. In 1919, the red scare, a wave of national hysteria about communism, swept the nation. In 1920, Harding's administration supposedly marked the return to normalcy, but it was short-lived. With the 1929 stock market crash, the nation entered a severe economic depression, and a new era of reform began. In these conditions the modern period of adult education had its start.

A New Agency. In the 1920s, Everett Dean Martin of the People's Institute of New York City observed that adult education was everybody's business and interest—so much so that he called adult education a mass movement. He believed, however, that the movement lacked direction. From 1918 to 1941—the end of World War I to the beginning of World War II—the central adult education focus was the attempt to determine the direction of this movement (Stubblefield, 1988). Educators, intellectuals, foundation executives, civic reformers, and others began to consider adult education as a new agency in American life.

In promoting adult education as a new agency, the efforts of the Carnegie Corporation dwarfed those of all others. How the Carnegie Corporation came to be interested in adult education is a matter of dispute. Recent scholarship indicates that it grew out of the early-twentieth-century concern for diffusing expert knowledge to the widest possible audience—a concern that preceded Frederick Keppel, who served as president of the Carnegie Foundation from 1923 to 1941. Thus, adult educators' emphasis on the importance of Keppel to the initiation of Carnegie support of adult education is more mythical than real. In 1926, the Carnegie Corporation facilitated the organization of the American Association for Adult Education (AAAE), financed the AAAE's administrative operation, and used it as the funding agency for the Carnegie Corporation's study, research, and demonstration projects.

Beyond a general belief that the adult public needed to be brought up-to-date in its thinking, the early advocates held differing views about what adult education, as a new agency in American life, should accomplish. Clearly the point of greatest contention centered on the extent to which adult education should be associated with social action. In the 1920s, Morse A. Cartwright, the executive director of the AAAE, attempted to keep adult education neutral by refusing to identify AAAE efforts with any of the special interest groups promoting adult education for specific purposes. When the depression came, Cartwright took his stand with liberal education—individual enlightenment and understanding—and opposed education for social action. Cartwright believed that America was a classless society in which no group should be denied opportunity.

Others, such as Joseph K. Hart, Harry Overstreet, and Eduard C. Lindeman, advanced a conception of adult education as social education. Adult education could not be disassociated from the study and critique of social institutions, including institutionalized racism. Lindeman, for example, regarded adult education as a method by which adults became intelligent about their situations in life. To him, adult education attained its greatest power and relevancy when associated with the work of functional groups and not when it was divorced from social action.

Federal Involvement. For a brief period in the 1930s, the federal government entered the fields of adult education and culture (art and theater) through the federal emergency relief programs. The programs had lasting impact upon individual participants and through the products they produced; but the programs ended with the beginning of World War II, and the efforts resulted in no permanent federal involvement in adult education. This brief experiment, nevertheless, raised many questions about the appropriateness of a federal role in adult education, questions that recur periodically.

Post–World War II and Toward the Present

Interest in adult education and activities to promote its expansion greatly increased after World War II. Three aspects of these activities seem particularly important in assessing what adult education has become in the almost half century since the war ended.

Adult Education and Economic Development. One pattern has been the growing use in government, higher education, and the workplace, of adult education for economic development. The federal government involvement began during the war. To reduce the impact of returning service men on the economy, Congress passed the Servicemen's Readjustment Act in 1944. Popularly known as the G.I. Bill, this act subsidized higher education and vocational training for over two million veterans.

In the 1960s, the federal government, in response to an economic recession, began retraining initiatives. Following President Kennedy's assassination in 1963, President Johnson initiated a broader federal initiative in massive programs with the War on Poverty and the Great Society. Initiated partly in response to the civil rights movement, partly in response to poverty, and partly in response to racial unrest, the programs included job retraining and adult basic education. A short-lived Community Action Program sought participation of the poor in administering these programs. With the election of President Nixon in 1968, the federal government's commitment to the poor diminished. Under the Reagan administration, only the adult basic education program has maintained its level of funding. The redefinition of the Comprehensive Employment and Training Act (CETA) to the Job Training Partnership Act (JTPA) under President Reagan gave a large part of the educational role of training and retraining to private corporations. This was a distinct policy change.

Higher education institutions have played an increasingly important role in economic development. They have greatly expanded their services for the working adult to meet the desires for credentialing and continuing education. Adults now have greater accessibility to degrees through nontraditional arrangements and greater opportunities for continuing education through residential centers, noncredit courses, and continuing professional education. The continuing education unit makes it possible to measure noncredit participation. Information systems have been developed to provide information about postsecondary educational opportunities, and educational brokering agencies have been organized to connect adults with educational providers, to provide career guidance, and to serve as client brokers. By 1975, adult learners were the new majority in higher education.

In the 1960s, community colleges became a powerful educational force. In the time of the Great Society reforms, the community colleges provided an open door to social and economic opportunities for minorities and the disadvantaged. But some critics maintained that these opportunities were limited in effect and were used to settle social unrest.

Higher education forged linkages with the workplace, and the workplace itself became a school for adults. The history of training in the workplace has not yet been written, but the key event came in the early part of this century when Taylor's creation of scientific management made the process of work itself an object of study. After World War II, the United States became a knowledge economy in which the acquisition and application of information was the foundation of work. Persons who engage in knowledge work require continuing education to keep up with new developments in their fields and to learn new skills and disciplines that are best learned in adulthood rather than through extended schooling.

In the 1950s, corporations moved aggressively into the training and development field, establishing training departments and providing a wide range of educational programs. Enhancing productivity is the driving force for training in the workplace. And workplace training has been made more urgent by international competition, by the need for continual retraining, by the growing participation of workers in decision making in some industries, and by the need to provide basic education for a large number of the workforce inadequately educated by the public school system.

Adult Education and an Alternative Vision. A wave of national hysteria over communism followed World War I, and it recurred after World War II, reaching its peak in the 1950s. Much of American foreign policy has been directed at containing communism abroad. As a response to American intervention in Vietnam in the 1960s and early 1970s, and in Central America in the late 1970s and 1980, dissenting Americans responded with protest movements. Through study and action, they sought an alternative to an interventionist policy; they focused attention on America's role in the world and on how democracy should be spread.

In the 1950s and 1960s, several groups of Americans—blacks, women, Native Americans, and Mexican-Americans—pressed their case for social, political, and economic justice. These social movements contained an essential educational component through which those who struggled for justice came to understand their situation and to gain a sense of their own power to change it. National coordinating organizations were formed to guide these movements. Among these were the Southern Christian Leadership Conference, the National Organization for Women, the American Indian Movement, and the National Farm Workers Association.

An example from the civil rights movement shows the role of adult education in a way not usually included in a consensus history approach (Morris, 1984). The Highlander Folk School, founded by Myles Horton in 1932 in Tennessee, was one of several movement halfway houses. Highlander brought together black leadership, created an integrated institution so that blacks and whites attending Highlander had a vision of a new society, and developed through its experiences resources for social change. Perhaps Highlander's most important contribution was the development of a mass educational program called *citizenship schools*. Organized first in Johns Island, South Carolina, to teach literacy to blacks, the schools used the participants' own experiences as the basis for learning. Beyond teaching literacy, the schools also helped blacks understand the white power structure and their rights in a democracy. In 1961, the Southern Christian Leadership Conference took over operation of the schools.

Education Beyond Schooling. The debate over the direction of adult education—what kind of education do adults as adults need?—was not resolved in the 1920s and 1930s, nor was it resolved immediately after World War II. However, the National Training Laboratory in Group Development, organized in 1947, did make progress in charting new directions in adult resocialization, analysis of adult situations, participative techniques of learning, and a dynamic interpretation of adult learner behavior.

In the 1950s, new initiatives in liberal education occurred with the Great Books programs of Robert Hutchins and Mortimer Adler. An even broader vision of liberal adult education to equip adults as citizens in a free society underlay the Ford Foundation's sponsored Fund for Adult Education. The fund's Test Cities programs, for example, sought to create both a program and a community-based structure for liberal education. And the fund sponsored Grattan's (1971) history of liberal adult education, still relevant and very readable. The Association of University Evening Colleges sought to broaden the scope of its liberal education for adults, and in 1951 organized, with initial financial help from its Fund for Adult Education, a quasi-independent organization called the Center for the Study of Liberal Education for Adults. This center outlasted by seven years the Fund for Adult Education.

With the organization of the Adult Education Association of the U.S.A. (AEA) in 1951 came a more comprehensive approach to adult education. The AEA attempted to serve the various segments of the adult education field by promoting the development of professional competencies, institutional cooperation, and adult education as a social good.

From its inception, the AEA had to contend with diverging conceptions of adult education. Group dynamic advocates held prominent positions, and the Fund for Adult Education provided financial support for eight years in return for some emphasis on liberal education. With the changing social conditions of the 1960s, new ways of thinking about adult education began to appear under labels such as lifelong education, lifelong learning, and recurrent education. Each of these in some way reflected an attempt to make adult education an object of public policy.

Conclusion

As adult educators contemplate the directions that adult education will take in the last decade of the twentieth century and into the twenty-first century, they will not find a road map in the study of history. Instead, they may find new ways of thinking about adult education, the forms it has taken, and the purposes—both liberating and oppressing—it has served. Those who read with care the history of adult education in the United States may avoid being trapped in the vise of the present and may emerge with new understandings.

References

Carlson, R. A. *The Quest for Conformity: Americanization Through Education.* New York: Wiley, 1975.

Dauenhauer, R. "Conflicting Visions in Alaskan Education." Xerox occasional paper no. 3. Fairbanks: Center for Cross-Cultural Studies, University of Alaska, 1980.

Evans, S. M., and Boyte, H. C. *Free Spaces: The Sources of Democratic Change in America.* New York: Harper & Row, 1986.

Galeson, D. W. *White Servitude in Colonial America.* New York: Cambridge University Press, 1981.

Grattan, C. H. *In Quest of Knowledge: A Historical Perspective on Adult Education.* New York: Arno Press and *The New York Times,* 1971.

Haskell, T. L. *The Emergence of Professional Social Science.* Urbana: University of Illinois Press, 1977.

Lockridge, K. A. *Literacy in Colonial New England.* New York: Norton, 1974.

McGee, L., and Neufeldt, H. *Education of the Black Adult in the United States: An Annotated Bibliography.* Westport, Conn.: Greenwood Press, 1985.

Morris, A. D. *The Origins of the Civil Rights Movement: Black Communities Organizing for Change.* New York: Free Press, 1984.

Oleson, A. "Introduction: To Build a New Intellectual Order." In S. C. Brown, *The Pursuit of Knowledge in the Early American Republic.* Baltimore, Md.: Johns Hopkins University Press, 1976.

Stubblefield, H. W. *Towards a History of Adult Education in America.* London: Croom-Helm, 1988.

4

Purposes and Philosophies of Adult Education

Hal Beder

This chapter discusses the purposes and philosophies of adult education. Purposes, as defined here, are the basic reasons for conducting adult education; purposes are translated into practice. In some cases, purposes are derived from ideals, to abet the so-called good society or to help individuals achieve their true potential, for example. In other cases, however, purposes derive from more operational concerns such as making a profit or improving organizational effectiveness.

Philosophies are the beliefs about the way in which adult education should be conducted and the general principles that guide practice. As Elias and Merriam (1980, p. 3) point out, philosophies are integrated sets of propositions and "are the foundations or basic structures by which phenomena, events and realities are understood." The study of the philosophy of adult education is systematic and essentially intellectual. Clearly, purposes and philosophies are interrelated. Yet they are also conceptually distinct.

One might take the position that philosophy is the guiding principle behind practice, and that being so, the chapter should begin with philosophy as the focus and proceed to demonstrate how purposes derive from philosophy. Indeed, such an approach is defensible, and authors such as Elias and Merriam, who discuss liberal, progressive, behaviorist, humanistic, radical, and analytical approaches, have aptly taken this course. In a similar vein, Apps (1985) argues that philosophy should guide practice and goes on to demonstrate how the application of philosophical inquiry could improve practice.

However, after reviewing the general professional books of the field from the 1920s to the present, I have concluded that the reverse may be a more accurate description of the field's development in North America. Philosophy, for the most part, has developed from purpose, because adult education has been more affected by the social function it serves than by the thought systems associated with it. Adult education exists as a field of practice and inquiry today because it serves a vital social function. To be sure, adults have always been educated. Yet in American society, formal, systematic, institutionalized adult education has become indispensable because the extension of formal learning beyond youth is necessary if society is to function. This need derives in part from the growth of mass society and social dynamism and in part from the great increase in technical knowledge brought about by the scientific revolution.

As societies become larger, a specialized division of labor is required to maintain the economic, distribution, and governance systems upon which the social order depends. Given specialization, not all that one needs to learn in order to function can be learned during youth, because the general and theoretical knowledge learned during youthful education must be refined through application if adult tasks are to be performed competently. At the same time, rapid social change has meant that knowledge quickly becomes irrelevant, and hence what one learns during childhood must constantly be updated, revised, and supplemented.

Along with the trend toward a mass society, and related to it, has been what is often referred to as the scientific revolution. Scientific reasoning has enabled us to understand the physical universe to a degree never before known, and advances in knowledge have been constantly translated into technological development. Technological development stimulates social change and makes constant retraining in the workplace a requisite for productivity. As Cremin (1970) suggests, the roots of this social imperative for adult education go back to colonial times and "take off" during the Industrial Revolution.

Adult education was first recognized as a vital component of our educational system during the 1920s. During this decade, the term *adult education* first came into general usage (Hart, 1927), and the adult education movement was launched. If the purposes of adult education derive primarily from its social function, it is more fruitful to organize this chapter around purposes and to discuss philosophy in respect to them. This is the course I have chosen.

Over the years, many authors have proposed purposes for adult education. Reviewing the literature, Hallenbeck (1964) notes Bryson's functions, which are remedial, relational, liberal, and political; Halsey's functions, which are remedial, assimilative, mobility promoting, and compensatory; and Peers's function, which is developing responsible citizens in a democratic society. Verner (1964) divides purposes into expansional, participational, integrational, and personal, and Darkenwald and Merriam (1982) categorize aims and objectives as cultivation of the intellect, individual self-actualization, personal and social improvement, social transformation, and organizational effectiveness.

As one reviews the functions and purposes proposed by others, however, it becomes clear that the basic purposes of adult education can be collapsed into four major categories: (1) to facilitate change in a dynamic society, (2) to support and maintain the good social order, (3) to promote productivity, and (4) to enhance personal growth. These categories of purpose are interrelated. Success or failure in achieving one affects all others.

To Facilitate Change in a Dynamic Society

So much has been said about the need for lifelong learning in the age of "knowledge explosions," knowledge "half-lives," rapid technological change, and "future shock" that we sometimes are led to believe that such concerns are purely contemporary. They are not. As Hart (1927, p. vii) notes in one of the first books with the words *adult education* in the title, "Within the last century, education, having become more or less completely identified with schooling, has been allocated almost exclusively to the period of childhood and youth. This has enabled adult generations to avoid and escape education. All this has taken place in a century of unprecedented industrial and social change—a century that should, because of those changes, have devoted a major part of its energies to the education of adults for intelligent living in this changed world."

This theme is echoed throughout the literature from Hart's time to the present. As noted earlier, this purpose of education derives from adults' need to remain current in the wake of rapid change and increasing knowledge. It has two dimensions, one social, the other material.

On the social dimension, as values, attitudes, and beliefs change, so do social role expectations. As role expectations change, so must the behavior of adults change, for if it does not, inappropriate role behavior results (Mortimer and Simmons, 1978). Inappropriate role behavior is generally sanctioned negatively, thus making life quite difficult for the adult who fails to comprehend social change and to act accordingly. The need to comprehend changes in expected role behavior and to change accordingly has been the basic purpose behind much of the adult education that developed within the women's movement. It has also been a propelling force behind parent education and in many continuing professional education programs in fields such as medicine, law, and nursing.

Rapid change in a material sense pertains to the rapid change in knowledge needed to perform specialized tasks—change so rapid that adults must continuously update themselves if tasks are to be performed adequately. This is perhaps most true in the scientific and technical occupations in which there has been a phenomenal growth in technical knowledge and a concomitant increase in industrial training, staff development, and continuing professional education. The burgeoning of knowledge and constant need for updating is not restricted to technical fields alone, however, for increases in the objective knowledge of science and technology in turn affect the more relational aspects of the workplace and society in general. For example, as the amount of technical knowledge increases, no one person can comprehend it all. Hence, fields of knowledge break down into specialties, and work becomes organized into specialized functions. This specialization dramatically increases the need for communication and coordination among specialized units and results in a demand for more efficient management and management training.

To Support and Maintain the Good Social Order

Obviously, the way in which the good social order is maintained and supported depends on what is considered to be good. In the American tradition, it has generally been accepted that the good order is embodied in democracy. True democracy, however, is considered by most authors to be an ideal that can be achieved only through conscious effort.

That a major purpose of adult education is to promote the democratic order is an idea with strong roots in the early adult education movement. The logic was as simple as it was powerful: Democracy can work only if the citizenry exercises rational, informed, choice, for in the absence of informed, rational choice, propaganda prevails, and democracy lapses into totalitarianism.

Furthermore, true democracy requires active participation on the part of the citizenry. Since the electorate are adults, it is the purpose of adult education to assist in informing and developing critical skills. Lindeman (1926, p. 46) recognized the relationship between adult education and democracy when he wrote, "We do not acquire freedom—we grow into freedom." Baker (1936, p. 11) expanded on that theme: "The preservation of our civilization depends upon the ability of our democracy to suspend judgement until all the facts are known, to resist prejudices, to permit intellect to rule over feelings. The sort of education that cultivates such ability must be continuous and common to all people through the whole of the United States."

Although an informed, critical-thinking citizenry is necessary for democracy, it is not sufficient. Participation is also required, and this too was considered to be a purpose of adult education. As Sheats, Jayne, and Spence (1953, p. 21) wrote, "If democracy means government by the governed, we can not delegate citizenship! Every individual competent to pull his own load must reserve a spot in his life for direct participation in the management of his political and economic affairs, and it should be a major objective of adult education to assist adults to manage these affairs with competence."

The participation theme is echoed by Bergevin (1967, p. 35) who wrote, "There is little doubt that, if democracy is to survive, citizens must participate intelligently in the affairs of the various institutions that constitute democratic society. And intelligent participation is predicated on learning."

Another theme that persists from Hart (1927) to Brookfield (1984a) is the notion that the good democratic society requires good community relationships. One product of the advent of mass society is the breakdown of communities based on face-to-face relationships (*gemeinshaft*) into communities based on impersonal organization (*gesellshaft*). As Sheats, Jayne, and Spence and others note, this breakdown can result in alienation and social disenfranchisement. The task of adult education then, is to assist in building groups within communities that identify common problems and that participate together in solving them. The themes of enlightening the citizenry, participation, and community are central to the notion of the good democratic order espoused by most of the authors who identify with the adult education movement. In the Johnson era, however, a different but compatible theme seemed to gain more currentness, and that was the notion of equality as embodied in economic opportunity.

The logic behind economic opportunity is that American society had produced an underclass of persons who could not rise in the system because social requisites such as education had been denied them. For a society to be democratic, all members should have an equal chance for socioeconomic success. Hence, the conditions that had produced unequal opportunity, such as prejudice and unequal access to resources, should be eliminated.

Economic opportunity, as a purpose of adult education, found expression in the Economic Opportunity Act of 1964, which provided the first substantial federal funding for adult literacy. In 1966, responsibility for adult literacy was transferred from the Office of Economic Opportunity to the Office of Education by the Adult Education Act (Title III of the 1966 Amendments to the Elementary and Secondary Education Act).

Generally speaking, mainstream adult educators have considered the American system to be basically good, albeit capable of improvement through adult education. Given this general perspective, in this country there has not been an extensive radical tradition that has sought to eliminate the current system and to replace it with another. This is not the case in many developing countries, where the radical ideas of Paulo Freire (1970, 1973) and others have had great impact.

To Promote Productivity

The third general purpose of adult education, to promote productivity, is manifest on two levels. The first is the organizational or institutional level where adult education is conducted to enhance individual performance as a means toward increasing organizational effectiveness. Adult education at this level is typically termed training, staff development, or human resource development, although the term *human resource development* frequently includes other development strategies in addition to education—strategies such as compensation.

Adult education is also used to promote productivity at the societal level, the second level discussed here. At this level human capital theory comes to the fore and is used to justify public subsidy of adult education programs that enhance the productivity of the general economy.

The Organizational Level. Ideas about adult education at the organizational level, particularly in the workplace, have changed substantially since the beginning of the adult education movement in the 1920s. Thinkers such as Lindeman were more concerned with the personal development of the worker than they were with productivity and profit. As Lindeman (1926, p. 26) wrote, "We stand in need of a revolution of the mind—not a mere exchange of power-groups—before an economic revolution can transform industry into a cooperative enterprise, before 'power over' is transposed into 'power with' in industry." Intellectuals such as Lindeman, Hilda Smith, and others believed that a failure to understand the workplace and its relation to society weakened workers and that an understanding of economics, sociology, and politics in relation to real experience would empower the working class. This notion persisted into the 1950s when John Walker Powell (1956, p. 134) wrote, "What should a man know about his means of livelihood? Well, does he know the role of his industry or business or profession within the nation's whole economy? Does he think about what his work contributes to that industry or business or profession? . . . These are samples of what one might suppose would be concerns of the thinking worker."

Today the intellectual tradition of education in the workplace has given way to a utilitarian vision that seeks to maximize organizational effectiveness through the enhancement of employee or member competence. Nadler (1982) distinguishes among *training,* which is designed to improve employees' performance in their present jobs, *education,* which prepares employees for future, well-defined positions in the organization, and *development,* which is learning for the general growth of the individual or organization. Training, which is oriented toward a specific job, is highly systematic in Nadler's Critical Events Model, and in the designs of most other training-oriented adult educators as well. The training process generally begins with job or task analysis which results in setting precise learning objectives. Then methods are selected, training is conducted and evaluated, and the results of evaluation are fed back into the design process. Most authors in the training field caution that training should be used only as an organizational strategy when the problem to be solved results from the worker's inability to perform a task because of a lack of skills or knowledge.

The Societal Level. At the societal level, human capital theory is often used as a justification for the public subsidy of adult education. The logic is that human skills and knowledge attained through education, as well as monetary capital, are vital to economic growth. It follows that public subsidy of education, which promotes general productivity, is a form of social investment because society benefits as well as the individual learner. Public subsidy is warranted when the net benefit to society is more than the individual's private benefit (Beder, 1981). Adult literacy, the Cooperative Extension Service, and adult vocational education have benefited from this point of view.

Adult literacy is a particularly good case in point. For economic growth to occur, a basic infrastructure must be in place. This includes a transportation system, since raw materials must get to the point of production and to the consumer, once produced. The infrastructure also includes an energy delivery system to distribute power production. Most important for adult literacy, however, an adequate infrastructure requires an efficient communication system that can accumulate knowledge as well as transmit it—a system that depends on the written word and spoken English. As a society, we are willing to allocate public monies for adult literacy because in doing so, everyone benefits from the economic growth an efficient communication system promotes.

To Enhance Personal Growth

The notion that the purpose of adult education is to facilitate personal growth is a recurrent theme in the literature of the field and has several manifestations. An idea prevalent in the early adult education movement was that the objective of personal growth was the production of "the whole person" (Jacks, 1936, p. 4). The whole person concept derives from traditional liberal education. The whole person is one who can think rationally and critically, who has a refined aesthetic sense, who is of high moral character, and who maintains good physical conditioning. In the whole person, these qualities are synthesized into a total unity. While production of whole persons had previously been relegated to youth, the early writers on adult education felt the goal should be lifelong.

Similar to the notion of the whole person is the notion that the objective of personal growth is maturity. As Bergevin (1967, p. 7) expressed, "The term 'maturity' is used here to mean the growth and development of the individual towards wholeness in order to achieve constructive spiritual, vocational, physical, political and cultural goals. A maturing person is continually advancing towards understanding and constructive action in the movement from mere survival (the state of lower animals) to the discovery of himself both as a person and responsible member of society." Knowles (1980, p. 29), following Overstreet (1949), noted that maturity includes "linkages with life," personal growth but within a social context. Indeed, the concept of maturity focuses heavily on humans as social animals who must live productively and responsibly within society to be whole and fully functioning.

In the 1950s and early 1960s, the field of adult education was influenced by the humanist school of psychology. The concepts of personal growth espoused by thinkers such as Maslow and Rogers find expression in one of the most widely read books on adult education in the last twenty years, Knowles's *The Modern Practice of Adult Education* (1980). For those of the humanist school, the object of adult education is to assist learners in exercising the quality that separates humans from other animals—the ability to choose. Given this goal, adult education becomes highly learner centered, and the adult educator functions primarily as a facilitator. Maslow (1954) interjected the concept of self-actualization as a goal of personal growth—becoming all one is capable of becoming.

More recently, Mezirow (1981) has proposed the concept of *perspective transformation* as a very significant purpose of adult education. Building on the work of the German philosopher Jurgen Habermas, Mezirow theorizes that through education, adults can (and often need to) undergo entire shifts in consciousness that result in their perceiving themselves and society in completely new and more productive ways.

Personal growth oriented programs operate on at least three levels—on what Bryson (1936) terms the *relational level,* on the *self-actualization level,* and on the *enrichment level.* Relationally oriented programs assist the learner to develop more effective relationships with others—family, co-workers and so on. This type of program includes, for example, leadership training, sensitivity training, and parent effectiveness training. Self-actualization programs attempt to help learners to understand their own potentials and to actualize them. Women's reentry programs are an example. Finally, enrichment programs assist learners in making creative use of leisure time. Many general purpose public school and community college programs are directed toward this purpose.

Philosophy

For the sake of simplifying the complex, the discussion of philosophy here is divided into three traditions: the liberal-progressive, the countercritique, and the personal growth traditions. Each proposes different ends for adult education, and each differs somewhat in its vision for the good society.

Liberal-Progressive. The liberal-progressive tradition of adult education has been part of mainstream thought at least since the 1920s and represents an amalgam of liberal and progressive views. The centrality of this tradition to North American adult education is evidenced by the purposes of adult education discussed in the first portion of this chapter. Having given considerable attention to the liberal-progressive tradition earlier, the treatment will be more brief here.

Liberal and progressive educators generally agree on the prescribed ends for adult education. Adult education has a decidedly social role; its purpose is to abet the democratic order, which, although it is good, can be improved. These ends are evident in many of the authors previously cited such as Hart (1927), Lindeman (1926), Sheats, Jayne, and Spence (1953), and Knowles (1980).

At times, liberals and progressives seem to speak with one voice. Both liberals and progressives provided intellectual leadership in the early adult education movement, and the thinking of many adult educators was influenced by both perspectives. Yet, while both espouse similar ends, there is frequently a difference of opinion with regard to means. Liberal adult educators focus on cultivation of the intellect, which, as Elias and Merriam (1980) point out, includes a knowledge of facts, a systematic grasp of a subject matter or discipline, and the ability to critically assess and analyze. All three characteristics are considered essential if the learner is to achieve the ultimate goal—wisdom. In liberal education, the teacher is viewed as the master of the subject matter who is charged with transferring knowledge to neophyte learners.

Traditionally, liberal education predominated in the realms of secondary and higher education, and many of the early intellectual leaders of adult education, such as Nicholas Murray Butler and James Russell, hailed from this milieu. Many felt that the critical skills fostered by liberal education were essential if adult citizens were to make the informed choices upon which the democratic order depended. Hence it was incumbent upon adult educators to extend liberal education to the masses of adults who had not attended institutions of higher learning or who had been too immature to benefit from it. The Great Books Program was probably the best known liberal adult education program (Elias and Merriam, 1980).

While agreeing that the good democratic society should be the goal of adult education, the progressives believed that learning should proceed from experience—from the situations of adults themselves rather than from abstractions or discipline-based subject matter. This belief mandated a highly learner-centered form of education involving the teacher as a guide and facilitator rather than as the guardian of knowledge. Eduard Lindeman was perhaps adult education's most eloquent proponent of the progressive tradition. His influence on more contemporary adult educators such as Malcolm Knowles has been profound (Knowles, 1987), and Lindeman mounted a consistent critique of liberal education, which he believed to be elitist (Stewart, 1987).

The Countercritique. What has been termed the *countercritique* here owes so much of its substance to Karl Marx that there is a temptation to refer to this tradition as Marxist. However, to do so may not do justice to some from the reproductionist school and to Paulo Freire. Like the thinkers of the liberal-progressive tradition, the countercritique focuses on the relation of education to society. However, unlike the liberal-progressive tradition, those associated with the countercritique consider capitalist democracy to be inherently flawed by structural inequalities that can be redressed only by substantial reordering of the social system.

Although it is difficult to discuss adequately the contribution of Marxist thought to the countercritique in the space provided, it is impossible to ignore Marx. As Carnoy (1982, p. 80) notes, a Marxist vision of society is class based. "Individual behavior is the product of historical forces, rooted in material conditions. As material conditions change, through class conflict, so do relations between individuals in different social positions, positions determined by the social organization of production and each person's relation to production." For Marx, the class structure is a product of the capitalist means of production, and society is necessarily unequal as the dominant bourgeoisie (ruling class) uses its control over the means of production to exploit the proletariat (working class). Resulting social inequality results in endemic class conflict. Youngman (1986) notes that in practice Marxist societies have taken two directions, socialism from above and socialism from below. In the first case, as in the USSR, the emphasis is on state direction through the bureaucratic apparatus. In the second case, as in Cuba perhaps, the emphasis is on mass mobilization of the population. Youngman also notes two intellectual traditions of Marxism. One stresses economic determinism and the eventual collapse of capitalism, while the other, often termed *Marxist humanism,* stresses that humans possess the power of choice and can therefore determine their own fate.

Marx, in fact, said little about education, and the extension of Marxist ideas into education has been left to others. One of them is Gramsci (1971) who theorizes that dominance of the ruling class is exercised through ideological hegemony. More than coercing the proletariat through manipulation of social structure, the dominant class controls the ideological structure of society, which is passed on to subsequent generations through social institutions, most notably education. Intellectuals play a major role in this process. Traditional intellectuals abet the forces of hegemony, while intellectuals who maintain a connection with the working class can, at times, play a major role in formulating a counter hegemony that leads to substantial social reorganization (Carnoy, 1982). It might be said, by extension, that the role of adult education in a Gramscian perspective is to support and assist in the production of intellectuals who are oriented toward the working class.

Following Gramsci's analysis of the role of education in capitalist society, more contemporary writers have focused on the way in which the social structure reproduces itself through education. Apple (1982) notes two traditions. Authors such as Bowles and Gintis (1976) have focused primarily on the relationships among the economic means of production, class structure, and education, and they are decidedly Marxist in orientation. Others, Bourdieu and Passeron (1977) for example, focus more on the reproduction of culture. Reproductionist arguments note that capitalist society must reproduce the class structure, skills, values, and belief systems upon which the system depends. Schooling operates as a filter through which individuals are slotted into various positions in the social order. While some are slotted into working class positions, others are destined to become managers and executives. Bourdieu and Passeron's concept of cultural capital provides insight into how the process works. Through basic childhood socialization, some individuals learn the behavior patterns required of those at the top of the social hierarchy while others learn the behaviors required to function at lower social strata. Language structures, deference behavior, and organizational skills are examples. These behaviors function as cultural capital. Those endowed with more cultural capital have a great advantage in the competition for spaces at the top of the social hierarchy while those with little cultural capital are impoverished in their efforts to rise.

Much of the countercritique of education has focused on the role of elementary, secondary, and higher education. In fact, it might be asked, if individuals are already "reproduced" by the time they have reached adulthood, what is the role of adult education in a reproductionist framework?

The answer may lie in the concept of empowerment, which is central to the thought of Paulo Freire.

Freire is a Brazilian adult educator whose philosophy was developed in relation to the oppression he witnessed in Latin American society. Freire (1970) believes that the oppressed lack critical consciousness of the forces that control their lives, and lacking that consciousness, they are powerless to redress the oppression that dominates their lives. The role of adult education is, through dialogue with learners, to facilitate acquisition of critical consciousness. Once learners become conscious of the forces that control their lives, they become empowered, and empowerment leads to action.

In summation, those of the countercritique consider North American society to be inherently unequal, because the system perpetuates the dominance of favored groups over the less favored. Society, therefore, must be transformed, and one way to achieve this transformation is through adult education, which empowers learners to act in their own behalf.

Personal Growth. While thinkers associated with the personal growth tradition share with those of the liberal-progressive tradition the belief that society is essentially good, they tend to focus on the individual rather than on the society. An orientation to personal growth is closely associated with what Elias and Merriam (1980) call humanism. Humans, as opposed to animals, have the ability to choose; choice implies that learners are responsible for their own actions. The objective of adult education is to assist learners in making choices that maximize their human potential. Since learners are responsible for their actions, they should control learning content, process, and evaluation. As with the progressive tradition, humanist education is highly learner centered, and the educator is more properly a facilitator of learning than a conveyor of knowledge.

An orientation toward personal growth became very evident in the 1950s as the group dynamics movement developed. And Malcolm Knowles (1980), whose ideas are also influenced by progressivism, popularized personal growth ideas with his technology of andragogy in the 1970s.

Recent Trends. An analysis of the literature of adult education leads to the conclusion that thought regarding the purposes and philosophies of adult education has generally revolved around social philosophy, an investigation into the relationship between adult education and human problems. This emphasis remains and is evidenced by new attention to the work of Lindeman (Brookfield, 1984b; Stewart, 1987). Yet, while the thinkers of the early adult education movement generally perceived society as being good, in recent years there has been a more concerted critique of the very foundations of society as embodied in the thought of the reproductionists, neo-Marxists, and Paulo Freire (1970). The thought of those associated with the countercritique, while still retaining its critical element, has started to develop into an operational pedagogy (Freire, 1973; Youngman, 1986). The personal growth tradition also has received recent attention in the work of Mezirow (1981), who, following the German philosopher Jurgen Habermas, has developed a critical theory of adult education focusing on perspective transformation.

While attention to social philosophy still predominates, consideration has also been given recently to analytical philosophy (Lawson, 1979; Patterson, 1979) and to phenomenology (Stanage, 1987). Yet, while currents and crosscurrents, critiques and countercritiques abound in the thought of adult education, it is still possible to derive a set of core principles that form the basic foundation of the field:

1. Whether society is basically good or is inherently flawed, it can and should be improved. In this, adult education can and should play a major role.
2. If individuals, and ultimately society, are to prosper, learning must continue throughout life.
3. Adults are capable of learning and should be treated with dignity and respect.
4. All adults should have access to learning the things required for basic functioning in society.
5. Although adults may or may not differ from preadults in respect to the basic cognitive processes of learning, the context of adult education differs substantially from the context of preadulthood. Hence adults should be educated differentially from preadults.

References

Apple, M. "Reproduction and Contradiction in Education: An Introduction." In M. Apple (ed.), *Cultural and Economic Reproduction in Education: Essays in Class Ideology and the State*. Boston: Routledge & Kegan Paul, 1982.

Apps, J. W. *Improving Practice in Continuing Education*. San Francisco: Jossey-Bass, 1985.

Baker, N. D. "To Base Our Judgement on Facts." In M. Ely (ed.), *Adult Education in Action*. New York: George Grady Press, 1936.

Beder, H. W. "Adult Education Should Not Require Support from Learner Fees." In B. W. Kreitlow and Associates, *Examining Controversies in Continuing Education*. San Francisco: Jossey-Bass, 1981.

Bergevin, P. A. *A Philosophy for Adult Education*. New York: Seabury Press, 1967.

Bourdieu, P., and Passeron, J. *Reproduction*. Beverly Hills, Calif.: Sage, 1977.

Bowles, S., and Gintis, H. *Schooling in Capitalist America*. New York: Harper & Row, 1976.

Brookfield, S., *Adult Learners, Adult Education and the Community*. New York: Teachers College Press, 1984a.

Brookfield, S. "The Meaning of Adult Education: The Contemporary Relevance of Eduard Lindeman." *Adult Education Quarterly,* 1984b, 34 (4), 185–196.

Bryson, L. *Adult Education.* New York: American Book Company, 1936.

Carnoy, M. "Education and the Capitalist State: Contributions and Contradictions." In M. Apple (ed.), *Cultural and Economic Reproduction in Education: Essays in Class Ideology and the State.* Boston: Routledge & Kegan Paul, 1982.

Cremin, L. *American Education: The Colonial Experience.* New York: Harper & Row, 1970.

Darkenwald, G., and Merriam, S. *Adult Education: Foundations of Practice.* New York: Harper & Row, 1982.

Elias, J., and Merriam, S. *Philosophical Foundations of Adult Education.* Melbourne, Fla.: Kreiger, 1980.

Freire, P. *Pedagogy of the Oppressed.* New York: Herder & Herder, 1970.

Freire, P. *Education for Critical Consciousness.* New York: Seabury Press, 1973.

Gramsci, A. *Selections from Prison Notebooks.* New York: International Publishers, 1971.

Hallenbeck, W. "The Role of Society in Education." In G. Jensen, A. Liverwright, and W. Hallenbeck (eds.), *Adult Education: Outlines of an Emerging Field of Study.* Washington, D.C.: Adult Education Association of the U.S.A., 1964.

Hart, J. K. *Adult Education.* New York: Crowell, 1927.

Jacks, L. P. "To Educate the Whole Man." In M. Ely (ed.), *Adult Education in Action.* New York: George Grady Press, 1936.

Knowles, M. S. *The Modern Practice of Adult Education.* (Rev. ed.) New York: Cambridge Books, 1980.

Knowles, M. S. "Foreword." In D. Stewart, *Adult Learning in America: Eduard Lindeman and His Agenda for Lifelong Learning.* Melbourne, Fla.: Kreiger, 1987.

Lawson, K. H. *Philosophical Concepts and Values in Adult Education.* (Rev. ed.) Milton Keynes, Eng.: The Open University Press, 1979.

Lindeman, E. *The Meaning of Adult Education.* New York: Republic, 1926.

Maslow, A. H. *Motivation and Personality.* New York: Harper & Row, 1954.

Mezirow, J. D. "A Critical Theory of Adult Learning and Education." *Adult Education,* 1981, *32* (1), 3–24.

Mortimer, J. T., and Simmons, R. G. "Adult Socialization." *Annual Review of Sociology,* 1978, *4,* 421–454.

Nadler, L. *Designing Training Programs.* Reading, Mass.: Addison-Wesley, 1982.

Overstreet, H. A. *The Mature Mind.* New York: Norton, 1949.

Patterson, R.W.K. *Values, Education and the Adult.* Boston: Routledge & Kegan Paul, 1979.

Powell, J. W. *Learning Comes of Age.* New York: Association Press, 1956.

Sheats, P. H., Jayne, C. D., and Spence, R. B. *Adult Education: The Community Approach*. New York: Dryden Press, 1953.

Stanage, S. *Adult Education and Phenomenological Research*. Melbourne, Fla.: Kreiger, 1987.

Stewart, D. W. *Adult Learning in America: Eduard Lindeman and His Agenda for Lifelong Learning*. Melbourne, Fla.: Kreiger, 1987.

Verner, C. *Adult Education*. Washington, D.C.: Center for Applied Research in Education, 1964.

Youngman, F. *Adult Education and Socialist Pedagogy*. London: Croom-Helm, 1986.

5

The Sociology
of Adult Education

Kjell Rubenson

There is an enormous body of general sociological literature that could be included in a discussion of the sociology of adult education. One way would be to present various basic sociological concepts like stratification, mobility, organizational behavior, group behavior, and so on. Valuable as it may be, this approach will not be attempted here. First, because only a superficial presentation could be provided in the space available, and second, because the sociology of adult education is not about how to use sociological concepts in adult education. Instead, as Bernstein (1971) suggests, its purpose is to explore the ways in which a society classifies, transmits, and evaluates knowledge. Richardson (1986), in the preface to the *Handbook of Theory and Research for the Sociology of Education,* makes a similar observation when he suggests that the force that unifies the modern sociology of education is a preoccupation with two interrelated questions: To what extent does education make society better by making it more egalitarian, and to what extent does education legitimate, and even enhance, existing social and economic inequalities? The purpose of this chapter is to discuss these two questions in relation to adult education. The analysis begins with an overview of two predominant paradigms within the sociology of adult education and a discussion of the concept of hegemony. The purpose of this section of the chapter is to provide a framework in which to address Richardson's two questions focusing on adult education.

Another major difficulty in addressing the topic of this chapter is that the sociology of adult education is not an established scholarly field with a well-defined body of knowledge. In fact, only recently has the North

American adult education literature moved to discuss the sociological aspects of the field. Compared with their European colleagues, North American adult educators, to a larger extent, have defined and conceptualized their research problems within a predominantly psychological framework.

Despite this psychological orientation, there have been sporadic attempts to introduce sociological considerations into the field of adult education in North America. Without entering into historical analysis, it is worth pointing out the change in direction that seems to have occurred in the way sociology and social questions are treated in the field. While the early writing, particularly of Eduard Lindeman, focuses on adult education as a social and collective phenomenon (Lindeman, 1929, 1945), some forty years later a rather different picture emerges. Jack London's chapter in the so-called Black Book (London, 1964) emphasizes the relevance of the study of sociology to adult education practice, and its focus is on the individual. One issue that seemed to disappear in the interim between Lindeman and London was the social or collective aspect of the earlier work—concern for how society develops and analysis of the role of adult education in this process. In its place London presented sociological concepts as technical tools for analysis, devoid of any deeper reflection on adult education as a social phenomenon. Two factors help explain this change in focus. First, Lindeman and London adhere to different theoretical schools. Although not a Marxist, Lindeman applies a perspective that discusses both social structure and class. London's sociology, with its roots in social-interactionism, seems based in what Giddens (1984) would call psychological imperialism. Second, in the 1920s, adult education was not yet professionalized, and it was unusual to write with a professional clientele in mind, whereas the opposite was true at the time of London's chapter. As Jensen argued (1964), adult education is a practical discipline whose ultimate goal is to give to adult education practitioners better control over factors associated with the problems they face. Knox (1985, p. 183), reviewing the situation in the United States twenty years after Jensen's commentary, reflects the same ethos when he states, "One major reason for adult education research is to produce findings the practitioner can use to improve practice."

Recently, there has been an increased interest in the societal aspects of adult education. Several books have been published on this topic in Europe, and some North American scholars now pay serious attention to the critical theory of the Frankfurt School and of Jurgen Habermas. This surge in interest can be attributed to three factors: the increasing importance of adult education within all forms of society, the impact of Third World development on adult education, and the changing perspectives in the social sciences in general and in sociology of education in particular.

The conceptual base for North American educational policies and practice previously emanated from a structural-functional framework emphasizing consensus. Merritt and Coombs (1977) argue that this conceptualization, which supported the notion that educational reform had little to do with politics and social structure, was the greatest stumbling block that had to be removed. Its removal forced social scientists to reconsider both the theoretical frameworks with which they work and their conceptualizations of the phenomena under study. With this loss of political innocence, social scientists had to recognize that the importance of conflict and ideology had been underestimated in their consensus paradigms. The resulting crisis in the social sciences in general, and in the sociology of education in particular, led to the introduction of several alternative paradigms on the relationship between education and society. This shift has not passed unnoticed in adult education (see, for example, Griffin, 1987; Jarvis, 1985).

However, some have argued that as these theories and concepts are based on preadult education, they are not directly applicable to adult education (see, for example, Boyd and Apps, 1980; Kranjc, 1987). With regard to such arguments, two points will be made. The first is that educational sociologists have almost totally ignored education that takes place outside the formal system. As Simon (1985) argues, this affects their conclusions regarding education and social change. For example, by ignoring the less traditional areas of trade unions, popular movements, and voluntary associations, the sociology of education does not account for the role adult education plays as an alternative channel for social mobility.

The second observation, one seldom addressed by adult educators, is that the sociology of education and social theory in general have much to offer adult education. Principles underlying theories on the relationships among education, social structure, and social change hold equally true for preadult and adult education (Alanen, 1978). Not only do the two fields of the sociology of education and adult education have much to offer each other, but they are mutually dependent. It is from this perspective that this chapter is written.

The Two Paradigms Within the Sociology of Adult Education

There are two main contrasting positions in the sociology of education and adult education that determine how issues within this field of study are approached and interpreted: the consensus paradigm and the conflict paradigm. Historically, the consensus approach in the form of functionalist theories has dominated, especially in North America. However, in the past fifteen years, there has been a renewed interest in the conflict paradigm. These two paradigms offer fundamentally different views of the structure of society, and they differ widely in their notions of inequality. Thus they afford two different potential sketches of the role of adult education in society as it relates to stratification, mobility, and social control—that is, who gets what kind of adult education.

A fundamental assumption on which the consensus paradigm rests is that societies cannot survive unless their members share at least some perceptions, attitudes, and values in common (Lenski, 1966). Consensus theories emphasize common beliefs and values; conflict is secondary, and coercion is seen either as temporary or as benefiting society as a whole. Davis (1949, p. 3) sums up the functionalist perspective on inequality this way: "Social inequality is thus an unconsciously evolved device by which societies insure that the most important positions are conscientiously filled by the most qualified persons."

According to this paradigm, an unequal society does not arise out of the vested interests of single individuals or of groups, but out of the needs of society as a whole. Thus inequality is seen not only as inevitable but also as necessary and beneficial to all, since individual survival is contingent upon the survival and well-being of society (Lenski, 1966). In addition, the system of classification in any society is essentially an expression of the value system of that society. The rewards accruing to certain positions are a function of the degree to which their quality, performance, and possessions measure up to the standards set by society.

Those working within the conflict paradigm approach questions of social change, inequality, mobility, and stratification, and hence adult education, from the standpoint of the various individuals and interest groups within society. Social inequality is seen as an expression of the struggle for power, privileges, and goods and services that are in short supply. Conflict theorists emphasize competing interests, elements of domination, exploitation, and coercion. The world *conflict* somewhat erroneously gives the impression that the theory focuses only on dramatic events such as revolution, war, and other forms of open conflict. Its main argument, however, is not simply that society consists of conflict but that open conflict is only the tip of the iceberg (Collins, 1985).

The intellectual contribution of the work of Marx and Engels lies at the core of the conflict paradigm. In classical Marxism, the so-called forces and relations of production are central to class conflict. Material conditions determine human consciousness, and social classes see the world differently depending on their economic interests and on the social conditions to which they are exposed. While classes may see the world differently, the dominant ideas in any society are those of the ruling class.

A common conclusion regarding classical Marxist theory is that because its theory of economic production has proven inadequate, the whole theory is invalidated. However, as Collins points out, the approach developed by Marx and Engels does not have to be abandoned completely, given that their work facilitates an understanding of the political conditions under which it is possible to have liberal reforms, class rights, and the representation of working-class interests.

The two paradigms present different views on the social functions of education. Parsons (1959), the leading consensus theorist, sees schools as instruments of selection. They function as agencies of socialization whose role is the allocation of manpower to appropriate positions. Socialization, in turn, is broken up into the two constituent areas of (1) commitment to the broad values of society, and (2) commitment to the performance of a specific type of role within that society. According to Parsons, the main process of differentiation and selection through education takes place along the axis of achievement. Achievement is different for different people, and it is differentially valued by different people. So, from society's point of view, according to Parsons, allocation of human resources through differentiation and selection, based on widely shared values, is considered fair. Parsons (p. 30) states, "Probably the most fundamental condition underlying this process is the sharing of common values by the two adult agencies involved, the family and the school. In this case, the core is the shared valuation of achievement. It includes, above all, recognition that it is fair to give differential rewards for different levels of achievement, so long as there has been fair access to opportunity, and fair chance that these rewards lead to higher-order opportunities for the successful."

As Parsons notes, this view of education embodies the fundamental value of equality of opportunity in its emphasis on initial equality of access and, at the same time, sanctions selection through differential achievement.

The structural-functionalist view of socialization has been criticized because it treats education as a unified, coherent mechanism in a world of consensus. The functionalist framework is based upon the implicit assumption that the pedagogic actions of families from different social classes, as well as the actions of the schools, work together in a harmonious way to transmit a cultural heritage which is considered the property of the whole society. The assumption is that the educational system promotes mobility in a fair and equal way (Bourdieu, 1977).

In contrast, the conflict theorists maintain that the structure of symbols and of knowledge in educational institutions is that of the dominant culture and is therefore intimately related to the principles and practices of cultural and social control (Apple, 1982). Instead of regarding the education system as being fair and equal, serving society at large, they view education as an instrument for domination that perpetuates the inequalities of society—inequalities reflected in the selection and lack of mobility that occur. According to this perspective, then, schools reproduce and legitimate the ubiquitous power structures of today's society.

Althusser (1971), in his influential essay "Ideology and Ideological State Apparatuses," suggests the school as the most important source in the reproduction of capitalist society. It is through the school that one comes to accept as real one's class identity and thereby one's relation to the mode of production. While the school is seen as relatively autonomous from the economy, it is part of the state apparatus and through this it transmits the ruling ideology. According to Althusser, it is through instruction, social interaction, and other school experiences that ideological and class positions are transmitted.

In the work of Bowles and Gintis (1976), the education system is viewed as an integral element in the reproduction of the prevailing class structure

of society. Because of the structural correspondence between social relationships in the educational system and relationships of production in the economic system, education integrates pupils into the system of the economy.
According to the authors, the structure of social relations in education not
only inures students to the discipline of the workplace, but it also develops
modes of self-presentation, self-image, and social class identification that are
considered crucial in hiring and that therefore work to preserve the division
of labor.

     A third perspective on reproduction is provided in the work of Bour-
dieu (Bourdieu, 1977; Harker, 1984). Bourdieu examines the role of culture
in the reproduction of class hierarchies, and further links culture, class, and
domination. Bourdieu maintains that the culture of the school system is that
of the dominant group, those who control political, economic, and social
resources. According to Bourdieu, then, we have also to talk of cultural
capital. Educational institutions are seen as favoring those who through their
family background already possess cultural capital, which then acts as a selective filter in the reproductive process.

     The extent to which reproduction theories have influenced percep-
tions of how the relationship between education and society is perceived can
be charted in the shift from the overly optimistic, almost naive approach
of the 1950s and 1960s to the critical vision of the 1970s. Nonetheless, there
has been reaction from radical quarters against the determinism of reproduction theories, especially as it is developed in structuralist versions of Marxism. Their criticism suggests that the reproduction thesis does not sufficiently
take into account human agency, people's capacity to act in order either
to resist or to change situations (Giroux, 1983; Simon, 1985). They further
maintain that reproduction theories do not address the possibility of what
Gramsci would call counterhegemonic education. Gramsci's concept of
hegemony is crucial to an understanding of the functions of education and
of the relationship between education and social change—particularly with
regard to adult education.

Hegemony

     The notion of hegemony refers to the way one social class exercises
political, cultural, or economic influence over other classes. However, according to Entwistle and Gramsci (1979), it is the establishment of a moral
or cultural influence, rather than physical coercion or political power, that
is the basis of Gramsci's concept of hegemony. Social control occurs through
wide-ranging consent to and acquiescence in the culture and ideas of the
dominant hegemony. In Marxian terms, hegemony is the base of the false
consciousness of the working class, and, according to Williams (1975), the
importance of Gramsci's work lies in his exploration of ways to break the
bourgeois hegemony over workers' minds.

     Debate in the sociology of education around the notion of counter-
hegemony is mainly concerned with how teachers within the formal educa-

tional system can create similar liberatory strategies (see Giroux, 1983; Shor and Freire, 1987). As Entwistle points out, while Gramsci's writings refer to the schooling of children, the key to his theory of counterhegemonic education lies in the education of adults, especially workers; that is, Gramsci saw counterhegemonic education primarily as something imbricated with the political education of adults. It is with this realization that the distinctive nature of some forms of adult education start to appear, and a base in social theory can be found to justify claims for the uniqueness of adult education. It is important to recognize how this argument differs from previous attempts to claim unique status for adult education.

Most prior claims about the uniqueness of adult education are made on the basis of certain assumptions about the adult learner. As Darkenwald and Merriam (1982, p. 11) pointed out, "there is an increasing agreement that the maturity of the adult learner and the needs and problems of adulthood are what gives adult education its special quality." The theoretical foundation for this line of reasoning is to be found in the tenets of developmental psychology and its importation into the adult education canon, primarily by those working within an andragogical framework (see Jarvis, 1984; Knowles, 1980).

An alternative view, and the one presented in this chapter, has its roots in social theory and concerns human action, social institutions, and their mutual interaction. This view departs from the assumption that adults directly can change social structure, whereas children cannot. This statement should not be interpreted as a defense of subjectivism (which stresses the knowledgeable human agent) as superior to objectivism (which emphasizes the predominance of society over the individual). As Giddens (1984, p. xxi) argues in his analysis of structuration theory, we need to formulate a coherent account of change that acknowledges both structure and agency if we are to come to terms with Marx's aphorism that "men make history but not in circumstances of their own choosing."

Giddens' point, as well as Gramsci's concept of counterhegemony, is well illustrated by a Swedish study on local struggle for industrial democracy that addresses the relationship between adult education and social change. Figure 5.1 represents the situation before the organization of work was radically changed and reflects the link between structure and agency.

In the process of changing the workplace, employees, who were the subjects of the research, came together in study circles to explore ways in which they could strengthen their influence over the organization of work. During this process, the workers created what Svensson calls their own critical knowledge, and their meetings acted to strengthen solidarity among the union members (all workers were unionized). As the workers' solidarity and critical awareness increased, they gradually managed to achieve a more fully realized industrial democracy. This in turn resulted in a further strengthening of solidarity and increased critical insight into the conditions of labor. According to some of the workers interviewed in Svensson's study, the most important element in this spiraling process of solidarity and insight was adult

Figure 5.1. Relationship Between Work Organization,
Knowledge, and Personality Before Democratization.

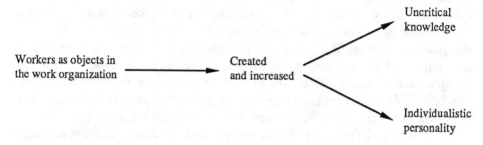

Source: Svensson, 1985, p. 99

education that occurred in the study circles. The workers' point of departure was their own experience, which they related to course material on industrial democracy, and which in turn led them to visualize alternatives to the system in which they were working. These alternatives, the practical result of the interplay of study circle material and everyday experience, were then presented to the employer under the auspices of the local union.

The structural changes that occurred in their workplace also affected the workers' sense of agency; their values, expectations, and demands were higher, and their class awareness and sense of solidarity with the working class was greater. It can be argued that the democratization of the workplace led to the emergence of a local workers' culture that arose out of the development of collective knowledge.

The Svensson study is but one recent example of how, for generations, various groups within social movements have engaged collectively in special kinds of nonformal educational activities as part of their struggle to transform society. Svensson's study offers a vivid illustration of exactly how adult education can be involved in the creation of counterhegemonic knowledge.

In discussing counterhegemony, the role of adult education as an integral part of social movements' broader struggles for change is central. While Scandinavian literature gives considerable attention to this topic, North American literature does not (see Welton, 1987).

However, as Paulston (1980) reminds us, it is important also in North America to examine the extent to which adult education is used by social movements in the struggles to heighten members' consciousness and commitment to their dreams and goals for social change and social justice.

The discussion so far returns us to the old problem of defining adult education, and to the problem of determining what part of adult education can be considered counterhegemonic. In the following section, this issue will be addressed briefly, and the discussion will conclude with an analysis of the social functions of adult education—an analysis informed by the prior discussions of conflict and consensus paradigms and hegemony.

The Boundaries of Adult Education

Most adherents to the tenets of andragogy discuss the uniqueness of adult education in generic terms. Because learning principles stem from assumptions regarding the individual, the context of education is less relevant. Thus when Knowles presents his andragogic principles, the context of education is largely ignored; a social phenomenon, education, is thereby reduced to a psychological phenomenon, learning. If, however, the uniqueness of adult education is defined from a sociological viewpoint, context and structure becomes critical, and any claim for uniqueness of adult education would be specific to certain conditions under which adult education can be considered to be counterhegemonic.

There are various ways of classifying education, including adult education, and one of the most common of these is Philip Coombs's (1973) tripartite division into the formal, nonformal, and informal. By formal education, Coombs refers to the hierarchically structured, chronologically graded education system running from primary school through the university. Coombs does not address noncredit activities for adults occurring within public schools, community colleges, and universities. However, from the point of view of the way in which society classifies and transmits its public knowledge, these activities are part of the same structure as the regular formal system. Nonformal education refers to systematic, organized, educational activity outside the established formal system. By contrast, he associates informal education with all residual educational activity not covered by formal or nonformal education, for example, self-education. There is, however, another category not directly addressed by Coombs—the incidental or unintentional learning that takes place during daily experience.

From the perspective of the conflict paradigm, formal adult education is subject to the same hegemony that governs the preadult education system, although the paradigm does not deny that adults differ in many respects from their counterparts in preadult education.

In adult education and in the lifelong learning literature, nonformal education often is promoted as a liberatory force. However, merely because the education takes place outside the formal system does not mean that it is counterhegemonic. Research on nonformal education and national development in Third World countries has shown that while nonformal education can serve to accelerate political participation, it can also produce a "cooling out" function, lowering aspiration levels and reinforcing existing disparities (Bock and Papagiannis, 1983; La Belle, 1986). The potential ambivalence of nonformal education is obvious if one considers that organized educational activities of both social movements and in-service training belong to this category. As discussed above, educational activities organized through a social movement are the most distinct examples of counterhegemonic activities that can be found. Looking at the other extreme, the findings of the 1983 Smith's survey of employer-sponsored education in the United States reflect a different situation. Education for broad general skills or knowledge was rare and confined generally to white collar workers. Manual workers not only received a disproportionately small share of organized educational activities, but also the training they did receive was more specifically job related. In this context it is interesting to note that despite the uneven access to employer-sponsored education, job-related training is still the dominant form of education among blue collar workers with a short formal education (Morrison and Rubenson, 1987).

Turning to a discussion of informal education, Thomas (1983) touches on a crucial boundary issue. Based on Tough's research on learning projects (1978) and on the philosophy of lifelong education promoted by UNESCO (Cropley, 1980), there has been a change in emphasis, especially in North America, from education to learning. The change is so notable that a recent governmental committee on paid educational leave in Canada recommended that all adults have the right to learn, not the right to an education as might have been expected (Employment and Immigration Canada, 1983). Similarly, in 1985 the World Conference on Adult Education recommended the right to learn (United Nations Educational, Scientific, and Cultural Organization, 1985).

There are several problems with the recent developments. First, learning in this sense is an internal psychological process that is separate from the effort to learn and from the organization of the activity that is supposed to create the circumstances for learning. Second, there are problems resulting from studies purporting to measure the extent of self-directed learning, or self-education. For example, the results of the work of Tough and his followers are interesting in that they show the differences among social groups participating in self-directed learning to be trivial (see Tough, 1978). In this study, self-directed learning appears to be universal and individual without any directly observable effect on the position of disadvantaged groups. But it seems rather useless to establish the existence of self-directed knowledge without isolating its effect on the individual and without examining its potential importance to society.

Ira Shor and Paulo Freire make some valuable observations related to this issue. Discussing the concept of self-directed learners, Freire denies the possibility of individual self-empowerment. If the sense of freedom is not social, then the only thing being exercised is an individualist attitude toward empowerment or freedom. Shor sees the emphasis on self-education in the American educational context as a reflection of the deep roots of individualism, the utopian devotion to "making it on your own" (Shor and Freire, 1987).

It is interesting to relate these comments by Shor and Freire to historical accounts of self-education—accounts reflecting the collective purpose of various social movements. For example Edward Thompson (1963), in *The Making of the English Working Class,* makes reference to the crucial role that self-education played in consciousness raising in radical circles.

In summary, when analyzing adult education and social change, it is important (1) to focus on the extent to which adult education is directed toward either the collective or the individual, (2) to realize that organized adult education, as well as self-education, can be of a collective or individual nature, and (3) to question the extent to which the educational activities are connected to a broader social and political struggle.

To date, two paradigms on education and social change have been reviewed—the concept of hegemony, and boundary issues in adult education. These paradigms provide a rough conceptual framework for the discussion of the social function of adult education in North America as reflected in the organizational structure of adult education, in participation patterns in these activities, and in the consequences for mobility, selection, and reproduction.

Social Functions of Adult Education

From a functionalist perspective it is obvious that adult education does not play the same role in socialization that preadult education does. However, socialization is not only a question of the transmission of knowledge or of the cultural tradition from one generation to the next; it also involves the lifelong process of interaction with the world through which individuals obtain their identities.

According to Brim (1966), the most important differences between childhood and adult socialization involve shifts in emphasis from motivation to ability and knowledge, and from concern with values to a concern with behavior. Society assumes that adults know the values to be pursued in different roles, that they want to pursue them by the socially appropriate means, and that all that remains is to teach them what to do. That this consensus interpretation of adult socialization governs the perceived functions of adult education is obvious in the following quotation from Coolie Verner (1964, p. 88): ''For the purposes of adult education, at least, we can say, therefore, that an adult is a person who has come into that state of life in which he has assumed responsibility for himself and usually for others, and who has concomitantly accepted a functionally productive role in his community . . . This distinction defines the character of adult education, sets the boundaries for research into the changing patterns of responsibility in adult life, and identifies the corresponding functions which adult education should perform. An important problem for research is to formulate learning objectives which are functionally related to the emerging tasks that create the need for learning and provide the motivation for participation in adult education.''

Although adult education has a lesser role to play in the development of values and attitudes, it nonetheless does have a role to play. This role varies from country to country, depending on historical, economic, political, and cultural factors. Societies that are in a revolutionary phase take a view of socialization different from the one proposed by Brim and evident in Verner's writings. Adult education within the formal as well as nonformal system is described and consciously used as an instrument for transmitting new values and for creating a sense of motivation. Where its intent is to break down an older society and to build a new one, moral education becomes a learning priority (see Paulston, 1972).

An emphasis on basic values in general socialization emerges quite clearly in adult education documents from East European countries. Skalka (1977, p. 79) states, "It is in the very system of lifelong communist education that adult education fulfills its significant irreplaceable function," and he further notes that "it raises the qualifications of the working people, contributes to the formation of their ideological, political, specialist and cultural level and the socialist way of life." In these countries, political education forms a major part of adult education (see Fukasz, 1978). The use of adult education to transmit certain desired values and attitudes is also clear in many Third World countries, where a central concern is to dismantle the colonial system. Frequently, mass literacy campaigns have strong ideological roots, as is the case in Algeria, Cuba, Tanzania, and Vietnam.

Dominant groups in countries such as Canada and the United States are not concerned with this type of general resocialization, and consequently adult education is seldom looked upon or referred to as an instrument to influence basic values. The exception is adult education with a marked component of resocialization—for example, immigrant education in America of the 1920s. So predominant were the Americanization programs that adult education became virtually synonymous with Americanization (Knowles, 1977; see Selman, 1987, for information regarding Canada). Other settings where education's influence on certain values is important are remedial education and prison education. The state is the main sponsor for these activities.

Economic-Skilled Labor. In the consensus paradigm, exemplified in the work of Talcott Parsons (1959), young people come to develop a commitment to the performance of a specific role within the structure of society through their interactions in the family and at school. As previously noted, this process of selection and allocation is performed along the axis of achievement and is considered fair. Turning to adult education, in a consensus paradigm, one important function of adult education for an already selected group is the provision of the knowledge and ability needed to maintain an efficient performance of one's allocated adult role for the good of society at large. Thus a pronounced social function of adult education is to maintain and upgrade the human capital necessary for the competitive and efficient economy to work for society's good.

The large increase in the number of adult students in the last twenty-five years is closely linked to changes in the economy and to the influence of two interrelated developments: the increased importance of human capital theory in educational planning and the increased demand for adult education by people wanting to be more competitive in the labor market. The latter is especially true of women, whose increased numbers in credit-granting programs is reflected in their increased labor force participation.

It is in the above perspective that the general worldwide trend toward greater involvement on the part of the formal system of adult education should be understood. This trend is reflected in the following data from the United States. At the beginning of the 1960s, about 36 percent of adult students participated in courses sponsored by community organizations, and 21 percent participated in college and university courses (Johnstone and Rivera, 1965). Since then, the role of community organizations has diminished while that of adult education in formal educational institutions has increased. According to official U.S. statistics, only 9 percent of the adult students participated in courses offered by community organizations, whereas 40 percent attended colleges and universities. Between 1970 and 1980, the number of college students under the age of twenty-five increased by approximately 22 percent, but enrollment for students twenty-five years and older increased nearly 100 percent (Rubenson, 1987).

A recent survey in Canada also points to the central role of formal adult education (Secretary of State, 1984). As many as 50 percent of those identified as participating in organized adult education activities did so within the formal system: public schools, colleges, and universities. From a conflict perspective, this development toward the relatively greater importance of the formal system implies that the dominant culture has taken a firmer grip on North American adult education.

Due to developments linked to the information economy, the economic function of adult education is becoming increasingly important. These days, a nation's competitiveness in the world market is dependent on its human resources, particularly a knowledgeable, skilled intelligentsia. Indicative of this trend is the major international study on education and effective economic performance currently being conducted on behalf of the ministers of finance—not education—under the auspices of the Organization for Economic Cooperation and Development (OECD). This study has focused attention on the further training and education of adults. The demand for this kind of adult education will further increase due to demographic changes that will have a major effect on the availability of labor. With fewer young people entering the labor force, industry will have to rely on retraining of older workers. (For a discussion on population trends, see Chapter One.) Given its predominant emphasis on job-related training (Schutze and Istance, 1987), such education can hardly be considered counterhegemonic in the Gramscian sense, because of its structural situation.

Mobility and Leisure Consumption. In discussing the social functions of adult education, one also has to take into consideration the participation pattern and what it reflects with regard to mobility and the use of adult education as a form of leisure consumption. One profound difference between preadult and adult education is that, with rare exceptions, the latter is governed by self-selection; that is, it is the individual's choice to participate in adult education. Given this, the issue of participation is paramount to our understanding of the social functions of adult education. The general conclusion arrived at by Johnstone and Rivera (1965, p. 231) in their comprehensive study in 1965 is this: "One of the most persistent findings emerging from the inquiry is that a great disparity exists in the involvement in continuing education of segments of the population situated at different levels of the social hierarchy."

A close look at different forms of adult education reveals that the better an education pays off in terms of income, status, occupation, political efficacy, cultural competence, and similar matters, the greater the differences in socioeconomic status between participants and nonparticipants (Rubenson, 1980). The smallest degree of difference is found in self-directed activities of the kind measured by Tough, and the largest is in high-status adult education university programs. In fact, there is evidence to support the argument that elite university programs for adults may prevent social mobility. For mobility to occur, some must be downwardly mobile while others are upwardly mobile. Data show that adults who are on a downward trend (having occupations of a status lower than those of their parents) are using these elite adult programs to reverse this trend (Hopper and Osborn, 1975; Rubenson, 1980).

In short, the institutional structure and participation pattern in formal and nonformal adult education in North America reflects the influence the dominant culture has on the way society classifies, transmits, and evaluates knowledge. The extent to which a social movement selects, classifies, distributes, transmits, and evaluates the movement's knowledge through organized adult education is more limited. One conclusion is that there is no strong visible counterhegemonic adult education structure. This situation reflects what Marx and Engels saw as the dominant class's control over the mental production.

The vast differences among various social groups in their participation in organized adult education cannot entirely be explained by the social functions of adult education. One also has to take into account adult education as a form of cultural consumption. Bourdieu's concept of *habitus* provides a fruitful perspective on this phenomenon. Through socialization within the family, in the school and, later on, in working life, a positive disposition toward adult education becomes a part of some groups' habitus but not of others. It is this phenomenon that Bergsten (1977) refers to when he shows that non-competency-oriented adult education is linked to a leisure style consisting of types of cultural activities usually found in the middle and upper classes. The relationship between habitus and conceptions of adult education is further elaborated by Larsson (1986). He found that nonskilled workers who had short formal educations, and who were occupied in work that offered limited possibilities for growth, were characterized by a very restrictive conception of adult education. According to this restricted view, it is only when participation in adult education results in better and higher paying work that it is meaningful.

Participation has to be understood in relation to the processes that govern the social construction of attitudes toward adult education and in relation to the social functions that adult education is allocated in society. A system of adult education that implicitly takes for granted that the adult is a conscious, self-directed individual in possession of the instruments vital to making use of the available possibilities for adult education—a system that relies on self-selection to recruit the participants—will by necessity widen, not narrow, the educational and cultural gaps in society.

From a consensus point of view, this widening gap can be seen as inevitable and acceptable as long as there has been prior equality of opportunity and as long as the selection is based on achievement. It is this very notion of equality of opportunity that is questioned by the conflict perspective. The latter will argue that the subsequent stress on achievement serves only to legitimate inequality. Pointing to the vicious circle of poor childhood conditions, short formal education, repetitive jobs, reduced opportunities to participate in political life, and so on, conflict theorists maintain that factual opportunities to participate are far from equal.

A crucial issue related to the social functions of education and inequality is the link between supply of and demand for adult education—the processes that govern who gets what kind of adult education. Broström and Ekeroth (1977) claim that in order to understand why the effects of adult education on equity are so small we have to look at the way in which demand determines the adult education supply. They claim that the activities of adult education organizations have been a response to manifest social and individual demands rather than to the needs stemming from inequalities in society. A policy for equity would imply a striving for equalization, which, in turn, entails a wish or a conception that certain groups will consume a supply. This policy raises two problems that are very seldom solved. The first is the stimulation of demand among the groups for which a measure is taken. The second is the understimulation of demand from groups that are not direct objects of a measure. Very probably, the prevailing market forces will make the desired policy impossible to achieve.

Conclusion

In the introduction, I suggested that the two fields of the sociology of education and adult education have much to offer each other. I hope that the discussions in this chapter on adult education as a counterhegemonic force and on the sociologically based claim for uniqueness of adult education, as well as presentation of data on the structure of adult education in North America, have convinced the reader of the fruitfulness of such a connection. Further it should be evident that the focal issue is not a simple question of adult education borrowing concepts, but is rather an examination of the phenomenon of adult education that can provide new insights into the sociology of education and social theory.

A point of departure for this chapter was that a sociology of adult education had to address two questions: To what extent does education make society better by making it more egalitarian, and to what extent does education legitimate, and even enhance, existing social and economic inequalities?

By now it ought to be obvious that scholars working within a conflict perspective will answer differently from those working within a consensus perspective. The former have, through their work, seriously questioned many of the basic assumptions on which the dominant liberal views on adult education are based. In fact, much of the North American data on the structure and participation pattern of adult education seem to support a conflict perspective. However, this does not imply that one has to accept simplistic structuralist theories that do not take human agency into account. The challenge is to develop a perspective that incorporates the imperialism of the subject found in interpretative sociologies with the imperialism of the social object found in functionalism and structuralism (see Giddens, 1984).

The discussion of hegemony questions the usefulness of talking about adult education in a generic sense. As was pointed out above, the answers to the questions become different depending on what kind of adult education one is looking at. The fact that a collectively oriented adult education or self-education seems to play a minor role in North America while the formal system has increased in importance implies that adult education is more a force for maintaining the present power structure than it is a force for changing it.

The psychological domination that characterizes much of North American scholarship in adult education prevents a serious and much needed penetration of the theoretical and empirical problems addressed in this chapter. The sociology of adult education is not something that should be seen as esoteric and separate from main issues in adult education. Instead it can provide a fruitful additional perspective on the teaching process, on program planning, and on participation in adult education.

References

Alanen, A. "Adult Education and Pedagogy." *Adult Education in Finland,* 1978, *15* (1), 3–17.

Althusser, L. "Ideology and the Ideological State Apparatuses." In L. Althusser, *Philosophy and Other Essays.* London: New Left Books, 1971.

Apple, M. *Education and Power.* Boston: Routledge & Kegan Paul, 1982.

Bergsten, W. *Adult Education in Relation to Work and Leisure.* Stockholm: Almquist & Wiksell International, 1977.

Bernstein, B. "On the Classification and Framing of Educational Knowledge." In M.F.D. Young (ed.), *Knowledge and Control.* London: Collier-Macmillan, 1971.

Bock, J. C., and Papagiannis, G. J. *Nonformal Education and National Development: A Critical Assessment of Policy Research and Practice.* New York: Praeger, 1983.

Bourdieu, P. "Cultural Reproduction and Social Reproduction." In J. Karabel and A. G. Halsey (eds.), *Power and Ideology in Education.* New York: Oxford University Press, 1977.

Bowles, S., and Gintis, H. *Schooling in Capitalist America: Educational Reform and the Contradiction of Economic Life.* New York: Basic Books, 1976.

Boyd, R. D., and Apps, J. W. "A Conceptual Model for Adult Education." In R. D. Boyd and J. W. Apps (eds.), *Redefining the Discipline of Adult Education.* San Francisco: Jossey-Bass, 1980.

Brim, O. G. "Socialization Through the Life Cycle." In O. G. Brim and S. Wheeler (eds.), *Socialization After Childhood: Two Essays.* New York: Wiley, 1966.

Broström, A., and Ekeroth, G. *Vuxenutbildning och Fördelningspolitik* [Adult Education and Redistribution Politics]. Uppsala, Sweden: Sociologiska Institutionen, Uppsala Universitet, 1977.

Collins, R. *Three Sociological Traditions.* New York: Oxford University Press, 1985.

Coombs, P. *New Path to Learning.* New York: International Council for Education and Development, 1973.

Cropley, A. J. *Towards a System of Lifelong Education.* Elmsford, N.Y.: Pergamon Press, 1980.

Darkenwald, G., and Merriam, S. B. *Adult Education: Foundations of Practice.* New York: Harper & Row, 1982.

Davis, K. *Human Society.* New York: Macmillan, 1949.

Employment and Immigration Canada. *Learning and Living in Canada.* Ottawa: Minister of Supply and Services Canada, 1983.

Entwistle, H., and Gramsci, A. *Conservative Schooling for Radical Politics.* Boston: Routledge & Kegan Paul, 1979.

Fukasz, G. *Adult Education in Hungary.* Prague: European Center for Leisure and Education, 1978.

Giddens, A. *The Constitution of Society.* Berkeley: University of California Press, 1984.

Giroux, H. *Theory and Resistance in Education.* South Hadley, Mass.: Bergin & Garvey, 1983.

Griffin, C. *Adult Education as Social Policy.* London: Croom-Helm, 1987.

Harker, R. K. "On Reproduction, Habitus and Education." *British Journal of Sociology of Education,* 1984, *5* (2), 117–127.

Hopper, E., and Osborn, M. *Adult Students: Education Selection and Social Control.* London: Francis Pinter, 1975.

Jarvis, P. "Andragogy—A Sign of the Times." *Studies in the Education of Adults,* 1984, *16,* 32–38.

Jarvis, P. *The Sociology of Adult and Continuing Education.* London: Croom-Helm, 1985.

Jensen, G. "How Adult Education Borrows and Reformulates Knowledge of Other Disciplines." In G. Jensen, A. A. Liveright, and W. Hallenbeck (eds.), *Adult Education.* Washington, D.C.: Adult Education Association of the U.S.A., 1964.

Johnstone, J., and Rivera, R. *Volunteers for Learning*. Hawthorne, N.Y.: Aldine, 1965.

Knowles, M. *A History of the Adult Education Movement in the United States*. Melbourne, Fla.: Krieger, 1977.

Knowles, M. *The Modern Practice of Adult Education*. (Rev. ed.) Chicago: Follett, 1980.

Knox, A. "Adult Education Research: United States." In T. Husen and T. N. Postlethwaite (eds.), *The International Encyclopedia of Education*. Vol. 1. Elmsford, N.Y.: Pergamon Press, 1985.

Kranjc, A. "Research in Adult Education: Major Areas of Theory and Inquiry." In C. Duke (ed.), *Adult Education: International Perspectives from China*. London: Croom-Helm, 1987.

La Belle, T. J. *Nonformal Education in Latin America and the Caribbean*. New York: Praeger, 1986.

Larsson, S. *Arbetsupplevelse och Utbildningssyn hos icke Facklärda* [Work Experience and Conceptions of Education Among Nonskilled Workers]. Göteborg, Sweden: Göteborg's Studies in Educational Sciences, 1986.

Lenski, G. *Power and Privilege: A Theory of Social Stratification*. New York: McGraw-Hill, 1966.

Lindeman, E. C. "The Meaning of Adult Education." *Progressive Education*, 1929, *6* (1), 35–39.

Lindeman, E. C. "The Sociology of Adult Education." *Journal of Educational Sociology*, 1945, *19*, 4–13.

London, J. "The Relevance of the Study of Sociology to Adult Education Practice." In G. Jensen, A. A. Liveright, and W. Hallenbeck (eds.), *Adult Education*. Washington, D.C.: American Education Association of the U.S.A., 1964.

Merritt, R., and Coombs, F. "Politics and Educational Reform." *Comparative Education Review*, 1977, *21* (2–3), 247–273.

Morrison, I., and Rubenson, K. *Recurrent Education in an Information Economy*. Toronto: Canadian Association of Adult Education, 1987.

Parsons, T. "The School Class as a Social System: Some of Its Functions in American Society." *Harvard Educational Review*, 1959, *29* (3), 297–318.

Paulston, R. G. "Cultural Revitalization and Educational Change in Cuba." *Comparative Education Review*, 1972, *16* (4), 474–485.

Paulston, R. G. *Other Dreams, Other Schools: Folk Colleges in Social and Ethnic Movements*. Pittsburgh, Pa.: University Center for International Studies, University of Pittsburgh, 1979.

Richardson, J. G. (ed.). *Handbook of Theory and Research for the Sociology of Education*. Westport, Conn.: Greenwood Press, 1986.

Rubenson, K. "Background and Theoretical Context." In R. Hoeghielm and K. Rubenson (eds.), *Adult Education for Social Change*. Lund, Sweden: Liber, 1980.

Rubenson, K. "Adult Education Research: In Quest of a Map of the Territory." *Adult Education*, 1982, *32* (2), 57–74.

Rubenson, K. "Adult Education in Industrialised Countries: Perspectives and Approaches." in C. Duke (ed.), *Adult Education: International Perspectives from China.* London: Croom-Helm, 1987.

Schutze, H. G., and Istance, D. *Recurrent Education Revisited.* Stockholm: Almquist & Wicksell International, 1987.

Secretary of State. *One in Every Five.* Ottawa: Education Support Sector, Secretary of State, 1984.

Selman, G. "Adult Education and Citizenship." In F. Cassidy and R. Faris (eds.), *Choosing Our Future.* Toronto: Ontario Institute for Studies in Education, 1987.

Shor, I., and Freire, P. *A Pedagogy for Liberation.* South Hadley, Mass.: Bergin & Garvey, 1987.

Simon, B. *Does Education Matter?* London: Lawrence & Wishart, 1985.

Skalka, J. "The Theory of Adult Education in the CSSR." In J. Skalka and E. Livecka (eds.), Adult Education in the Czechoslovak Socialist Republic. Prague: European Centre for Leisure and Education, 1977.

Smith, G. "Employer-Sponsored Program." In H. Levin and H. Schuetze (eds.), *Financing Recurrent Education.* Beverly Hills, Calif.: Sage, 1983.

Svensson, L. *Arbetar Kollektivet och Facket* [Worker Collective and the Union]. Lund, Sweden: Lund University, 1985.

Thomas, A. *Learning in Society.* Occasional paper no. 41. Ottawa: Canadian Commission for UNESCO, 1983.

Thompson, E. P. *The Making of the English Working Class.* Middlesex, Eng.: Penguin Books, 1963.

Tough, A. "Major Learning Efforts: Recent Research and Future Directions." *Adult Education,* 1978, *28* (4), 250–263.

UNESCO (United Nations Educational, Scientific, and Cultural Organization) *Final Report International Conference on Adult Education.* Paris: UNESCO, 1985.

Verner, C. "Definition of Terms." In G. Jensen, A. Liveright, and W. Hallenbeck (eds.), *Adult Education.* Washington, D.C.: Adult Education Association of the U.S.A., 1964.

Welton, M. "On the Eve of a Great Mass Movement: Reflections on the Origins of the Canadian Association of Adult Education." In F. Cassidy and R. Faris (eds.), *Choosing Our Future.* Toronto: Ontario Institute for Studies in Education, 1987.

Williams, G. *Proletarian Order.* London: Pluto Press, 1975.

6

International and Comparative Adult Education

Peter S. Cookson

This chapter has as its purpose the definition and conceptualization of the terms *international adult education* and *comparative adult education*. Although these terms have much in common, notable differences in their meanings preclude their being used interchangeably. To explain the relevance of these terms, this chapter is subdivided into the following four parts: (1) definition of terms, (2) contributions of comparative education, (3) overview of international dimensions of adult education, and (4) brief comment on the value of international and comparative adult education for adult educators.

Definitions

There is much ambiguity and confusion regarding the meaning of international adult education and comparative adult education. This section presents the definitions not only of these key terms, but also of a related term, *international studies* (in adult education).

International Adult Education. Building upon a definition of adult education proposed by Houle (1972), two distinct though interrelated definitions are proposed:

1. International adult education is the process whereby men and women (in individual, group, or institutional settings) participate in or implement organized learning activities that have been designed to increase their knowledge, skill, or sensitiveness, and that take place across international borders. This definition refers to international adult education as a field of practice in other countries.

2. International adult education is the systematic study of the process whereby men and women (in individual, group, or institutional settings) participate in or implement organized learning activities that have been designed to increase their knowledge, skill, or sensitiveness, and that take place across international borders. This definition refers to international adult education as a field of research that focuses on adult education as it is manifest in other countries.

Comparative Adult Education. This second term is defined as the area of study that (1) focuses on provision of organized learning activities for men and women across international or intercultural boundaries, and (2) utilizes comparative methods of study. Given the relatively few individuals worldwide who are actively and continuously engaged in such studies, comparative adult education could not yet, with any accuracy, be considered a field of study; hence the more appropriate reference to an area of study that constitutes a subset of each of two parent fields: (1) international comparative education and (2) adult education.

Virtually all comparative adult education research may be considered international adult education research, but the converse would only be true to the extent comparative methodologies are used. From the point of view of observers in other countries, cross-cultural adult education studies could properly be cited as instances of both comparative and international adult education research. One notable example would be Roberts's (1982) comparison of adult education policies and practices in the Canadian provinces of Alberta and Quebec.

International Studies (in Adult Education). The term *international studies* refers to organized educational activities designed to assist men and women to become more knowledgeable about and sensitive to the cultures and people of other lands and the global issues that affect human life. Although understanding the foreign policy of one's own country, familiarity with world affairs, and awareness of international interdependence are aspects that permeate each of the concepts defined above, for international studies, they are a central focus.

Contributions of Comparative Education

If what people in international and comparative education say and do is any indication, it is clear that those fields exclude from their purview organized learning activities outside of schools by people beyond the normal age of school attendance. This is not to say that the contributions of international and comparative education to international adult education have not been substantial. Some of the more important contributions are described in the following list.

1. The process of adoption of new practices and the conducting of studies of education in other countries can be improved by following systematic

procedures developed through the study of international and comparative education.

2. Specific research methods that have been developed and refined by comparative educationists can be applied to the field of adult education.
3. The sizeable international community of social science scholars and educational policymakers and practitioners who share a common commitment to the improvement of education (despite the preponderant emphasis on schooling for children and youth) may form alliances based on international and comparative adult education.
4. Publication outlets for comparative education materials leave open the possibilities for submissions relating to education across the human life cycle. (For several years the *Comparative Education Review* has featured references to adult education topics in its international and comparative education bibliography, which appears in each issue.)

According to Noah and Eckstein (1969), the development of comparative education has been marked by five distinct linear and historical stages: (1) travelers' tales, (2) educational borrowing, (3) international cooperation, (4) factors and forces, and (5) social science explanation. Although these so-called stages lack conceptual precision and nonmutual exclusivity (Epstein 1983), they can still serve as a set of developmental orientations toward the field of comparative education, as well as possible analogues for the development of international adult education.

International Dimensions of the Adult Education Movement

The aim of this section is to highlight the interface between the historical development of international and comparative adult education. The same five stages Noah and Eckstein used to categorize elements in the development of comparative education are used as a framework within which to note different orientations in the development of international and comparative adult education.

Travelers' Tales. Although the documentary record is fragmentary, first- and second-hand, in-person means of dissemination of information about programs and practices of adult education in other countries have been supplemented in three primary ways: (1) publications of international periodicals such as the *Internationales Jahrbuch der Erwachsenenbildung (The International Yearbook of Adult Education),* edited by Joachim H. Knoll (1986) in West Germany, and *Convergence,* the journal published by the International Council for Adult Education; (2) presentations and symposia at national and international conferences by American adult educators who have traveled to other countries, as well as by adult educators from other countries; and (3) travel and study tours for adult educators organized both by national adult education organizations and by programs of graduate programs in adult education at major U.S. and Canadian universities.

Educational Borrowing. Pre-Industrial Revolution forms of adult education such as self-directed study, apprenticeship, practical how-to-do-it handbooks, autonomous group study, early mass literacy campaigns, military training, literacy institutes, and newspapers were developed and widely diffused throughout Europe. Many of those responsible for replanting these practices in the New World were immigrants who desired to retain valued features of their Old World culture. Many of the English and European nineteenth and early twentieth century institutions that were brought to the New World (for example, the mechanics' institute, the Young Men's Christian Association, university extension, and the Workers' Education Association) did not flourish. Although the inflexibility of the mechanics' institute led to its demise everywhere, the YMCA not only survived but prospered similarly in countless countries. North American university extension at first suffered a fate similar to early English university extension, only to resprout in a markedly different form two decades later and, in that form, to extend worldwide.

The borrowing of ideas led to the establishment of at least two significant national adult education associations in North America. Although adult education in Britain was recognized as an instrument of public social policy with publication of the so-called 1919 Report (Adult Education Committee, Ministry of Reconstruction, 1919), the term *adult education* was practically unknown in the United States. But Frederick P. Keppel, then serving as president of the Carnegie Foundation, was impressed by the potential for adult education as described in the 1919 Report and by a book of essays, *The Way Out* (Stanley, 1923), as well as by what he had learned from visiting Danish folk high schools. Keppel decided to raise the question of the extent and importance of the field in the United States. He and his staff subsequently appointed an advisory committee on adult education which, with financial backing from the Carnegie Foundation, went on to form, in 1926, the American Association for Adult Education, one of the organizational predecessors to the American Association for Adult and Continuing Education. In 1932, the Carnegie Foundation extended similar support for the founding of the Canadian Association for Adult Education.

Despite the success of the Scandinavian folk high school movement pioneered in Denmark during the last century by Bishop N.F.S. Grundtvig, efforts to transplant that innovation to North America were futile. The Danish folk high school, however, served as inspiration to Miles Horton, a young American theology student eager to launch a school for oppressed people. In 1931, he went to Denmark where he learned Danish and "studied the trade union movement, the farmers' cooperatives, and the folk colleges" (Adams, 1979, p. 217). Returning to Tennessee, he won sufficient support to found the Highlander Folk School, a residential educational center which was to become an influential and controversial catalyst in the South for workers' education and union organizing efforts in the thirties, for the civil rights movement in the fifties and sixties, for community organizing in Appalachia in the seventies, and for the environmental movement in the eighties.

Yet another North American example of the power of borrowing ideas is provided by the experience of Father Jimmy Tompkins who, in 1921, while on the faculty of St. Francis Xavier University in Nova Scotia, wrote a fiery tract to arouse to action the economically depressed fishermen, miners, and farmers of the Maritime Provinces in Canada. He drew inspiration not only from the Danish folk high schools, but also from university extension styled after the University of Wisconsin, from the workers' education movement in England, from cooperativism, and from the credit union movement in Quebec. That tract, "Knowledge for the People," (Tompkins, 1921), and his tireless devotion to its implementation, led to a subsequent lifelong collaboration with the charismatic Father Moses Coady and to the founding of the Antigonish Movement, which was reported to have transformed the Maritimes' rural economy for countless mining, fishing, and farming communities in the 1930s. A lasting part of the Tompkins and Coady legacy includes the world-renowned Coady Institute which, since the 1950s, has been engaged in the dissemination of cooperativism and adult education for community development throughout the Third World.

Other twentieth century innovations that have been borrowed by the United States and Canada from England include the Workers' Education Association and various forms of the British Open University. The Open University was begun in England by Lord Harold Wilson, leader of the Labour Party, who drew inspiration from correspondence courses, from the use of radio in Russian higher education, and from teaching films by the *Encyclopedia Britannica* (McArthur, 1974). Innovations that have been diffused from North America to other parts of the world include correspondence instruction, American-style university extension, agricultural extension, human resource development, community schools, and experiential learning. While with the World Council of Churches in the middle to late 1970s, Brazilian Paulo Freire's (1970) ideas concerning conscientization (the heightening of one's critical awareness) through dialogue and praxis challenged many literacy and adult basic education practitioners in both Canada and the United States. Freire's influence was further disseminated via the work of World Education, a private, nonprofit development assistance agency that grew out of training programs at India's Literacy House. It was founded in 1951 to focus on design and implementation of community-level education projects—at first overseas, and subsequently in North America, to help teachers of adults adopt consciousness-raising strategies. Yet another example of ideas borrowed from outside North America is the efforts of the Kettering Foundation to encourage application of Swedish study circle techniques to citizenship and workers' education in North America (Oliver, 1987). (See also Chapter Thirty-Five.)

International Cooperation. This third orientation, treated in detail elsewhere (Cookson, 1987), has been manifest in the joint involvement of adult educators from nations throughout the world in international governmental and nongovernmental organizations, international conferences, and other cooperative ventures. One pioneering but short-lived experiment to "bring into cooperation and mutual relationships the adult education movements and institutions of the world" (Jennings, 1984, p. 55) was the World Association for Adult Education, founded in 1919 with headquarters in London. Unfortunately, "It never really came alive as an international organ, since its membership was composed largely of individuals, in the absence of effective national organizations for adult education in most of the countries from which they came" (Peers, 1958, p. 247).

Before the World Association disappeared in the 1930s, the American Association for Adult Education, one of its staunch supporters, sent delegates to world conferences and had representatives on the executive board, giving force to the mission statement of the Association as explained in Article II of its constitution: "Its object shall be to promote the development and improvement of adult education in the United States and to cooperate with similar associations in other countries" (Cartwright, 1935, p. 17).

After World War II, interest in cooperation with adult educators in other countries was manifest by the support given in North America to the formation of the United Nations Educational, Scientific, and Cultural Organization (UNESCO), for which one central plank was cooperation among nations. At that organization's first two world assemblies, resolutions were approved for the sponsorship of an international conference on adult education. In spite of the worldwide tensions caused by the cold war between East and West, UNESCO-sponsored international conferences promoted a central theme of international cooperation among adult educators (Hely, 1962; Kidd, 1974). At the first international conference on adult education in the postwar period, attended by participants from twenty-nine countries at Elsinore, Denmark in 1949, cooperation was perceived as a way to achieve peace and mutual understanding among nations, especially those of Eastern and Western Europe. At the second conference in Montreal in 1960, attended by representatives from fifty-one countries, recommendations were approved to promote cooperation to combat more effectively the worldwide specter of illiteracy (UNESCO, 1985a).

Four years after the third international adult education conference at Tokyo, attended by nearly 400 representatives from eighty-five countries, the UNESCO General Session in Nairobi approved a "Recommendation on the Development of Adult Education." The recommendation called for exchange of information, dissemination of research findings, and sharing of experience and expertise (UNESCO, 1985b). At the fourth conference, in 1985 at Paris, attended by representatives from 122 member states, exchange of information among member states was identified as a way to resolve the major problems of the contemporary world (UNESCO, 1985c). Additional forms of international cooperation and exchange stressed at the Paris conference included international conferences to address those problems, pooling of experience and expertise, dissemination of research findings, and international cooperation in the provision of aid and assistance.

Another way UNESCO facilitated cooperation and exchange was to disseminate international adult education directories (Giere and Maehira, 1980; UNESCO, 1982; UNESCO, 1984; UNESCO, 1985d) that listed national boards and councils, training and research institutions, information and documentation services, and adult education periodicals. To promote international cooperation, UNESCO circulates a newsletter, *UNESCO Adult Education Information Notes,* available without charge to adult educators worldwide.

Other contributions of international quasi-governmental organizations to international adult education cooperation and exchange during the past twenty years include the concepts of *lifelong education,* once claimed by UNESCO (Faure, 1972) to be the overarching concept for all education throughout the entire life cycle; *recurrent education,* which has been promoted by the Organization for Economic Cooperation and Development (1973); and *education permanente,* which has been a central focus of the Council of Europe (1973).

One nongovernmental organization that has promoted international cooperation has been the International Congress of University Adult Education (ICUAE) organized by university adult educators from the United States, Canada, and other countries immediately prior to the Montreal UNESCO conference. At its 1965 conference, the ICUAE stressed the importance of studies of adult education and called for a conceptual framework to facilitate such comparative study. In 1966, the ICUAE organized the first international conference on comparative adult education at Exeter, New Hampshire (Bennet, Kidd, and Kulich, 1975; Liveright and Haygood, 1968).

International cooperation has also been the watchword at four world assemblies of adult education convened by the International Council for Adult Education, a unique international, nongovernmental, voluntary partnership of people—both national and regional adult education organizations "working together for the education of adults for responsible, human-centred social and economic development" (International Council for Adult Education, n.d.). Founded in 1973 by the internationally respected Canadian adult education professor J. Roby Kidd, the organization maintains a small secretariat in Toronto, Ontario, and has grown to include national adult education organization members from more than eighty countries. Based on the premise that "adult education must involve itself with the critical social issues that affect the lives of people everywhere" (International Council for Adult Education, n.d.), the ICAE focuses on issues such as peace; the advancement of women; self-reliant advancement of marginal, oppressed peoples; universal literacy; and universal access to education, basic services, and employment. A central tenet is that people should be empowered to act locally and think globally. As explained by Sullivan (1985, p. 2657), "The work of the Council is carried out in all regions of the world through member associations, networks, and collaborative projects that are supervised by individuals in various countries. It includes research, training, information exchange, and advocacy. It involves the organization of international seminars and workshops, comparative studies, the publication of a quarterly journal (*Convergence*), occasional papers, reports, and a newsletter.''

The pace of international cooperation appears to have quickened during the 1980s—particularly between adult educators in North America and Western Europe and among adult educators who belong to global informal networks affiliated with the International Council for Adult Education. The combined efforts of the Canadian Association for the Study of Adult Education, the International Adult Education Unit of the American Association of Adult and Continuing Education (as well as the International Adult Education Sections of its two organizational predecessors), the International Task Force of the North America-based Commission of Professors of Adult Education, and the Standing Conference on University Teaching and Research in the Education of Adults resulted in publication of the *International Adult Education Exchange and Cooperation Directory* (Cookson, 1984). This directory contains the indexed names of 235 adult educators who indicated a commitment to support multiple forms of exchange and cooperation with counterparts in other countries. Yet another organization, the International League for Social Commitment in Adult Education (1987), which was founded in 1984, has facilitated the formation of informal networks in different countries to support each others' efforts (1) to raise consciousness about social issues, (2) to engage in action that promotes social commitment, and (3) to support the work of affiliated groups and chapters throughout the world with information and assistance. ILSCAE activities include a newsletter, annual international conferences, and support of informal issues-oriented networking among adult education (*educación popular*) practitioners in both industrialized and Third World countries.

Forces and Factors. Most writing pertaining to adult education in other countries has fallen into the category of international adult education rather than comparative adult education. The pattern appears to have been set early in the history of the field with publication in 1929 of the *International Handbook of Adult Education* by the World Association for Adult Education, in which serial descriptions by adult educators in twenty-eight countries constituted the main thrust. Similarly in his *Quest of Knowledge: A Historical Perspective on Adult Education,* Grattan (1955) traced the history of the movement in Britain and the United States, but nowhere did he analyze or discuss the common factors and forces responsible for the differences and similarities noted on both sides of the Atlantic.

A notable exception to the generalization that comparisons are rare is Peers's (1958) *Adult Education: A Comparative Study* in which he detailed the history of the adult education movement in Britain and then compared it with "international aspects of adult education work" worldwide (p. 249). Likewise, in her *Patterns of Adult Education,* Ulich (1965) sketched the historical development of adult education in four countries: Denmark, England, the Federal Republic of Germany, and the United States. Her overall conclusion

was simply that adult education reflects the social conditions in each country—
"even more than do the other levels of education" (p. 202). In his *Strategies for Adult Education: Practices in Western Europe,* Titmus (1981) serially mapped the adult education terrain in nine Western European countries. Except for a brief introductory chapter, he left it for the reader to compare the different adult education systems. Such works comprise examples of international rather than comparative adult education.

More in the realm of international adult education than comparative adult education, one of the most ambitious projects in recent years has been the "Adult Education in Europe" series sponsored by the European Centre for Leisure and Education in Czechoslovakia, with financial backing from UNESCO. At least twenty volumes were published from 1977 to 1984, each featuring a country in either Central or Western Europe. Presumably the aim was for each national study to follow a similar outline, but, varying greatly in their academic rigor, several merely echo official governmental and political party ideology rather than demonstrate dispassionate, critical analysis. Numerous country descriptions of adult education also appeared in Husen and Postlethwaite's (1985) *The International Encyclopedia of Education.* Three recent compilations of commentaries regarding selected aspects of adult education in one country are *Adult Education in China,* edited by St. John Hunter and Keehn (1985), *Adult Education: International Perspectives from China,* edited by Duke (1987), and *China: Lessons from Practice,* edited by Wang, Lin, Sun, and Fang (1988).

Other researchers have focused on a single institution in one or more countries. One such thorough study of a national adult education form, social education, is J. E. Thomas's (1985) *Learning Democracy in Japan: The Social Education of Japanese Adults.* Similarly focusing on a single institution, Taylor, Rockhill, and Fieldhouse (1985), in their *University Adult Education in England and the U.S.A.,* compared university extension programs in relation to the liberal tradition in both English and U.S. societies. In her study, *Between Struggle and Hope: The Nicaraguan Literacy Crusade,* Miller (1985) described the historical and ideological context for a nation's efforts to rid itself of mass ignorance resulting from decades of oppression by the U.S. government-sanctioned Somoza dictatorship.

Three works at the beginning of the 1980s demonstrated a truly comparative research vein. Peterson and others (1982) introduced a framework that enabled the authors in *Adult Education and Training in Industrialized Countries* to focus on principal components of adult education opportunities for particular population groups: workers, older persons, women entering the labor force, parents, and undereducated adults. Following his synthesis and comparative analysis, Peterson highlighted implications for national adult education policy in the United States. In *Comparative Adult Education: Practice, Purpose and Theory,* Harris (1980) not only detailed what he called the "comparative perspective" and the "international comparison and method," but he also exemplified such analysis in various types of case studies. In *Com-*

paring Adult Education Worldwide, edited by Charters (1981), almost all of the chapter authors (from nine countries) fulfill a dual purpose of presenting specific global issues while at the same time demonstrating a particular approach to comparative adult education research.

Taking a global problems and issues (forces and factors) orientation, Lowe's (1975) *Education of Adults: A Global Perspective* constitutes one of the most comprehensive comparative adult education studies. The initial basis for the book was Lowe's analysis of country reports submitted prior to UNESCO's third international conference in Tokyo; but in his subsequent discussions of numerous international issues, he goes far beyond those reports. A more recent discussion of global problems and issues was presented by Knox (1988) in his *International Perspectives on Adult Education.*

Social Science Explanation. Most works classified as either international adult education or comparative adult education tend to rely on common sense interpretation of events rather than on social science explanations. One notable exception, which draws on political science concepts and analysis, is Styler's (1984) *Adult Education and Political Systems* in which he explores and compares the role of the state in the development of adult education in what he calls the "liberal first world democracies," the "communist states," and the "developing countries." A second example, which draws on both political science and sociological analysis, is Rubenson's (1980) analysis of the role of adult education in promoting social, cultural, economic, and political equality in North American and Swedish contexts. In contrast to the other orientations guiding international and comparative adult education work, this social science explanation is far less developed vis-a-vis those whose focus is international aspects of child and youth education.

In sum, although many adult educators appear to be intensively involved in different forms of international adult education, relatively few are actively engaged in comparative adult education. Several reasons account for international adult education and comparative adult education not being more developed as an area of study: (1) Financially strained governments tend not to value the collection of statistics relative to adult education provision. (2) Because so much of adult education, particularly in the industrialized democracies, occurs in voluntary association and in non-government settings, efforts to collect data on such efforts are sometimes fiercely resisted. (3) In many countries, particularly poorer countries, information relative to adult education is often nonexistent. (4) There is a lack of equivalence in parallel data sets and there is confusion arising from the use of common words to refer to highly dissimilar activities in different countries, as has been amply illustrated by the term *community education,* which in the United States refers to liberal school-based education, while in the United Kingdom it refers to liberating education (Brookfield, 1985). (5) Few of those who are engaged in adult education have an academic grounding in the social sciences. Hence, their explanations of adult education phenomena tend to rely on educational and common sense explanations, rather than on social science analyses. Being grounded in the field of practice, such practitioners do not typically place a high priority on empirical research.

Value of International and Comparative Adult Education Studies

For adult education, the value of international adult education as an area of practice and as an area of study, and of comparative adult education as an area of study, is incalculable. This review of some of the international dimensions of the adult education movement suggests that the adult education movement itself is intertwined with experiences obtained on other shores—both in the past and continuing into the future. Kidd (1981) provided a thoughtful response to the question, "Why study adult education?" To the extent that adult education practitioners and scholars are knowledgeable about adult education elsewhere and to the extent to which they themselves are engaged in systematic, comparative analysis of their own and others' practice—both within and beyond their own national boundaries—to that same extent they are empowered to (1) continuously develop their overall adult education philosophy; (2) initiate meaningful reforms needed to confront fundamental issues surrounding the practice and study of adult education; and (3) introduce improvements in the ways they conceptualize the process of adult education.

References

Adams, F. "Highlander Folk School: Social Movements and Social Change in the American South." In R. G. Paulston, *Other Dreams, Other Schools: Folk Colleges in Social and Ethnic Movements.* Pittsburgh, Pa.: University Center for International Studies, University of Pittsburgh, 1979.

Adult Education Committee, Ministry of Reconstruction. *The 1919 Report: The Final and Interim Reports of the Adult Education Committee of the Ministry of Reconstruction.* London: His Majesty's Stationery Office, 1919.

Bennet, C., Kidd, J. R., and Kulich, J. (eds.). *Comparative Studies in Adult Education: An Anthology.* Syracuse, N.Y.: Syracuse University Publications in Continuing Education, 1975.

Brookfield, S. "Community Adult Education: A Comparative Analysis of Theory and Practice." *Comparative Education Review,* 1985, *29* (2), pp. 232-239.

Cartwright, M. A. *Ten Years of Adult Education: A Report on a Decade of Progress in the American Movement.* New York: Macmillan, 1935.

Charters, A. N., and Associates. *Comparing Adult Education Worldwide.* San Francisco: Jossey-Bass, 1981.

Cookson, P. S. *International Adult Education Exchange and Cooperation Directory,* Vancouver: Adult Education Research Centre, University of British Columbia, 1984.

Cookson, P. S. "The Case for International Cooperation and Exchange." In C. Klevins (ed.), *Materials and Methods in Continuing Education*. Los Angeles: Klevens Publications, 1987.

Council of Europe. Council for Cultural Cooperation. *Permanent Education: Final Report*. Strasbourg, France: Council of Europe, 1973.

Duke, C. (ed.). *Adult Education: International Perspectives from China*. London: Croom-Helm, 1987.

Epstein, I. "Currents Left and Right: Ideology in Comparative Education." *Comparative Education Review*, 1983, *27* (1), 3-29.

Faure, E. *Learning to Be*. Paris: UNESCO, 1972.

Freire, P. *Pedagogy of the Oppressed*. New York: Seabury, 1970.

Giere, U., and Maehira, Y. *Directory of Writers on Lifelong Education*. Hamburg, W. Ger.: UNESCO Institute for Education, 1980.

Grattan, C. H. *In Quest of Knowledge: A Historical Perspective on Adult Education*. New York: Association Press, 1955.

Harris, W.J.A. *Comparative Adult Education: Practice, Purpose and Theory*. London: Longman, 1980.

Hely, A.S.M. *New Trends in Adult Education*. Paris: UNESCO, 1962.

Houle, C. O. *Design of Education*. San Francisco: Jossey-Bass, 1972.

Husen, T., and Postlethwaite, T. N. (eds.) *The International Encyclopedia of Education*. Elmsford, N.Y.: Pergamon Press, 1985.

International Council for Adult Education. *A Partnership in Development*. Pamphlet. Toronto, Ontario: International Council for Adult Education, n.d.

International League for Social Commitment in Adult Education. *Newsletter*, 1987, *1* (4), 1-8.

Jennings, B. "Albert Mansbridge and the First World Association for Adult Education." *Convergence*, 1984, *17* (4), 55-63.

Kidd, J. R. *A Tale of Three Cities: Elsinore-Montreal-Tokyo: The Influence of Three UNESCO World Conferences upon the Development of Adult Education*. Syracuse, N.Y.: Syracuse University Publications in Continuing Education, 1974.

Kidd, J. R. "Research." In A. N. Charters and Associates, *Comparing Adult Education Worldwide*. San Francisco: Jossey-Bass, 1981.

Knoll, J. H. *Internationales Jahrbuch der Erwachsenenbildung* [The International Yearbook of Adult Education]. Frankfurt, W. Ger.: Bohlau Verlag Koln Wien, 1986.

Knox, A. B. *International Perspectives on Adult Education*. Columbus: ERIC Clearinghouse on Adult Vocational and Career Education, Ohio State University, 1988.

Liveright, A. A., and Haygood, N. (eds.). *The Exeter Papers: Report of the First International Conference on the Comparative Study of Adult Education*. Boston: Center for the Study of Liberal Education for Adults, 1968.

Lowe, J. *Education of Adults: A Global Perspective*. Paris: UNESCO, 1984.

McArthur, B. "An Interim History of the Open University." In J. Tunstall (ed.), *The Open University Opens*. Boston: Routledge & Kegan Paul, 1974.

Miller, V. *Between Struggle and Hope: The Nicaraguan Literacy Crusade*. Boulder, Colo.: Westview Press, 1985.

Noah, H. J., and Eckstein, M. A. *Toward a Science of Comparative Education.*
New York: Macmillan, 1969.

Oliver, L. P. *Study Circles: Coming Together for Personal Growth and Social Change.*
Washington, D.C.: Seven Locks Press, 1987.

Organization for Economic Cooperation and Development. *Recurrent Education: A Strategy for Lifelong Learning.* Paris: Organization for Economic
Cooperation and Development, 1973.

Peers, R. *Adult Education: A Comparative Study.* Boston: Routledge & Kegan
Paul, 1958.

Peterson, R. E., and others. *Adult Education and Training in Industrialized Countries.* New York: Praeger, 1982.

Roberts, H. *Culture and Adult Education: A Study of Alberta and Quebec.* Edmonton: University of Alberta Press, 1982.

Rubenson, K. "Background and Theoretical Context." Unpublished manuscript, University of British Columbia, 1980.

St. John Hunter, C., and Keehn, M. M. (eds.). *Adult Education in China.*
London: Croom-Helm, 1985.

Stanley, O. *The Way Out.* Oxford, Eng.: Oxford University Press, 1923.

Styler, W. E. *Adult Education and Political Systems.* Nottingham, Eng.: Department of Adult Education, University of Nottingham, 1984.

Sullivan, J. "International Council for Adult Education." In T. Husen and
T. N. Postlethwaite (eds.), *The International Encyclopedia of Education.* Vol.
5. Elmsford, N.Y.: Pergamon Press, 1985.

Taylor, R., Rockhill, K., and Fieldhouse, R. *University Adult Education in
England and the U.S.A.: A Reappraisal of the Liberal Tradition.* London: Croom-
Helm, 1985.

Thomas, J. E. *Learning Democracy in Japan: The Social Education of Japanese
Adults.* London: Sage Publications, 1985.

Titmus, C. *Strategies for Adult Education: Practices in Western Europe.* Chicago:
Follett, 1981.

Tompkins, J. J. "Knowledge for the People." Pamphlet originally published
1921. In J. R. Kidd (ed.), *Learning and Society.* Toronto: Canadian Association for Adult Education, 1963.

Ulich, M. E. *Patterns of Adult Education: A Comparative Study.* New York:
Pageant Press, 1965.

UNESCO (United Nations Educational, Scientific, and Cultural Organization). *Directory of Adult Education Training and Research Institutions.* Paris:
UNESCO, 1982.

UNESCO. *Directory of National Adult Education Co-ordinating Bodies.* Paris:
UNESCO, 1984.

UNESCO. *The Development of Adult Education: Aspects and Trends.* Paris: UNESCO,
1985a. (ED 85/CONF.210/3)

UNESCO. *Adult Education Since the Third International Conference on Adult Education, Tokyo, 1972: Round-up Replies to the Survey Carried Out by UNESCO Among*

National Commissions with a View to Gathering Information on the Development of Adult Education. Paris: UNESCO, 1985b.

UNESCO. *Final Report.* Fourth International Conference on Adult Education, Paris: UNESCO, 1985c.

UNESCO. *Directory of Adult Education Periodicals.* Paris: UNESCO, 1985d.

Wang, M., Lin, W., Sun, S., and Fang, J. (eds.). *China: Lessons from Practice.* New Directions for Continuing Education, no. 37. San Francisco: Jossey-Bass, 1988.

World Association for Adult Education. *International Handbook of Adult Education.* London: World Association for Adult Education, 1929.

7

Adult Education and International Development

D. Merrill Ewert

Development planners have viewed education as a vehicle for social change since time immemorial. The debate continues, however, as to the nature of this educational process, its specific role in change, and its application to practice.

This chapter examines the historical evolution of development as a construct and the emergence of nonformal education as a strategy for national and community development. It concludes by highlighting several conceptual themes in current programs and by identifying several barriers to practice.

Although nonformal education gained currency during the 1960s, Coombs's taxonomy of education provided it with conceptual clarity in the 1970s. This discussion is based on Coombs's definition of nonformal education as "any organized educational activity outside the established formal system . . . that is intended to serve identifiable learning clienteles and learning objectives" (1973, p. 11). For a fuller discussion of definitions, consult Chapters Two and Five.

Development in Perspective

Development is best understood in juxtaposition to the related processes of relief and rehabilitation. *Relief* refers to the provision of short-term emergency aid in response to natural or human-made disasters. Governments and nongovernmental organizations respond to earthquakes, famines, or typhoons, for example, with emergency food, clean drinking water, medicines, blankets, and shelter. Wars and political insurrections frequently dislocate civilian populations who are malnourished and need health care. This transfer of urgently needed commodities and provision of basic services typically lasts for only a few months following the initial crisis. A second response, *rehabilitation,* follows the relief stage and concentrates on restoring the quality of life to predisaster conditions. Examples include the resettlement of Kampuchean refugees in Thailand following the fall of Pol Pot, postearthquake housing schemes in Mexico City, and afforestation projects in drought-stricken Ethiopia. This form of intervention, usually lasting a year or two, combines material and technical assistance designed to help people and communities rebuild their lives.

By contrast, *development* is a long-term process that addresses poverty and suffering, seeking to solve the basic problems of society through some direct intervention. The role of nonformal education in social change must be viewed within the broader context of debates among planners over development philosophy, theory, and practice. Nonformal education designed to promote development largely emerged in direct response to problems and limitations of earlier models of social change. Development has been understood in several different ways by those involved in planning and implementing development programs. Few dispute that education has a role in development; the only question is the form it should take.

Defining the Problem

Although the word *development* became part of the popular lexicon following World War II, the notion of modernizing indigenous societies goes back to colonial times. European nations imposed Western political rule, introduced cash crops, and organized extractive industries that linked these colonies to the world economy. Coerced by taxation, government regulations, and physical force, farmers produced cash crops for overseas corporations even at the risk of famine and impoverishing the land (Crowder, 1987, p. 13).

At the same time, Western missionaries brought Christianity to the Third World. Missions started schools, built dispensaries and hospitals, and introduced technologies designed to promote agricultural and industrial production. Missions also collaborated with colonial administrators to build transportation and communications infrastructures.

Some call this confluence of the interests of Western missions, colonial administrations, and multinational corporations the "unholy trinity" (Young, 1965). Their combined efforts both provided a structure for social welfare and subverted indigenous institutions and local initiatives.

North American assistance abroad before this century came primarily through missionary efforts, the development of the Red Cross, and an array of ad hoc responses to particular events (Sommer, 1977). Development as public policy is primarily a postwar phenomenon growing out of the

Marshall Plan's success in the reconstruction of Europe. These historical forces generated an emphasis among Western planners on economic growth and industrialization. This process was capital intensive, emphasized technology transfer, and led to the creation of new institutions. Everett Rogers's diffusion of innovation studies promoted extension as the mechanism for modernization and social change in the 1960s, the first "development decade" (Rogers and Shoemaker, 1971). The World Bank's Training and Visit System (Benor, 1977) became the sine qua non of national development policy in many nations.

In spite of high expectations, the results of this focus on development as modernization were disappointing. Third World economies did not develop rapidly. The introduction of green revolution technologies (hybrid seeds, fertilizers, and irrigation) increased production but also exacerbated social inequalities in many areas of the world. Studies showed that while production increased dramatically in some areas, so did the concentration of society's resources in the hands of its elite (Murdoch, 1980). Small farmers were unable to compete with wealthy landowners who could afford the capital-intensive inputs that make agriculture more productive and cost-effective. Many began to doubt that the poor had, in fact, benefited from the economic growth that accompanied the process of modernization. While the contrasts between the rich and poor have been recognized for centuries, the magnitude of the difference is now much greater than before (Cole, 1981), and so is people's awareness of these differences.

Schools and Development. If the diffusion and adoption of technological innovations was one leg of the developmental policies of Third World nations, schools were the other. "Education for nation building" became the popular rallying cry of newly independent nations. The African states participating in a 1961 UNESCO conference in Addis Ababa agreed that "education is not only a good thing, it is a paying thing" (Makulu, 1971, p. xvi). Tugbiyele (1973) called education a necessary investment and a key to overall national development. Postindependence African leaders reflected this belief in addresses bearing titles such as "Education and Social Progress," "Education for Self-Reliance," and "Our Students Must Participate in the Development of the Country" (Ewert and Heisey, 1979, p. 1).

Many countries assumed that universal primary education could be achieved in 20 to 25 years, even though industrialized countries required 100 to 150 years (Timar, 1983). Coombs' 1968 book, *The World Educational Crisis,* reflected this optimism. The Faure Commission report to UNESCO posited scientific humanism as the path toward a learning society through which people are prepared to address new and more complex problems (Faure, 1972). Many of these hopes were not realized. Coombs, in a 1985 assessment of the state of education after two development decades, tempered his expectations with a more modest and realistic view.

Schools promoted basic skills, but they also became sifting and sorting mechanisms through which a fortunate few rapidly moved up the social ladder. Critics such as Illich (1970) denounced schools as elitist institutions that inappropriately promote a consumer mentality which developing nations cannot afford. Furthermore, the economies of many Third World nations have been unable to absorb the volume of their new graduates.

Schools also have not benefited everyone equally. Women have consistently had less access to education than their male cohorts (Lele, 1986). A United Nations Department of Public Information (1985) report, *The State of the World's Women 1985*, concluded that the world not only does not expect girls to succeed but systematically schools them for failure. Rural children and school leavers, according to Coombs (1973) are other neglected groups. Thus, nonformal education programs were proposed as an alternative to schools that failed to carry out adequately the development agenda (Srinivasan, 1984).

Economic pressures have limited educational expenditures. If formal education is the engine of development, as some had assumed, it ran out of fuel in the 1970s when the commodity market collapsed. Third World nations that depended upon the export of copper, palm oil, cotton, coffee, and sugar suddenly lost their primary source of hard currency needed to sustain costly educational systems. The burden of national debts, high interest rates, reduced foreign aid, and pressure by donors to control public sector expenditures has limited the resources available for education (Lewin, 1986).

Adult Literacy. An emphasis on adult literacy programs paralleled the commitment of many nations to the expansion of formal education. Governments justified large expenditures for adult literacy as the means to transform subsistence economies into industrial societies. With population growth, the absolute number of illiterates in the world has continued to grow (Hall and Stock, 1985). This has encouraged large-scale literacy campaigns along with the more modest efforts of private voluntary organizations.

Although the effects of literacy programs have not been well studied, Bhola (1981) suggests that newly literate individuals become more independent, objective, analytical, and able to think abstractly. Literacy's impact on the family and community are unclear, but its effects on the economic, social, and political development of society has been strongly argued by Bhola. St. John Hunter (1987) points out, however, that, historically, literacy has followed industrialization rather than the other way around. It is a myth, she says, that the Third World is poor because most of the population is illiterate. Literacy as a body of technical skills is much less important than first believed.

Coombs (1985) suggests development planners were wrong in attaching a special mystique to mechanical literacy skills. UNESCO's Experimental World Literacy Program was initiated with a broad commitment to social, cultural, and intellectual development that went beyond economic change and growth. The realities of the field, however, proved to be more complex than anticipated, and the special mystique attached to mechanical literacy skills proved unwarranted. The problems, Coombs concludes in retrospect, were less pedagogical than cultural, psychological, and political. These are issues that conventional literacy programs were unequipped to address.

Dependence. In Latin America, the failure of modernization theory led to a redefinition of the problem of development in the late 1960s. Frank (1978) argued that the most important obstacles to development can be found in the structure of international political and economic relationships. The industrialization of a metropolitan center implies the underdevelopment of its periphery, both within a country and between nations.

The Commission on International Development began its report to the World Bank in 1969 assessing two decades of development by describing "the widening gap between the developed and developing countries" as the "central issue of our time" (Pearson, 1969, p. 3). The commission called for a new partnership between the developed and developing nations. Books such as *Rich Against Poor: The Reality of Aid* examined the plight of "nations and peoples whose destinies became subject to the will of European peoples and their Japanese imitators" (Hensman, 1971, p. 86). Hensman argued that Third World poverty is not a historical tradition but a created social product of a process he calls "antidevelopment" (p. 122). The benefits of economic growth have been unevenly distributed, with income concentrated in the hands of the industrial sector. Writing on Peru, Hensman (p. 137) concludes that there has been "little or no progress towards more adequate levels of income for the peasantry, the landless rural laborer or the unskilled urban laborer."

Critics of modernization schemes have also shown that such assistance is often counterproductive. Lappe's (1980) *Aid As Obstacle* argues that food aid diverts attention from the process of addressing the underlying causes of hunger and malnutrition. Many development planners mistakenly promote relief solutions to basic structural problems. Good intentions not withstanding, the result has often been increased dependency on outside resources.

Technical Assistance. The Western world's enthusiasm for technological solutions to Third World problems has generated a new type of professional—the development consultant. Many government and multilateral aid programs define the problem of development as the lack of technical assistance; they therefore invest their resources in hiring specialists to plan and implement development schemes. Adult educators with planning, evaluation, and training skills have been in considerable demand for these roles.

Some of the most spectacular development failures, such as the Tanzania groundnut scheme, were the work of foreign experts who did not understand local conditions or aspirations. Plans called for the cultivation of three million acres of groundnuts through the application of new technologies. After ten years, the project was abandoned because of miscalculations in the amount of annual local rainfall, the abrasiveness of the soil, which ruined metal plows, and the presence of plant diseases in the region. All these conditions were well-known to local farmers (Fuglesang, 1984). The failure of planners to consider the cultural and historical dimensions of contemporary problems led many scholars to redefine the problem of development.

In a survey of "successful" U.S. Agency for International Development (USAID) projects in 1973, William and Elizabeth Paddock (1973) synthesized their findings in the title of their report, *We Don't Know How*. The underlying problem of technical assistance has been the failure to involve people in their own development. The belief that development goes beyond technological change to address basic societal structures has generated new strategies for nonformal education that promote learning and change.

Strategies for Nonformal Education

Nonformal education programs have emerged in response to different cultural, social, and political contexts. Cookson discusses some of the dynamics of this process in the preceding chapter. The applications of nonformal education concepts have taken several forms.

Critical Consciousness. Paulo Freire's *Pedagogy of the Oppressed* (1970) redefined development and redirected the efforts of many adult educators working for social change. Highly critical of most education and development efforts, Freire proposed an alternative paradigm based on the development of critical consciousness. He organized "circles of culture" that engaged the oppressed in dialogues regarding their own problems and their underlying causes. Skillful facilitators led discussions of generative themes conceptualized as pictures that reflected community problems.

People who are trapped in a "culture of silence," Freire says, lose hope and internalize the low opinion that society holds of them. Through critical reflection, however, they go through what Mezirow (1978) calls "perspective transformation," no longer blaming their problems on their own inherent inferiority. Freire found that as a result of this new consciousness, people proposed specific actions through which they addressed the problems they had defined. These actions were often political, making government agencies responsive to their needs. In this process, they gained a new belief in their own capacity to transform the conditions in which they lived. The translation of Freire's ideas into other languages spread them throughout the world.

Community-based education, as Freire has shown, can be an empowering process. (See Chapter Thirty-Three.) A community health program among low-caste people in rural India featured various health promotion activities ranging from teaching simple techniques to cure common problems to promoting health education. The program was based on the dialogical process of reflection and action. When evaluating the project, the staff asked participants to describe how their lives had changed through their involvement in this program. Anticipating responses regarding reduced morbidity and mortality, the staff were surprised to hear people say, "We can now look people in the eye." The process of participation had transformed their perspective, giving them hope, confidence, and a belief in themselves, which they had lacked before.

An integrated community development project in Zaire used proverbs, parables, and metaphors as codifications to stimulate critical reflection. Farmers, frustrated that palm oil factories were no longer processing fruit, discussed their problems and the possible actions they could take. At first, these farmers expected local development agencies to solve their problems for them. "You are our father and mother. You tell us what to do" (Ewert, 1981, p. 35). However, community discussions regarding the collapse of the palm oil industry led farmers to take several individual and collective actions. Some adopted improved agricultural practices. Families participated in a health promotion program, and the community repaired and reopened a road leading into the area that had been closed for months. The discussions also shifted the responsibility for addressing local problems from the development program to people in the community themselves.

While Freire's is a revolutionary pedagogy dedicated to structural transformation, his proposal of an educational process designed to promote critical consciousness has inspired development workers to apply these principles to other contexts. It has shifted attention away from the adoption of new behaviors and technologies to the promotion of economic and social justice. Freire's emphasis on dialogical education based on people's own knowledge and values has led to a reexamination of the teaching and learning process in development. Community educators influenced by the Freire paradigm facilitate learning by posing questions that stimulate reflection leading to action, rather than by sharing technical information that addresses local problems.

This view of education as an empowering process has become an underlying premise of national development strategies in several countries. Its application to practice will be discussed in the next section.

Education for Mobilization. In a 1967 white paper on educational policy entitled *Education for Self-Reliance,* Tanzania's President Nyerere called for an authentic educational process appropriate to an independent and free society. In introducing the *First Five Year Development Plan,* Nyerere proposed a focus on education for adults, the impact of which would be felt immediately rather than after five, ten, or twenty years. "The people must understand the plans for development of this country; they must be able to participate in changes which are necessary, only if they are willing and able to do this will this plan succeed," Nyerere suggested (Ahmed, 1984, p. 227).

This educational process included mass education emphasizing adult literacy and universal primary education designed to promote self-reliance. Though Tanzania is one of Africa's poorest countries, a nationwide literacy drive reduced illiteracy from 70 percent to 21 percent in the decade between 1970 and 1981. The momentum of this campaign has been sustained by workshops for writers, the development of rural newspapers, the creation of rural libraries, educational radio campaigns, folk development colleges, and a variety of postliteracy training opportunities. Similarly, from 1970 to 1975, primary school enrollments increased from 54 percent to over 90 percent (Ahmed, 1984), a remarkable record.

The program combined a clearly articulated philosophy, a political commitment at the policy level, an organizational structure making heavy use of volunteers, and a viable support system. This approach extended the teaching and learning process from a national campaign to a sustained educational program.

The National Literacy Crusade in Nicaragua, following the 1979 revolution, mobilized the nation around a new set of national goals. These ranged from the eradication of illiteracy to improved health of the population and reinforcement of the country's historical, cultural, and ecological heritage (Le Boterf, 1984, p. 250). Based on Freire's pedagogy of critical consciousness, an army of volunteers facilitated community dialogues based on primers created to promote reflection on cultural themes. During a five month period in 1980, adult illiteracy was reduced from 50 percent to 13 percent (Le Boterf, 1984). In addition to new literacy skills, the program fostered new types of relations between teachers and learners and between class and age groups. It also promoted an appreciation among Nicaraguans for their own cultural heritage.

Popular Education. The term *popular education,* first widely used in Latin America, is another application of Freire's concept of education for critical consciousness. From Highlander in Tennessee (Adams, 1975), to Nepal (Parajuli, 1986), the Philippines (Evans, 1985), Botswana (Kidd, 1984), Sierra Leone (Malamah-Thomas, 1987), Canada (Castellano, 1986), and Latin America (Buttedahl, 1985), popular education is a response to the problems of development. It begins with people's experience within the larger political and social context (Hall and Stock, 1985). Its goal is to mobilize peasants, workers, and other marginalized people in need of psychological or political empowerment (Buttedahl, 1985). (See also Chapters Thirty-Three and Thirty-Four.)

At Highlander, Myles Horton developed a new kind of school, a school for problems (Adams, 1975). Though it taught basic skills such as reading and writing, its central purpose was to empower politically the victims of poverty and injustice. New literates could register, vote, and participate in the political system. They became first-class citizens in the process (Tjerandsen, 1983). In Nicaragua, people not only developed basic literacy skills but also learned to participate in collectives, trade unions, and other social organizations, leading Freire to call the country "one big popular school" (Parajuli, 1986, p. 31).

Philosophically, popular education is a grass-roots movement addressing society's underlying structural problems. Methodologically, it draws on people's own art forms—theater, dance, storytelling, music, songs, poetry, and art—to stimulate reflection and analysis. As this educational process provides a sense of hope and mobilizes the disadvantaged to political action, it becomes a transforming tool for development.

Evans (1985) describes a popular theater movement in the Philippines designed to transform people's perspectives of themselves. Instead of viewing themselves as the passive objects of someone else's history, the program sets people to the task of creating their own culture and telling their own stories. Evans (p. 142) concludes: "It is a culture of hope and dignity, of people taking responsibility for their lives. It is a culture in which people see themselves as the subjects of their own history."

Integrated Community-Based Development. In the middle 1980s, the specter of starvation in Africa moved the world. Aid of unprecedented proportions poured into the continent in an attempt to alleviate human suffering. Governments and private relief and development agencies struggled to find lasting solutions to endemic problems. The food crisis, however, has no single explanation nor universal cure (Berry, 1984). Children die because their families lack wells, hoes, and purchasing power. The conditions in many places perpetuate drought, disease, and famine (Chandler, 1986). Attempts to address these underlying causes of human misery have resulted in new strategies for development that integrate health, education, nutrition, agricultural production, clean water, and the delivery of health care services at the community level. The process is an educational one with people learning how to prevent disease and to promote health through changed behavior. It becomes political when people attempt to change those structures that are ultimately responsible for the existence of these problems.

David Werner's work in Mexico redefined integrated, community-based development. His book, *Where There is No Doctor* (1982) showed how nonliterate people could improve their own health through limited training in their own communities. With Illich, Werner believes that those who control health information—physicians, health care institutions, and so on—manipulate this control to their own advantage. He therefore demystified health knowledge by showing people how they could improve their own health at home. People learned to treat diarrhea by mixing oral hydration solution. They prevented disease by practicing good hygiene and by improving nutrition. They promoted health through environmental sanitation, improved food production, clean water, and family planning.

Demystification and dissemination of technical information regarding health and agriculture is one aspect of community-based development. Perhaps a more important element is the training of local villagers in organizational skills. This "implants among the poorest precisely those social resources that hold the key to their empowerment" (Gran, 1983, p. 167). The contribution of adult education's community-based experience to health development is reflected in the International Council for Adult Education's International Network for Primary Health Care and Popular Education. This group seeks to strengthen the links between popular educators and nongovernmental groups promoting local initiatives and training community health workers.

Studies show that a mother's level of schooling is highly correlated with infant and child mortality. Maternal education improves the health of children and reduces infant mortality (Lewin, Little, and Colclough, 1983).

As mothers understand principles of nutrition, hygiene, and preventive health care, family health improves. This process of learning also happens outside the school under certain conditions. Adult education, in and of itself, has little effect but can play a role in reducing poverty. It is, Duke (1983) suggests, a necessary but insufficient condition for development to occur at either local or national levels. Hall and Stock (1985, p. 26) echo this conclusion suggesting that while poverty and oppression are complex and persistent, "adult education has a critical role to play even if it is not the key role we might once have claimed." Adult education can build self-esteem, provide hope, and raise awareness of political structures that limit one's options. Through education, people can understand how to address the structures of power and how to take political action.

An indigenous organization in Latin America asked a health and development agency to intercede with government authorities on its behalf. The people wanted to protest a particular government policy but felt impotent; so they requested help from expatriates who they thought would gain an official hearing. Instead of interceding with the government directly, the development agency organized seminars to teach the people how the decision-making apparatus of the government worked so they could make their own intervention. Participants also learned how to write letters of protest and how to make personal appearances in government offices to appeal political decisions. The community's challenge forced a change in public policy. Subsequently, they defended their own interests in other matters as well.

Nonformal education programs now stress integrated development encompassing health, agriculture, and political action at the community level. Gran (1986), writing on famine in Africa, argues that real development, and thus the end of starvation, will occur only through an informed participation by those who matter most—the small farmers who produce the food. "Marginalized, assetless, unorganized poor people will never be efficient producers and consumers. . . . Development thus begins with people: consciousness raising, mobilization, and empowerment through self-directed organizations" (p. 278). While concerned with the structural issues underlying the causes of poverty, many working at the local level also focus their attention on the practical issues of preventing disease, increasing food production, teaching needed skills, and dealing with community concerns. Paulo Freire shares this concern about local problems but addresses it from a more conceptual and political perspective by promoting a sense of critical consciousness.

These four paradigms—Freire's perspective of critical consciousness, the mobilization of societies for transformation, the rise of popular education, and the emergence of integrated development programs—share several common themes examined in the next section.

Common Themes in Nonformal Education for Development

Although nonformal education has always been part of the development process, several themes have emerged.

Process Instead of Projects. Government and private agencies typically have organized development activities into projects designed to meet specific behavioral objectives. Almost by definition, these are short-term interventions based on measurable goals selected by external agents. Planning documents, such as USAID's logical framework, spell out precise indicators of social change and detail budgetary constraints and specific implementation schedules. The result is an emphasis on information acquired, skills learned, and behaviors adopted.

Nonformal educators influenced by Freire and by the popular education movement emphasize the development of critical consciousness rather than the transfer of skills and technology. People who understand history and recognize their own potential are more likely to take actions that will improve their own lives than are those who lack such a perspective.

Nonformal Education as an Empowering Process. Although development practice began by addressing technical problems, it now goes far beyond to address social and political issues that deeply affect people's lives. Development has been redefined, and nonformal educators are focusing their energies on empowering people to take increasing control over their own lives. Development is becoming more political, and the idea of empowerment contrasts sharply with the opinion of some that the poor and oppressed must be controlled and manipulated for their own good.

This process of empowerment through which people learn to analyze their own problems, to propose solutions, and to take collective action, has been called mobilization or development from the bottom up (Nesman, 1981).

Participation. No principle is more central to the adult education literature than the importance of people's participation in the design and implementation of their own learning experiences. Freire's (1970) process of conscientization begins with people identifying their own themes. In Hall's (1975) work in the United Republic of Tanzania, he adopted the concept of *participatory research,* which was designed to involve people in examining their own problems and implementing their own solutions. Instead of being viewed as the objects of study or as the beneficiaries of a development process, the people became the subjects of study and the initiators of change. This method contrasts with both traditional social science and contemporary development practice. (See Chapter Twelve.)

Those committed ideologically to participation in the design and implementation of development projects, however, frequently underestimate its difficulties. Participatory planning is often misunderstood, sometimes raising unrealistic expectations (Pigozzi, 1982) and it can also unleash a political response more oppressive than the original problem (Ewert, 1982).

Rise of Voluntary Initiatives. When the specter of famine in Africa mobilized the popular consciousness of the world, an explosion of activity occurred in the private sector in support of development objectives. Private voluntary agencies of all kinds, including religious, civic, and political groups, invested their efforts in nonformal educational activities on behalf of development work. These kinds of agencies are known for being relatively efficient, innovative, flexible, nonbureaucratic, cost-effective, and people oriented (Kassam, 1986). As a result, they are increasingly attracting government and multilateral agency funds.

Problems and Issues in Nonformal Education and Development

One of the major problems facing many development efforts is the politicization of aid. For example, a USAID official described to representatives of nongovernmental organizations his agency's development strategy as a collaborative relationship with the private sector. He defined as its goals the pursuit of U.S. foreign policy objectives. USAID provides financial support to many voluntary agencies, and this aid goes to those who support activities consistent with U.S. foreign policy. By contrast, the Canadian International Development Agency (CIDA) has largely separated its government's private sector aid support from its foreign policy objectives.

International aid is increasingly being called international cooperation, but that term raises the issue of whether or not a genuine partnership is possible in a power relationship. Have donors, Kassam (1986) asks, abandoned their own economic interests in an aid relationship? Is the partnership real or is it a facade?

Economic Constraints. Many Third World nations have felt the financial pressures caused by the collapse of international commodity markets and by the rise of oil prices, which have eaten up their hard currency reserves. Nonformal education initiatives are costly, often competing with schools for the same resources and forcing governments to make difficult choices. The alternative is to try to do more with less.

External Funding. Third World nations forced to rely on outside resources do not control their development agendas. Countries such as Zaire, Egypt, and Israel receive a disproportionate amount of their aid from the United States and might find it difficult to survive without such assistance. Following the famine in Ethiopia, money was spent not so much on long-term solutions as on high-profile relief programs that gave immediate evidence of success but failed to address underlying causes.

Gap Between Theory and Practice. Although the world is full of white papers, policy statements, and five-year plans, many are not translated into meaningful practice. The rhetoric of agencies on the needs of the poorest of the poor is not matched by the direction of their resources. The burgeoning literature on nonformal education and development is also long on theoretical formulation, but relatively few firsthand accounts document how principles of nonformal education translate into practice.

Underserved Populations. Although many nations have directed their efforts at disadvantaged populations, promoting change for minority populations is still difficult. Women, rural communities, and lower classes are not participating proportionately in development.

Fragmentation of Development Efforts. Many countries divide the development task among agencies with different agendas. An integrated strategy of development, Hollnsteiner (1982) suggests, is easier in community-based development countries such as China, Ethiopia, Tanzania, and Vietnam than in capitalist societies in which people are more likely to pursue their own goals. Similarly, private agencies are often reluctant to coordinate their activities with national development plans, particularly in noncapitalist societies.

Conclusion

Nonformal education is a participatory and empowering process through which people gain control over, and substantively improve, the quality of their own lives. Freire's emphasis on critical consciousness has shaped the agendas of many development planners dedicated to addressing the underlying causes of poverty. Mass campaigns and popular education programs have mobilized entire societies to bring about integrated social change.

References

Adams, F., with Horton, M. *Unearthing Seeds of Fire: The Idea of Highlander.* Winston-Salem, N.C.: John F. Blair, 1975.

Ahmed, M. "The Education Revolution in Tanzania." *Assignment Children,* 1984, (65–68), pp. 225–245.

Benor, D. *The Training and Visit System.* Washington, D.C.: The World Bank, 1977.

Berry, S. S. "The Food Crisis and Agrarian Change in Africa: A Review Essay." *African Studies Review,* 1984, *27* (2), 59–112.

Bhola, H. S. "Why Literacy Can't Wait: Issues for the 1980s." *Convergence,* 1981, *16* (1), 6–23.

Buttedahl, P. "Training of Adult and Popular Educators in Latin America." *Convergence,* 1985, *18* (3–4), 94–102.

Castellano, M. B. "Collective Wisdom: Participatory Research and Canada's Native People." *Convergence,* 1986, *19* (3), 50–53.

Chandler, W. U. "Child Health, Education and Development." *Prospects: Quarterly Journal of Education,* 1986, *16* (3), 285–299.

Cole, J. P. *The Development Gap: A Spatial Analysis of World Poverty and Inequality.* New York: Wiley, 1981.

Coombs, P. H. *The World Crisis in Education.* New York: Oxford University Press, 1968.

Coombs, P. H. *The World Crisis in Education: The View from the Eighties.* New York: Oxford University Press, 1985.

Coombs, P. H., with Prosser, R. C., and Ahmed, M. *New Paths to Learning for Children and Youth.* New York: International Council for Educational Development, 1973.

Crowder, M. "Whose Dream Was It Anyway? Twenty-Five Years of African Independence." *African Affairs,* 1987, *86* (342), 7–24.

Duke, C. "Adult Education and Poverty: What Are the Connections?" *Convergence,* 1983, *16* (1), 76–83.

Evans, D. "Training Popular Theatre Workers in the Philippines." *Convergence,* 1985, *18* (3–4), 140–142.

Ewert, D. M. "Proverbs, Parables and Metaphors: Applying Freire's Concept of Codifications to Africa." *Convergence,* 1981, *14* (1), 32–43.

Ewert, D. M. "Involving Adult Learners in Program Planning." In S. B. Merriam (ed.), *Linking Philosophy and Practice.* New Directions for Continuing Education, no. 15. San Francisco: Jossey-Bass, 1982.

Ewert, D. M., and Heisey, N. "Nonformal Education in Africa: The Past as Prologue." Paper presented at Lifelong Learning Research Conference, College Park, Md., Jan. 1979.

Faure, E., and others. *Learning to Be: The World of Education Today and Tomorrow.* Paris: UNESCO, 1972.

Frank, A. G. *Dependent Accumulation and Underdevelopment.* London: Macmillan, 1978.

Freire, P. *Pedagogy of the Oppressed.* New York: Herder & Herder, 1970.

Fuglesang, A. "The Myth of People's Ignorance." *Development Dialogue,* 1984, (1–2), pp. 42–62.

Gran, G. *Development by People: Citizen Construction of a Just World.* New York: Praeger, 1983.

Gran, G. "Beyond African Famines: Whose Knowledge Matters?" *Alternatives,* 1986, *15,* 275–296.

Hall, B. "Participatory Research: An Approach for Change." *Convergence,* 1975, *8* (2), 24–31.

Hall, B., and Stock, A. "Trends in Adult Education Since 1972." *Prospects: Quarterly Journal of Education,* 1985, *15* (1), 13–26.

Hensman, C. R. *The Rich Against the Poor: The Reality of Aid.* Cambridge, Mass.: Schenkman, 1971.

Hollnsteiner, M. R. "The Participatory Imperative in Primary Health Care." *Convergence,* 1982, *15* (3), 56–66.

Illich, I. *Deschooling Society.* New York: Harper & Row, 1970.

Kassam, Y. "Adult Education, Development and International Aid: Some Issues and Trends." *Convergence,* 1986, *19* (3), 1–12.

Kidd, R. *From People's Theatre for Revolution to Popular Theatre for Reconstruction: Diary of a Zimbabwean Workshop.* The Hague, Netherlands: Center for the Study of Education in Developing Countries, 1984.

Lappe, F. M., and others. *Aid as Obstacle: Twenty Questions About Our Foreign Aid and the Hungry.* San Francisco: San Francisco Institute for Food and Development Policy, 1980.

Le Boterf, G. "The Challenge of Mass Education in Nicaragua." *Assignment Children,* 1984, (65–68), 247–266.

Lele, U. "Women and Structural Transformation." *Economic Development and Cultural Change,* 1986, *34* (2), 195–221.

Lewin, K. "Educational Finance in Recession." *Prospects: Quarterly Review of Education,* 1986, *16* (2), 215–230.

Lewin, K., Little, A., and Colclough, C. "Effects of Education on Development Objectives." Part One. *Prospects: Quarterly Journal of Education,* 1983, *13* (3), 1983.

Makulu, H. F. *Education, Development and Nation Building in Independent Africa.* London: SCM Press, 1971.

Malamah-Thomas, D. H. "Community Theater with and by the People: The Sierra Leone Experience." *Convergence,* 1987, *20* (1), 59–68.

Mezirow, J. "Perspective Transformation." *Adult Education,* 1978, *28* (2), 100–110.

Murdoch, W. W. *The Poverty of Nations: The Political Economy of Hunger and Population.* Baltimore, Md.: Johns Hopkins University Press, 1980.

Nesman, E. G. *Peasant Mobilization and Rural Development.* Cambridge, Mass.: Schenkman, 1981.

Nyerere, J. *Education for Self-Reliance.* Dar Es Salaam, Tanzania: Government Printer, 1967.

Paddock, W., and Paddock, E. *We Don't Know How: An Independent Audit of What they Call Success in Foreign Assistance.* Ames: Iowa State University Press, 1973.

Parajuli, P. "Grassroots Movements, Development Discourse and Popular Education." *Convergence,* 1986, *19* (2), 29–40.

Pearson, L. *Partners in Development.* New York: Praeger, 1969.

Pigozzi, M. J. "Participation in Non-Formal Education Projects: Some Possible Negative Outcomes." *Convergence,* 1982, *15* (3), 6–18.

Rogers, E. M., and Shoemaker, F. F. *Communication of Innovation.* New York: Free Press, 1971.

St. John Hunter, C. "Myths and Realities of Literacy/Illiteracy." *Convergence,* 1987, *20* (1), 1–8.

Sommer, J. G. *Beyond Charity: U.S. Voluntary Aid for a Changing Third World.* Washington, D.C.: Overseas Development Council, 1977.

Srinivasan, T. N. "Development, Poverty, and Basic Human Needs: Some Issues." In P. K. Ghosh (ed.), *Third World Development: A Basic Needs Approach.* Westport, Conn.: Greenwood Press, 1984.

Timar, J. "The New Crisis in Education Seen in the Developing Countries." *Prospects: Quarterly Journal of Education,* 1983, *13* (4), 397–411.

Tjerandsen, C. "The Highlander Heritage: Education for Social Change." *Convergence,* 1983, *16* (2), 10–22.

Tugbiyele, E. A. "Education for Rural Development." *Prospects: Quarterly Review of Education,* 1973, *3* (2), 246–251.

United Nations Department of Public Information. *The State of the World's Women 1985.* New York: United Nations Department of Public Information, 1985.

Werner, D. *Where There Is No Doctor.* Palo Alto, Calif.: The Hesperian Foundation, 1982.

Young, M. C. *Politics in the Congo.* Princeton, N.J.: Princeton University Press, 1965.

8

The Voluntary Sector and Adult Education

Paul J. Ilsley

This chapter begins with the assumption that volunteerism is central to the mission of adult education. From the inception of our field, adult educators have recognized the importance of voluntary learning, the contributions of voluntary organizations that perform adult-education-related activities, and the value of learning that occurs as a result of community service within a variety of volunteer contexts. One cannot fail to be impressed by the remarkable diversity of learning opportunities available to people through community involvement in volunteer-based institutions. In recent years the voluntary sector has evolved so that it is now characterized by a higher degree of organization from within and by burgeoning interest from the governmental and corporate sectors. Owing to increased professionalization of voluntary institutions and to governmental policies directed toward the voluntary sector, voluntarism is undergoing a profound reorganization. Terms such as *voluntarism, voluntary action,* and *volunteer* have become ambiguous. I will argue here that the meaning of voluntarism to adult education is shifting accordingly, and that a critical examination of the shift is warranted.

To accomplish this purpose, I will make a historical link between adult education and voluntary action, clarify terms based on these analyses, present an investigation of the field of voluntary action and voluntary institutions, and examine significant themes of modern voluntary action. For now, let us assume that voluntarism is organized selfless commitment to the greater good. We can expect this definition to be challenged later, though first the historical link must be made.

Voluntary Action and Adult Education

The partnership between voluntary action and adult education has endured throughout the history of organized adult education and is based on conceptual similarities; they have actually been conceptually linked through several historical epochs. In religious, agricultural, remedial, leisure, and even military adult education, programs have relied heavily on volunteer involvement. In other instances, volunteers have worked alongside professionals. Perhaps more notably, attention has been given to the voluntary learning ethic, replete with examination of trends of voluntary learning. (See Chapter Five.) It would not be an exaggeration to say that the history of adult education has been a history of voluntary activity and voluntary association. Likewise, many of the characteristics that make the voluntary movement unique are related to adult education, such as the emphases on program planning and training and the inherent assumption that many volunteers are motivated by learning.

Adult Educators Practice Voluntary Action. Many of the greatest accomplishments of voluntary movements have involved adult educators. The influence of Jane Addams, and those who worked with her, was an educating influence, not only on people in the Hull House neighborhood, but on the consciousness of America as a whole, especially with regard to her dedication to the peace movement (Addams, 1927). Frank Laubach's (1970) worldwide literacy campaign by voluntary teachers and learners has already had an impressive impact on global illiteracy. His influence continues directly through Laubach Literacy International and, in North America, Laubach Literacy Action. Saul Alinsky (1971) was successful in organizing volunteers participating in Chicago-based community groups because of his ability to educate people both inside and outside his organizations.

Much of modern adult education traces its roots back to Josiah Holbrook's National American Lyceum. The legacy of the lyceum includes local historical societies, improved town government, public libraries, and free public education for juveniles (Bode, 1956). In its earliest days, the ideal of the lyceum was mutual self-education. Group discussion and group decision making were a part of the lyceum spirit. Though not every volunteer institution nor every adult education program operates this way, most adult educators are comfortable with the same ethic today.

According to Reichlin (1982), it was Dewey who provided the most enduring rationale for voluntary action. Equating voluntarism with strong citizenship, and strong citizenship with a strong democracy, Dewey promoted the concept that voluntary organizations provide arenas for civic service, social participation, and self-enlightenment. In recruitment efforts to this day, volunteers are often persuaded to join organizations based on the dual benefit of developing potential while helping the nation. Reichlin goes on to point out that the connection between voluntarism and adult education is paramount in recruitment efforts. Nearly 40 percent of randomly selected voluntary organizations in the Boston area mention training in their brochures as incentives to attract volunteers who seek paraprofessional training.

Recognition of the singularly unique connection between voluntary action and adult education does not confine us to a handful of people, nor is it specific to the United States or Canada. *The 1919 Report* of the Adult Education Commitee of the Ministry of Reconstruction (p. 17) shows the same awareness: "A second principle which is maintained in the Report is the essential importance of trusting and encouraging voluntary efforts. It is characteristic of the growth of education in these islands that it has till the last few years depended almost exclusively on voluntary effort inspired by religious or humanitarian motives." Thus, in recognition that citizens participate in a cause out of a commitment to spiritual, educational, or civic ideals inspired by their rights of involvement and by the quest for learning, *The 1919 Report* called for the sustained provision of voluntary efforts on a national basis.

Perhaps the most consistent proponent of a broad concept of voluntarism in adult education was Eduard Lindeman (1928). His work brings forth the full implications of problems such as overprofessionalism and specialization, the transference of decision-making power from individuals to professional authorities, and a chronic reliance on specialized expertise. Lindeman was not only concerned with the wastefulness of the pofessionalization process; he also perceived that, for some tasks, volunteers are the only ones who can accomplish the job. Examples include town meetings, civic forums, and religious institutions. Lindeman regarded voluntary citizen participation as an antidote to increasing bureaucratization and institutional rigidity, provided that voluntary action itself avoids the temptations of professionalization.

Conceptual Connections Between Voluntary Action and Learning. Viewing volunteer participation as a learning activity, it makes sense that the free will of volunteers governs their level of involvement. Volunteers find meaning from direct participation in voluntary enterprises, from problem solving, and from significant decision making. Viewed this way, voluntary agencies are essentially settings for adult education because, in order for significant involvement to occur, volunteers first must be placed in situations of deliberate and sustained learning. Museum volunteers, whose duration of service exceeds that of other groups of volunteers, for example, most commonly learn large amounts of information, whether it be policy, historical aspects of exhibits, or the specifics of the collections. It is not unusual for volunteers to perform instrumental organizational functions, such as hiring of paid staff and exhibit design. In museums, there is a firm connection between the quality and amount of learning of volunteers and their involvement in the decisions of the organization.

Organizations vary as to the kind of learning opportunities available to volunteers. Research of various contexts of voluntary action, such as the peace movement, Red Cross, public access media, hospitals, volunteer literacy organizations, and corporate voluntarism supports the notion that commitment to a cause and the type of learning volunteers do are linked. Put another way, the will to participate is influenced by the amount of learning available to volunteers. Accordingly, the kind of learning opportunities provided to volunteers influences their commitment and, therefore, their duration of service. Additionally, the conclusion is supported that motives for volunteering, and hence individuals' needs and patterns of learning, evolve. The original motive for volunteering may give way to new motives as volunteers become acculturated to the norms and values of an organization. In this sense, voluntary enterprises are complex settings for adult education because effective management of volunteers depends upon correct identification of learning needs of volunteers and upon the provision of opportunities that encourage volunteers into higher levels of participation and learning.

Thus, three simple but pervasive concepts provide a basis for analysis of the link between voluntary action and adult education: (1) voluntary action provides learning potential for adults, (2) volunteers' learning needs evolve over time, and (3) volunteers remain in service longer, and exhibit a higher commitment, when permitted to participate in the decision making of their institutions.

Understanding Voluntary Action

Understanding of voluntary institutions requires a comprehension of the general field of voluntary action and of the most common definitions of terms such as *volunteer* and *voluntarism*. Historical analyses often cast volunteer activities in the light of the pioneer barn-raising ethic (Scattschneider, 1984)—activities in which people give time and service in response to a need. Popular literature depicts volunteering as neighborly selfless commitment to the greater good (Bellah and others, 1985). As popular as these conceptions may be, they fail to take into account the juxtaposition of voluntarism to the organizational or historical context. Voluntarism has meant different things during different historical epochs and in different volunteer contexts.

What is the meaning of voluntarism in a modern technological culture? Karl (1984) believes that the term *volunteer* belongs to a class of terms that can be compared with an opposite term, such as good is to bad. He says that for centuries voluntarism stood as opposite to religious doctrine and, later, opposite to military service. Then, during Wilson's presidential term, it was voluntarism as opposed to bureaucracy, a distinction that lasted through World War II and beyond. ''The belief that the public's willingness to give generously to support the war and its victims was easily translated into a peacetime belief that such energies could be marshaled for all of society's catastrophes, from natural disasters to the very existence of poverty itself'' (Karl, 1984, p. 503). Whether people volunteer as a response to an emergency situation, such as a depression or war, or out of compassion for the poor, voluntary action "can be said to be an acknowledgment of the perpetual nature of the need for service—that there will always be the poor and the sick to tend as effectively and as systematically as possible" (p. 508). Today voluntarism seems to be the opposite of professionalism. With the advent of professionalism, and the attending certification and licensing, professionals began to replace volunteers. That volunteers are still present in our society may be indicative of an anomaly in the professions. As Karl puts it, "Our use of 'volunteer' has become a distinction between public subvention and private, as though the source of the money were the real difference. Yet it is inconceivable that a return to volunteer service is the answer for modern industrial society. . . . For American society, perhaps more than in most societies in modern history, has a commitment to service that is part of self-interest. That commitment is an essential part of the materialist ethic that we have made work" (p. 522).

Voluntarism Defined. Upon reflection, the ambiguity of what constitutes voluntary action may result from stubborn belief in obsolete notions. Some theorists argue that voluntarism is not a function of altruism, but rather that it provides some direct benefit in a quid pro quo arrangement to the volunteer—for example, the chance to learn something new, an opportunity for career rehearsal, or the realization of some other psychic benefit (Smith, Macaulay, and Associates, 1980; Gidron, 1983). Organizationally, voluntary action makes the most sense not in individual terms, but in formal bureaucratic terms—specifically with regard to recruiting, training, placement, and monitoring volunteers. There is a discrepancy between the meaning of volunteering to individuals and the meaning to organizations. The very act of organizing volunteers in specified roles, which is perhaps a necessary feature of many modern volunteer-based organizations, places restrictions on the free will of volunteers for the sake of channeling their energy, gaining organizational efficiency, or striking a level of consistency.

Though much of modern voluntary action is characterized by organizational formality, the experience to the volunteers themselves represents an opportunity to engage in worthwhile activity that would otherwise be of a high risk nature if tried elsewhere. Given this, a more reasonable definition of a volunteer is one who chooses to commit oneself to a cause or to others in a deliberate spirit of service, in response to one or more perceived social needs, within an organizational context, and in return for some psychic benefit. For our purposes, a successful volunteer experience hinges on mutual satisfaction of volunteer and organizational needs.

Scope. According to a study by the Gallup Organization (1985), nearly one in four Americans over the age of fourteen has volunteered in a recognizable sustained way during the year. Moreover, of those volunteering, nearly 50 percent put in three or more hours per week, while 20 percent logged more than six or more hours. Though an exact figure is impossible to calculate, these figures translate roughly into a staggering 170 million volunteer work hours per week and close to nine billion hours per year in North America.

For whom do they volunteer and what do they do? They volunteer in settings such as health, education, and religious organizations. They participate in social services, civic, social, and fraternal associations, community action, recreation, arts and culture, work-related organizations, and in various political organizations. They perform duties such as assisting the elderly, tutoring illiterate adults, raising funds for local organizations, assisting paid employees, teaching Sunday school, serving on boards and committees, answering or making phone calls, leading a recreational activity, driving people from one place to another, ushering in church, or greeting visitors. A vast majority (93 percent) of those surveyed have at least one reason for continuing voluntary service—for example, they enjoy it, they have free time, they want to learn something new and gain experience, they want to keep taxes down, or they want to do something useful for others.

It is instructive that a similar survey was conducted in 1981. During the four years between the first and second surveys, several notable trends developed. One is that the ratio of male to female volunteers leveled out, though more women than men continued to volunteer (55 to 45 percent). Another trend was that participation of young adults eighteen to twenty-four years old, urban volunteers, and volunteers among middle-income households ($20,000 to $39,000) declined (Gallup Organization, 1981, 1985) To characterize voluntary participation today, those most likely to volunteer are white women under the age of fifty who are employed (especially part-time), who have upper-level incomes, who are formally educated, and who possess large houses in the suburbs or rural areas.

Classifying Types of Voluntary Action. There are many ways to classify volunteer programs. The task is analagous to sorting a room full of toys. One way to approach the task is to sort them according to color, with all the blue ones grouped together, all the green ones together, and so forth. Another way is to sort them according to locomotion (stationary, wheels on ground, airborne, water-bound), and still another way to classify them is by size. Of course, one classification scheme is no more correct than another. But one system may be more useful than another. The usefulness of the sorting process depends on the reason for the classification scheme in the first place—to understand the diversity of the items, to better understand differences and similarities, or to conceptually depict the scope of the items. Perhaps the best typologies lead one to action, as in the case of sorting the toys according to safety factor or in some other way that promotes consumer awareness.

A variety of classification schemes appear in the volunteer literature (Schindler-Rainman and Lippitt, 1985; Smith, 1981; Ilsley and Niemi, 1981; Ilsley, 1985a, 1985b). In most cases, these typologies present variations on a theme by pointing out differences of institutional form, context, purpose, or structure. A typology following the institutional form scheme might list out types such as the arts, education, religion, environment, health, human service, international institutions, and public or societal benefit organizations. In this typology, voluntary action is seen to be as broadly based as human action itself. A typology following the volunteer context scheme might list out examples such as traditional, political action, and social movement; mutual aid or self-help groups; and consumer groups. By organizing voluntary agencies this way, the political purpose becomes explicit. Either a voluntary organization seeks to preserve the status quo, as in the case of many traditional agencies, or it seeks to change it, as is the case with the other types listed.

A typology delineating purpose might be as action oriented as the examples in the following listing: to assist disadvantaged adults, to care for the needy, to promote community development, to provide early childhood education and child welfare, to foster unity among people, to provide skill training, or to comfort the infirmed. Here only a sample of purposes are listed, though the possibilities are numerous. Volunteer-based institutions have a variety of broad purposes: education, religion, justice, social change, health, and leisure, among others.

A typology developed according to organizational structure might include types such as charismatically based, hierarchical-bureaucratic, task specific, and individually oriented. Some voluntary agencies are connected to larger, nonvoluntary agencies, and some are tightly structured while others are not.

The following typology presented in Table 8.1 is an attempt to combine aspects of the points mentioned above and is organized by four types of volunteer contexts. To distinguish the four types, an emphasis is placed on learning, including the kind of learning, the content, and the method. In this way it is hoped adult educators will have a starting point for discussion of the purposes and types of voluntarism.

By analyzing factors such as the object of commitment, the type of learning, volunteers' objectives, content of learning, and method of learning, it is possible to discern four types of voluntary action organizations: (1) institutionally directed organizations, (2) volunteer-group-directed organizations, (3) problem-directed organizations, (4) social-change-directed organizations. Although the model recognizes that other types may be found and that these four overlap, it underscores the importance of placing voluntary action in a sociopolitical and education-oriented context. Moreover, the model emphasizes the importance of understanding voluntary participation from a bottom-up as well as from a top-down perspective. That is, to understand voluntary action, it is necessary to consider both volunteer and organizational perspectives.

Themes in Voluntary Action. Two persistent themes influence the quality and purposes of voluntary action. First is the professionalization of the field of voluntary action, and second is the networking and formulation of partnerships between and among institutions of volun-

Table 8.1. A Typology of Volunteer Learning.

Volunteer Context	Commitment	Type of Learning	Volunteers' Objectives	Content of Learning	Method of Learning
Type I Institution-directed organizations	To organization	Instrumental-Didactic (uniformity)	Meeting organizational goals	Task-specific skills and knowledge for role	Skill instruction rehearsal
Type II Volunteer group-directed organizations	To volunteer group	Social-Expressive	Social goals and organizational values	Role of volunteers and tolerance of differences	Group socialization
Type III Problem-directed organizations	To mission of organization	Problem-Solving	Accomplishing mission	Teamwork and group process	Experiential learning and goal accomplishment
Type IV Social change-directed organizations	To social ideals and vision of future	Critical-Reflexive	Social change empowerment	Political processes and sacrifice	Praxis

tary action and organizations in the private and governmental sector.

Voluntary action is attractive because it can serve different political purposes. This characteristic has led to multipartisan support of its growth and professionalization. Relatively few people oppose voluntary action, though some resist service volunteering because of its link with oppression of women, while others oppose social movement volunteering because of its tendency to disrupt the status quo. During recent years, unmistakable professional influences have appeared in the field of voluntary action. Currently, there are associations, journals, degree-granting programs, conventions, certification schemes, and even licensing of volunteers or administrators of volunteers. Some believe voluntary action is growing as a "distinct management discipline" (Ellis, 1986, p. 181). Accordingly, managers of volunteers are advised to visit resource centers such as voluntary action centers, local boards of volunteer administrators, state and provincial offices and associations, and even national organizations such as the Association for Volunteer Administration, VOLUNTEER: The National Center, and the Association of Voluntary Action Scholars. Newsletters and workshops abound and provide administrators with a broad array of methods and techniques of managing voluntary service.

Perhaps more important, the professionalism of voluntary action has meant new visions of organizing and structuring volunteer programs. Texts on the subject of volunteer management commonly refer readers to highly structured plans for recruitment, retention, and training of volunteers. In this sense, technical rationality has become a guiding principle for managers of volunteers. Many assume that the workplace metaphor, especially the professional workplace metaphor, best fits the volunteer scene. People can now be "hired" into volunteer positions, trained and certified, contracted, and evaluated according to performance criteria that appear on job descriptions. The professional workplace metaphor is useful for drawing attention to the need for efficiency and consistency, not to mention reducing conflict between volunteers and paid staff, especially professional staff. However, present in the metaphor are distinct assumptions about the need for control, about motivation of volunteers, and about how people learn.

Pearce (1982, 1983) suggests that the employment model is unnecessary for volunteers. By interviewing volunteers and paid staff from comparable organizations, she discovered that volunteers are less dependent on the organization than are paid staff, and that differences in motivation depend more on the type of work than on the relative status levels. Clary and Miller (1986) concur, and they suggest that duration of service and commitment on the part of volunteers depend less on the rules and procedures of the volunteer institution and more on the nature of the volunteer role. That is, length of service and commitment depend on how nurturing volunteers are asked to be and on the cohesiveness of the volunteer group.

The second theme, new partnerships in voluntary action, is related to the first. As professionalization of voluntary action develops, partnerships that lend an air of credibility to voluntary action are forming. Perhaps the newest participants in voluntarism are corporations. Corporate volunteering is seen as a mutually beneficial collaboration whereby voluntary organizations receive badly needed help from local business leaders, and, in exchange, corporations receive reputational benefits. Owing to recently enacted tax initiatives, many corporations have created voluntary service offices, which often are attached to personnel departments. Employees are encouraged to volunteer (often on released time) through such offices and to reach out into the community with their time and talents. The result has been well-structured programs of community involvement and excellent participation and duration of corporate volunteers. (Corporate Volunteers Coordinators Council, 1984)

Another partner in the professionalizing process is the government. In the United States, the federal government has shown unprecedented interest in voluntarism by enacting the Volunteer Services Act; by creating the umbrella agency ACTION, which coordinates the Peace Corps, RSVP, and VISTA; and by launching voluntary programs for seniors, students, and the disabled. Moreover, state and provincial governments have established offices of voluntary action to assist with the development and extension of voluntary action. Voluntarism is, in this way, viewed as a corrective enterprise that pays close attention to those groups of people most in need. These offices give attention to the creation of coalitions of voluntary groups that work together to solve pressing social ills.

Despite the attention and growth, critics worry that co-optation will occur as voluntary action becomes just another arm of the government or of a corporate enterprise (Langston, 1981; Van Til, 1987). Specifically, Langston fears a trend toward increased bureaucratic practice, accompanied by increasing centralization of services, that may result in diminished advocacy on the part of voluntary organizations. Moreover, Langston expects excessive governmental regulations in the not-too-distant future. Such warnings are not only applicable to the voluntary sector; they are also proper warnings for governmental and even private sector organizations. Extending the argument, Van Til points out that these trends underscore a muddling of the so-called sectors: businesses are not really private anymore; voluntary agencies are doing governmental work in many cases; and corporations are entering the social services. The distinctions among the public, private, and voluntary sectors are becoming blurred. Van Til raises doubts as to whether voluntarism in particular means the same thing it once did for the preservation of a democratic society.

Future Trends of Voluntary Action

Recent trends in voluntary action evoke the corporate image of efficiency and consistency. With the rise of governmental influence and the formulation of coalitions, one is drawn to the belief that voluntarism is becoming bureaucratic, technical, and professional. The disturbing aspect of this trend is that, in the process, voluntary action may become more narrowly focused and less responsive to the needs of the citizenry and of volunteers. Of course, there is no knowledge of what will happen in the future. A scenario can be neither right nor wrong. With that in mind, the following points are meant to spur discussion:

1. Voluntary action is becoming technicist. Technicism is the rise of the use of and obedience to tools. In a technicist practice, tools define the problem, as opposed to the problem calling for the right tool. Technicists promote a pigeonholing of human problems that disguises those problems with technical language and places the power of problem solving into the hands of experts. Voluntary action will be defined as technicist because there will be an overreliance on statistical, measurable data, and on certification schemes. Language will become increasingly unfriendly to volunteers as we continue to borrow metaphors from the corporate culture and from the military. We see this trend in the increased use of terms such as *bottom line, marketing segments, target population,* and *strategic maneuvers.* And, finally, training programs will become standardized and mandatory.

2. National organizations will form megacoalitions that will be responsive to governmental funding. These megacoalitions will be strongly represented in the legislative halls and will influence the next trend of human service. Such organizations will be immune to critical questioning because the agenda will be set in collaboration with the governmental-corporate-voluntary nexus—an arrangement too huge for citizens to influence.

3. The voluntary sector will be seen to be just another powerful arm of corporations and governments, removed from the needs of the people and ensconced in its own professional ethics, values, norms, and cultural traits.

4. Democracy will suffer a serious blow because many of the forums of participation will be removed from easy access, and instead will reside in the domain of expertise. Entry requirements into policy-making organizations will be restricted and the neighborhood ''voice'' will be channeled through larger civic organizations.

5. In the meantime, voluntarism on the local level, in unorganized fashion, will continue in rural areas, in clubs, and in social gatherings. Though less definable than the massive organizations of voluntary action, non-formal voluntarism will confront the challenge to counteract the influence of highly organized, large-scale, bureaucratic voluntary organizations.

Conclusion

In this chapter, I have argued that voluntary action serves different values at the same time, whether they be the values of volunteers, voluntary organizations, corporations, or governments. Moreover, I have suggested

that increased professionalization of the field of voluntary action is changing the face of voluntarism and may in fact weaken the distinctions among
the voluntary, public, and private sectors. What does this mean to the field
of adult education? Historically, adult educators have been committed to
giving people a voice and to providing people with an environment conducive to learning. It is not enough merely to assign training, tasks, and
roles to volunteers. To do so relegates our mission to mere technical form,
void of the social purposes of our roots. Rather, for the link between adult
education and voluntary action to continue, adult educators will need to have
an expanded social imagination and to look ahead to see how voluntary efforts bring us closer to solving our societal problems.

References

Addams, J. *Twenty Years at Hull House*. New York: Macmillan, 1927.

Adult Education Committee, Ministry of Reconstruction. *The 1919 Report:
The Final and Interim Reports of the Adult Education Committee of the Ministry
of Reconstruction*. London: His Majesty's Stationery Office, 1919.

Alinsky, S. *Rules for Radicals*. New York: Random House, 1971.

Bellah, R. N., and others. *Habits of the Heart*. Berkeley: University of California Press, 1985.

Bode, C. *The American Lyceum*. New York: Oxford University Press, 1956.

Clary, E. G., and Miller, J. "Socialization and Situational Influences on
Sustained Altruism." *Child Development*, 1986, *57*, 1358–1364.

Corporate Volunteers Coordinators Council. "The Virtues of Volunteering." *Personnel Journal*, 1984, *63*, 42–48.

Ellis, S. J. *From the Top Down: The Executive Role in Volunteer Program Success*.
Philadelphia: Energize Associates, 1986.

The Gallup Organization. *Americans Volunteer: 1981*. Princeton, N.J.: The
Gallup Organization, 1981.

The Gallup Organization. *Americans Volunteer: 1985*. Princeton, N.J.: The
Gallup Organization, 1985.

Gidron, B. "Sources of Job Satisfaction Among Service Volunteers," *Journal of Voluntary Action Research*, 1983, *12* (1), 20–35.

Ilsley, P. J. *Adult Literacy Volunteers: Issues and Ideas*. Columbus, Ohio: ERIC
Clearinghouse on Adult, Career, and Vocational Education, 1985a.

Ilsley, P. J. "Toward a Typology of Literacy Voluntarism Programs." Paper
presented at the Standing Conference of University Teaching and Research
in the Education of Adults, Sheffield, Eng., 1985b.

Ilsley, P. J., and Niemi, J. *Recruiting and Training Volunteers*. New York:
McGraw-Hill, 1981.

Karl, B. D. "Lo, the Poor Volunteer: An Essay on the Relation Between
History and Myth." *Social Service Review*, 1984, *54* (4), 493–552.

Langston, S. "The New Voluntarism." *Journal of Voluntary Action Research*,
1981, *10* (1), 8–20.

Laubach, F. *Forty Years with the Silent Billion.* Old Tappan, N.J.: Fleming H. Revell, 1970.

Lindeman, E. C. *The Meaning of Adult Education.* Montreal: Harvest House, 1928.

Pearce, J. L. "Leading and Following Volunteers: Implications for a Changing Society." *Journal of Applied Behavioral Science,* 1982, *16,* 385–394.

Pearce, J. L. "Job Attitude and Motivation Differences Between Volunteers and Employees from Comparable Organizations." *Journal of Applied Psychology,* 1983, *68,* 646–652.

Reichlin, S. "Volunteering and Adult Education: A Historical View." In E. M. Greenberg (ed.), *New Partnerships: Higher Education and the Nonprofit Sector.* New Directions for Experiential Learning, no. 18. San Francisco: Jossey-Bass, 1982.

Scattschneider, E. E. *The Semi-Sovereign People: A Realist's View of Democracy in America.* New York: Holt, Rinehart & Winston, 1984.

Schindler-Rainman, E., and Lippitt, R. *The Volunteer Community: Creative Use of Human Resources.* Fairfax, Va.: NTL Learning Resources, 1985.

Smith, D. H. "Altruism, Volunteers and Volunteering." *Journal of Voluntary Action Research,* 1981, *10* (1), 21–36.

Smith, D. H., Macaulay, J., and Associates. *Participation in Social and Political Activities.* San Francisco: Jossey-Bass, 1980.

Van Til, J. "The Three Sectors: Voluntarism in a Changing Political Economy." *Journal of Voluntary Action Research,* 1987, *16* (1–2), 50–63.

9

Professional Associations
for Adult and
Continuing Education

Ralph G. Brockett

Who should provide leadership to the adult and continuing education field? Schroeder (1980, p. 42) has suggested that leadership systems
"furnish guidance and direction to the field by establishing broad goals and
policies, allocating resources, training leaders, and generating knowledge."
He identifies four types of leadership systems: (1) state, regional, and national governments; (2) private foundations; (3) adult education graduate
programs; and (4) professional associations. Fellenz (1981, p. 228) has argued
that the professional success of the field to date can be attributed to "the
efforts of individual leaders" and that continued growth of the field will result
"to the extent that professional adult educators are willing to unite and furnish collaborative leadership in continuing education." This collaborative
leadership, according to Fellenz, is achieved by individuals working through
their professional associations.

According to Houle (1972, pp. 229–230), an association is a "structured body of members who join together, more or less freely, because of
a shared interest, activity, or purpose, and who, by the act of joining together,
assume the same basic powers and responsibilities held by other members."
While the terms *association* and *organization* are frequently used interchangeably, Houle distinguishes between the concepts by noting that authority in an
association is temporary, based on election of officers, while the authority
structure within an organization is hierarchical and relatively permanent.
Associations are designed to benefit the membership while organizations are
directed at serving "their owners, a defined clientele outside their own
membership, or the public at large" (p. 234).

This chapter will examine the role of professional associations in the field of adult and continuing education in the United States and Canada. Beginning with a look at some of the benefits that can be derived through such associations, emphasis will then shift to consideration of the different types of associations. A scheme will be presented that classifies associations according to role and scope. Finally, several issues of relevance to the future of professional associations will be discussed. While a detailed survey of specific associations is beyond the scope of the chapter, a number of associations will be mentioned in the context of illustrations throughout the chapter.

Why Professional Associations?

Professional associations serve a variety of functions. Some of the functions identified by Houle (1980, p. 171) include fulfilling "a need for status, a sense of commitment or calling, a desire to share in policy formation and implementation . . . a feeling of duty, a wish for fellowship and community, and a zest for education." In addition, associations in some professional fields, such as medicine, social work, and law, serve a regulatory function. In adult and continuing education, professional associations historically have played an important leadership role (Knowles, 1977). Today, these associations offer many potential benefits to individuals, to the field, and to the larger society.

Benefits to Individuals. Darkenwald and Merriam (1982) have suggested that the most important function provided by associations may be opportunities for professional development. Through conferences, workshops, and publications, associations help people within the field to keep abreast of new developments, current issues, and changing practices. By providing opportunities for leadership, associations also assist members in developing new skills and in shaping the directions they wish their fields to take in the future.

In addition to these more formal functions, professional associations provide a vital informal benefit to their members. The networks that individuals can form through their affiliations with other members often serve as an invaluable resource for sharing ideas, gaining new perspectives, and learning from one another. So often, the high point of attending conferences comes not so much from the formal sessions as from the opportunity to exchange ideas and insights with professional colleagues on an informal basis and to establish networks that serve as valuable resources long after the conference has ended.

Benefits to the Field. Within the field of adult and continuing education, professional associations have played an important role in the United States since the 1920s when the Department of Adult Education of the National Education Association (DAE, NEA) and the American Association for Adult Education (AAAE) were founded. Professional associations benefit adult and continuing education by contributing to the identity of the field.

For instance, McClusky (1982a, p. 8) has suggested that the establishment of the AAAE in 1926 "constituted the decisive and formative first step in giving both substantive and programmatic identity to the field." Similarly, associations can provide outlets for increasing professionalization and play a major advocacy role for adult and continuing education within the broader realm of education. While adult and continuing education continues to be viewed as marginal activity in some circles, professional associations can help to inform others about the importance of the role played by educators of adults and, in doing so, contribute to the strength of the field.

Benefits to Society. Still another function of professional associations involves creating greater awareness of adult learning throughout the larger society. It would probably be safe to say that, at present, most people outside of education do not realize that a field of adult and continuing education even exists. Through efforts to expand this awareness, it is possible for us, as a field, to play a greater advocacy role by educating society about the myths and realities surrounding the adult learner. National Adult and Continuing Education Week is one example of efforts already being made. Another aspect of the advocacy role is political involvement. Griffith (1976) has argued that if educators of adults are to play a major role in shaping opportunities for adult learning, it will be necessary to be actively involved in the political process and in policy-making. Many associations have legislative committees that work to promote adult education policy issues. Thus, one way in which professional associations can benefit society is by playing a leadership role in educating legislators at the national and state levels with regard to adult learning issues.

The Role and Scope of Professional Associations

Many types of associations exist within adult and continuing education. In attempting to understand how these associations fit within the large picture of adult and continuing education, it is possible to look at ways of classifying these associations. Griffith (1970), for example, used the work of Houle as a basis for a typology of associations. According to Griffith, professional associations within the field can be classified according to five criteria: (1) shared interest in a specific content area, such as adult basic education; (2) affiliation with a certain type of sponsoring agency, such as university continuing education or cooperative extension; (3) emphasis on a delivery method, such as external degree programs; (4) geographic location, such as a region, state, or metropolitan area; and (5) identification with a specific clientele, such as education for the aging. These categories are not mutually exclusive; thus, one can often classify an association according to two or more of these criteria.

Another way of categorizing associations is according to the type of the membership served. Smith, Eyre, and Miller (1982) suggest that three types of professional associations in adult and continuing education can be differentiated on the basis of membership emphasis. The first type is individual-membership-based associations. These groups derive most of their operational budgets from individuals and, similarly, are noted primarily for providing services to individual members. The American Association for Adult and Continuing Education (AAACE) and the American Society for Training and Development (ASTD) are examples of this type of association.

A second type of association is what Smith, Eyre, and Miller refer to as "institution-based." Here, the emphasis is on providing services that directly benefit institutions of adult and continuing education. Thus, financial support comes from institutional sources as opposed to individual membership fees. The National University Continuing Education Association (NUCEA) and the American Association of Community and Junior Colleges (AACJC) are examples of this association type.

Finally, some associations are, in fact, associations of associations. Organization-based associations, according to Smith, Eyre, and Miller, (1982, p. 386), "link several individual and institutional-based associations in order to aid their member associations in more effectively carrying out their respective responsibilities." Examples of these associations, which generally receive their financial support from other associations, include the Coalition of Adult Education Organizations (CAEO) and the International Council for Adult Education (ICAE).

There are numerous ways to classify professional associations of adult and continuing education. Given the diversity of these groups, it should be clear that there is no single ideal way to make such a classification. Yet drawing the distinction among different types of associations remains a worthwhile activity because it can help us gain insights into the breadth of our field and, as a result, into the problems of professional identity that have so often pervaded the field. Therefore, I am proposing an alternative approach to the classification of adult and continuing education professional associations. In this approach, associations are classified according to two criteria: the major role performed by the association and its scope or breadth of service. This two-way classification is illustrated with specific examples in Table 9.1.

Role. Determining the role played by a professional association centers around assessing its major purpose or focus. The five criteria addressed by Griffith (1970) identify a number of different roles for associations of adult and continuing education. For purposes of this discussion, however, professional associations are assumed to serve one of two primary roles: unification of the field or meeting the specialized needs of the field.

A key mission of many associations is the unification of the adult and continuing education field. In discussing the legacy of the Adult Education Association of the U.S.A. (AEA/USA) relative to the future of the AAACE, McClusky (1982b, p. 5) argued for the role of the association as a "unifying and integrating force in the field." Such a role is viewed as beneficial to the field because it can serve to strengthen both the power and knowledge bases of adult and continuing education. With regard to the power base,

Table 9.1. Examples of Adult and Continuing Education
Professional Associations According to Role and Scope.

	Role	
Scope	Unification	Specialization
Local	Metropolitan Washington Association for Adult and Continuing Education	Central New York Chapter of the American Society for Training and Development
	Milwaukee Council for Adult Learning	
State/ Provincial	Montana Association for Adult and Community Education	California Association for Re-Entry Education
	Connecticut Association of Adult and Continuing Education	British Columbia Association of Continuing Education Administrators
Regional	Mountain Plains Adult Education Association	Regional Groups of the National University Continuing Education Association
	Missouri Valley Adult Education Association	
National	American Association for Adult and Continuing Education	Commission on Adult Basic Education
	Canadian Association for Adult Education	Association for Continuing Higher Education
International	International Council for Adult Education	International League for Social Commitment in Adult Education

McClusky (p. 6) noted that ''the practice of adult education will never achieve the power of which it is capable if the agencies of adult education persist in performing in isolation. . . . Power will be much more likely when the programs of the separate agencies are supported by a common structure in pursuit of a generic goal. Separation leads to weakness while unification leads to strength.'' Similarly, McClusky suggested that only through a unified view will it be possible to build the knowledge base in terms of common areas across the field. Associations such as the AAACE and the Canadian Association for Adult Education (CAAE), which strive to serve a broad membership, exemplify this role.

Although the arguments in favor of unification stress the common bond among adult and continuing educators, the fact remains that the field is a vastly diverse one, with ideologies and issues covering a broad spectrum. In fact, the only thing one can say with certainty about a common bond among those who practice in the field is that we all share a concern for serving the adult learner. Therefore, it is only through working within specialty areas that we can truly develop the practices and issues that are more or less specific to particular practice settings. Just as issues related to the awarding of college credit will have little direct relevance to the administrator of a noncredit program in a public school district, the teaching of basic reading and writing skills is normally not within the domain of those educators who provide continuing education for professional groups such as social workers, physicians, or accountants. It is through opportunities for specialization that we can continue to forge ahead with issues and practices unique to certain segments of the field. The Commission on Adult Basic Education, the Association for Continuing Higher Education, and the Commission of Professors of Adult Education exemplify associations that meet specialized needs and, in fact, provide an outlet that can help to keep the special interests of any one segment of adult and continuing educators from dominating a larger organization.

Balancing Unification and Specialization. Darkenwald and Merriam (1982, p. 29) suggest that "the profusion of associations of adult educators might be interpreted as an example of healthy pluralism or as a symptom of parochialism and fragmentation." They suggest that it can be both. But I suggest that if professional associations are to have maximum influence on the field, there will need to be concern for both the unification and specialization aspects. Without broad "umbrella" associations, the field will inevitably continue to suffer from fragmentation and lack of professional identity. At the same time, without opportunities to associate professionally among those with specific shared concerns, we run the risk of failing to move beyond general themes to the particular issues that are germane to certain segments of the field. I therefore suggest that both unification and specialization are valuable roles for professional associations in the field. Balance between associations serving these two roles can provide maximum benefit to the field.

Scope. Another dimension that can contribute to understanding of professional associations is the level at which the association functions. How broad is the scope of the audience served by the association? Clearly, the level at which an association functions will impact the purposes it can strive to meet, the services it can provide, and the kinds of members it is likely to attract. Five levels of associations—local, state or provincial, regional, national, and international—illustrate the broad scope that such groups serve.

Historically, local adult education groups have served to link those individuals who practice in a particular community (Kotinsky, 1940). Today, local associations continue to thrive in some communities, such as Milwaukee and metropolitan Washington, D.C. More often, however, local associations function as informal networks rather than as formal organizations. Local associations, whether formal or informal in structure, serve an important function in that they are more in touch with concerns of adult and continuing educators in the context of a specific community than is possible in the other levels of associations.

At the state or provincial level, a major function of professional associations is to influence legislation relative to adult education. This is most often seen in the area of adult basic and secondary education. Across the United States and Canada, state and provincial associations vary considerably in terms of their breadth, influence, and effectiveness. In many areas, these associations play a major role in professional identity and in the development of its members. Often, associations at this level are a joint effort between two related groups such as adult and community education. This cooperation can lead to increased strength in numbers and minimal duplication of effort. Montana, for instance, operated separate adult and community education associations for several years. However, given the geography and demography of the state, many of the same individuals were providing leadership for both groups. The establishment of a joint association in 1985 has made it possible to maximize human and financial resources, while still serving the special needs of each field.

Regional associations such as the Mountain Plains Adult Education Association (MPAEA) and the Missouri Valley Adult Education Association (MVAEA) provide a link between state and national level associations. Similarly, some national associations, such as the National University Continuing Education Association (NUCEA), also have regional associations. Based on common concerns throughout a geographical region, these groups play a valuable role in professional development, particularly among those individuals who are unable to afford travel to national conferences. A particularly noteworthy effort at the regional level has been the publication of a refereed journal by the MPAEA since the early 1970s. While not all regions of the United States and Canada are currently represented by regional associations, these groups have potential to play a key role, particularly in geographically isolated and sparsely populated areas.

National associations have been central to the U.S. adult and continuing education movement for over six decades. Because these associations have a broad-based membership, they have a resource base much broader than local, state, or regional groups. Publications, education, and legislative relations are three of the major services of these associations. If there is to be a coordinated field of adult and continuing education, it can be argued that such an effort will need to take place at the national level.

Finally, the scope of international associations extends beyond the boundaries of a single nation. These groups strive to deal with issues of relevance on a global scale. Perhaps since international associations are less concerned with day-to-day issues of practice in specific institutions, membership of these associations is not as broadly based as membership at the other levels. Yet, international associations are vital to the field, for they help us to understand better and to work toward action on issues that affect our global society such as literacy, peace, and human rights.

The Future of Professional Associations in Adult and Continuing Education

As we look toward the next century, it will be important to consider the role that professional associations will play in the adult and continuing education field. To do this, it is necessary to realize that most people who will be practicing in the year 2000 are already in the field today. Thus, it is up to us to create the kind of future that we would like our field to have (Brockett, 1987). The position taken in this chapter is that professional associations have made a vital contribution to the development of the adult and continuing education field. However, it would be shortsighted not to recognize some of the issues that have often led to controversy within professional associations, particularly at the national level. To create a desirable future for adult and continuing education associations, it will be helpful to consider several of these issues and their potential impact on the future.

The Role of Professionalization. Few issues in adult and continuing education have been more controversial than whether the field should strive toward greater professionalization. This issue is addressed by Galbraith and Zelenak in Chapter Ten; thus, an extensive discussion of the pros and cons of professionalization is beyond the scope of this chapter. However, for those concerned with providing leadership to associations, professionalization will be a central theme. Whether the field moves toward a traditional model of professionalization, such as can be found in medicine, law, social work, and numerous other fields, or whether it adopts an alternative model such as one proposed by Cervero (1987), the issue inevitably will be linked to the role of professional associations in terms of questions such as the following: Should professional associations develop and administer some sort of certification process for adult and continuing educators? If such a process were to be adopted, which associations would have a role in establishing and enforcing standards? Could increased professional status allow associations to have greater influence in the process of seeking legislative support for adult and continuing education programs?

Elitism. Inextricably linked to the professionalization issue is the question of whether associations should strive to maintain open membership policies or whether membership should be restricted to individuals on the basis of certain criteria. Indeed, the issue of elitism has long been central to associations of adult and continuing education. In fact, as McClusky (1982a, p. 8) pointed out, it was "the 'elitist' and centralized character of its operation that enabled the AAAE to come into existence" in the late 1920s. Conversely, the rise of the AEA/USA, as can be seen in the process by which the association was founded and in the policies through which it operated, grew out of a desire to democratize participation in the association. Yet the ideal did not always parallel the practice. As Liveright (1968, p. 31) observed, "the very organizational structure of the newly formed Adult Education Association contained seeds of division." Indeed, the decision of public school adult educators to initiate a move away from the AEA through the establishment of the National Association of Public School Adult Educators only one year after the merger of the AAAE and the DAE, NAE, is evidence that these seeds of division had taken root.

Perhaps the questions that revolve around issues of elitism and representativeness are necessary elements in any discussion of the umbrella association concept. While the term *umbrella* implies inclusiveness, the fact remains that the adult and continuing education field is so vast and ideologies are so varied that, in many cases, all that is shared by various segments is a concern for working with adult learners. This does not negate the potential value of umbrella associations; however, it does make necessary the clear definition of the parameters of such groups. The myth of being all things to all people will inevitably lead to greater confusion, fragmentation, and elitism within organizations intended to bring together various elements of the field. So, it is important for associations designed to unite the field to strive toward the identification and promotion of common ground. Conversely, it is within the associations designed to meet specialized needs that the seeds of division should be freely planted. The distinction among the types of roles played by associations, therefore, has the potential to address and minimize concerns over elitism and representativeness.

Clearly, the issue of elitism will be crucial in the future development of professional associations. Shall adult and continuing education associations, for example, strive to seek a broad membership base or shall they limit membership to those who meet qualifications as so-called professionals? Should key leadership opportunities be open to all members or should they be restricted to certain groups within the membership, such as professors or state directors of adult education? How can the problems that have contributed to fragmentation and elitism in the past be minimized or eliminated in the future?

Publications. A major function of professional associations, particularly at the national level, is the development of a knowledge base in adult and continuing education. This is achieved primarily through the publication of professional journals. A perennial debate within the AAACE and its predecessor associations has been over the degree to which publications of the association should emphasize theory and research over practice. Those who favor the latter position argue that a more practical publication will be used more widely by those involved in direct practice. On the other hand, Beder (1985, p. 2) makes a convincing argument that "professional journals are the building blocks of our emerging profession" and, thus, should be treated as valuable tools. What should be the major function of professional publications in adult and continuing education? To what extent can and should publications help to define adult and continuing education as a professional field? The issue of publications is addressed in greater detail by Imel in Chapter Eleven.

Educational Role of Professional Associations. Houle (1980) has noted that associations are one of the major providers of continuing education to professional groups. If we are to consider adult and continuing education as a profession or as an emerging profession, clearly this educational function will be central to the function of professional associations. While much of the educational role of associations is of an informal nature, through mechanisms such as conferences, publications, and networking with colleagues, associations will need to think about their positions relative to more formal continuing education activities. If the field moves toward increased professionalism, two questions that have been raised by Hohmann (1980, pp. 84–85) become especially relevant: "If influence over members' professional behavior is a legitimate function of the association, by what mechanism should it operate? How can the effectiveness of that mechanism be regularly and reliably evaluated?"

Alternative Associations. Although the focus of this chapter has been on associations that exist more or less within the mainstream of adult and continuing education, it is important to recognize the important role played by many informal networks found throughout the field. These groups are generally formed for one of two purposes: (1) to represent positions or issues not prevalent within existing associations, or (2) to serve as a medium for the informal exchange of ideas or information. An example of the former is Basic Choices, Inc., a network based in Madison, Wisconsin, designed to provide for the exchange of alternative viewpoints about adult and continuing education, particularly related to issues of social responsibility. Though Basic Choices has operated with a minimum level of financial support and a handful of dedicated supporters, including founder and organizer John Ohliger, the organization has provided an invaluable consciousness-raising function about a host of social issues. For example, in the late 1970s and early 1980s, Basic Choices played a key role in bringing debate about the issue of mandatory continuing education to the forefront of the field. This debate forced many educators to rethink their positions on the issue and on the basic assumptions underlying this position.

A second type of informal network is reflected in the recent development of the Adult Education Network (AEDNET) at Syracuse University through support from the W. K. Kellogg Foundation. AEDNET is a worldwide network of adult educators who use the computer as a primary medium of communication. It is designed to provide a forum for discussion of issues and to provide worldwide access to a wide range of resources for educators of adults. In addition, AEDNET provides a means for electronic exchange, publishes an electronic journal, and serves as an interface to high-speed electronic networks that are emerging across the world.

Although Basic Choices and AEDNET serve very different purposes, groups such as these do, in fact, share a common goal of serving as outlets for the exchange of ideas and information not widely represented in the structures of existing associations. Often, such groups are formed around the desire to advocate a given set of issues or practices. Basic Choices, for instance, was organized around a concern for issues of social commitment in adult and continuing education. On the other hand, AEDNET is the result of an effort to utilize technology in linking educators of adults with a wide range of resources for professional development. While alternative associations are often not characterized by the same type of structures typically found in more traditional professional associations, they nonetheless serve an important function—one that frequently goes wanting in more formal associations. For this reason, these less formal groups hold much potential for the future of the field.

Conclusion

Professional associations have played a vital role in the development of the adult and continuing education field in the United States since the 1920s. Yet confusion over the role and scope of such associations, as well as debate within the field over the issue of professionalization, has often diminished the influence of these associations. In considering the future of professional associations of adult and continuing education, it will be essential to address such questions. Given the diversity of the field, it would seem appropriate to support a wide range of associations so that such groups will be able to serve both unification and specialization roles within local, state, regional, national, and international spheres.

References

Beder, H. "Defining the We." *Lifelong Learning: An Omnibus of Practice and Research,* 1985, *8* (5), 2.

Brockett, R. G. (ed.). *Continuing Education in the Year 2000.* New Directions for Continuing Education, no. 36. San Francisco: Jossey-Bass, 1987.

Cervero, R. M. "Professionalization as an Issue for Continuing Education." In R. G. Brockett (ed.), *Continuing Education in the Year 2000.* New Directions in Continuing Education, no. 36. San Francisco: Jossey-Bass, 1987.

Darkenwald, G. G., and Merriam, S. B. *Adult Education: Foundations of Practice.* New York: Harper & Row, 1982.

Fellenz, R. A. "The National Leadership Role Belongs to Professional Adult Educators." In B. W. Kreitlow (ed.), *Examining Controversies in Adult Education.* San Francisco: Jossey-Bass, 1981.

Griffith, W. S. "Adult Educators and Politics." *Adult Education,* 1976, *26* (4), 270–297.

Griffith, W. S. "Adult Education Institutions." In R. M. Smith, G. F. Aker, and J. R. Kidd (eds.), *Handbook of Adult Education.* New York: Macmillan, 1970.

Hohmann, L. "The Professional Associations." In H. J. Alford (ed.), *Power and Conflict in Continuing Education: Survival and Prosperity for All?* Belmont, Calif.: Wadsworth, 1980.

Houle, C. O. *The Design of Education.* San Francisco: Jossey-Bass, 1972.

Houle, C. O. *Continuing Learning in the Professions.* San Francisco: Jossey-Bass, 1980.

Knowles, M. S. *The Adult Education Movement in the United States.* (Rev. ed.) Melbourne, Fla.: Krieger, 1977.

Kotinsky, R. *Adult Education Councils.* New York: American Association for Adult Education, 1940.

Liveright, A. A. *A Study of Adult Education in the United States.* Boston: Center for the Study of Liberal Education for Adults, 1968.

McClusky, H. Y. "The Legacy of the AEA/USA: Implications for the Future of Adult and Continuing Education." Part 1. *Lifelong Learning,* 1982a, *6* (1), 8–10.

McClusky, H. Y. "The Legacy of the AEA/USA: Implications for the Future of Adult and Continuing Education." Part 2. *Lifelong Learning,* 1982b, *6* (2), 4–6.

Schroeder, W. L. "Typology of Adult Learning Systems." In J. M. Peters, and Associates (eds.), *Building an Effective Adult Education Enterprise.* San Francisco: Jossey-Bass, 1980.

Smith, W. L., Eyre, G. A., and Miller, J. W. "Join Your Professional Organizations." In C. Klevins (ed.), *Materials and Methods in Adult and Continuing Education.* Los Angeles: Klevens Publications, 1982.

10

The Education of Adult and Continuing Education Practitioners

Michael W. Galbraith
Bonnie S. Zelenak

The dynamic growth of adult education and the plethora of agencies and institutions that provide adults with educational opportunities are perhaps strengths as well as limitations when trying to confront the issue of educating competent adult and continuing education (ACE) practitioners who will implement the field's mission. Although the nature of the field of adult education can be characterized (Long, 1987), the characteristics and training of adult educators are less evident (Boshier, 1985).

Constraining Characteristics of ACE Practitioners

One of the primary issues that confront ACE practitioners is their lack of a common identity. The problem is related to the diversity of job titles, to the responsibilities of individuals who are providing adult education, and to their lack of association, in many cases, with the field or with its professional organizations. Many providers do not characterize themselves as ACE practitioners nor do they hold a common set of assumptions, educational backgrounds, training, or philosophies about their roles and responsibilities. The question of whether ACE practitioners have a professional identity, and just what that identity is or should be, has been debated at least since the inception of the American Association for Adult Education in 1926, and the debate will certainly continue into the 1990s. Merriam (1985, p. 86) suggests that "Without a common identification as adult educators, many are likely to lack the incentive to be trained as adult educators."

Roles and Educational Backgrounds of ACE Practitioners. In an effort to define accurately who ACE practitioners are, scholars in the field have created typologies to classify them according to the roles they play and the characteristics they possess. Boshier (1985) maintains that nearly all adult educators work as planners or teachers. Knox (1979) classifies practitioners as administrators, teachers and counselors, and policymakers. Houle (1970) uses the shape of a pyramid to describe ACE practitioners—the lay leadership at the base, the practitioners in the middle, and, at the apex of the pyramid, those who have made adult education their primary career. Today's ACE practitioners work in both paid and voluntary positions, work part-time and full-time, and include paraprofessionals as well as professionals. They practice their craft in formal, nonformal, and informal settings.

The numerous job titles and responsibilities associated with ACE practitioners, the diversity of their academic backgrounds, the degrees they hold, and the academic fields in which they hold those degrees contribute simultaneously to the richness and to the marginality of the field. According to a survey conducted by the Learning Resources Network (LERN), "The typical practicing adult educator is new to the position, has little or no coursework in adult education, comes from a field outside of adult education, and is likely to leave it in five years, and works very hard" (Hartman, 1983, p. 4). Survey results also revealed that at least 65 percent of the respondents held their highest degrees in something other than education. A full 43 percent had not taken a single academic credit course in the field of education. Richmond (1983) found that individuals holding continuing professional education positions had experienced a similar lack of training in the field of adult education. Most people received their expertise through on-the-job training (57 percent) while only 12 percent were trained in adult education.

Competencies of ACE Practitioners. Various studies have been produced in an attempt to identify the competencies needed by educators of adults. Most of the studies seek to identify the competencies of adult education teachers and administrators (Grabowski, 1976; Knox, 1979) although one study addressed the skills and knowledge needed by adult educators in the future (Rossman and Bunning, 1978). The *Models for Excellence* study (American Society for Training and Development, 1983) produced a list of thirty-one competencies and identified fifteen roles performed by training and development professionals who work mostly with the business and industry sector. The majority of such studies are concerned with the identification of specific roles or settings in adult education; however, several writers have attempted to address the issue of what competencies and proficiencies all ACE practitioners should possess (Grabowski, 1976; Knox, 1979).

Grabowski (1976) suggested that the competent ACE practitioner should have the following abilities:

- Understand and take into account the motivation and participation patterns of adult learners
- Understand and provide for the needs of adult learners
- Be knowledgeable in the theory and practice of adult learners
- Know the community and its needs
- Know how to use various methods and techniques of instruction
- Possess communication and listening skills
- Kow how to locate and use education materials
- Have an open mind and allow adults to pursue their own interests
- Continue his or her own education
- Be able to evaluate and appraise a program

Knox (1979) investigated proficiencies of educators of adults and proposed three core proficiencies needed by practitioners, regardless of institutional and role specifications. He suggested that all adult educators need to possess an understanding of the field of adult education, of various aspects of adult development and learning, and of the development of personal qualities such as commitment to lifelong learning, the effectiveness of interpersonal relations, and the desire for the improvement of practice through innovative strategies.

Professional Development of ACE Practitioners

The purpose of professional development is to help ACE practitioners acquire the knowledge, skills, attitudes, and behaviors needed to achieve the purposes of their jobs and to improve their performance. Professional development does not end with one course or with a series of workshops. Professionals must continue to acquire needed skills and behaviors throughout their careers. Learning activities must be available to practitioners who hold voluntary, part-time positions as well as to those who have made adult education their primary careers. Knox (1979, p. 2) suggests, "Perhaps the primary challenge of the coming decade in continuing education of adults revolves around defining and increasing the professional proficiency of workers in the field." That challenge continues into the 1990s.

Boshier (1985) recommends that ACE practitioners receive training determined by the roles they play, by the desired outcome, and by whether their role as adult educator is of primary or secondary professional concern. That is, training should follow function. He suggests that training is currently available through experience in the field, through short-term and in-service opportunities, and through graduate study. The primacy of the role performed must dictate the amount of training that can be provided. The quality of the experience should be similar for all who receive training.

Quality professional development for ACE practitioners may provide the means to reduce the marginality of the field, to increase the probability of creating a common bond among practitioners, and to ensure that they develop specific proficiencies. Phillips (1987) suggests that training changes performance in continuing education, resulting in benefits to the clients. In addition, professional development enhances the process of professionalization, the dynamic process whereby the field of adult education can be observed to change in certain crucial characteristics in the direction of a profession (Farmer, 1974). However, not all theorists accept the argument that the professionalization process is in the best interest of ACE practitioners or of the field of adult and continuing education (Ohliger, 1974; Carlson, 1977). They believe that the exclusionary practices and rigid standards associated with professionalization are inconsistent with the informal and voluntary nature of the field. Cervero (1987, p. 75) suggests that we should look "at the practice of continuing education rather than the process of training" and that the "field should professionalize in ways that are consistent with central beliefs about what it means to be continuing educators."

Although there is little empirical evidence to suggest that those who have been trained in adult education provide better services to participants than those who have not (Griffith, 1986), there is adequate reason to believe that involvement in learning activities and interactions with individuals who are willing to explore issues leads to enhanced learning and changed performance. Good training models and strategies for their implementation are worthy of continuing development, and the potential for enriching the lives of learners and the performance and critical thought of practitioners outweighs the concern that there is a lack of proof regarding their direct impact on these populations.

Forms of Training

The forms of training typically experienced by ACE practitioners are reflected in Houle's pyramid of leadership (1970). The forms of training that practitioners receive are largely dependent on the roles they play. Those at the base of the pyramid, the lay leadership, are inclined to learn on the job, through community-based providers and in alternative nonformal settings (see Chapter Eight). Those at the intermediate level, who perform adult education services as one part of their job, are likely to receive in-service training. Those at the top of the pyramid who have made adult education their primary career are more likely to receive formal training in the field; but even among this population, it is still the minority of full-time ACE practitioners who receive formal training. Self-directed learning is not limited to any of the levels of the pyramid; all practitioners are capable of developing learning experiences related to their needs.

On-the-Job Training. The primary means by which the lay leaders who serve as volunteers in a variety of community settings develop the skills or proficiencies needed for their particular roles is through on-the-job experience. Richmond (1987) and the LERN survey (Hartman, 1983) both reveal that the majority of practicing ACE practitioners gain needed skills and knowledge through experience, trial and error, modeling, peer groups, collegial contacts, and collaborative efforts, as well as through self-directed study that utilizes human and material resources. Learning planned by the individual must be considered a key factor in the development of ACE practitioners. These individuals engage in independent learning through networking, professional conferences, reading of the professional literature, and through questioning, self-assessment, decision-making, and self-evaluation processes, as well as through collaborative efforts (see Chapter Sixteen).

In-Service Training. Another form of preparing ACE practitioners is through in-service training, which is typically sponsored by employing agencies, corporations, professional associations (see Chapter Nine), colleges and universities, resource centers, or private consultants. Such training, usually short-term in nature, is conducted by a human resource developer or trainer whose purpose is to focus on learning that advances the development of specific job-related competencies, behaviors, and attitudes needed or desired by the sponsoring organization (Marsick, 1987). ACE practitioners who participate in in-service training are usually involved in some aspect of adult education as part of their work or supplemental activities. Volunteers, part-time employees, and paraprofessionals make up the largest segment of people who implement adult education procedures in a variety of settings, and they typically receive training through in-service activities sponsored by provider organizations—activities that directly relate to specific tasks they must perform.

Graduate Education Degree Programs. A formal educational mechanism by which individuals can acquire education and professional development is the graduate degree program in adult education. Nearly six decades ago, Rowden (1934) described courses in adult education offered by institutions of higher education. Since that time, others have addressed the issue of graduate degree programs in adult education (Jensen, Liveright, and Hallenbeck, 1964; Houle, 1970; Ingham and Hanks, 1981), and since the awarding of the first doctoral degrees in the 1930s, the number of graduate programs has increased substantially. According to a list of graduate programs in adult education compiled by the Commission of Professors of Adult Education (1986a), ninety-four universities and colleges in the United States and nine universities in Canada offered degrees. Jones and Galbraith (1985) found that 165 universities and colleges in the United States and Canada provided degree programs or offered course work in adult education that provided education or professional development to persons interested in adult education. In their study, twenty-eight different areas of concentration were available in the various programs such as adult basic education, administration, comparative education, continuing professional education, educational gerontology, extension education, human resource development, instructional design, and labor education. This variability in the major areas of study demonstrates the diversity of the graduate degree programs.

The typical core curriculum of adult education graduate programs consists of adult learning and development, program planning and administration, methodology, and foundational courses (Knox, 1973), with courses in research and related areas incorporated into the core curriculum (Merriam, 1985). The typical core curriculum is directed at the development of technical competence and skill. The ideological base, however, varies among graduate programs; so the core curriculum may reflect the ideology and desired outcomes of a specific department which might focus on sociopolitical change, social responsibility, or social integration, and not on technical skill acquisition.

The Commission of Professors of Adult Education (1986b) has attempted to differentiate between master's and doctoral levels in terms of beginning and advanced graduate study by suggesting that the core curriculum at the master's level should include the following subject matter:

- An introduction to adult education
- Adult learning and development
- Adult education program processes (planning, delivery, evaluation)
- Historical, philosophical, and sociological foundations
- An overview of educational research

At the doctoral level the core areas include study that is "more far-ranging and more intensive than study at the master's level" (p. 3). Therefore, at the doctoral level the core areas should include the following subject matter:

- Advanced study of adult learning
- In-depth analysis of social, political, and economic forces that have shaped the historical and philosophical foundations of adult education
- Study of leadership, including theories of administration and management
- Study of issues that impinge on policy formation
- Advanced study of methods of inquiry, in order to conduct adult education research

The differentiation of master's and doctoral level core curricula seems only to be divided by the degree of intensity. The best combination of theory and practice that should be acquired by persons preparing for or being trained in adult education has not been determined.

Brookfield (1985, p. 300) suggests that graduate programs are reflective of their broader host culture, and that therefore "such programs can only be fully understood if they are seen as socio-cultural products." Graduate education programs, both in the United States and in Canada, are expected to stress research, but most adult education degree programs are directed at the enhancement of the realization of individual strengths and therefore are focused on the development of technical and practical skills. The technical and practical skills orientation can be seen in the typical core curriculum of adult education graduate degree programs. Graduate programs with a technical and practical skill orientation will generally reflect the cultural and political ideologies and intellectual emphases of university organizations in which they are housed. And graduate programs that are directed at some other orientation will reflect the specific ideological emphases of their universities.

Conclusion

The focus of this chapter has been on the constraining characteristics of ACE practitioners and on the forms of training in which they engage. Because training experiences are often linked to occupational role and status, it must be recognized that the amount of control the field of adult education has over the training received by ACE practitioners is limited. Training is largely dependent upon the primacy of the role that the practitioner plays. For the majority of ACE practitioners who hold voluntary positions in a number of community settings, the bulk of training received is informal and on-the-job. The field of adult education has little or no control over the quality or type of training received by this group or over the outcomes of the training they experience. When training is provided to this group, it is skill oriented. To the extent that it has any philosophical orientation, training for volunteers may include information intended to develop a commitment to the goals of the specific agency.

For ACE practitioners who perform adult education as a function of their job, it is possible to have a fairly high level of control over the in-service training they receive. Properly planned and implemented, the specific goals for the training, as well as the quality, content, and training procedures, can be controlled. By narrowing the focus of training to those who can be reached through their jobs and through supervisors who support this overall purpose, it becomes possible to help selected segments of ACE practitioners improve their job-related knowledge and skills and to expand their understanding of how they fit into the broad network of adult educators. In-service training with this emphasis can help to develop a common bond among ACE practitioners and to decrease the marginality of the field.

Finally, for those who have adult and continuing education as their primary career, a higher level of control over the quality of training is possible through preservice graduate education programs and in-service activities. However, expecting a high level of control over the quality of practice and performance of ACE practitioners, even at this level, is not practical due to the manner in which they enter the field.

Despite the inherent limitations on the amount of control possible over the training received by ACE practitioners and the resultant quality of practice, the goal of developing well-qualified, competent educators is worthy of continuing pursuit. The single most important strategy that can lead toward reducing the marginality of the field and toward enhancing the education of ACE practitioners is the development of a professionalization process that is framed around the questions of what good practice is and what beliefs ACE practitioners should hold (Cervero, 1987). From this perspective, each new member entering adult and continuing education is made aware of principles of good practice and of the central accepted beliefs. Individuals involved in the education of ACE practitioners can influence the type of outcome desired from each specific form of training.

To address some of the constraining characteristics of ACE practitioners, a component of the professionalization process may be a voluntary professional certification program (Galbraith and Gilley, 1986). While some believe that such a program may be too bureaucratic and too rigid for a field as diverse as adult and continuing education (Fahs, 1987), it does have the potential of enhancing the identity and reducing the marginality of the field. A well-developed professional certification program administered by the major professional association representing ACE practitioners could address the issues of who the field comprises, the functions they perform, and the competencies they should possess to carry out each identified role. Professional certification should be performance oriented and not academic oriented. Such a program could instill in the ACE practitioner the expectations associated with the role—the level of competency that must be acquired. This kind of program could provide a mechanism for demonstrating whether practitioners were performing at a proficient level, and it should include a continuing education component to focus upon remaining current and competent (Galbraith, 1987). Professional certification would be entirely compatible with the professionalization process in which each member is made aware of the central beliefs and principles of good practice for each specific subfield that constitutes adult education.

Another central component of the professionalization process should be the development of a code of ethics that addresses the principles of good practice and the central beliefs to which ACE practitioners should adhere. Such a code of ethics can help to introduce new members of adult and continuing education to the beliefs and expectations of the field. Something that has been rather informal and implicit may become more formal and explicit, thus helping educators design the various forms of training. A code of ethics may contain guiding principles that all ACE practitioners should follow and that translate to good practice in areas such as administration, program planning, marketing, evaluation, research, instruction, and social responsibility (Brockett, 1988).

This chapter has reviewed the constraining characteristics of ACE practitioners as they relate to the diversity of roles they play and the training they receive. It has suggested that the marginality of the field and lack of control over the training of the practitioners, and thus the quality of their performance, may be improved through a professionalization process. This process must include a focus on the identification of good principles of practice and on the identification or definition of the role of competent practitioners—

factors that must be inherent in all forms of training received by ACE practitioners. The development of the professionalization process, with its voluntary professional certification program and related code of ethics, would clarify and codify our guiding principles. The field and its practitioners both would be the beneficiaries.

By focusing on the mechanisms for identifying good principles of practice and by disseminating those principles through the various forms of training and related literature, the field has the opportunity to enhance the performance of practitioners. Ultimately, the quality of the performance of the practitioners, not the quantity of training provided to them, is most important. Although the quantity may vary among the various forms of training, it is important to ensure that the quality of that training remains consistent. All forms of training should be designed to lead to the enhanced performance of ACE practitioners.

References

American Society for Training and Development. *Models for Excellence: The Conclusions and Recommendations of the ASTD Training and Development Competency Study.* Washington, D.C.: American Society for Training and Development, 1983.

Boshier, R. "Conceptual Framework for Analyzing the Training of Trainers and Adult Educators." *Convergence,* 1985, *18* (3-4), 3-22.

Brockett, R. G. (ed). *Ethical Issues in Adult Education.* New York: Teachers College Press, 1988.

Brookfield, S. D. "Training Educators of Adults: A Comparative Analysis of Graduate Adult Education in the United States and Great Britain." *International Journal of Lifelong Education,* 1985, *4* (4), 295-318.

Carlson, R. A. "Professionalization of Adult Education: An Historical-Philosophical Analysis." *Adult Education,* 1977, *28* (1), 53-63.

Cervero, R. M. "Professionalization as an Issue for Continuing Education." In R. G. Brockett (ed.), *Continuing Education in the Year 2000.* New Directions for Continuing Education, no. 36. San Francisco: Jossey-Bass, 1987.

Commission of Professors of Adult Education. *Graduate Programs in Adult Education: United States and Canada.* Hollywood, Fla.: American Association for Adult and Continuing Education, 1986a.

Commission of Professors of Adult Education. *Standards for Graduate Programs in Adult Education.* Hollywood, Fla.: American Association for Adult and Continuing Education, 1986b.

Fahs, G. M. "Bureaucracy Does Not Assure Quality." *Lifelong Learning: An Omnibus of Practice and Research,* 1987, *11* (2), 25, 28.

Farmer, J. A. "Impact of Lifelong Learning on the Professionalization of Adult Education." *Journal of Research and Development in Education,* 1974, *7* (4), 57-67.

Galbraith, M. W. "Certification Would Advance Professional Practice." *Lifelong Learning,* 1987, *11* (4), 15, 18.

Galbraith, M. W., and Gilley, J. W. *Professional Certification: Implications for Adult Education and HRD.* Information Series no. 307. Columbus, Ohio: ERIC Clearinghouse on Adult, Career, and Vocational Education, 1986.

Grabowski, S. *Training Teachers of Adults: Models and Innovative Programs.* Syracuse, N.Y.: National Association for Public Continuing and Adult Education and ERIC Clearinghouse in Career Education, 1976.

Griffith, W. "Challenging the Future: The Professionalization of the Major Segments of Adult and Continuing Education." In L. Lewis and J. Neimi (eds.), *Commission of Professors of Adult Education: Proceedings of the 1986 Annual Conference.* Hollywood, Fla.: Commission of Professors of Adult Education, 1986.

Hartman, M. "Some Surprises Found in National Survey of Adult Educators." *The Learning Connection,* 1983–1984, *5* (1), 4–6.

Houle, C. O. "The Educators of Adults." In R. M. Smith, G. F. Akers, and J. R. Kidd (eds.), *Handbook of Adult Education.* New York: Macmillan, 1970.

Ingham, R. J., and Hanks, G. "Graduate Degree Programs for Professional Adult Educators." In S. M. Grabowski and Associates, *Preparing Educators of Adults.* San Francisco: Jossey-Bass, 1981.

Jensen, G., Liveright, A., and Hallenbeck, W. (eds.). *Adult Education: Outlines of an Emerging Field of University Study.* Washington, D.C.: Adult Education Association of the U.S.A., 1964.

Jones, G. E., and Galbraith, M. W. "Adult Education: A Study of Graduate Programs in the United States and Canada." Unpublished manuscript, Central Community College, Grand Island, Nebr., 1985.

Knox, A. B. *Development of Adult Education Graduate Programs.* Washington, D.C.: Adult Education Association of the U.S.A., 1973.

Knox, A. B. *Enhancing Proficiencies of Continuing Educators.* New Directions for Continuing Education, no. 1. San Francisco: Jossey-Bass, 1979.

Long, H. B. *New Perspectives on the Education of Adults in the United States.* New York: Nichols, 1987.

Marsick, V. (ed.). *Learning in the Workplace.* London: Croom-Helm, 1987.

Merriam, S. "Training Adult Educators in North America." *Convergence,* 1985, *18* (3–4), 84–93.

Ohliger, J. "Is Lifelong Education a Guarantee of Permanent Inadequacy?" *Convergence,* 1974, *7* (2), 47–58, 74.

Phillips, L. E. "Is Mandatory Continuing Education Working?" *MOBIUS, 1987, 7* (1), 57–63.

Richmond, K. *Professional Association Educators Survey.* Athens: Georgia Center for Continuing Education, University of Georgia, 1987.

Rossman, M. H., and Bunning, R. L. "Knowledge and Skills for the Adult Educator: A Delphi Study." *Adult Education,* 1978, *28* (3), 139–155.

Rowden, D. "Courses in Adult Education." In D. Rowden (ed.), *Handbook of Adult Education in the United States, 1934.* New York: American Association for Adult Education, 1934.

11

The Field's Literature and Information Sources

Susan Imel

The knowledge base of a field is represented through written materials. Usually referred to as its literature, this body of knowledge is important not only because it contains the information that makes the field unique—thus separating it from other disciplines—but also because it demonstrates what is known about the field of practice (Boshier and Pickard, 1979; Sork and Buskey, 1986). Since 1926, the field of adult education has developed a literature base that has helped it attain status as a profession. The first section of this chapter reviews the development of the literature of adult education. After a brief discussion of what constitutes that literature, some historical aspects of its development are noted. The section concludes with a review of some research and writing that examines the literature.

As the literature of adult education has grown and expanded, knowing how to access or locate the literature has become a critical skill. The second section of the chapter discusses information sources for adult educators and describes information data bases, libraries, and clearinghouses that organize and make available the literature of adult education. The chapter concludes by raising some issues related to the literature and to information sources.

The Literature of Adult Education

The literature comprises those materials that represent the knowledge base of the field of practice and distinguish it from other fields or disciplines. According to Dickinson and Rusnell (1971, p. 177), "One of the hallmarks of the emergence of adult education as a distinct profession has been the development of an organized body of knowledge.'' Although any type of written material may be considered to be a part of the literature of the field, those items that add to or enhance the understanding of existing information are considered more important because they enhance the knowledge base.

As the field has grown and expanded, so has its literature base. The literature of adult education is very much like the field itself: it covers a vast array of topics and is available in many different formats (Verner, 1960). The most common forms of adult education literature include books, periodicals, dissertations, and so-called fugitive materials.

Many books have been written about adult education, beginning with Pole's *A History of the Origin and Progress of Adult Schools,* first issued in England in 1816. Because books are durable and because libraries have systematic procedures for collecting and classifying them, much of the literature of adult education is available in this format. Due to their specialized nature, however, books about adult education are generally purchased only by large public or university libraries, and many books considered to be classics, such as Lindeman's *The Meaning of Adult Education* (1926), remain virtually inaccessible to large numbers of adult educators.

Periodicals, including journals or newsletters, are an important source of adult education literature. In commenting on their significance, Long and Agyekum (1974, p. 101) said ''journals are a chief medium for the diffusion of emerging and developing areas of concern in the discipline.'' As the field has expanded, so has the number of periodical publications devoted to it. Also, many articles about aspects of adult education frequently appear in nonadult education periodicals. Although adult educators may have access to some current periodical literature through personal subscriptions, institutional libraries, or resource centers, a comprehensive range of adult education periodical literature is usually available only in large public or university libraries.

More than 3,000 doctoral degrees have been awarded in adult education (Long, 1987). The dissertations that have been written to fulfill the requirements for these degrees represent a major form of adult education literature. *Dissertation Abstracts International* makes information about dissertations available through both on-line computer searching and print indexes.

Much of the literature of adult education is available in a form known as fugitive materials. So named because its availability is not well-known or publicized, or because it may be difficult to acquire, fugitive material includes items such as pamphlets, brochures, conference proceedings and papers, research studies, and reports of government-funded projects. Although much of it is ephemeral in nature, many fugitive materials have made important contributions to the adult education literature base. With the advent of the Educational Resources Information Center (ERIC) in 1966, fugitive materials became much more accessible. ERIC's role in this respect is discussed in the chapter's section on information sources.

The Development of the Literature Base. Following Pole's book recording the adult school movement, the literature base of adult education began to develop. Two other significant pieces of adult education literature originating in Great Britain were *The 1919 Report* (see Adult Education Committee, Ministry of Reconstruction, 1919) and *W. E. A. Education Year Book 1918* (Workers' Education Association, 1918). *The 1919 Report,* which was produced by the Adult Education Committee of the Ministry of Reconstruction, provided a comprehensive survey of the history and organization of adult education in Great Britain and included a series of recommendations that were instrumental in shaping its development between the world wars. In the introduction to *A Design for Democracy,* an abridged version of the original report, Waller (1956, p. 15) suggested that it is "probably the most important single contribution ever made to the literature of adult education." *The W. E. A. Education Year Book 1918,* produced by leaders of the Workers' Educational Association, provided an account of the adult education system from the perspective of a number of prominent intellectuals and writers including George Bernard Shaw and H. G. Wells. Fortunately, both *The 1919 Report* and *The W. E. A. Year Book* have been reprinted by the Department of Adult Education at the University of Nottingham.

The American Association for Adult Education (AAAE), founded in 1926 with support from the Carnegie Foundation, is generally credited with laying the foundation for the development of a professional literature base (Brockett, 1987; Grattan, 1955; Hilton, 1981; Knowles, 1977). AAAE engaged in a publications program that "was probably more responsible than any other factor for establishing the adult educational field as a respectable and definable field of study" (Knowles, 1977, p. 256).

Because of its commitment "to try to make something more of adult education" (Grattan, 1955, p. 277), the Carnegie Foundation provided funds for studies of adult education during the period in which it was supporting the organization of AAAE. Publications resulting from these studies included books such as *New Schools for Older Students* (Peffer, 1926), *Correspondence Schools, Lyceums, Chautauquas* (Noffsinger, 1926), *Educational Opportunities for Young Workers* (Evans, 1926), *The University Afield* (Hall-Quest, 1926), and *Adult Learning* (Thorndike and others, 1928). Peffer (p. 7) commented on the literature's status during that period by observing that he cited few references in his book "because there are so few. . . . There is no literature of adult education in the United States or of adult education enterprises."

In addition to those produced with support from the Carnegie Foundation, there were other significant books published during the period AAAE was being organized. Most notable among these was Eduard Lindeman's *The Meaning of Adult Education* (1926), considered by many to be the book that laid the philosophical foundations for the field of adult education. Two other books of note were *Adult Education* by Joseph K. Hart (1927) and *The Meaning of a Liberal Education* by Everett Dean Martin (1926).

After its founding, AAAE demonstrated its commitment to developing the knowledge base of adult education by producing works such as *Adult Education and the Social Scene* (Kotinsky, 1933), *Adult Education in Action* (Ely, 1936), and *The Literature of Adult Education* (Beals and Brody, 1941). It was also responsible for initiating the *Handbook of Adult Education* series, publishing the first volume in 1934 and issuing subsequent volumes in 1936 and 1948.

Although many of the books published by AAAE are still regarded as classics, it is generally agreed that its most important contribution to the literature was *The Journal of Adult Education,* published from 1929 to 1942. The journal's contributors included many of the most respected thinkers and intellectuals of the day (Hilton, 1981). According to Morse Cartwright (1935, p. 65), AAAE's executive director, the journal was a "most unifying force in the field of adult education . . . [and] within and without the Association its influence [was] a definite factor upon quality of effort."

In 1942, both the name and the emphasis of the journal changed. It became the *Adult Education Journal,* and news from and about the field of adult education took precedence over general cultural issues, philosophical topics, and social problems. Professional adult educators became the major contributors with this change in focus. In 1950, the *Adult Education Journal* merged with the *Adult Education Bulletin,* published by the National Education Association (NEA), and became known simply as *Adult Education* (Knowles, 1977).

Although no other group or organization had such a singular impact upon the development of the literature base of adult education as did AAAE, there were other significant contributors during the field's formative years. In 1952, AAAE merged with the NEA Department of Adult Education to form the Adult Education Association of the U.S.A. (AEA). As the professional association succeeding AAAE, AEA also continued the tradition of contributing to the literature base through its publications program. AEA took over the publication of *Adult Education.* Although the emphasis of that journal changed to a focus on research during the thirty years it was published by AEA, it retained the same title.

AEA also published a number of other items during this period including the Leadership Series, collections of articles from *Adult Leadership* known as *Leader's Digest,* and a number of monographs developed in conjunction with the ERIC Clearinghouse on Adult Education, which was located at Syracuse University. AEA's Commission of Professors of Adult Education produced *Adult Education: Outlines of an Emerging Field of University Study* (Jensen, Liveright, and Hallenbeck, 1964), a book that "was the product of collective thinking about the conceptual foundations of adult education as a field of university study" (Niemi, 1987, p. 119). Another significant publication produced by AEA was *Last Gamble on Education* (Mezirow, Darkenwald, and Knox, 1975), a grounded research study of adult basic education. AEA also continued AAAE's tradition of publishing, bringing out single volumes in 1960 and 1970 and an eight-volume set in 1980.

The Fund for Adult Education (FAE), established by the Ford Foundation in 1951, also made significant contributions to the literature during this period. The FAE made grants to AEA for special publications including the 1960 edition of the *Handbook* and *Adult Leadership,* a monthly publication designed to develop communication between AEA and its nonmembers who functioned in some adult education capacity (Fund for Adult Education, n.d.; Knowles, 1977). *Adult Education: Issues in Dispute* (Powell, 1960), a collection of articles from the journal's *Adult Leadership* and *Adult Education,* was also published by AEA with support from the FAE. Developed by AEA's Committee on Social Philosophy, this publication is notable because it reprinted several articles by its editor, John Walker Powell.

The FAE also provided funding for the Center for the Study of Liberal Education for Adults (CSLEA), an organization that developed publications devoted to higher adult education. CSLEA's monographs, which included the series "Notes and Essays on Adult Education" and "Reports," "were soon recognized as outstanding contributions to the literature and professional standards" (Whipple, 1967, p. 22). Two publications related to adult education literature developed by CSLEA were *On Behalf of Adult Education: A Historical Examination of the Supporting Literature* (Cotton, 1968) and *The Literature of Liberal Adult Education 1945–1957* (Mezirow and Berry, 1960).

By 1960, the field of adult education had established a literature base of some significance, one that was beginning to demonstrate its "growing maturity" (Verner, 1960, p. 171). In the *1960 Handbook of Adult Education,* Coolie Verner (p. 171) observed that "the literature of adult education is rapidly moving out of the phase of impressionistic propaganda and intuitive reports into more carefully structured research." In the thirty years since Verner's assessment, the literature has developed at a rapid pace. A number of factors have contributed to its growth including a "growing cadre of professional scholars, researchers, and trained leaders" (DeCrow, 1970, p. 78), federal legislation supporting educational programs for adults (Long and Agyekum, 1974), and growing recognition by publishers that adult education is a significant field of practice.

The growth of the literature has been supported by a number of activities, some examples of which are cited below. Journals such as *Convergence* and the *International Journal of Lifelong Education* have emerged to provide a forum for comparative and international adult education. In 1979, the commercial publisher Jossey-Bass initiated the New Directions for Continuing Education series, which supplemented its extensive publications program in adult and continuing education. Literature related to Canadian adult education has been produced and disseminated by a number of sources including the Canadian Association for Adult Education, which in 1987 began publishing the *Canadian Journal for the Study of Adult Education* to supplement its monograph series; the Ontario Institute for Studies in Education; and the University of British Columbia's Centre for Continuing Education. Research conferences such as the Adult Education Research Conference, the Lifelong Learning Research Conference, and the Midwest Research-to-Practice Conference in Adult and Continuing Education have produced and made available conference proceedings.

Literature About the Literature. As the literature has developed, numerous efforts have been made to analyze it. Although most of the literature about the literature examines only certain aspects of it, two common themes emerge from this body of research—the evolution of a knowledge data base for adult education and the quality of that data base. Following a brief review of two publications of historical interest, these themes are discussed.

As a part of its contribution to the development of the literature, AAAE sponsored a review of the field's early writing, *The Literature of Adult Education* (Beals and Brody, 1941). Concentrating primarily on the period between 1929 and 1939, Beals and Brody (pp. xiv, xv) reviewed adult education literature "of potential usefulness to the 'serious student'" giving preference "to titles that indicate[d] the scope of the study or methods of investigation characteristic of the field." Despite the fact that this book is more descriptive than analytical, it is important because of its coverage of the literature developed during the field's early years.

In 1959, with support from the Fund for Adult Education, the AEA published *An Overview of Adult Education Research* (Brunner and others, 1959). Like Beals and Brody, Brunner and his associates looked at the literature produced primarily since the organization of the field in 1926. However, their review included only research studies that met specific criteria, and it was much more critical and analytical. They concluded that the status of adult education research was "rather chaotic" and that "a few pertinent areas . . . [had] been explored far more thoroughly than others" (p. 2).

Since 1970, additional research and writing related to the development of the adult education literature have been produced. Two general themes have emerged from this body of material. The first has to do with the evolution of a knowledge base for adult education and the second with the adequacy or quality of that knowledge base.

A number of studies have investigated the emergence of a knowledge base for the field of adult education by examining portions of its literature (Allcorn, 1985; Boshier and Pickard, 1979; and Dickinson and Rusnell, 1971). These studies used the journal literature in an attempt to answer the question, "Is there a distinct knowledge base for the field of adult education?" All concluded that adult education is creating or generating a unique body of knowledge.

Although most adult educators would agree that the field does possess a distinct knowledge base, there has been great debate about the adequacy or quality of that literature. One of the most frequently cited problems related to the literature has to do with the failure of contributors to develop a cumulative knowledge base (Allcorn, 1985; Boshier and Pickard, 1979; Fingeret, 1984; Ilsley, 1985; Long, 1987; Plecas and Sork, 1986; and Sork and Buskey, 1986). Those engaged in developing the literature do not build on existing research and theory. The result is a literature base that lacks depth, is repetitive, and lacks a well-developed theoretical basis. Because of the failure to develop a cumulative knowledge base, Plecas and Sork (1986, p. 55) concluded that "what we end up with is a discipline uncertain of direction, moving in several directions, and building its knowledge base outward but not upward."

During its formative years, the field of adult education was concerned with developing or generating a distinct knowledge base. There were many contributors to that process, and the field now has a literature available in many forms. More than sixty years after its formal organization, a sign of the field's maturity is that it can turn its attention to improving the adequacy or quality of that literature.

Information Sources for Adult Educators

Although there is a growing body of adult education literature, individuals may not know how to access or locate it. This section of the chapter describes three sources of adult education literature or information: libraries, information data bases, and clearinghouses or resource centers.

Libraries. Libraries, especially college and university libraries located at institutions with graduate programs in adult and continuing education, are sources of adult education literature. Although there are several outstanding collections of adult education literature in unversity libraries within the United States, the collection at Syracuse University is particularly notable. Known as the Syracuse University Resources for Educators of Adults (SUREA), it is the largest collection of adult education materials in the world. SUREA contains a number of special collections including archival materials from groups such as FAE, AEA, and AAAE and from individuals such as A. A. Liveright, Paul Sheats, Coolie Verner, and Frank Laubach; the largest media collection of adult education materials including the Omnibus series produced by the Ford Foundation and Columbia Broadcasting System (CBS); and more than 10,000 photographs (Hilton, 1985). SUREA makes accessible a "rich collection of materials about many of the organizations and individuals who have played a significant role in the development of adult education in the United States" (Stubblefield, 1980, p. 7). In September 1986, Syracuse University launched a five-year research project related to SUREA. Funded by the Kellogg Foundation, the Syracuse University Kellogg Project has two primary goals: (1) to provide access to the University's collection of adult education materials using laser disk and computer technologies, and (2) to promote information exchange through computer-mediated and nonelectronic means of communication (Syracuse University Kellogg Project, n.d.). Individuals once had to travel to Syracuse, New York, to make use of SUREA. Now, using information technologies, the Kellogg Project will make the materials accessible throughout the world.

Information Data Bases. Information data bases store collections of related information that can be retrieved via computer using information retrieval software. Although many information data bases are useful to adult educators, the Educational Resources Information Center (ERIC) data base is considered to be the primary source for adult education due to both its purpose and its history of service to the field. Currently funded by the U.S. Department of Education's Office of Educational Research and Improvement, ERIC is designed to put the results of educational research into the hands of researchers, practitioners, policymakers, and others interested in information about education. Since 1966, ERIC has been collecting and classifying all types of educational materials, focusing on the fugitive types that were described earlier. In addition to fugitive or document literature, ERIC also contains information about journal literature. More than 700 education-related journals are scanned regularly to select articles for inclusion in ERIC, including all major adult education journals published both in the United States and abroad (Niemi and Imel, 1987).

Generally, searches of ERIC are conducted by a trained searcher. However, the availability of microcomputers has made ERIC more accessible to individuals, and many are choosing to search ERIC using their own equipment. In addition, the packaging of the ERIC data base in CD-ROM (compact disk-read only memory) format makes it available to individuals who have access to CD-ROM equipment. A subject search of ERIC results in bibliographic information plus an abstract of all information in the ERIC data base on the topic. Most documents in ERIC are available in either microfiche or paper copy from the ERIC Document Reproduction Service (EDRS), but journal articles must be obtained through other sources such as journal reprint services or libraries.

Since 1966, more than 12,500 items whose major topic is related to adult education have been selected for inclusion in the ERIC data base. Types of adult education materials contained in ERIC include reports and materials produced by projects funded under Section 310 of the Adult Education Act; conference proceedings from the Adult Education Research Conference, the Lifelong Learning Research Conference, and the Midwest Research-to-Practice Conference in Adult and Continuing Education; papers and presentations given by the American Association for Adult and Continuing Education Conference; and reports of government-funded research projects related to adult education. ERIC also contains a wide variety of international adult education materials including publications produced by the Canadian Association for Adult Education, UNESCO, the Adult Literacy and Basic Skills Unit in London, the Australian National University's Centre for Continuing Education, and the International Council for Adult Education. Some of the historical materials discussed earlier are also available through ERIC, including CSLEA's series "Notes and Essays on Adult Education" and AEA's Leadership Series.

Clearinghouses and Resource Centers. A number of clearinghouses and resource centers disseminate information about adult education to a variety of audiences including administrators, teachers, researchers, students, and the general public. Some of these organizations, such as the ERIC Clearinghouse on Adult, Career, and Vocational Education (ERIC/ACVE), serve international audiences. Others, such as the Dissemination Network for Adult Education in California, are state-level organizations. Clearinghouses and resource centers serve a variety of functions such as providing on-line searches of information data bases like ERIC, information about resources and materials, collections of materials and resources, and referral to other agencies and organizations serving adult learners. Many also develop and make available newsletters and free or inexpensive materials related to adult education resources. *Directory of Clearinghouses* (U.S. Department of Education, Division of Adult Education, 1987) lists clearinghouses and resource centers that provide information about adult education in the United States. Information about international resources can be found in the *International Handbook of Resources for Educators of Adults* (Charters and Dengel, 1986). This publication contains a section on information organizations that covers networks, information centers, clearinghouses, and resource centers throughout the world.

Issues Related to the Literature and Information Sources

Although the literature base of the field is expanding and becoming more accessible through a variety of sources, several issues emerge from an examination of the current status of the literature and information sources. The chapter concludes by raising four of these issues: nature of the literature base, adequacy of the literature base, access and equity, and selection of appropriate information.

Nature of the Literature Base. Since the literature base reflects what is known or accepted about the field, it is important to examine its nature. For example, how is new knowledge or information created? Are existing practices in knowledge development adequate? Rubenson (1982) suggested that in their knowledge development activities, adult educators have focused on using more sophisticated methodologies rather than on conceptualizing essential problems. As a result, theory development that will "give answers to vital questions" has been neglected (p. 64). Another aspect of this issue has to do with the representativeness of the literature base. Does it reflect only the values and perspectives of the dominant culture? To what extent does it include and accommodate varying perspectives on issues, problems, and questions? The issue of its nature poses critical questions for the future development of the adult education knowledge base.

Adequacy of the Literature Base. Closely related to its nature is the issue of the adequacy of the literature base. Now that the field of adult education has established a knowledge base, questions about its adequacy or quality are being raised. As discussed earlier, the major concern related to quality or adequacy has to do with the failure to build on the existing literature. The adequacy of the literature in the future will depend to a great extent upon the commitment of researchers to use the existing knowledge base as a foundation for their work. The existing literature should become a point of departure for future work. Long (1987, p. 154) proposed the use of critical, integrative, analytical reviews of research and other existing literature as a means of "pointing out gaps in research, conflicts or contradiction, points of agreement, trends, and additional hypotheses." Use of this type of review, also referred to as metanalysis, can help ensure that the future literature will be founded on the existing knowledge base and thus will be built upward rather than outward (Plecas and Sork, 1986).

Access and Equity. The issue of access and equity refers to the accessibility of the literature and the appropriateness of the available information. Questions related to this issue include the following: "how accessible is the literature?" "Are there certain groups who do not have equal access to literature and information sources?" and "Is the kind of information that users need available and does it represent all perspectives?" The fact that some adult education literature, such as periodicals and historical items, is not widely accessible was discussed earlier. Although information data bases such as ERIC have made adult education literature more accessible, there is concern that the use of information technologies will only widen the gap between those who have access to information and those who do not (Gooler, 1987). The appropriateness of available information is also a part of this issue. Sources of literature and information such as libraries, information data bases, and clearinghouses do not have unlimited capacities for making information available, so critical decisions are made about which material to select and to disseminate. Criteria for making these decisions determine the extent to which appropriate information is available to users.

Selection of Appropriate Information. The growth of the literature base combined with its increasing accessibility results in a fourth issue: the selection of the most appropriate information. Related questions include, "How can individuals learn to select the most appropriate information for their needs?" and "What is the role of information providers in this process?" As the adult education literature expands, individuals not only must become familiar with methods of accessing the literature but also must learn to select those sources that are most appropriate for their needs. Making decisions about the most appropriate information sources is a complex process, one that requires knowledge about the range of information available as well as the ability to assess individual sources. Although information providers can help users select appropriate sources, individuals need to develop skills that will allow them to make these decisions on their own.

Summary

Since 1926, the field of adult education has engaged in developing a literature base. Individuals have access to this literature through a number of avenues including libraries, information data bases, and clearinghouses and resource centers. The field of adult education has a distinct knowledge base, and, in addition, other issues are related to it. Four that were raised here are the nature of the literature base, its adequacy, its accessibility and equity, and selection of appropriate information or literature.

References

Adult Education Committee, Ministry of Reconstruction. *The 1919 Report: The Final and Interim Reports of the Adult Education Committee of the Ministry of Reconstruction.* London: His Majesty's Stationery Office, 1919.

Allcorn, S. "The Knowledge Gap of Adult Education." *Lifelong Learning,* 1985, *8* (5), 12–16.

Beals, R. A., and Brody, L. *The Literature of Adult Education.* New York: American Association for Adult Education, 1941.

Boshier, R., and Pickard, L. "Citation Patterns of Articles Published in *Adult Education* 1968–1977." *Adult Education,* 1979, *30* (1), 34–51.

Brockett, R. G. (ed.). "1926–1986: A Retrospective Look at Selected Adult Education Literature." *Adult Education Quarterly,* 1987, *37* (2), 114–121.

Brunner, E., and others. *An Overview of Adult Education Research.* Chicago: Adult Education Association of the U.S.A., 1959.

Cartwright, M. *Ten Years of Adult Education.* New York: Macmillan, 1935.

Charters, A. N., and Dengel, R. E. *International Handbook of Resources for Educators of Adults. English Language Materials.* Syracuse, N.Y.: Syracuse University Publications in Continuing Education, 1986. (ED 283 971)

Cotton, W. E. *On Behalf of Adult Education: A Historical Examination of the Supporting Literature.* Brookline, Mass.: Center for the Study of Liberal Education for Adults, 1968.

DeCrow, R. "Information Resources and Services." In R. M. Smith, G. F. Aker, and J. R. Kidd (eds.), *Handbook of Adult Education.* New York: Macmillan, 1970.

Dickinson, G., and Rusnell, D. "A Content Analysis of *Adult Education.*" *Adult Education,* 1971, *21* (3), 177–185.

Ely, M. (ed.). *Adult Education in Action.* New York: American Association for Adult Education, 1936.

Evans, O. D. *Educational Opportunities for Young Workers.* New York: Macmillan, 1926.

Fingeret, A. *Adult Literacy Education: Current and Future Directions.* Information Series no. 284. Columbus: ERIC Clearinghouse on Adult, Career, and Vocational Education, National Center for Research in Vocational Education, Ohio State University, 1984. (ED 246 308)

Fund for Adult Education. 1951–1961. A Ten-Year Report of the Fund for Adult Education. New York: Ford Foundation, n.d.

Gooler, D. "Using Integrated Information Technologies for Out-of-Classroom Learning." In J. A. Niemi and D. D. Gooler (eds.), *Technologies for Learning Outside the Classroom.* New Directions for Continuing Education, no. 34. San Francisco: Jossey-Bass, 1987.

Grattan, C. H. *In Quest of Knowledge*. New York: Association Press, 1955.

Hall-Quest, A. L. *The University Afield*. New York: Macmillan, 1926.

Hart, J. K. *Adult Education*. New York: Crowell, 1927.

Hilton, R. J. "The Short, Happy Life of a Learning Society: Adult Education in America, 1930–39." Unpublished doctoral dissertation, Department of Administrative and Adult Studies, Syracuse University, 1981.

Hilton, R. J. "SUREA: The Grand Canyon of Adult Education Research." *Lifelong Learning*, 1985, *8* (7), 16–18, 27.

Ilsley, P. *Adult Literacy Volunteers: Issues and Ideas*. Information Series no. 301. Columbus: ERIC Clearinghouse on Adult, Career, and Vocational Education, National Center for Research in Vocational Education, Ohio State University, 1985. (ED 260 303)

Jensen, G., Liveright, A. A., and Hallenbeck, W. (eds.). *Adult Education: Outlines of an Emerging Field of University Study*. Washington, D.C.: Adult Education Association of the U.S.A., 1964.

Knowles, M. S. *A History of the Adult Education Movement in the United States*. Melbourne, Fla.: Krieger, 1977.

Kotinsky, R. *Adult Education and the Social Scene*. East Norwalk, Conn.: Appleton-Century-Crofts, 1933.

Lindeman, E. *The Meaning of Adult Education*. New York: New Republic, 1926.

Long, H. B. *New Perspectives on the Education of Adults in the United States*. London: Croom-Helm, 1987.

Long, H. B., and Agyekum, S. K. "*Adult Education* 1964–1973; Reflection of a Changing Discipline." *Adult Education*, 1974, *24* (2), 99–120.

Martin, E. D. *The Meaning of a Liberal Education*. New York: Norton, 1926.

Mezirow, J. D., and Berry, D. (comps.). *The Literature of Liberal Adult Education 1945–1957*. Metuchen, N.J.: Scarecrow Press, 1960.

Mezirow, J., Darkenwald, G., and Knox, A. *Last Gamble on Education: Dynamics of Adult Basic Education*. Washington, D.C.: Adult Education Association of the U.S.A., 1975. (ED 112 119)

Niemi, J. "Review of *Adult Education: Outlines of an Emerging Field of University Study*." In R. Brockett (ed.), "1926–1986: A Retrospective Look at Selected Adult Education Literature." *Adult Education Quarterly*, 1987, *37* (2), 114–121.

Niemi, J., and Imel, S. "Information Retrieval." In C. Klevins (ed.), *Materials and Methods in Adult and Continuing Education*. Canoga Park, Calif.: Klevens Publications, 1987.

Noffsinger, J. S. *Correspondence Schools, Lyceums, Chautauquas*. New York: Macmillan, 1926.

Peffer, N. *New Schools for Older Students*. New York: Macmillan, 1926.

Plecas, D. B., and Sork, T. J. "Adult Education: Curing the Ills of an Undisciplined Discipline." *Adult Education Quarterly*, 1986, *37* (1), 48–62.

Pole, T. *Pole's History of Adult Schools*. (Reprint of the 1816 edition with introduction and bibliographical notes by C. Verner.) Washington, D.C.: Adult Education Association of the U.S.A., 1967.

Powell, J. W. (ed.). *Adult Education: Issues in Dispute*. Washington, D.C.: Adult Education Association of the U.S.A., 1960.

Rubenson, K. "Adult Education Research: In Quest of a Map of the Territory." *Adult Education*, 1982, *32* (2), 57–74.

Sork, T. J., and Buskey, J. H. "A Descriptive and Evaluative Analysis of Program Planning Literature, 1950–1983." *Adult Education Quarterly*, 1986, *36* (2), 86–96.

Stubblefield, H. "An Archives for Adult Education: Syracuse University Provides a Library for a Wealth of Adult Education Literature." *Lifelong Learning*, 1980, *4* (1), 7.

Syracuse University Kellogg Project. *Information Brochure*. Syracuse, N.Y.: Syracuse University Kellogg Project, n.d.

Thorndike, E. L., and others. *Adult Learning*. New York: Macmillan, 1928.

U.S. Department of Education, Divison of Adult Education. *Directory of Clearinghouses: Resource Centers and Clearinghouses Serving Adult Educators and Learners*. Washington, D.C.: U.S. Government Printing Office, 1987.

Verner, C. "The Literature of Adult Education." In M. S. Knowles (ed.), *Handbook of Adult Education in the United States, 1960*. Washington, D.C.: Adult Education Association of the U.S.A., 1960.

Waller, R. D. "1919–1956: The Years Between." In Adult Education Committee, Ministry of Reconstruction, *A Design for Democracy*. New York: Association Press, 1956.

Workers' Education Association, The. *The W. E. A. Education Year Book 1918*. Nottingham, Eng.: University of Nottingham, Department of Adult Education, 1918.

Whipple, J. B. *A Critical Balance: History of CSLEA*. Brookline, Mass.: Center for the Study of Liberal Education for Adults, Boston University, 1967.

12

Adult Education Research: Issues and Directions

David Deshler
with Nancy Hagan

The primary purpose of this chapter is to provide an introduction to current disputes and issues surrounding and embedded in research efforts in adult education. Following a brief historical statement of the evolution of adult education research, several major disputes will be discussed in turn. These disputes concern differing perspectives and values regarding (1) philosophies of science, (2) purposes of research, (3) control and ownership of the research enterprise, (4) strategies appropriate for mapping the field, and (5) research directions that are potentially promising.

Brief Historical Statement

Adult education, although a field of practice throughout history, is a young field of study that has experienced a rapid increase in research since World War II (Peters and Banks, 1982). The narration of that unfolding knowledge base can be traced through the work of Brunner (1959), Kreitlow (1960, 1970), Knox (1965), and Jensen, Liveright, and Hallenbeck (1964). more recently the works of Knox (1977), Long, Hiemstra, and Associates (1980), Long (1983b), and Darkenwald and Merriam (1982), have continued that tradition of providing research overviews for the field.

The expansion of research has occurred as the number of graduate programs has increased. Approximately 2,500 doctorates in adult education have been awarded since the 1930s. Professors of adult education increased in number from approximately 25 in 1930 to over 275 in 1988. Their research productivity is reported not only in *Adult Education,* the primary

North American research journal for the field, but also in over 300 different journals (Dickinson and Rusnell, 1971; Long, 1977).

Several research efforts have been conducted to characterize the changing nature of this expanding knowledge base (Miller, 1967; Dickinson and Rusnell, 1971; Long and Agyekum, 1974; Boshier, 1979; Grabowski, 1980; Peters and Banks, 1982; Long, 1983a; and West, 1985). From these reviews of articles appearing in *Adult Education,* published doctoral dissertations, and presentations at sessions of the Adult Education Research Conference (AERC), three somewhat overlapping phases of research history can be discerned. The first phase emphasized a theoretical program description (Miller, 1967; Dickinson and Rusnell, 1971; and Long and Agyekum, 1974). The second phase emphasized improvement of research methods and designs patterned after the natural sciences (Boshier, 1979; Grabowski, 1980; West, 1985). The third phase, which is currently underway, emphasizes theory building and definition of research territory (Grabowski, 1980; Peters and Banks, 1982). With this brief overview of the history of adult education research, let us now turn to some of the current issues in dispute.

Which Philosophy of Science Should Ground Research?

Probably the most fundamental question among adult education researchers is what constitutes social science research. During one phase of adult education's growing sophistication, an increasing number of adult education researchers appropriated research assumptions of the natural sciences. These positivist philosophical assumptions about science (Popper, 1959, 1965) were fully spelled out in standard social science research works (Campbell and Stanley, 1963; Fox, 1969; Kerlinger, 1973; Smith, 1975) that described science as an empirical process of discovering knowledge. Apps (1979, pp. 179–180) summarized this dominant research paradigm with several assumptions regarding knowledge:

1. We live in a knowable world, which has an objective reality, not the creation of the human mind. Knowledge is out there awaiting human discovery.
2. Knowledge is discovered principally through empirical means, that is, through sensory experience. If one can't see, smell, touch, or hear something, its existence is questionable.
3. The validity of knowledge is based on repeatability.
4. Knowledge is measurable and usually convertible to numbers.
5. Knowledge occurs in patterns. Objects and events in the world are marked by likeness.
6. Objects, events, and people do not appreciably change their basic characteristics over time. . . . This allows researchers to draw generalizations with some assurance that the generalizations will hold for some time.

7. Objects and events may be broken into discrete parts. . . . It is assumed that what is discovered in studying the discrete parts can be added together to provide an understanding of the whole from which the parts were originally derived.

8. The researched is an object for study. . . . The researcher assumes that it is important to maintain distance from that which is researched in order to maintain objectivity.

9. The situation that exists between the researcher and the researched is objective and value-free.

10. Only the researcher has responsibility for discovering knowledge.

11. Because of formal training and experience, the researcher is profoundly more qualified than the researched to discover knowledge.

Beginning in the 1970s, alternatives to positivist perspectives on research began to appear in a substantial number of presentations at Adult Education Research Conferences. A counterpart to this shift in adult education research occurred among some math and science school education researchers, who began calling themselves constructivists (Goodman, 1978). Other postpositivists began to call their research naturalistic. The debate at that time polarized on what now is considered to be a false dichotomy—the relative merits of qualitative versus quantitative research methods (Howe, 1985). However, underlying the debate were major differences regarding philosophies of science. More research and evaluation described as naturalistic continued to be reported. Some of it referred to the grounded theory approach of Glaser and Strauss (1967). Other studies derived their perspectives from the Chicago school of sociology (Bruyn, 1966; Blumer, 1969; Becker, 1970; Denzin, 1970). More recently studies have referred to the naturalistic methods of Guba and Lincoln (1981), Lincoln and Guba (1985), Miles and Huberman (1986), and Williams (1986). Others base their research on ethnographic methods of Spradley (1980), Fetterman (1984), Goetz and LeCompte (1984), Whyte (1984), and Agar (1986). Still others describe the merits of phenomenology (Stanage, 1987). Although there is no consensus among the naturalistic researchers, the following statements provide a starting point for appreciating this alternative view of social science:

1. Knowledge is the creation of the human mind. It is not out there to be discovered. Rather, reality is created by perceiving through constructs that are selected by the researcher.

2. Knowledge continually changes; new constructs permit new perspectives and subsequent knowledge claims.

3. Knowledge is social; its meaning should be interpreted within specific social settings and traditions.

4. Knowledge is both quantitative and qualitative. The qualitative uniqueness of persons, objects, and events or of in-depth internal subjective

understanding is as important as their external, objective, quantitatively described similarities and differences.

5. Objects, events, and especially people are continuously changing. The process of that change is as important to study as is the description of what can be viewed as having continuity.

6. Reductionism or the distortion that comes from breaking objects, events, and people into discrete parts is to be avoided by emphasizing systems and the viewing of the whole.

7. Intimate, unique, in-depth knowledge is made possible through researcher involvement with subjects rather than only through objective, detached observation.

8. The values of the researcher and the researched (teachers, learners, administrators, policymakers) are essential to interpret the meaning of the research effort.

9. Human subjects participate as researchers in creating knowledge.

Those who hold these postpositivist, interpretive, or naturalistic research assumptions argue that the process of one human being studying another is not as straightforward as the process of one human being studying a potato, a clam, or even a solar system, as we would in the natural sciences. To study adult education, distinctive research approaches appropriate to the nature of the enterprise are required. Apps (1972, pp. 12–13), for instance, has argued that "the predominant tendency to define all valid research as necessarily empirical (that is, if we can't smell something, see something, touch something, or hear something, it doesn't exist) is too narrow a definition for research in adult education." He called this tendency the "scientism trap" with its adherence to a ritualistic positivist method. Forest (1972) and Farmer (1980) echoed Apps's view that adult educators may be caught up in empiricism and should be open to naturalistic research.

Nevertheless, the positivist or empiricist view is still the most pervasive educational research approach in higher education. One of the reasons that much adult education research is influenced by positivist assumptions is that it is conducted through graduate education programs that are located in schools of education, most of which adhere to the positivist paradigm of science. However, reports of naturalistic interpretive studies are increasing at the American Educational Research Association (AERA) conferences, and at the Adult Education Research Conferences (AERC), as well as in journal publications. Dialogue between those subscribing to these two paradigms promises to be vigorous in the future.

There are several research orientations, according to Collins (1986), that are compatible with naturalistic approaches to social science. They include conceptual (linguistic) analysis, phenomenology, hermeneutics, and critical theory. In the future, we can expect to see a broad range of research approaches in addition to historical studies, experiments, and descriptive surveys.

Which Purposes Should Research Serve?

Should adult education research focus on applied research, creating knowledge that solves problems of practitioners, or focus on basic research, building a theoretical knowledge base? This tension is partially due to adult education's being both a field of research and a profession. Those who give priority to the field of research view the purpose of research as intrinsic, that is, to create theoretically based knowledge for a discipline. Those who give priority to the profession view the purpose of research as adjunct to the practice needs of the profession, that is, to invent remedies and solve practitioner problems. This gap or tension between basic and applied research priorities is long-standing and fundamental to the composition of adult education research.

Kreitlow (1970), in his review of research within the field, described the practical orientation of most of the research efforts reported in *Adult Education* between 1960 and 1970. At that time he advocated a research focus on functions of adult education such as evaluation, program planning, and methods and techniques—all practical orientations rather than theoretical. The 1970 *Handbook of Adult Education* reflected an orientation that viewed research as flowing out of the identification of problems of practice. Kreitlow's (1965) list of needed research also reflects this orientation as does the work of Knox (1965, 1977).

As research productivity increased, a growing concern, on the part of some professors, for theory generation was strongly expressed by the Commission of Professors of Adult Education (CPAE), part of what is now the American Association for Adult and Continuing Education. In 1976, the CPAE established task forces composed of members who wanted to pursue various areas of interest. One group called itself the Research Needs Task Force and set about identifying practitioner needs that should be given high research priority. Another group of professors, assuming that research in the field would best be served by addressing the building of theory in order to inform practice, organized a Theory Building Task Force. The two approaches represented the tension between the practical and theoretical perspectives on the purpose of research and between different assumptions about how to improve practice through research. It was not until the annual meeting of the CPAE in 1987 that the commission voted to combine the two task forces, after observing that each of the two groups had worthwhile considerations and contributions.

The gap between research and practice is long-standing. Most of the researchers who have addressed this gap have advocated a linking of inquiry and application. For instance, Suttle (1982) suggested that successful practitioners should not view their successes as something achieved strictly in the practice domain, independent of a theoretical base. On the contrary, he declared, the extent to which one's teaching practice is successful is the degree to which one is employing sound educational theory. Concomitantly, he thought it was absurd to claim something might be good in theory but would not work in practice. He thought researchers should identify the theory behind successful practice. Another name for this is *theory-in-use*.

Perhaps a central task of adult education research should be to integrate theory and practice through research. Both sides are beginning to appreciate that both deductive (beginning with theory and testing it) and inductive approaches (beginning with practice and building theory) are legitimate and required (Kenny and Harnisch, 1982), and this suggests that the polarity between theory building and applied research is not an either-or matter.

This move to blend inductive and deductive approaches has led to the practice of action research in adult education. Action research is a form of investigation with interactionist requirements for the researcher—not simply as a participant observer, but as an active change agent (Schein, 1987). According to Bryant and Usher (1986), action research has become the preferred style of adult education research in England. They give several reasons for this. The first is that action research more readily facilitates links between research and practice, stimulating practitioner-based inquiry, which is congruent with andragogical models. Second, research funders, desiring greater value for money spent, are now requiring relevant, practical, and real world research.

However, Bryant and Usher go on to cite inherent problems with the implementation of action research. There are disagreements among stakeholders regarding where to place the emphasis at any given time. There are differences regarding who should be included in the action research effort. As the action research progresses, contracts for change should be revised, but sometimes provision of resources to produce the desired change may not be available. There is often a contradiction between the formal reporting required by the funders and the formative evaluation that is useful for the improvement of the program. Funders usually require researchers to show results in as short a time as possible, but the client system requires time for reflective analysis and consideration of competing claims and viewpoints.

Clearly, conclusions are not viewed in the same way by the different stakeholders and audiences. Professional audiences want sound and statistically significant education findings while clients want immediate program improvement. These requirements are difficult to reconcile. Research reports that accurately portray what happened, yet at the same time adequately reflect the value of the project to all interested parties, are difficult to write.

Positivist-oriented researchers have responded to action research with questions such as, Has action research made research indistinguishable from practice? Are findings recognizably research? Is there anything that is generalizable from this type of research that can be disseminated as practical knowledge? Will funders recognize the proper limitations of findings and not attempt to spread practice fads to inappropriate settings? Is there any academic accountability or peer review for research beyond pleasing the client system? The dialogue has just begun.

Who Owns and Controls Research?

Advocates of participatory research have presented another challenge to the positivist view of research. Positivist research typically begins with researchers selecting or generating theory and then testing it. Participatory research, on the other hand, begins with learners or participants who engage in their own inquiry for the sake of empowerment. Participatory research is an old idea with a new name. Cooperative extension agents in North America advocated its use in the first part of this century. More recently it has been introduced as an adjunct to popular education and education for development in the Third World. It has been articulated and promoted by Hall (1975) of the International Council for Adult Education. An annotated bibliography by Ohliger and Niemi (1975) provides an introduction to this literature.

Kassam (1985, p. 1) defined participatory research as a three-pronged activity aimed at bringing about progressive social change for the betterment of the poor and the oppressed: "(1) It is an approach to social investigation and analysis with the full and active participation of the community in the entire research process; (2) a means of taking collective action for the benefit of those among whom research is conducted; and (3) an educational process of mobilization for development. In practice, the combination of these three processes cannot be separated. Their integration gives participatory research its unique strength and power, and it is this very integration that baffles the understanding of the conventional researchers and invokes their discomfort and criticism."

Participatory research advocates (Reason and Rowan, 1981; Hall, 1975, 1981, 1985; Kassam, 1985; Gaventa, 1985; Cassara, 1986, 1987) declared that what was at issue in the research-to-practice gap was ownership and control of knowledge. Who defines the research problem? they asked. Who pays? They pointed out that those who control research determine the content (what is studied) as well as the outcome of research (who benefits). They asked why some things were studied and not others, and why learners and the powerless were not engaged in their own research. They suggested that the process of information gathering and analysis by researchers leads to learning and skill building (creation of knowledge) on the part of the educated elite, who control the dissemination of findings on behalf of organizations they choose to benefit. At the same time, powerless adult education learners and participants are viewed as objects to be studied. Participatory research advocates charged that the elitist approaches to research contribute to social inequality especially through the growth of the "knowledge industry," with its increasing centralization of knowledge production and dissemination under corporate ownership (Kassam and Mustafa, 1982; Gaventa, 1985).

A common reaction of conventional positivist researchers is that participatory research is fine as a device to encourage reflection, learning, and action, but that it does not constitute research since it does not follow positivist natural science research assumptions. Participatory research advocates typically respond to this criticism by asserting naturalistic assumptions regarding science. However, it should be pointed out that participatory research could be and probably has been conducted using positivistic assumptions regarding science. Debate regarding the virtues and limitations of participatory research will likely continue for the immediate future.

Since 1980, participatory research exchanges and groups have been established in many countries including Brazil, Canada, England, Germany, India, Italy, the Philippines, Tanzania, and the West Indies. They share examples of their efforts and encourage investigations of injustice, health hazards, and unfair working conditions.

Defining the Research Territory: Which Strategies?

Early efforts to map the territory of adult education research included differentiation of research according to the types of objects or events that were the focus of study. Typical classifications included the following: adult learning, including self-directed learning (Caffarella and O'Donnell, 1987); instruction and teaching methods, including distance education and educational technology; program development; organization and administrative studies; community development and education for public decisions; and adult education policy studies. Gowin (1981) has identified four commonplaces that, he claims, comprise all education inquiry: teaching, learning, curriculum, and governance. The above classifications can be subsumed under Gowin's commonplaces as one way to structure the territory.

Another way of categorizing research is according to setting—home and family, workplace, recreation site—or according to program area—adult basic education, literacy, health education, human resource development, educational gerontology, religious education, continuing professional education, self-help groups, and so on. In this handbook, most of the chapters that describe program areas can be viewed as categories of research associated with those types of adult education programs. However, none of these approaches, although helpful in distinguishing the focus of research activity, adequately defines the theoretical territory of research.

Boshier (1979) and others, particularly during the middle 1970s, decried the atheoretical nature of much adult education research and called for efforts to define the territory theoretically. That call has, for the most part, been heeded. What is in dispute today is how to do it. Five alternative strategies have been discerned in the literature. Using these strategies, researchers have endeavored to do the following: (1) generate theory unique to adult education, (2) build on critical theory, (3) borrow theory from different disciplines, (4) test theory through international comparative research, or (5) synthesize theory through metaresearch. Each of these strategies will be described briefly.

Generate Theory Unique to Adult Learning and Development. One of the most long-standing efforts in adult education has been to identify what is unique about adult learning in contrast to child or youth learning. It was reasoned that if this difference could be identified, the research territory of adult education could then be based on those theoretical distinctions that would serve as boundaries. This effort gave rise to the term *andragogy,* the practice of helping adults learn, as distinct from *pedagogy,* the practice of instructing children. The term *andragogy* was first used in 1883 by Kapp, a German (Davenport and Davenport, 1985), and was introduced in the United States by Lindeman in the 1920s (Brookfield, 1984). It was popularized by Knowles (1970). The debate over the adequacy of the concept as a basis for adult education research is unresolved (Davenport and Davenport, 1985; Yonge, 1985). However, parts of the concept have led to other theoretical bases for research. For instance, one of the characteristics of adulthood that Knowles emphasized in his work is self-directedness. This concept has generated a line of research that defines itself as particularly unique to adult learning (Tough, 1971; Brookfield, 1984; Caffarella and O'Donnell, 1987).

Build on Critical Theory. Another characteristic of adults is the capacity to learn through self-criticism and through reflective consciousness focusing on the relationship between the self and society. This capacity is generally acknowledged to be quite limited in children prior to adolescence. Those who are constructing theory from this premise claim that learning through reflecting on the self and on the way society defines the self is the essence of adult learning. This process exemplifies the highest developments in human learning and optimally leads to human liberation and empowerment. This line of inquiry, which has come to be known as *critical theory,* has been articulated through the sociology and philosophy of the Institute for Social Research in Frankfurt, Germany, beginning in the 1930s, interrupted by World War II, and continuing to the present. (See Chapter Five.)

Reacting to the rise of fascism and nazism, on the one hand, and to the failure of orthodox Marxism, on the other, the Frankfurt School developed critical theory to analyze the formal structure of consciousness in order to discover how a dehumanized society could continue to maintain its control over its inhabitants. They wanted to learn how it was possible that human beings could participate willingly at the level of everyday life in the reproduction of their own dehumanization and exploitation. These scholars sought to find a clue to understand the nature of society and the dynamics of ideological, cultural, and psychic domination. Critical thought or reflectivity became for them the precondition for human emancipation and freedom from the servitude of human existence (Giroux, 1983, 1985.) The Frankfurt School, under the leadership of Horkheimer (1972), Adorno and Horkheimer (1972), Marcuse (1968, 1972), and more recently Habermas (1971, 1975)

have drawn upon the work of Gramsci (1985) who believed that adult education was a crucial vehicle for exposing exploitation through critical reflection on the ideological legitimation of the ruling class (hegemony) (Armstrong, 1987). Giroux (1981) has interpreted the importance of critical theory
for schooling, particularly through the idea of the *hidden curriculum*—the
messages, values, and social practices that schools employ to impart cultural
reproduction to support the status quo and social injustice. Freire (1985)
is probably the best known adult educator who has drawn implications from
critical theory and has popularized these ideas for the practice of adult education for empowerment.

Mezirow (1981, 1985) has drawn upon the work of critical theorists,
particularly the work of Habermas (1971). Mezirow (1985, p. 149) holds
that "the use of discourse or dialogue as a basis for consensual validation
of our views of self and society is the central unique function of adult education. He asserts that adult educators should have a function of helping adults
free themselves from dependency producing constraints by assessing relevant experience, becoming aware of cultural contradictions (false consciousness) that oppress them, researching their own problems, building confidence,
examining action alternatives, identifying resources, anticipating consequences, and fostering participation and leadership." The most significant
task of adult education for Mezirow is to "precipitate and facilitate this kind
of learning for perspective transformation" (p. 149). This research and
theory-building strategy is viewed as the unique task and domain of adults,
educators, and researchers.

Based on observations at recent sessions of the Adult Education Research Conference in North America and at other research conferences, it
is anticipated that an increasing number of adult education researchers will
pursue a critical theory perspective. The direction of this theory-building
enterprise is unpredictable, since there are many positions and the vocabulary
is complex and rich in diverse meaning. However, it is forecast that vigorous
dialogue will occur over the importance and nature of this strategy for defining
the field of adult education research.

Borrow and Reformulate Theory from Different Disciplines. Jensen
(1964) first encouraged adult education researchers to borrow and to reformulate knowledge from other disciplines as the major strategy for generating
a research base for adult education. Most researchers at that time were university professors who came from various social science disciplines other than
education, so it made sense that their disciplinary perspectives would be
transferred to their new field of research interest.

Which disciplines have provided theoretical sources for adult education research? In North America the answer has to be psychology, particularly
the research thrusts on participation. Cookson (1987, p. 25) complains that
"because the contributors to the unique body of knowledge in adult education tend to overemphasize and overly depend upon psychology in particular
as the basis of their theoretical and empirical work, the North American

literature demonstrates a condition which might be referred to as 'psychological reductionism.' Indeed, we find a remarkable predilection to explain adult education behaviors in terms of the relative salience of a cluster of psychological variables, with only passing reference to one or more social background (sociological) variables, usually selected to stand as proxy measures for more substantive variables excluded from the analysis."

For instance, the structure of sociological theory (Turner, 1978) can make a major contribution to understanding the relationships between adult education and the following: social order, stability or social change, distribution of knowledge, social networking, and interorganization relations. Articles and books on the sociology of adult education are now beginning to appear (Jarvis, 1985). More recently Darkenwald and Valentine (1985) have conceptually moved beyond the psychological variables of motivation for participation to include sociological variables of deterrents to participation.

Disciplines with theories from which adult educators have not extensively borrowed include anthropology, political science, and economics (Hunter, Borus, and Marrian, 1974; Cohn, 1979). Other promising fields of study from which adult education may borrow include communications, systems theory, and administrative science. The humanities, including literature, have been mined by a few researchers for insights parallel to those found in the empirical research literature (Merriam, 1983).

All too few adult educators outside of the United Kingdom have become historical researchers; all too few historians have written adult education histories. In either case, the field could benefit from adult education historical research that integrates the relationship between adult learning and historical development and change.

Borrowing and reformulating theory from other disciplines itself is not very controversial. What is at issue is whether such borrowing may produce research that suffers from a view that is narrow, incomplete, discipline-bound, and restricted, as in the case of North America, to a predominant view of reality (Cookson, 1987). Cookson calls for an awareness of parallel streams of research in other fields of study, for creation of a cumulative research knowledge base, and for generation of comprehensive integrative theories or models that make possible the categorization and explanation of relationships between adult-education-related behavior and a full range of possible independent or dependent variables. In other words, we need to move from research bound to a single discipline to multidisciplinary and interdisciplinary approaches. To be interdisciplinary is no longer to be innovative; it is the only way we can be responsible to the disciplines themselves. We in adult education have an opportunity to create an interdisciplinary atmosphere of intellectual and personal exchange that is simultaneously professional and academic.

Test Theory Through International Comparative Research. One of the major benefits of conducting international comparative research is that researchers very soon become aware that much of adult education in another historical, political, cultural, and social setting poorly fits conceptual maps created from a single culture. Through comparative research, we are made aware of the limitations of generalizations, of the inadequacies of categories and concepts, and particularly of aspects we have neglected to research due to our cultural and social blindness and bias. For instance, Rubenson (1982), noting the uneven development of adult education research in different countries, suggested that the neglect of certain questions of research may be due to cultural tendencies not to want to delve into various areas of knowledge. In contrasting adult education research in Sweden with that of North America, he pointed to the Swedish focus on policy studies that reflect the historical role of adult education in the support of a socialist society. Rubenson exclaimed that North Americans almost have reduced the problems concerning their adult education research territory to psychological ones. The North American tendency to view the adult education enterprise as serving individual or organizational interests rather than societal or political interests may have led to the psychological focus discussed earlier.

Rubenson's observations of international comparative adult education led him to question the "tunnel vision" of what constitutes a map of the research territory of adult education. He challenged North Americans to include political and sociological perspectives in their research on participation rather than continuing to practice a form of reductionism that looks only for psychological motives to explain participation. In addition, he declared that most journals in adult education are provincial in their perspectives, reflecting national definitions of the map of the research territory. Because comparative research is very likely to challenge limited definitions, research questions, methodologies, and research traditions, a more comprehensive map of the research territory is more likely to develop when international comparative adult education research is given a higher priority.

During the 1980s, an increasing number of researchers from other countries have attended North American research conferences and sessions of the Commission of Professors of Adult Education (CPAE). The International Task Force of the CPAE also has been active in encouraging international comparative research. These efforts led to an international research conference at the University of Leeds, England in 1988. The conference was sponsored jointly by the Adult Education Research Conference, the Standing Conference on University Teaching and Research in the Education of Adults (Great Britain), and the Canadian Association for the Study of Adult Education.

Relationships between European and North American scholars also have been supported by the formation of a Kellogg-International Council of Adult Education Research Exchange Working Group composed of twenty-eight American and Canadian scholars committed to conducting international comparative adult education research. These scholars test research assumptions and conceptualizations through their international comparative research activities. The group was later expanded to include a total of sixty scholars from North America, Europe, Latin America, and Africa who met following the Leeds conference with the financial assistance of the Kellogg Foundation. The expanded group formed the transformative Research Network, affiliated with the International Council of Adult Education.

Synthesize Through Metaresearch. Another strategy for creating theoretical maps of the research territory is to synthesize theory through metaresearch. Sork (1985, p. 4) defined metaresearch as the "systematic study of the processes and products of inquiry which characterize a discipline or field of study, or, more simply, research on research." To aid the efforts of metaresearch, Sork (1985) compiled a listing of adult education metaresearch published in North America through 1984. His typology of metaresearch includes the following six types.

Type 1—*Inventories or registers of research* are listings of research studies that range in complexity from simple bibliographic entries that include the name of the investigator, title of the study, and sources of additional information to compilations that provide a complete abstract of each study and arrange them by topic for more efficient access.

Type II—*General reviews of research* are analyses of findings spanning the domain of a field of study for the purpose of judging the progress of knowledge production within the field.

Type III—*Critical or interpretive reviews of research on specific topics* are state-of-the-art reviews designed to analyze, to systemize, and to evaluate studies dealing with a single concept, topic, issue, or question.

Type IV—*Research agenda or taxonomies of needed research* are listings of research questions or topics that should receive more attention from researchers and, by implication, from those who fund research.

Type V—*Focused critiques of research methodology* are systematic analyses and reflective commentaries on the means used to study phenomena of interest to a field.

Type VI—*Frameworks of paradigms for understanding and improving research* are studies intended to help researchers better understand the nature of the research enterprise and through such understanding to improve the process and products of inquiry.

The bibliography that accompanies this typology can be helpful to adult education researchers who undertake metaresearch.

Space limitations of this chapter prevent the inclusion of examples from all the categories. However, two examples will serve to show the type of work that can be done as a Type III metaresearch effort.

Cookson (1987) has outlined a comparison of three different theories of voluntary participation in adult education (Miller, 1967; Rubenson, 1982; Boshier, 1977). Miller proposed a force field analysis of why people participate, using variables drawn from both psychology and sociology to explain differences between social class participation. A competing theory of participation is that of Rubenson (cited in Cross, 1981) whose expectancy-valence model is based on interaction theory in sociology. Alternatively, Boshier's theory holds that motives for participation are related to social, psychological, and other variables, and that motivational orientations are surface manifestations of psychological states related to age and socioeconomic factors.

Merriam (1987) has provided a second example of mapping the territory by comparing competing theories (Type III—Critical or interpretive reviews of research on specific topics). She reviewed the research on adult learning theory and clustered the theories according to (1) those that are based on adult learner characteristics (Knowles, 1973, 1980, 1984; Cross, 1981), (2) those that emphasize the adult's life situation (McClusky, 1963, 1970, 1971; Knox, 1980, 1985) and (3) those that focus upon changes of adult consciousness (Freire, 1970a, 1970b; Mezirow, 1981). These comparisons highlight differences in conceptualization as well as potential points of synthesis or integration.

Metaresearch can be an effective means for generating comprehensive, integrative maps of the territory of adult education research. However, at this stage of adult education research history, it is limited by the lack of sustained and cumulative research efforts, since few researchers build from others' work (Boshier and Pickard, 1979). This situation should change in the future.

It is anyone's guess which of the five strategies for creating maps of the research territory will prove to be the most helpful: (1) generating theory unique to adult education, (2) building on critical theory, (3) borrowing theory from different disciplines, (4) testing theory through international comparative research, or (5) synthesizing theory through metaresearch. Perhaps these strategies can be viewed as making a complementary contribution. The first three strategies assist in conceptualizing research; the fourth and fifth strategies assist in integrating adult education research.

Promising Directions for Adult Education Research

Although accurately forecasting human activity is always precarious, we anticipate that during the next decade considerable progress will be made in attempts to map the territory of adult education research. Moreover, we anticipate that the focus of research will expand to include greater effort in (1) historical research, (2) research on life span development and learning, (3) research on gender issues, (4) research on education related to economic and social development, (5) research on education for public decisions, (6) research on learning in the workplace, and (7) research on knowledge systems.

Historical Research. An increase in historical research is forecast mostly because it is long overdue. Large expenditures of public money for adult education have been made throughout the world. The history and patterns of these efforts are likely to spur a historical perspective before continued investment is warranted. It is hoped that those with a historical research interest will increase their networking and publishing efforts.

Research on Life Span Development and Learning. Although we anticipate that research on self-directed learning and on the unique perspectives of special groups of learners, such as young adults, women, minorities, and older adults, will continue to be emphasized in North America, this research effort is likely to be combined with life span development perspectives within specific social and cultural contexts. The findings from developmental psychologists and educational psychologists combined with the perspectives of sociologists will contribute to a holistic understanding of adult development and learning.

Research on Gender Issues. The women's movement has led to wide recognition that gender issues are crucial in all cultures around the globe. All too little is known about gender differences in different cultures and the extent to which they are socially or biologically based. This research area is promising, and the political aspects of it will sustain further research related to adult learning and the formation of public educational policy.

Research on Education Related to Economic and Social Development. Uneven economic and social development, not only in the Third World, but everywhere, is challenging public officials and researchers to question the relationship between investments in specific types of adult education and returns on those investments. This research agenda will raise fundamental questions regarding the relationship of adult education to unemployment, economic productivity, social class differences, and development theory. Most of this research will take the form of evaluations of adult education public policy and finance.

Research on Education for Public Decisions. Those who have studied social movements in recent years emphasize the increasing role of education as a central strategy, particularly in the human rights movement, the environmental movement, the peace movement, and the women's movement. In addition, the public may become more interested in forecasting, impact analysis, and the process of "futures invention"—all ways in which futurists approach the study of public decision making. Although research on learning for individual development will continue to be important, research on learning related to decisions for public policy will become increasingly important.

Research on Learning in the Workplace. This next decade will mark extensive efforts in adult education related to the world of work. Greater complexity, diversity, and uncertainty in the high-technology workplace will require more human resource development, particularly in North America. Moreover, China is launching a major adult education effort in the workplace. Most human resource education will not be voluntary but will be initiated by employers and governments. Research into the nature of learning occurring in workplace environments will become essential in order to appreciate the relationships among forces initiated by the individual and those directed toward socialization, as well as those whose goal is technical proficiency and those seeking human liberation and empowerment.

Research on Knowledge Systems. The explosion of knowledge, the technology of knowledge storage and retrieval, the sociology of knowledge, and the spread of knowledge and technology all will open new issues for the focus of research as well as new methods for conducting it. Insight into how knowledge travels and who has or does not have access to it is basic for making programmatic, large-scale interventions in adult education. This type of research undoubtedly will be helpful to social movements, extension systems, and governments. This research will be based on understanding systems of knowledge including indigenous knowledge.

Viewed historically, adult education research has come a long way during the last forty years. The types of issues in dispute today, the differences over strategies for defining the theoretical territory, and the promising directions mentioned briefly in this chapter are evidence of vitality and opportunity for research creativity for the future.

References

Adorno, T. W., and Horkheimer, M. *Dialectic of Enlightenment.* (J. Cummings, trans.) New York: Seabury, 1972.

Agar, M. H. *Speaking of Ethnography.* Beverly Hills, Calif.: Sage, 1986.

Apps, J. W. "Toward a Broader Definition of Research." *Adult Education,* 1972, *23* (1), 59–64.

Apps, J. W. *Problems in Continuing Education.* New York: McGraw-Hill, 1979.

Armstrong, P. F. "L'Ordine Nuovo: The Legacy of Antonio Gramsci and the Education of Adults." Paper presented at the Adult Education Research Conference, Laramie, Wyo., May 1987.

Becker, H. *Sociological Work.* Hawthorne, N.Y.: Aldine, 1970.

Blumer, H. *Symbolic Interactionism.* Englewood Cliffs, N.J.: Prentice-Hall, 1969.

Boshier, R. A. "Motivational Orientations Revisited: Life-Space Motives and the Educational Participation Scale." *Adult Education,* 1977, *27* (2), 75–88.

Boshier, R. A. "A Conceptual and Methodological Perspective Concerning Research on Participation in Adult Education." In J. A. Niemi (ed.), *Viewpoints on Adult Education Research.* Columbus: National Center for Research in Vocational Education, Ohio State University, 1979.

Boshier, R., and Pickard, L. "Citation Patterns of Articles Published in *Adult Education* 1968-1977." *Adult Education,* 1979, *30* (1), 34–51.

Brookfield, S. "The Contribution of Eduard Lindeman to the Development of Theory and Philosophy in Adult Education." *Adult Education Quarterly,* 1984, *34* (4), 185–196.

Brunner, E. S., and others. *An Overview of Adult Education Research.* Chicago: Adult Education Association of the U.S.A., 1959.

Bruyn, S. *The Human Perspective in Sociology.* Englewood Cliffs, N.J.: Prentice-Hall, 1966.

Bryant, I., and Usher, R. "Tension Points in Adult Education Research." Paper presented at the annual meeting of the Standing Committee of University Teaching and Research in the Education of Adults, University of Hull, Hull, Eng., June 1986.

Caffarella, R. S., and O'Donnell, J. M. "Self-Directed Adult Learning: A Critical Paradigm Revisited." *Adult Education Quarterly,* 1987, *37* (2), 199–211.

Campbell, D. T., and Stanley, J. C. *Experimental and Quasi-Experimental Designs for Research.* Skokie, Ill.: Rand McNally, 1963.

Cassara, B. *Participatory Research: Self-Directed Learning for Social Transformation.* Electronic Publication Series. Athens: Adult Education Department, College of Education, University of Georgia, 1986.

Cassara, B. "The How and Why of Preparing Graduate Students to Carry Out Participatory Research." *Educational Considerations,* 1987, *14,* 39–42.

Cohn, E. *The Economics of Education.* Cambridge, Mass.: Ballinger, 1979.

Collins, M. "Philosophy and the Role of the Adult Educator." Paper presented at the annual meeting of the American Association for Adult and Continuing Education, Hollywood, Fla., Oct. 1986. (ED 277 859).

Cookson, P. S. "The Nature of the Knowledge Base of Adult Education: The Example of Adult Education Participation." *Educational Considerations,* 1987, *14* (2–3), 24–28.

Cross, K. P. *Adults as Learners.* San Francisco: Jossey-Bass, 1981.

Darkenwald, G. G., and Merriam, S. B. *Adult Education: Foundations of Practice.* New York: Harper & Row, 1982.

Darkenwald, G. G., and Valentine, T. "Factor Structure of Deterrents to Public Participation in Adult Education." *Adult Education Quarterly,* 1985, *35* (4), 177–193.

Davenport, J., and Davenport, J. A. "A Chronology and Analysis of the Andragogy Debate." *Adult Education Quarterly,* 1985, *35* (3), 152–159.

Denzin, N. K. (ed.). *Sociological Methods: A Sourcebook.* Hawthorne, N.Y.: Aldine, 1970.

Dickinson, G., and Rusnell, D. "A Content Analysis of *Adult Education.*" *Adult Education,* 1971, *21* (3), 177–185.

Farmer, J. "The Conduct of Inquiry Relative to Adult and Continuing Education." Paper presented at a symposium conducted at Adult Education Research Conference, Vancouver, B.C., May 1980.

Fetterman, D. (ed.). *Ethnography in Educational Evaluation.* Beverly Hills, Calif.: Sage, 1984.

Forest, L. B. "Beyond Scientific Empiricism in Adult Education Research." Paper presented at Adult Education Research Conference, Chicago, Apr. 1972.

Fox, D. J. *The Research Process in Education.* New York: Holt, Rinehart & Winston, 1969.

Freire, P. "Cultural Action for Freedom." *Harvard Educational Review* monograph series, no. 1, 1970a.

Freire, P. *Pedagogy of the Oppressed.* New York: Herder & Herder, 1970b.

Freire, P. *The Politics of Education: Culture, Power and Liberation.* South Hadley, Mass.: Bergin & Garvey, 1985.

Gaventa, J. "The Powerful, the Powerless and the Experts: Knowledge Struggle in an Information Age." In P. Park, B. Hall, and T. Jackson, *Participatory Research in America.* Toronto: International Council for Adult Education, 1986.

Giroux, H. A. *Ideology, Culture, and the Process of Schooling.* Philadelphia: Temple University Press, 1981.

Giroux, H. A. *Theory and Resistance in Education: A Pedagogy for the Opposition.* South Hadley, Mass.: Bergin & Garvey, 1983.

Giroux, H. A., and Aronowitz, S. *Education Under Siege: The Conservative, Liberal and Radical Debate Over Schooling.* South Hadley, Mass.: Bergin & Garvey, 1985.

Glaser, B., and Strauss, A. *The Discovery of Grounded Theory: Strategies for Qualitative Research.* Hawthorne, N.Y.: Aldine, 1967.

Goetz, J., and LeCompte, M. *Ethnography and Qualitative Design in Educational Research.* Orlando, Fla.: Academic Press, 1984.

Goodman, N. *Ways of Worldmaking.* Indianapolis: Hackett, 1978.

Gowin, D. B. *Educating.* Ithaca, N.Y.: Cornell University Press, 1981.

Grabowski, S. M. "Trends in Graduate Research." In H. B. Long, R. Hiemstra, and Associates (eds.), *Changing Approaches to Studying Adult Education.* San Francisco: Jossey-Bass, 1980.

Gramsci, A. *Selections from Prison Notebooks.* (Q. Hoare and G. Smith, eds. and trans.) New York: International Publishers, 1985.

Guba, E. G., and Lincoln, Y. S. *Effective Evaluation: Improving the Usefulness of Evaluation Results Through Responsive and Naturalistic Approaches.* San Francisco: Jossey-Bass, 1981.

Habermas, J. *Knowledge and Human Interests.* Boston: Beacon Press, 1971.

Habermas, J. *Legitimation Crisis.* Boston: Beacon Press, 1975.

Hall, B. L. "Participatory Research: An Approach for Change." *Convergence,* 1975, *8* (2), 25–28.

Hall, B. L. "Participatory Research, Popular Knowledge and Power: A Personal Reflection." *Convergence,* 1981, *14* (3), 6–17.

Horkheimer, M. *Critical Theory.* New York: Seabury, 1972.

Howe, K. R. "Two Dogmas of Educational Research." *Educational Researcher,* 1985, *14* (8), 10–18.

Hunter, J. M., Borus, M. E., and Marrian, A. *Program of Studies in Non-Formal Education: Study Term Reports.* East Lansing, Mich.: Institute for International Studies in Education, 1974.

Jarvis, P. *Sociology of Adult and Continuing Education.* Dover, N.H.: Croom-Helm, 1985.

Jensen, G. "How Adult Education Borrows and Reformulates Knowledge from Other Disciplines." In G. Jensen, A. A. Liveright, and W. Hallenbeck (eds.), *Adult Education: Outlines of an Emerging Field of University Study.* Washington, D.C.: Adult Education Association of the U.S.A., 1964.

Jensen, G., Liveright, A. A., and Hallenbeck, W. (eds.) *Adult Education: Outlines of an Emerging Field of University Study.* Washington, D.C.: Adult Education Association of the U.S.A., 1964.

Kassam, Y. "Participatory Research: Adult Education and Empowerment." Paper presented at the first annual conference of the International League for Social Commitment in Adult Education, Ljungskile, Sweden, July 1985.

Kassam, Y., and Mustafa, K. *Participatory Research: An Emerging Alternative Methodology in Social Science Research.* Toronto: International Council for Adult Education, 1982.

Kenny, W. R., and Harnisch, D. L. "Developmental Approach to Research and Practice in Adult and Continuing Education." *Adult Education,* 1982, *33* (1), 29-54.

Kerlinger, F. N. *Foundations of Behavioral Research.* New York: Holt, Rinehart & Winston, 1973.

Knowles, M. S. *The Modern Practice of Adult Education.* New York: Association Press, 1970.

Knowles, M. S. *The Adult Learner: A Neglected Species.* Houston, Tex.: Gulf, 1973.

Knowles, M. S. *The Modern Practice of Adult Education: From Pedagogy to Andragogy.* (2nd ed) Chicago: Follett, 1980.

Knowles, M. S. *Andragogy in Action.* San Francisco: Jossey-Bass, 1984.

Knox, A. B. "Current Needs in Adult Education Research." *Journal of Education,* 1965, *147* (3), 21-31.

Knox, A. B. *Current Research Needs Related to Systematic Learning by Adults.* Occasional paper, no. 4. Urbana: Office for the Study of Continuing Education, College of Education, University of Illinois, 1977.

Knox, A. B. "Proficiency Theory of Adult Learning." *Contemporary Educational Psychology,* 1980, *5,* 378-404.

Knox, A. B. "Adult Learning and Proficiency." In D. Kleiber and M. Maehr (eds.), *Advances in Motivation and Achievement.* Vol. 4: *Motivation in Adulthood.* Greenwood, Conn.: JAI Press, 1985.

Kreitlow, B. W. "Research in Adult Education." In M. S. Knowles (ed.), *Handbook of Adult Education in the United States.* Washington, D.C.: Adult Education Association of the U.S.A., 1960.

Kreitlow, B. W. "Needed Research." *Review of Educational Research,* 1965, *35* (2), 240-245.

Kreitlow, B. W. "Research and Theory." In R. M. Smith, G. F. Aker, and J. R. Kidd (eds.), *Handbook of Adult Education.* New York: Macmillan, 1970.

Lincoln, Y. S., and Guba, E. G. *Naturalistic Inquiry.* Beverly Hills, Calif.: Sage, 1985.

Long, H. B. "Publication Activity of Selected Professors of Adult Education." *Adult Education,* 1977, *27* (3), 173–186.

Long, H. B. *Adult Learning: Research and Practice.* New York: Cambridge University Press, 1983a.

Long, H. B. "Characteristics of Adult Education Research Reported at the Adult Education Research Conference, 1971–1980." *Adult Education,* 1983b, *33* (1), 79–96.

Long, H. B., and Agyekum, S. K. "Reflections of a Changing Discipline." *Adult Education,* 1974, *24* (2), 99–120.

Long, H. B., Hiemstra, R., and Associates. *Changing Approaches to Studying Adult Education.* San Francisco: Jossey-Bass, 1980.

McClusky, H. Y. "The Course of the Adult Life Span." In W. C. Hallenbeck (ed.), *Psychology of Adults.* Washington, D.C.: Adult Education Association of the U.S.A., 1963.

McClusky, H. Y. "An Approach to a Differential Psychology of the Adult Potential." In S. M. Grabowski (ed.), *Adult Learning and Instruction.* Syracuse, N.Y.: ERIC Clearinghouse on Adult Education, 1970.

McClusky, H. Y. *Education: Background.* Report prepared for the 1971 White House Conference on Aging, Washington, D.C., 1971.

Marcuse, H. *Negations: Essays in Critical Theory.* Boston: Beacon Press, 1968.

Marcuse, H. *Counter-Revolution and Revolution.* Boston: Beacon Press, 1972.

Merriam, S. B. *Themes of Adulthood Through Literature.* New York: Teachers College Press, 1983.

Merriam, S. B. "Adult Learning and Theory Building: A Review." *Adult Education Quarterly,* 1987, *37* (4), 187–198.

Mezirow, J. "A Critical Theory of Adult Learning and Education." *Adult Education,* 1981, *32* (1), 3–27.

Mezirow, J. "Concept and Action in Adult Education." *Adult Education Quarterly,* 1985, *35* (3), 142–151.

Miles, M. B., and Huberman, M. A. *Qualitative Data Analysis: A Sourcebook of New Methods.* Beverly Hills, Calif.: Sage, 1986.

Miller, H. L. *Participation of Adults in Education: A Force-Field Analysis.* Boston: Boston University, Center for the Study of Liberal Education for Adults, 1967. (ED 011 996)

Ohliger, J., and Niemi, J. A. "Annotated and Quotational Bibliography on Participatory Research." *Convergence,* 1975, *8* (2), 82–87.

Peters, J. M., and Banks, B. B. "Adult Education." In H. E. Mitzel (ed.), *Encyclopedia of Education.* (5th ed.) New York: Free Press, 1982.

Popper, K. R. *The Logic of Scientific Discovery.* New York: Harper & Row, 1959.

Popper, K. R. *Conjectures and Refutations: The Growth of Scientific Knowledge.* New York: Harper & Row, 1965.

Reason, P., and Rowan, J. (eds.). *Human Inquiry.* New York: Wiley, 1981.

Rubenson, K. "Adult Education Research: In Quest of a Map of the Territory." *Adult Education,* 1982, *32* (2), 57–74.

Schein, E. H. *The Clinical Perspective in Fieldwork.* Beverly Hills, Calif.: Sage, 1987.

Smith, H. W. *Strategies of Social Research.* Englewood Cliffs, N.J.: Prentice-Hall, 1975.

Sork, T. J. "A Bibliography of Adult Education Meta-Research Published in North America Through 1984." Paper presented at the Adult Education Research Conference, Tempe, Ariz., Mar. 1985.

Spradley, J. *Participant Observation.* New York: Holt, Rinehart & Winston, 1980.

Stanage, S. M. *Adult Education and Phenomenological Research: New Directions for Theory and Practice.* Melbourne, Fla.: Krieger, 1987.

Suttle, B. "Adult Education: No Need for Theories?" *Adult Education,* 1982, *32* (2), 105–107.

Tough, A. M. *The Adult's Learning Projects: A Fresh Approach to Theory and Practice in Adult Learning.* Research in Education Series, no. 1. Toronto: Ontario Institute for Studies in Education, 1971.

Turner, J. H. *The Structure of Sociological Theory.* Homewood, Ill.: Dorsey Press, 1978.

West, R. F. "A Power Analytic Investigation of Research in Adult Education: 1970–1982." *Adult Education Quarterly,* 1985, *35* (3), 131–141.

Whyte, W. F. *Learning from the Field.* Beverly Hills, Calif.: Sage, 1984.

Williams, D. D. *Naturalistic Evaluation.* New Directions for Program Evaluation, no. 30. San Francisco: Jossey-Bass, 1986.

Yonge, G. D. "Andragogy and Pedagogy: Two Ways of Accompaniment." *Adult Education Quarterly,* 1985, *35* (3), 159–163.

13

Public Policy and the Financing of Adult Education

William S. Griffith
with Pamela J. Fujita-Starck

Learning opportunities in Canada and the United States are provided by an array of institutions, organizations, associations, and government agencies, each of which defines its own target audience and secures the funds to operate from a variety of sources, both public and private. Public policy in the financing of adult and continuing education (ACE) includes the formal governmental priorities and corresponding levels of support as well as the nongovernmental provision of support from a variety of sources. Each government decides the level of support it will give to each variety of ACE, and the entire infrastructure of providing bodies must adjust to those provisions. Legislatures have the responsibility and authority to decide which programs are contributing to the general welfare and are therefore deserving of financial support from the public treasury. Adult and continuing educators have the responsibility of informing those policymakers to enable them to make wise decisions based on sound data.

In this chapter, the discussion of public policy that affects financing of ACE draws examples from both Canada and the United States—first by describing the problem of image and by addressing some of the assets and liabilities associated with the diversity of this field. Following a presentation of the forms of funding employed by governments and providers of ACE, the examination turns to factors that influence the funding process. Subsequently, the sporadic and episodic nature of ACE funding is described and this description is followed by a discussion of efforts that have been organized to influence the process. Next, problems arising from the conflicting and competing missions of ACE providers and the approaches to dealing with these problems are described. Finally, the chapter concludes with a discussion of standards and essential steps that are required if there is to be a consistent public policy on the financing of ACE in Canada or the United States.

An Unclear Image

Public policy and the financing of adult and continuing education are complicated by the diversity of definitions of adult and continuing education (see Chapter Two) and by the necessity for legislation to contain restrictive definitions that guide the provision of funds. For example, in the United States, the Adult Education Act authorizes only adult basic and adult secondary education and refers to these as adult education. The Higher Education Act refers to postsecondary level adult education as continuing education (Delker, 1987). Each act with its guidelines deals with one or more sectors of the ACE education panoply of concerns and sets forth definitions, but neither act deals with all the issues ("Higher Education Funds . . . ," 1988).

P. H. Christoffel (1978), a researcher who has studied the funding of various sectors of ACE for over twenty years, observes that there is no single federal policy toward lifelong learning. She notes that a number of policies have been developed through the years, but not as part of an overall design and, in some cases, "almost by accident" (p. 357). Alan M. Thomas (1987b), professor of adult education at the Ontario Institute for Studies in Education, believes that the current state of affairs with adult education legislation is simply unavoidable because of the necessary and desirable involvement of ACE in every phase of development and in every sector. The multiplicity of uses for ACE ensures that it will be employed widely and often for the achievement of purposes other than education.

The most highly publicized adult education programs involve a relatively minor part of the total federal effort. The 1988 fiscal year appropriation for adult education as defined by the Division of Adult Education of the U.S. Department of Education (Adult Literacy Initiative and Division of Adult Education, U.S. Department of Education, 1988, p. 5) was $134 million, an increase of $21 million over the 1987 appropriation. Although this is the highest funding level for the Adult Education Act, just a decade earlier the federal government was spending much more on adult and continuing education—over $14 billion on more than 270 federal programs dealing with ACE in twenty-nine cabinet level departments and agencies (Christoffel, 1978, pp. 350–351). At least nineteen committees in the U.S. House of Representatives and sixteen in the Senate are responsible for programs dealing with various aspects of ACE (p. 351). And while the federal government spent in excess of $14 billion, it has been estimated that the private sector spends over $40 billion annually for ACE (Rivera, 1987, p. 18).

Estimates of government expenditure for ACE are debatable. J. Lowe (1982, p. 175) lamented, after examining national reports on funding for adult education, that, "To obtain reliable figures for adult education expenditure is exceedingly difficult even in highly industrialized countries. Much expenditure in both public and private sectors is hidden under a variety of budgetary headings.'' Countless programs whose primary purpose is not education depend upon adult education to achieve their objectives, yet they are not regarded as ACE by their sponsors and sometimes not even by those who carry them out. We will not attempt here to identify the totality of the programs and portions of appropriations that have been enacted to support all aspects of ACE.

The search for an overarching policy and the philosophy that informs it is daunting, but some researchers have sought to grasp the totality. R. E. Anderson (1982), who studied the costs and financing of adult education and training in the United States, believes that public policy with regard to program support in adult education has been thoughtfully pursued. He argues that public funds should not be used to replace private resources, but instead should be used to leverage them. Christoffel (1978, p. 357) surmised, based on her study of some 270 federal programs involving adult and continuing education, that, ''We have a policy of support for general education and training for selected subgroups of the population, but it has been shown that the federal government spends substantially more on advantaged than on disadvantaged persons.'' The decision to support programs is usually based on the predicted economic benefits.

Who Should Pay

A key issue in any policy discussion about ACE is who should pay the costs of providing programs. The prevailing sentiment in both the United States and Canada is that while the education of children should be fully paid from tax funds, the education of adults should be paid by those who directly receive the benefits.

Professional adult educators have the option of designing programs that qualify for government support or programs that must be paid for by the participants (Roberts, 1982). They can exercise limited control by subsidizing certain activities with residuals from other service-for-fee programs that generate revenues in excess of expenses or by influencing governments or other potential sources of funding. Employers convinced of the direct benefits their firms derive from employees' participation may assume part or all of the costs of job-related programs. Private sources of funding such as foundations may underwrite the costs of selected programs that serve a particular audience or that deal with a subject of particular interest to them. Business and industry may fund selected programs in order to improve their images with the general public.

Sources of Financial Support

J. L. Wattenbarger and P. Clark (n.d.) identified five major sources of financial support for institutions and programs: self-sustaining or tuition-based support; local taxes; state taxes; federal taxes; and gifts, endowments, or grants. In general, basic skills programs, adult secondary education, and vocational education are heavily supported in the United States by both state and federal funds, while recreational, personal enrichment, and professional development programs usually are supported with program fees. It should be noted, however, that so-called self-support programs often receive some state or local support in the form of personnel, facilities, and administrative support services. In Canada the federal government is permitted to support only vocational education, and the provinces traditionally have been responsible for other kinds of education. Nevertheless, dollars provided by the federal government are routinely used for supporting provincial educational programs.

Cyril O. Houle (1968), in an analysis of the evolution of federal policies on ACE in the United States, noted that although the idea of general aid for adult education has been warmly espoused since at least 1914, when the time comes for Congress to fund programs, ACE programs are funded to achieve a specific objective or mission. He identified four mechanisms employed by the federal government to fund adult education: grants-in-aid, contracts for service, direct operation, and aid to students. A grant-in-aid is given to the states or directly to institutions to carry out continuing programs such as basic education or cooperative extension. A contract for service is used to support training such as training for VISTA volunteers. The direct operation of programs is used to provide in-service training for government employees or to fund public information programs on health or conservation. Aid to students is provided through mechanisms such as benefits for veterans and for members of the armed forces and scholarships for teachers of selected subjects.

Influencing the Legislative Process

If professional adult educators are to influence the decision making of elected officials regarding the funding of specific ACE programs, they must learn to appreciate the nature of legislation and its inherent restrictions. The common viewpoint of adult educators has been aptly described by Alan M. Thomas (1987a), who stated that in the past thirty years in Canada, the attitude toward ACE could be called "the more joy in heaven" perspective from which any increase in students or classes has been regarded as good per se. He believes that adult educators have not been particularly helpful in policy-making because they have not comprehended the fundamental, unavoidable conflict between the language of learning and the language of legislation, regulation, and rules. While the former is intended to open possibilities and to expand definitions, according to Thomas, the latter is intended to limit and to fix definitions.

National, state, and provincial legislation is typically drafted in optimistic terms, expressing the belief that a problem situation can be corrected by the application of funding to pay for educational programs. It is not often that legislation is drafted that openly acknowledges the problem situation has been in existence for many years and only a partial solution can be anticipated. The understandable desire of legislators to demonstrate to their constituents that they are really solving a problem once and for all should not be overlooked by those who seek to influence the legislative process.

It is more desirable educationally to have the public become better informed about the nature and history of the problems than it is to have the public swayed by a simplified description of a problem and its supposed solution. The eradication of illiteracy may appear to be an attractive goal, yet the problem is not one that will be solved by a package of ACE programs (Hawaii Governor's Council for Literacy, 1987). So-called cures are rarely adequate to produce the desired results, and the public, which has a very limited attention span, is frequently distracted by a new burning issue.

Social Problems May Stimulate Financial Support

ACE professionals find that their programs often benefit from the increased public awareness of problems, insofar as the programs are perceived as suitable means of counteracting social problems. For example, current public concern about the acquired immune deficiency syndrome (AIDS) has made it possible for groups such as Planned Parenthood and the Sex Information and Education Councils of Canada and of the United States (SIECAN and SIECUS) to conduct educational programs that had previously been regarded as unsuitable. Because of the public alarm, university funds are being provided to sponsor public forums and workshops. State and provincial health departments are funding public education programs. Clearly, adult education is given public support when the public can see the connection between education and the solution to a threatening situation. But public interest is episodic and often unpredictable.

The Episodic and Sporadic Nature of Support

Federal, provincial, and state support for specific adult and continuing education programs tends to be episodic, and policies evolve incrementally. As R. K. Loring (1980, p. 138) observed, "An examination of public support of continuing education, whether at the federal, state, or local level, shows no single guiding policy or organizational structure, but rather reveals a decentralized, fragmented, uncoordinated, and sporadic effort developed over a long period of time as a result of accepted political lobbying-based processes." Each year and each decade has its special concerns. One of the tasks of the adult educator is to draw upon the interest stimulated by these concerns to provide the interested audiences with the kinds of responsible and realistic educational programs that the educator believes are potentially of marked benefit but which may have had only limited appeal prior to the sudden expression of public opinion regarding the particular issue of the year. A creative adult educator finds ways of using these expressions of concern to advertise program offerings in ways that clearly demonstrate their relevance to the particular public concern (National Conference on Continuing Professional Education, 1986).

As early as 1964, the Canadian Association for Adult Education (CAAE) issued a white paper on the education of adults in Canada in which the total picture of adult education in Canada was seen as "an opportunistic, short-term sporadic enterprise exploited by the nation in times of crisis and left to private and desperate chance when the emergency is past" (p. 1). In dealing with policy regarding the financing of adult education, the CAAE stated, "There are two major principles in educational finance: one is to subsidize institutions which in turn recruit their own students, the other to subsidize students who will then choose their institutions. Obviously we cannot and should not choose one of these to the total exclusion of the other. Institutions requiring continuity and large capital outlays cannot be left to the vagaries of student choice; nor should students over the school leaving-age be left entirely at the mercy of institutions" (p. 8). Sound financing of ACE serves the targeted groups of learners and supports the infrastructure required to maintain effective programs.

Federal funding cannot be understood without considering the division of responsibility between it and the states or provinces. Audrey M. Thomas (1983, p. 66), commenting on the situation in Canada, noted that "the federal government has influenced adult basic education (ABE), but only insofar as ABE is a part of manpower policy. Through cost-sharing agreements and grants, the federal government does support educational activity, but for literacy training the responsibility rests with the provinces. Each province has jurisdiction over education within its boundaries and has built its own system which can be quite different from those in other provinces." Clearly, the situations in Canada and the United States are parallel.

National governments may engage in what has been called "continuous bribery" in dealing with the states or provinces. Through the use of programs that provide 90 percent federal support and require only 10 percent matching funds from the states, the federal government may persuade state or provincial governments to give priority to federal programs. Similarly, states or provinces may use funding to entice smaller political units to engage in particular types of programs. Gordon Selman (n.d.) has reported on the Continuing Education Projects Fund in the Province of British Columbia which was used by the Ministry of Education to encourage college and school districts to devise means of reaching and serving disadvantaged groups. Although the total funds provided in any one year did not exceed a half million dollars, the targeted use of those funds was successful in encouraging the districts to devise projects to qualify for such assistance.

A New Thrust in Literacy

Although it may be popularly believed that the role of the government is to support programs that the public have requested, there are clear instances of leadership being taken by government to stimulate the public. As a part of the Adult Literacy Initiative, which began in September 1983, the National Diffusion Network and the Division of Adult Education Services of the U.S. Department of Education work together to disseminate publications about literacy programs and to provide state facilitators to assist school districts and other agencies interested in developing programs.

In commenting on the fourth year of the Literacy Initiative, Karl Haigler (1986, p. 1) noted that, "It is clear that the main perception of the Initiative's role has been as an advocate for volunteerism and private sector donations to the cause." The government is attempting to stimulate public awareness of the literacy situation and to stir individuals and businesses to volunteer to assist with literacy efforts. Further, officials of the Department of Education hold discussions with policymakers, corporate leaders, and foundation representatives about ways in which they might contribute to the campaign to reduce illiteracy in America.

In Canada, private initiatives seek similar goals. The Canadian Business Task Force on Literacy was established to spread the concern for adult illiteracy and to fund various support groups in need of money (Chandler, 1986). Canadian booksellers have established a Canadian Give the Gift of Literacy Foundation to raise money from public donations to support literacy training groups.

Legislators' Knowledge as a Factor Influencing Funding

Financing levels reflect the perception legislators have of the relative importance of ACE programs in relation to other societal concerns. The knowledge a legislator has about any given issue is a function of several factors: the legislator's own level of expertise in the area; the legislator's staff's knowledge and interest in the topic; the amount of concern shown by the legislator's constituents; and the individual and collective efforts of adult educators, and of others, to present their perceptions of the needs. Adult education associations give attention to public education not only because of their belief in public enlightenment, but also because they know that if the constituents become concerned about a problem, some of them are likely to share that concern with their elected representatives.

Adult education programs have been mounted to increase the ability of adult educators to influence the shaping of public policy regarding financing of ACE. The University of Georgia has been conducting a Biennial Institute for Legislators for nineteen years to afford an opportunity for new and incumbent legislators to discuss, with specialists, policy issues they expect to face in upcoming sessions of the legislature (Governor Addresses Biennial Institute . . . , 1987). It is not a coincidence that the Georgia legislature has been particularly generous in supporting the adult education work of the university. In addition, the administrators of the Georgia Center for Continuing Education and of the university have been among the most successful applicants for financial assistance for ACE from the W. K. Kellogg Foundation.

National Associations for Adult and Continuing Education

Adult educators are organized on the national level both in Canada and in the United States, and these associations reflect national characteristics. In Canada there are two national organizations of adult educators. For the Anglophones there is the Canadian Association for Adult Education, and for the Francophones there is the Institut Canadien d'education des Adultes (ICEA). In the United States, one organization strives to play the role of umbrella organization for ACE. The American Association for Adult and Continuing Education (AAACE) and the Canadian Association for Adult Education (CAAE) have devised approaches to influence public policy regarding the funding of adult learning opportunities.

Education of Legislative Staff and Association Members. Officers and staff of the AAACE and of the CAAE give both public and private testimony as well as helpful information to legislators and to their staffs. In addition, these national associations endeavor to educate their members about the need for similar educative activity on both the federal and state levels. In 1987, the AAACE held its annual Leadership and Legislative Seminar where, for the first time, they addressed the nature of the process of informing elected officials and their staffs regarding public policy formation in both the United States and Canada. Such programming acquaints emerging leaders in both countries with common concerns faced by adult educators in both presidential and parliamentary forms of government.

A Legislative Network. Of immediate practical concern to those who are eager to exert influence is the Legislative Network established by the AAACE to alert concerned adult educators throughout the United States when legislation concerning adult education is being drafted, debated, or rewritten. This network provides timely information to the U.S. Congress to increase the likelihood that the opinion of the AAACE will be considered by staff members and by elected officials who are trying to act wisely with regard to adult education legislation.

Conflicting and Competing Missions

Each year, the number of persons participating in ACE grows. At least 50 percent of American adults participate in some form of organized training, and ACE is expected to continue its growth well into the 1990s (Hodgkinson, 1983). To a large extent, this expected increase can be attributed to the growing number of adults in the population as well as to their increasing desire to continue their education. Professional associations and certifying boards are requiring ongoing education, and changing technologies and the generation of new knowledge are necessitating it. The desire for personal enrichment, a better job, or a higher income also prompts many adults to seek additional training. Because of the increased demand, ACE programs are being provided by an ever-increasing number of institutions and organizations, as described in Chapters Twenty-One through Thirty-Two. The target audiences and the program emphases change and expand, as noted in Chapters Twenty-Three through Forty-Five.

Problems of blurred and overlapping missions become widespread, and those institutions and agencies that serve the public compete for the same students. Thus, there is duplication and omission of effort, and individuals or groups who are less inclined or less able to participate are commonly overlooked unless third-party funding is provided. While there may be no segment of the public that can be considered oversupplied with learning opportunities, there are segments for which the provision of such opportunities is seriously limited or nonexistent. This is particularly true for economically disadvantaged adults, as well as for those who live in geographically remote and sparsely populated areas. Economic forces encourage programming that serves those best able to pay and to attend, while others' pressing needs are ignored because no practical way has been found to cover the costs of providing them with the programs they want.

States are grappling with issues of control and coordination of adult education, and, as pointed out by Cross and McCartan (1984, p. 1), "Responses to the issues raised vary enormously from state to state. Some adopt a hands-off stance, because they are unaware of the issues or their alternatives. Others take a laissez-faire approach either to avoid controversy or to implement the choices of a free market. Most, however, seem to be striving for coordination and cooperation among providers."

Federal legislation is being used in an effort to encourage and to stimulate cooperation among agencies, institutions, and organizations engaged in providing ACE. For example,

> Since 1978, Section 306(b)(8) of the [Adult Education] Act has required states to be involved in a host of nonpublic school agencies and organizations in developing and carrying out its program. Regulations implementing this requirement specify those to be involved: The SEA [State Education Agency] shall describe the means by which one or more representatives of each of the following agencies and groups were involved in the development of the state plan and how they will continue to be involved in carrying out the plan: (1) The business community; (2) Industry; (3) Labor unions; (4) Public educational agencies and institutions; (5) Private educational agencies and institutions; (6) Churches; (7) Fraternal/Sororal organizations; (8) Voluntary organizations; (9) Community organizations; (10) State manpower and training agencies; (11) Local manpower and training agencies; (12) Adult residents or rural areas; (13) Adult residents of urban areas with high rates of unemployment; (14) Adults with limited English language skills; (15) Institutionalized adults; (16) Other entities concerned with adult educa-

tion, such as basic skills programs, libraries, and organizations offering education programs for older persons and military personnel and their adult dependents [Delker, 1987, pp. 70–71].

As the number of adult students increases along with their demand for education, state policymakers will find it increasingly difficult to maintain a hands-off stance. State as well as provincial governments are becoming increasingly sensitive to the economic value of knowledge and training, as well as to their responsibility to protect the public from unsound and poor quality education programs. Although the hands-off approach seems inappropriate, efforts to centralize adult education may also prove self-defeating as the state's authority is often unclear and providers report to a wide variety of authorities (Cross, 1984).

At various times, proposals have been made for tidying up ACE through coordinating schemes. Such schemes have not won support from theoreticians or from practitioners partly because the sources of funding are so diverse and partly because few experienced adult educators have been able to envision a sufficiently effective coordinating mechanism that would not stifle creativity and innovativeness in its search for tidiness and predictability.

The ability of the field to respond to disparate groups is partly a function of the absence of coordination and central direction. Those who sense a need typically set out to satisfy that need. Others may question or even deny needs felt by members of groups with whom they do not interact. To retain flexibility in adult education programming, the right of new groups to organize programs and to offer them to the public should be protected. If increased support could be secured only through sacrificing the right to improvise, then that support should be rejected as too expensive. It should be possible to provide the basic level of funding for those programs that are defined as essential continuing programs without insisting upon such strict control as to stifle fresh attempts to serve those populations who are institutionally underserved with socially significant programs.

An International Standard

In its recommendations on the development of adult education, UNESCO (1980, p. 11) stated, "The proportion of public funds, and particularly of public funds earmarked for education, allocated to adult education, should match the importance of such education for social, cultural and economic development, as recognized by each Member State within the framework of this Recommendation. The total allocation of funds to adult education should cover at least: (a) provision of suitable facilities or adaptation of existing facilities; (b) production of all kinds of learning materials; (c) remuneration and further training of educators; (d) research and information expenses; (e) compensation for loss of earnings; (f) tuition, and, where necessary and if possible, accomodation and travel costs of trainees.'' Further, as a guiding principle, UNESCO (p. 11) stated that, ''for the individual, lack of funds should not be an obstacle to participation in adult education programs. Member States should ensure that financial assistance for study purposes is available for those who need it to undertake adult education. The participation of members of underprivileged social groups should, as a general rule, be free of charge.'' Unfortunately, too little was said about the potential sources of these funds.

An Approach to the Future

Successful shaping of public policy to increase the amount of funding available for providing adult and continuing education depends upon (1) a sustained systematic means of keeping abreast of developments within the legislative bodies concerned, (2) an appreciation of the episodic nature of funding, (3) an awareness of the tendency of legislation to be drafted to solve or to eliminate problems, (4) legislators' and legislative staffs' knowledge of issues and information relevant to the issues at hand, (5) the formulation of well thought out position papers that reflect the best thinking of the associations of adult educators, (6) the avoidance of unnecessary conflict in testimony provided by the representatives of various associations who take responsibility for testifying before legislative hearings, (7) the awareness of special interest groups regarding potential programs and their possible benefits, and (8) public awareness of and concern for the problems as reflected in their efforts to alert their representatives to the need to take action.

Twenty years ago, A. A. Liveright (1968, p. 114), who had undertaken a study of adult education in the United States funded by the U.S. Office of Education, concluded, ''Because clarity is lacking, terms must first be defined so that national goals may be established.'' Sixteen years later, the Commission on Higher Education and the Adult Learner (1984, p. 1), composed of forty leaders from education, business, labor, and the community, asserted, ''For reasons of national interest embedded in the economic, political and social determinants of the quality of life, the fostering of learning by adults is an immediate and compelling national need, a need requiring a lucid and forthright statement of national policy and immediate attention by the nation's colleges and universities.'' To stimulate new and more effective adult learning programs that can be replicated, and to assure access regardless of the individuals' economic status, the Commission (p. 13) endorsed ''a multi-faceted approach consisting of support of research and innovation; strengthening of institutional capacity; elimination of discrimination against needy adult learners in access to student financial assistance; revisions in tax policy to encourage rather than discourage productive use of learning resources by the nation's work force; and creation of the information, counseling and guidance services that are necessary to make access and equity a reality.'' Similar and combined approaches would be appropriate for other sectors of ACE.

W. V. Bell (1960, p. 139), in analyzing what he regarded as the cause for inadequate public funding for adult education, asserted that, "The basic trouble lies in public failure to realize the need for and power of adult education. Its cure will come when leaders have presented a picture of adult education sufficiently convincing to bring about the necessary public affirmation, and to elicit from private and public pockets the sums essential to unleash the ultimate potential of adult education." Today, public policy regarding the financing of ACE continues to evolve as educators and legislators at provincial, state, and federal levels learn new uses for education and as they work together, sometimes following and sometimes leading the Canadian and American publics to a more abundant life through learning.

References

"Advisory Council Zapped: Another May Go Soon." *Adult and Continuing Education Today*, Feb. 29, 1988, p. 1.

Anderson, R. E. "Overview and Implications." In R. E. Anderson, E. S. Kasl, and others, *The Costs and Financing of Adult Education and Training*. Toronto: Heath, 1982.

Bell, W. V. "Finance, Legislation and Public Policy for Adult Education." In M. S. Knowles (ed.), *Handbook of Adult Education in the United States*. Washington, D. C.: Adult Education Association of the U.S.A., 1960.

Butler, E. P., Hahn, A., and Darr, J. *The Literacy-Employment Equation: Education for Tomorrow's Jobs—A Policy Options Monograph*. Unpublished report, Far West Laboratory for Educational Research and Development, San Francisco, 1985.

Canadian Association for Adult Education. *A Canadian Policy for Continuing Education*. Toronto: Canadian Association for Adult Education, 1964.

Chandler, M. "Groups Assemble to Combat Illiteracy." *British Columbia School Trustees' Association Report*, 1986, *82* (18), 3.

Christoffel, P. H. "Current Federal Programs for Lifelong Learning: A $14 Billion Effort." *The School Review*, 1978, *86* (3), 348–359.

The Commission on Higher Education and the Adult Learner. *Adult Learners: Key to the Nation's Future*. Columbia, Md.: The Commission on Higher Education and the Adult Learner, 1984.

Cross, K. P., and McCartan, A. *Adult Learning: State Policies and Institutional Practices, No. 1*. Washington, D. C.: Clearinghouse on Higher Education and Association for the Study of Higher Education, 1984.

Delker, P. V. "United States Federal Government Planning for Adult Basic and Adult Secondary Education." In W. M. Rivera (ed.), *Planning Adult Learning: Issues, Practices and Directions*. London: Croom-Helm, 1987.

"Governor Addresses Biennial Institute for Georgia Legislators." *Georgia Center Quarterly*, 1987, *2* (3), 6.

Haigler, K. O. Letter to persons involved in or concerned with literacy work, Office of the Under Secretary, United States Department of Education, Washington, D.C., Nov. 1986.

Hawaii Governor's Council for Literacy. *Together We Can End Illiteracy by the Year 2001.* Honolulu, Hawaii: Governor's Council for Literacy, 1987.

"Higher Education Funds in Fiscal 1989 Budget." *Chronicle of Higher Education,* Feb. 24, 1988, p. A25.

Hodgkinson, H. L. "Guess Who's Coming to College." *Academe,* 1983, *69* (2), 13–20.

Houle, C. O. "Federal Policies Concerning Adult Education." *The School Review,* 1968, *76* (2), 166–189.

Liveright, A. A. *A Study of Adult Education in the United States.* Boston: Center for the Study of Liberal Education for Adults, 1968.

Loring, R. K. "Dollars and Decisions." In H. J. Alford (ed.), *Power and Conflict in Continuing Education.* Belmont, Calif.: Wadsworth, 1980.

Lowe, J. *The Education of Adults: A World Perspective.* (2nd ed.) Toronto: Ontario Institute for Studies in Education, 1982.

MacNeil, T. "Popularizing Public Policy: The Social Context." In F. Cassidy and R. Faris (eds.), *Choosing Our Future: Adult Education and Public Policy in Canada.* Toronto: Ontario Institute for Studies in Education, 1987.

National Conference on Continuing Professional Education. *A Call to Action.* Report of the National Conference on Continuing Professional Education. Pennsylvania State University, University Park, Sept. 28–Oct. 1, 1986.

Rivera, W. M. "Adult Learning: Nomenclature, Systems, Politics and Planning." In W. M. Rivera (ed.), *Planning Adult Learning: Issues, Practices and Directions.* London: Croom-Helm, 1987.

Roberts, H. *Culture and Education: A Study of Alberta and Quebec.* Edmonton: University of Alberta Press, 1982.

Selman, G. "The Leadership Function of Government: The Case of Adult Education in British Columbia 1976–1983." Unpublished paper, Administrative, Adult and Higher Education Department, University of British Columbia, n.d.

Thomas, A. M. *Adult Illiteracy in Canada: A Challenge.* Ottawa: Canadian Commission for UNESCO, 1983.

Thomas, A. M. "Government and Adult Learning." In F. Cassidy and R. Faris (eds.), *Choosing Our Future: Adult Education and Public Policy in Canada.* Toronto: Ontario Institute for Studies in Education, 1987a.

Thomas, A. M. "Policy Development for Adult Education: The Law." In A. M. Rivera (ed.), *Planning Adult Learning: Issues, Practices and Directions.* London: Croom-Helm, 1987b.

UNESCO (United Nations Educational, Scientific, and Cultural Organization). *Recommendation on the Development of Adult Education.* Occasional Paper no. 34. Ottawa: Canadian Commission for UNESCO, 1980.

Wattenbarger, J. L., and Clark, P. "Financing Adult Education." Unpublished paper, Department of Higher Education, University of Florida, n.d.

Part 2

Adult Learners and the Educational Process

Chapters in Part I on the setting, history, philosophy, literature, preparation of practitioners, and so on, presented an overview of adult education as a field of professional practice. In addition to sharing many of the same goals and purposes of adult education, all agencies, programs, and personnel in adult education exist to assist adults in the educational process. It is this focus on adult learners, in fact, which unites an otherwise extraordinarily diverse field of practice, and which serves to differentiate adult education from other forms of education. Beginning with a chapter on the adult learner, Part II focuses on learners and on the learning transaction itself.

The adult learner is at the heart of any learning transaction. Understanding who adults are as learners, what changes adults go through as they age, what motivates adults to seek learning experiences, and how adults accommodate the role of learner in addition to their other life roles is crucial to designing meaningful educational programs and to facilitating the learning that takes place. Boucouvalas and Krupp's chapter, on adult development and learning, and Brookfield's chapter, on facilitating adult learning, address these questions and provide a basis for the next five chapters related to the design of educational programs.

Certainly one major way in which adult students differ from children is that adults add on the role of student to their other life roles. Going to school does not, in most cases, mean giving up being a parent, a spouse, a community member, or a worker. An adult learner still does all that he or she has done before, but with the added responsibility of being a student.

Providers of educational opportunities for adults are responding in creative ways to the unique situations of their learners. Taken into account more and more by providers of adult education are adult schedules, responsibilities, past experiences, and preferred modes of learning. Rose's chapter, on nontraditional education and the assessment of prior learning, and Garrison's chapter, on distance education, explore some of the creative responses of institutions and agencies.

The last three chapters in Part II directly address the planning, management, and evaluation of adult education programs. Sork and Caffarella discuss the role of planning models and then carefully review the basic steps in the planning process including analyzing the context, assessing needs, developing program objectives, formulating an instructional and administrative plan, and designing an evaluation. Controversial issues related to each of these steps are also discussed. The authors note that some well-designed programs fail because of lack of attention to administrative details such as funding and recruitment. These administrative details—the overall management of a continuing education organization—are the subject of Smith and Offerman's chapter. Using a systems perspective, these authors discuss four basic tasks characteristic of adult education—programming, financing, staffing, and marketing. These tasks are carried out through the three managerial functions of planning, organizing, and evaluating.

Much is written in adult education literature about the importance of evaluation, and there are more than fifty different models of program evaluation that an educator might use with his or her program. Nevertheless, many programs go unevaluated due to lack of time, money, interest, or knowledge of evaluation on the part of the program planner or administrator. Steele's chapter on evaluation deals with yet another dimension of this part of the educational process—the complexity of many of the issues central to the evaluation process. For example, one must determine the purpose of the evaluation, how it is to be carried out, and what the results mean to those who have a stake in the process. Although evaluation is a complex and difficult component to include in the educational process, its systematic use can inform and enhance the practice of adult education.

14

Adult Development and Learning

Marcie Boucouvalas
with Judy-Arin Krupp

The terms *adult* and *adulthood* form a pivotal axis upon which adult education revolves as a field of both study and practice. Concerted study of adulthood, however, as a distinct period of life, has evolved only within recent decades. Emergence of this field was preceded by studies of the development of children, adolescents, and senior citizens, but adult development is now established as a field in its own right. It is a field that, according to reviews by Lasker, Moore, and Simpson (1980) and Merriam (1984), can inform the practice and study of adult education. For Merriam, the system of andragogy (the art and science of facilitating adult learning) set forth by Knowles (1968, 1980, 1984; Knowles and Associates, 1984) represents a well-developed link between adult development and adult learning.

An adult developmental perspective poses the question of how one changes during adulthood. The voluminous literature in this area characterizes adult life as one of continual change not restricted just to biological decrement. Some change is simple accretion or drift, while other change is considered growth oriented. The term *development,* however, is characterized by unevenness of usage. While some writers are content to use the terms *change* and *development* interchangeably, others, such as Basseches (1984) argue that, although life tasks and crises provide opportunities for development, they do not necessarily ensure development itself. These writers advise caution in the use of the term. At issue in the literature, therefore, is the question of how much (quantity) and what kind (quality) of change must take place to constitute development.

The concept of *change* also seems integral to conceptualizations of adult learning that range (depending upon one's philosophical orientation) from changes in behavior to changes in internal consciousness. Whether one deliberately or incidentally changes awareness, perception, behavior, or ways of knowing, learning entails both acquiring the new and letting go of the old.

But how does one define adulthood? Chronological age alone is insufficient as a descriptor or determinant. Researchers have defined adulthood by biological, social, psychological, and existential age (Troll, 1976), as well as by functional measures of age such as biological, behavioral, subjective, interpersonal, social, and other indices (Kastenbaum, 1985).

Adult development and learning, then, require a multidisciplinary understanding. Moreover, learning, when broadly defined, approaches synonymity with development, but in narrower terms takes on the character of acquiring information, knowledge, skills, attitude, and wisdom. Whatever focus one takes, however, change of a fairly lasting nature is implied. Change is thus the linchpin between the terms *adult development* and *learning*. External events may cause internal change, and internal events may cause external change. An understanding of the complexity of this territory is the focus of this chapter. Development leads to changes in the nature, modes, interest, and content of learning, and learning often leads to further development. Accordingly, an examination of adult change in different arenas of life over time is offered first and leads into a discussion of perspectives on understanding the adult learner. Implications for adult education are suggested throughout the chapter. A concluding section offers a recapitulation of the highlights and notes additional resources for continuing inquiry.

Developmental Change in Adult Learners

So much literature abounds within the area of developmental change in adults that it is difficult here to be comprehensive. Consequently, this discussion illustrates major patterns, trends, movements, and issues that emerge within the literature of adult development and learning as it potentially impinges upon the study and practice of adult education.

One major theme in the literature posits predictable sequential progressions in an individual's life course or, at least, in selected domains or aspects of it. Here we present a selected review of the literature within this theme, along with caveats and concerns related to the material, and we offer other approaches for conceptualizing and understanding development.

Throughout the chapter, however, the reader should bear in mind the dynamic interplay of biological, social, psychological, historical, and environmental or contextual factors influencing an adult's life course and one's capacity for and involvement with learning.

Sequential Perspectives. The concept of *stage* is integral to discussions of sequential progression, but the term may pose a dilemma to the reader interested in conceptual precision because of its multiplicity of usages. While some authors prefer to reserve the term only for a specific hierarchical invariant sequence, others use the term more loosely to refer to age-related periods and tasks in life.

Accordingly, many writers have offered categorizations in an effort to bring order to the territory (for example, Cross, 1981; Troll, 1982). Kohlberg and Armon (1984) offer a particularly useful typology suggesting distinctions among three types of stage models: functional, soft structural, and hard structural. Their cognitively oriented frame of reference led Kohlberg and Armon to use the internal structure of Piagetian stages of cognitive development discussed later (which they consider hard) as a template against which to compare other stage approaches. Each stage approach is discussed below.

Kohlberg and Armon use the work of Erikson (1963, 1982) as an example of the functional stage models which, they emphasize, are not hierarchical in nature, although researchers disagree about this claim. Essentially, a new set of functions emerges at each period, and the adult experiences new sociocultural spheres and roles.

Erikson's well-known model portrays development as the resolution of a series of dualities that emerge at critical periods across the life span. Resolution of each duality leads to ego strengths, such as wisdom from integrity and despair. Erikson stresses integrating the themes of love and work when resolving each duality (Smelser and Erikson, 1980).

The term *psychosocial* connects the self, or development of the psyche, to the world. Erikson's establishment of this psychosocial sequence of stages for development remains the scaffolding for many of what Lasker, Moore, and Simpson (1980) have called phase studies (Levinson and Gould) as well as for other research efforts (Neugarten and Havighurst).

The findings of Levinson and others (1978), Levinson (forthcoming), and Gould (1978), based on clinical data, describe the relationship between age and the tasks or problems encountered across the life span. No hierarchy, however, is implied. Levinson's work also emphasizes the role that mentoring seems to play in adult development and learning, an area futher pursued by others (Bolton, 1980; Daloz, 1986; Merriam, 1983). Gould's developmental model, on the other hand, requires adults to relinquish childhood consciousness. Women, researched more recently, appear to experience the same phases and tasks at approximately the same ages, but the way women work on these tasks differ, as do their outcomes (Levinson, forthcoming; Roberts and Newton, 1987).

Neugarten (1979) and Neugarten and Neugarten (1987) suggest that the timing of a life task or event determines its effect on development. Off-time events precipitate crises, while on-time occurrences allow for rehearsal and anticipation of the change. Unlike on-time events, off-time events usually are unexpected given one's age or station in life. For example, an injury that forces one into early retirement or the death of one's child would be considered an off-time event.

For Havighurst ([1952] 1972), "developmental tasks" vary with one's social roles. Although the content of his work may be dated, his concept of each developmental task creating a "teachable moment" has great import for adult educators. When working in an international context, one might keep in mind that developmental tasks may be different for each society and subculture.

Returning to the typology of Kohlberg and Armon (1984), these functional stage models address different functions—roles, responsibilities, spheres, and tasks emerging at each period. They deal with the structure of neither consciousness nor cognition as do the soft and hard structural stage models, respectively. Consequently, they remain more culture-bound.

Soft and hard structural stage models have in common more stagelike properties, particularly properties of a hierarchical progression. The criteria of stage development the authors put forth include the following: (a) "Stages imply a . . . qualitative difference in structures . . . that still serve the same basic function . . . at various points in development. (b) The different structures form an invariant sequence. . . . Cultural factors may speed up, slow down, or stop development, [but] they do not change its sequence." (c) Each [stage] forms a "structured whole." An underlying "thought organization" is represented, not just "familiarity with the task" at hand. (d) "Stages are hierarchical integrations." Each stage represents a "differentiated and integrated structure" that subsumes the lower stages (Kohlberg and Armon, pp. 384–385). One might add that the stages do not necessarily relate to age and that one may have difficulty understanding or functioning at a stage that one has not yet achieved.

The hard structural stages, with Piaget as prototype, meet all of the criteria. The soft structural stages, however, exhibit some, but not all, of the criteria. The specific criteria met differ among the models. A commonality, however, among soft-structured models involves "an ego or self consciously making meaning for itself" (p. 384). Emphasis is on self-reflection. Soft stages, in effect, "depend upon formal reflection" (p. 393). Each stage is associated with a different perspective on reality and way of being. A few examples follow. Loevinger (1976) studied ego development (ego defined as that which strives to master, integrate, or create meaning from experience and maintains stability by focusing on life factors related to one's present being). Descriptions of the term *adult stages* range from self-protective to integrated, and are being extended by the research of Cook-Greuter (1987) to a universal stage where one's motives lie beyond only personal self. An understanding of the developmental progression of the ego's defense mechanisms is offered by Vaillant (1977).

For Kegan (1982), the way individuals respond to a particular life event is based on the meaing one has constructed both for the event and for the self in relation to the event. Each individual constructs his or her own reality and that reality is the only reality possible for that person at that time. Similarly, meaning achieves centrality in Fowler's (1981) research on faith development (a vision or way of seeing meaning in our lives). One moves from a faith that conforms to the expectations of others to universalizing faith.

Common to many of these studies is the emergence of individuals who have integrated and balanced self-systems—that is, autonomous and homonomous dimensions of self are developing and harmonizing. These people are being all they can be as separate, unique individuals, yet as connected selves they are deriving meaning from being and feeling—identifying with part of a greater whole. Likewise, a developmental pattern emerges characterized by movement from self-centeredness to an understanding, acceptance, and embracing of others and their perspectives. One's developmental level may, in effect, determine how one navigates through life. It seems that adult educators would profit by reflecting upon how one can respond to, as well as contribute to, a learner's further development, keeping in mind that some learners may develop beyond the stage of the educator.

Many developmental researchers suggest that growth may be predicated upon one's stage of cognitive development. Piaget (1972), with his hard structural stages, provides the seminal research in the area of cognitive development. Each stage represents a structural logic, a way of thinking, and a form of reasoning. One moves through qualitatively different ways of thinking from sensorimotor to formal operations that include metacognition, or thinking about thinking (Weinert and Kluwe, 1987). The hard stage criteria of the Piagetian model are, according to Kohlberg and Armon (1984), also fulfilled by Kohlberg's stage model of moral development, given that justice is the "parallel in the social world to the structure of logical thought in the physical world" (p. 390). The authors conclude, however, that the rational thought of the hard stage models may prove inadequate to address the wisdom and experience of adulthood—a domain in which the soft structural models have promise.

An Expanded Perspective on Developmental Stages. A network of scholars have further advanced stages of cognitive development beyond that of Piaget's formal operations, and they call it postformal thinking. Beyond formal thought lies relativistic thinking and beyond that dialectic thinking, whereby one is able to reconcile previously considered antithetical thoughts into a greater whole (Commons, Richards, and Armon, 1984; Commons, Sinnott, Richards, and Armon, 1989). Postformal thinkers can reconcile contradictions and understand knowledge as temporary (Rybash, Hoyer, and Roodin, 1986). They apparently work within an open-system framework, as did Prigogine and Stengers (1984). Logic is viewed as only one stage in human development, which can progress further. At issue, however, in other caches of the literature is the question of whether, from a developmental perspective, logic must precede other ways of knowing (Broughton, 1984). Also, Rybash, Hoyer, and Roodin (1986) suggest that adults might operate at one cognitive stage in their domain of expertise but at other stages in domains in which they are more novice. Debate still continues as to whether such advances observed in thinking and thought processes indeed constitute a stage.

Wilber (1986) suggests a nine-stage developmental model of consciousness that draws equally on Western and Eastern approaches and expands on Piaget's work. He fully describes the self-system, which is developing in each stage. The fifth stage, formal reflexive mind, he compares to Piaget's formal operations, and stage six (vision-logic) parallels in part the postformal thinkers discussed above. Stages seven through nine deal with transpersonal development, during which perceptual power arises from inner sight rather than from thought, as is the case in the stages of personal development.

Integration of the person self, then, becomes a step along the way to full humanness. Wilber points out ''neglect of most conventional researchers for the transpersonal stages of development'' (p. 78), perhaps because such understanding becomes difficult if one employs thought or intellect alone. Experience seems critical. Consequently, study of transpersonal experiences (for which one's personal self is not a central motivator) may be of import to adult education. While transpersonal stages pertain to a small portion of the population, transpersonal states or moments occur in the lives of most people. An example is the theta level of consciousness, which occurs just before sleeping and just prior to full waking. Theta is good for problem solving since self-censors on creativity are often suspended. Based on research at the Menninger Foundation (Green and Green, 1977), one can learn how to lengthen one's time in this territory.

The structures of cognition, then, are viewed as only one way of knowing. Philosophers through the ages have emphasized the balance between cognitive, analytical, intellectual ways of knowing and the contemplative approach, both of which may have relevance to a more comprehensive understanding of the adult as a learner. The research of Brown (1986) offers an understanding of deep structures of consciousness (six stages forming an invariant sequence) revealed through meditation practices across traditions and cultural contexts. Brown defines meditation as ''simply a form of intensive attention training . . . triggering an atypical sequence of adult development . . . atypical only in the sense that the path . . . is not available to all adults, only those who rigorously train attention'' (p. 266). Internal changes of consciousness, changes in cognition and perception, as well as behavioral changes, result from such attention training. As we move toward the next millennium, adult educators might well consider ways to cultivate, both in themselves and in learners, cognitive, contemplative, and other ways of knowing.

Individuals do not develop in vacuums. Researchers have documented developmental change in contexts such as intimate relationships in which one moves from a power struggle, blame-game way of relating to a cocreative stage (Campbell, 1980) or in organizational contexts such as the Environmental Quality (EQ) Scale of Gibb (1978). Such environmental influences range from punitive to cosmic, and, accordingly, fulfill or frustrate needs of individuals at various places in the developmental continuum.

Learning often involves relating to another and frequently occurs within an organizational context. What kind of relationships will adult learners develop and what relationships in their lives are already defining them and setting a context for learning? A relationship with a mentor is one that some research suggests leads to learning and development, albeit differently defined. What is the quality of this and other kinds of learning relationships? As posited by Campbell, might a relationship turn into a power struggle for the person in the early stages of intimacy or can it reach the cocreative stage? Moreover, what questions should one ask as an adult educator or adult learner about the environmental quality of an organization?

Caveats and Cautions. Although the stage concept is a commonly used perspective in the adult development literature, not all researchers accept it. Some find the search for invariant and unidirectional development less useful than a search for stability and change. Many warn against viewing stage theory and development as a purely linear process. Particularly at issue is whether movement is abrupt or fluid between stages. Yet others question the validity of the whole concept of stage. Other concerns include the following: (1) small qualitative samples have been used studying mostly the middle class, white, and married; (2) research is just beginning to address the influence of one's cultural norms on the developmental pattern—an area in which anthropological literature is particularly germane (for example, Keith, 1980); (3) earlier research emphasized male development, but more recent research is achieving a balance by targeting females (Belenky and others, 1986; Caffarella and Freeman, 1985; Bardwick, 1980; Harris, Ellicott, and Holmes, 1986).

Gilligan (1982) has been on the vanguard of this movement with her thesis that women tend to strive for attachment and connections and men for separation. At issue, however, is whether and to what extent one can generalize claims about adult development and learning on the basis of a biological sex construct—male or female. Another perspective on balance is provided by the literature on psychological androgyny, and psychosocial construct of gender—that is, psychological traits that are stereotypically assigned as masculine or feminine. Androgynous beings embody both characteristics and sometimes blend opposite traits into one act (for example, firing someone with compassion). An understanding of this literature may be relevant to adult education endeavors, particularly since the literature on adulthood suggests that integration, reconciliation, and transcendence of such dualities are characteristics of continued development.

The Perspective of the Individual and Society. As the discussion proceeds, it should become evident that an understanding of adult developmental learning rests on both individual differences (such as biology and neurology, personality and emotional systems, cognition and intelligence) and the interaction between these variables and social or cultural factors (such as social class, ethnic group, educational level, political system, subculture, relationships, organizations, and environment). Influential also are historical factors (cohort expectations or behaviors and major historical events). Historical and social events seem to affect patterns of development for whole groups as well as for individuals (Felton and Shaver, 1984; Schaie and Willis, 1986). The life-span development approach (Kastenbaum, 1985; Schaie and Willis,

1986) may be particularly useful in understanding the multidisciplinary nature of this territory and the continuous nature of development throughout life. An understanding of adult development and learning, therefore, must take into account individual differences as they affect and are affected by psychosocial, sociocultural, sociopolitical, and historical factors.

Even individual differences interact dynamically. Personality variables such as openness to new experiences and flexibility (Hooper and Colbert, 1984; Schaie and Willis, 1986; Malatesta and Izard, 1984) correlate positively with one's intellectual functioning. The question of personality change over the years, however, becomes a function of how one defines personality. Aspects such as temperament and character traits (disposition) appear to remain stable while values and self-esteem may change (McCrae and Costa, 1984). One's personality, however defined, affects one's preferences and approaches to learning.

Intellectual functioning in adulthood itself has been a well-researched topic since the seminal studies of Thorndike (1928). This foundational thrust and the advances made beginning in the 1930s by Lorge and others (1965) on the power to learn have been amply discussed, for example, by Robinson (1936), Brunner (1959), Kidd (1973), Knox (1977), and Long (1983). Knowledge is still incomplete, but Rybash, Hoyer, and Roodin (1986) offer an encapsulated model of the various approaches to the study of adult knowing, thinking, and information processing—including, but not limited to, both the stage perspective and the psychometric movement. For a discussion of cognitive and learning styles, the reader should refer to Long (1983) and to Bonham (1988).

Certainly the physiological-neurological domain of development clearly influences one's capacity for and involvement with learning. As reviewed by Thompson (1982), decline in sensory acuity and reaction time is indisputable, and decline in motor functions and their cognitive and behavioral correlates is predictable (Joseph, 1988). The straightforwardness of this information has resulted in the decrement perspective on adulthood and adult learning. Debates still rage, however, as to the nature and extent of age-related declines. Decline in speed of response and short-term memory seem evident, but stability and even increase in verbal fluency, for example, have been reported.

Recent research from neurosciences also provides potential evidence that all is not decremental in the adult years, although one should exercise caution in interpreting such findings. Researchers still acknowledge neuronal loss but report the continuous development and strengthening of synapses and cortical connections during adulthood. Neurons communicate via synapses and thus process information.

Such claims, guided by the research on neuroplasticity of the brain (that is, modifiability in the structure and physiology of neurons) suggest that, by providing enriched, appropriate environments even in adulthood, the capacity for learning, in neurological terms, can continue to develop.

Moreover, active involvement in learning seems to create cortical connections (Milgram, MacLeod, and Petit, 1987; Renner and Rosenzweig, 1987; Winlow and McCrohan, 1987). Conversely, too much stimulation can possibly cause synapses to shut down, thus interfering with learning (Sinclair, 1986). Further, boredom may result from an overload of processing such meaningless information (Klapp, 1986). Likewise, meaning becomes central in memory research. Findings suggest that meaningful information tends to be processed at a deeper level, thus retrieved and remembered more easily (Cermak and Craik, 1979). Schaie and Willis (1986) question whether the issue of meaning, and a consequent lack of motivation, may also be at work in intelligence testing when, for example, adults fail at memorizing ten numbers backward.

Some neurological mechanisms, however, involved in the fluid intelligence configuration of Horn and Cattell (1967) appear to decline with age, but performance on tasks requiring crystallized intelligence increases (Horn and Donaldson, 1980). The innate and biologically based fluid intelligence factor, represented in rote memory and reaction time, is independent of experience and education. Its apparent decline with age is often compensated for and in many cases superseded by crystallized intelligence—the knowledge, strategies, and experience that accumulate with age and that are reflected in judgment and wisdom.

Beyond neurological and cognitive capacities, seeming decrements observed in adults may also be a function of world views, values, internal and external environments, and disposition of the individual. As the findings of Lundberg (1974) suggest, social class itself might sustain values that mitigate against one's development and further learning.

According to Schaie and Willis (1986), decline is predicated on two factors: disease and lack of environmental stimulation. While one's health affects the capacity for and quality of learning, recent evidence from the field of psychoneuroimmunology suggests that the mind may actually play a role in keeping the body healthy (Locke and others, 1985).

Training seems successful in attenuating loss from disuse. Gains become apparent as a result of intervention strategies such as physical exercise, diet, or learning of cognitive strategies (such as linking one's experience to the present learning). Adult learning capacity also expands as one learns how to learn (Smith, 1982, 1983, 1988)—a concept that is gaining acceptance and momentum. Learning to learn is helping adults increase their appreciation of the following learning skills: (1) deriving maximum benefit from material and human resources; (2) recognizing one's own proclivities in the manner and form of learning; (3) understanding cognitive, social, affective, and other factors facilitating and inhibiting one's learning; and (4) developing adaptive and facilitating strategies and attitudes in learning.

So, the capacities of adults appear to remain relatively stable given continued use, absence of disease, and absence of time constraints. Based on longitudinal studies, intelligence seemingly can continue to increase during adulthood (Jarvik, Eisdorfer, and Blum, 1973; Schaie and Willis, 1986), particularly in domain-specific areas of expertise (Rybash, Hoyer, and Roodin, 1986) for adults open to new experiences (Malatesta and Izard, 1984). Yet, performance deficits have been observed repeatedly. Some are due, however, to fast pacing, to motivational issues, or to the element of cautiousness that manifests itself in many adults as they grow older.

Stability, growth, and decrement all characterize adult life. Social variables such as gender, social class, and culture also are influential. In fact, attention to the social context is indispensable to a fuller understanding of how adults learn from both formal and informal settings (Ingham, 1987; Jarvis, 1987a, 1987b). This understanding of how adults and adult learners change over time should better equip the reader to understand the adult learner.

Better Understanding the Adult Learner

Early efforts to understand the adult learner dealt with the question, can adults learn? Studies gradually have revealed age as only one factor to consider when investigating learning ability. Variables such as education, experience, social background, cultural background, personality, physical condition, roles, and relationships all contribute.

Once adults' ability and power to learn was established (Thorndike, 1928; Lorge, 1965), studies began to address the questions of who learns, and what, where, why, and how do they learn? Much of the data have come from multidisciplinary sources and, more recently, from the field of adult education itself. Gibb (1960) and Lasker, Moore, and Simpson (1980) review the way major learning theories interface with adult learning and education, and Knowles (1984) offers an understanding of the differences between propounders and interpreters of the learning theory literature.

Within the field of adult education, participation, as well as barriers to it, has been a widely investigated topic for decades. Many studies, including the EPS (Education Participation Scale) of Boshier (1982) and Boshier and Collins (1985), have emerged from the foundational work of Houle (1961) on goal-oriented, activity-oriented, and learning-oriented learners. An attempt to understand and enhance motivation continues (Cross, 1981; Long, 1983; Wlodkowski, 1985), as does a focus on learning how to learn (Smith, 1982, 1983, 1988). Recent strides also have been made in understanding and facilitating the access of the developmentally disabled adult learners, the topic of Chapter Forty-Five.

Tough (1971, 1982) enlarged the literature base on the population of adult learners making intentional changes to include adults who plan, design, and pursue their own learning projects. More recently, the emphasis has expanded beyond deliberate learning to include incidental learning and learning from experience and life in both conscious and nonconscious ways (Rossing and Russell, 1987; Ingham, 1987). Of related importance is the area of tacit, unspoken, and untaught learning (Polanyi, 1976). Sternberg and Caruso (1985, p. 147), for example, argue that "most of the practical knowledge adults acquire is tacit." Such tacit knowledge evidently is vital to "real-world pursuits" (Wagner and Sternberg, 1985).

Self-direction in learning now has become an issue of discussion and debate with controversy still apparent on definitional and conceptual issues. State-of-the-art reviews are available from Caffarella and O'Donnell (1987) and Long and Associates (1988).

Merriam (1987) has managed to sort through the material within the field of adult education and to delineate a three-fold framework of the kinds of models adult educators are proposing in order to understand and explain adult learning—models based on adult characteristics (Knowles, 1980, 1984; Knowles and Associates, 1984; Cross, 1981), (2) adult life situations (McClusky, 1970; Knox, 1980, 1986), and (3) changes in consciousness (Mezirow, 1981, 1985; Freire, 1970). Brookfield's (1985, 1986) transactional encounter and Candy's (1982) personal paradigm transition both follow this lead.

These perspectives emanate from the field of adult education after a systematic and thoughtful analysis by individuals who have worked with and studied adult learners and adult learning. Commonalities and discrepancies have stimulated healthy discussion. Individually and collectively these perspectives resonate with the growing multidisciplinary contribution to an understanding of adulthood. Sometimes, however, adult educators do not have a full awareness of relevant findings from other disciplines and fields. In the future, adult educators should work toward a more unified understanding of adult development and learning and of the contributions that many disciplines make toward this end.

Summary and Conclusions

Since present space constraints preclude a comprehensive rendition of the constantly burgeoning areas of adult development and learning, references were selected with an eye to providing resources for further inquiry. The reader can keep abreast of the various handbooks (for example, Binstock and others, 1985; Birren and Schaie, 1985; Finch and Schneider, 1985) that provide constantly updated companion reading to this handbook and particularly to this chapter. Also, the annual serial publication of *Lifespan Development and Behavior,* as well as other periodicals, should prove useful. Readers, as continual lifelong learners, should consider the authors of this chapter and other chapters in the handbook as human resources with whom to communicate for further dialogue and update.

In summary, then, adults can and do change—sometimes consciously and other times unconsciously or unintentionally as a by-product of an event or activity. While some change brings role gain or adds to one's being, other modifications result in loss. Still other changes result in development involving alterations in the structures of consciousness and cognition.

The question of the relevance of this knowledge about adult change, development, and learning to the study and practice of adult education is one for both individual and collective pursuit and reflection. Many disciplines contribute to a better understanding of adult development and adult learning, and they create a broad base to serve as a foundation for practice. Because adult education is founded on such a multidisciplinary base, adult educators can and perhaps should form a personal approach to practice.

The literature on adult development and learning offers guidelines as well as challenges. Understanding the life tasks of various periods can afford a broader perspective on one's own life trajectory and those of learners—if one exercises caution in understanding the cultural relativity of various developmental tasks, roles, and functions. Similarly, observed differences between males and females in socialization and ways of knowing may be instructive if one does not fall into the trap of social stereotyping. Not all males or all females fit the norm. Further, as the literature on psychological androgyny suggests, a blending of purportedly "male" and "female" strengths is possible in one person. In general, the ability to integrate dualities and reconcile disparities seems a characteristic pattern of development. Self-reflection acts as a catalyst in this process and deepens the meaning in one's life path and perspectives. Such meaning is central to adult learning endeavors.

Whether one functions as a learning facilitator, consultant, counselor, program designer, or administrator, the more one understands the developmental process the greater the likelihood of being able to relate better to a spectrum of learners. As educators, it also is imperative that we be able to recognize those learners whose development extends beyond the educator, acknowledging that one's perception remains limited by one's own developmental stage and issues. In this vein, one might also want to remain open to the various ways of knowing. Adult learning, then, involves a network of interrelated factors. Each individual's physical and neurological condition, cognitive and intellectual structures, psychological disposition and characteristics, and social roles and attributes all interact and influence his or her capacity for and involvement with learning. Although advancing age brings decline in sensory and motor functions, adult learning continues— barring disease and disuse.

This dynamic constellation of factors influences and is influenced by one's environment—including relationships, organizational affiliations, levels of involvement, and the larger cultural context. All are inextricably intertwined with one's place in time and space and with the greater historical context. An understanding of the amazingly complex manner by which adults change over time and of the nature of adults as learners provides a foundation for better facilitating adult learning—the topic of the next chapter.

References

Bardwick, J. M. "The Seasons of a Woman's Life." In D. McGuigan (ed.), *Women's Lives: New Theory, Research and Policy.* Ann Arbor: University of Michigan Center for Continuing Education of Women, 1980.

Basseches, M. *Dialectical Thinking and Adult Development.* Norwood, N.J.: Ablex Publishing, 1984.

Belenky, M. F., and others. *Women's Ways of Knowing: The Development of Self, Voice, and Mind.* New York: Basic Books, 1986.

Binstock, R. H., and others (eds.). *Handbook of Aging and the Social Sciences.* (2nd ed.) New York: Van Nostrand Reinhold, 1985.

Birren, J. E., and Schaie, K. W. *Handbook of the Psychology of Aging.* (2nd ed.) New York: Von Nostrand Reinhold, 1985.

Bolton, E. B. "A Conceptual Analysis of the Mentor Relationship in the Career Development of Women." *Adult Education,* 1980, *30* (4), 195–207.

Bonham, L. A. "Learning Style Use: In Need of Perspective." *Lifelong Learning,* 1988, *11* (5), 14–17, 19.

Boshier, R. *The Education Participation Scale.* Vancouver, B.C.: Learning Press, 1982.

Boshier, R., and Collins, J. B. "The Houle Typology After Twenty-Two Years: A Large-Scale Empirical Test." *Adult Education Quarterly,* 1985, *35* (3), 113–130.

Brookfield, S. "A Critical Definition of Adult Education." *Adult Education Quarterly,* 1985, *36* (1), 44–49.

Brookfield, S. *Understanding and Facilitating Adult Learning.* San Francisco: Jossey-Bass, 1986.

Broughton, J. M. "Not Beyond Formal Operations but Beyond Piaget." In M. L. Commons and others (eds.), *Beyond Formal Operations: Late Adolescent and Adult Cognitive Development.* New York: Praeger, 1984.

Brown, D. "The Stages of Meditation in Cross-Cultural Perspective." In K. Wilber, J. Engler, and D. P. Brown (eds.), *Transformations of Consciousness: Conventional and Contemplative Perspectives on Development.* Boston: New Science Library, 1986.

Brunner, E. S., and others. *An Overview of Adult Education Research.* Washington, D.C.: Adult Education Association of the U.S.A., 1959.

Caffarella, R. S., and Freeman, S. "Women in Their Thirties: The In-Between Generation." In W. M. Rivera and S. M. Walker (eds.), *Lifelong Learning Research Conference Proceedings.* College Park: University of Maryland, 1985.

Caffarella, R. S., and O'Donnell, J. M. "Self-Directed Learning: A Critical Paradigm Revisited." *Adult Education Quarterly,* 1987, *37* (4), 199–211.

Campbell, S. *The Couple's Journey: Intimacy as a Path to Wholeness.* San Luis Obispo, Calif.: Impact, 1980.

Candy, P. C. "Personal Constructs and Personal Paradigms: Elaboration,

Modification and Transformation.'' *Interchange on Educational Policy,* 1982, *13* (4), 56–69.

Cermak, L. S., and Craik, F. I. (eds.). *Levels of Processing in Human Memory.* Hillsdale, N.J.: Erlbaum, 1979.

Commons, M. L., Richards, F. A., and Armon, C. (eds.). *Beyond Formal Operations: Late Adolescent and Adult Cognitive Development.* New York: Praeger, 1984.

Commons, M. L., Sinnott, J., Richards, F. A., and Armon, C. (eds.). *Adult Development: Comparisons and Applications of Developmental Models.* New York: Praeger, 1989.

Cook-Greuter, S. R. "The Nature of Stages 5/6 (Post-Autonomous) and 6 (Universal) in Ego Development Theory and Their Practical Identification in Responses to Loevinger's Sentence Completion Test." Paper presented at the third Beyond Formal Operations Symposium: Positive Development During Adolescence and Adulthood, Cambridge, Mass., Harvard University, June 25–27, 1987.

Cross, P. *Adults as Learners.* San Francisco: Jossey-Bass, 1981.

Daloz, L. A. *Effective Teaching and Mentoring: Realizing the Transformational Power of Adult Learning Experiences.* San Francisco: Jossey-Bass, 1986.

Erikson, E. H. *Childhood and Society.* (Rev. ed.) New York: Norton, 1963.

Erikson, E. H. *The Life Cycle Completed: A Review.* New York: Norton, 1982.

Felton, B., and Shaver, P. "Cohort Variations in Adults' Reported Feelings." In C. Z. Malatesta and C. E. Izard (eds.), *Emotion in Adult Development.* Beverly Hills, Calif.: Sage, 1984.

Finch, C. E., and Schneider, E. L. (eds.). *Handbook of the Biology of Aging.* New York: Van Nostrand Reinhold, 1985.

Fowler, J. *Stages of Faith: The Psychology of Human Development and the Quest for Meaning.* New York: Harper & Row, 1981.

Freire, P. *Pedagogy of the Oppressed.* New York: Herder & Herder, 1970.

Gibb, J. R. "Learning Theory in Adult Education." In M. S. Knowles and E. Dubois (eds.), *Handbook of Adult Education in the United States.* Washington, D.C.: Adult Education Association of the U.S.A., 1960.

Gibb, J. R. *Trust: A New View of Personal and Organizational Development.* Los Angeles: Guild of Tutors Press, 1978.

Gilligan, C. *In a Different Voice: Psychological Theory and Woman's Development.* Cambridge, Mass.: Harvard University Press, 1982.

Gould, R. *Transformations: Growth and Change in Adult Life.* New York: Simon & Schuster, 1978.

Green, E., and Green, A. *Beyond Biofeedback.* New York: Delta, 1977.

Harris, R. L., Ellicott, A. M., and Holmes, D. S. "The Timing of Psychosocial Transitions and Changes in Women's Lives: An Examination of Women Aged 45 to 50." *Journal of Personality and Social Psychology,* 1986, *51* (2), 409–416.

Havighurst, R. J. *Developmental Tasks and Education.* (3rd ed.) New York: McKay, 1972. (Originally published 1952.)

Hooper, S. G., and Colbert, K. K. *Personality and Memory Correlates of Intellectual Functioning: Young Adulthood to Old Age.* Vol. 11: *Contributions to Human Development.* Basel, Switz.: Karger, 1984.

Horn, J. L., and Catell, R. B. "Age Differences in Fluid and Crystallized Intelligence." *Acta Psychologica,* 1967, *26,* 107–129.

Horn, J. L., and Donaldson, G. "Cognitive Development in Adulthood." In O. G. Brim and J. Kagan (eds.), *Constancy and Change in Human Development.* Cambridge, Mass.: Harvard University Press, 1980.

Houle, C. *The Inquiring Mind.* Madison: University of Wisconsin Press, 1961.

Ingham, R. "Context and Learning." In W. Rivera and S. Walker, (eds.), *Lifelong Learning Research Conference Proceedings.* College Park: University of Maryland, 1987.

Jarvik, L., Eisdorfer, C., and Blum, J. E. *Intellectual Functioning in Adults.* New York: Springer, 1973.

Jarvis, P. *Adult Learning in the Social Context.* London: Croom-Helm, 1987a.

Jarvis, P. "Meaningful and Meaningless Experience: Towards an Analysis of Learning from Life." *Adult Education Quarterly,* 1987b, *37* (3), 164–172.

Joseph, J. A. (ed.). *Central Determinants of Age-Related Declines in Motor Function.* Annals of the New York Academy of Science, Vol. 515. New York: New York Academy of Science, 1988.

Kastenbaum, R. "Life Span Development." In T. Husen and T. M. Postlethwaite (eds.), *The International Encyclopedia of Education: Research and Studies.* Vol. 5. Elmsford, N.Y.: Pergamon Press, 1985.

Kegan, R. *The Evolving Self: Problem and Process in Human Development.* Cambridge, Mass.: Harvard University Press, 1982.

Keith, J. "The Best Is Yet to Be: Towards an Anthropology of Age." *Annual Review of Anthropology,* 1980, *9,* 339–364.

Kidd, J. R. *How Adults Learn.* (2nd ed.) New York: Association Press, 1973.

Klapp, O. E. *Overload and Boredom: Essays on the Quality of Life in the Information Age.* New York: Greenwood Press, 1986.

Knowles, M. S. "Andragogy, Not Pedagogy." *Adult Leadership,* 1968, *16,* 350–352, 368.

Knowles, M. S. *The Modern Practice of Adult Education: From Pedagogy to Andragogy.* (2nd ed.) Chicago: Association/Follett, 1980.

Knowles, M. S. *The Adult Learner: A Neglected Species.* (3rd ed.) Houston, Tex.: Gulf, 1984.

Knowles, M. S., and Associates. *Andragogy in Action: Applying Modern Principles of Adult Learning.* San Francisco: Jossey-Bass, 1984.

Knox, A. B. *Adult Development and Learning.* San Francisco: Jossey-Bass, 1977.

Knox, A. B. "Proficiency Theory of Adult Learning." *Contemporary Educational Psychology,* 1980, *5,* 378–404.

Knox, A. B. *Helping Adults Learn.* San Francisco: Jossey-Bass, 1986.

Kohlberg, L., and Armon, C. "Three Types of Stage Models Used in the Study of Adult Development." In M. Commons, F. A. Richards, and

C. A. Armon (eds.), *Beyond Formal Operations: Late Adolescent and Adult Cognitive Development.* New York: Praeger, 1984.

Lasker, H., Moore, J., and Simpson, E. L. *Adult Development and Approaches to Learning.* Washington, D.C.: National Institute of Education, U.S. Government Printing Office, 1980.

Levinson, D. J. *The Seasons of a Woman's Life.* New York: Knopf, forthcoming.

Levinson, D. J., and others. *The Seasons of a Man's Life.* New York: Knopf, 1978.

Locke, S., and others. *Foundations of Psychoneuroimmunology.* Hawthorne, N.Y.: Aldine, 1985.

Loevinger, J. *Ego Development: Conceptions and Theories.* San Francisco: Jossey-Bass, 1976.

Long, H. B. *Adult Learning: Research and Practice.* New York: Cambridge University Press, 1983.

Long, H. B., and Associates. *Self-Directed Learning: Application and Theory.* Athens: Department of Adult Education, University of Georgia, 1988.

Lorge, I., and others. *Adult Learning.* Washington, D.C., Adult Education Association of the U.S.A., 1965.

Lundberg, M. J. *The Incomplete Adult: Social Class Constraints on Personality Development.* Westport, Conn.: Greenwood Press, 1974.

McClusky, H. Y. "An Approach to a Differential Psychology of the Adult Potential." In S. M. Grabowski (ed.), *Adult Learning and Instruction.* Syracuse, N.Y.: ERIC Clearinghouse on Adult Education, 1970.

McCrae, R. R., and Costa, P. T. *Emerging Lives, Enduring Dispositions: Personality in Adulthood.* Boston: Little, Brown, 1984.

Malatesta, C. Z., and Izard, C. E. *Emotion in Adult Development.* Beverly Hills, Calif.: Sage, 1984.

Merriam, S. B. "Mentors and Proteges: A Critical Review of the Literature." *Adult Education Quarterly,* 1983, *33* (3), 161–173.

Merriam, S. B. *Adult Development: Implications for Adult Education.* Columbus, Ohio: ERIC Clearinghouse on Adult, Career, and Vocational Education, 1984.

Merriam, S. B. "Adult Learning and Theory Building: A Review." *Adult Education Quarterly,* 1987, *37* (4), 187–198.

Mezirow, J. "A Critical Theory of Adult Learning and Education." *Adult Education,* 1981, *32,* 3–27.

Mezirow, J. "Concept and Action in Adult Education." *Adult Education Quarterly,* 1985, *35* (3), 142–151.

Milgram, N. W., MacLeod, C. M., and Petit, T. C. *Neuroplasticity, Learning and Memory.* New York: Liss, 1987.

Neugarten, B. "Time, Age, and the Life Cycle." *American Journal of Psychiatry,* 1979, *136,* 887–893.

Neugarten, B., and Neugarten, D. "The Changing Meaning of Age." *Psychology Today,* 1987, *21* (5), 29–33.

Perry, W. G., Jr. *Forms of Intellectual and Ethical Development in the College Years.* New York: Holt, Rinehart & Winston, 1970.

Piaget, J. "Intellectual Evolution from Adolescence to Adulthood." *Human Development,* 1972, *15,* 1–12.

Polanyi, M. "Tacit Knowing." In M. Marx and F. Goodson (eds.), *Theories of Contemporary Psychology.* New York: Macmillan, 1976.

Prigogine, I., and Stengers, I. *Order Out of Chaos: Man's New Dialogue with Nature.* Boulder, Colo.: New Science Library, 1984.

Renner, M. J., and Rosenzweig, M. R. *Enriched and Impoverished Environments: Effects on Brain and Behavior.* New York: Springer-Verlag, 1987.

Roberts, P., and Newton, P. M. "Levinsonian Studies of Women's Adult Development." *Psychology and Aging,* 1987, *2* (2), 154–163.

Robinson, J. H. "Can People Go on Learning?" In M. L. Ely (ed.), *Adult Education in Action.* New York: American Association for Adult Education, 1936.

Rossing, B., and Russell, R. "Informal Adult Experiential Learning: Reality in Search of Theory." In W. M. Rivera and S. M. Walker (eds.), *Lifelong Learning Research Conference Proceedings.* College Park: University of Maryland, 1987.

Rybash, J. M., Hoyer, W. J., and Roodin, P. A. *Adult Cognition and Aging: Developmental Changes in Processing, Knowing, and Thinking.* Elmsford, N.Y.: Pergamon Press, 1986.

Schaie, K. W., and Willis, S. L. *Adult Development and Aging.* (2nd ed.) Boston: Little, Brown, 1986.

Sinclair, J. D. "The Rest Principle: An Alternative Rule for How the Strength of Neural Connections is Controlled." *Integrative Psychiatry,* 1986, *4* (3), 186–190.

Smelser, N. J., and Erikson, E. H. *Themes of Work and Love in Adulthood.* Cambridge, Mass.: Harvard University Press, 1980.

Smith, R. M. *Learning How to Learn: Applied Learning Theory for Adults.* Chicago: Follett, 1982.

Smith, R. M. (ed.). *Helping Adults Learn How to Learn.* New Directions for Continuing Education, no. 19. San Francisco: Jossey-Bass, 1983.

Smith, R. M. (ed.). *Theory Building for Learning How to Learn.* DeKalb: Educational Studies Press, Northern Illinois University, 1988.

Sternberg, R. J., and Caruso, D. "Practical Modes of Knowing." In E. Eisner (ed.), *Learning and Teaching the Ways of Knowing.* 84th yearbook, part 2. Chicago: University of Chicago Press, 1985.

Thompson, D. "Adult Development." In H. E. Mitzel (ed.), *Encyclopedia of Educational Research.* Vol. 1. New York: Free Press, 1982.

Thorndike, E. L., and others. *Adult Learning.* New York: Macmillan, 1928.

Tough, A. M. *The Adult's Learning Projects: A Fresh Approach to Theory and Practice in Adult Learning.* Toronto: Ontario Institute for Studies in Education, 1971.

Tough, A. M. *Intentional Changes: A Fresh Approach to Helping People Change.* New York: Cambridge University Press, 1982.

Troll, P. B. "The Nature of the Adult Client: Developmental Needs and Behavior." In N. C. Seltz and H. V. Collier (eds.), *Meeting the Educational and Occupational Planning Needs of Adults.* Bloomington: School of Continuing Studies, Indiana University, 1976.

Troll, P. B. *Continuations: Adult Development and Aging.* Monterey, Calif.: Brooks/Cole, 1982.

Vaillant, G. E. *Adaptation to Life.* Boston: Little, Brown, 1977.

Wagner, R. K., and Sternberg, R. J. "Practical Intelligence in Real-World Pursuits: The Role of Tacit Knowledge." *Journal of Personality and Social Psychology,* 1985, *49* (2), 436–458.

Weinert, F. E., and Kluwe, R. H. (eds.). *Metacognition, Motivation, and Understanding.* Hillsdale, N.J.: Erlbaum, 1987.

Wilber, K. "The Spectrum of Development." In. K. Wilber, J. Engler, and D. P. Brown (eds.), *Transformation of Consciousness: Conventional and Contemplative Perspectives on Development.* Boston: New Science Library, 1986.

Winlow, W., and McCrohan, C. (eds.). *Growth and Plasticity of Neural Connections.* Wolfeboro, N.H.: Manchester University Press, 1987.

Wlodkowski, R. J. *Enhancing Adult Motivation to Learn.* San Francisco: Jossey-Bass, 1985.

15

Facilitating
Adult Learning

Stephen D. Brookfield

The ascendancy of facilitation in North American adult education during the past two decades says much about the ethos of the field. The concept has been interpreted in a number of ways, and various metaphors and role descriptors have been proposed to describe the activity of facilitation. At its base is a vision of education that assumes the equality of teachers and learners and the interchangeability of teaching and learning roles. Facilitators usually are described in terms that imply they will assist rather than direct learners. In contrast to descriptions of the teaching function that emphasize instructional roles or the transmission of information, descriptions of facilitators are most frequently expressed in terms such as *resource persons* and *helpers*. To some (Hostler, 1982; Lenz, 1982) facilitation is an artistic enterprise which can never be reduced to a set of rules routinely applied in all learning environments. Facilitators as artists draw upon their powers of creativity, improvisation, innovation, and sensitivity. To others, facilitators are counselors (Brockett, 1983) employing skills of attending and responding. Those viewing facilitators as helpers (Tough, 1979) see them as accepting of learners, as having a high regard for learners' self-planning abilities, as being engaged in an equal dialogue with learners, and as open to change and new experiences. Facilitators are sometimes described as *andragogues* (Knowles, 1984), who treat adult learners in ways very different from the ways they would treat children. Despite recent critiques of the empirical soundness and epistemological validity of the concept of andragogy (Nottingham Andragogy Group, 1983; Hartree, 1984; Tennant, 1986), this concept has had an enormous and far-reaching influence on the field of adult education practice. Central to the practice of andragogy is the fostering of adults' capacity for self-direction (Knowles, 1975; Brookfield, 1985; Long and Associates, 1988), and many adult educators see the fostering of self-directedness as the chief purpose of facilitation.

One stream of research views facilitators as learning analysts, concerned with helping learners become aware of their preferred learning styles (Smith, 1982, 1983; Cell, 1984). In helping adults learn how to learn, facilitators develop learners' metalearning skills of awareness and self-reflection rather than skills of content transmission. Some regard facilitators as critical analysts (Mezirow, 1981; Daloz, 1986; Brookfield, 1986; Shor and Freire, 1987) engaged in presenting alternative ways of thinking and acting, drawing attention to contradictions and ambiguities, and prompting a scrutiny of previously unchallenged and uncritically accepted assumptions. As critical analysts, facilitators help learners to locate their personal troubles within the context of wider social forces and structures. In French Canada the concept of the *animateur* (or social animator) describes this function. These varying interpretations of the concept of facilitation can be seen to fall within one of three dominant paradigms of facilitation—the behaviorist, the humanist, and the critical.

The Behaviorist Paradigm

SKINNER

The behaviorist paradigm is drawn from the thought of Skinner, and, in adult education, it has been influential in the development of competency-based adult education. Its application is widely observable in sectors of adult education such as the armed forces, nursing and health education, and training within business and industry. The assumption behind the behaviorist paradigm is that the facilitator's task is to ensure that learners attain previously defined learning objectives, many of which are specified in terms of clearly observable, behavioral outcomes. Learning activities are sequenced so that learners move through a series of carefully designed, progressively complex operations. The educational activity is evaluated as successful to the extent that the previously defined learning objectives are demonstrably achieved.

characteristics of behaviorism

This paradigm of facilitation is seen most prominently in contexts where the objectives to be attained are unambiguous, where their attainment can be judged according to commonly agreed upon criteria of successful performance, and where a clear imbalance exists between teachers' and learners' areas of expertise. Examples might be learning to give an injection, learning a computer program, learning accountancy procedures, learning to swim, or learning to operate a sophisticated machine. Although no learning is without elements of reflection or emotive dimensions, these examples are all located primarily in the domain of task-oriented, instrumental learning, and it is this domain that fits most easily with the behaviorist

concerns

approach. The paradigm is far less suited to contexts in which learners are trying to make sense of their worlds, to develop self-insight, to scrutinize

critically the assumptions underlying their thoughts and actions, or to interpret, and to find meaning within, their experiences. This kind of critically
reflective learning is often reported as occuring unexpectedly; that is, the
skills developed, knowledge acquired, and insights realized could not have
been anticipated, or planned for, at the outset of an educational activity (Boyd
and Fales, 1983; Daloz, 1986; Belenky, Clinchy, Goldberger, and Tarule,
1986).

If much significant learning occurs unexpectedly, and is not actively
sought or anticipated by learners, this calls into question the predetermined-
outcomes, behaviorist model of facilitation. For facilitators, this means they
should not regard as irrelevant those skills, knowledge, and insights exhibited
by learners just because they were not part of their previously determined
objectives. Facilitators must be alert to those teachable moments when   *Practice*
learners' attentions are engaged in some unanticipated way and, being alert   *principle*
to these moments, facilitators should build on them. They should recognize
the charge and excitement of such occasions and be ready to depart from
the script of their planned activities. They should value spontaneity and should
encourage risk taking—both for themselves and for their learners. According to the predetermined-objectives model of facilitation, such behavior
is likely to be labelled unprofessional, yet it is precisely this readiness of
facilitators to risk departing from the lesson script that can be so conducive
to learning. Recent research on self-directed learning reminds us that learners
regard much of their most useful learning as serendipitous and unplanned—
learning in which they take advantage of chance events as they occur (Spear,
1988; Danis and Tremblay, 1988). Sticking rigidly to a preplanned format
because it is prescribed as the official syllabus can be inimical to learning.
It may be the safest and most institutionally approved mode of facilitation,
but it may inhibit rather than enhance adults' learning.

2. The Humanistic Paradigm

The humanistic paradigm is the predominant paradigm of practice
within the literature of North American adult and continuing education.   MASLOW
Drawn from the work of humanistic psychologists (Rogers, 1961; Maslow,
1968; Allport, 1955), and finding its most noted exponent in Malcolm   KNOWLES
Knowles (1984), this paradigm comprises a number of assumptions regarding teaching and learning that have profoundly influenced the field. The
activity of facilitating learning is conceived as being essentially collaborative,
with strong emphasis on learners and teachers negotiating objectives, methods, and evaluative criteria. Facilitators in this tradition respect the integrity
of learners and grant learners' interests and demands a great deal of validity.
Adult education is seen as a democratic, cooperative venture, with facilitators
assuming no particular status within a learning group simply by virtue of
their knowledge or experience. This tradition of liberal humanism has a long
and proud history in America and Canadian adult education and is deeply

rooted in a view of education as a partnership rather than as an authoritarian transmission of information from the expert to the ignorant. Facilitators devote themselves to assisting learners' quests for self-actualization by helping learners realize their deeply felt needs.

CONCERNS

A danger inherent in this conceptualization is the tendency to think that all educational encounters should resemble a trouble-free voyage along a smoothly flowing river of increasing self-actualization, with no whirlpools or eddies of conflict, self-doubt, anxiety, or challenge. In reality, facilitating learning is often the educational equivalent of white water rafting. Periods of placidity alternate with episodes of turbulence during which the self-concepts of teachers and facilitators are challenged. Reflection and analysis are balanced by active inquiry. At times, tentative agreement is reached on matters of interpretation, on curricula to be explored, or on acceptable methods to be employed. At other times major disagreements emerge on these issues.

At the root of the humanistic paradigm is the felt-needs rationale. This rationale, briefly stated, holds that good practice in adult education is equated with meeting learners' felt needs, that is, with satisfying the educational demands and wants expressed by learners in the manner they prescribe. This rationale is appealing; when curricula, methods, and evaluative criteria are determined by the learners, it might seem to be an admirable embodiment of principles of democratic education. Yet such a rationale can be overly consumerist. It stresses giving learners what they say they want.

2 misassump-
tions abt.
felt-needs

Two fundamentally erroneous assumptions are embedded in the consumerist interpretation of the felt-needs rationale. The first is that a good facilitator is one who pleases learners by meeting their declared needs in the manner requested. The second is that learners are always the best judges of their own interests. One possible consequence of these two assumptions is that the facilitator's role could be reduced to that of an educational customer service manager whose activities are determined solely by learners' expressed desires. This would mean that facilitators would have to quell those ideas, experiences, and insights that would not somehow contribute to meeting learners' declared wants. Good facilitators, according to this rationale, are those who please learners. And since pleasing learners sometimes entails pandering to their prejudices or helping them stay comfortable by avoiding the painful, critical scrutiny of personal, occupational, and political realities, it is entirely possible that facilitators might never encourage learners to explore alternative ways of thinking and acting.

the problem

This limited facilitator role would make it easier for learners to remain within their own narrow, familiar, reassuring paradigms of thinking and acting. But this would not be an acceptable outcome. Since it is very difficult to generate alternative ways of thinking about (and acting in) the world entirely as a result of one's own self-will, an important task of facilitators is to encourage learners to explore alternatives to their current ways of thinking and acting (Meyers, 1986; Brookfield, 1987).

PRACTICE
PRINCIPLE

3. The Critical Paradigm

The critical paradigm of facilitation, drawn from the work of Freire, *FREIRE* and interpreted in North American adult education by writers such as Heaney *MEZIROW* (1981), Mezirow, (1981), Noble (1983), and Shor (1987), focuses on facil- itators encouraging learners to scrutinize critically the values, beliefs, and assumptions they have uncritically assimilated from the dominant culture. Critical facilitators emphasize that social and political reality is constructed, that values and beliefs are contextually created, and that these values and beliefs frequently serve the interests of dominant groups in society. They challenge learners to engage in a critical scrutiny of the assumptions, values, and norms undergirding their ideas and actions. At times, the expectations, learning styles, and personalities of facilitators and learners do connect. Often, however, there will be significant divergences in how different learners and facilitators define appropriate content and method (Shor and Freire, 1987; Daloz, 1986). The educational activity is often described in terms of a dialogue between facilitators and learners who bring to the conversation markedly diverging experiences, expectations, perspectives, and values. Within this learning conversation, the particular function of the facilitator (where this *PRACTICE* is not being performed by other members of the learning group) is to challenge *PRINCIPLE* learners with alternative ways of interpreting their experiences. Prompting people to scrutinize their previously unexamined values, actions, and ideas is difficult and intimidating for even the most experienced facilitators. Yet in doing this, facilitators can help adults to become critical thinkers engaged in a continual process of inventing and reinventing their personal, occupa- tional, and political worlds.

Two problems are embedded within the critical paradigm. First, its *CONCERNS* proponents promote a dualistic image of critically sophisticated facilitators in possession of a fully authentic, objective perception of the nature of op- pressive reality, and critically naive learners who are constantly bemused and duped by Machiavellian mind manipulators. This image is untrue and is insulting to the dignity of adult learners. Those under oppression are usually all too aware of their condition, but they may blame this condition on per- *PRACTICE* sonal inadequacy or fate instead of connecting their personal troubles to *PRINCIPLE* broader social forces and structures. Making explicit this connection is an important objective for the practice of adult education (Brookfield, 1987).

Second, there is sometimes an unacknowledged ideological bias under- lying the concepts of critical thinking and critical awareness. Proponents of this paradigm take as self-evident the view that a critically aware learner will naturally subscribe to left-of-center political values. Proponents believe, in other words, that having become aware of the nature of oppressive reality and of the distorting, hegemonic power of dominant cultural values, learners will commit themselves to perspectives and movements that challenge these values. This may well happen, but it is not inevitable. A learner can perceive how power relationships operate to maintain inequality and decide to join the oppressive class, or he or she can simply refuse to acknowledge the truth of this reality and those engaged in making it explicit as unpatriotic subversives.

Learners' Perceptions of Facilitation

A number of studies have been conducted in which adults have been encouraged to talk about their own life histories as learners and about the importance of facilitators to this learning (Boyd and Fales, 1983; Daloz, 1986; Belenky, Clinchy, Goldberger, and Tarule, 1986; Boud and Griffin, 1987). Several themes are apparent within these studies, all of which have important implications for how facilitation is conceived. First, the learners involved reported that the educational activities most meaningful for them were those in which they could make a direct connection to their past experiences or current concerns. For facilitators, this is a reminder of the importance of grounding curricula and methods in terms that learners can appreciate and understand and that allow them to make connections between these activities and their experiences or concerns. Second, learning episodes the learners recalled as being of greatest personal significance were those in which they had to confront and work through some kind of challenge. They did not recall vividly or proudly those times when developing skills, acquiring knowledge, or realizing insights came easily and quickly. Instead, they spoke proudly of how they had come to resolve contradictions, to appreciate ambiguities, or to develop problematic skills, overcoming their fears and poor self-images as learners in the process.

In studies of adults' transformational learning (Daloz, 1986; Mezirow, 1977; Keane, 1987; Weiser, 1987), reflective learning (Boyd and Fales, 1983), connected and constructivist knowing (Belenky, Clinchy, Goldberger, and Tarule, 1986), dialectical thinking (Basseches, 1984), and the use of embedded logic in adulthood (Labouvie-Vief, 1984), we find that learners speak vividly and passionately of their encounters with ambiguity, of how they came to fuse relativistic and universal modes of reasoning, and of their realization of the constructed and malleable nature of reality. For facilitators, these testaments to the significance of encounters carry an important message. They should be wary of falling into the trap of assuming that learners will resist, shy away from, or completely reject activities or situations characterized by challenges, contradictions, and ambiguities. For those under the spell of the felt-needs rationale, it is easy to avoid setting problematic tasks for fear of irrevocably alienating learners. It is salutary to remember, then, that learners recall with pride, and in vivid detail, those episodes and moments when they faced, contended with, and resolved some activity, task, or circumstance that was challenging and problematic.

Summary

Facilitating adult learning is a highly complex psychosocial drama in which the personalities and learning styles of the learners and facilitators involved, the divergent experiences and expectations they bring to the educational encounter, and the prevailing institutional and wider political climates are all important. It is apparent that there is no Holy Grail of facilitating adult learning and no one way to instructional enlightenment. Indeed, facilitators who are critically alert and sensitive to altered contexts will be immediately skeptical of standardized concepts or models that purport to be replicable in all possible situations. Different approaches will be called for depending on the class, ethnicity, cultural conditioning, and personality characteristics of learners. The demands of the context within which learning is occurring are paramount—in particular, the subject matter and learning domain involved, the varying levels of expertise and sophistication in a group, and the conflicting motives of teacher and learners. Given this complexity of variables, a degree of ambiguity should be expected as a constant feature of attempts to facilitate learning.

PRACTICE PRINCIPLE

Because every group of people engaged in learning will exhibit a formidable diversity of abilities, experiences, personalities, and preferred learning styles, it follows that facilitators should be ready to try a range of different approaches. It is important that facilitators vary their methods, have a range of materials (visual and written) on hand, and make efforts to individualize their curricula and evaluative criteria when appropriate. Shor and Freire (1987) describe this approach as employing parallel pedagogies. Nothing is more guaranteed to frustrate facilitators, and ultimately to hinder their efforts, than to seek always to achieve some neatly predictable, perfect outcome of their efforts. Nothing is more likely to prevent facilitators from working in a relaxed but effective manner than is their expectation that they must somehow exemplify the model of a perfect facilitator. Facilitators will never meet all the needs of their learners to their full satisfaction. They will never connect directly, simultaneously, and dramatically with all their group members. While it is essential to have some clear purpose and rationale directing their efforts, facilitators should avoid the mistake of crucifying themselves on the cross of perfection.

PARALLEL PEDAGOGIES

One of the most frequent mistakes made in evaluating the worth of any educational endeavor is to judge its relative success by the indicator of participants' satisfaction. Significant advances in people's learning often arise out of periods of frustration and struggle (Keane, 1987; Weiser, 1987; Cowan, 1988). People may realize important insights long after they have left a workshop, retreat, or course, and yet these realizations may be directly connected to earlier participation in those activities. If facilitators feel they are successful only when people leave their activities feeling pleased with what happened, they may hold back from challenging learners and asking them to face some uncomfortable or confusing ambiguities. Good facilitators of adult learning are ready and willing to take risks. In particular, they are eager to build on the excitement generated at those teachable moments when some serendipitous occurrence captures the imagination of group members. These emotionally charged occasions can prompt some of the most memorable episodes in a facilitator's career. It is important to remember, however, that risk taking also entails the possibility of failure, or of only partial success, and facilitators need to be ready for their departures from a previously planned exercise to fall short of what they had hoped to achieve. They also need to remember that one less-than-successful venture in risk taking does not invalidate for the future all other attempts to build upon unexpected teachable moments.

References

Adult Literacy Initiative and Division of Adult Education, U.S. Department of Education. *Adult Literacy: A Newsletter for the Adult Literacy and Learning Community,* Feb. 1988 (entire issue).

Allport, G. W. *Becoming: Basic Considerations for a Psychology of Personality.* New Haven, Conn.: Yale University Press, 1955.

Basseches, M. *Dialectical Thinking and Adult Development.* Norwood, N.J.: Ablex, 1984.

Belenky, M. F., Clinchy, B. M., Goldberger, N. R., and Tarule, J. M. *Women's Ways of Knowing: The Development of Self, Voice, and Mind.* New York: Basic Books, 1986.

Boud, D., and Griffin, V. (eds.). *Appreciating Adults Learning: From the Learner's Perspective.* Toronto: Ontario Institute for Studies in Education, 1987.

Boyd, E. M., and Fales, A. W. "Reflective Learning: Key to Learning from Experience." *Journal of Humanistic Psychology,* 1983, *23* (2), 99–117.

Brockett, R. "Facilitator Roles and Skills." *Lifelong Learning: The Adult Years,* 1983, *6* (5), 7–9.

Brookfield, S. D. (ed.). *Self-Directed Learning: From Theory to Practice.* New Directions in Continuing Education, no. 25. San Francisco: Jossey-Bass, 1985.

Brookfield, S. D. *Understanding and Facilitating Adult Learning.* San Francisco: Jossey-Bass, 1986.

Brookfield, S. D. *Developing Critical Thinkers: Challenging Adults to Explore Alternative Ways of Thinking and Acting.* San Francisco: Jossey-Bass, 1987.

Cell, E. *Learning to Learn from Experience.* Albany: State University of New York Press, 1984.

Cowan, J. "Struggling with Self-Assessment." In D. Boud (ed.), *Developing Student Autonomy in Learning.* (2nd ed.) London: Kogan Page, 1988.

Daloz, L. A. *Effective Teaching and Mentoring: Realizing the Transformational Power of Adult Learning Experiences.* San Francisco: Jossey-Bass, 1986.

Danis, C., and Tremblay, N. A. "Autodidactic Learning Experiences: Questioning Established Adult Learning Principles." In H. B. Long (ed.), *Self-Directed Learning: Application and Theory.* Athens: Department of Adult Education, University of Georgia, 1988.

Hartree, A. "Malcolm Knowles's Theory of Andragogy: A Critique." *International Journal of Lifelong Education,* 1984, *3* (3), 203–210.

Heaney, T. W. "Action, Freedom, and Liberatory Education." In L. Suransky and V. Suransky (eds.), *Paulo Freire in Ann Arbor*. Vol. 2. Ann Arbor: School of Education, University of Michigan, 1981.

Hostler, J. "The Art of Teaching Adults." *Studies in Adult Education*, 1982, *14*, 42-49.

Keane, R. "The Doubting Journey: A Learning Process of Self-Transformation." In D. Boud and V. Griffin (eds.), *Appreciating Adults Learning: From the Learner's Perspective*. Toronto: Ontario Institute for Studies in Education, 1987.

Knowles, M. S. *Self-Directed Learning*. New York: Cambridge Books, 1975.

Knowles, M. S. *Andragogy in Action: Applying Modern Principles of Adult Learning*. San Francisco: Jossey-Bass, 1984.

Labouvie-Vief, G. "Logic and Self-Regulation from Youth to Maturity: A Model." In M. L. Commons, F. A. Richards, and C. Armon (eds.), *Beyond Formal Operations: Late Adolescent and Adult Cognitive Development*. New York: Praeger, 1984.

Lenz, E. *The Art of Teaching Adults*. New York: Holt, Rinehart & Winston, 1982.

Long, H. B., and Associates. *Self-Directed Learning: Application and Theory*. Athens: Department of Adult Education, University of Georgia, 1988.

Maslow, A. H. *Toward a Psychology of Being*. New York: D. Van Nostrand, 1968.

Meyers, C. *Teaching Students to Think Critically*. San Francisco: Jossey-Bass, 1986.

Mezirow, J. "Perspective Transformation." *Studies in Adult Education*, 1977, *9* (2), 153-164.

Mezirow, J. "A Critical Theory of Adult Learning and Education." *Adult Education*, 1981, *32* (1), 3-27.

Noble, P. *Formation of Freirean Facilitators*. Chicago: Latino Institute, 1983.

Nottingham Andragogy Group. *Toward a Developmental Theory of Andragogy*. Nottingham, England: Department of Adult Education, University of Nottingham, 1983.

Rogers, C. R. *On Becoming a Person: A Therapist's View of Psychotherapy*. Boston: Houghton Mifflin, 1961.

Shor, I. *Critical Teaching and Everyday Life*. (2nd ed.) Chicago: University of Chicago Press, 1987.

Shor, I., and Freire, P. *A Pedagogy for Liberation*. South Hadley, Mass.: Bergin and Garvey, 1987.

Smith, R. M. *Learning How to Learn: Applied Theory for Adults*. New York: Cambridge Books, 1982.

Smith, R. M. (ed.). *Helping Adults Learn How to Learn*. New Directions for Continuing Education, no. 19. San Francisco: Jossey-Bass, 1983.

Spear, G. "Beyond the Organizing Circumstances: A Search for Methodology for the Study of Self-Directed Learning." In H. B. Long (ed.),

Self-Directed Learning: Application and Theory. Athens: Department of Adult
Education, University of Georgia, 1988.

Tennant, M. "An Evaluation of Knowles' Theory of Adult Learning."
International Journal of Lifelong Education, 1986, *5* (2), 113–122.

Tough, A. M. *The Adult's Learning Projects: A Fresh Approach to Theory and Practice
in Adult Learning.* Austin, Tex.: Learning Concepts, 1979.

Weiser, J. "Learning from the Perspective of Growth of Consciousness."
In D. Boud and V. Griffin (eds.), *Appreciating Adults Learning: From the
Learner's Perspective.* Toronto: Ontario Institute for Studies in Education,
1987.

16

Nontraditional Education and the Assessment of Prior Learning

Amy D. Rose

Adults returning to school are often faced with many hurdles, in terms of both bureaucratic and curricular requirements. The nontraditional education movement, and especially its manifestation in the assessment of prior learning, has enabled institutions to expand access while providing alternatives to all students, but most notably to adults.

Nontraditional education has been defined as a "set of learning experiences free of time and space limitations" (Hartnett, 1972, p. 14). Many different methods and approaches have been developed, but they all share a common emphasis on what the student knows—not where he or she learned it (Cross and Valley, 1974). This "Copernican Shift," as Wedemeyer (1981, p. 78) terms it, involves a "shift of gravity from the inputs of schools and teachers to the outputs of learning and learners." This shift has resulted in several areas of real innovation within education. While these changes are the results of many different factors, together they present a potential means for revitalizing North American education.

For adult students, the new practices provide both greater institutional flexibility and the possibility for a more meaningful and relevant educational experience. In addition, as adults, with many informal and unaccredited learning experiences, they are in the best situation to take full advantage of the new approaches.

The changes have occurred on all levels of instruction, evaluation, curriculum reform, and, of course, bureaucratic procedures. One result of the shift in emphasis has been closer attention to different modes of delivery. These include individualization through the use of learning modules, contract learning, cassette instruction, credit for prior learning, proficiency examinations, distance learning, and external degree programs (Campbell, 1984). (See Chapters Seventeen, Twenty-Three, Twenty-Four, and Twenty-Eight.)

But the most important result has been the reorientation placing greater emphasis on learning than on the process or delivery of that learning. This reorientation has resulted in attempts to move education outside of the classroom and a growing recognition of non-school-based educational experiences that might influence an individual's learning. This interest has led to a new emphasis on the measurement and evaluation of learning.

One of the earliest manifestations of this attempt to measure learning was the emergence of equivalency degrees on both the secondary and post-secondary levels. Such degrees allow individuals the opportunity to earn diplomas by taking a series of tests. If they pass, they are entitled to a degree, regardless of where they did their learning. The General Equivalency Diploma (GED) in the United States and the madureza in Brazil are examples of such approaches on the high school level (Perraton, 1982). (See Chapters Twenty-Three, Twenty-Four, and Twenty-Eight.)

Such equivalency degree programs are based on a standardized and generally accepted body of knowledge. They evince little interest in how this knowledge was obtained, although almost all such programs have added study components for those unable to complete the examinations without assistance. The issues that surface when such approaches are used relate to the measurement of specific outcomes (Perraton, 1982).

In contradistinction to the outcome orientation, experiential learning with its emphasis on the process of learning has also become an important aspect of nontraditional education. Although arriving at a definition is fraught with difficulty, experiential learning generally refers to learning that takes place outside the classroom. When translating such experiences into credit, the principal issues of contention are the structuring of such experiences and how they should be evaluated (Keeton, 1976).

While present at all levels of education, experiential education has proved to be particularly important as a potential means of revitalizing higher education. It expands the educational possibilities for traditional college-aged students, moving them outside the classroom and allowing them to apply what they had previously learned only theoretically. In addition, experiential education is one way of providing access to education for those groups previously excluded. Thus individuals who did not possess the common language necessary for more traditional study could learn this language in a nonthreatening atmosphere (Gartner, 1976). Experiential learning also serves as a means of vocational training by providing students a taste of the real world.

On the college and university level, the inclusion of experiential learning raises questions about the nature and meaning of a college education and of the credit system. The necessity of establishing an equitable system of awarding credit for experiential learning has led institutions to reconsider their current methods of awarding all credit. Instead of creating separate spheres, some colleges have begun to examine the assumptions underlying the granting of all credit and have moved to clarify the learning expected in all aspects of a student's program (Keeton, 1976, 1981; Kirkwood, 1976; Kolb, 1984). (See Chapter Twenty-Four.)

For adult students, experiential learning has additional attractions. Many returning students turn to higher education in order to advance themselves on the job. They are seeking the combination of a vocational education and a credential. They want to learn how to do something as quickly as possible (Shipton and Steltenpohl, 1981). Experiential education offers these students the opportunity to ease their transition to the world of higher education while gaining valuable and, from their point of view, immediately transferable skills.

Prior Learning

The growing acceptance of prior learning on both the college and secondary levels is directly related to the increasing interest in opening up educational institutions and in providing different kinds of learning experiences to those enrolled. The periods from 1973 to 1974 and from 1981 to 1982 saw a dramatic increase in the number of such credits being awarded (Kolb, 1984). In general, prior learning refers to that learning gained outside of the traditional classroom prior to matriculation. This learning could have been gained through myriad activities ranging from in-service training courses to voluntary activities or hobbies or the work experience itself.

The concept of prior learning involves recognition of the fact that people learn in many different ways and places. Instead of focusing on the process of learning, this approach emphasizes the outcome. That is, it does not matter how individuals acquire particular pieces of knowledge as long as they can demonstrate what they have actually learned.

Some programs, such as those at Empire State College in New York and Athabasca University of Alberta, offer students the possibility of acquiring a degree that is substantially assessment based (Wedemeyer, 1981). Such institutions assess individual learning in a variety of ways. While most popular on the postsecondary level, assessment-based degrees are also proliferating on the high school level (Nickse, 1980).

While many institutions have been willing to accommodate adults with evening classes, registration, child care, and so on, actual changes in the curriculum have been rarer. The use of prior learning credits, although limited, represents one of the few institutional acknowledgments of informal or unaccredited learning efforts. It provides adult students with an opportunity to examine their lives and to gain recognition for their learning, no matter how they gained it. For institutions, the introduction of prior learning assessment often leads to broader internal discussion about the nature of the degree being awarded and about the kinds of learning expected. (See Chapters Twenty-Three and Twenty-Four.)

Antecedents. Although the immediate impetus for the current growth of prior learning programs is rooted in the changes of the 1960s and 1970s, the first efforts go back to World War II. In 1944, as American colleges and universities geared up for the influx of veterans returning to school under the aegis of the G.I. Bill, there was much discussion of how the potential problems could be eased. There was a fear that the veterans would bring to the campus major psychological problems and that they would have difficulty adjusting to civilian life. These soldiers would be entering school with many more experiences than the typical college student, and administrators anticipated that the traditional college curriculum and especially the college life would not be appropriate. In addition to the actual experiences of war, the veterans had lived in other countries, had experienced other cultures, and had taken armed forces training courses. They thus entered college with far richer life experiences than the typical eighteen year old (Olson, 1974).

The colleges had two primary concerns. First, they wanted to maintain campus tranquillity and harmony. This meant absorbing the returning students quickly, placing them in appropriate courses, and making sure they adjusted with alacrity. In addition, the colleges wanted to move the students out as quickly as possible. One way of achieving both of these goals was to give the veterans college credit for what they had already learned. The most common mechanism for doing this was the acceptance of armed forces courses that had been evaluated by the American Council on Education (ACE). These courses included aspects of army training, specialized courses, and even courses offered in POW camps. According to one 1948 poll of academic deans, over 90 percent of their institutions accepted ACE credit recommendations, as listed in the so-called Tuttle Guides (Olson, 1974).

In addition, many colleges offered students a testing option for placing out of courses. Brooklyn College is often presented as the model for this type of program (Houle, 1976). The returning veteran could petition a department for credit, and each department was responsible for conducting its own evaluation. This evaluation was usually completed by means of a written or oral examination or some form of discussion. The catalog description was considered the learning outcome statement and was used as the basic criterion for evaluation. In the 1950s, the adult population at Brooklyn College expanded as refugees flooded into the area, and this process of awarding so-called life experience credit was continued to meet the needs of this group (Hruby, 1980). After the crisis of the returning veterans and other postwar dislocations had passed, many colleges cut back on the opportunities for evaluation of prior learning, although these were not entirely eliminated.

The experience with the G.I. Bill set an important precedent in establishing administrative flexibility for dealing with returning veterans. But the learning being evaluated still conformed to traditional course material. There was no notion of permanently changing the college curriculum; instead the colleges saw the evaluation process as a temporary measure taken to meet an emergency situation.

While some colleges maintained certain aspects of the evaluation process, such as the acceptance of ACE evaluated courses and some testing options, there was little growth in this area of life experience credit until the late 1960s and 1970s.

Assessment of Prior Learning. Although by no means universally accepted, some type of prior learning model has been adopted by many colleges as they attempt to attract adult students to campus (Sweet, 1980). But this limited acceptance has not been without pitfalls. The biggest problem has been the measurement and evaluation of prior learning. The central questions have become, what serves as acceptable college-level learning, and how can it be evaluated?

Currently used in many programs throughout North America, the evaluation of prior learning has several different configurations. Most commonly it is offered as an option within a traditional college curriculum with anywhere from nine to ninety credits being awarded. The rules and procedures vary considerably. Many colleges use the Brooklyn College precedent of evaluating learning on a course basis. Students may also test out of particular courses on the basis of standardized tests such as those offered by the College Level Examination Program (CLEP). In addition they may receive credit for sponsored learning that has been evaluated through the American Council on Education. This includes armed forces study as well as some in-service training courses.

Many schools allow students to pursue individualized evaluations for particular course work that might not be covered through the CLEP. This is done through the amassing of a portfolio. In either case, the process of evaluation is similar, involving an evaluation of the individual's learning and a recommendation about the credit to be awarded.

Individualized Approach to Evaluation. While the individualized assessment process allows students the greatest flexibility in defining their own learning and having it evaluated, there are enormous variations in the willingness of institutions to embark on this time-consuming process. Some have developed an abbreviated assessment process that relies heavily on external criteria for evaluation. While this approach helps to alleviate some of the problems of assessment, it limits the student's ability to define his or her own learning.

Evaluation of learning experiences is usually done through a formal evaluation of each student's learning. Proponents of prior learning are united in stressing that, in general, credit should not be awarded for an experience, but only for the actual learning gained. Measuring this learning has become the most difficult aspect of prior learning assessment. This assessment process has been developing continuously since the mid-1970s, and there are now many variations depending on the institution. Some procedures, however, are widely accepted.

Initially, the Cooperative Assessment of Experiential Learning (CAEL) Project identified six steps in the individualized assessment process (Forrest,

Knapp, and Pendergrass, 1976). In the first step, the student identifies the learning to be evaluated. This is not as simple as it may initially seem. Students may have a wide range of experiences, but have no immediately apparent way of categorizing their learning. The first task must be reflection on one's life activities and on how these might be considered college-level learning.

The second step involves an analysis of this identified learning and an assessment of its articulation with the rest of a student's program of study. Prior learning is generally thought to be an important part of the entire planning process. Students need to assess where they have been, what they have learned, and how this learning fits in with their future goals.

In the third step, students amass a portfolio that includes as much documentation as possible about the nature of their experiences and learning. In the early days of prior learning evaluation, this portfolio included all of the material gathered by the student in order to document learning experiences and accomplishments. This usually meant the inclusion of an autobiography and verification of all experiences through the inclusion of letters from supervisors and colleagues. But the format for the portfolio has undergone changes as the emphasis has shifted from verification of experience to further measurement of learning. Now much of this step is considered unnecessary and expendable (Shipton and Steltenphol, 1981). Instead the present emphasis is on the measurement and evaluation of learning (Knapp and Gardiner, 1981). In any event, the portfolio was never meant to be the method for measuring the learning, but rather a means of organizing students' experiences.

The fourth step is the measurement of learning. This may involve any number of techniques. The submission of a product such as a musical composition, a painting, or a short story is one popular means of measurement. Other measurement tools include examinations (either applied or theoretical) or simulation of a relevant situation. But perhaps the most widely used measurement technique is the interview. It allows the evaluator time to probe for clarification of learning and to follow up if there are further questions. No one measurement technique is better than the others. In fact, it is highly recommended that the evaluator consider using two or more techniques in order to ascertain most thoroughly the extent and depth of each student's learning (Forrest, Knapp, and Pendergrass, 1976).

The fifth step in the assessment process is evaluation. At this stage, the evaluator makes a recommendation about the nature of the student's learning and about the amount of credit that should be granted. The pivotal question here is the justification of credit awarded. Without the time-honored concept of homework and without time spent in class, the amount of credit each learning component is worth is difficult to determine.

The final step in the assessment process is transcription. Forrest, Knapp, and Pendergrass (1976) maintain that the traditional transcript is misleading because it simply translates everything into credit hours. They advocate instead the development of some type of narrative transcript that would include an actual description.

Problems. The development of assessment-based degrees and, in fact, most aspects of nontraditional education have provided many exciting innovations within higher education. At the same time, they have raised many issues and problems yet to be resolved. Of primary importance is the disparity between institutional and individual aims and goals. Most North American institutions of higher learning maintain their vision of a generalized bachelor's degree, although there are many differences of opinion about what this means. Very often, students, and especially adults, enter college for vocational reasons even though the institution maintains a clear liberal arts orientation. This disparity may translate into continuous misunderstandings and friction as the student attempts to negotiate the system (Shipton and Steltenpohl, 1981).

In terms of prior learning assessment, there may be a considerable difference between student expectations of credit awards and those actually given. Students often find it difficult to identify learning that is appropriate for evaluation (Shipton and Steltenpohl, 1981). For example, it is common for women to feel that they do not have any prior learning. The task for the adviser becomes one of helping students to reflect on their lives and to see that they have indeed learned things that could be appropriately included in a college curriculum.

On the other hand, it is not unusual for students to enter college with unrealistic expectations about the kinds of credit they will be awarded. This lack of realism often results from a lack of knowledge about what is considered college-level learning, and this lack of knowledge is compounded by the lack of clarity among faculty members as they attempt to define college-level learning. Without a clear understanding of what college-level learning is, neither the student nor the evaluator can assess whether or how much credit should be awarded.

In fact, there is little agreement about what college-level learning is, especially when this learning takes place outside of the classroom. Some hold that college-level learning involves generalizable knowledge—that is, students must have reflected on their learning to the extent that they are able to apply it to situations other than those that they immediately face. According to the characteristics described by Willingham (1977, p. 12), college-level learning must include "a conceptual as well as a practical grasp of the knowledge or competencies acquired." In addition, it must be applicable outside the specific context in which it was acquired, and it should be subject matter usually included in the college curriculum. However, these caveats only begin to address the problems; there are no clear criteria for implementing the definition.

Many courses already offered within colleges and universities do not include learning that goes beyond the practical (Sachs, 1980). In addition, different colleges have different minimum standards. Most students who have learned something experientially will not have developed clearly differentiated categories. Generally, they will not be familiar with major arguments for and against particular approaches, even if they have learned these different approaches. The learning in effect will be quite different from book or course learning. How are equivalencies to be established? Should they be? Are there other ways of assessing learning without resorting to course equivalents?

Because there are no guidelines for deciding whether something is college level, it is difficult to arrive at a fair measurement of that learning. Without having the student produce the equivalent of a course's work, how is one to decide whether learning has indeed taken place and whether credit should be awarded for this learning? Clearly, institutions must answer these questions on the basis of their own standards or norms. But within the institution, some consistency is necessary.

The problem of standards is a common one that must be addressed, particularly since it is often raised by faculty members and administrators, who are themselves hesitant to adopt prior learning credits (Hruby, 1980; Sachs, 1980). The measurement tools discussed in the previous section are inadequate in that they still follow standard academic procedure.

Consistency also becomes a critical issue when discussing individualized evaluation. There is always the fear that evaluators are not objective and that because the evaluations are not standardized, they are not replicable. There is the additional problem of defining what is being assessed. Would different students with different abilities to express themselves, but with equal learning, receive the same credit? How is the evaluation process to be evaluated?

On an administrative level the most important problem is the form the evaluation should take. There has been criticism that the transcripts of many institutions are unclear and difficult to understand. In addition, the transcript is not always clear about the source of the learning or about the nature of the assessment process (Martorana and Kuhns, 1979). Most important perhaps, such credit awards are not easily transferred, thus raising questions about the academic respectability of institutions offering such credits.

From the opposite side, some proponents have voiced concern that the search for academic respectability has led some institutions to abdicate their responsibility to nontraditional education by disproportionately emphasizing standardized testing. For example, in evaluating a student's knowledge of literature, it is important to decide what one is assessing. While present standardized tests focus on authors, titles, and plot, a truer assessment of the state of the student's knowledge would probably be gained through an evaluation of the individual's analysis and reaction to specific pieces (Dressel, 1980). Critics therefore see the movement for the acceptance of prior learning as one that has become diverted from its initial quest to redefine higher education.

Conclusion

Nontraditional education, with its emphasis on moving learning outside of the classroom, provides the opportunity for educational innovation on all levels. It combines an outcomes orientation with the concern for process embodied in the experiential learning movement.

The adoption of this approach implies the acceptance of the notion that people learn in many different ways and in many different circumstances. The difficulties arise in the measurement and evaluation of this learning. The principal concerns are with the ability of evaluators to evaluate fairly and equitably this type of learning. The present models are not adequate.

For adult learners, the acceptance of prior learning credit signals a real attempt by colleges and universities to adapt the curriculum to meet their needs. The recognition of nontraditional learning allows greater flexibility in developing a college program while enabling students to build on their pasts. One result of this approach is the possibility of speeding up the acquisition of a college degree. For adults this can become a critical aspect of the accessibility of higher education.

While nontraditional education has created many new opportunities for all learners, adults have gained the most. New delivery systems, coupled with the growing emphasis on learning, have created the possibility for institutional recognition of learning, no matter where it takes place. Conversely, the concomitant development of individualized programs and assessment techniques allows greater flexibility in meeting the diverse needs of adult students. The assessment of prior learning not only allows students the possibility of earning credit, but also the opportunity to assess properly what they know and what would be most appropriate to study. While there are still many problems, the considerations of nontraditional education indicate a new commitment on the part of some institutions to rethink some of the accepted meaning of education and particularly of a college degree.

References

Campbell, D. D. *The New Majority: Adult Learners in the University.* Edmonton: University of Alberta Press, 1984.

Cross, K. P., and Valley, J. R. "Non-Traditional Study: An Overview." In K. P. Cross, J. R. Valley, and Associates (eds.), *Planning Non-Traditional Programs.* San Francisco: Jossey-Bass, 1974.

Dressel, P. L. "Models for Evaluating Individual Achievement." *Journal of Higher Education,* 1980, *51* (2), 194–206.

Forrest, A., Knapp, J. E., and Pendergrass, J. "Tools and Methods of Evaluation." In M. T. Keeton and Associates (eds.), *Experiential Learning: Rationale, Characteristics, and Assessment.* San Francisco: Jossey-Bass, 1976.

Gartner, A. P. "Credentialling the Disenfranchised." In M. T. Keeton and Associates (eds.), *Experiential Learning: Rationale, Characteristics, and Assessment.* San Francisco: Jossey-Bass, 1976.

Hartnett, R. T. "Non-Traditional Study: An Overview." In S. B. Gould and K. P. Cross (eds.), *Explorations in Non-Traditional Study.* San Francisco: Jossey-Bass, 1972.

Houle, C. O. "Deep Traditions of Experiential Learning." In M. T. Keeton and Associates (eds.), *Experiential Learning: Rationale, Characteristics, and Assessment.* San Franciso: Jossey-Bass, 1976.

Hruby, N. J. "The Faculty as Key to Quality Assurance—Fact and Mystique." In M. T. Keeton (ed.), *Defining and Assuring Quality in Experiential Learning.* New Directions for Experiential Learning, no. 9. San Francisco: Jossey-Bass, 1980.

Keeton, M. T. "Credentials for the Learning Society." In M. T. Keeton (ed.), *Experiential Learning: Rationale, Characteristics, and Assessment.* San Francisco: Jossey-Bass, 1976.

Keeton, M. T. "Assessing and Credentialing Prior Learning." In A. W. Chickering and Associates (eds.), *The American College.* San Francisco: Jossey-Bass, 1981.

Kirkwood, R. "Importance of Assessing Learning." In M. T. Keeton (ed.), *Experiential Learning: Rationale, Characteristics, and Assessment.* San Francisco: Jossey-Bass, 1976.

Knapp, J. E., and Gardiner, M. "Assessment of Prior Learning: As a Model and in Practice." In J. Knapp (ed.), *Financing and Implementing Prior Learning Assessment.* New Directions for Experiential Learning, no. 14. San Francisco: Jossey-Bass, 1981.

Kolb, D. A. *Experiential Learning Experience as the Source of Learning and Development.* Englewood Cliffs, N.J.: Prentice-Hall, 1984.

Martorana, S. V., and Kuhns, E. (eds.). *Transferring Experiential Credit.* New Directions for Experiential Learning, no. 4. San Francisco: Jossey-Bass, 1979.

Nickse, R. "A Comparison and Analysis of Four Alternative High Schools' Credentialing Programs." *National Association of Public and Continuing Adult Education Exchange,* 1980, *3* (2), 11–13.

Olson, K. W. *The G.I. Bill, the Veterans, and the Colleges.* Lexington: University Press of Kentucky, 1974.

Perraton, H. "The Scope of Distance Teaching." In H. Perraton (ed.), *Alternative Routes to Formal Education: Distance Teaching for School Equivalency.* Baltimore, Md., and London: World Bank, 1982.

Sachs, M. P. "The Tasks of Administrators in Assuring Sound Assessment Practices." In M. T. Keeton (ed.), *Defining and Assuring Quality in Experiential Learning.* New Directions for Experiential Learning, no. 9. San Francisco: Jossey-Bass, 1980.

Shipton, J., and Steltenpohl, E. "Relating Assessment of Prior Learning to Educational Planning." In J. Knapp (ed.), *Financing and Implementing Prior Learning Assessment.* New Directions for Experiential Learning, no. 14. San Francisco: Jossey-Bass, 1981.

Sweet, D. "Building Adult Student Enrollments: Actions to Take Now." In R. G. Moon, Jr. and G. R. Hawes (eds.), *Developing New Adult Clienteles by Recognizing Prior Learning.* New Directions for Experiential Learning, no. 7. San Francisco: Jossey-Bass, 1980.

Wedemeyer, C. A. *Learning at the Back Door: Reflections on Non-Traditional Learning in the Lifespan.* Madison: University of Wisconsin Press, 1981.

Willingham, W. W. *Principles of Good Practice in Assessing Experiential Learning.* Columbia, Md.: Cooperative Assessment of Experiential Learning, 1977.

17

Distance Education

D. Randy Garrison

Writings on the subject of distance education traditionally have placed considerable emphasis on the separation of teacher and student. In the past, students had little choice but to cope with the isolation of distance education or to discontinue—which they did at a worrisome rate. Recently, however, the emergence of new communications and computer technology has marked a new era of distance education. As a result of the new distance education methods made possible by these technologies, adult educators now have a variety of means for reaching out to adult learners to provide increased access and support. The focus is no longer on distance education but on education at a distance.

What follows is a description and discussion of the structural and process characteristics of distance education. I will describe the structure of distance education from a technological and institutional perspective, and I will argue that to understand the educational transaction in distance education is to understand the two-way communication process between teacher-facilitator and student-learner. From this description will evolve a discussion of various issues confronting adult educators.

Distance Education Described

Before proceeding with a description of distance education, a comment regarding the concept of education is required. It must be emphasized that our primary concern is with learning in an educational situation—learning that is intentional and planned. This kind of learning is a collaborative process between teacher and student; that is, it is concerned with both teaching and learning. While the teacher may present information and manage the activities, the perspectives and ideas of both teachers and learners must be valued and examined. The crucial element in this process is the two-way communication between teacher and learner, so it will be a central concern throughout this discussion of distance education.

Perhaps one of the most difficult tasks of any field of practice is to define the field with some precision without being excessively restrictive. In the field of distance education, this problem has been magnified in recent years due to its expansion resulting from the adoption of new communications technology, so special caution must be exercised to avoid being overly restrictive in attempting to define it.

Over the years, various definitions of distance education have been proposed and have served useful purposes. Some have stressed the structural characteristic of distance education with its separation of teacher and student (Holmberg, 1985), while others have focused upon the process of delivering education at a distance (Moore, 1973). Yet another approach was provided by Keegan (1986), who, through his review of the literature, incorporated various characteristics of previous definitions. However, Keegan's descriptive and comprehensive definition has been criticized by Garrison and Shale (1987a) as being too restrictive and focused on an independent print-based form of distance study.

In an attempt to describe distance education without defining it in too restrictive a manner, an approach by Garrison and Shale (1987a, p. 10) provided a minimum set of criteria to be used as a guide or standard "while leaving open the likelihood that other criteria may be added as our understandings or purposes change." The following three criteria are proposed as being the minimum for characterizing the distance education process:

1. Distance education implies that the majority of educational communication between (among) teacher and student(s) occurs noncontiguously.
2. Distance education must involve two-way communication between (among) teacher and student(s) for the purpose of facilitating and supporting the educational process.
3. Distance education uses technology to mediate the necessary two-way communication [Garrison and Shale, 1987a, p. 11].

The first criterion notes the structural separation of teacher and student, but it also includes the possibility of using face-to-face methods. The second and third criteria are essentially corollaries of the first. They emphasize the necessity of two-way communication in an educational transaction and the reliance on technology to mediate this communication. The third criterion is tautological in the sense that, if teacher and student are noncontiguous and two-way communication is a necessity, then some form of technology must mediate the communication process. It is the technology of distance education that we turn to next.

Distance Education Technologies

Correspondence education represents the roots and foundation of distance education. Organized correspondence education is, according to Holmberg (1986), at least 150 years old. While the first documented case of correspondence education occurred in Boston in 1728, it was not until the late 1800s that the movement gained considerable momentum (Holmberg, 1986).

The first significant distance education effort in North America was part of the Chautauqua movement. The Chautauqua movement was based upon John Vincent's belief that education should be available to all—not to just the privileged few. In 1878, Vincent established a home reading circle that was considered to be the "most successful attempt at adult continuing education up to that time" (Swanson, 1988, p. 40). William Rainey Harper joined the Chautauqua movement in 1883, and that same year the Chautauqua University received its charter. Within the Chautauqua University, the College of Liberal Arts was mainly a correspondence school under the principalship of Harper. Subsequently, in 1892, as president of the University of Chicago, Harper incorporated many of his ideas of distance education into that institution's extension division. As a result of Harper's pioneering efforts, he has been referred to as the father of correspondence education in North America.

One of the motivating goals of correspondence education was to provide access to education for those who, for a variety of reasons, were unable to attend traditional classroom instruction. Correspondence education was an attempt to break the hegemony of formal traditional classroom instruction and to reach out to learners regardless of socioeconomic or educational background. Not only did correspondence education increase access to education, but it provided educational independence for the learner. As Wedemeyer (1981, p. 50) states, "Correspondence study was the first formally structured method for independent study." Correspondence education is by its nature an individual activity with considerable student control over the learning process, but it also is accompanied by the constraints of independent study.

Mediated two-way communication already has been identified as a distinguishing criterion of distance education. In correspondence study, the message is in the form of print, and the delivery mode is by mail. While print is a very cost-effective medium, the two-way communication can only be described as slow and, therefore, not always educationally supportive. Holmberg (1986, p. 56) states that "The great weakness of distance education has in most cases been the slowness of the communication process caused by the correspondence method dominating this kind of education.'' For this reason, many of the larger print-based distance education institutions assign a tutor to be contacted when the learner requires help. Even with the help of a tutor, motivation is difficult to sustain over time, and this difficulty may partly explain the high dropout rates in correspondence-based distance education programs (Garrison, 1987).

Dropout in correspondence courses has ranged from 40 percent to 90 percent (Baath, 1984; Persons and Catchpole, 1987). Most distance educators do not see this as a natural and expected phenomenon, but rather consider these dropout rates to be serious and frustrating (Rekkedal, 1985). While correspondence study provides access to education and freedom to study when and where students wish, these learners must possess considerable motivation and learning ability to succeed. Independence alone does not ensure that students will successfully reach worthwhile educational goals. Appropriate support and feedback are also required in an educational transaction to counteract one of the major complaints of correspondence students—the sense of isolation and need for affiliation (Persons and Catchpole, 1987).

The problem of slow and irregular feedback in the correspondence educational transaction has caused distance educators to explore the use of rapidly evolving communications and computer technology. The adoption of these new technologies in some situations has changed drastically the educational transaction at a distance and certainly has made distance education a more complex and exciting field of practice. To reflect this influence of new technologies, the International Council for Correspondence Education changed its name in 1982, to the International Council for Distance Education.

The change in our view of distance education was precipitated by telecommunications technology; in particular, audio teleconferencing represented the first and most profound departure from correspondence study. Audio teleconferencing in North America came into its own in the mid-1960s, largely as a result of the University of Wisconsin-Extension educational telephone network (Olgren and Parker, 1983). While audio is the most prevalent form of teleconferencing in distance education, video and computer teleconferencing also are available. The unique aspect of teleconferencing is that it is a group method of distance education that can support immediate two-way communication. Discussions among teachers and students across wide geographic areas are possible. As a result, a new range of instructional techniques are available to support and sustain the educational transaction.

Teleconferencing can be viewed as a distinct generation of distance education (Garrison, 1985). It is seen from a generational perspective because it builds upon correspondence capabilities of the first generation of distance education. Teleconferencing for educational purposes invariably is supported by print materials. The combination of print and telecommunications technology makes teleconferencing a unique and successful method of delivering education at a distance.

Teleconferencing has experienced a phenomenal growth in recent years. It is safe to say that some form of teleconferencing has been used or seriously considered in a majority of states and provinces in North America. The two major reasons for its proliferation are its group method of instruction and its ready access through communications technology such as telephone and satellite service. A number of studies have demonstrated that achievement and attitude measures in teleconference study are equivalent to or better than face-to-face instruction (Haaland and Newby, 1984; Robertson, 1987; Shaeffer and Roe, 1985). There are, however, serious concerns with the supposed need to compare distance education outcomes with those resulting from conventional methods. The first issue is the quality of the specific design and the teaching that apparently affects learning (Clark, 1983). Second, and perhaps more important, since most distance learners do not have the luxury of choosing between distance and conventional methods, the comparisons are mostly meaningless. For many would-be learners, the choice is distance education or nothing.

To increase the range of choice and opportunity for learning, a third generation of distance education is on the horizon. It is based upon the most promising and pervasive information processing advancement of this century—the microcomputer. From the perspective of distance education, the microcomputer has the potential of supporting both real and simulated communication by way of computer messaging and conferencing as well as by intelligent computer assisted learning (ICAL) tutorials. While quality ICAL courseware currently exists largely in experimental form, the future regarding both hardware and courseware developments is very promising. With the advent of these technological capabilities, true individualization becomes possible for studying at a distance. In the near future, distance learners not only will be able to study when and where they like, but they will be able to choose how they wish to learn and to have all the guidance and support they require or request, thereby acquiring maximum control of the educational transaction.

Before concluding this discussion of distance education technologies, we cannot ignore a class of media used for delivering education at a distance. Technological media such as audiocassettes, videocassettes, laser videodiscs, and broadcast radio and television, while powerful and useful, must be seen as ancillary media because of their inability or inadequacy to support two-way communication in the educational transaction. Such media must be integrated with the technological tools of distance education as discussed previously. For example, broadcast radio and television routinely enhance correspondence education, and audiocassettes and videocassettes can support audio teleconferencing. And when a laser videodisc is interfaced with a microcomputer, one of the most promising and powerful educational technologies is created.

New communication technology has "the potential not only to alter distance education radically but also conventional higher education" (Bates,

1985, p. 3). Smith (1988, p. 38) believes "that through these technologies in their broadest sense, distance education has had an impact on educational methods in general, and will continue to be in the vanguard of educational change." These technologies of communication have influenced the current structuring of distance education organizations and also have begun to be integrated into conventional higher education organizations.

Distance Education Organizations

Discussion of distance education technology is concerned with the microlevel structural dimensions and issues. To complete the discussion regarding the structure of distance education and to provide another perspective at a macrolevel, a classification of distance education institutions has been developed. The classification presented here is drawn from Keegan (1986).

Keegan's classification of distance education institutions consists of five types—(I) public and private correspondence schools, (II) distance teaching universities, (III) independent study divisions of conventional schools, (IV) the consultation model, and (V) the integrated mode. The first two types are autonomous, while the other three types are found within the structure of a conventional institution. The distinguishing feature of the two autonomous institutions is their use of media and support for learning. In practice, Type I institutions are the more traditional correspondence study institutions, and Type II institutions are typically modeled after the British Open University, which marked a new era of utilizing sophisticated media and course development teams (Holmberg, 1985). Type III institutions are seen by Keegan as independent study divisions within conventional colleges or universities. They may use a variety of delivery technologies and media, and course development is usually done by university faculty on an overload basis. A didactic or consultation model characterizes Type IV institutions. Often, they bear little resemblance to correspondence study in that they begin "with a residential seminar on campus after which students study at home from the learning materials provided" (Keegan, 1986, p. 152). Home study is then supplemented with periodic one-day on-campus consultations. Type V institutions are represented by the Australian integrated mode. The integration of distance education staffing and course development with the university as a whole attempts to preserve as many of the on-campus provisions as possible. The university's lecturers teach both external and internal students through independent study materials and face-to-face instruction.

Another organizational structure that is becoming increasingly prevalent is the consortium of distance education institutions. The basic reason for this trend is cost-effectiveness. A broader range of courses and delivery technologies can be made available when institutions share the costs of course development and communication systems. There are several consortia in

Canada, but perhaps the best example is the Open Learning Consortium of British Columbia. This consortium includes all degree-granting institutions in the province, along with the satellite-based Knowledge Network. In the United States, good examples are the Association for Media Based Continuing Education for Engineers (AMCEE) and the National Technological University (NTU). Together they offer credit and noncredit courses and form the AMCEE/NTU Satellite Network.

Mediated Communication

Communication is referred to by Holmberg (1985) as the core or cornerstone of distance education. In fact, as has been noted previously, communication is essential in any educational transaction. The great difference in distance education is that communication is usually mediated by technology that often limits the form, frequency, and immediacy of the messages. By understanding mediated communication, we can understand this most important feature of distance education, which links all components of the educational process.

A distinct and important difference exists between one-way and two-way communication. One-way communication simply stimulates the receiver who, after receiving the message, is expected to act in a particular manner. According to Rowntree (1975), this is essentially manipulative. Two-way communication, however, is facilitative and "allows room for the negotiation of meaning and the prospect of mutual learning through dialogue and discussion" (Rowntree, 1975, p. 284).

To this point, distinctions have been made between one-way and two-way communication and between direct (that is, face-to-face) and mediated communication. Garrison and Shale (1987b) summarize various communication modes for distance education, and, in addition to the previous distinctions, they suggest two different types of two-way mediated communication—communication that is immediate, as in teleconferencing, and communication that is delayed, as in correspondence study. With advances in ICAL tutorials, another distinction must be addressed—the distinction between real and simulated two-way communication that the ICAL technology makes possible. It has been argued elsewhere that ICAL tutorials have the potential to meet the basic requirements of two-way communication (Garrison and Shale, 1987b).

Although space does not permit further explication of these various forms of communication, the point is that considerable thought must be given to the communication process in distance education. Since learning in an educational situation is so dependent upon the interaction between teacher and student (Rothkopf, 1970; Clark, 1983), and given the separation of teacher and student in distance education, every effort must be made to understand the communication process and to use it in optimal ways that benefit adult learners, keeping in mind that adult learners appear to benefit the most when they have control of the educational transaction.

Control and Communication

Brookfield (1983, p. 24) stated "that the physical separation of teacher and student clearly did not grant cognitive independence to the latter." On the contrary, correspondence education often tends to be rigidly prescriptive, allowing for little control over the content and method of learning. The troubling part of this situation is that distance education (especially correspondence study) has been cited as supporting and developing student independence (Holmberg, 1985, 1986). To some, independence is highly attractive, yet this term can be misleading if the nature of the educational transaction is not understood. The question that must be addressed is whether control can be achieved by simply granting independence and freedom, or whether independence without the consideration of ability and resource issues is an illusion.

In attempting to understand the issues surrounding independence, Garrison and Baynton (1987) have suggested the more inclusive concept of control. According to Garrison and Baynton, control in the learning process is determined by the dynamic balance of independence, power, and support. In an educational context, independence is the freedom to choose objectives and methods of learning. Power is concerned with the various abilities of the learner to cope with the educational activity. Support, the third dimension of control, refers to the range of resources available to the learner. Each of these dimensions must be considered for the effective and efficient achievement of worthwhile educational goals. It would be naive or even irresponsible to grant independence to learners without serious consideration of their abilities and skills (power) as well as the necessary human and physical resources (support) available to achieve intended educational outcomes. While control is shared to varying degrees by teacher and student, it must be emphasized that students can gain control by accepting guidance and support. That is, students will more readily and likely achieve the intended learning goal. In a collaborative educational transaction, control has nothing to do with coercion and domination. True control is concerned with the likelihood that students will achieve intended and worthwhile educational outcomes.

Manifesting control in an educational transaction is achieved through two-way communication. Control of the educational transaction must be determined through an awareness of its dimensions and a commitment to constructive negotiation and dialogue between teacher and student. Considering only the narrow concept of independence in distance education is simplistic and does not take into account the abilities and resources of the learner. The challenge in distance education is to facilitate the negotiation of control as opposed to accepting the illusion of independence. A more holistic view of adult and distance education is required to continue to meet the changing educational needs of adult learners.

Participation and Distance Education

Adult education has long been concerned with democratizing education and encouraging greater rates of participation. One of the characteristics of the early days of adult education in North America was the reaching out to individuals and groups in society regardless of location and educational background. This reaching out is evidenced by the agricultural extension programs pioneered by Seaman Knapp, by William Rainey Harper's work in the Chautauqua movement and with correspondence study, by Canada's Frontier College founded by Alfred Fitzpatrick, and by the National Farm Radio Forum broadcasts on the Canadian Broadcasting Corporation in the 1940s. Each was a unique attempt by adult educators of the time to meet the learning needs of adults beyond the walls of formal institutional structures.

Some of the basic assumptions underpinning adult education are that adults tend toward self-directedness, that adult learning needs are generated by real-life problems, and that adults wish to apply acquired knowledge and skills (Knowles, 1980). A survey of adult learning activities by Johnstone and Rivera (1965) resulted in findings to support these assumptions and was the basis upon which Darkenwald and Merriam (1982, p. 124) stated that the "intimate relationship between learning and living is in our view the hallmark of adult education." If this is indeed true, then what method has more potential than distance education for increasing participation through the integration of learning into the lifespace of the adult?

Distance education methods have the ability to overcome the barriers of time and location, cited by Cross (1981), that prevent participation in adult education programs. These methods also can provide the support that many self-directed learners would welcome in planning and conducting their learning projects (Tough, 1979). For adult educators to have any hope of reaching the majority of adult learners who do not participate in formal educational programs, distance education methods and technologies will have to be employed. Zigerell (1984, p. 1) states that distance education technologies portend "not only an extension and transformation of the field of adult education, but also a broadening of the role of adult educators . . . to develop programs for the adult who must, or chooses to, study at a distance."

Another concept intimately related to this discussion of adult and distance education is that of lifelong learning. The use of lifelong learning as a concept and policy has become widespread. Before discussing the concept in relation to distance education, we must appreciate that lifelong "merely signifies an adjective describing the temporal context for an independently defined meaning of education" (Wain, 1985, p. 109). We are, as with adult and distance education, talking about the phenomenon of education—only spread over the lifespan of the individual learner. While some feel that adults are continuously engaged in purposeful learning, and that therefore lifelong learning already exists (Brookfield, 1986), there is still a question of whether we are facilitating and supporting this learning adequately.

Distance education methods and technologies clearly have much to offer adult and lifelong education in terms of access and support. The future will see increased efforts to integrate adult and distance education, both conceptually and in practice, in realizing lifelong education. As Moore (1987, p. 39) states, "Within a decade, distance education will have become a very significant part of the universe of adult, continuing and higher education. It will cease to be a subject of special comment and be no longer a curiosity. The distinctions between distance and traditional education, adult, continuing and higher education will become blurred and recede in memory. This will coincide with the growing acceptance by both educators and public of the notion of universal lifelong education."

Conclusion

This discussion has attempted to describe distance education's potential and capability to extend opportunities for learning. However, this is not to say there are not contentious issues that surround distance education. One of the fundamental issues is the relationship between distance and conventional education. The question is whether distance education is simply a cost-effective means of offering existing educational programs or whether distance education will serve those students who would not normally attend conventional institutions.

While distance education methods are usually adopted to extend or to enhance the quality of existing programs, there is a danger that distance education methods could be used to replace conventional methods and simply duplicate the rigidity and hegemony of much of conventional education. To allow this to happen would negate the great potential of distance education to reach the isolated and disadvantaged learner. This is not to say that distance education methods should not be used for traditional continuing education programs. But, if we are to expand our base of participants in adult education, distance education must also be used to reach new audiences through provision of equal access to and adequate ongoing support for these learning efforts. Such was the motivation of Vincent and Harper at Chautauqua in their use of distance education to extend learning opportunities. It is clear that distance education is again becoming a major component of adult education provision with the increased power and availability of new communication technology.

References

Baath, J. "Research on Completion and Discontinuation in Distance Education." *Epistolodidaktika*, 1984, *12*, 31–43.

Bates, A. W. *New Technology and Its Impact on Conventional Distance Education.* Papers on Information and Technology, no. 237. Walton, Eng.: Open University, Institute of Educational Technology, 1984. (ED 268 966)

Brookfield, S. D. *Adult Learners, Adult Education and the Community*. Milton Keynes, Eng.: Open University Press, 1983.

Brookfield, S. D. *Understanding and Facilitating Adult Learning*. San Francisco: Jossey-Bass, 1986.

Clark, R. "Reconsidering Research on Learning from Media." *Review of Educational Research*, 1983, *53* (4), 445–459.

Cross, K. P. *Adults as Learners*. San Francisco: Jossey-Bass, 1981.

Darkenwald, G. G., and Merriam, S. B. *Adult Education: Foundations of Practice*. New York: Harper & Row, 1982.

Garrison, D. R. "Three Generations of Technological Innovation in Distance Education." *Distance Education*, 1985, *6* (2), 235–241.

Garrison, D. R. "Researching Dropout in Distance Education: Some Directional and Methodological Considerations." *Distance Education*, 1987, *8* (1), 95–101

Garrison, D. R., and Baynton, M. "Beyond Independence in Distance Education: The Concept of Control." *American Journal of Distance Education*, 1987, *1* (3), 3–15.

Garrison, D. R., and Shale, D. "Mapping the Boundaries of Distance Education: Problems in Defining the Field." *American Journal of Distance Education*, 1987a, *1* (1), 7–13.

Garrison, D. R., and Shale, D. "The Communication Process as a Unifying Concept in Distance Education." Unpublished manuscript, University of Calgary, 1987b.

Haaland, B. A., and Newby, W. G. "Student Perception of Effective Teaching Behaviors: An Examination of Conventional and Teleconference-Based Instruction." In L. A. Parker and O. H. Olgren (eds.), *Teleconferencing and Electronic Communications III*. Madison: University of Wisconsin-Extension, 1984.

Holmberg, B. *Status and Trends of Distance Education*. Lund, Sweden: Lector, 1985.

Holmberg, B. *Status and Trends of Distance Education*. London: Croom-Helm, 1986.

Johnstone, J. W., and Rivera, R. J. *Volunteers for Learning: A Study of the Educational Pursuits of American Adults*. Hawthorne, N.Y.: Aldine, 1965.

Keegan, D. *The Foundations of Distance Education*. London: Croom-Helm, 1986.

Knowles, M. S. *The Modern Practice of Adult Education: From Pedagogy to Andragogy*. (2nd ed.) New York: Cambridge Book, 1980.

Moore, M. G. "Toward a Theory of Independent Learning and Teaching." *Journal of Higher Education*, 1973, *44*, 661–679.

Moore, M. G. "Distance Learning in the United States: The Near Future." *Distance Education*, 1987, *8* (1), 38–46.

Olgren, C. H., and Parker, L. A. *Teleconferencing Technology and Applications*. Dedham, Mass.: Artech House, 1983.

Persons, H., and Catchpole, M. "The Addition of Audio-Teleconferencing to Interactive Telecourses: An Experimental Analysis of Drop-Out Rates." *Distance Education*, 1987, *8*, 251–258.

Rekkedal, T. *Introducing the Personal Tutor/Counsellor in the System of Distance Education*. Stabekk, Norway: NKI-skolen, 1985.

Robertson, B. "Audio Teleconferencing: Low-Cost Technology for External Studies Networking." *Distance Education*, 1987, *8* (1), 121–130.

Rothkopf, E. "The Concept of Mathemagenic Activities."*Review of Educational Research*, 1970, *40*, 325–336.

Rowntree, D. "Two Styles of Communication and Their Implications for Learning." In J. Baggaly, H. Jamieson, and H. Marchant (eds.), *Aspects of Educational Technology*. Vol. 8: *Communication and Learning*. London: Pitman, 1975.

Shaeffer, J. M., and Roe, R. G. "Effective Teaching Behaviors as Perceived by Students in a Face-to-Face and Teleconferencing Course." In L. A. Parker and C. H. Olgren (eds.), *Teleconferencing and Electronic Communications IV*. Madison: University of Wisconsin-Extension, 1985.

Smith, P. "Distance Education and Educational Change." In P. Smith and M. Kelly (eds.), *Distance Education and the Mainstream: Convergence in Education*. London: Croom-Helm, 1988.

Swanson, B. "An Early American Experiment in Distance Education." *International Council for Distance Education Bulletin*, 1988, *16*, 39–42.

Tough, A. *The Adult's Learning Projects: A Fresh Approach to Theory and Practice in Adult Learning*. (2nd ed.) Toronto: Ontario Institute for Studies in Education, 1979.

Wain, K. A. "Lifelong Education and the Philosophy of Education." *International Journal of Lifelong Education*, 1985, *4* (2), 107–118.

Wedemeyer, C. A. *Learning at the Backdoor: Reflections on Non-Traditional Learning in the Lifespan*. Madison: University of Wisconsin Press, 1981.

Zigerell, J. *Distance Education: An Information Age Approach to Adult Education*. Information Series no. 283. Columbus, Ohio: ERIC Clearinghouse on Adult, Career, and Vocational Education, 1984.

18

Planning Programs for Adults

Thomas J. Sork
Rosemary S. Caffarella

Since the publication of Tyler's *Basic Principles of Curriculum and Instruction* (1949) and Knowles's *Informal Adult Education* (1950), dozens of books, chapters, and articles have been written about the process of planning programs for adult learners. Interest in the literature on systematic planning has remained high throughout the intervening years because of the need to design educational programs—a complex decision-making process that can be substantially aided by the models or frameworks found in this literature. Although there are some important differences in approaches to planning as described over this forty-year period, the major elements of planning described by London in the 1960 *Handbook of Adult Education* can be found in most of the literature published since that time (Sork and Buskey, 1986).

In its most general sense, planning refers to the process of determining the ends to be pursued and the means employed to achieve them. In adult education, planning is a decision-making process and a set of related activities that produce educational program design specifications for one or more adult learners. It is important to recognize that the literature on planning is largely normative. That is, the literature consists mostly of descriptions of how planning should be done rather than descriptions of how planning is done. These descriptions are sometimes accompanied by detailed justifications for adopting the approach suggested, but more often they simply present an approach to planning that the author believes is best. Models based on an analysis of how planning is done can be found in Mazmanian (1980) and in Pennington and Green (1976).

Defⁿ of PLANNING (handwritten margin note)

Our intention in this chapter is to present the basic elements of planning as found in the literature, to identify controversial or contentious issues related to each of the major phases or steps of planning, and to point out areas in which there remain substantial gaps between what theorists say should be done and what practitioners do.

Role of Planning Models

A planning model is a tool used to help understand and to bring order to a complex decision-making process. The typical planning model consists of a set of steps (which imply a preferred sequence or order to the planning process) or elements (which imply a more interactive or dynamic process) that suggest decisions that must be made and dependent relationships that exist between the various decisions. Any effort to summarize the complexities of planning—whether using steps or elements—is bound to oversimplify the process as it occurs in practice. Indeed, anyone who claims that a planning model accurately represents how planning occurs in practice either has a naive understanding of what planning involves or is concerned with only a narrow range of adult education settings. But models do make the underlying logic of a planning process explicit and provide verbal or graphic cues to help practitioners systematize their work. For examples of interactive models of planning, see Simpson (1987) and Murk and Galbraith (1986).

We have elected to use a six-step basic model to organize discussion of the process and to illustrate the most common planning logic found in the literature. The steps are consistent with a similar model used by Sork and Buskey (1986) to evaluate the literature on program planning—although we have consolidated their nine steps into six. The model is basic because each step includes more than one task or set of decisions. The six steps are (1) analyze planning context and client system, (2) assess needs, (3) develop program objectives, (4) formulate instructional plan, (5) formulate administrative plan, and (6) design a program evaluation plan.

In the sections to follow, we will describe the tasks included within each of the six steps, and we will explain unresolved or contentious issues related to each. Before elaborating on each of the steps, however, we should reveal a few key beliefs we have about planning programs for adults—beliefs that influence our understanding of the process.

First, although the practice of planning rarely follows a linear pattern in which decisions related to one step are made before decisions about the next are considered, the process can best be understood in a stepwise fashion whereby the logic of one step preceding or following another step is explained. However, loops operate in practice to make it possible to skip steps temporarily, to work on several tasks simultaneously, and to make decisions that appear to defy logical sequence. We agree with Houle (1972) that educational design is a complex of interacting elements; yet, at the same time, we adopt his technique of explaining the process one element at a time while presenting the logic that suggests a preferred sequence.

Second, we believe that direct participation of client or learner in planning is desirable but not essential. Conventional wisdom in adult education supports the principle that adult learners should always have the opportunity to participate in planning their own learning experiences. Although research supports the practice of actively involving the learner in instruction once the program begins, there is inconclusive evidence to support the assertion that direct participation of the learner in planning consistently enhances learning, motivation, or attitudes toward the program. Lest we be accused of heresy, we should acknowledge that there may be compelling philosophical or practical reasons for always involving learners in planning, as, for example, in cases in which community development (see Chapter Thirty-Three) or empowerment are goals.

Third, we believe that systematic planning is a powerful tool for designing effective, efficient, relevant, and innovative educational programs. There are weaknesses in the rational, needs-based approach to planning that must be acknowledged (see Boshier, 1986), but, on balance, systematic planning is a more powerful tool than any of the alternatives presented thus far.

Steps in the Planning Process

The first step is to analyze the planning context and the client system. Planning occurs within a milieu, the characteristics of which can substantially influence the process. In most cases, programs are planned within organizations and institutions that have histories, traditions, philosophical orientations, policies, and operating procedures that affect how planning proceeds. Those who work within these settings usually understand how contextual factors influence their work, and they constantly assess whether decisions made are consistent with the constraints imposed by the nature of the organization. Both the approach to planning and the degree of commitment to planning processes are strongly influenced by this context.

The purpose of analyzing the planning context is to identify internal and external factors or forces that should be taken into account during planning. Internal factors of particular concern are (1) the history and traditions of the organization, (2) the current structures that govern the flow of communication and authority, (3) the mission of the organization, (4) the resource limits, (5) the standard operating procedures, and (6) any philosophical constraints that limit who can be served or what types of needs can be addressed. External factors include (1) the relationships (competitive or cooperative) between the organization and others that serve the same client groups, (2) any comparative advantage enjoyed by the organization that makes it easier to respond to needs, and (3) the attitudes toward the organization held by influentials in the community. The analysis provides a baseline of information that can be used in making decisions about the planning milieu.

Analysis of the client system is the second task in this first step of planning. It involves collecting information about those individuals who are eligible for the attention of the program planner—information that may have implications for later steps of planning. Although relevant information will vary from one planning situation to another, the following items represent a sampling from the literature: age, educational attainment, cultural background, facility with written language, economic status, history of participation in education, geographic distribution, and social affiliations.

A client system analysis should accomplish two important functions. First, it should specify the undisputed boundary of the client system. That is, there should be an unambiguous determination of who is and who is not eligible for the attention of the program planner. Only when this is accomplished can a needs assessment be properly focused. Second, a client system analysis should reveal any characteristics of the client group that may have important implications for later steps of the planning process. For example, the analysis may reveal that lack of time and money is a formidable barrier to participation for most of those in the client group. This piece of information has important implications for several subsequent steps of planning. Without this knowledge, serious errors could be made in the design, pricing, and promotion of the program. Although research has helped us develop a rudimentary understanding of why people do and do not participate in programs, identification of all the planning implications of specific contextual factors or client characteristics is still difficult.

Assess Needs. The concept of need as a basis for justifying and focusing the planning process has been misunderstood and maligned for years. Literally every program planning model published in the past thirty-five years includes a step or element referred to as *needs assessment,* or labeled with an accepted synonym (Sork and Buskey, 1986). Yet there has been so much disagreement and confusion about what a need is that some authors (Mattimore-Knudson, 1983) have argued for purging the concept from the lexicon and replacing it with a more serviceable term. Yet, because the term is so well entrenched in the planning literature, and because there is a modest degree of consistency in how it is defined, it seems premature to propose a substitute that may produce no less confusion. After conducting one of the most comprehensive reviews of the literature yet reported, Witkin (1984, p. 6) concluded that, ''In the context of needs assessment . . . the term *need* is properly used only as a noun with the denotation of a discrepancy or gap between some desired or acceptable condition or state of affairs and the actual or observed or perceived condition or state of affairs.'' This discrepancy definition of need is found in various forms in the work of Leagans (1964), Knowles (1980), and Knox (1986), among others.

Most often confused with the definition is the conception of need as that which is required or desired to bring about a change in the condition or state of affairs of the learner. These definitions are mutually exclusive. In the case of the discrepancy definition, needs assessment involves establishing the existence and determining the priority of gaps between present and desired capabilities, proficiencies, outcomes, and so on. In the case of the second definition, the focus of the assessment is on finding solutions or means of altering the situation of the learner. Adopting the discrepancy definition of need means that value judgments are an integral part of the needs assessment process because identifying needs requires the specification of a more desirable condition or state of affairs. Determining the present condition is usually based on data acquired through observations, questionnaires, tests, performance analyses, self-assessment instruments, record reviews, and other means of documenting current levels of capability, performance, proficiency, and so on. But there is no equivalent set of concrete tools that can be used to construct a description of the desired condition. The present condition is determined empirically; the desired condition must be constructed based on the values and aspirations of those involved in planning. Creative use of so-called futuring techniques (such as futures invention, trend extrapolation, Delphi, scenario construction, cross-impact analysis, technology assessment) can enrich the process of specifying the desired condition so that the program is oriented to a dynamic, changing environment rather than to the past or present (see Chapters Forty-Five, Forty-Six, and Forty-Seven).

Once needs are specified, they should be presented in a format that makes both the present and the more desirable condition as explicit as possible. The following is a sample needs statement that contains both essential elements:

> *Present State of Affairs:* Fifteen percent of adult community residents know how to influence the legislative process.
> *Desired State of Affairs:* At least 30 percent of adult community residents should know how to influence the legislative process.

Needs assessments usually produce more needs than can be addressed with existing resources. When this happens, there must be some technique used to determine priorities. Although priority setting remains a somewhat neglected topic in the literature, useful discussion of techniques can be found in Caffarella (1988), Kemerer and Schroeder (1983), and Witkin (1984). Most techniques require the specification of criteria to be used to determine priorities and the systematic application of criteria to all the needs identified. Knowles (1980) uses a filter analogy and three criteria to establish priority. Other authors use ranking, rating, and graphic representation systems to make these decisions. The purpose of priority setting is to provide a rational resource allocation basis that will be acceptable to those to whom the planner is accountable.

Although the centrality of needs assessment in the planning literature is undisputed, there is a growing number of scholars and practitioners who urge a revision in thinking about the importance of needs assessment to effective educational planning. Practitioners argue that they rarely have time to conduct needs assessments. More often than not they justify offering programs based on potential demand (which may or may not have anything to do with need) or based on the availability of the resources required to offer the programs (such as an instructor or a classroom filled with microcomputers). There appears to be a serious gap between the process as described in the literature and the actual practice of needs assessment. Reducing this gap will require either a revision of planning theory or substantial changes in the behavior of practitioners. As Mattimore-Knudson (1983) and Sork (1986), among others, have suggested, it may be time to revise planning theory so that it takes into account more of the contextual circumstances confronted by practitioners—circumstances that limit the practical utility of needs assessment and offer other legitimate means of justifying and focusing programs.

Develop Program Objectives. Some adult educators have argued that program objectives should be done away with completely (Jones, 1982). Even those who agree that program objectives are important disagree about the level of specificity at which these objectives should be stated. Despite these controversies, the literature generally supports the notion that program objectives—statements of the anticipated results of the program—are a necessary element in the planning process.

Program objectives may be broad in scope, such as descriptions of the outcomes of a comprehensive adult education program, or they may have a much narrower focus, such as outlines of the results of one specific workshop or conference. Program objectives are often divided into two major categories: (1) educational objectives that focus on the participants' learning as a group, and (2) organizational or operational objectives that relate to the maintenance and improvement of the educational function itself or to the organization in which the program is housed (Boyle, 1981; Knowles, 1980). One of the major purposes for having program objectives is to provide concrete guidelines for further program development. In addition, these objectives can serve as benchmarks for measuring the progress and achievements of a program and can provide motivation to get the job done.

Program objectives should flow from the needs that have been identified and should be as explicit as possible. They should be presented in a format that captures the desired state of affairs and has meaning for all parties involved, including the educator, other key organizational staff, and potential clientele. The following is the desired state of affairs presented in the section above with a corresponding program objective derived from the need:

> *Needs Statement (Desired State of Affairs):* At least 30 percent of adult community residents should know how to influence the legislative process.
>
> *Program Objective:* At the conclusion of a year-long series of community forums and workshops, at least 30 percent of adult community residents will be able to describe at least one means they can use to influence the legislative process at the local level.

As alluded to earlier, a number of authors have questioned the assumption that program objectives should be fixed entities, determined prior to the start of a program. Apps (1985), for example, raises the issue of whether it is always important or even possible to identify expected outcomes before an educational program begins. When viewed in this light, program objectives can be seen as somewhat open-ended so that unanticipated but important outcomes of the program can be noted. The notion that educationally oriented program objectives should be stated primarily in behavioral or performance terms is also in dispute. Both Apps (1985) and Brookfield (1986), among others, believe that this type of program objective supports only one type of learning—instrumental or technical learning—and thus leads program planners to ignore other categories of learning, such as emancipatory or reflective learning.

Formulate Instructional Plan. Approaches to the design of instruction can be placed on a continuum with systematic (some would say mechanistic) approaches at one end and artistic or creative approaches at the other. Whatever approach is taken along this continuum, formulating these plans is often done by a person or persons other than the program planner—a person such as a course instructor or workshop leader—although in adult education the instructor and the planner may be the same person. For example, the director of a hospital-based community education program may decide that the hospital will offer a program, but the content and format for each individual session will be determined by a nurse educator who specializes in maternity care.

Developing instructional plans involves preparing instructional objectives (or, for the more artistic end of the continuum, at least thinking about what the end product might be), selecting and ordering content, designing the instructional process, selecting appropriate resources, and determining evaluation procedures. Instructional objectives describe the outcome or result of a specific learning segment or activity and are written from the perspective of the individual learner. Three categories of learning outcomes are usually identified: knowledge acquisition, skill building, and a change in the attitudes or values of a person. These objectives provide the starting point for selecting the specific content to be learned. Tracey (1984) suggests preparing a rough draft of the content for each objective and then expanding this until a detailed outline is achieved.

Although there is no one set way to order the content, the following general guidelines may be helpful to instructors. First, provide a framework for learners to assist them in organizing their learning. Second, where possible, start with material that may be familiar to the learners so their experience and background can become a part of the learning process. And third, where applicable, integrate practice applications as part of each learning segment (Tracey, 1984).

Selecting the instructional processes goes hand in hand with determining the content. It is just as important for instructors of adults to choose carefully how they will teach the materials as it is for them to choose the materials to be taught and the instructional resources (books, worksheets, videotapes, computer programs, and so on) to be used. The underlying assumption here is that there is no one best way of assisting people to learn. Again the instructional objectives provide a good starting point for choosing the instructional strategies and resources. Other factors to consider are the capability of the instructor; the background and experience of the learner; the time available; and the space, equipment, and materials needed.

The last component of the instructional plan—determining evaluation procedures—involves planning a way to find out how well the learners have achieved the instructional objectives. This can be done in a number of ways, depending on the nature of the proposed learning outcome, from formal testing to observation to product review.

One of the major issues related to the instructional process that continually surfaces revolves around the use and form of instructional objectives. The questions posed are similar to those raised about developing program objectives: Should emphasis continually be placed on determining instructional objectives prior to commencing an educational activity? Can behavioral or performance-based objectives capture all levels and types of learning? Is the learning process enhanced by using objectives, and, if not, under what conditions should their use not be encouraged (Apps, 1985; Brookfield, 1986)?

A second issue centers on how adult educators should design the actual instructional process. There seems to be a constant pull between the content of instruction and the process of instruction. Should we as adult educators primarily be facilitators of the learning process, with the emphasis on helping learners become more self-directed in their learning endeavors? Or, should we be more content oriented, and thus be largely concerned with whether learners gain new knowledge and skills or with whether they change their values or attitudes in some way. Brookfield (1986) recently has added new fuel to this controversy by challenging the accepted way in which the role of facilitator has been conceived.

Formulate Administrative Plan. One of the reasons for the failure of well-designed programs is the lack of attention paid by some program planners to administrative details such as advanced publicity and program financing. Thus, it is incumbent upon the planner to outline how the administrative tasks will be addressed. It is often helpful, especially when developing larger programs, to have an administrative checklist of things to do prior to, during, and immediately after the program and to assign a specific person to be responsible for each item. Assuring participation in the program is one of the first administrative tasks that must be handled by the planner. Although not all adult education programs need to be promoted, many potential audiences must be convinced of a program's value before they will attend.

Most adult education programs cost money, and some programs are even expected to generate revenue for their sponsoring organizations. Therefore, it is important that program planners know what the program will cost and how it will be financed. Three basic costs are associated with educational programs: development costs, delivery costs, and evaluation costs (Laird, 1985). Staff salaries and benefits, instructional materials, equipment, food, and facilities are examples of typical program expense items. The primary sources of income include sponsoring organization subsidy, participant fees, grants and contracts, and government funds (Matkin, 1985). In addition to the financing of programs, there are numerous other administrative tasks that must be taken care of, depending on the requirements of a specific program—requirements such as obtaining facilities and equipment and arranging for meals, lodging, and transportation.

One of the major unresolved issues related to formulation of administrative plans revolves around the financing of programs. When adult educators are expected to operate programs on a cost-recovery or profit-making basis, the need to fill classrooms or workshops with paying customers—instead of the educational needs of the citizenry at large—tends to become the major force that drives programs. But what of the underserved population—those who, for the most part, unless some outside funding is available, cannot pay their own way? Will access to adult education programs for these hard-to-reach populations become even further limited than it is currently? The choice of whom to serve is a difficult one for practitioners, especially in this era of scarce resources.

Partially due to this market-driven practice of program planning, a renewed concern with ethics has also arisen among adult educators. Should our programs be driven primarily by economics or by educational needs? What are our responsibilities as adult educators to those hard-to-reach adult learners? Exploration of these and many other ethical issues associated with program planning can be found in Brockett (1988) and in Singarella and Sork (1983).

Design a Program Evaluation Plan. There are many different ideas about what evaluation is and how it should be done. To some, evaluation means determining whether people enjoyed a program by using so-called happiness indicators. Others test people to determine if gains have been made in knowledge or skill levels, while still others observe changes in people's performance after a program is completed. Deshler (1984) posits two kinds of evaluation: Formative evaluations focus on improving programs, and summative evaluations focus on measuring and appraising the results or outcomes of programs.

Although each of these ways of gathering data may be important, evaluation is more than just a process for providing data. Rather, the essence of evaluation, as defined in this chapter and in much of the literature, is making judgments about the value or worth of a program.

Deciding what to evaluate is a critical part of the evaluation process. A good way to start is to frame the evaluation questions and issues within the context of the program objectives. Adult educators should always be concerned about whether programs produce expected learning results. In addition, planners may also be interested in (1) people's reactions to programs, (2) the impact of people's learning on specified aspects of their lives (work, home, family, and so on), (3) the policies, procedures, and practices of the adult education program, and (4) the impact of the program on the sponsoring organization or on the community. The next steps in the evaluation process include determining the evaluation design, planning the collection of data, specifying data analysis procedures, and establishing evaluation criteria. The most widely used means of collecting evaluation evidence are written questionnaires, tests, interviews, observations, product reviews, and examinations of organizational records.

Resource constraints often force program planners to choose a less than ideal design and methodology. This is true whether the evaluation is quantitative or qualitative in nature, or a combination of both. Knox (1986) has noted that one of the most frequent flaws in the evaluation process is inadequate planning of data analysis procedures. This part of the process tends to be overlooked until after the data have been collected, rather than carefully thought through ahead of time. The most serious problem that may arise when procedures are not determined beforehand is that data may not be analyzable in the form in which they were collected, and thus they are unusable. Whatever analysis procedures are chosen should flow naturally from the type and amount of data that will be gathered.

One of the most challenging and most often neglected tasks of the evaluation process is establishing criteria by which to judge the program. Measurable criteria, such as numbers of people served, learning gains as determined by test scores, and budgetary goals, are fairly easy to develop and manage. The results produced by the program either meet the stated criteria or they do not. The criteria more difficult to establish are those related to less tangible program outcomes, such as changes in values, the ability to critically analyze, or empowerment of the adult learner.

Houle (1972) has stressed that in interpreting and using evaluation data, both the successes and failures of the program should be examined. Too often only the successes are highlighted while the failures are forgotten. A potentially useful tool, termed the *postmortem audit,* has been developed by Sork, Kalef, and Worsfold (1987) to analyze these program failures. The primary purpose for conducting the audit is to reduce the incidence of preventable program failures by strengthening planning and administrative procedures within educational organizations.

A question has been raised by Knowles (1980) and others as to the value of the whole evaluation process. Do educators and especially policymakers really want or need proof that their programs are producing verifiable results? The actions of practitioners appear to be in accord with the sentiment that evaluation of adult education programs is either not important or not feasible (Brookfield, 1986; Laird, 1985; Pennington and Green, 1976), at least in its present form.

The assumption that program evaluations need to be systematic and precise has been disputed, as has the assumption that quantitative data are preferable to demonstrate the value and worth of a program. For example, it is argued by both Brookfield (1986) and Forest (1976) that the very nature of adult education programs calls for alternative evaluation strategies such as more naturalistic approaches. In addition, Knowles (1980, p. 199) has pointed out that, in general, "human behavior is too complicated and the number of variables affecting it are too numerous for us to be able to prove that it is our program alone that produces the desired change." For a more detailed treatment of the evaluation process, see Chapter Twenty.

Toward a Firmer Foundation for Planning

In this chapter we characterized the current state of planning theory, and we identified unresolved or contentious issues associated with the process. The literature is normative in character—it describes an idealized process that may or may not fit with the realities of practice. Although we possess no data to confirm it, we have the impression that the gap that has always existed to some degree between theory and practice has widened since the publication of the last *Handbook of Adult Education* in 1980. Several possible explanations may account for this widening: (1) practitioners take shortcuts in planning in order to get the job done; (2) contextual factors largely determine how planning is done; (3) planning theory is increasingly irrelevant to practice.

It seems to us that there are shortcomings in the planning literature that need to be addressed. Building a theory that takes into account the exigencies of day-to-day responsibilities of practitioners will require a collaboration between scholars and practitioners that is much closer than is usually found in adult education. Reflective practice, as described by Schön (1983), should reveal the major discrepancies. Scholars, working with practitioners, can then go to work refining theory so that it takes into consideration the contextual factors that affect planning. Only by reducing these discrepancies will theory become more relevant to practitioners and will the complexities of planning as it occurs in practice be understood and appreciated by scholars.

References

Apps, J. W. *Improving Practice in Continuing Education.* San Francisco: Jossey-Bass, 1985.

Boshier, R. "Proaction for a Change: Some Guidelines for the Future." *International Journal of Lifelong Education,* 1986, *5* (1), 15–31.

Boyle, P. G. *Planning Better Programs.* New York: McGraw-Hill, 1981.

Brockett, R. G. (ed.) *Ethical Issues in Adult Education.* New York: Teachers College Press, 1988.

Brookfield, S. D. *Understanding and Facilitating Adult Learning.* San Francisco: Jossey-Bass, 1986.

Caffarella, R. S. *Program Development and Evaluation Resource Book for Trainers.* New York: Wiley, 1988.

Deshler, D. (ed.). *Evaluation for Program Improvement.* New Directions for Continuing Education, no. 24. San Francisco: Jossey-Bass, 1984.

Forest, L. B. "Program Evaluation: For Reality." *Adult Education,* 1976, *26* (3), 167–177.

Houle, C. O. *The Design of Education.* San Francisco: Jossey-Bass, 1972.

Jones, R. K. "The Dilemma of Educational Objectives in Higher and Adult Education: Do We Need Them?" *Adult Education,* 1982, *32* (3), 165–169.

Kemerer, R. W., and Schroeder, W. L. "Determining the Importance of Community-Wide Adult Education Needs." *Adult Education Quarterly,* 1983, *33* (4), 201–214.

Knowles, M. S. *Informal Adult Education.* New York: Association Press, 1950.

Knowles, M. S. *The Modern Practice of Adult Education: From Pedagogy to Andragogy.* (Rev. ed.) Englewood Cliffs, N.J.: Prentice-Hall, 1980.

Knox, A. B. *Helping Adults Learn.* San Francisco: Jossey-Bass, 1986.

Laird, D. *Approaches to Training and Development.* (2nd ed.) Reading, Mass.: Addison-Wesley, 1985.

Leagans, J. P. "A Concept of Needs." *Journal of Extension,* 1964, *2* (2), 89–96.

London, J. "Program Development in Adult Education." In M. S. Knowles (ed.), *Handbook of Adult Education in the United States.* Washington, D.C.: Adult Education Association of the U.S.A., 1960.

Matkin, G. W. *Effective Budgeting in Continuing Education.* San Francisco: Jossey-Bass, 1985.

Mattimore-Knudson, R. "The Concept of Need: Its Hedonistic and Logical Nature." *Adult Education,* 1983, *33* (2), 117–124.

Mazmanian, P. E. "A Decision-Making Approach to Needs Assessment and Objective Setting in Continuing Medical Education." *Adult Education,* 1980, *31* (1), 3–17.

Murk, P. J., and Galbraith, M. W. "Planning Successful Continuing Education Programs: A Systems Approach Model." *Lifelong Learning,* 1986, *9* (5), 21–23.

Pennington, F., and Green, J. "Comparative Analysis of Program Development Processes in Six Professions." *Adult Education,* 1976, *27* (1), 12–23.

Schön, D. A. *The Reflective Practitioner: How Professionals Think in Action.* New York: Basic Books, 1983.

Simpson, E. L. "An Interactive Model of Program Development." In C. Klevins (ed.), *Materials and Methods in Adult and Continuing Education.* Los Angeles: Klevens Publications, 1987.

Singarella, T. A., and Sork, T. J. "Questions of Value and Conduct: Ethical Issues for Adult Education." *Adult Education Quarterly,* 1983, *33* (4), 244–251.

Sork, T. J. "Yellow Brick Road or Great Dismal Swamp: Pathways to Objectives in Program Planning." In *Proceedings of the Twenty-Seventh Annual Adult Education Research Conference.* Syracuse, N.Y.: Syracuse University Press, 1986.

Sork, T. J., and Buskey, J. H. "A Descriptive and Evaluative Analysis of Program Planning Literature, 1950–1983." *Adult Education Quarterly,* 1986, *36* (2), 86–96.

Sork, T. J., Kalef, R., and Worsfold, N. E. *The Postmortem Audit: A Strategy for Improving Educational Programs.* Vancouver, B.C.: Intentional Learning Systems, 1987.

Tracey, W. R. *Designing Training and Development Systems.* (Rev. ed.) New York: AMACOM, 1984.

Tyler, R. W. *Basic Principles of Curriculum and Instruction.* Chicago: University of Chicago Press, 1949.

Witkin, B. R. *Assessing Needs in Educational and Social Programs.* San Francisco: Jossey-Bass, 1984.

19

The Management of Adult and Continuing Education

Douglas H. Smith
Michael J. Offerman

The desire to serve adult learners successfully is the common thread that binds the widely divergent organizations involved in adult continuing education (ACE).* Within this overarching purpose, specific goals may differ from organization to organization. However, each organization is ultimately judged by whether it has effectively served its purpose in terms of its selected goals. Every member of the organization's staff shares in that effort, but it is the ACE manager who is specifically responsible for planning, organizing, and evaluating the organizational activities that will achieve the goals.

Since managers must rely upon others to carry out the necessary activities, the process of managing is interpersonal and complex. The person-oriented approach to management is the style most in keeping with the philosophical assumptions of adult and continuing education in planning, organizing, and evaluating the learning experiences of adults.

Management is the art and science of achieving goals through people. Management differs from administration, which is more concerned with carrying out tasks than it is with working with people (Langerman and Smith, 1979). Literature in educational administration often uses the terms *management* and *administration* interchangeably. However, review of recent writings reveals the emergence of *management* as the preferred term (Freedman, 1987; McCorkle and Archibald, 1982; Matkin, 1985; Simerly, 1987). The term

---

*In this chapter the adult continuing education organization or unit, and the adult continuing education manager, will be referred to as the ACE organization or unit, and the ACE manager, respectively.

leadership is also used interchangeably with *management*. However, leadership is not limited to those charged with managing an organization. Leadership is the capacity to exceed the minimum expectations of one's role (Katz and Kahn, 1978). Thus, leadership is provided by all members of the organization.

The Management of Adult and Continuing Education:
A Systems Perspective

This chapter provides an effective framework for the management of adult continuing education in the 1990s. Based on a systems perspective (Kast and Rosenzweig, 1984), the ACE organization is a system consisting of five components or subsystems: (1) mission and goals—the purpose or mission, and long-range goals of adult continuing education; (2) structural—the tasks to be done and their formal and informal division and coordination; (3) psychocultural and sociocultural—individual behavior and motivation, group dynamics, and cultural and political behavior; (4) technical—the techniques for transforming program needs and ideas into courses, workshops, seminars, and so forth; and (5) managerial—the central and coordinating subsystem that sets the goals and objectives, designs the structure, implements policies, facilitates the group dynamics of the organization, and establishes the control processes. "It is the subsystem that thinks about the overall plan and implements its thinking" (Churchman, 1968, p. 8).

The managerial system is also the focus of this chapter. Chapters One, Two, Four, and Five discuss areas germane to mission and goals. The next section on institutions and organizations examines the various structures of adult and continuing education. The section on program areas specifies various technical areas of required program expertise.

Figure 19.1 presents a framework for examining the management of adult continuing education. Four basic tasks or jobs characteristic of adult continuing education—programming, financing, staffing, and marketing—are carried out through effective implementation of three managerial functions—planning, organizing, and evaluating. These tasks and functions are performed in a specific environment, the ACE unit, but the unit must be sensitive to other environments within which it operates—the parent organization, the community, and the larger human learning system.

The literature in educational administration and management is rich with various lists of management functions and roles. A common list for adult continuing education would include planning, organizing, staffing, leading, and controlling (Langerman and Smith, 1979). The framework presented in Figure 19.1 distinguishes between managerial tasks (the things needing to be done) and functions (the steps through which the tasks are done and assessed). Leadership, while important, is not an exclusive managerial function because leadership needs to be practiced by all the staff, as previously mentioned. Evaluation replaces controlling because evaluation

Figure 19.1. Tasks, Roles, and Environments of Adult Continuing Education Management.

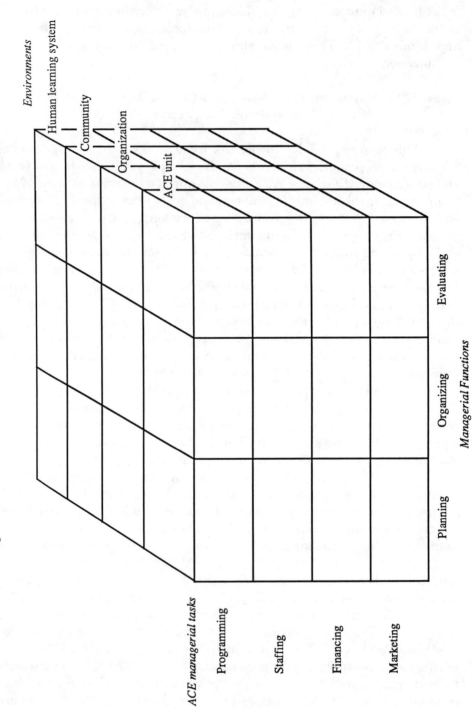

provides for mutuality in program evaluation, without the assumption of a supervisor-subordinate relationship inherent in controlling.

Specific Tasks in Managing an Adult Continuing Education Unit

The four tasks of programming, financing, staffing, and marketing are basic to adult continuing education. These tasks are described in order of priority. The major commitment should be to programming for adult learners—the primary purpose of adult continuing education. Programs are implemented by the staff and are made possible by financing. Marketing, while last on the list, requires creative leadership of the ACE manager in promoting the programs—usually on a limited budget.

Programming. Programs, more than any other factor, create the image of the organization and the basis upon which it is judged and supported. Programming produces the organization's product, its identity. The ACE staff that produces responsive, quality programs will contribute greatly to the parent organization and will assure a healthy, vigorous, and succcessful ACE program (Offerman, 1987).

The programming responsibilities of ACE managers are different from those of other organization members. ACE managers must provide for adult learners a general direction and a sound philosophical base for programming (Apps, 1979). The manager must assure that programs (1) reflect the mission and strengths of the ACE unit and of the parent organization, (2) are designed and conducted at a proper educational level, and (3) provide quality in all aspects of the program (Freedman, 1987). Managers must have the knowledge and skills to conduct needs assessments of diverse adult populations, to involve the adult learners in decision making, to plan and to evaluate programs and delivery systems, and to do all this within effective adult learning theory and practices (Knox, 1985).

Staffing. Since management is the achievement of organizational goals by working with and through its people, managerial success hinges upon an effective staff. The staffing function consists of recruiting, inducting, developing, and retaining good people. Thus, while programming is the core of the ACE mission, staffing is the most crucial of the managerial tasks. Staffing is also discussed in Chapter Eight within the framework of the role of volunteers in adult continuing education.

Increasingly, the staffs of ACE organizations are highly trained and skilled people. Managers must provide leadership by enabling and empowering these colleagues to perform at their peak in their areas of strength (Smith, 1987). Such enablement is congruent with adult and continuing education theory. It is the best way to create a dynamic, vital organization built upon staff expertise and excellence. While all managers have the designated authority or power, the wise manager is the one who acknowledges that true power and leadership is within the staff.

Managers also have a responsibility for their own enablement through a personal program of professional development. Ideally, this would be a mix of self-directed learning and reading, participation in key seminars, and involvement in professional associations. This mix can provide external contacts and new ideas, as well as thinking time for introspection. Professional development of ACE managers and staff, and professional organizations of adult continuing education, are discussed at length in Chapters Nine and Ten.

Financing. A primary concern for all organizations is the sources of funding. Ranging from program tuition and fees to grants to government funding, the typical ACE program relies on many sources of funds. Programming, marketing, and staffing are all directly affected by and, in turn, affect the sources and amount of funds. The manager is responsible both for securing the necessary funds and for budgeting these funds in accord with organizational goals and program objectives. The financing of adult continuing education is further discussed in Chapter Thirteen.

Marketing. Marketing is a concept only now coming into broad acceptance within the educational community. Too often, managers have failed to recognize its relevance in the nonprofit sector. Kotler's (1982) discussion of marketing of nonprofit organizations emphasizes that marketing is neither selling nor promotion, but is rather the assurance of maximum service. Consistent with adult and continuing education philosophy, the purpose of marketing is to inform, to stimulate, and to meet the needs of clients. Marketing is not the role of an isolated department or individual. It is an attitude that should permeate the organization. Everyone in the organization must become client oriented. The entire staff must engage in dialogue and planning with targeted client groups to assure mutual communication, promotion, and evaluation (Walshok, 1987).

The Functions of Management

While many functions are ascribed to management, there is general agreement that the three primary functions are planning, organizing, and evaluating. These functions are, in one respect, linear. That is, planning precedes organization, and evaluation flows from both planning and organizing. However, they are also simultaneous, dynamic, and interwoven. Planning does not end with organizing, nor does evaluating wait until planning and organizing are complete.

Planning. All ACE programs have a purpose and an idea of how to accomplish that purpose. Planning is the process of setting objectives and selecting steps to attain the objectives through analysis and evaluation of alternatives (McCorkle and Archibald, 1982). Planning sets a basic direction for the organization. It stimulates collective action by the staff toward goals and objectives evolving from the plan.

A specific approach to planning is strategic planning, a model conducive to the comprehensive concept of management presented in this chapter and Chapter Eighteen. It is an alternative to the quick fix orientation of popular management publications.

Strategic planning is a methodology that considers all environmental and organizational opportunities and constraints. (Keller, 1983; Simerly, 1987). Its purpose is to develop strategies that include both functional objectives and operational plans for the staff. There are five basic steps of strategic planning. First, define the mission of the organization (How do we serve our adult clientele?). Second, identify the strengths of the organization (What do we do well, and why?). Third, describe the present and potential clientele and their environment (What adult learners do we serve, could we serve, and how much do we know about them?). Fourth, consider both internal and external factors likely to affect the organization (What resources do we have or need from the organization and the community?). Fifth, develop an operational plan (What needs to be done in programming, staffing, and marketing, and how will it be financed?).

Planning is a balance governed by the organization's mission, programming, staffing, marketing, and financial capabilities (Strother and Klus, 1982). If too narrowly defined, a plan is a constraint on full effectiveness. If too broadly defined, a plan can sap organizational resources and ultimately fail. Planning is more valuable than the plan itself (Vicere, 1985). As President Eisenhower is reputed to have said, "A plan is nothing, but planning is everything."

Organizing. As plans are developed, they need to be carried out. To organize is to develop a system of roles and responsibilities and to delegate tasks and resources that provide maximum performance, clear expectations, and effective decision making.

The most successful organizations have a basic, uncomplicated organizational structure that allows for flexibility and rapid adaptation (Kilmann, 1984; Peters and Waterman, 1982). The intent is to align the ACE organizational resources in the strategic direction the organization plans to pursue, and in a manner that allows it to function effectively (Beder, 1984).

Evaluating. As the planning process progresses, and resources are organized, it is necessary to evaluate the process to ensure accomplishment of the goal and objectives. Evaluation provides information the ACE staff can use to compare actual activities with the intended plan, or, if deviations occur, to change the plan itself or to change the organization in order to achieve the plan.

The evaluation methods selected should be based on their ability to provide useful information and ease of implementation. The methods should also be as accurate as possible and should protect people's basic rights (Joint Committee on Standards for Educational Evaluation, 1981). Evaluations are conducted through data analysis, client (adult learner) interviews, and program audits. Most important, however, evaluations are best conducted through careful, continuous personal observation. A full discussion of evaluation is presented in Chapter Twenty.

To summarize, as illustrated in Figure 19.1 and as discussed above, the four general tasks of adult continuing education—programming, staffing, financing, and marketing—are carried out through the three managerial functions of planning, organizing, and evaluating. Both tasks and functions, however, are conducted within an organizational and community environment that, at the same time, helps and limits the managerial functions.

The Environments Within Which
Adult and Continuing Education Functions

All organizations operate within multiple environments that affect and are affected by the organization. The adult continuing education unit is itself a system consisting of many persons and parts. It is also a subsystem of at least three larger systems: the parent organization, the community at large, and the human learning system.

To maximize organizational effectiveness, ACE managers must continuously assess these multiple environments and adjust program plans and strategies to deal with environmental factors. These factors may affect resource availability, programming demands, and political support.

The Adult Continuing Education Unit. The most immediate environment demanding management sensitivity is the organizational climate of the adult continuing education unit. To improve the service and quality of the staff, it is essential that an efficient and supportive workplace be provided. The organizational climate has a tremendous influence on how people view their work and on how they carry it out. Effective programming and quality service will more likely result from a climate that emphasizes mutual respect and support.

The Parent Organization. Most adult and continuing education programs are part of a larger organization that does not have adult education as its primary purpose. Yet, the parent organization greatly influences the availability of resources and the stability of the ACE unit (Knox, 1981). It is essential that the ACE unit know as clearly as possible the culture and dynamics of the parent organization. It should understand its own role within it and should carry out its programs in a manner consistent with the overall purposes and values. Equally important are effective interpersonal relationships with people in the other units of the parent organization. If all these activities are successfully performed, adult continuing education will more readily obtain the required resources and produce the desired results.

The Community. When referring to the external environment, ACE staffs usually refer to the community in which they work. It includes adult learners, client organizations and groups, other providers, critics, and supporters. To derive usable information, a process is needed to scan appropriate aspects of the community. Environmental scanning provides the basis for identifying developing trends and events that affect adult continuing education. Major factors or forces in the community are categorized, and information under each classification is collected and analyzed. The data collected are integrated into the strategic plan, as discussed previously. Kotler and Fox (1985) have developed one data classification scheme which categorizes demographics, economics, natural resources, technology, politics, and culture. The appropriate categories selected by a specific ACE unit should be tested by the unit before using the collected data.

The Human Learning System. Finally, in addition to considering the general community, ACE managers need to consider the organization as a subsystem within a larger learning system. They need to recognize adult continuing education's role within the entire human learning system—family, community, church, workplace, media, schools, colleges, and universities (Niebuhr, 1984). As a subsystem within this communitywide learning system, relationships and interdependencies affect the role of adult and continuing education. These subsystems continuously interact formally and informally. In the 1990s it will become increasingly important for the manager to be aware of all these components and interactions.

Managing Adult and Continuing Education in the 1990s

The basic principles of management are applicable to managing any organization. What makes management a tremendous challenge is applying these principles to specific organizations, particularly in the coming decade and into the twenty-first century. The remainder of this chapter identifies and describes trends and issues confronting ACE managers in the 1990s. They are presented within the managerial tasks described above (refer to Figure 19.1).

Our nation and the world are evolving into a new era, variously called the information age, the service society, the computer age, and the new-age economy—all collectively noting the rapid shift to high technology, intense international competition, media-based communication, an increased involvement of minority populations, high individualism, and a loss of established social values and family stability. The primary educators of the human learning system in this new age are the workplace and the media (Niebuhr, 1984). The family, church, and community are minimal providers. Schools and colleges provide basic educational skills upon which human resource developers in organizations can further educate their employees. And the media are at a crossroads of either assuming their designated role as a contributor to learning, or continuing to provide programming that primarily entertains rather than educates the public.

It is within this learning environment of the 1990s that ACE managers will lead a staff that must provide courses and workshops of expected high quality. How will they do it? Returning to the managerial system, the functional activities within programming, marketing, financing, and staffing provide a framework for identifying key trends and issues confronting the ACE manager and guidelines for developing effective management practices.

Programming. ACE managers must be sensitive to the following trends that will strongly affect programming decisions in the 1990s:

- The workplace will be a learning center for the majority of the population. Organizations will assume increasing responsibility for making the work environment more learner centered.
- The competition for adult learners will be intense. Consulting groups, with sophisticated marketing, will be the dominant providers. These groups will possibly include persons and units in the same organization but separate from the ACE section.
- The increasing multicultural and heterogenous population will require highly diverse instruction at a variety of learning levels. This subject is extensively discussed in Part Three of this book.

Three critical programming issues confront the ACE manager in this decade:

- Planning will be increasingly difficult because of increasing needs, diverse populations, and continued limited resources.
- ACE must be adaptive to these needs and populations, but most ACE units will operate within an organization that is tradition-bound and usually not oriented to adult learning and programming.
- ACE will have increasing competition from providers outside and inside the organization.

The ACE unit must move from being education oriented toward being learner oriented. If the primary locus of learning is to be the workplace, adult continuing education must get out of the school and into the office, shop, training center, executive suite, and corporate retreat center. Programs must be more custom designed, more high tech and computer based, and more individualized.

The increasingly diverse adult population will require more involvement of adult learners in program planning. The time of ACE staffs fully knowing the needs of their adult clientele and paying lip service to involving learners in planning has passed. Advisory committees and dialogue and focus groups need to be more fully implemented.

Evaluation systems that define performance-based learning benefits to the learner-worker and productivity benefits to the organization should be developed. While specific results can be stated for skill-based training, specific results usually cannot be realistically isolated for managerial and behavioral learning (Gordon, 1987). Nevertheless, adult and continuing education programs must measure and articulate intended outcomes of all programs.

Staffing. Three primary trends will impact the staffing of ACE units and programs:

- The pool of qualified staff will increase as more people complete degrees in adult education.

- The ACE staff will be more knowledgeable about their jobs, which will require innovative leadership and management.
- While income will be important, other factors such as job satisfaction, adequate challenges, and self-leadership will be increasingly important.

From these trends, three staffing issues evolve for the ACE manager:

- Staff turnover will increase as skilled ACE professionals are pirated by businesses and consulting firms.
- The persistent culture and traditions of many parent organizations will continue to place the ACE unit and staff in marginal roles within the organization.
- These two issues, along with moderate salaries and heavier workloads, will cause increased stress and burnout of the ACE staff.

All managers must realize that "they are being paid for enabling people to do the work for which those people are being paid" (Drucker, 1980, p. 24). A critical role of managers is to assign persons where their full potential can be realized. The organization should be flexible enough to accommodate the strengths of the staff.

This orientation and commitment to the staff is a positive, motivational approach that will attract quality people to adult and continuing education—a field in which high salaries are not likely. Managers who are supportive and sensitive to the professional growth of their staffs will attract both up-and-coming professionals wanting to gain helpful experience and experienced professionals who are wanting a new challenge, but who are not needing a high salary. The strength or power of this kind of ACE manager lies within the individual performance and collective productivity of the staff. The manager serves the staff by facilitating their effectiveness, and they in turn serve the adult learner, the ultimate leader of the staff and manager.

Financing. Three trends will have impact upon the financing of ACE units:

- The population will continue to get older, and the demand for publicly funded recurring education (lifelong learning) will increase.
- However, the pressure for other services, such as crime and drug prevention, will continue to limit increased educational funding.
- Within education, persistent problems such as illiteracy and high dropout and low retention rates will demand more funds.

Three financial issues are of special interest to the ACE manager:

- Funds, in real dollars, for adult and continuing education will likely not increase for the forseeable future, and decreases are quite probable.
- The pressure for ACE to become financially self-sustaining will greatly increase.

- Most central administrations will maintain the perception of ACE as a "cash cow" that should return some profit to the general fund.

Many ACE programs should be revenue-producing, profit-making entrepreneurial enterprises. However, the term profit must be defined. So-called profit that is income above direct program expenses is not really profit but is instead a resource that covers normal, nonprogram expenses such as office and classroom space, utilities, and salaries. If profit is defined as revenue above all unit overhead expenses, then it should be a resource to be invested in future growth and development of the ACE program—not to be returned to a general fund. As Smith (1987, p. 83) states, "profit is the cost of staying in business. It is the 'seed corn' for tomorrow, the investment funds for the healthy continuing education program in the twenty-first century."

Marketing. Three trends in marketing will have impact upon the ACE program:

- Marketing is becoming more service driven and less product or sales driven as developed countries become more service oriented.
- Advertising will continue to be increasingly targeted and sophisticated, using all kinds of media and strategies.
- One of the best forms of advertising, word-of-mouth, will increase as networking increases.

Because of these trends, the ACE manager will need to deal with three basic issues:

- The need for marketing expertise will increase, but not the funds available to purchase it.
- Time will need to be spent by the entire staff in developing comprehensive marketing strategies with a high service focus.
- ACE units must wrestle with viewing learners as customers.

Rare is the ACE manager with adequate expertise in marketing. If the marketing plan previously discussed in this chapter is implemented in the extremely competitive adult learning market of the 1990s, it will require the full-time attention of a professional. Equally important will be the need to assign enough funds to carry out the marketing plan.

Acknowledging that such professional staff and funds will be difficult to get, ACE managers will need innovative marketing strategies and carefully developed plans maximizing the strengths of the ACE unit. The strongest programs and learning resources should be promoted, with focused marketing strategies and creative advertising geared to specific, receptive populations.

While a major emphasis of adult continuing education marketing should be on the working learner, marketing strategies aimed at other learners should continue. Serious consideration should be given to the so-called learning circle approach. Learners are consumers. They select and purchase those activities that they perceive will meet their individual needs. Designing learning activities for small groups, or learning circles, will enable adult and continuing education managers to tap a common core of general programs and learning resources. They can then design and market them to very specific populations—young professionals, retirees, professional associations, health clubs, county extension programs, service groups, and chambers of commerce. The possibilities are limited only by the manager's creativity.

The most effective marketing will be a quality program that is creatively learner centered. The successful adult and continuing education program will be a learning enterprise that the learners know and appreciate.

The trends having an impact on ACE managers in the 1990s and the issues they will have to address effectively and creatively are those that make being a manager the most difficult yet the most important position in adult and continuing education. If the trends are acknowledged, the issues aggressively addressed, and the tasks effectively executed, it is likely the manager will not reap the reward directly. The real reward of good management is the vicarious benefits—the pure pleasure of leading an effective and productive staff that is providing quality programming.

Summary: The Central Role of Management

This chapter provides a framework for the management of adult continuing education, the most important job in the field. Managers have the responsibility of making resources as productive as possible. They must effectively carry out the three managerial functions of planning, organizing, and evaluating within the four adult continuing education tasks of programming, staffing, financing, and marketing. The opportunities for ACE management in the 1990s are tremendous and challenging, but long-range program planning will be difficult. Developing succinct programs for specific learners will be more useful if they are guided by carefully designed general goals and by operational objectives of the ACE organization.

The following ten guidelines, which ACE managers should consider, illustrate and summarize the strategies that have been stressed in this chapter.

1. Identify clearly the "business" the parent organization is in and the unique strengths adult continuing education brings to this business.
2. Have a good understanding of how continuing adult education is perceived by the organization and of the relationships between the adult continuing education program and the other program areas of the organization.
3. Accept the facts that additional funds from the parent organization will not increase and that the ACE unit will be required to generate more of their own funds.
4. Consider profit, be it grant funds or fees, as a source of funds for investment in the future of adult continuing education.

5. View most adult continuing education programs as entrepreneurial activities providing quality, custom-designed programming to clearly identified populations.
6. Do less planning based solely on today's trends. Rather, develop strategies that identify and use the opportunities of tomorrow.
7. Actively pursue programmatic and consultative relationships with outside organizations, maximizing the unique strengths the adult continuing education unit can provide.
8. In consultation with the staff, develop a personal and professional plan for everyone—professional staff, clerical staff, part-time staff, and volunteers—that facilitates growth and productivity.
9. Develop a plan for self-development that includes futures thinking, strategic planning, high tech applications in adult and continuing education, and future studies.
10. Finally, learn to give up leadership. Encourage people to be their own leaders. Adopt the Zen concept that one learns in order to do better what one already knows how to do well.

References

Apps, J. W. *Problems in Continuing Education.* New York: McGraw-Hill, 1979.

Beder, H. W. (ed.). *Realizing the Potential of Interorganizational Cooperation.* New Directions for Continuing Education, no. 23. San Francisco: Jossey-Bass, 1984.

Churchman, C. W. *The Systems Approach.* New York: Dell, 1968.

Drucker, P. *Managing In Turbulent Times.* New York: Harper & Row, 1980.

Freedman, L. *Quality in Continuing Education.* San Francisco: Jossey-Bass, 1987.

Gordon, J. "Romancing the Bottom Line." *Training,* 1987, *24* (6), 31–42.

Joint Committee on Standards for Educational Evaluation. *Standards for Evaluations of Educational Programs, Projects and Materials.* New York: McGraw-Hill, 1981.

Kast, F. E., and Rosenzweig, J. E. *Organization and Management.* (3rd ed.) New York: McGraw-Hill, 1984.

Katz, D., and Kahn, R. *The Social Psychology of Organizations.* (2nd ed.) New York: Wiley, 1978.

Keller, G. *Academic Strategy: The Management Revolution in American Higher Education.* Baltimore, Md.: Johns Hopkins University Press, 1983.

Kilmann, R. H. *Beyond the Quick Fix: Managing Five Tracks to Organizational Success.* San Francisco: Jossey-Bass, 1984.

Knox, A. B. "The Continuing Education Agency and Its Parent Organization." In J. C. Votruba (ed.), *Strengthening Internal Support for Continuing Education.* New Directions for Continuing Education, no. 9. San Francisco: Jossey-Bass, 1981.

Knox, A. B. *Leadership Strategies for Meeting New Challenges.* New Directions for Continuing Education, no. 13. San Francisco: Jossey-Bass, 1982.

Knox, A. B. "Strengthening Leadership of Continuing Higher Education." *Continuum,* 1985, *49* (2), 135–139.

Kotler, P. *Marketing for Nonprofit Organizations.* Englewood Cliffs, N.J.: Prentice-Hall, 1982.

Kotler, P., and Fox, K. *Strategic Marketing for Educational Institutions.* Englewood Cliffs, N.J.: Prentice-Hall, 1985.

Langerman, P. D., and Smith D. H. (eds.). *Managing Adult and Continuing Education Programs and Staff.* Washington, D.C.: American Association for Adult and Continuing Education, 1979.

McCorkle, C. O., Jr., and Archibald, S. O. *Management and Leadership in Higher Education.* San Francisco: Jossey-Bass, 1982.

Matkin, G. W. *Effective Budgeting in Continuing Education.* San Francisco: Jossey-Bass, 1985.

Niebuhr, H., Jr. *Revitalizing American Learning.* Belmont, Calif.: Wadsworth, 1984.

Offerman, M. J. "Matching Programmatic Emphases to the Parent Organization's Values." In R. G. Simerly (ed.), *Strategic Planning and Leadership in Continuing Education.* San Francisco: Jossey-Bass, 1987.

Peters, T. J., and Waterman, R. H., Jr. *In Search of Excellence: Lessons from America's Best-Run Companies.* New York: Harper & Row, 1982.

Simerly, R. G. (ed.). *Strategic Planning and Leadership in Continuing Education.* San Francisco: Jossey-Bass, 1987.

Smith, D. H. "Changing Practices in Continuing Education Management." In R. G. Brockett (ed.), *Continuing Education in the Year 2000.* New Directions for Continuing Education, no. 36. San Francisco: Jossey-Bass, 1987.

Strother, G. B., and Klus, J. P. *Administration of Continuing Education.* Belmont, Calif.: Wadsworth, 1982.

Vicere, A. A. "Creating Order from the Chaos: Academic Integrity in Continuing Professional Education." *Adult Education Quarterly,* 1985, *35* (4), 229–236.

Walshok, M. L. "Developing a Strategic Marketing Plan." In R. G. Simerly (ed.), *Strategic Planning and Leadership in Continuing Education.* San Francisco: Jossey-Bass, 1987.

20

The Evaluation
of Adult and
Continuing Education

Sara M. Steele

   The literature of program evaluation has changed substantially since
the 1950s when the Adult Education Association of the U.S.A. published
a monograph that defined the term *evaluation* as measurement of the attainment of objectives. Legislation requiring evaluation of federally funded social
programs in the 1960s found that definition of evaluation too limited.

Usable Evaluation

   One of the greatest changes in evaluation since the 1950s has been
the emphasis on useful evaluation. Evaluation should use information in
such a way that the process improves adult education programs. The concept of *usefulness* is complex and illusive. Usefulness can be visible or invisible, and it can be specific or pervasive (Glaser, Abelson, and Garrison, 1983).
It can challenge, clarify, or reinforce a rationale and a general understanding, or it can directly influence decisions and action. Regardless of the form
usefulness takes, use-governed evaluation requires new thinking about evaluating adult education programs. It turns evaluation into a dynamic, positive
force for enhancing programs and for increasing understanding of effective
education of adults rather than turning it into a sacred cow, a product for
export, or an amulet worn to ward off evil spirits.
   The field of professional program evaluation is diverse, still growing,
and still maturing (Cronbach and others, 1980; Worthen and Sanders, 1987).
Today, adult educators choose selectively from evaluation literature developed
for other educational and social programs. But the concepts and approaches

chosen must be consistent with adult education philosophy and beliefs. One of the major issues today is whether adult educators' beliefs and practices in regard to evaluation really are consistent with their beliefs about adult education (Apps, 1985). And other issues emerge as we go beyond empirical research traditions. This chapter stresses going beyond tradition into evaluation approaches that best fit adult and continuing education. It will briefly review the following areas: multiple perspectives, needs, and models; mental and social process; sound grounding in adult education; definitions of successful programming; multiple methods; documenting versus measuring; multiple versus single reality; and broader standards for evaluation.

Multiple Perspectives, Needs, and Models

Administrators, coordinators, teachers, and program participants all can benefit from evaluation. However, frustration results when each expects something different from the same evaluation. Administrators need evaluations that summarize quality, results, and value of total programs carried out by several teachers and coordinators (Knox, 1969). Federal and state administrators need information that summarizes programs as carried out in many locations. Teachers are primarily interested in the quality and results of their own work (Deshler, 1984; Grotelueschen, 1980), and participants are primarily interested in evaluation that helps them understand their progress in relation to that of others and to that which is expected.

Evaluation literature usually takes the administrator's side and emphasizes evaluation for accountability. Managerial evaluation examines the use of resources and the amount of yield for the resource investment. Its strong emphasis on management by objectives assumes that the only important consideration is whether the program did what it said it would. Managerial evaluation ignores the question of whether the original objectives were important. Evaluation has been so tightly tied to management that it is hard to imagine other perspectives.

Adult education is a leader among other social fields in the use of a consumer perspective. Program examination often concerns qualities important to the consumer—value for time and money invested, the amount of help received, whether the program was stimulating, and whether participating was pleasant.

By contrast, because of their accountability responsibilities, adult educators are especially interested in evaluation that results in enhanced programs and in increased professional competence. Limited resources for evaluation dictate that the greatest possible value must be secured from any investment in evaluation. Although the distinction between the concepts of *formative evaluation* as evaluating while a program is in process to improve the program and *summative evaluation* as evaluating the completed program for accountability has blurred over the past twenty years, summative evaluation is still more relevant to accountability. While formative evaluation concentrates on program improvement, summative evaluation is designed (1) to account for program decisions and investments, (2) to identify ways to enhance future offerings, and (3) to determine further needs.

Although evaluation models usually have little relationship to perspectives or needs, more than fifty models of program evaluation have emerged and have gained some acceptance. Hunting for the one perfect model of program evaluation is like hunting for the pot of gold at the end of the rainbow. Most models show relationships rather than the ideal way to do evaluation, and many of the models help give us a better understanding of programs rather than a better understanding of evaluation (Madous, Scriven, and Stufflebeam, 1983). Adult educators should learn from models but not be limited to any one.

Mental and Social Process

Traditionally, evaluation is viewed as a technical process of collecting and statistically analyzing data. But usable evaluation is also a process of interpreting data and forming conclusions and recommendations. Whether the evaluation is mental reflection or a five-year study, evaluation of adult education programs goes beyond technical data manipulation. Evaluation requires (1) thinking skills, (2) social skills, (3) management skills, and (4) communication and teaching skills.

Thinking Skills. Creative thinking, critical thinking, and reasoning are essential in using evaluative information. Creativity and vision are needed for maximum understanding of what has occurred and what needs to occur. Critical thinking tests those creative ideas for accuracy and practicality. Reasoning underlies both; logical relationships must be clear. Although these three mental skills are central, evaluation also requires many other mental skills, such as discrimination, comparison, organization, synthesis, and analysis (Brookfield, 1987; Patton, 1981).

Social Skills. The evaluator must be skilled in relating to people at all stages of the evaluation—from working with people in designing the evaluation to skillfully stimulating action as a result of the evaluation. Evaluators need skills in listening, group processes, and influencing others.

Adult educators also need to understand how society and groups within society define and influence evaluation. For example, society, government, and professional groups are the entities that operationally define the terms *evaluation* and *program success.* Criteria, critical questions, and value traits, as well as conclusions, recommendations, and implications are developed by people, and since both programs and evaluations occur in social settings, those settings need to be understood.

Management Skills. Management requires both mental and social skills. Even the simplest reflective evaluation involves controlling time and concentrating attention. Formal evaluation requires careful use of limited resources. In particular, time should be treated as a scarce commodity and a time schedule maintained in order for the results of the evaluation to reach users at the best possible time. Schedules must include time for thinking and discussing and time for interpreting, communicating, and facilitating use of the evaluation.

Communication and Teaching Skills. Although some evaluations are used only by those doing the evaluation, most (including reports to administrators) require skillful and timely communication. Larger evaluations must be communicated in such a way that people understand and act upon recommendations (Boyle, 1981). Adult education principles are involved. For example, the communication must fit the potential user's preferred means of securing information (written, oral, graphic, anecdotal, statistical, or testimonial), and it must fit his or her information processing style. The user should set the bounds for the amount of data collected and the kind of analysis used.

Some Grounding in Adult Education

The evaluator must have a sound background in adult learning and in program development. Knowing standard evaluation procedures is not enough. Some believe that any evaluator who is well trained in data procedures can evaluate any program regardless of his or her background in the specific program. But when the critical component is providing information that is meaningful to the user, the evaluator must know the standards of quality and success in the particular field. Similarly, each adult educator needs an evaluative framework of beliefs about what constitutes successful, high quality programs and about the kind and extent of results to be expected. This framework, drawn from research, experts, and personal experience, establishes a base for all evaluative activities. (Chapters in the first section of this handbook suggest content for such a framework.) Evaluators need a framework for understanding results of adult education programs and for understanding the theory that relates input and process to results in different contexts.

Evaluators designing programs, and those evaluating, need to understand categories of results and relationships among those categories (Bennett, 1975; Bloom and others, 1956). Most expected outcomes can be categorized into general groups. The classification indicates how best to document or to measure the results. For example, gain in knowledge is examined by tests, but change in attitude is measured by attitude scales. The relationship of one category to another also needs to be clearly identified. The following is an example of a simple classification system.

Level 1: Learning. The most frequent categories of results facilitated by adult educators include (1) cognitive (knowledge) gains, (2) affective (attitude and value) changes, (3) skill development (physical, social, and mental), and (4) conative changes (changes in aspiration). Often more than one kind of learning is involved. For example, in order to build skill, one must know what to do, how to do it, and when to do it. Whether one retains and applies knowledge often has an affective component related to the strength with which one believes the information.

Level 2: Action. Some programs have action objectives: adopting a new practice or taking part in some form of social action. For that action to occur, the learner has to have internalized appropriate information, to have built a strong belief in the value of the action, to have developed the skills necessary, and to have seen the action as fitting his or her aspirations. A lack in any one of the learning categories is likely to result in no action or in incomplete or inaccurate action.

Level 3. Effects. Some programs have goals that identify the kind of result that will occur because program participants take action. For example, some programs have goals of changing professional practice or improving net income. These goals cannot be achieved unless the learning that makes possible the necessary action has already occurred.

Level 4: Value. A few programs have goals from which others derive value because of the actions of the program participants. For example, some programs have goals of improving communities or the economy. Those programs are directed toward providing the kind of learning opportunities needed to bring about the action and the effects that are of value to society in general.

The evaluator who has a categorization system such as this, and who understands relationships, is able to analyze the evaluation task more efficiently and to make better decisions about evidence.

Indicators and patterns help us assess complex phenomena. Specific learning changes can be examined directly, but improving generalizable ability (such as management or leadership) and ascertaining effects of action are much more complex. In some instances it is not feasible to examine the broad goal other than by looking at changes that indicate the broad goal was accomplished. Such indicators are specific behaviors accepted as evidence. For example, if an assertiveness program includes a general objective such as standing up for oneself firmly and tactfully, the evaluator must decide upon indicators that demonstrate this objective has been reached.

Indicators of a broad goal should be arranged in a pattern that shows the relationship of each indicator to the broader goal. Specific behavioral objectives also need to be arranged in patterns that show the larger objective attained through specific behaviors. For example, ten specific objectives, each relating to knowing a part of a gasoline engine, have the most meaning when the student can see how they relate to each other, thereby providing a more complete understanding of that engine. Without such patterning, indicators and specific behavioral objectives look like a bunch of pick-up sticks.

The evaluator also needs a thorough knowledge of program theory, including (1) adult education principles that make a program meaningful and relevant to adults, (2) factors that enhance or inhibit learning and use of learning, and (3) elements needed in a program to achieve the expected results (Bickman, 1987). For example, theory states that lecturing usually does little to increase students' skill. Demonstration helps. But skill is developed most efficiently when each student has sufficient time to practice the skill in a supportive learning setting.

The evaluator needs a clear picture of CIPP relationships. CIPP stands for context, input, process, and product. It was first proposed as a modeling of four basic areas of programmatic decisions, and it identifies four key aspects of programs that should be considered singularly and in relation to each other. An evaluation may focus on any one of the four arenas, but the other three need to be described to create greater understanding.

Before CIPP, many adult educators evaluated only process or results (product) and failed to relate the two. The addition of input (amount of time and other resources) and context greatly increases understanding. An understanding of expected (program theory) relationships between the amount and kind of input and the process within a context is important in understanding the results of a program. For example, the amount of time (input) and kind of teaching approaches (process) needed to facilitate learning of dropouts (context) may be quite different from the input and process needed in continuing education of professionals.

The process of so-called evaluability assessment examines these relationships before starting an evaluation. Such an assessment determines whether the program can be evaluated adequately by examining the theory upon which the program is built and by determining (1) whether the program has been carried out as planned and what changes must be taken into consideration in the evaluation, (2) whether stakeholders agree on the purpose of the program and of the evaluation, (3) whether the program design is likely to yield the results expected, and (4) whether there is likely to be sufficient use of evaluation findings to justify the cost. The evaluator gains a much better understanding of the program and of the context of the evaluation by doing an evaluability assessment.

Definitions of Successful Programming

Evaluation needs to consider much more than the attainment of objectives. Some people would dispute this assertion, but others long ago accepted attainment of objectives as an important criterion against which adult education programs are judged—although they also agree that much more needs to be considered.

Matrix Model for Examining Results. One of the first changes to come out of evaluation in the 1960s was the recognition that evaluation needs to look for both expected results (objectives) and unexpected results and that evaluation also needs to look for both positive results and negative results. In the matrix model, a matrix is formed where expected or unexpected results are juxtaposed with positive and negative results, thus providing a four-cell categorization.

Definitions of Success Should Match Philosophy. Adult education includes diverse purposes and philosophies, and it is not nearly as cohesive as most other fields of education, so it is especially important in adult education to relate evaluation design and procedures to the purpose and philosophy of the program. Definitions of success must be compatible with philosophy.

Need Identification and Problem Solving. Those adult education programs that emphasize need identification and community or societal problem solving should be evaluated on how well the program helps meet needs or solve problems. The evaluation should go beyond specific results and should compare the results to the need or problem that prompted initiation of the program.

Learner-Centered Programs. If a program is learner centered, the evaluation should identify each learner's objectives and the extent to which each was helped to meet his or her objectives. The learner's freedom to accept or reject learning should be considered in interpreting data about results.

Adult Development. When agencies or adult educators believe all programs, regardless of topic, should help adults develop generalizable skills, such as improved communication, management, or reasoning, program evaluations should be based on the extent to which they help participants develop such skills. If the emphasis is on relating specifics to broader areas of knowledge, programs should be evaluated on the learners' ability to relate as well as on the specifics—for example, not just knowing the basic food groups but understanding nutrition's role in health.

Self-Knowledge. When an agency or adult educator believes education should help adults better understand themselves, the program should be evaluated on the extent to which understanding is increased. Most content knowledge fosters self-understanding as well as understanding of the external world. For example, a short course on poetry may open discussion about emotion through which the participants better understand their own emotions.

To Cope or to Challenge. Some programs aim at helping people cope with barriers in their lives; others aim at helping them challenge and eliminate such barriers. For example, the definition of success for a consciousness raising program might be quite different than that of success for a management-mandated training program.

Issues. Philosophies also differ in terms of the educator's responsibility for helping adults identify and deal with issues. An agricultural educator can simply teach how to apply pesticides safely, or he or she can also point out issues regarding the use of pesticides. If a program focuses on issues, it should be evaluated in terms of how well people understand and take appropriate action in issue areas rather than on traditional learning criteria.

Learning and Information Processing Styles. If the agency or adult educator believes there are differences in how adults learn and in how they process information, the program should be evaluated to determine whether it has facilitated different learning and information processing styles.

Source of Knowledge. Definitions of success also need to be consistent with views of the appropriate knowledge base for the program. Some agencies or adult educators view the knowledge base as resting solely with the teacher. He or she is always teaching new material to learners. Others feel the role of the teacher is to help the student integrate some new knowledge into what the individual already knows. Other programs concentrate on helping the learner activate and apply what he or she already knows—for example, programs dealing with very difficult behavior like controlling weight, or giving up smoking or substance abuse. Standards of success for a program designed as transformational education should differ from the evaluation of a program designed for dissemination.

Evaluation should examine the program within its existing purpose and philosophy and examine whether that purpose and that philosophy are appropriate.

Multiple Methods

There is no one best way to do evaluation, nor is there any one best concept of program evaluation. Evaluation needs to encompass diverse activities and to be designed to fit specific users and evaluation situations. Evaluation includes four major kinds of activities: (1) program reviews, (2) evaluative studies, (3) continuous monitoring, and (4) reflection on experience. Each of these activities, if used appropriately, can have considerable value in adult education.

Reviews. Program reviews are sometimes called program assessment or accreditation. They involve people in judging a program, and they emphasize conclusions and recommendations based on accurate information.

The review process can vary considerably. The review may be done by professionals or by representative clientele. Some adult education programs are subject to periodic reviews by accrediting agencies; others are reviewed by their advisory groups. Some reviews require extensive self-study prior to meeting the reviewers. Others arrange for early involvement of reviewers who spend considerable time talking with program participants and personnel.

Studies. Studies look at a program at one or two points in time. Evaluation studies use applied research techniques including a review of previous studies, a design suited to the evaluation's purpose, data collection and analysis, and a summary. Some evaluative studies simply provide information. Others form conclusions and recommendations. Evaluation studies differ from research in that they are designed to answer immediate questions about programs, regardless of whether those answers contribute new knowledge to a discipline.

Continuous Monitoring. Management information systems (MIS) permit adult educators to continuously monitor progress. Such systems include enrollment, attendance, and budget components. End-of-meeting reactions and result follow-ups can be built into the system. Well-designed systems document trends, compare the same program with different clientele, and compare different programs with the same clientele.

Reflection on Experience. Probably the evaluative activity most important to the program participant, teacher, and program coordinator is reflection on experience (Schön, 1987). This is the way most people evaluate what they have given and what they have received from a program. End-of-meeting reaction sheets are the tools most often used in this activity to try to capture the extent to which program participants value the experience they have had. Often ignored by the literature of evaluation, reflection on practice is gaining new respect from some researchers.

Focusing an Evaluation

The four major approaches to evaluation are not mutually exclusive alternatives. None is automatically better than the others. Adult educators need to use all four wisely in a complete system. Most of the approaches can be used with any of the following foci: proof of effect, judgment against criteria, critical questions, and valuing.

Proof of effect is the oldest way of focusing an evaluation. Its objective is to prove that results are caused by the program rather than by chance. Social science researchers use the traditional laboratory science mode of testing causality—experiment and control groups, before and after measurements, statistical analysis—to test whether a particular program, a treatment, causes an effect. This construct does not fit adult education very well because (1) it assumes that all people will do exactly the same thing as a result of the treatment—an assumption diametrically opposed to adult educators' beliefs in individual differences; (2) it assumes that the participants can be kept isolated from sources other than the treatment; and (3) it assumes that treatment is randomly given or denied (Suchman, 1967). The most serious limitation, however, is that the proof-of-effect approach often does not look at the actual results to examine whether they are sufficient.

Judgments against criteria, exemplified by so-called criteria-focused evaluation, is probably the second most traditional approach to evaluation. It compares what is with what should be. What should be is expressed in terms of conceptual criteria and levels of expected performance. This focus is illustrated in accreditation, personnel evaluation, and behavioral objectives. Certain qualities or levels of performance are set, and the program is compared to those standards and levels. The emphasis is excellence rather than causality. Criteria and standards codify a group's view of which qualities are most important and most valuable. Criteria help administrators, teachers, and students understand each other's beliefs about good programs. But the focus on criteria is a static approach to evaluation in that the criteria usually are difficult to change.

Focusing on critical questions is a much more dynamic approach. The evaluation focuses on those questions that stakeholders—funders, administrators, program personnel, or participants—see as being most important at the particular time. For example, funders often ask questions that have little to do with either proof of causality or excellence. They may ask about duplication with other agencies, the proportion of the target clientele reached, or the difference it would make if the program were no longer funded.

Some of their questions merely need a descriptive response, but others seek a comparative or evaluative answer. This critical-questions approach is more dynamic because the questions keep changing.

Valuing is the least traditional of the evaluation foci even though evaluators often define the term *evaluation* as determining worth. Few evaluations examine the kind and amount of economic, social, psychological, or aesthetic value of the results of programs or the percentage of those eligible who secure this value. Research-driven evaluators have viewed valuing as subjective and inappropriate. Using a valuing approach is often difficult because different people value the same thing differently.

Increasing proficiency in each of the four main foci can help adult educators to improve their program effectiveness as well as to protect their programs and positions through good accounting.

Documenting Versus Measuring; Multiple Reality Versus Single Reality

All evaluation requires careful examination of evidence, but that evidence may take many forms. Issues about the processes of gathering and examining evidence are most likely to arise when new concepts challenge the old. In the case of evaluation, the traditional approach to evidence has been measurement; and measurement has traditionally taken the quantitative approach (or single approach) to reality. Moreover, evaluation studies often focus on only one perspective and one information source.

Measurement or Documentation. Educational evaluation traditionally has emphasized the writing of measurable objectives. Helpful as this approach may be, both in learning and in evaluating, it becomes an issue if it leads teachers to abandon any area or goal that cannot be easily measured. Some of the most important outcomes—mental skills, aesthetic appreciation, character building, developing psychological strength and mental health—are very difficult to measure. Such measurement often require complex research instruments that take so much time they disrupt the adult education process.

Traits that cannot be easily measured often can be documented by description and testimony. People can describe what they believe. Simulations can be developed or actual situations observed in which people have the opportunity to demonstrate growth in relation to the less tangible goal. For example, appreciating the beauty of a sunset can be documented through an individual's description of that sunset, but such appreciation usually cannot be measured in a quantified way. Both measurement and documentation are important in evaluation (Guba and Lincoln, 1981; Patton, 1980; Smith, 1981; Williams, 1986).

Multiple Realities. Traditional quantitative approaches are based on one reality, and data collection requires participants to fit that reality. For example, in a quantitative approach, each step on a rating scale is carefully defined in an attempt to ensure that every participant defines each rating in exactly the same way. Qualitative approaches, on the other hand, accept multiple realities and view reality as personal perception (Bogdan and Taylor, 1975). Qualitative rating scales may use a term like *a lot* for the top of the rating scale and not define it. It is irrelevant that a lot for one person is a little for another. The relevant fact is that some people found the program a lot of help according to their own perception.

Qualitative approaches attempt to understand each response in terms of the individual's own perception and life situation; such approaches are consistent with adult educators' beliefs in individual differences. Qualitative approaches include case studies, historical examinations, perceptual data (how much have you gained?) and ethnographic studies. They usually result in rich descriptions and verbal information. However, even numerical data can be used in a qualitative way when they examine ranges and differences in responses. Quantitative approaches using numeric data, on the other hand, focus on central tendency and usually are numeric, and these methods may be helpful in examining the extent of similarity in the realities of those involved in a program.

Triangulation. Assuming there is a fixed limit on time or money resources to invest in a particular evaluative study, should the evaluator invest all of those resources in collecting and analyzing data according to one particular design? Or should two or three approaches be used? For example, should an evaluator both study case examples and complete a structured survey? Information about the same program secured through two or more independent means often provides better understanding and sounder conclusions than one large study. In the same fashion, viewing a program or its results from several perspectives—those of students, those of prospective employers, and those of community leaders—gives a better understanding of the value of the program.

Broader Standards for Evaluation

One of the greatest challenges for the research-trained evaluator is that of establishing appropriate definitions of quality in user-focused evaluation. The very process of this kind of evaluation precludes some of the previously described actions believed to increase objectivity. In particular, the evaluator can no longer remain remote from the program.

In order for an evaluation to be accepted, the users must have trust in both the evaluation and the evaluator. Usually staff are more likely to trust and use evaluations done by someone in their own agency or someone who they are sure thoroughly understands their situation. By contrast, funders usually trust someone not directly involved in the program. Agencies deal with this difference by having one evaluator monitor the other—either by having someone who is truly conversant with the program complete the evaluation and then having outside experts review the plans, process, and conclusions for objectivity, or by having an outsider complete the evaluation and then having it reviewed by an inside group.

Partially to increase trust and partially to increase the possibility of action, many recommend that an evaluator work closely with program personnel and participants in designing and carrying out evaluation. The so-called stakeholder approach prescribes that a variety of people be consulted in the design of an evaluaion as well as in the interpretation of findings and the development of conclusions (Bryk, 1983). Participatory evaluation requires that both program personnel and program participants be involved throughout the evaluation process and that they have considerable control of that process (American Council of Voluntary Agencies for Foreign Service, 1983). Again, adult education processes must be consistent. If an agency or adult educator believes strongly that local people should be involved in planning a program, the same people should be equally involved in summative evaluation.

Scientific standards such as validity and reliability used to be the only standards applied to evaluation. Now utility standards are as important as, or more important than, scientific standards. Timeliness, relevance, understandability, credibility, and usefulness determine whether an evaluation will be used. In 1980, professional evaluator groups proposed thirty criteria for high quality evaluation. The criteria were grouped under the following headings: utility standards, feasibility standards, proprietary standards, and accuracy standards (Joint Committee on Standards for Educational Evaluation, 1980). Trade-off and balancing are often needed in determining the degree to which each criterion can be met in the same evaluative activity.

Summary

The last twenty years have shown considerable growth in general understanding of the use of evaluation as a less threatening, more valuable tool in improved programming. Issues like those identified in this chapter need to be analyzed and debated in the process of finding the most useful ways of evaluating adult and continuing education programs. It is not sufficient to follow tradition blindly or to copy new approaches used in other social programs. Adult education practitioners can draw both from tradition and from other programs, but they must be sure that evaluation is consistent with their program philosophy and theory. As adult educators, they need to be more assertive in sharing their unique views of evaluation and their ways of ensuring evaluation is used by those in other educational and social fields. Adult educators are in the best position to demonstrate that an evaluator can be an educator.

References

American Council of Voluntary Agencies for Foreign Service. *Evaluation Sourcebook.* New York: American Council of Voluntary Agencies for Foreign Service, 1983.

Apps, J. W. *Improving Practice in Continuing Education.* San Francisco: Jossey-Bass, 1985.

Bennett, C. "Up the Hierarchy." *Journal of Extension.* 1975, *13*, 7–12.

Bickman, L. (ed.). *Using Program Theory in Evaluation.* New Directions for Program Evaluation, no. 33. San Francisco: Jossey-Bass, 1987.

Bloom, B. S., and others. "Taxonomy of Educational Objectives." In B. S. Bloom (ed.), *Handbook I: Cognitive Domain.* New York: McKay, 1956.

Bogdan, R. C., and Taylor, S. J. *Introduction to Qualitative Research Methods: A Phenomenological Approach to the Social Sciences.* New York: Wiley, 1975.

Boyle, P. G. *Planning Better Programs.* New York: McGraw-Hill, 1981.

Brookfield, S. D. *Developing Critical Thinkers.* San Francisco: Jossey-Bass, 1987.

Bryk, A. A. (ed.). *Stakeholder-Based Evaluations.* New Directions for Program Evaluation, no. 17. San Francisco: Jossey-Bass, 1983.

Cronbach, L. J., and others. *Toward Reform of Program Evaluation.* San Francisco: Jossey-Bass, 1980.

Deshler, D. (ed.). *Evaluation for Program Improvement.* San Francisco: Jossey-Bass, 1984.

Glaser, E. M., Abelson, H. H., and Garrison, K. N. *Putting Knowlege to Use.* San Francisco: Jossey-Bass, 1983.

Grotelueschen, A. B. "Program Evaluation." In A. B. Knox and Associates, *Developing, Administering, and Evaluating Adult Education.* San Francisco: Jossey-Bass, 1980.

Guba, E. G., and Lincoln, Y. S. *Effective Evaluation.* San Francisco: Jossey-Bass, 1981.

Joint Committee on Standards for Educational Evaluation. *Standards for Evaluations of Educational Programs, Projects, and Materials.* New York: McGraw-Hill, 1980.

Knox, A. B. *Continuous Program Evaluation.* National Association for Public School Adult Education, 1969.

Madaus, G. F., Scriven, M., and Stufflebeam, D. L. *Evaluation Models: Viewpoints on Educational and Human Services Evaluation.* Boston: Kluwer-Nijhoff, 1983.

Patton, M. Q. *Qualitative Evaluation Methods.* Beverly Hills, Calif.: Sage, 1980.

Patton, M. Q. *Creative Evaluation.* Beverly Hills, Calif.: Sage, 1981.

Schön, D. A. *Educating the Reflective Practitioner.* San Francisco: Jossey-Bass, 1987.

Smith, N. L. *New Techniques for Evaluation.* Beverly Hills, Calif.: Sage, 1981.

Suchman, E. A. *Evaluation Research.* Beverly Hills, Calif.: Sage, 1967.

Williams, D. (ed.). *Naturalistic Evaluation.* San Francisco: Jossey-Bass, 1986.

Worthen, B. R., and Sanders, J. R. *Educational Evaluation.* New York: Longman, 1987.

Part 3

Major Providers of Educational Programs for Adults

The staggering number of diverse institutions and organizations that sponsor educational programs for adults mystifies observers outside the field and occasionally frustrates those in the system itself. Some educators have called for coordination of these efforts at the national level to ensure equal access to these opportunities, to account for effective use of public funds, and to provide quality service. Others maintain that there is no guarantee that a unified system will ensure these factors are accounted for and that such a system may in fact rob the field of its vitality and responsiveness.

For whatever reason, a single system of adult education does not exist in North America. Rather, providers of adult education range from proprietary schools to the armed forces, to museums, to employers. The ability to grasp the span of institutions, agencies, and organizations that offer adult learning opportunities necessitates having some sort of organizing framework—a template that can be placed upon the field of adult education. Many such frameworks have been proposed. The first chapter in this section of the handbook reviews the frameworks that have been developed over the past years and introduces a new one that takes into account the present situation in adult education.

The first of four categories in the framework suggested by Apps in Chapter Twenty-One includes those agencies and institutions that are fully or partially tax supported. These include public schools and community adult education, four-year colleges and universities, community and technical schools, cooperative extension, libraries and museums, state and federal public educational agencies, armed forces, and correctional facilities. Part

Three of the handbook contains a chapter on each of these providers.

A second category in Apps's framework is that of nonprofit, self-supporting agencies and institutions. Religious institutions fall under this classification. The third category of providers includes those that are for profit. Information has become a commodity that can be bought and sold; hence we see a proliferation of for-profit providers. Proprietary schools and the educational programs of business and industry fall into this category. It is estimated, in fact, that more money is spent on education in business and industry than is spent in the public school system. Part Three concludes with chapters on proprietary schools and on business and industry.

The fourth category of providers suggested by Apps in Chapter Twenty-One is that of nonorganized learning opportunities such as those found in traveling, in recreational and leisure-time activities, and in the family setting.

Whether tax supported, nonprofit, or for profit, providers of adult education share some of the same concerns. Delivering quality programs, meeting the needs of adult learners, guaranteeing access by various segments of the adult population, determining a balance between collaboration and competition, and so on, are issues that cut across the diversity of delivery systems in the field. These and other issues are discussed in the individual chapters in Part Four.

21

Providers of Adult and Continuing Education: A Framework

Jerold W. Apps

Developing a framework for understanding adult education is no easy task. Those trying to describe adult education as a field of educational activity often have been frustrated. Lyman Bryson (1936, p. 13) said, "[Adult education] has always been carried on by a wide variety of agencies, for a variety of purposes, and with many different kinds of people. For this reason, some critics have called it formless and without direction."

More than fifty years after Bryson wrote those words, adult education continues to be called, at least by some critics, formless and without direction.

Historical Categories

Bryson traces adult education in the United States to four major providers: lyceums, chautauquas, women's clubs, and correspondence schools. Lyceums, a system of public lectures, began in 1826 in Massachusetts. Chautauquas started in 1874, at Chautauqua Lake, New York, and soon spread throughout the country. They included programs on music, art, drama, and current problems. Chautauquas also included study groups and correspondence study.

Women's clubs, which started in the 1870s, included discussion groups and led to the formation of the League of Women Voters, the American Association of University Women, and business and professional women's clubs.

Correspondence schools, a part of formal education in Europe at least a generation before coming to America, formally started in this country in 1873 with the formation of the Society to Encourage Studies at Home (Bryson, 1936).

In 1936, Bryson said the agencies of adult education were: (1) the public schools, (2) national public programs including agricultural extension and government vocational classes resulting from the Smith-Hughes Act of 1917, (3) federal emergency programs such as the Civilian Conservation Corps, (4) colleges and universities including extension and alumni programs, (5) libraries, (6) museums, (7) religious bodies, (8) workers' groups, and (9) parent-teacher groups.

In the 1948 *Handbook of Adult Education* (Ely, 1948), the authors said adult education was organized around six areas of interest activity and need: (1) vocational efficiency (including educational activity of corporations, private correspondence schools, and hospitals), (2) economic understanding (labor-management, worker's, and consumer education), (3) civic participation and responsibility (immigrant education, education for Native Americans, and safety education), (4) better human relations and community improvement (cooperative extension and intercultural education), (5) group interest (education for later maturity and education of young adults), and (6) personal growth and self-realization (creative arts, recreation in adult education, adult health education, and music as an educational and recreational field for the adult).

And six categories of institutional resources were listed: (1) religious institutions and organizations, (2) public schools, (3) colleges and universities, (4) libraries, (5) museums, and (6) schools for adults, such as the Bread Loaf Writer's Conference and the Chautauqua Institute.

In the 1960 *Handbook of Adult Education in the United States* (Knowles, 1960), seventeen chapters described institutional programs and resources. Agencies and institutions discussed ranged from business and industry to labor unions, international organizations, and voluntary organizations. No attempt was made to categorize or to classify the various providers of adult learning opportunities.

The 1970 *Handbook of Adult Education* (Smith, Aker, and Kidd, 1970) included descriptions of eleven categories of adult education providers from the armed forces to hospitals and proprietary schools. But, more important, Wayne Schroeder (1970) attempted a classification system of adult education agencies. Schroeder described four categories of agencies:

> *Type I Agencies established to serve the educational needs of adults—adult education is a central function.* Proprietary schools, which . . . include business schools, correspondence schools and technical schools, [as well as] independent residential and nonresidential centers [fit within this category]. . . .

Type II Agencies established to serve the educational needs of youth which have assumed the added responsibility of at least partially serving the needs of adults—adult education is a secondary function. Included here are the public schools (adult evening or day programs), junior colleges (community service or adult education divisions) and colleges and universities (general extension divisions, evening colleges, residential centers and Cooperative Extension Service).

Type III Agencies established to serve both educational and non-educational needs of the community—adult education is an allied function employed to fulfill only some of the needs which agencies recognize as their responsibility. Libraries, museums and health and welfare agencies constitute examples of agencies which, though established to serve the more general needs of a community, become involved with adult education as one means of satisfying part of their total purpose.

Type IV Agencies established to serve the special interests (economic, ideological) of special groups—adult education is a subordinate function employed primarily to further the special interests of the agency itself. Generally agencies in this category (examples being business and industry, labor unions, government, churches and voluntary associations) are concerned with adult education to the extent that such education contributes to the effectiveness of the agency in fulfilling its primary purpose—governing, selling and spreading a doctrine [p. 37].

Meanwhile, others attempted to conceptualize the field of adult education. Coombs (1973) drew a distinction among formal learning (schools and universities), informal learning (from everyday interactions), and nonformal learning (organized learning outside the formal system).

Coombs introduced informal learning as a legitimate source of adult learning, equal in importance to learning opportunities provided in formal, full-time study settings.

Richard Peterson (1979, p. 14) went a step further. He developed a two-part framework which he called simply "deliberate education and learning" and "unintentional learning."

Peterson's framework makes several contributions to understanding learning opportunities within adult education. First, he puts adult education into the context of the rest of education when he includes preprimary, elementary, and secondary schools in his list of schools. Second, he recognizes the power of the self-directed learner who chooses a wide variety of approaches to learning, including travel as a deliberate source of learning. Third, Peterson underlines the importance of unintentional learning in the home, at work, from friends, from the mass media, and beyond.

In 1980, *Building an Effective Adult Education Enterprise,* (Peters and Associates, 1980) was published as part of the Adult Education Association Handbook series. This volume included a chapter by Knowles and another by Schroeder, both discussing approaches to understanding adult education. Knowles (1980, p. 13) said, "The term *adult education* has been used in the literature with three different meanings: (1) a field of operations that encompasses all the organized activities in which mature men and women engage for the purpose of learning, usually under the auspices of an institution; (2) a process of self-directed inquiry through which individuals systematically learn from their daily experiences and other resources in their environment; and (3) a social movement that encompasses the whole spectrum of mature individuals learning in infinite ways under innumerable auspices the many things that make life richer and more civilized and is dedicated to the improvement of the process of adult learning, the extension of opportunities for adults to learn, and the advancement of the general level of our culture" (p. 13).

Schroeder (1980, p. 46) listed three operating systems in adult education: "(1) institutional agencies; (2) voluntary associations, and (3) individual agents." Within the category *institutional agencies,* Schroeder placed (1) autonomous adult education agencies—proprietary schools, consulting firms, and so on, (2) youth education agencies—community colleges, public schools, four-year colleges, and universities, (3) community service agencies—libraries, museums, health agencies, and recreational centers, and (4) special interest groups—military, business and industry, and religious groups.

Schroeder included the following groups within the category *voluntary associations:* (1) pressure groups—labor unions and farmer organizations, (2) community betterment organizations and service clubs—League of Women Voters and Rotary Clubs, (3) mutual benefit societies and social clubs—Moose and Elks, and (4) professional organizations—American Bar Association, American Medical Association, American Association for Adult and Continuing Education.

Within the category *individual agents,* Schroeder included entrepreneurs providing their knowledge to others for profit and volunteers who share their knowledge for personal satisfaction and service.

The most recent attempt by the U.S. Department of Education (1986) to classify adult education lists nine categories of providers of instruction. The list includes the following: (1) four year colleges or universities, (2) two-year community colleges, junior colleges, or technical institutes, (3) vocational, trade, or business schools (including hospitals and trade schools), (4) elementary or high schools, (5) other schools, (6) private community organizations (churches, synagogues, YMCA, Red Cross), (7) governmental agencies (federal, state, county, or local), (8) labor organizations or professional associations, and (9) tutors, private instructors, or others. The U.S. Department of Education focuses on adult education courses, and its survey asks people how many courses they have taken recently. No attempt is made to obtain information about self-directed learning activities or even about participation in conferences, workshops, and the hundreds of other learning opportunities that are not courses.

In recent years, the breadth of learning opportunities for adults has increased greatly. And several major changes have taken place affecting what opportunities are offered, who offers them, and how they are offered.

A Provider Framework

Having reflected on the various frameworks of adult education providers developed over the past years, and having considered the present situation in adult education, I suggest the framework presented in Figure 21.1 as a tool for understanding the educational opportunities available to adults.

Figure 21.1. Provider Framework.

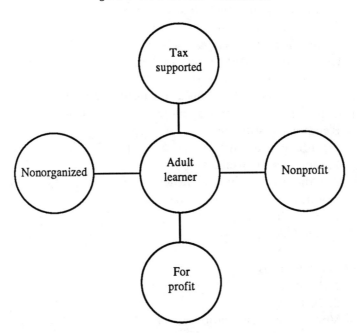

The framework is based on the assumption that adult learners have choices for learning opportunities—a long-standing characteristic of the adult education field. It should be noted, however, that although almost all adult learners have some element of choice, some adults are mandated by their professions, or by governmental units, to participate in learning activities.

Self-directed learning is not listed as a separate category. But within the framework, a self-directed learner may deliberately choose to learn something from any of the four categories of providers, including the nonorganized category.

For all learners, there can be both deliberate and nondeliberate learning, within all four categories. Deliberate learning is planned for or sought. Nondeliberate learning occurs serendipitously. Sometimes the learner is well aware of nondeliberate learning—for instance, some new idea or insight gained beyond that which the learner had set out to learn. Other times, the learner may not be aware of everything he or she is learning, as some learning will occur subliminally. Examples of subliminal learning can occur in any of the four areas of the framework, but it is most likely to occur through the mass media, such as television.

The framework reflects the situation of adult education in North America in the late 1980s. The following examples illustrate how various forms of adult education fit within the framework.

I. Fully or partially tax-supported agencies and institutions
    A. Public school adult education
    B. Four-year colleges and universities
    C. Community and technical colleges
    D. Cooperative extension
    E. Armed forces
    F. Correctional institutions
    G. Libraries and museums
    H. State and federal public adult education agencies
II. Nonprofit, self-supporting agencies and institutions
    A. Religious institutions
    B. Health institutions
       1. Courses on wellness
       2. Courses on physical fitness
    C. Community-based agencies
       1. Red Cross
       2. YMCA
       3. YWCA
    D. Service clubs
       1. Kiwanis
       2. Rotary
    E. Voluntary organizations
       1. League of Women Voters
       2. Sierra Club
    F. Professional organizations—national, state, and local
    G. Worker education programs (for example, union leadership training programs)
    H. National adult education clearinghouses and conference providers (for example, the Learning Resources Network in Kansas)
III. For-profit providers
    A. Correspondence schools (for example, the Writer's Digest School for writers)

       B.   Proprietary schools
          1. Truck driving schools
          2. Electronics schools
          3. Hairdresser schools
       C.   Private tutors and teachers (for example, piano teachers)
       D.   For-profit, degree-granting colleges and universities
       E.   Consultant and workshop providers
       F.   On-line data base services
       G.   Publishers of how-to books, videotapes, and audio tapes
       H.   Computer software publishers
       I.   Business and industry sponsored programs
          1. Arthur Little management degree program
          2. Instructional courses offered by craft stores
       J.   Business and industry human resource development programs for employees (The firms are profit making, and the educational programs are designed to increase a firm's profits.)
       K.   Conference centers (for example, the Xerox International Center for Training and Management Development)
IV.   Nonorganized learning opportunities
       A.   Television viewing and other mass media
       B.   Work setting
       C.   Family
       D.   Travel
       E.   Recreational and leisure-time activities

Current Trends

Several trends influence how the field of adult education is viewed today.

Blurring Between Higher Education and Adult Education. The number of older students enrolling in degree-credit programs is increasing. In 1982, adults twenty-five years of age and older made up 39 percent of the students enrolled in higher education's two-and four-year colleges. Demographers predict that, by 1992, 49 percent of higher education's students will be twenty-five years of age or older. Nineteen percent of higher education's students will be thirty-five years old and older, and 85 percent of these students will study part-time (U.S. Bureau of Census, 1985, p. 150).

Colleges and universities will, of necessity, be forced to offer more of their degree-credit work in evenings, on weekends, and at off-campus locations. And they will be using educational technology such as computers. The senate of the University of Alberta recently completed a study to examine the ways in which the Province of Alberta could better use nontraditional learning methods such as off-campus courses, learning-at-a-distance technology (including correspondence courses), and regular on-campus courses offered at nontraditional times to meet the needs of the growing number of adult students (University of Alberta, 1986). Other colleges and universities across North America are conducting similar inquiries.

The clear distinction that some like to make between higher education and adult education is disappearing. For others, the distinction never existed.

Education for Profit. Many educators dislike talking about profits. But clearly, the motive for many providers of adult learning opportunities is profit. Tax money is drying up for providers such as college and university extension services. They are forced to charge fees that cover instructor costs, overhead, and even more. Most college and university extension divisions are officially nonprofit providers. But continuing education directors know that at year's end their profit and loss statements must be written in black ink. At some institutions, top level administrators use the profits from adult and continuing education programs to bail out less successful, and often more traditional, college and university programs that have suffered declining enrollments.

New colleges and universities are popping up, organized as for-profit businesses, and are providing educational opportunities for adult learners. The Electronic University Network in San Francisco is an example. Through the Electronic University Network, people from throughout the country can enroll in credit courses and earn degrees, without having to leave their homes.

Adult education entrepreneurs are on the increase. In 1972, the consultant directory published in the *Training and Development Journal* listed 190 firms specializing in training. The 1988 *Training* marketplace directory listed 1,254 companies offering educational programs, activities, and materials in 124 educational areas ranging from affirmative action to women at work and remedial writing skills. Their offerings included prepackaged, off-the-shelf programs a company or organization can purchase; custom programs developed around a firm's needs; and a host of classroom programs, cassettes (audio and video), films, slides, books, and computer courseware.

Publishing houses increasingly are providing how-to books and videotapes on a far-ranging list of topics. Fitness and health-related tapes and general self-improvement tapes have been big money-makers for them.

According to *Nation's Business* ("Managing Your Business: Girth of a Nation," 1986), 65 million Americans are dieting and spending upwards of $31 billion on diet foods and weight-loss classes. Organizations such as Diet Center and Weight Watchers, Inc. attract thousands of overweight men and women to their classes.

Other adult education businesses doing well include Dale Carnegie and Berlitz Language Training, long established adult education businesses. New adult education for-profit businesses spring up regularly, offering programs that go well beyond those appealing only to businesses. For example, The Learning Annex, a New York-based adult education company, offers so-called quick hit courses ranging from flying helicopters and making sushi to a course called "How to Strip Your Mate" (Gill, 1987).

Influence of Information Technology. Adult educators have long talked about educational technology, and in many instances they have been on the forefront of adopting new approaches to providing educational opportunities.

Great technical advances have been made in information storage, retrieval, and transmittal. The compact disc read only memory (CD-ROM) allows one to store some 250,000 pages of information on a disc, and to find it readily. By connecting a CD-ROM to one's computer, it is possible to have an encyclopedia-sized information resource available at one's fingertips. On-line computer data bases have increased phenomenally during the past several years. Some 3,369 data bases are now available worldwide and offer over 528 on-line data base services (The Online Access Guide,'' 1987). Anyone with a computer, a modem, and the money to pay the on-line costs has access to almost unlimited information.

Degree programs such as those offered by the Electronic University Network in California offer an on-line library for students enrolling in their courses. The courses themselves are on computer discs, and students contact their instructors through electronic bulletin boards.

The National Technological University in Colorado offers its graduate degree engineering programs via satellite to firms around the world. The courses are videotaped. And students can contact their instructors via electronic bulletin boards and through teleconferencing.

Present information technology is allowing many new approaches to adult education. The new technology is particularly beneficial to the adult learner who, because of geography, work, or family, cannot travel to a provider site. Canadian adult education providers have been quick to adopt technology. A 1984 report indicates that twenty of Canda's seventy-one universities and thirty of the 196 Canadian colleges use teleconferencing in their credit and noncredit programs. Teleconferencing, according to this report, was most developed in Newfoundland, Quebec, Alberta, and British Columbia (Tobin and Sharon, 1984). Other technologies such as Telidon, which links libraries, schools, and other educational providers with satellite communication and videodisc, are widely used in Canada.

Many other forces influence adult education activity. Space does not permit a discussion of the influence of population trends (the number of older learners outnumbering younger learners), the global community (other countries' great influence on what happens in the United States), illiteracy rates (continuing high in the United States), and a shift from an industrial to a service economy (major economic changes resulting in thousands of displaced workers seeking new skills and careers).

Implications and Questions

The four circle framework in Figure 21.1 is a reflection of adult education in North America today. It helps us understand the nature of providers, and it helps us understand the new adult education field that is emerging. There are several dimensions to the new field. First, information, once considered by educational providers as something to be shared free, or as inexpensively as possible, has become a commodity. Information is bought and sold on the marketplace. Thus we see the proliferation of adult education for-profit providers.

For-Profit Adult Education. Interestingly, some of the most innovative and interesting adult education is coming from the for-profit providers. For-profit providers must be attractive and must meet needs and wants in order to survive and to make a profit. Thus we see for-profit providers often taking the lead with new formats, new technology, and explorations into helping adults learn in a variety of settings.

In many instances, traditional providers, such as higher education, are simply not keeping up. They are not meeting the demands, the wants, and the needs of adult learners. So these adult learners, willing to pay for their learning, are flocking to the for-profit providers.

The framework also recognizes that great amounts of learning occur through travel, through leisure-time activity, through family activities, through television viewing, and through one's work activity. This is not organized learning, but it must be recognized. The amount of time adults spend on organized learning is likely to be an infinitesimal percentage of the time spent watching television, of the time at work, and so on. For many adults, nonorganized learning is their primary source of learning. So we at least ought to recognize its existence, and, as educators of adults, we should begin thinking about the possibilities of helping people take better advantage of their nonorganized learning. Some would argue, however, that we have no business trying to help people make sense of their unorganized learning, and that our time, as adult educators, would be better spent improving the organized programs for which we have responsibility.

Today, the for-profit segment of adult education is the fastest growing. Bryson (1936) did not even include for-profit agencies and institutions in his definition of adult education. Is the field of adult education creating a larger gap between those who can and those who cannot afford to pay for educational opportunity? Requirements for payment are everywhere: fees for workshops and courses, the cost of computer modems, compact disc players, and on-line computer charges. What learning opportunities will be available for low-income adults? Will low-income people have access only to the governmentally sponsored remedial programs, which may soon make up a large segment of tax-supported adult education activity?

From an organizational perspective, what will happen to institutions that must earn greater and greater percentages of their keep? Will they cease to be important providers of educational opportunities for adult learners? Will they become providers for only those adults who can pay, and thus be in competition with other providers who depend on paying customers for their existence—that is, college and university extension divisions, museums, vocational technical schools, and a host of others?

Impact of Information Technology. Educational technology, long of interest to adult educators, has become a major force in the last half dozen years, particularly since the advent of the microcomputer and satellite communication. Information technology excels in storing, transmitting, and retrieving information. But there is many a slip between a fact gathered and an idea gained. Unfortunately, information accumulation is too often passed off as learning. Many topics of importance to adult learners require careful assessing of information, relating of information to previous learning and to present situations, combining of facts, sorting, thinking about, trying out, and discarding. In-depth learning requires more than information gathering. In fact, an overload of information may prevent important learning from taking place.

A more clearly positive impact of the new information technology is the ability to learn at home, without travel and without having to meet face to face with other learners. But even this is both a boon and a bane. For some topics, face-to-face learning is required. Such face-to-face learning sessions prepare people for the give-and-take required in community and governmental decision making. If large numbers of people will not have the opportunity to practice human relations skills through their learning activities, what will this do to the fabric of societal decision making? Such democratic decision making is based on assumptions of personal interaction skills, often gained through adult education activity.

Quality Control. With so many learning opportunities available, the question of quality and quality control becomes increasingly important. On the one hand are those who favor letting the market work. They claim that those programs that are not of high quality will not survive, as long as the learner-consumer has the freedom to choose where he or she wishes to learn.

On the other hand are those who want to register or license or somehow control every provider of adult learning opportunities. The learners must be protected, say advocates of this position. They claim that, just as we have national standards that automobile manufacturers must follow and requirements for food, drug, and a host of other manufacturers, we must have controls over educational providers.

The question of quality will become the issue of the 1990s. The issue has been heating up for some time. It has been fueled by diploma-mill colleges that exist on paper only and by workshop organizers producing shiny brochures and shoddy workshop sessions. The issue will be inflamed by hundreds of disappointed learners who will put down their money and then discover that the only thing they learn is that they threw away hard-earned dollars. Such experiences will accumulate, and the pressure for regulation will rise—unless adult education providers can themselves work out a system for quality control.

Freedman (1987) says that continuing higher education absolutely must keep its quality high, and the same should be said of all adult learning providers.

We are entering a new era in adult education, and we must change our thinking about how it is organized. The framework presented here is a reflection of adult education today and of the direction in which the field appears to be headed. The question we must ask ourselves is whether this is the direction we believe adult education should be going. If it is not, what steps should we take to change it?

References

Bryson, L. *Adult Education.* New York: American Book, 1936.

"Consultant Directory." *Training and Development Journal,* 1972, *26* (11), 20–42.

Coombs, P. H. *New Paths to Learning.* New York: International Council for Educational Development, 1973.

Ely, M. L. (ed.). *Handbook of Adult Education.* New York: Institute of Adult Education, Teachers College, Columbia University, 1948.

Freedman, L. *Quality in Continuing Education.* San Francisco: Jossey-Bass, 1987.

Gill, M. "The Secret of the $1,000 Suit: How Style Helped Bill Zanker Conquer the Adult Education Market." *Success,* Sept. 1987, pp. 66–67.

Knowles, M. S. *Handbook of Adult Education in the United States.* Washington, D.C.: Adult Education Association of the U.S.A., 1960.

Knowles, M. S. "The Growth and Development of Adult Education." In J. M. Peters and Associates, *Building an Effective Adult Education Enterprise.* San Francisco: Jossey-Bass, 1980.

"Managing Your Business: Girth of a Nation." *Nation's Business,* Dec. 1986, pp. 50–51.

"Marketplace Directory 1987–1988." *Training: The Magazine of Human Resources Development,* 1988, *25* (supplement), entire issue.

"The Online Access Guide." *Online Access,* Sept.–Oct. 1987, pp. 58–76.

Peters, J. M., and Associates. *Building an Effective Adult Education Enterprise.* San Francisco: Jossey-Bass, 1980.

Peterson, R. E. *Lifelong Learning in America.* San Francisco: Jossey-Bass, 1979.

Schroeder, W. L. "Adult Education Defined and Described." In R. M. Smith, G. F. Aker, and J. R. Kidd (eds.), *Handbook of Adult Education.* New York: Macmillan, 1970.

Schroeder, W. L. "Typology of Adult Learning Systems." In J. M. Peters and Associates, *Building an Effective Adult Education Enterprise.* San Francisco: Jossey-Bass, 1980.

Smith, R. M., Aker, G. F., and Kidd, J. R. (eds.). *Handbook of Adult Education.* New York: Macmillan, 1970.

Tobin, J., and Sharon, D. *New Technologies in Education in Canada: Issues and Concerns.* Toronto: Ontario Educational Communication Authority, 1984.

University of Alberta. *Task Force Inquiry into Needs for the Delivery of University Education.* Edmonton: The Senate, University of Alberta, 1986.

U.S. Bureau of Census. *Statistical Abstract of the United States 1985.* Washington, D.C.: U.S. Government Printing Office, 1985.

U.S. Department of Education. *Participation in Adult Education.* Washington, D.C.: U.S. Department of Education, Center for Statistics, Office of Educational Research and Improvement, 1986.

22

Public Schools and Community Education

Paul F. DeLargy

This chapter provides an overview of community education based in public school systems. In an effort to foster the reader's understanding of the concept of community education, I will discuss several definitions as well as the historical development of community education in the public schools. Presenting a historical perspective illustrates the evolution of the development of community education in the United States and, to a limited extent, in Canada. Also included in the chapter are discussions of the relationship between community education and lifelong learning and, finally, some issues perceived as critical by practicing community educators.

Defining Community Education

Historically there has been a great deal of misunderstanding or confusion regarding community education. Oftentimes, only limited portions of the community education concept are used in a definition, without acknowledgment of the overall pattern or organized configuration of experiences, activities, or acts necessarily included in an accurate description of community education. An effective means used by Minzey and LeTarte (1972) to define community education was to describe not only what it is, but also what it is not. Their technique is used in the following paragraphs to dispel some misconceptions.

Community education is not entirely programmatic; it does not consist only of social activities, recreation programs, or enrichment courses. But a misconception frequently arises because of the many immature community education programs that lack process activities—programs that feature only enrichment, social, cultural, or recreational programs, or informal and formal education courses, mostly at night, for adults. Any or all of these activities can be part of a community education program. In most cases, when community education is limited to only one of these activities, the fault lies in the weakness of a particular community education implementation process. Frequently, especially in rural communities, community education begins with an emphasis on recreation and never develops much further.

Community education is not a poverty program or a program for the disadvantaged only—however great the need may be for meaningful community education programs and activities for these segments of any community's population. This misconception of community education as a program for the poor arose from the many community education programs that were started in communities with limited resources. These communities were able to obtain federal or state funds for programs for their specific populations, thereby causing community education in low-income areas to be labeled a program for the disadvantaged.

The neighborhood school concept and community education are not the same. The misconception that they are the same has, in some instances, engendered negative attitudes toward community education development because of the conceptual association of the so-called neighborhood school with racial segregation.

The term *community education* does not have the same meaning as the term *community school*. While many people use these terms interchangeably, they actually denote different ideas. The term *community school* is older and was widely used during the early developmental stages of community education to describe both a philosophy and a place. However, current usage is different. For the purposes of this chapter, the term *community education* means the philosophy or concept, and *community school* means the place in which much of the community education takes place.

That is enough of what community education is not. Now, what is it? Its meaning is not clear to a majority of people, and community educators are continuously confronted with the difficult task of adequately defining community education.

In search of a definition of community education in the United States, one can go as far back as the Massachusetts Act of 1642, which prescribed that schools and curricula be designed in terms of utility in the community and support of community traditions (Solberg, 1970). The evolution of the community education movement has generated differing definitions over the years.

Two important yet differing definitions were published in 1969. The Board of Directors of the National Community School Education Association (NCSEA) (1969, p. 6) issued a definition adopted for their organization: "Community School Education is a comprehensive and dynamic approach to public education. It is a philosophy that pervades all segments of education planning and directs the thrust of each of them toward the needs of the community. The community school serves as a catalytic agent by providing leadership to mobilize community resources to solve identified community problems. This marshalling of all forces in the community helps to bring about changes as the school extends itself to all people.''

In the same year, Weaver's (1969, p. 19) newly published book on community education administration contained the following definition: ''Community Education is an attempt to marshall all the educational resources within the community to create a laboratory for management of human behavior. . . . Community Education is a theoretical construct—a way of viewing education in the community, a systematic way of looking at people and their problems. . . . It is based upon the premise that education can be made relevant to people's needs and that the people affected by education should be involved in decisions about the program. It assumes that education should have an impact upon the society it serves. It requires that all who are worthy of the name 'Community Educator' are involved in all facets of the community at large.''

The 1969 definitions attest to the comprehensiveness of the community education concept as viewed by leaders in the field. Another definition that has had great impact and acceptance in the United States and Canada is that proposed by Minzey and LeTarte (1972, p. 19): ''Community Education is a philosophical concept which serves the entire community by providing for all the educational needs of all of its community members. It uses the local school to serve as the catalyst for bringing community resources to bear on community problems in an effort to develop a positive sense of community, improve community living, and develop the community process toward the end of self-actualization.''

A key phrase in the Minzey and LeTarte definition is, ''It uses the local school''—a phrase that implies decentralization. In the opinion of this writer, decentralization as part of the community education process is essential; the use of public schools allows process and programs to take place at a local, or community, level. This use of public schools also serves to differentiate community education from community college education and continuing education. Continuing or community college educators generally bring people to the program whereas community educators try to bring the program to the people—centralization as compared with decentralization. (See Chapter Twenty-Four.)

In order to clarify their definition, Minzey and LeTarte (1972, pp. 24–29) suggested community education objectives. They stated that, ''Community Education attempts . . . (1) to develop a number of community programs . . . , (2) to promote interaction between school and community . . . , (3) to survey community resources and to coordinate their interaction . . . , (4) to bring about a better relationship between social and governmental agencies . . . , (5) to identify community problems and ferret out the needs of the community . . . , (6) to develop a process by which the community can become self-actualized.''

Following Minzey and LeTarte's definition of community education, there has been a trend to interpret community education more comprehensively. Many new dimensions have been included in local community programs, such as school-business partnerships, at-risk-youth programs, intergenerational activities, and latchkey programs for children.

The identification of goals has also helped clarify the concept of community education. Community education goals have been identified through the research of Weaver (1972), DeLargy (1973, 1981), and Kaplan (1974). These studies represent the first extensive attention directed toward community education goal statements that could be tested, challenged, and even modified over time.

A second trend affecting definition is the maturing of the philosophy beyond a community school movement toward a community education philosophy. Kerensky and Melby (1971), Hiemstra (1972), and Bremer (1975) have all expressed conceptualizations that extend beyond the schooling context.

Minzey and LeTarte (1972) initiated a third trend that continues to the present: an emphasis on process, which they explained by using a so-called program to process paradigm. A national study by DeLargy (1981) affirmed this trend by indicating an increase in the importance of process goals from 1973 to 1981. The 1981 Delphi study generated four new goal classifications: (1) encourage community development, (2) address environmental, ecological, and energy issues, (3) provide training in community education, and (4) develop community-based K–12 programs.

These definitions and trends, as well as others, exemplify the slowly evolving nature of the concept of community education. Although the definitions cited above differ in focus, each indicates that the local schools have a mission beyond teaching children. Another important ingredient in each definition is a strategy for mobilizing the community to meet its needs and to solve its problems.

According to Shoop (1980, p. 15), community education faces three serious dangers related to definition: "The danger of being defined so broadly that it loses clarity and effectiveness; the danger of being defined so narrowly that it becomes just another program; and the danger of becoming centralized, with the decision making power resting in the hands of the professionals."

My own definition of community education is a process that identifies the community's educational needs, assesses available community resources, and uses these resources to develop appropriate programs and activities to meet the identified needs. Community education is primarily conducted in public schools, which can be called community schools.

Historical Overview

Community education is not a new concept; indeed, basic elements of it can be traced back to the ancient Greeks and Romans. American education from the beginning, influenced by colonial development and frontier living, included components of community education, but early education was by no means preoccupied with social change. Early New England colonies created public schools to carry on social and religious traditions brought over from Europe. The curriculum included religious education, vocational training, and literacy skills, but there was little emphasis on general education (Solberg, 1970).

Although the new United States government was committed to public education, no real progress was made to include the community until after the Civil War, when land-grant laws encouraged community involvement in public education development. However, the early nineteenth century did see scattered instances of public schools being used for adult education, principally in Providence, Rhode Island, and in Chicago (Cubberly, 1934). One of the earliest publications describing what is now considered community education philosophy was Henry Barnard's 1845 "Report of the Conditions and Improvements of Public Schools in Rhode Island (Nashlund, 1953, p. 256). This report described the role of the school in improving community and individual living.

Several influences encouraged the schools to become more involved with community problems. The settlement houses of the late nineteenth and early twentieth centuries became models of community partnerships aimed at meeting the social, educational, and economic needs of newly arrived immigrants. Another strong influence was that of John Dewey (1949, p. 47), who emphasized the importance of making "each one of our schools an embryonic community life, active with types of occupations that reflect the life of the larger society and permeated with the spirit of art, history, and science."

One of Dewey's followers, Joseph K. Hart (1924, p. 382) emphasized the role of the community even more by writing, "Education is not apart from life. . . . The democratic problem in education is not primarily a problem of training children; it is a problem of making a community within which children cannot help growing up to be democratic, intelligent, disciplined to freedom, reverent to the goals of life, and eager to share in the tasks of the age. Schools cannot produce the result; nothing but the community can do so." The democratic educational philosophy espoused by Dewey, Hart, and other writers caused communities to be increasingly referred to as educative agencies and to be held more accountable for providing leadership for social change. This philosophy had a strong impact on the development of community schools, the first of which was developed in 1929 by Elsie Clapp in Kentucky (Olsen and Clark, 1977).

Another influence on schools and communities during the first half of the present century was the Great Depression. Schools became the centers of home economics, adult citizenship, and agricultural education programs as well as centers for community education, which provided other than K–12 programs (Berridge, 1973). The conditions caused by the depression had an affirmative and practical effect on the historical pattern of community education, because efforts were aimed at getting maximum good from available resources and encouraging people to work together to achieve common goals (Boo and Decker, 1985).

From 1936 to the present, a more rapid succession of events has added momentum to the community education movement. Without a doubt, the greatest impact was made by the Charles Stewart Mott Foundation, which, in 1936, initiated support of the Flint, Michigan Community Schools Program led by Frank J. Manley. From Flint, the community school idea spread to other Michigan areas in the 1940s and 1950s, and visitors came to Flint to observe community education in action.

Clapp's (1939) classic publication, *Community School in Action,* Seay's (1945) "The Community School Emphasis in Post War Education: American Education in the Post War Period," from the fourty-fourth yearbook of the National Society for the Study of Education, and Olsen and others' (1945) teacher education textbook on community education, *School and Community,* all added impetus to the community education movement in public schools. Additional impetus came from the Sloan Foundation's experiments in Kentucky, Florida, and Vermont to measure the impact of the schools on the improvement of community life (Goodykoontz, 1953).

An increasing interest in technology after World War II, and newly emphasized mathematics, science, and foreign language curricula for both elementary and secondary schools following Sputnik in 1957, caused community schools to decline markedly. According to Olsen and Clark (1977, p. 69), "The barely emerging life-concerns curriculum orientation was quietly superceded. The whole traditional, academic-subject curriculum pattern was again entrenched."

In the 1960s, the Mott Foundation began an outreach effort to advance community education awareness and development in all fifty states by establishing community education centers in universities and in state departments of education (Boo and Decker, 1985). By 1978, there were fifteen regional centers, seventy-nine cooperating centers, and a National Center for Community Education located in Flint, Michigan, all funded by the Mott Foundation (Storey and Rohrer, 1979). Currently there are 122 university centers and state department agencies for community education (Mott Foundation, 1988). An emphasis on the training of professional community educators, combined with increased efforts to make citizens more aware of the community education concept, has yielded positive results for the movement. The number of community schools grew from five started in 1936, in Flint, Michigan, to 5,833 across the nation in 1978, 2,912 of which were added between 1973 and 1977 (Storey and Rohrer, 1979). This increase was a result of a major effort funded by the Charles Stewart Mott Foundation to promote the community education concept by providing for the training of community education professionals and by supporting their placement into public school systems.

Currently in the United States, 14,851 community schools have at least one designated community education professional on the staff (Mott Foundation, telephone interview with research specialist, Mar. 1988), whereas, according to the 1985 U.S. *Statistical Abstract* (U.S. Bureau of Census, 1985), 80,556 public schools claimed to have community education programs.

The Mott Foundation figure of 14,851 community schools as compared with the U.S. Statistical Abstract figure of 80,556 public schools claiming to have community education is a clear example of the discrepancy among definitions of community education programs—especially when these figures are compared with the U.S. Department of Education Center for Education Statistics figures, which indicate that in the fall of 1982 there were 82,715 public schools in the United States. That would mean that, using the Mott figure based on their definition, 18.0 percent of all public schools claimed to be community schools, but, using the U.S. Statistical Abstract figure, 97.4 percent of all schools in the United States claim to have community education.

The formation of a national professional association in 1967 further institutionalized the field of community education. The National Community Education Association, initially formed as the National Community School Education Association, has a current membership of over 1,500, including 150 institutional members. In addition, state community education associations have been organized in forty states and now have a total membership of more than 8,000 individuals (Council of Chief State School Officers, 1986).

This historical overview supports Decker's (1980, p. 48) contention that the implementation of the community education concept "has been neither steady nor continuous." Contemporary conditions, however, have generated new interest in the concept. The following facts, documented by the Council of Chief State School Officers (1986), indicate that much progress has been made in the recent past:

- Twenty-nine state school boards have approved resolutions supporting community education.
- Twenty-three states have passed legislation supporting the community education concept.
- Forty-nine states have designated one or more persons reponsible for community education development at the state department of education level.
- Twenty states provide state funding for community education.
- State community education advisory councils operate in twenty-three states.
- Community education is an approved federal purpose eligible for current Chapter 2 funding and was recognized and supported by the U.S. Congress and by the President in federal legislation adopted in 1974 and 1978.

The democratic philosophy inborn in the community education concept historically has encouraged grass-roots-level involvement. Therefore, the public school's position in the educational hierarchy makes it an appropriate agent to achieve the goals of community education. According to Decker (1980, p. 22), the public school has become the implementation agent because it "has played the traditional role of common denominator in our society and today is an institution truly representative of all classes, creeds, and colors." He further points out that the physical plants of the schools, representing a huge community investment, are perfectly suited for community recreation and education and that the use of these facilities eliminates the need for costly duplication. Moreover, their geographic locations and ready accessibility to all citizens makes them suitable neighborhood centers for recreation, education, and democratic action (Mott, 1959). Public schools historically have provided a neutral meeting place for community members, and even though schools are not always nonthreatening places for people who have experienced failure in school, they can serve as a base from which to administer programs and activities in other nonthreatening locations.

Development of Community Education in Canada

According to Janet Eaton, director of the Community Education Research and Development Program at Dalhousie University in Halifax, Nova Scotia, community education development reached a peak throughout Canada in the 1960s and 1970s, followed by a decline in interest and a decline in support by the educational community. Only in the past few years has there been evidence of renewed interest.

The development of community education in Canada suffers severely from a lack of funding. There is little federal funding, and the local programs that have started have done so generally because of the leadership provided by local school or community leaders committed to the community education concept. This statement can also be made about the development of community education in the United States.

Community education programs are scattered rather sparsely nationwide; however, approximately half of the Canadian provinces now have professional associations for community education. The Canadian Association for Community Education was formed in 1986. There is only one Center for Community Education now operating, and that is at Dalhousie University with the support of some Mott Foundation funding (Janet Eaton, telephone interview with the author, Mar. 1988).

According to Eaton, in contrast to the more school-based community education programs in the United States, Canadian community education programs are associated much more with nonprofit organizations such as community economic development agencies or community development corporations. In Nova Scotia, only one of the twenty-one school systems has a community education program. Saskatchewan has community education programs in their Native schools. Good community education programs exist in Ottawa and Winnipeg, and Toronto is reputed to have an exemplary program, but one that is quite different from the Flint, Michigan model.

Relationship Between Community Education and Lifelong Learning

In *A Nation at Risk,* the National Commission on Excellence in Education (1983) cited the need for educational reform focused on the goal of creating a learning society—a society giving all members the opportunity to stretch their minds to full capacity, from early childhood through adulthood, learning more as the world changes. The learning society described by the commission has been the goal of community educators for more than fifty years. Community education reflects the belief that learning is a lifelong process.

The philosophies of lifelong learning and community education are similar in that they both support the beliefs that persons of all ages can learn and change, that learning is a continuous process, that education should be community based, and that a pragmatic, client-centered approach to learning based on needs is essential. In addition to the philosophical bases, both philosophies are similar by definition, as evidenced in the legislation of the Community Schools Act of 1974 and the Lifelong Learning Act of 1976. Both community education and lifelong learning are relatively new as fields of focus in education. They have similar target groups, and they use like methods to attain their parallel objectives.

There are several inhibiting factors in the relationship between community education and lifelong learning, however. They are frequently seen as competing programs. The Coalition of Adult Education Organizations (CAEO) (1979, p. 48), a panel of eleven specialists in the field of Community and Adult Education, claims that, "The language of both is too vague, too flexible, and too subject to manipulation. They are both referred to as 'programs,' but are defined as concepts. Both are misunderstood as being concerned only with adult populations. They are misunderstood by the general public in terms of target groups, territorial rights, definition, and funding priorities." Since the time of the CAEO's 1979 statements, however, some of the inhibiting factors have been overcome by efforts to make the public aware of the basic roles of community education and lifelong learning and by the encouragement of interaction between community educators and adult-lifelong learning professionals.

An analogy can be drawn between the evolution of the terms *community school concept* to *community education* and *adult education* to *lifelong learning*. Both lifelong learning and community education are largely undefined and mean different things to different people. Moreover, they both suffer from having interpretations that are too general or too specific.

"Lifelong learning is not synonymous with adult education but is more comprehensive in nature and scope. Neither is community education synonymous with adult education. All three—lifelong learning, community education, and adult education—have separate elements as well as areas of overlap," according to the CAEO (Coalition of Adult Education Organizations, 1979, p. 50).

Historically, there have been a number of areas in which adult education and community education have had close relationships. For example, eight state departments of education have joint offices for adult and community education. Likewise, there are large numbers of local school systems that operate their programs of adult and community education as joint ventures. Many local school systems, especially rural school systems, employ persons to serve as joint adult and community educators.

The roles of a community educator are that of facilitator of process, initiator of programs, coordinator of resources, supporter of lifelong learning, catalyst or linkage agent, and assessor of community needs. Community educators carrying out these roles in cooperation with adult educators could impact the problem of illiteracy; the community educator acting as facilitator to aid the adult educator's role as teacher would have a synergetic effect.

Critical Issues

There are many issues facing the field of community education in public schools, and there is little consensus on which are the most critical. The following broad issues are deemed by this writer to be among the most important to be addressed.

The Future Course of Community Education Development. In order to address this issue, there needs to be an examination of those forces or events that professional community educators can control as well as an analysis of the influences external to community education. Shoop (1980) has pointed out the dangers related to practitioners' definitions that are too broad, too narrow, or too centralized in nature. In his article, "Remember, We're Not Selling Snake Oil," he warns, "In the rush to enlist support for community education, the professionals in the field are running the risk of being charged with quackery" (p. 15)—by promising a quick and easy remedy for community problems. He states that some community educators oversell the concept and then "pack up their wagons and move down the road" (p. 15). Because each community is different, community education programs should not be standardized. Successful programs work because they are designed by local residents to meet local needs.

The process aspect of community education requires a long-term commitment and arduous effort. It includes assessment of community needs, identification of resources, prioritization of needs, development and implementation of relevant programs or activities, and evaluation of community education programs and processes used. The question is, to what degree are community educators prepared to make such commitment and effort?

The question of adequate leadership is an internal problem as well. There is a high rate of attrition related primarily to two factors: burnout or lack of commitment. Highly committed practitioners can soon burn out from their conscientious efforts to meet community needs while often neglecting their own personal and family needs. Conversely, many able leaders with low commitment to community education use it as a stepping stone to higher level administrative positions. Additionally, there is a problem in filling professional community education positions with adequately trained persons who are knowledgeable and skilled enough to provide the leadership necessary for developing a comprehensive community education program (Fallen and Miller, 1981).

Besides the internal issues affecting the development of community education, there are outside influences on local communities that are likely to continue to increase and change in the immediate future. According to Warden (1985, p. 23), there is likely to be "a decline in direct services provided by the current array of vertical agencies and organizations that are in the business of community education by name. Community education centers will decrease in number. State departments of education may no longer have staff roles associated with community education. The Mott Foundation may decrease its direct dollar support of community education." These statements have been proven true in the years since they were made by Warden.

Community educators must examine themselves, their philosophy, and their practice in order effectively to come up with answers regarding the future development of community education.

The Ability of Community Education to Address Pressing Community Problems Identified by Educators and Citizens. According to Richard Remy (1979), issues identified almost a decade ago by educators as major ones affecting schools and communities were the following:

- Loss of public faith in schools
- Demand for student competency
- Increased citizen participation in policy-making
- General economic conditions
- Declining school enrollments
- Changes in the family structure
- Decline of a sense of community
- New demands on education facilities

Four major issues raised by citizens a decade ago were the following (Clasley, 1979):

- Declining school enrollment
- Transitions in family life
- Fiscal constraints
- Taxpayers' unrest

We must ask how effective the efforts of community educators have been in addressing the foregoing issues during the past decade, and how effective they can be in the future. And we must strive to ensure that community education can make an impact on the followng issues that were identified at a recent issues conference of the National Community Education Computer Network.

- Illiteracy
- Problems of aging
- Crime

- At-risk youth
- The homeless
- Poverty
- Environmental problems
- Rural and urban schools
- Economic development (including school-based development enterprises)
- Preschool and after-school child care

A review of these issues reveals that they include problems of individuals and problems of communities. According to Fantini, Laughran, and Reed (1980, p. 12), "To say . . . that community development is as important as individual development to the emerging definition of community education is to imply that the delivery system must also be pluralistic. No one agency can encompass such diversity. Only a concept that is inclusive and expandable can inform an effort to help develop a community. Thus, community education must be a process, not a program. No one program or series of programs is adequate; rather, a series of highly complex processes must be developed that are better able to address [these community issues]."

If this is true, then another question is to be answered: Can community education provide the resources—mainly the leadership and research—to facilitate effective community and individual problem-solving processes?

Providing Appropriate Programs to Meet the Needs of the Elderly. The percentage of adults over sixty-five years of age in both Canada and the United States is predicted to rise faster than other age groups. This age group will increase to 13 percent of the population in the United States and to 12 percent in Canada by the year 2000, according to the National Gerontology Resource Center in Washington, D.C. (U.S. Bureau of Census, 1988). In the United States, the 1987 elderly population was 29.8 million and is expected to increase to 34.9 million by the year 2000. This means that in the near future, the elderly population will be as large as the present school-age population.

Community educators need to be aware of the magnitude of the demographic changes taking place with the elderly, and they need to respond. With over 70 percent of the taxpayers not having children in school and a large percentage being elderly taxpayers, involvement of the elderly with the public schools is essential to maintain community support. We must consider the impact community education can have on employment, poverty, housing, education, and health problems of the elderly. (See Chapter Forty.)

A Strong Commitment to the Implementation of Community Education. There are some indications that the commitments to implement community education are becoming stronger. According to the Council of Chief State School Officers' *State Educators Agency Community Education Survey* in 1987, more states had increased funding than in their 1984 report. Of forty-five states responding, seven states and the District of Columbia now commit more than $1 million each per year to community education activities at the state level. Minnesota led in funding in 1987 with $14.9 million, as opposed to its $2.0 million in 1984 (Council of Chief State School Officers, 1987). Other leaders included North Carolina, $5.9 million ($2.8 million in 1984); Maine, $3.0 million ($1.8 million in 1984); Florida, $2.4 million ($2.2 million in 1984); New York, $2.0 million ($120,000 in 1984); Maryland, $1.5 million (did not respond in 1984); and the District of Columbia, $1.3 million (did not respond in 1984). In 1984, Alaska's budget for community education was $4.1 million contrasted with $818,000 in 1987. The Texas budget was $2,205,000 in 1984; Texas did not respond in 1987.

The survey found other indications of additional support. More state educational agencies had full-time staff. Of forty-five states there were fifty-seven full-time and twenty-five part-time staff members in 1987. In 1984, with forty states responding, there were forty-nine full-time and forty-three part-time staff members. Of forty-five states in 1987, nineteen had state education functions related to school-business partnerships. In 1984, with forty states responding, seventeen reported school-business partnerships. In 1984, twenty-one states out of forty had some form of legislation to support community education. In 1987, twenty-two out of forty-five had some form of community education legislation. At least three more states had legislation for community education in 1987.

Even so, it has been difficult for public school educational leaders to adopt the community education concept to the point where they think of their educational leadership responsibility as being for the entire community rather than being limited to students of elementary schools, middle schools, or high schools. It has also been difficult for many educators to adjust to a year-round use, and longer daily use, of schools by the community. And institutions of higher education generally have had only limited success through their educational programs for teachers and administrators in fostering a strong commitment to implementation of community education or adult education.

Educators and public school systems generally have not embraced the community education philosophy, have not eagerly sought to fund community education, have not developed training programs and career opportunities to encourage community education development, and have not dealt with the high burnout rate of community educators. However, the implementation of community education is taking place in some states, and a much stronger awareness of the community education concept is developing in many other states.

The potential of a comprehensive, well-implemented community education program delivered through the public schools to improve the quality of life has not yet been realized. The pressing need is for an awareness of this potential and a commitment to community action.

Summary

This chapter has attempted to provide an overview of public-school-based community education. The public school can extend itself to all people and can help marshal the forces and energies of the community. It can also provide leadership and facilitate a process for mobilizing community resources to identify and to solve community problems. When the public school takes the role of community school, it serves as a catalyst for community problem solving. It then becomes "a unifying force of the community rather than merely a social institution in the community" (Hanna and Nashlund, 1953, p. 55).

Community schools also accommodate the trend toward offering services in decentralized locations—a trend related to growth in the number of programs for adults. As larger numbers of adults (52 percent of students in college credit courses in 1980 were over twenty-five years old) attempt to enroll in classes of all kinds, offering decentralized services becomes more important. Studies have shown that bringing a service to people, rather than forcing people to go to the service, will increase use of the service by about 25 percent (Kliminski, 1983).

Community education, although it may be ill-defined and sometimes uneven in practice, has the potential for making a positive impact on the quality of life in local communities. M. Donald Thomas (1984), South Carolina Deputy Superintendent of Schools for Public Accountability, and former Superintendent of Salt Lake City Public Schools, predicts that, "By the year 2000 community education will be the basis for creating community coherence and common purposes. Community education will create what America needs most: a community of character, a coherence of values, a unity of purpose—if not perfect, at least in the making. . . . There is no social agency other than our public schools to do that."

References

Berridge, R. I. *The Community Education Handbook*. Midland, Mich.: Pendell, 1973.

Boo, M. R., and Decker, L. E. *The Learning Community*. Alexandria, Va.: National Community Education Association, 1985.

Bremer, J. A. *A Matrix for Modern Education*. Toronto: McClelland & Stewart, 1975.

Clapp, E. R. *Community School in Action*. New York: Viking Penguin, 1939.

Clasley, M. *The Role of the Schools in the Community: Community Perspectives*. Washington, D.C.: U.S. Department of Education, 1979.

Coalition of Adult Education Organizations. "The Relationship Between Community Education and Lifelong Learning." In V. M. Kerensky and J. D. Logsdon (eds.), *A New Foundation: Perspectives on Community Education*. Washington, D.C.: U.S. Department of Education, 1979.

Council of Chief State School Officers. *Community Education and State Education Agencies: Initiatives, Activities and Leadership*. Washington, D.C.: Council of Chief State School Officers, 1986.

Council of Chief State School Officers. *State Education Agency Community Education Survey*. Washington, D.C.: Council of Chief State School Officers, 1987.

Cubberly, E. P. *Public Education in the United States.* Boston: Houghton Mifflin, 1934.

Decker, L. E. *Foundations of Community Education.* Charlottesville, Va.: Community Collaborators, 1980.

DeLargy, P. F. "Identification of Community Education Goals by Use of the Delphi Technique." Unpublished doctoral dissertation, College of Education, University of Georgia, 1973.

DeLargy, P. F., DeLargy, C. B., and Dickey, P. D. *National Community Education Goals: A Comparative Study.* Valdosta, Ga.: Center for Community Education, Valdosta State College, 1981.

Dewey, J. *The School and Society.* Chicago: University of Chicago Press, 1949.

Fallen, J. A., and Miller, S. L. "How Community Leaders Perceive the Issues." *Community Education Journal,* 1981, *8* (3), 31.

Fantini, M. D., Laughran, E. L., and Reed, H. B. "Toward a Definition of Community Education." *Community Education Journal,* 1980, *7* (3), 11–14.

Goodykoontz, B. "Selected Studies Relating to Community Schools." In N. B. Henry (ed.), *The Community School.* Fifty-second yearbook of the National Society for the Study of Education, part II. Chicago: University of Chicago Press, 1953.

Hanna, P. R., and Nashlund, R. A. "The Community School Defined." In N. B. Henry (ed.), *The Community School.* Fifty-second yearbook of the National Society for the Study of Education, part II. Chicago: University of Chicago Press, 1953.

Hart, J. K. *The Discovery of Intelligence.* New York: The Century Company, 1924.

Hiemstra, R. *The Educative Community.* Lincoln, Nebr.: Professional Educators Publications, 1972.

Kaplan, M. H. "A Comparative Analysis of the Ratings of Community Education Goals Assigned by Four Groups: Regional and Cooperating Center Directors; and Principals, Superintendents, and Community Education Directors in Minnesota Community School Districts." Unpublished doctoral dissertation, College of Education, Michigan State University, 1974.

Kerensky, V. M., and Melby, E. O. *Education II.* Midland, Mich.: Pendell, 1971.

Kliminski, G. "Demographics and the Use of Public Facilities." In D. H. Schoeny and L. E. Decker (eds.), *Community Education and Social Impact Perspectives.* Charlottesville: University of Virginia Printing Office, 1983.

Miller, S. "NCEA Report." *Community Education Journal,* 1980, *7* (3), 29.

Minzey, J. D., and LeTarte, C. *Community Education: From Program to Process.* Midland, Mich.: Pendell, 1972.

Mott, C.S.H. "The Flint Community School Concept as I See It." *Journal of Educational Sociology,* 1959, *23* (4), 141.

Mott Foundation. *1988 Guide to Community Education Resources.* Flint, Mich.: Charles Stewart Mott Foundation, 1988.

Nashlund, R. A. "The Impact of the Power Age on the Community School Concept." In N. B. Henry (ed.), *The Community School.* Fifty-second yearbook of the National Society for the Study of Education, part II. Chicago: University of Chicago Press, 1953.

National Commission on Excellence in Education. *A Nation at Risk: The Imperative for Educational Reform.* U.S. Government Printing Office, 1983.

National Community School Education Association. *Second Annual Directory of Membership.* Flint, Mich.: National Community School Education Association, 1969.

Olsen, E. G., and Clark, P. A. *Life Centering Education.* Midland, Mich.: Pendell, 1977.

Olsen, E. G., and others. *School and Community.* Englewood Cliffs, N.J.: Prentice-Hall, 1945.

Remy, R. C. *The Role of the School in the Community: The Educator's Perspectives.* Washington, D.C.: U.S. Department of Education, 1979.

Seay, M. F. "The Community School Emphasis in Post War Education, American Education in the Post War Period." In M. F. Seay (ed.), *Curriculum Reconstruction.* Forty-fourth yearbook of the National Society for the Study of Education, part I. Chicago: University of Chicago Press, 1945.

Shoop, R. J. "Remember, We're Not Selling Snake Oil . . . " *Community Education Journal,* 1980, *7* (3), 15.

Solberg, J. R. "The Evaluation and Implementation of the Community-School Concept." Unpublished doctoral dissertation, College of Education, University of Michigan, 1970.

Storey, D. S., and Rohrer, K. H. *The Historical Development of Community Education and the Mott Foundation.* Mt. Pleasant: Central Michigan University Center for Community Education, 1979.

Thomas, M. D. "It's Time for Community Education to Be a Full-Fledged Member of the Education Family." *Community Education Journal,* 1984, *11* (2), 4–6.

U.S. Bureau of Census. *U.S. Population Estimates by Age, Sex, and Race, 1980–1987.* Population Report P25, no. 1022. Washington, D.C.: U.S. Government Printing Office, 1988.

U.S. Bureau of Census. *Statistical Abstract of the United States 1985.* Washington, D.C.: U.S. Government Printing Office, 1985.

Warden, J. "Outside Influences on Community Education." *Community Education Journal,* 1985, *12* (2), 21–23.

Weaver, D. C. "Community Education—A Cultural Imperative." In National Community Schools (ed.), *The Community School and Its Administration.* Midland, Mich.: Ford Press, 1969.

Weaver, D. C. "The Emerging Community Education Model." Presidential address to the National Community Education Association, Flint, Mich., 1972.

23

Four-Year Colleges and Universities

Thomas M. Hatfield

This chapter describes the particular qualities and features of adult and continuing education in four-year colleges and universities in the United States. An accurate description is difficult because the United States government neither collects all pertinent statistics nor maintains separate data on adult and continuing education in this type of institution. Therefore, primary source information must be based on survey research, personal observation, interviews, and information provided voluntarily to professional associations by member colleges and universities. This chapter also includes information about adult and continuing education in Canadian universities, derived mostly from publications of the Canadian Association for University Continuing Education.

Terminology

The reader of college and university publications will find a variety of terms used to describe adult and continuing education programs. Such differences in terminology usually reflect only minor differences in concept or in philosophy because an aim of virtually all adult and continuing education programs is to provide an organized learning experience for individuals who are beyond usual college age and who are not regularly enrolled students in a college or university. Some individuals may be regularly enrolled students, but their participation in such programs is normally supplemental to their other studies. Variations in terminology probably indicate preferences of administrators who believe that certain terms have become dated or that other terms will have greater appeal, either to potential enrollees or to higher-level decision makers within the institution. This terminological variation should not cause serious confusion, but it deserves a brief exposition.

Educational historians generally accept that the first formally organized, university-based, adult education occurred in 1873 at Cambridge University in England with the formation of a syndicate of local lecturers consisting of professors who held classes beyond the university. Later the name was changed to extramural studies, having the literal meaning in Latin, outside the walls (Welch, 1973). The idea was quickly transported to the United States, and the term *extension,* already being used in England, became widely accepted (Adams, 1901).

After the passage of the Smith-Lever Act in 1914, wherein Congress created the Cooperative Extension Service for agricultural education, the term *university extension* gained acceptance to differentiate nonagricultural extension activities from agricultural extension. (See Chapter Twenty-Five, "The Cooperative Extension Service.") It is therefore no accident of terminology that when nonagricultural extension educators met at Madison, Wisconsin in March 1915, to form an organization, they named it the National University Extension Association. The term fared well until about midcentury, when many university extension educators concluded that the term *extension* was antiquated or too easily confused with *co-op extension* for agriculture.

Another term, *continuing education,* had surfaced in the meantime. It probably derived from the Center for Continuation Study, the name given to the first university residential facility for adults with lodging, food service, and meeting rooms under one roof. This facility opened at the University of Minnesota in 1936 ("Adult Education Gets New Impetus," Oct. 25, 1936, Sec. 2, p. 4). The term *continuing education* came gradually into use as an apt phrase to describe the ongoing and advanced education necessary for professionals to stay abreast of the knowledge explosion then emerging in many fields of practice. Continuing education captured the imaginations of academicians and the literate society as the new generic term for university-based adult education. The term spread rapidly after the W. K. Kellogg Foundation began making grants to certain universities for the construction of residential continuing education centers, the first of which opened at Michigan State University in 1951 (Alford, 1968). By the mid-1970s, the term *extension* had been discarded by most professional organizations, as well as by colleges and universities—save some that had been leaders in developing and implementing the concept, notably Harvard and the Universities of Minnesota, Wisconsin, and California.

By the early 1980s, however, the exclusive identification of continuing education with academic institutions had been lost. The reason was that department stores, garden clubs, and churches used the term to describe their teaching-learning activities for adults. College and university leaders then sought to distinguish their adult programs from noncollegiate providers by using terms such as *continuing studies, nontraditional study,* and *lifelong education,* often without reconceptualizing programs and practices. Given the wide variety of terms now in use, one must look hard to find a four-year college or university that uses the term *adult education* to designate its educational programs for adults, unless designed for literacy training. (See Chapter Thirty-Five, "Adult Basic Education.") In the mid-1980s, not a single Canadian university's continuing education administrative unit included the word *adult* in its title (Brooke and Morris, 1987).

Institutional Context

Within four-year colleges and universities, adult and continuing education occurs under many and varied conditions. Some institutions may have a school or division of continuing education administered by a dean or a director, and other institutions may offer part-time degree programs under the auspices of an office for older students. Still others may offer continuing education through the alumni association or under the aegis of a special office in the institution's central administration. In Canada, organizational pluralism also prevails, most often with a center for (or division of) continuing education administered by a dean or director who reports to a vice-president for academic affairs (Brooke and Morris, 1987). Many institutions provide some continuing education without any formal organizational structure and without official acknowledgment of its existence. Nearly every institution has externally minded and public-spirited faculty members who delight in presenting useful and interesting knowledge outside academe. Thus, many colleges and universities have programs for adults independent of an organizational unit designated to develop adult programs. Such offerings are the work of a few persons who sense particular educational needs or respond to new forces in society.

Often, too, institutions are not aware of the extent to which middle-aged and older adults, who previously have been considered continuing education students, are enrolling in regular courses and thus are integrating themselves with the student body. Conversely, many young adults are enrolling for courses planned as continuing education for their elders. These trends are more pronounced in some institutions than in others, but how they play out by the year 2000 in terms of administrative organization, curricula, and instruction will be perhaps the most interesting spectacle of the decade in the field of collegiate adult and continuing education (Chickering, 1981; Brickell, 1987).

A brief glance at an institution may not provide an accurate indication of the level and quantity of continuing education. Significant activities may not be obvious because of the delivery system utilized or because of the administrative organization of the institution. Even in an institution with a highly visible organizational component for continuing education, programs for adults may be carried on under the administration of another department of the institution—a department whose name does not reveal its orientation toward an adult clientele. Further, there are always efforts of consequence by individual faculty members. An example is the engineering professor engaged in consultation with an electronics firm who updates practitioners on the latest research findings, leaving no institutional record of the presentation as would have happened if the professor had lectured at a workshop in the university's continuing education center. Similarly, a history professor speaking before a historical society may give insights into the evolution of a state or province, thereby providing continuing education to the audience in a manner that may be replicated by many professors in many fields across the college—all without inclusion in the official records of the institution.

A 1988 inquiry seeking information at two leading American technology institutes from officers by any title with responsibility for continuing education found that no one with such responsibility could be identified in the institutional directory. However, an examination of publications in component departments revealed that considerable and creative attention had been given to the importance of reaching out to practitioners in cognate fields. Thus, much continuing education is invisible, spread across the institutional landscape, existing in places and quantities frequently unknown even by the college or university responsible for it.

The extent to which an institution is visibly and formally engaged in continuing education is determined by the perceived importance of its clientele to the well-being of the institution and by the philosophy of the institution. The rationale for continuing education in many institutions might be summed up as survival and service. Many continuing educators consider their work to be primarily furthering their institution's public service function rather than the teaching and research functions. However, the emerging perspective is that continuing education, undergraduate education, and graduate education are three categories of instruction, and that "public service is not a function but a *principle* which animates and guides the basic work" (Mawby, 1987, p. 27) of the institution, whether manifest as instruction or as research.

As a rule, the greater a college's or university's investment in science and technology, including both facilities and faculty, the more likely it is that the institution's continuing education programs will be focused on professional practitioners or on academic colleagues with highly specialized and advanced educational needs, and the less likely it is that a comprehensive continuing education program that enables the public to share in the richness of the university will develop. There are exceptions, but institutional prominence in the form of faculty Nobel Laureates or numerous memberships in the National Academy of Science and the National Academy of Engineering may not correlate positively with the institutional profile in continuing education. Within the culture of institutions with potential for significant research, those faculty who do respectable research are treated with greater precedence than those who are respectable teachers and who seek to disseminate established knowledge. As a consequence, continuing education suffers unless there are stable and accepted institutional traditions and structures for carrying it on. Why is this so? One explanation is that institutional stature follows faculty stature, and a reasonably good researcher can become known throughout the world, while an excellent teacher may hardly be known beyond the campus. Further, one institutional dollar spent on research may generate five additional dollars in external subvention that shows clearly on an accountant's ledger sheet, whereas the return on money spent on continuing education may be notable but not so easily measurable.

The more prominent the liberal arts in an institution, even in the presence of great strengths in science and technology, the greater the tendency to develop continuing education programs for a broad spectrum of the public or general audiences. Essential to the development of any substantial program are a minimal number of accessible clients and a capable faculty and staff (with adequate financing) who commit themselves to the success of the program and who exert the will to see it through. Such ingredients have brought forth many exemplary programs in the humanities, conspicuously at St. John's College in Annapolis, Maryland, and at Washington University in St. Louis, Missouri. St. John's College awards a master of arts in liberal studies upon the completion of a curriculum based on questions pertaining to civilization. Sixty percent of the students are teachers or administrators. Other representative occupations are physicians, lawyers, and business people. Washington University awards a master of liberal arts for thirty credits, at least twelve (four courses) of which must be selected from colloquia specifically designed for the program. A thesis is optional in lieu of six credits of coursework. Business people have made up a plurality of the enrollment, with teachers, homemakers, and professionals in health and in law constituting most of the remainder (Gabor and House, 1987).

Noncredit personal enrichment courses are common offerings at all categories of institutions. The research universities place high value on continuing education that extends the academic strengths of the institution—in contrast to institutions that address the needs of a client even if it means instruction on topics outside the organic capability of the institution (Lord, 1979). Although a wide array of personal enrichment continuing education programs may be offered, the high-quality professional programs taught by regular faculty members are usually the foundation of credibility within research institutions that enables personal interest programs to exist. The greater the value placed on eminent research in a university, the greater the value placed on continuing education programs that convey research findings and, correspondingly, the less emphasis on personal enrichment programs. Ironically, the very narrowness of the many college curricula today is a major reason why the personal enrichment aspect of continuing education is important; college graduates need the opportunity to be occasional part-time students in order to complete the basic liberal arts education they did not acquire as undergraduates.

Programs

Generally, continuing education programs in four-year colleges and universities are of three types: credit, primarily for the purpose of formal professional credentialing and less frequently for personal enrichment; noncredit, for professional development, and noncredit, for personal enrichment. Credit programs consist of individual courses for semester or quarter credits. Such courses are normally applicable to academic degrees, are listed on transcripts, and are indistinguishable from other courses offered for academic credit for the institution. Frequently, such courses will be pursued by adults who do not have an academic degree, or by individuals in the process of changing careers and obtaining certification, or by those who simply desire additional education and want their achievement recognized by another academic degree.

Noncredit courses or programs are organized educational activities that do not represent credit toward academic degrees. They are characterized by a wide array of formats including, but not limited to, conferences, workshops, short courses, symposia, weekend courses, correspondence study, travel study, and lecture series. Noncredit courses have two primary purposes: professional development and personal enrichment. As the term indicates, professional development courses are primarily for professionals—such as accountants, architects, dentists, engineers, lawyers, nurses, pharmacists, physicians, social workers, and teachers—who have a recurring need to update themselves in their fields. Many professions require their members to participate in pertinent continuing education for a minimum number of hours each year in order to maintain their licenses to practice. Quality assurance measures in such courses are typically rigorous; otherwise, the classroom may be empty when the course is offered again. In addition, many new programs offering certification have developed in specialized professional fields, both in the credit and noncredit contexts. Adults opting for such programs often already have degrees and are usually interested in a new career.

For the purposes of connoting distinction and standardizing noncredit instruction, the continuing education unit (CEU) has been developed as another measure of noncredit instruction, both within and outside of colleges and universities. Standards adopted by the Council on the Continuing Education Unit (1986, p. iii) define one CEU as "ten contact hours of participation in an organized continuing education experience under responsible sponsorship, capable direction and qualified instruction."

Noncredit personal enrichment continuing education has, as its primary clientele, adults whose educations have been narrowly focused on career goals and adults who desire to develop their intellects further by study of the arts and humanities. Another considerable group are adults and children who enroll in so-called life skills courses. For adults, such courses may mean learning experiences aimed at improving interpersonal relationships or making better consumer decisions; for children, such courses may teach swimming or first aid practices. Many four-year colleges and universities also have organized basic adult education programs aimed at mitigating illiteracy. In 1987, about 740 four-year colleges and universities in the United States and sixty universities in Canada enrolled approximately 67,500 retired persons in Elderhostel, a week-long noncredit, collegiate-level academic program on personal enrichment topics (Elderhostel, 1988). And many other institutions also were offering programs for the older population. (See Chapter Forty, ''Education for Older Adults.'')

An indeterminate number of four-year colleges and universities offer nontraditional degree options to adult students. The Commission on Non-Traditional Study's 1973 definition of nontraditional education is valid: ''more an attitude than a system, puts the student first and the institution second, concentrates more on the [student's] need than the [institution's] convenience, encourages diversity of individual opportunity, de-emphasizes time, space and even course requirements in favor of competence and performance'' (Cross, Valley, and Associates, 1974, p. ix). Often, traditional programs are labeled nontraditional, and vice versa. In reality, most programs fall between the two extremes, leaving observers to reach their own judgments about the extent to which a program is nontraditional.

The discerning student may be aided by Houle's conceptualization of external degrees involving three types on a continuum with each type more nontraditional than the previous: extension, adult, and assessment (Houle, 1973). The extension degree simply extends the curriculum to another time and place with little or no difference from the traditional curriculum. The adult degree is a distinctive curriculum based on principles of adultness: maturity, responsibility, and the perceived uniqueness of the adult learner. Roosevelt University's bachelor of general studies is an example of this type of degree. The organizing principle of assessment degrees is the separation of instruction from the awarding of credit. This means that where and when learning occurs is not as important as assessing what has been learned. The DePaul School of New Learning's baccalaureate degree requirements are expressed in competencies, and students may use both old and new learning to fulfill those requirements (Cunningham, 1988).

Degree programs by means of nontraditional study are viewed suspiciously in many quarters. Institutions would be ill-advised to initiate nontraditional study programs in the belief that they will be less expensive than traditional programs. If an institution provides the nontraditional program with the same quality assurance it does for the traditional program, the nontraditional program will probably not cost less (Cross, Valley, and Associates, 1974).

Administrative Organization

The forms of administrative organization for continuing education in colleges and universities range from the highly centralized organizational structure to the complete lack of any deliberate organization. Between these two extremes are degrees of decentralization that occur either by design or by neglect. Pennsylvania State University has a deliberate correlated administrative organization in which the planning, marketing, budgeting, and administration of continuing education are handled by a central unit, and academic aspects are the responsibility of the relevant departments. Penn State leaders attribute their institution's enviable success in continuing education to its organizational structure. The University of Southern California centralizes policy formulation and decentralizes budgeting, program planning, and implementation. The University of Texas, Austin employs a hybrid of centralization and decentralization.

The more complex the institution in terms of its role, scope, and size, the greater the tendency toward decentralization in continuing education, as well as in other activities such as fund raising and research. A comprehensive university with many sources of income may be able to afford decentralization, whereas a small institution may not be able to afford the duplicative cost of decentralization. Indeed, a small institution may not be able to afford any formal administrative organization for continuing education.

Empirical evidence indicates that broad constituencies are better served by a degree of centralization that assures programs are generally representative of the faculty as a whole and not merely of professional schools. The happenstance approach to an institution's administrative organization for continuing education almost always assures that the university's professional schools, which serve the more financially rewarding professions, will collect most of the income—to the relative neglect of the arts, humanities, and less wealthy professions such as social work, public administration, and teaching. (See Chapter Thirty-Nine, "Continuing Education for the Professions.")

A public university, in particular, owes the public the right of reasonable and organized access to its educational and cultural resources, including its faculty. Notable examples of state universities that have maintained centralized continuing education, not without some erosion, are the University of Georgia and all the campuses of the University of California. Such an administrative organization has enabled university extension at the University of California's Los Angeles (UCLA) campus to act as a bridge to the community with a massive breadth of personal enrichment programs balanced by numerous offerings in the university's professional schools, such as medicine and business. UCLA enrolls annually about 100,000 predominantly college-educated individuals in more than 4,500 courses.

Private Colleges and Universities

Although public colleges and universities far surpass the private institutions in continuing education enrollments, the contributions of private colleges has been important, if not indispensable. When founded in 1892, the University of Chicago formally incorporated extension education into its organization. This innovation seized the imaginations of leaders in the emerging state universities of the Midwest and is reflected still in the continuing education strengths of those universities, paradoxically to a greater extent than in the University of Chicago itself.

In few fields has Harvard University's leadership been so significant as in adult and continuing education. In 1910, Harvard broke new ground by offering bachelor of liberal arts degrees to extension students, featuring open enrollment, coeducation for all ages, modest tuition, and instruction primarily by Harvard-affiliated faculty in the historic Harvard Yard. Graduates of Harvard's baccalaureate extension degree have subsequently earned advanced degrees from all professional schools in the university. In addition to the baccalaureate, a student in Harvard extension can opt for an associate of arts degree, master of liberal arts in nineteen fields of concentration, and certificates of advanced or special study in administration, management, applied sciences, and public health.

New York University (NYU) is notable for the broad array of continuing education opportunities, credit and noncredit, that it has provided in Manhattan since the early 1900s. One of NYU's more significant contributions was to make noncredit professional education academically acceptable in the 1940s with the initiation of an institute for accountants on federal taxation.

Brigham Young University (BYU), with a strong denominational affiliation, has the largest continuing education enrollment of any institution in the United States. In the 1986–1987 academic year, BYU enrolled more than 376,000 students, two-thirds of them in outreach programs involving faculty lecturers serving church congregations in North America. George Washington University, in Washington, D.C., has enjoyed a unique relationship with the federal government, particularly regarding military personnel in the District of Columbia and in Virginia, with part-time graduate degree programs in engineering, administration, management, and education. Syracuse University has a long history of operating off-campus centers and external master's degree programs that attract a nationwide clientele of professionals in graphic arts, business, engineering, and computer sciences. Johns Hopkins University's School of Continuing Studies is unique among similar administrative units in offering doctoral degrees, which it does in two areas—communications and counseling.

In private institutions particularly, the alumni associations often have greater visibility in the continuing education community than in the college or university itself. Examples of such prominent alumni associations are Stanford University, Dartmouth College, Princeton University, and the California Institute of Technology. This phenomenon is mostly unknown in public institutions, although their alumni associations may sponsor events labeled lifelong learning or continuing education.

Methods of Finance

The primary sources of income for college and university continuing education are participants' fees, usually with limited financial support from the parent institution. Institutional support may be direct, with cash supplements from endowments or from other income-producing activities. Or support may be indirect, with the provision of staff benefits, building space, janitorial services, and utilities. In the case of public institutions, state legislatures may appropriate funds designated for continuing education. With the exception of the Cooperative Extension Service, seldom is there a continuing education program without the requirement of a fee from participants. Other exceptions to the fee requirement may occur in programs that enjoy subsidies from a foundation or from a governmental agency, as is the case with some basic literacy programs.

An important matter in the finance of collegiate continuing education is the ability to carry over participant fee income from one fiscal year to the next. Generally, to the extent that a continuing education operation is dependent on participant fee income, the more important it is to carry over funds from one year to the next. Dependence on fee income means that continuing education is subject to fluctuations in the economy and must constantly engage in new program development. Under such conditions, continuing education assumes more aspects of a business, and if it cannot use surpluses from one year in the following year, it may lack the capital and staying power to develop new programs and to retain quality employees in economic downturns. Finally, dependence on participant fee income also compels continuing education to be market driven by its programs, as opposed to being academically driven—a harsh fact with academic and financial implications that are not always understood in higher academic councils. In Canadian universities, about 50 percent of total funds for continuing education are allocated by the central administration.

Questions and Issues

Six pervasive and global questions in adult and continuing education are the following: Who is to be taught? Who is to teach? What will be taught? How will teaching occur? Who will pay for it? How will learning be assessed? Within these profound questions are four specific issues for four-year colleges and universities in the last decade of the twentieth century: Is continuing education best provided as credit, noncredit, or both? What shall be the role of four-year colleges and unversities in professional continuing education? To what extent will so-called adult developmentalization based on life-cycle theory affect collegiate administration, curricula, and instruction (Chickering, 1981)? Can continuing education best perform its function in the academic mainstream of the institution, from the cultural margin, or both?

Credit instruction enables the adult student to earn academic degrees and to obtain entry into the professions; and noncredit instruction is a method of satisfying recurring educational needs, both professional and personal. With the exception of occasional compressed-time courses, credit courses are usually of several months' duration, and practicing professionals (or persons who are fully occupied with activities other than schooling) do not normally have the discretionary time necessary for such courses. Noncredit programs tend to be short-term and complete in themselves, whereas credit courses tend to be building blocks in lengthy curriculum. Content modifications are more easily made in noncredit programs—an important characteristic given the interdisciplinary nature of most continuing education. These characteristics augur well for noncredit instruction, a forecast supported by trends of the fifteen-year period from 1969 to 1984, as reported by the U.S. Department of Education (1985). In 1969, the majority of courses in colleges and universities were taken by adults for some type of credit. By 1984, only about one-third of the courses taken by adults were for credit.

Competition is constant among professional societies, private entrepreneurs, and colleges and universities over which group will provide professional continuing education to practitioners (Stern, 1983). Large corporations provide continuing education to retailers of their products, although conflicts of interest are often apparent. For example, a pharmaceutical manufacturing firm providing continuing education to pharmacists or to physicians may yield to the temptation to promote its products rather than convey objective information. Colleges and universities would seem the logical providers of professional continuing education, but obligations of their faculty to undergraduate and graduate teaching assignments and research often leave continuing education to other providers of professional continuing education. But, in some cases, faculty may teach part-time for these providers, whether professional societies, entrepreneurs, or corporations. And, although some effects of this competition may be positive for these other providers, the basic strengths of colleges and universities augur well for the stability and quality of their continuing education: they generally have firm credibility with the public and with the client group; they are nonprofit and relatively free of conflicts of interest; and through their faculties they have the inherent capability of ongoing program development. (See Chapter Twenty-One, "Providers of Adult and Continuing Education: A Framework.")

Effective university continuing educators are actively involved in academic processes within their institutions and with their clients outside the institution, both as groups and as individuals. Continuing educators occupy territory in which the academic culture and the nonacademic culture meet and overlap—territory that has characteristics of both cultures. Thus, continuing educators often are perceived, or believe they are perceived, as marginal members of the academic culture—an ambiguous status that can foster a sense of insecurity and isolation. There are, however, positive aspects of marginality, such as relatively more freedom and motivation to innovate and to improve customary practices (Marksbury, 1987). Innovation has been a hallmark of continuing education throughout its history.

A continuing educator must maintain standing in the prevailing academic community and must also communicate effectively with the external market. Many continuing educators believe their most productive position is to have a foot in both camps, which may mean that each camp views the continuing educator with suspicion. Standing up to a substantial nonacceptance in the culture of the parent institution may require strong personal conviction of the continuing educator and a transcending professional belief in continuing education as a major part of the institutional mission. Some analysts of university continuing education hold that the first courses in such diverse fields as computer sciences, gerontology, labor studies, and social work came from continuing educators who capitalized on their marginal status and developed new subject matter that subsequently became socially and economically important as well as academically respectable. History shows that continuing higher education has made its finest contributions from the creative and pragmatic margin, not from the central core. As it moves toward the core, there will remain that creative margin, which has been its strength from the beginning.

References

Adams, H. R. "Educational Extension in the United States." In *Report of the U.S. Commissioner of Education for 1899–1900*. Washington, D.C.: U.S. Government Printing Office, 1901.

"Adult Education Gets New Impetus." *New York Times,* Oct. 25, 1936, sec. 2, p. 4.

Alford, H. J. *Continuing Education in Action: Residential Centers for Lifelong Learning*. New York: Wiley, 1968.

Brickell, H. M. "Mainstreaming of Adult Students: Change and Opportunity." *Management of Lifelong Education Alumni Bulletin*, 1987, *1* (1), 1–3.

Brooke, W. M., and Morris, J. F. *Continuing Education in Canadian Universities: A Summary Report of Policies and Practices-1985*. Ottawa, Ont.: Canadian Association for University Continuing Education, 1987.

Chickering, A. W., and Associates. *The Modern American College*. San Francisco: Jossey-Bass, 1981.

Commission on Non-Traditional Study. *Diversity by Design*. San Francisco: Jossey-Bass, 1973.

Council on the Continuing Education Unit. *The Continuing Education Unit: Criteria and Guidelines*. Washington, D.C.: Council on the Continuing Education Unit, 1986.

Cross, P. K., Valley, J. R., and Associates. *Planning Non-Traditional Programs*. San Francisco: Jossey-Bass, 1974.

Cunningham, P. M. "Non-Traditional Programs: The Adult Learner." In North Central Association of Colleges and Schools, *A Collection of Papers on Self-Study and Institutional Improvement*. Chicago: North Central Association of Colleges and Schools, 1988.

Elderhostel. "1987 Program Survey." Memorandum. Boston: Elderhostel, 1988.

Gabor, S. C., and House, D. B. "Final Report: Exemplary Humanities Programs for Adults." A project funded by the National Endowment for the Humanities, School of Continuing Studies, Johns Hopkins University, March, 1987.

Houle, C. O. *The External Degree*. San Francisco: Jossey-Bass, 1973.

Lord, C. B. "Continuing Education: Organization and Purpose." *Journal of Continuing Higher Education*, 1979, *27* (4), 2-6.

Marksbury, R. A. "Marginal Dwellers: A Positive Role for Continuing Education." *The Journal of Continuing Higher Education*, 1987, *35* (2), 2-5.

Mawby, R. G. "Public Service." In G. F. Hudgins (ed.), *The Green Sheet*. Washington, D.C.: National Association of State Universities and Land Grant Colleges, 1987.

Stern, M. R. (ed.). *Power and Conflict in Continuing Professional Education*. Belmont, Calif.: Wadsworth, 1983.

U.S. Department of Education. *Trends in Adult Education*. Washington, D.C.: U.S. Government Printing Office, 1985.

Welch, E. *The Peripatetic University: Cambridge Local Lecturers, 1873-1973*. Cambridge, Eng.: Cambridge University Press, 1973.

24

Community Colleges

Ronald W. Shearon
Terrence A. Tollefson

Community colleges in the United States and Canada have evolved into major community-based adult education institutions. To a substantial degree, community colleges represent mirrors of their local communities and of the larger society surrounding them. Dominant social, technical, and economic trends that will extend beyond the year 2000 include greater urbanization, increasing numbers and proportions of minority persons, a decline in the number of eighteen to twenty-two year olds, increasing rates of technological change, more senior citizens, more women in the work force, and greater economic competition internationally. Other apparent but less conclusively documented trends are shifts in financial support from local to state funding sources and corresponding shifts in the control of community colleges. We believe community colleges that anticipate such changes accurately and deal with them effectively will flourish, and others will decline and possibly go out of existence. The historical context of the community college is important to the future, as many of its traditions are embodied in laws and in human value systems.

Evolution of Community Colleges

For almost every generalization that can be made about community, junior, and technical colleges in the latter part of the twentieth century, numerous exceptions can be found. Two-year colleges were established at different times by different people for different purposes, and they evolved in response to many local, state, and national needs. Moreover, they continue to bear different generic names, such as community, junior, and technical college, institute, and, in at least one case, university. We will employ the generic term *community college*. Despite differences in individual institutions, some general patterns and trends can be discerned.

The idea that secondary schools in the United States should offer the first two years of traditional university baccalaureate programs originated at least as long ago as 1851. Henry P. Tappan, who was then president of the University of Michigan, suggested that universities should shift the first two years of their programs to secondary schools (Palinchak, 1973).

In his 1969 inaugural address as president of the University of Minnesota, William W. Folwell elaborated upon the foregoing idea of a young person staying home and studying in a "high school or academy" until "somewhere near the end of the sophomore year," at which time he or she would "emigrate to a university" (Palinchak, 1973, p. 37). Folwell suggested a so-called new secondary department for this purpose, corresponding to the patterns of the German gymnasium and the French or Swiss lyceum.

The oldest public junior college in the United States is commonly believed to be Joliet Junior College, of Joliet, Illinois, which was founded in 1902 (Fields, 1967; Vaughan, 1985). The oldest public community college in Canada is believed to be Lethbridge Community College, Alberta, established in 1958 (Dennison and Gallagher, 1986).

Some scholars in community college education maintain that community college roots can be traced directly to the Morrill Acts of 1862 and 1890. This legislation created the land-grant system of educational institutions for the sons and daughters of working-class people in America. These institutions taught students and subjects (including agriculture and the mechanic arts) that had not been a part of traditional higher education. They were referred to as the people's colleges. They taught practical, applied, and basic subjects, and they advanced the idea of egalitarianism for all people. Clearly, the land-grant institutions have much in common with community colleges, which have been described as extensions of the land-grant idea (Vaughan, 1985).

A divergence of opinion exists regarding stages, periods, or generations of community college development in various American states and in the nation as a whole. Thornton (1966) labeled those periods as (1) the evolution of the junior college, 1850–1920, (2) the expansion of occupational programs, 1920–1945, and (3) the community college concept, 1945 to the present.

More recently, Deegan, Tillery, and Melone (1985) have divided the historical evolution of community colleges into five generations (1) extension of the high school, 1900–1930, (2) junior college, 1930–1950, (3) community college, 1950–1970, (4) comprehensive community college, 1970–1985, and (5) an unlabeled fifth generation beginning in 1985 and ending in 1995.

For our current purposes, we accept the Deegan-Tillery categorizations, and we label the fifth generation, The Search for a New Focus. The reasons for our proposed label will become clear as we proceed.

National Trends in Institutions and Enrollments

Most early junior colleges were private institutions. In 1900, there were eight private two-year colleges in the United States, and none was public. Not until the 1947–1948 academic year did the public two-year colleges (328) outnumber the private two-year colleges (322) in the United States. By 1980–1981, the number of private junior colleges had declined to 182—representing only 15 percent of the United States' total number of 1,231 two-year colleges (Cohen and Brawer, 1982, p. 10).

Two-year college enrollments in the United States reached their peak at nearly 4.8 million students in 1982 and declined to 4.5 million in 1985. Approximately 41 percent of two-year college students were age twenty-five or older in 1985, and about 63 percent were enrolled as part-time students in the fall of 1986. Further gradual declines to 4.4 million total students in 1992 are projected by the American Association of Community and Junior Colleges (AACJC). In the fall of 1985, women represented 54.6 percent of the full-time freshmen. In the fall of 1984, 2.1 million minority students were in higher education, and approximately 47 percent of all minorities were enrolled in community colleges (Association of Community College Trustees/American Association of Community and Junior Colleges, 1988). In 1982–1983, Canada had 123 community colleges and 44 other public postsecondary institutions fulfilling some of the same functions, with a total full-time enrollment of 478,000 (Dennison and Gallagher, 1986, pp. 285–294).

The roles, missions, and priorities of community colleges have varied over time. They also vary from one state or Canadian province to another and, possibly to a lesser degree, within a particular state or province. Such differences of focus are to be expected in a pluralistic and ever-changing society—particularly in institutions espousing a proud tradition of responding to community needs. In recent years, the intensity of the debate concerning the appropriate role, mission, and priorities of the community college has increased, at least partly in response to increased competition for tax dollars and for students. Community colleges have come under increasing attack for allegedly trying to be all things to all people.

In a review of current mission statements of numerous community college systems (Fountain and Tollefson, 1989), a common core of elements has been identified. They appear below in summary form:

1. Formal education consisting of courses and programs including college transfer, vocational-technical, remedial-developmental, and general education. With the possible exception of general education, these formal educational components have been designated by Cross (1985) and

by Carpenter and others (1987) as aspects of the vertical focus of the community college, which consists of formal education that has become the traditional bridge between high school and four-year college or university.

2. Services to students, such as counseling, diagnostic testing, and financial aid, that are designed to facilitate students' attendance and success in community colleges.

3. Continuing education consisting of scheduled noncredit courses in many areas ranging from literacy training to job enrichment to recreational topics.

4. Community services to individuals and organizations, including seminars, lectures, concerts, plays, and consultative activities intended to enhance community life. This component, in combination with number 3 above, is labeled the horizontal focus of the community college (Cross, 1985; Carpenter and others, 1987).

5. Clientele to be served including traditional freshmen and sophomore students, high school students enrolled for special purposes, older adults of all ages, women and minorities, educationally disadvantaged, and handicapped individuals.

6. Economic development. This component originated in some states as long as thirty years ago but has emerged nationally in recent years. It overlaps vocational-technical education in some respects, but also includes consultative services to present and potential employers in the community.

The differences in time, place, and situation of the origins of community colleges have spawned equally divergent patterns of governance or coordination structure, and funding from one state to another (Blocker, Plummer and Richardson, 1965; Fountain and Tollefson, 1989).

Five choices regarding missions and priorities have been identified by Cross (1985): (1) remain with the comprehensive mission and gamble that it can be done well, (2) improve the vertical focus and gamble that community colleges can compete with four-year institutions for students seeking the baccalaureate degree, (3) define a community-based horizontal mission and gamble that constituents and the community can be convinced to support and lobby for that function, (4) tackle the integrated focus and gamble that industry and students really want liberally educated workers and citizens, or (5) give renewed effort to remedial programs and gamble that confidence can be won and that the community college will continue to receive the major portion of funds marked for remedial services.

State Agencies for Public Community Colleges

In many states, individual public junior and community colleges were established without the types of specific enabling legislation that California enacted. Those early colleges typically were locally funded and locally controlled, frequently through local school boards, but sometimes through public universities or by their own governing boards. In some instances, state tax dollars were channeled through such agencies. As more colleges emerged, community college leaders began to advocate statewide planning and coordination for public two-year colleges. State master plans were developed in California and in a number of other states, either before or shortly after enabling legislation was enacted.

In a 1963 study, Martorana found five types of state-level organizations for public two-year colleges in the thirty-eight states that had such institutions at that time. They were (1) state departments of education, (2) state boards or superintendents of education, (3) state boards of higher education, (4) boards of universities, and (5) separate state junior college boards or commissions. He determined that twenty-six of those thirty-eight states had placed control of community colleges under state superintendents of education or under state boards of education. Eight states regulated two-year colleges through state boards of higher education; five states did so through university boards; and six had separate state boards or commissions for community colleges. This inconsistent pattern was deemed to indicate "that the image of the two-year college as a collegiate institution is not clearly delineated, at least insofar as agency control is concerned" (Blocker, Plummer, and Richardson, 1965, p. 82).

The types and degrees of both state funding and state control vary greatly from one state to another. Many writers contend that there is a correlation between the proportion of the institutional funds contributed by states to community colleges and the degree of state control. Several writers also have noted trends in the past decade toward proportionally less local funding, greater state funding (Tollefson, Adkins, and Buyse, 1980), and greater state control. Some authors and officials assert that the correlation between funding and control is appropriate and perhaps inevitable (Scott, 1987; Fischer, 1987).

In the years since the 1963 Martorana report, all twelve other states have established public two-year colleges. Their enrollments and supporting funds have increased dramatically, and state-level governance and coordination have responded in a number of ways, including expansion, to the growing importance of community colleges. The twenty-six states that regulated community colleges through state superintendents or boards of education appear to have declined to six. (Note that all figures in this section are approximate because of the complexities of agency names and because some states assign community college functions to more than one state agency.) States that include community college units under state boards, commissions, or departments of higher or postsecondary education have increased from eight to eleven. State boards, commissions, or departments of community colleges have increased from six to fifteen, and state university systems that are responsible for community colleges have increased from five to fifteen. Several states have still other patterns for state-level coordination or governance of community colleges, including Delaware and Rhode Island with one community college in each state, and others that combine community college state-level responsibilities with those for other vocational, technical, or adult education functions. From these and other indications, it is clear that community colleges are now identified nationally and internationally as postsecondary institutions.

Current Program and Services

The original and primary purpose of the community college was college transfer—to extend high school work to the thirteenth and fourteenth years or to provide the first two years of college. It was clearly a collegiate function with emphasis on the liberal arts. There is little doubt that what has become known generally as the transfer function dominated the early years of the junior college movement. The college transfer function of the community college continues to be an essential part of the overall comprehensive mission, even though enrollments and actual transfers to four-year institutions have declined (Kintzer and Wattenbarger, 1985). Studies have shown that "not more than one in twenty enrollees completes a two-year program and transfers in the succeeding term" (Cohen and Brawer, 1982, p. 54). One of the recommendations of the Brookings Institution report (Breneman and Nelson, 1981) called for community colleges to deemphasize the transfer function and to leave this function for the four-year institutions.

The main purpose of the college transfer program is to help students move from high school through the community college to the baccalaureate degree. The transfer curriculum is considered to be the most prestigious and most understood function of the community college (Cross, 1985). Some writers contend that traditional academic students have been neglected, and that the college transfer function is being vigorously reasserted by leaders in education (Zwerling, 1986).

Cohen and Brawer (1986–1987), drawing from a data bank of more than ten years from several national studies, trace the current status of the collegiate curriculum. They found that the collegiate curriculum accounts for more than 50 percent of the community colleges' credit course offerings. They report that, "English and mathematics, basic to all studies, enroll the most students, with history and the social sciences, and biology, the foundation of the health professions, following closely" (p. 13). Cohen and Brawer also noted two other findings that distinguish community college transfer courses and programs from their vocational-technical counterparts. They reported that a disproportionate share of courses in community college transfer programs are designated as being at the freshman level and that very few such courses have prerequisites. They characterize the typical transfer program as lateral rather than linear. James Palmer (personal interview with authors, Sept. 25, 1987) hypothesizes that the number of students who graduate with baccalaureate degrees after earning some credit in community college transfer programs may be substantially underestimated because conventional data collection efforts do not keep track of intermittent enrollments.

Vocational and Technical Education. Programs in vocational and technical education have been expanding in postsecondary institutions during the past decade. These programs are designed to prepare adults for immediate employment and job upgrading in local and regional job markets. They are influenced by occupational advisory committees, by licensure examinations, and by student and faculty interests. Accordingly, most community colleges offer programs in various health professions, engineering technologies, and business (Cohen and Brawer, 1986–1987).

Historically, vocational and technical programs have been considered terminal degree programs. However, more adults today are wanting to obtain or to improve employment as well as to be able to continue their educations. Thus, many transfer programs in technology have been developed to serve this need. Likewise, the integration of more general education courses with vocational studies is being emphasized in the curricula. Community colleges enroll over one-third of all students in higher education, and nearly one-half of these students are pursuing occupational degrees (Orris, 1985, p. 8).

Dale Parnell, president of AACJC, advocated a much closer linkage with the nation's high schools when he recommended the so-called 2 + 2 Tech-Prep/Associate-Degree Program for the ordinary students in the high schools. This alternative offers promise; however, it is worth noting that the past articulation efforts between high schools and community colleges would not fill a slim book (Parnell, 1985).

The National Roundtable on Economic Development, a consortium of leaders from government, the private sector, labor, and education, has made eleven major recommendations to community, technical, and junior colleges to foster economic development. Several of the important recommendations are summarized below.

1. These institutions have an essential role to play in economic development involving customized training for a changing work force.
2. Future students will be older; they may need to participate in expanded remediation programs, or they already may be college graduates returning for more skills training; they may need different learning environments; and they will include more immigrants, minorities, and women.
3. Literacy should be defined as the ability to read, write, compute, learn, unlearn, and relearn.
4. Community colleges should develop networks and partnerships with other educational delivery systems, both to facilitate technology transfer and to avoid unnecessary duplication of effort (Marsalis and McKenney, 1987).

These recommendations clearly challenge community, technical, and junior colleges to emphasize adult continuing education in combination with technical education for economic development in the twenty-first century. This direction has been backed up by strong leadership from the National Council for Occupational Education (NCOE). In its 1986 national study, the main conclusion was that the nation's colleges are beginning to reexamine the impact they have on economic development in communities they serve. Mission statements are being revised to include reference to economic development. Major initiatives for economic development were started in 1982 and 1984 by the American Association of Community and Junior Colleges and by the Sears-Roebuck Foundation—so-called Keeping America Working and Putting America Back to Work programs (National Council for Occupational Education, 1986; Hammond and Garrison, 1986). Both the AACJC and the Association of Community College Trustees (ACCT) received planning grants from the Sears-Roebuck Foundation in 1984 and 1985 for the Keeping America Working project (Parnell, 1987a).

General Education. An evolving thrust in community colleges may be occurring in general education—the integrated curriculum. General education focuses on developing a framework or cognitive map for organizing knowledge from numerous sources (Cohen and Brawer, 1982). It involves learning to think critically, developing values, understanding transitions and cultures, and, according to Cohen and Brawer, putting that knowledge to use.

Cross (1985) suggests that the integrated focus may be the "sleeper" with considerable potential (Cross, 1985). For example, increasing numbers of business and industry leaders are asking for workers who have a general education, good work attitudes, and the capacity to learn. The specific job training is increasingly done by many large employers. There does appear to be an adult market for general education if it is a truly integrated experience and not taught as preparation for academic majors.

Community Services and Continuing Education. Harlacher (1970, p. 220) characterized the community college as a "horizontal or distributed entity" that offers a wide variety of community services to adults throughout its district. This emerging focus of the community college emphasizes the community and its need for services: use of facilities, recreation, community forums and lectures, fine arts, noncredit short courses, seminars, workshops, conferences, institutes, and arts festivals. In the fifth generation of community colleges, there will likely be considerable reassessment of the commitment to community services, because the need for community services and non-formal continuing education probably will increase during the decade of the 1990s (Hankin and Fey, 1985).

The changing profile of demographic trends represents a major driving force for community services programs at the local community college. Americans are getting older. The median age is predicted to be thirty-four in 1990 and over thirty-seven by the year 2000. The average life expectancy is estimated to be 74.6 and is increasing each year due to better health care and education. This aging population will very likely place demands on community service programs in the areas of adjusting to retirement, leisure education, and volunteer opportunities (Hankin and Fey, 1985).

Changes are also taking place among minority groups and women. Blacks and Hispanics are increasing their proportion in the total population. In California, minorities increased from 15 percent in 1960 to 33 percent in 1980 and are projected to be 39 percent in 1990 and over 45 percent by the year 2000 (Smith, 1987).

Women are taking on new roles. Most new jobs are taken by women, and a majority of the working women have dependent children. Community colleges continue to help minorities and women enter the mainstream of American life by offering programs in English language training, job coping skills, adult basic education, women's reentry, and job and career training. They also offer counseling and placement services.

Life transitions represent another area of social change that is impacting on community services programming at the local community college. College Entrance Examination Board researchers have estimated that 126 million adults twenty-five years of age or older are in transition from one stage of adulthood to another (Aslanian and Brickell, 1980). Learning has been found to be important for making adjustments to numerous life transitions.

While the growth in and demand for community service programs continues to increase, most state systems and community colleges are reassessing this particular part of their mission. Critics have questioned the validity and quality of offerings, while some supporters still suggest that community services should be the central mission (Cohen and Brawer, 1982; Vaughan and Associates, 1983).

Remedial-Developmental Education. The community college has evolved into one of the major institutions trying to educate adult illiterates and insufficiently literate adults in American society. For many adults, the community college represents a second chance to learn basic academic skills that were not learned in the public schools. The community colleges are accessible because many operate under a so-called open-door or open-access policy of admitting any adult desiring instruction without regard to race, sex, religion, color, geographical location, or financial status. This egalitarian philosophy has resulted in the frequent reference to the community college as democracy's college, the people's college, or the opportunity college (Roueche, Baker, and Roueche, 1987).

Some studies have estimated that at least half of the adults entering community colleges are deficient in essential academic skills (Roueche, Baker, and Roueche, 1987). Developmental programs have been found to be helpful to students, especially in the areas of remediation. Dobson (1987) reported that students in developmental studies who needed and received remediation in specified skills subsequently attained higher grades in the areas in which they had received remediation than did adults who were assessed as not needing remediation. According to Roueche, Baker, and Roueche (pp.

22–26), "Early efforts at remediation proved marginal at best. Programs were poorly conceived, poorly designed, and even more poorly implemented. Today, there are working, observable community college models of how to succeed with entering students who are deficient in basic skills."

Cross (1985, p. 47) stated, "Although there is brave talk about improving the high schools to the point that remediation is no longer needed, most community college students are not coming directly from high school; and, even if high schools improve their teaching of basic skills greatly over the next decade, there will still be a great deal of 'catching up' to do. So far, remediation is a well-accepted part of the community college mission and funding has been protected reasonably well in most places for that critically important social function." Clearly, remedial and developmental education programs will continue to be a major task facing administrators and teachers in community colleges.

Student Services. Community colleges provide a myriad of support services to adult students. Even so, some leaders in the field believe the services are inadequate for a diverse adult student population. The changing needs of adult students have placed much stress on student services in most community colleges. Some changes that necessitate increased student services have been described by Matson and Deegan (1985). Perhaps the most troubling change is the increasing number of students underprepared for college-level work. Other trends include more part-time students; more off-campus delivery systems; more older students, especially women returning to college; an increasing number of displaced workers; new and complex developments in technology; more contract training programs; and more competition with business and industry in training and education.

The traditional functions of student services, according to Cohen and Brawer (1982), are the following: (1) counseling and guidance, (2) recruitment and orientation, (3) extracurricular activities, (4) residence halls, (5) financial aid, and (6) articulation. These types of student services appear to be more appropriate for credit or curriculum students than for students in community services and continuing education (Hankin and Fey, 1985). No real consensus exists regarding student service programs, but in many colleges there is a need to redesign student service programs for the working part-time adult student. New ideas, approaches, and models for adult students are needed.

Clientele

Community, technical, and junior colleges serve a broad base of constituent groups in communities throughout the nation. These institutions serve individual citizens, families, business and industry groups, local governments, and numerous community agencies. Clientele are as broad and diverse as the American society. There is clearly one common theme emerging in all the current literature on community colleges: these institutions serve adult learners from all walks of life who enroll for a variety of reasons. The five major program areas discussed in previous sections of this chapter have been developed to respond to the evolving educational needs of adults as learners— vocational and technical, remedial-developmental, community services and continuing education, college transfer, and general education. Community colleges are no longer just for the traditional eighteen to twenty-two-year-old college student. Today's community colleges are evolving into major adult education institutions offering credit and noncredit programs to a changing American society.

The Changing Demographics. Substantial evidence in the literature indicates that the demographics are changing in American society, and the implications for community colleges are broad and complex. The evidence indicates that retraining and lifelong education will be paramount. The following narrative presents a sampling of that evidence.

Parnell (1985) describes what he calls the neglected majority as the 60 to 70 percent of high school students who are not likely to pursue a baccalaureate degree program. Estimates indicate that roughly 80 percent of the nation's adult population does not hold a bachelor's degree and that 25 percent of students who start high school never finish. These figures illustrate the large gap between people who start high school and those who eventually complete a bachelor's degree.

Regarding the nation's work force, Parnell (1985) and Johnston (1987) suggest a shortage of skilled workers. The work force is aging, and the ratio of older workers to younger workers is increasing. On one hand, the number of people over sixty-five is growing about twice as fast as the population of the nation as a whole. And, on the other hand, Parnell (1987b) predicts a 21 percent decline in the number of young people who will be turning eighteen in the 1990s. When comparing the haves and have-nots, Parnell (1985) reports that two out of three adults meeting the federal definition of poverty are women, and that more than half of the poverty families are maintained by single women. The vast majority of the poor in American society are women with children. Three-fifths of all females over sixteen years of age will be working by the year 2000, and projections are that only 20 percent of new entrants into the labor force by the year 2000 will be native white males, compared with 47 percent today. Also by the year 2000, 29 percent of new entrants into the labor force will be nonwhite—about twice the current percentage. Moreover, immigrants are expected to increase both in the population and in the work force, especially in the South and the West. Nonwhites, women, and immigrants make up about one-half of the net additions to the work force today; however, by the year 2000, they will make up five-sixths of the net additions. Clearly, the work force will grow slowly while becoming older, more female, and more disadvantaged.

Another important demographic trend is increased urbanization. Four out of five Americans now live in population centers of 250,000 or more. Persons living in rural areas have the technical skills they need to live on the land but lack the skills necessary to attain a well-paying urban position. Thus, the migration pattern from rural to urban areas is creating at-risk populations of both rural and urban adults. Canada appears to be experiencing similar changes (Dennison and Gallagher, 1986).

Most of the new jobs and new wealth between now and the year 2000 will be created by service industries (Johnston, 1987). The expectation is that the new jobs in service industries will demand much higher skill levels in reading, in following directions, and in math. By the year 1995, three-fourths of all job classifications are expected to require some postsecondary education for entry into the workplace (Parnell, 1987b). Demographic trends in the work force, coupled with these increased skill requirements, will lead to more unemployment among the least-skilled people. It seems clear that both the work force and the institutions will need to be adaptable and willing to learn.

Adult Learner Profiles. A major change during the past decade has been the increase in part-time students on community college campuses. More than 50 percent of community college students today attend on a part-time basis. With the increase in part-time students, a noticeable decline in college transfer students has been reported (Kintzer and Wattenbarger, 1985). The impact on community college curriculum could be substantial, because part-time students appear to be more interested in career preparation and advancement than are the college transfer students.

Over the past decade, community colleges have enrolled more female students, more part-time students, and more older students. The population between the ages of eighteen and twenty-four is expected to decline by 15 percent between 1980 and 1990, and the twenty-five to forty-four year old group is expected to grow by 25 percent (Dearman and Plisko, 1980). The average age, as well as the number of part-time students, is expected to climb. And older students also tend to be less interested in general education courses and more interested in specific occupational training. The implications for the curriculum are clear.

In general, community colleges are enrolling a higher proportion of women, more part-time students with families and job responsibilities, more minorities, more academically underprepared students, and students who are primarily interested in occupational preparation and growth. These trends have been documented by several studies over the past decade (Shearon, Templin, and Daniel, 1976; Shearon and others, 1980; Warren, 1985). Community colleges must be prepared for the changes.

Emerging Agenda—A Search for a New Focus

Adults continuing their education by whatever means they choose represent a strong and potentially influential force in shaping a new focus for what has been characterized as the fifth generation of community colleges. At the very core of community colleges now and in the foreseeable future is a diverse and complex myriad of adults as learners. Terms such as *adult learning, recurrent education, self-directed learning, continuing education,* and *lifelong education* are being used extensively in adult education and community college literature. The emerging profiles of these adults as learners portray them as more likely to be women with families, older, employed, and taking credit or noncredit programs on a part-time basis either to advance in their jobs or to get a better job. As discussed in the preceding section, the age of these adult students is predicted to increase along with the proportion of minorities and immigrants, especially in the South and West.

Leaders in the field have identified several priorities to help in the search for a new focus for the evolving community college (Deegan, Tillery, and Melone, 1985; Deegan and Tillery, 1987). Increased fiscal, social, and political pressures have fueled the search for a new focus. The old paradigm of open-access, low-cost programs and a comprehensive mission of college transfer, occupational, remedial-developmental, community services, and continuing education will need to be examined as the fifth generation emerges. Already several authors (Deegan and Tillery, 1987; Alfred, 1984; Roueche and Baker, 1987; Smith, 1987, Mancha, 1987) are developing themes of excellence, quality, and productivity which will no doubt become a part of the debate and search for a new focus.

Some of the key priorities are as follows (Deegan and Tillery, 1987):

1. Community college leaders need to review and synthesize knowledge about outcomes (especially for older, part-time, and recurrent students) of a community college education.
2. More effective staff and organizational development programs need to be developed.
3. Community colleges need to resolve issues surrounding the comprehensive mission.
4. Community college leaders need to clarify and to resolve issues surrounding governance at local and state levels.
5. Effective strategic planning and coordination of community college curricula are needed to help achieve excellence and quality.
6. There is a need to restructure student service programs to meet more adequately the needs of the adult learner.
7. New and strengthened networks and linkages between community colleges and high schools, business and industry, and higher education are needed.

Community colleges have helped many adults prepare and retrain for meaningful work roles and experience a liberal education. These institutions have helped other adults prepare for life's transitions and experience life in a more meaningful way. Some have learned to read, to appreciate music and art, to speak a new language, or just to have fun. We hope and believe the next generation of community colleges will continue to help adults develop their abilities in liberal and practical ways for a better society. Previous generations of community college leaders persisted and overcame many adversities to achieve their ideals. Present and future generations can do the same. Within the umbrella of the comprehensive focus, individual colleges can assess local needs, values, and traditions to determine which parts of the overall comprehensive mission they most appropriately can emphasize.

Our conclusions are supported by the report of the national commission on the future of the community colleges (American Association of Community and Junior Colleges, 1988). This report strongly endorses maintaining the comprehensive mission of the community college and stresses the need for improved leadership and increased funding of community colleges.

References

Alfred, R. L. "Paradox for the Community College: Education in the '80s." *Community College Review,* 1984, *12* (1), 2–6.

American Association of Community and Junior Colleges. *Building Communities: A Vision for a New Century.* Washington, D.C.: American Association of Community and Junior Colleges, 1988.

Aslanian, C. B., and Brickell, H. M. *Americans in Transition: Life Changes as Reasons for Adult Learning.* New York: College Entrance Examination Board, 1980.

Association of Community College Trustees/American Association of Community and Junior Colleges. *Fact Book on Community Colleges.* Washington, D.C.: Association of Community College Trustees/American Association of Community and Junior Colleges, 1988.

Blocker, C. E., Plummer, R. H., and Richardson, R. C., Jr. *The Two-Year College: A Social Synthesis.* Englewood Cliffs, N.J.: Prentice-Hall, 1965.

Breneman, D. W., and Nelson, S. C. *Financing Community Colleges: An Economic Perspective.* Washington, D.C.: Brookings Institution, 1981.

Carpenter, D., and others. "The Future of Community Colleges." Unpublished memorandum from the National Council of State Directors of Community and Junior Colleges to members of the Commission on the future of Community Colleges, Apr. 21, 1987.

Cohen, A. M., and Brawer, F. B. *The American Community College.* San Francisco: Jossey-Bass, 1982.

Cohen, A. M., and Brawer, F. B. "The Collegiate Curriculum." *Community College Review,* 1986–1987, *14* (3), 13–20.

Cross, K. P. "Determining Missions and Priorities for the Fifth Generation." In W. L. Deegan and D. Tillery (eds.), *Renewing the American Community College: Priorities and Strategies for Effective Leadership.* San Francisco: Jossey-Bass, 1985.

Dearman, N. B., and Plisko, V. A. *The Condition of Education.* Washington, D.C.: National Center for Education Statistics, 1980.

Deegan, W. L., and Tillery, D. "Toward a Fifth Generation of Community Colleges: Seven Priorities for Action." *Community, Technical and Junior College Journal*, 1987, *57* (5), 36–40.

Deegan, W. L., Tillery, D., and Melone, R. J. "The Process of Renewal: An Agenda for Action." In W. L. Deegan and D. Tillery (eds.), *Renewing the American Community College: Priorities and Strategies for Effective Leadership*. San Francisco: Jossey-Bass, 1985.

Dennison, J. D., and Gallagher, P. *Canada's Community Colleges*. Vancouver: University of British Columbia Press, 1986.

Dobson, R. R. "Quality and Accessibility: Are They Mutually Exclusive?" *Community College Review*, 1987, *14* (4), 56–60.

Fields, R. R. *The Community College Movement*. New York: McGraw-Hill, 1967.

Fischer, R. G. "California Community Colleges: On the Road to Reform?" *Community College Review*, 1987, *15* (1), 13–20.

Fountain, B. E., and Tollefson, T. A. *Forty-Nine State Systems of Community Colleges in the United States*. Raleigh: North Carolina State University, 1989.

Hammond, P. K., and Garrison, D. C. *1985 Progress Report on the Sears Partnership Development Fund*. Washington, D.C.: American Association of Community and Junior Colleges, 1986.

Hankin, J. N., and Fey, P. A. "Reassessing the Commitment to Community Services." In W. L. Deegan and D. Tillery (eds.), *Renewing the American Community College: Priorities and Strategies for Effective Leadership*. San Francisco: Jossey-Bass, 1985.

Harlacher, E. L. "Community Colleges." In R. H. Smith, G. F. Aker, and J. R. Kidd (eds.), *Handbook of Adult Education*. New York: Macmillan, 1970.

Johnston, W. B. "Workforce 2000—Work and Workers for the Twenty-First Century." Indianapolis, Ind.: Hudson Institute, 1987.

Kintzer, F. C., and Wattenbarger, J. L. *The Articulation/Transfer Phenomenon: Patterns and Directions*. Horizons Issues Monograph Series, no. 25. Washington, D.C.: American Association of Community and Junior Colleges, Council of Universities and Colleges, and ERIC Clearinghouse for Junior Colleges, 1985.

Mancha, P. E. "Blueprint for the Future." *Community College Review*, 1987, 14 (4), 31–41.

Marsalis, W. C., and McKenney, J. F. *Report and Recommendations—The Role of Community, Technical, and Junior Colleges in Technical Education/Training and Economic Development*. Washington, D.C.: American Association of Community and Junior Colleges, 1987.

Martorana, S. V. "The Legal Status of American Public Junior Colleges." In *The American Junior Colleges*. Washington, D.C.: American Council on Education, 1963.

Matson, J. E., and Deegan, W. L. "Revitalizing Student Services." In W. L. Deegan and D. Tillery (eds.), *Renewing the American Community College: Priorities and Strategies for Effective Leadership*. San Francisco: Jossey-Bass, 1985.

National Council for Occupational Education. *Community College and Economic Development.* A report prepared by the Task Force on the Role of Community Colleges in Economic Development. Washington, D.C., October 17, 1986.

Orris, J. E. "General Education in the Community College: A Megatrendian View." *Community College Review,* 1985, *13* (1), 8-11.

Palinchak, R. S. *Evolution of the Community College.* Metuchen, N.J.: Scarecrow Press, 1973.

Parnell, D. *The Neglected Majority.* Washington, D.C.: Community College Press, 1985.

Parnell, D. (ed.). *American Association of Community and Junior Colleges Letter,* no. 257, Sept. 8, 1987a, pp. 1-4.

Parnell, D. "Preparing for the Next Century." *Community, Technical and Junior College Journal,* 1987b, *58* (1), 3.

Roueche, J. E., and Baker, G. A. *Access and Excellence: The Open Door College.* Washington, D.C.: Community College Press, 1987.

Roueche, J. E., Baker, G. A., and Roueche, S. O. "Open Door or Revolving Door?" *Community, Technical and Junior College Journal,* 1987, *57* (5), 22.

Scott, R. W. "Welcoming Remarks." Community College Instructional Administrators' Leadership Institute, Raleigh, N.C., June 1987.

Shearon, R. W., Templin, R. G., and Daniel, D. E. *Profile of Students in North Carolina Community Colleges and Technical Institutes.* Raleigh: North Carolina State University Press, 1976.

Shearon, R. W., and others. *Putting Learning to Work—A Technical Report.* Raleigh: North Carolina State University Press, 1980.

Smith, J. "Equity with Excellence." *Community, Technical and Junior College Journal,* 1987, *57* (4), 22-24.

Thornton, J. W., Jr. *The Community Junior College.* (2nd ed.) New York: Wiley, 1966.

Tollefson, T. A., Adkins, G. D., and Buysee, J. *National Survey of Funding and Accountability of Public Community, Junior and Technical Colleges, 1976-79.* Denver: Colorado State Board for Community Colleges and Occupational Education, 1980.

Vaughan, G. B. *The Community College in America.* Washington, D.C.: Community College Press, 1985.

Vaughan, G. B., and Associates. *Issues for Community College Leaders in a New Era.* San Francisco: Jossey-Bass, 1983.

Warren, J. "The Changing Characteristics of Community College Students." In W. L. Deegan and D. Tillery (eds.), *Renewing the American Community College: Priorities and Strategies for Effective Leadership.* San Francisco: Jossey-Bass, 1985.

Zwerling, L. S. (ed.) *The Community College and Its Critics.* New Directions for Community Colleges, no. 54. San Francisco: Jossey-Bass, 1986.

25

The Cooperative Extension Service

LaVerne B. Forest

Trying to describe the United States Cooperative Extension Service (CES) is analogous to the old story of four blind men describing an elephant. With one inspecting the leg, another the tusk, another the tail, and still another the ear, each formed an entirely different impression. CES also has been variously described, but because of its diversity, several perspectives are required to understand its mission, its clientele approaches, its successes, and its weaknesses as an adult education system. To begin, the Smith-Lever Act (Pub. L. No. 95–113, 91 Stat. 1011, 1018 [1977]), as amended in 1977, states the purposes of CES as follows: "to aid in diffusing among the people of the United States useful and practical information on subjects relating to agriculture, uses of solar energy with respect to agriculture, home economics, and rural energy and to encourage the application of the same. . . . Extension work shall consist of the giving of instruction and practical demonstrations in agriculture use, uses of solar energy with respect to agriculture, home economics, and rural energy and subjects relating thereto to persons not attending or resident in said colleges in the several communities."

But has CES fulfilled its educational mandate of providing practical, research-based information to people who will apply that information to their problems? It depends on who is answering the question. For instance, one perspective is offered by a typical pair of clients, Ann and Tony Oleson, a young farm couple in their early thirties with three children who are in the local, extension-supported 4-H club program. Both parents reflect positively on their own experiences in 4-H club work, which have influenced their decision to farm and to be 4-H volunteer leaders. On their 240-acre Corn Belt dairy farm, they have forty-two milking cows in the Dairy Herd Improvement Program, an extension program for improving dairy production and income. They are excited by the continued increase in the herd's annual average milk production (up to 19,450 pounds per cow) due to feeding and culling according to the extension recommendations in their monthly computer printout. Ann, a member of the local homemaker council, regularly receives training from the county home economics agent, and she passes on new information to other club members. Tony regularly goes to extension education meetings on land-use planning, forage production, and price forecasting. Using their computer, the Olesons keep farm records according to extension recommendations. They view extension as their key source of new research and knowledge on managing the farm and on raising their children. If you were to ask the Olesons, they would say extension is fulfilling its educational mandate, and they would hope CES will continue to do so.

Yet, in 1981, a U.S. congressional agricultural subcommittee (Department of Operations, Research, and Foreign Agriculture) said an oversight of CES was long overdue. The issues that the subcommittee listed for study implied that the answer to the question of whether CES is fulfilling its mission is inconclusive (contrary to the response the Olesons might give), especially as CES looks to the future. The issues were the following:

- What are the appropriate roles of the three primary investors (federal, state, and local governments)?
- How have demographic shifts affected CES programs?
- Does CES have a responsibility to provide services to a broad spectrum of national publics regardless of residence?
- Should CES transmit scientific findings or engage in practical research?
- Should CES continue to relate only to agriculture?
- How should CES adapt to using the new educational technologies?
- What should Congress expect from CES on program accountability?

Finally, a third perspective claims extension has failed to achieve its original mandate. In a very damning analysis, Hightower (1973) stated that extension policy and programs are determined on a daily basis at the county level by autonomous extension agents with little general oversight by state directors and the national administration. Hightower concluded that the effect of this local autonomy has been to isolate extension work from shifts in public priorities. A great deal of money left to the discretion of the local county agent, who consults a narrow group for advice, leads to very little program change at the local level. According to Hightower, the county agents just keep doing the same old things, day in and day out, preaching agricultural productivity and efficiency. He concluded that extension is largely irrelevant in today's rural America, certainly not warranting an investment of $332 million federal tax dollars.

The three different perspectives raise issues about CES as an adult education system for the future. If its mission is to disseminate practical new information to people who need it, has it been successful? If it has succeeded or not, is it time to reconsider priorities and goals, to shift to new clientele, to use new educational methods, or to obtain new modes of financing? Will the current CES staff be capable of addressing the possible program changes, and will they be appropriately accountable? This chapter's purpose is to review the past, to illustrate the present, and to address the future in the context of these issues.

The Past: CES's Origin and History

Disseminating new agricultural information to farmers who can use the ideas to improve farming probably goes back to the Chinese civilization and biblical times. Prawl, Medlin, and Gross (1984) recite the popular tale that the first agricultural agent was Squanto, a Native American who showed the Pilgrims how to place a fish below maize to enhance the plant's growth.

True (1929) provided perhaps the best and earliest documented history of extension. He stated that the Philadelphia Society was formed in 1785 and that the Massachusetts Society for Promoting Agriculture was formed in 1792. Those societies served as foundations for later county and state agricultural societies such as the Albemarle Society, organized by Thomas Jefferson, which, in turn, sponsored the state and local county fairs for competition, sales, and agricultural education. Between 1846 and 1850, Ohio state agricultural employees gave lectures in districts and towns. In 1854, the Massachusetts State Board of Agriculture initiated policies leading to establishment of farmer institutes.

These early efforts by both agricultural scientists and farmers provided the environment in which President Lincoln signed the Morrill Act of 1862, establishing land-grant universities and colleges in all of the states and territories. The act enabled the teaching of agriculture, mechanics, and other practical subjects.

During the remainder of the nineteenth century, farmer institutes continued. The Chautauquas, traveling agricultural entertainment and educational shows, evolved. In 1899, forty-seven states had farmer institutes with a total attendance of over 500,000 farmers.

Thus, much adult education was implemented by these early societies, fairs, institutes, and various agricultural organizations in response to the needs of the people in rural America—people primarily engaged in agriculture. However, the research was not keeping pace with the needs. Thus, in 1887, the Hatch Act was signed into law, establishing agricultural experiment stations in conjunction with each of the land-grant universities and colleges. This law provided federal funds, matching state and other dollars, to encourage increased practical agricultural research. The second Morrill Act, of 1890, established agricultural colleges throughout the southern United States for the black population.

Because of a growing perception among federal and state agricultural administrators that the increasing amount of research was not being applied by the farmers, a concerted effort was made around the turn of the twentieth century to increase extension activity. Seaman Knapp developed and carried out the demonstration method for controlling the boll weevil in Texas, Arkansas, and Louisiana in the late 1800s and early 1900s. The first county agent, W. C. Stallings, was hired in 1904, in Texas. Also during this time, the 4-H club program for youth and adults began in Ohio, Iowa, Minnesota, North Carolina, and in other states, focusing on corn growing, tomato canning, and cotton production. The philosophy of 4-H was to teach adult farmers through experiential, learn-by-doing 4-H youth programs—that is, involving adults as parents of 4-H youth was thought to be a way to reach adults. Chapters of the 4-H club were established in forty-seven states by 1915. And extension home economics education programs began in New York with an agent hired in Erie County in 1914.

In 1914, the Smith-Lever Act formally established the Cooperative Extension Service. The word *cooperative* in the name was derived from the unique three-way partnership among federal, state, and county governments. This act mandated that the land-grant universities' research also be disseminated and used by the rural populations.

Jenkins (1979) said that between 1914 and 1941, CES experienced much growth and increased acceptance. Early CES agents emphasized work with individual farmers, but CES helped establish many other agencies during the 1930s (for example, the Soil Conservation Service, the Tennessee Valley Authority, the Rural Electrification Association, the Farm Credit Administration, and Agricultural Adjustments offices), which, in turn, responded to the problems created by the Great Depression and general rural problems.

Jenkins pointed out that CES programs during World War II emphasized agricultural production but that they shifted to other social and economic concerns in rural and urban areas after the war. In 1954, based on an extension self-study report (Kepner, 1948), CES agressively strengthened its farm management programs by adding more farm management agents in 2,500 of the nation's 3,000 counties. Between 1961 and 1977, guided by another self-study report (Kearl and Copeland, 1959) and the 1968 *People and a Spirit* report (Watts, 1968), CES continued expanding its programs for urban areas, leading to serious questions from extension critics and federal and state officials about CES's priorities. The 1977 Federal Agricultural Act mandated that CES evaluate its social and economic consequences. General Accounting Office reviews and the House subcommittee eventually led to CES's fourth self-study, *Extension in the '80s* (Forest, 1983).

In summary, CES programs historically have been educational. They have helped people, especially farm families and others in rural communities, learn new practical research to solve the problems they face. Program priorities have shifted, depending on the needs of these primarily rural target clientele. As the U.S. population has increasingly migrated to urban areas, CES has attempted more and more urban-based programs to the dismay of both its traditional rural clientele who feel abandoned and public political stakeholders who have concluded that CES programs lack focus and relevancy. Thus, the last decade has been marked by CES searching for its image and priorities while continuing to respond educationally to local community and individual needs.

The Present: Cooperative Extension as Adult Education

The Cooperative Extension Service continues to be an educationally focused institution funded about equally by three cooperating levels of government—federal, state, and local. Programs vary by state and by local areas within states, depending on interests, needs, and priorities of the states, communities, and individual clients. Over 15,000 national, state, regional, and local extension staff work with over 1,000,000 volunteers in developing and implementing educational programs. The entire network of staff and volunteers are given guidance by the Extension Committee on Organization and Policy (ECOP), a subcommittee of the National Association of State Universities and Land-Grant Colleges (NASULGC) that consists of state extension directors and representatives of the federal partner. ECOP's many subcommittees set policy on needed legislation, programs, and training.

The organizational characteristics of CES are illustrated in the following series of events and anecdotes. In 1983, the Joint USDA-NASULGC Committee on the Future of Cooperative Extension (Forest, 1983, p. 1) stated, "The Cooperative Extension Service is a unique achievement in American education. It is an agency for change, a catalyst for individual and group action. . . . [It] is a vast partnership made up of local residents, the state land-grant universities, the U.S. Department of Agriculture [USDA], and county governments throughout the nation. All these groups share in planning, financing, and operating extension programs. Extension's job is education. . . . Extension's aim is to help people identify and solve problems."

The committee reiterated CES's basic mission: "to disseminate, and encourage the application of, research generated knowledge and leadership techniques to individuals, families, and communities" (p. 7). And to achieve the basic mission, the committee set program goals:

- To strengthen U.S. agriculture
- To enhance individual and group abilities in making decisions on nonrenewable resources
- To strengthen the home, family, and individual life skills
- To strengthen understanding of public policy issues
- To further understanding of international issues

Nationally, people representing the partners cooperated to reaffirm the CES mission, priorities, and goals. Since then, each state CES has involved its staff, public leadership, and clientele in clarifying its own mission emphasizing education. The following state mission illustrates this emphasis:

> CES links the state citizens to their county governments, to the University, . . . to the total land-grant university system, and to the United States Department of Agriculture . . . through a unique educational program and financial partnership. . . . Campus and county-based faculty work with volunteers and cooperating agencies to provide educational programs and leadership experiences . . . [and to] connect the resources and research of the University and total land-grant system with the high priority needs and concerns of . . . rural and urban citizens, groups, and communities. CES professionals provide this dynamic educational linkage by cooperatively identifying contemporary problems, sharing these problems with researchers and specialists on the campus, and distributing research findings and information through teaching and counseling, often through practical demonstrations, print media, computers, and audiovisual technology. CES's ultimate goal is achieved when citizens gain a better undrstanding of problems they face in their families, jobs, farms, businesses, and communities and when they apply knowledge that helps them solve those problems [University of Wisconsin Cooperative Extension Service, 1983, p. 1].

To implement the mission, this state established six criteria in 1983 for setting state extension program priorities: (1) evidence of future needs, demands, or problems, (2) potential impacts on and benefits to people, (3) extension's relative educational market strength, (4) adequacy of related research and knowledge bases, (5) qualifications and interests of faculty and staff, and (6) extension's ability to mobilize its resources. This state's mission and the priority-setting criteria agree with the broad general mission established by the 1983 national committee.

Further illustrating the current linkage and three-way partnership, Marathon County, Wisconsin, established citizen advisory committees to examine the relevancy of the state's eight priorities for the local county. The eight areas were economic improvement, environmental preservation, human development and relationships, food quality and marketing, food and fiber production, energy conservation, community and leadership development, and human health and nutrition. A one-day meeting attended by people representing all of the eight priority areas reviewed the local needs and priorities. Over 600 ideas and needs were generated using the nominal groups technique (Delbecq, Van de Ven, and Gustafson, 1975). Because only 20 of 600 solicited ideas were related to agricultural production, the area of natural environment and resource protection received highest priority for the next four years of educational programs. Accordingly, the county staff conducted water quality education programs during the next four years to achieve the following types of objectives: (1) Participating farmers will learn safe methods of pesticide container disposal. (2) Sixty percent of participating households will test private wells for coliforms and nitrates. (3) Forty percent of participants will understand principles of groundwater contamination.

The above series of needs analysis, priority setting, and goal setting occurs in some form in each of the fifty states (Forest, McKenna, and Donovan, 1986). Educational experiences at state, regional, and local levels to achieve these objectives have included the following examples: (1) computer programs on groundwater and surface water pollution, (2) water testing programs, (3) group teaching for government policymakers, (4) regional workshops on drinking water, (5) joint cooperation with local agribusinesses and financial institutions on teaching of water pollution and protection, and (6) individual family and household instruction. For each of the objectives, specific impact indicators were identified to guide follow-up measurements to determine whether the objectives had been reached after the educational programs were concluded.

Between 1983 and 1988, CES conducted hundreds of program-impact studies. Some of them were within states, and others were multi-state and coordinated nationally. These studies documented specific individual extension achievements, specific to counties. The studies measured the extent to which the clientele learned, applied, and changed in terms of the program objectives.

The above series of references and illustrations provides an example of how CES widely involves many different people at all levels in developing and implementing its educational programs. National initiatives and priorities and the local program priorities are connected. But local professional staff have the prerogative to be flexible in order to adapt to local concerns and needs.

The Future: Questions and Issues

In spite of achievements of the stated educational mission, learner satisfaction, and documented program impact and successes, CES continues to face critical issues regarding its future mission and priorities, funding and support, staff, methods, and clientele. Warner and Christenson (1984), the *Extension in the '80s* study (Forest, 1983), the 1987 *Extension in Transition* report by the Futures Task Force (Virginia Cooperative Extension Service, 1987), and the extension critics have all raised questions regarding these issues.

In 1987, the author asked a small, select sample of state extension directors to address these issues regarding extension's future (Forest, 1987). Their optimistic answers, quoted in this section, unanimously reaffirmed that CES has a bright future as an educational agency, but many barriers will have to be overcome and challenges met to reach its goals.

They said CES will increasingly be a responsive, critical link between university research and the issues and problems faced by people. At the same time, CES will continue its historical role of providing unbiased information people have come to trust. For instance, Walter Woods, director of the Kansas Extension Service, said "Absolutely. Cooperative Extension has a future if it is responsive to the educational needs of the citizens."

Perhaps the single most difficult challenge facing extension with its new clientele, needs, and methods, however, is dealing with the transition itself—that is, getting from the past traditions and expectations to the future. For example, Paul Larsen, director of the Utah Extension Service, said, "In my mind, every possible issue concerning extension has been addressed, dissected, and regurgitated. The problem is not who extension should address but whether it has the support, personnel, ability, and desire to address its current mandate and responsibilities. The problems are clearly there." Pat Borich, Cooperative Extension Service director in Minnesota, said, "Changing itself is its biggest challenge. Extension must create an image of being dynamic, educational, responsive, and relevant."

To make the transition, however, the directors agreed that the following were major issues needing resolution: (1) mission and goals, (2) clientele, (3) methods, (4) staffing, (5) financing, (6) accountability.

Mission and Goals. The directors' responses to these issues were explicit. Extension must be known as providing issue-oriented, research-based, relevant, practical, and future-oriented education. Extension must help people help themselves by helping put knowledge to work to solve problems and issues. This approach must be dynamic, responsive, and progressive. Extension has to be the essential link between university research and clientele. By boldly stating what CES is and what it is not, it will be better able to develop new constituencies and to retain the support and participation of past clientele.

Several quotes illustrate these conclusions. "Extension agents must be seen as faculty, scholars, educators," said Elwood Miller, director in Nevada. Ann Thompson, Alabama director, said, "Extension has to be known as learning for a lifetime, that it is self-help, and that it is oriented for the individual, group, and society."

These responses suggested extension has to set priorities. The directors said extension must increase formal and systematic planning according to explicit, understood, and accepted criteria.

For instance, Cindy Noble, director in New York, said, "Priority setting has to be opportunistic as well as future need oriented." Jerome Siebert, director in California, said, "We have no real effective priority setting process, particularly at the national level. With priority setting varying at the state level, we need to not only identify priorities but have a willingness to reallocate resources to meet the priorities." Borich of Minnesota strongly advocated that extension's priorities evolve in response to contemporary issues, and he has proceeded to lead Minnesota's extension service in that direction.

Clientele. The extension directors said CES cannot simply cease providing information to successful clients and work only with those who are not successful. It has to serve all people. For instance, Larsen of Utah cautioned, "Extension cannot disengage from its clientele who have, because of extension's educational services, become productive and successful. It would, at that point, cease to be extension." Tal DuVall, director in Georgia, said, "Our clientele will not necessarily change but they will be changed people—more educated, more demanding, more independent, and more affluent." Lamartine Hood, director in Pennsylvania, said extension has a responsibility "to serve all clientele that need extension education programming including the rural/urban, poor/rich, very educated/poorly educated. The challenge is to develop balanced educational programming for the clientele differences."

Methods. Gibson (1987, p. 1) writes, "Extension will increasingly use computers, video, audio, teleconferencing, dial-access audio, educational kiosks, but extension has to see the difference between information delivery and education. In many cases, people already have too much information and not enough knowledge. The educational process is only begun when people receive an educational bulletin in print or by computer, when they watch a video satellite program, or they listen to a four minute dial-access audio tape. Our most important role begins after our clientele have received the information."

Answers from several directors reinforce Gibson's conclusions that methods need to be educational as well as delivery oriented. "Electronic technology will be important. Extension must capitalize on the latest in electronic technology such as interactive video," said Robert Gilliland, director in New Mexico. Thompson of Alabama said, "We have to go beyond the one-to-one responsive approach, but we might not even know yet what will be the educational methods and media to be used in the future. Some are, in fact, not developed yet."

Staffing. Directors said CES must overcome the barriers of geographic lines and disciplinary lines. Multidisciplinary program teams; multicounty, regional, and multistate staff; and other staffing approaches will help overcome these barriers as extension looks to addressing multidisciplinary issues and problems more than to disseminating unintegrated research information.

Accordingly, extension staff will be different in the future. Many staff will be hired on an ad hoc or project basis as contrasted with hiring permanent employees. Several directors said CES should reduce its investment in personnel from the current 85 to 90 percent down to 60 percent. Staff will have to be skilled at working across disciplines and communicating on a variety of problems—with research specialists, with volunteers, and with clientele coming from different special interests. In fact, many more will have joint appointments to do research. Staff will be capable of using the new educational media and technology effectively.

Illustrative of comments by extension directors, H. R. Guenther, director in Idaho, said, "We have to work more on multistate, regional, and national bases to address the broader issues that impact the majority of the clientele we are serving. Idaho is moving in the direction of area or multicounty programs with less concern for county lines. CES will continue to have the county offices as the central local units. However, many staff will be working across county lines." Larsen, director in Utah, said staff will have to be experts in "communications as well as in science and technology."

Financing. The extension directors believe future federal funding will be much more limited. Extension services will come to depend on county and state budgets for support. User fees and private sector support will likely increase. Accountability for and achievement of project goals will increase. Grants and earmarked funding will likely increase in the future to replace general Smith-Lever formula funding. The grants and projects (Patton, 1987) will be contracted according to the issues which, in turn, will be the basis for extension's accountability.

For example, James Carpenter, director in Mississippi, said "Because of the federal deficit, the federal budget will likely see little or no increase, with increasing probability of reduction. Federal dollars will be restricted to high-priority needs identified by the federal partner. Counties are facing a constant task of doing more with less."

To counteract the reduced federal funding, however, Leo Lucas, director in Nebraska, said, "The average extension system in ten years will have at least 15 to 20 percent of their funds from user fees and grants."

Accountability. The extension directors agree with Forest, Rossing, and Coggins (forthcoming) who say the first step in CES accountability is to clarify its desired image and mission with the stakeholders to whom it is accountable. Extension must clarify this at the beginning, or as early in the program process as possible, so that at a later stage the people to whom extension is reporting will not have expectations different from extension's. More rigorous measurements, documenting the differences and benefits attributable to extension, and integral accountability and feedback through project reports will likely occur more in the future.

Representative of director comments, Thompson of Alabama said, "Accountability will be different, both formally and informally. We'll be out of business if we don't deliver what people perceive as a useful product." B. K. Webb, director in South Carolina, responded, "Extension must be more accountable in the future than ever before. We must document the cost-benefit ratios of our programs. If we are not or cannot be accountable, we should cease to exist." Miller of Nevada said, "Accountability will be formalized because stakeholders will demand it." Carpenter of Mississippi perhaps summarized everyone's feelings when he said, "Accountability will grow in importance. As dollars become more scarce, accountability will become more strict. If we cannot show quality use of dollars, then our chance of securing renewed funding is not good. Extension is probably one of the most accountable agencies around. Because it's a three-way partnership and funding coming from each level, accountability will continue to grow in importance."

Conclusion

The analysis of CES's past and current efforts provides some evidence that its successes have been due largely to its ability to shift program emphasis to new and emerging concerns of adult clientele who are at the teachable moment and to its ability to provide practical education on those concerns.

CES has had a clear mission and accepted goals, targeted clientele, effective educational methods, dedicated staff, sufficient responses, and adequate accountability. It has had a great deal of impact in the past, and recent studies suggest it is currently benefiting many people in spite of what critics say. It has effected these impacts and benefits using adult education in dealing with real needs and problems. But it increasingly has been asked to account to stakeholders providing funds.

Extension directors say CES in the future cannot rest on its achievements. The trophies sitting on the mantel do not impress current critics or future clientele. The question will continue to be asked, "What are you doing for me today?" CES will need to address not only relevant issues facing clientele but also the internal issues. Reasonable logic suggests CES will be here in the year 2000 as an effective adult education institution, with some modifications. The modifications are implied in the responses by state extension leaders.

Perhaps the most salient comment made by the state directors and leaders is that CES's main challenge is to deal pragmatically with the challenges themselves. For too long, CES and others have raised the same issues, challenges, and questions, only to conclude that, yes, there are problems and, yes, they ought to be addressed. CES is at a crossroads in 1990, having to make decisions with practical, pragmatic consequences in terms of its image, mission, goals, clientele, methods, staff, and accountability. The prediction here is that the system soon will make and implement these important, practical decisions, leading to an effective, contributing adult education institution in the year 2000.

References

Delbecq, A. L., Van de Ven, A. H., and Gustafson, D. H. *Group Techniques for Program Planning: A Guide to Nominal Group and Delphi Processes.* Glenview, Ill.: Scott, Foresman, 1975.

Forest, L. B. *Extension in the '80s: A Perspective for the Future of the Cooperative Extension Service.* Madison: Department of Continuing and Vocational Education, Cooperative Extension Service, University of Wisconsin, 1983.

Forest, L. B. *A Survey of Cooperative Extension's Future: What Do the Directors Say?* Unpublished report. Madison: University of Wisconsin, 1987.

Forest, L. B., McKenna, C., and Donovan, J. *Connections: A "How-To" Handbook for Developing Extension Long-Range Plans and Major Programs.* Madison: Cooperative Extension Service, University of Wisconsin, 1986.

Forest, L. B., Rossing, B. E., and Coggins, C. C. "Accountability." In D. J. Blackburn (ed.) *Foundations and Changing Practices in Extension.* Guelph, Ontario: Media Distribution, University of Guelph, forthcoming.

Gibson, T. "Delivery of Programs in an Electronic Technology Era." Preconference teleconference for the National Workshop on Extension Home Economics, Madison, Wis., Aug. 19, 1987.

Hightower, J. *Hard Tomatoes, Hard Times: A Report of the Agribusiness Accountability Project on the Failure of American's Land-Grant College Complex.* Cambridge, Mass.: Schenkman, 1973.

Jenkins, J. W. "Historical Overview of Extension." Unpublished manuscript. Program and Staff Development Office, Cooperative Extension Service, University of Wisconsin, Madison, 1979.

Kearl, B. E., and Copeland, O. B. (eds.) *A Guide to Extension Programs for the Future: The Scope and Responsibilities of the Cooperative Extension Service.* Raleigh: Agricultural Extension Service, North Carolina State University, 1959.

Kepner, P. U. (ed.) *Joint Committee Report on Extension Programs, Policies and Goals.* Washington, D.C.: U.S. Government Printing Office, 1948.

Patton, M. Q. "Tomorrow's Extension Professionals." *Journal of Extension, 1987, 25,* 40-42.

Prawl, W., Medlin, R., and Gross, J. *Adult and Continuing Education Through the Cooperative Extension Service.* Columbia: Extension Division, University of Missouri, 1984.

True, A. C. *A History of Agricultural Education.* Washington, D.C.: U.S. Government Printing Office, 1929.

U.S. Congress, House, Agricultural Subcommittee on Department Operations, Research, and Foreign Agriculture, *Issue Areas for Cooperative Extension System Oversight,* 97th Congress, 1st sess., 1981.

U.S. Department of Agriculture and National Association of State Universities and Land-Grant Colleges. *Joint Committee Report on Extension Programs, Policies, and Goals.* Washington, D.C.: U.S. Government Printing Office, 1948.

University of Wisconsin Cooperative Extension Service. *Strategic Directions: A Guide for Planning the Wisconsin Cooperative Extension Service in the Next Decade.* Madison: Cooperative Extension Service, University of Wisconsin, 1983.

Virginia Cooperative Extension Service. *Extension in Transition: Bridging the Gap Between Vision and Reality.* Report of the Futures Task Force to the Extension Committee on Organization and Policy. Blacksburg: Virginia Cooperative Extension Service, 1987.

Warner, P. D., and Christenson, J. A. *The Cooperative Extension Service: A National Assessment.* Boulder, Colo.: Westview Press, 1984.

Watts, L. (ed.) *A People and a Spirit.* Fort Collins: Colorado State University Press, 1968.

26

Armed Forces

Frank C. Veeman
Henry Singer

The concept of lifelong learning is an accepted objective of the armed services of the United States. By any comparison, the Department of Defense conducts the world's largest adult education activities. As each armed forces member enters the service, he or she attends basic training followed by a specialty occupation skill school. The specialty schools vary in length from a few weeks to longer than a year, depending on the required skill. In addition to correspondence schools, noncommissioned officers schools, officer candidate schools, command and general staff schools, to mention a few, there are specialty schools that provide new information and knowledge throughout an armed service member's career to enhance his or her professional military education.

The purpose of this chapter is to provide general information about the armed forces education programs conducted by the military services—which enroll nearly 700,000 undergraduate and graduate level college students (U.S. Department of Defense, 1987). The chapter also provides specific information to the reader about the interrelationship between the military and the colleges supporting the military in conducting an effective education program.

Voluntary Military Education

With the advent of the no draft–all volunteer military force in 1970, education programs received major command support, because it was determined through a series of surveys conducted by all the services that young people were primarily attracted to the service by opportunities for education and training. The service responded by hiring guidance counselors to support the existing education programs. Furthermore, the services initiated several new, exciting, and innovative programs to boost the concept of the voluntary education programs.

Education programs on military installations throughout the world have grown into a very large enterprise. Although programs may be attended by civilians working on military bases, or by military dependents and civilians living or working near the bases, the majority of students are in the military, attending classes during their normal off-duty, leisure time. Currently, the armed services provide substantial funds and support staff to the education program. The armed services, in addition to providing education administrative staff and education facilities, pay between 75 and 90 percent of the tuition for military students attending approved schools and colleges (U.S. Department of Defense, Office of the Assistant Secretary of Defense for Force Management and Personnel, 1987). Furthermore, the services provide additional incentives and opportunities for their members to participate in the off-duty education programs. The old G.I. Bill greatly benefited service members entering service prior to January 1, 1977. Those entering the service between January 1, 1977, and June 30, 1985, can receive benefits through the Veteran's Educational Assistance Program (VEAP). This program matches the individual's contribution on a two-to-one basis. The new Montgomery G.I. Bill (named after Representative G. V. Montgomery from Mississippi), which went into effect in July 1985, requires a $100 per month pay reduction for the first twelve months of active duty. Basic benefits are $300 per month for thirty-six months (based on a three-year or longer enlistment). Benefits can be used after two years on active duty or up to ten years after leaving the service. Eligible service members may receive up to $10,800 for this investment. In addition, the New Army College Fund (NACF) soldier may be eligible for another $14,400 depending upon enlistment, for a grand sum of $25,200 (Castrovilli, 1988). This fund is for service members employed in needed critical skill areas.

The military, recognizing that some of its members are not able to complete all their course work during off-duty hours or are not able to meet the appropriate residency requirements, have established so-called bootstrap programs. These bootstrap programs, although managed somewhat differently by the various branches of the service, generally provide for members to attend college full-time up to one year in order for those individuals to meet college graduation requirements. These programs include the Air Force's Airman Education and Commissioning Program (AECP) and the Marine Corps Commission Education Program (MCCEP), which allows qualified enlisted persons to attend college full-time in order to obtain a degree.

Based on surveys, the Army incorporated the Army Help for Education and Development (Project AHEAD) into its education programs. Project AHEAD provided a liaison between colleges and the Army so that an enlistee could identify with a hometown school, take courses anywhere in the world while serving in the Army, complete the course work, and graduate from the hometown school. The Navy designed the Navy Campus for Achievement, now shortened to Navy Campus. This system utilizes a network of professional civilian education advisers who help Navy personnel put together comprehensive packages consisting of on-duty and off-duty classes.

The Air Force took a different direction than did the other services in trying to find an education program that would be attractive to young people. In 1972, the Community College of the Air Force (CCAF) (1983) was officially opened. Without offering any courses itself, CCAF has managed to get most of the Air Force technical schools accredited by the Southern Association of Colleges and Schools, which in turn encourages enlisted people to supplement their Air Force technical instruction with relevant and voluntary off-duty education (Easterling, 1980). CCAF recently received another ten years of accreditation by the Southern Association of Colleges and Schools.

CCAF provides several major services to Air Force enlisted personnel. It breaks out the subject matter into understandable terms, and it allows enlisted personnel to work toward an associate of applied science degree, which CCAF grants when the appropriate course of study is accomplished. Moreover, it supplies a transcript for technical schools attended.

The Army-American Council on Education Registry Transcript System (AARTS) is designed to help soldiers receive academic recognition for learning acquired while in the Army. The AARTS transcript contains military educational experience including courses for which the American Council on Education (ACE) has made college-level credit recommendations. At present, AARTS service is available only for enlisted soldiers who entered active duty on or after October 1, 1981 (Castrovilli, 1988).

Military training can be translated into civilian educational credit. The American Council on Education (1986) publishes the ACE *Guide to the Evaluation of Educational Experiences in the Armed Services*. The ACE credit recommendations recognize learning from three sources: formal service school courses (longer than forty-five hours), military occupational specialties (MOS), and college-level tests such as the College Level Examination Program (CLEP). A separate guide containing pertinent information is published for each service. Department of Defense schools are also listed and evaluated. In addition, new course additions are continually being updated.

Each service has developed educational goals that are similar but involve vastly different operations. For example, training and education functions may be separate or together, depending on the services. As a result, comparison of education service offices is often difficult. The size of an office depends on the number of personnel served; the range of centers may be a remote site of six personnel geographically removed from any human contact, to an office in the Pentagon serving a huge population. The Navy has ships at sea ranging in size from a submarine, which may be out of contact with anyone six months of a year, to an aircraft carrier. Some Army and Marine units spend at least half their time in field training. All these units require educational services, and each service has developed unique processes to meet the needs of their unique clientele. Nevertheless, a fairly consistent pattern of educational opportunities has evolved through the years on military installations. Most installations offer a high school completion program, an undergraduate program, and a graduate program primarily for officers.

A legitimate question might be, to what extent are military personnel participating in the off-duty education programs? In the Air Force, for example, as of this writing, over 50 percent of the enlisted force were registered and participating at some level with the Community College of the Air Force. Due to the support of and efforts by the schools and colleges functioning on Air Force bases, the number of non-high school graduates was just over 1000, or only 0.24 percent of the total enlisted force. At the same time, 199,000 airmen, representing 40 percent of the total force in 1986, completed at least some college work. Air Force officers must have a bachelor's degree upon entry into the service, and it is interesting to note that currently over 40 percent of the officers hold graduate degrees (U.S. Air Force Education Office, 1983).

In an effort to minimize the impact of frequent transfers, the Department of Defense supported the development of a network of colleges and universities called the Servicemembers Opportunity College (SOC). The Servicemembers Opportunity College (SOC) is a consortium of 438 member colleges that have agreed to transfer of credit and modified residency requirements (Servicemembers Opportunity College, 1985). Through SOC, a specific associate degree program (SOCNAV for Navy, SOCAD for Army) was established. All institutions in these programs agree to accept course-by-course credits, in specific curricular areas, transferred from any other college in the network (Huff, Karasik, and Pratt, 1981). The Army has extended this concept to a program called Bachelor Degree for Soldiers (BDFS). Institutions involved must articulate course by course with each other in order for students to enter and to exit the program without loss of credit.

The Department of Defense also sponsors the Defense Activity for Nontraditional Education Support (DANTES). DANTES was created in 1974 after the dissolution of United States Armed Forces Institute (USAFI), which had served the needs of the military since World War II. Major services provided by DANTES include transcripts for tests and courses taken with either USAFI or DANTES. DANTES also provides a major testing program. DANTES provides cost free to military personnel the College Level Examination Program (CLEP), High School General Education Developmental Tests (HS GED), Standardized Subject Tests (SST), and a score of other popular tests. DANTES also provides a system that facilitates independent study programs through participating colleges (Defense Activity for Nontraditional Education Support, 1985).

Military educators have been major leaders in alternative delivery systems. DANTES's presence has encouraged and increased civilian institutions' recognition of the potential size of the military market. DANTES provides research studies and projects to help educators keep up with emerging technologies for delivering education programs. *DANTES Guide to Educational Delivery Systems* (U.S. Department of the Navy, 1987) identifies institutions that reach out to distance learners through audio programs, computerized programs, educational television (ETV) programs, satellite programs, and telecourse programs.

In order to maintain opportunities for men and women whose high school records do not adequately reflect their abilities, the services have developed several programs: (1) BOOST—Broadened Opportunities for Officer Selection and Training, (Navy), (2) Preparatory school before academy entrance (Navy, Marines, Army, and Air Force), (3) BSEP—Basic Skills Education Program, and (4) JSEP—Job Skills Education Program.

The BSEP program has increased basic skills proficiency needed to enhance the performance of a soldier within his or her military occupational specialty (MOS). Participation in BSEP may be voluntary or mandatory, however. Using on-duty time to learn basic skills has been criticized.

The JSEP program is an innovative Army computerized learning system being developed to accomplish basic skills learning by using elements of a soldier's MOS. If a soldier is diagnosed as needing mathematical skills, the instruction is constructed on the mathematics the soldier must use in his or her MOS. This innovative program shows promise in meeting needs identified by testing and in providing the means to develop immediate job skills.

Educational Programs of Reserve Forces

Opportunities previously limited to active duty personnel are now available, completely or partially, to members of Reserve and National Guard units. As part of the so-called total force concept, these units are now considered a vital part of the national defense. The Army Continuing Education System (ACES) has been open to the Army Reserve and Army National Guard since 1983. The Community College of the Air Force (CCAF) is available to both the Air National Guard and the Air Force Reserve. The services of the Defense Activity for Nontraditional Education Support (DANTES) have been available to all members of Reserve units since 1985. Guard and Reserve members who obligate themselves for six years are entitled by the Montgomery G.I. Bill to up to $140 per month for thirty-six months for a full-time student, with no dollar contribution from the student. The Army National Guard offers the Student Loan Repayment Program (SLRP) to members who enlist or extend enlistment. Repayments of 15 percent or $500 each year on certain federal loans, with a maximum repayment of $20,000, are allowed. The Marine Corps Reserve offers a variety of educational opportunities including professional education for both full-time and active-duty-for-training personnel.

K–12 Education

Also involved in military education is the overseas K–12 school system. The Department of Defense Dependent Schools (DoDDS) have approximately 150,000 students enrolled in 269 elementary and middle schools located in twenty foreign countries. So-called Section 6 schools are intended to provide for minor dependents of military personnel in locations where states are unable to provide suitable free public education. These schools are located in eighteen military installations (U.S. Department of Defense, Office of the Assistant Secretary of Defense for Force Management and Personnel, 1987).

Civilian Institutions

According to Castrovilli (1988), 3 percent of all students in higher education are currently using some form of the G.I. Bill. It has been projected that 10 percent of all students will be somehow related to veterans' programs throughout the 1990s. But Spikes (1983) has said that civilian educational institutions desiring to provide voluntary educational programs for military members face administrative and curricular challenges.

Each service has similar yet somewhat different processes involved in initiating and staffing programs. But general items of interest to all services are (1) institutional commitment and involvement, (2) student services, (3) administrative roles and structures, and (4) faculty. These areas of interest are necessary to any and all off-campus program operations, whether military or not.

U.S. Department of Defense (1987) directive number 1322.8, *Voluntary Education Programs for Military Personnel,* includes criteria for obtaining educational programs and services as well as criteria for selection of civilian institutions to deliver educational programs and services on military installations. Each branch of service maintains its own guidelines in the appropriate regulations. And each military installation has a designated Education Service Office staffed by an Education Service Officer (ESO), usually a civilian, who is assisted by guidance counselors and support staff. The ESO is normally the point of contact for inquiries and referrals. The mission of the ESO is to provide for the educational needs of active duty personnel at the installation.

Accreditation of civilian institutions is an important concern in the selection of an educational provider for a military installation. Regional accrediting agencies provide a service by comparing stated institutional goals with those reportedly being accomplished. Out-of-state institutions undergoing evaluation should be prepared to provide assurances concerning their capabilities to deliver service in compliance with the host state's approval criteria; each individual state determines the evaluation criteria an out-of-state provider must meet.

Quality, like beauty, is often in the eye of the beholder. Most of what has been written about quality assurance in off-campus programs applies to military base programs (Cross and McCartan, 1984). Bailey's 1979 report, *Academic Quality Control,* resulted in increased awareness of the need for demonstrated ability to ensure high-quality education. An institution that decides to serve a unique off-campus clientele such as the military should note that there is a difference in being apart from the campus and being a part of the campus. Such an institution must be vigilant to ensure uniform quality throughout the organization. Continual contact is necessary to demonstrate to campus administration and faculty that off-campus operations are consistent with those on the main campus. While operational differences may be necessary, the off-campus results must be as satisfactory or better than outcomes on the main campus.

Planned campus interaction must take place regularly. The "out of sight, out of mind" syndrome can easily occur without constant attention to interaction. A number of institutions (for example, Webster University in St. Louis, Missouri, Southern Illinois University in Carbondale, and Troy State University in Alabama) have well-defined programs of planned activities that require both campus administration and faculty to visit military installation sites on a regular basis. These innovative colleges with off-campus operations on military installations realize the importance of the support of a military education service office. They realize that, in identifying needed changes, the military is often on the cutting edge of ideas, programs, and technology.

When a specified curriculum is offered to a military installation, the courses in that curriculum should lead to a degree program. It is of increasing concern to military education offices that civilian institutions operating on installations provide programs of study leading to degrees. An offering of degree-related classes (classes that meet core or elective requirements for a degree or certificate) is much preferred to non–degree-related classes (classes not primarily designed to apply toward a degree). Due to a variety of factors, degree requirements are important when the intended audience is both mobile and working a full-time job; diversity in degree programs must be carefully planned. Important criteria measured by the military are (1) the number of class enrollments, (2) whether a class is technical in nature, (3) the number of degrees awarded, and (4) whether a course of study can be related to a military career.

Facilities and equipment are a concern to campus programs and even more so to military installations. Because these two items are so important to the success or failure of programs, a cooperative arrangement between the military service office and the educational institution may be necessary. If a specific need, such as laboratory facilities, is identified, communication of the resource requirements must be clear to both groups. A cooperative venture can then be developed to meet the identified need (lab facilities) only if both parties can understand what is needed.

A criterion often misunderstood and misjudged by colleges and universities is the distance of the provider institution from the military installation. A relatively close-by educational institution often questions how effectively a distant provider can deliver adequate education support. But often a local institution indicates that it can deliver needed services but does not attempt to modify its existing structure to include adult education as a goal in its military installation operation. A distant educational institution with an established track record of communication and the administrative structure to achieve on-installation successes should be considered the best choice by the military.

Assurance of the quality of military installation programs is closely associated with the quality of personnel working in the programs (NewMyer, 1981). Careful attention to all institutional representatives (administration, faculty, and staff) does much to ensure quality control of the program. It is important to remember that people are willing to invest their time, expertise, and reputations only in efforts they think will have a lasting value and impact on their own lives as well as on the institution (Marienau, 1985). Studies by Horgan and Parker (1985) provide relevant examples and describe the difficulties and successes of Saint Leo College's military programs as rapid expansion occurred. They also set forth planning guides for specific actions to develop defined quality.

Orientation of faculty to teach at a military installation is especially critical when an instructor's contact with the military has been limited. In addition to normal items such as textbooks, support materials, and course outlines, the history of the institution on the installation and the background of the students, including their branch of service, must be explained. A simple chart indicating the ranks of officers and enlisted personnel may answer a number of questions that faculty have concerning their students.

Typically, existing civilian student services can be extended or adapted to on-site military operations (Marienau, 1985). These services include (1) student recruitment, marketing, referrals, orientation, and college publications; (2) admission application and entrance processing; (3) registration, transcripts, data storage, and record retrieval; (4) financial aid counseling and application processing; (5) institutional resources including libraries, counseling, academic advising, bookstores, and academic skills support; and (6) tuition collection and billing and loan collections. Each of these areas should have specified methods of operation.

Each military installation has a unique situation with which to contend. But in all cases, instructional resources include several areas that involve institutional concerns (Harbert and Kowhler, 1982). For example, library support for graduate programs may require considerable study to ensure adequacy, and computer systems at sites linked to the main library can provide impressive library support if needed.

Academic advising is especially important to members of the military. On-site records should be available to advisers and students to ensure accuracy. Degree checks and policies on transfer and acceptance need to be addressed. The Servicemembers Opportunity College (SOC) and its relatives SOCAD (Army) and SOCNAV (Navy) allow an institution to examine necessary options in order to provide consistent standards of operation for military students. The American Council on Education (ACE) (1986) guide provides information on the acceptance of military education by other institutions. Winston and Associates (1984) offer suggestions on development of academic advising that are helpful in working with the service systems.

Scheduling classes for the military must be taken seriously, and the needs of the military student must be considered. Working with the education center, a college may elect to offer classes on a back-to-back schedule with the same instructor offering the same classes on succeeding nights to accommodate those service members working rotating shifts. This schedule may be followed with a selection of classes that start as early as 6:30 A.M. and continue until 10:20 P.M. if necessary. Classes may be offered in the mornings, during lunch hours, and in the early afternoons, in addition to the more popular classes offered during the evening hours. Some classes could be offered at odd times to accommodate needs expressed by some special units.

Research articles about military off-duty education programs are not plentiful. The National University Continuing Education Association (NUCEA) and the American Association for Adult and Continuing Education (AAACE) have separate branches for the military education community. The worldwide Military Conference, held at the University of Maryland in alternating years, is also helpful in providing current information on educational affairs. The Kansas State University annual national conference on Issues in Higher Education (Off-Campus Credit Programs) has continually been a forum for the exchange of ideas among professionals in delivering military education. Several states have created their own military educators associations. California and Florida are good examples of continuing education's formal associations based on military concerns.

Massey's quote on quality in 1980 is still valid today: "It needs to be recognized that certain environmental-organizational conditions must exist if off-campus programs are to be of high quality (p. 10)." He went on to state that this issue is one of the greatest challenges facing higher education. Whether it is meeting off-campus adult needs in the military or in other locations, the quest for quality and its elusive definition will continue. Educational institutions serving this unique clientele will continue to strive to meet and to surpass the quality of campus operations through innovation and cooperation.

Assuming that a participating college has institutional support to provide off-campus education and is fortunate enough to have appropriate funding to engage in these activities, and assuming that the college has put together appropriate programs that can be completed off-campus and has faculty to support these programs, the college still has to provide exceptional services and leadership if it is really going to be true to its mission. This fortunate state of affairs benefits all involved and clearly demonstrates that, through initiative, imagination, good leadership, and good will, outstanding education can be achieved throughout the world.

New Developments and Concerns

A new area of military interaction is the MOS training that postsecondary institutions, primarily community colleges, are contracting to do for National Guard and Reserve units. Handled by the individual states, this mode of MOS training is a significant change in normal operational procedure that could create new linkages altering old patterns.

The sheer number of armed forces personnel taking advantage of educational opportunities is staggering. Today more military personnel than ever are participating in the increasing numbers of high-quality educational programs offered in this country and abroad (Faux, 1988). The enrollment increases coupled with educational funding cutbacks have caused strain on tuition assistance funds. Several Army posts have had to eliminate tuition assistance because of a lack of funds. Other bases have shifted funding in order to maintain at least limited opportunities to use tuition assistance. The Air Force has indicated that it might maintain equal tuition assistance at all installations even if funding has to be cut back to less than 75 percent. A challenge in the future for armed forces will be to continue to find dollars to support tuition assistance and to maintain educational incentives as an effective recruitment and retention tool.

The benefits of adult education throughout an armed forces member's career seem to be taken as an article of faith by the leaders of our nation, as evidenced by the variety of options they have provided. Each program is tailored to encourage each service member to develop academic and occupational-technical skills and thus to increase the human capital and individual worth to the defense of our nation (U.S. Department of Defense, Office of the Assistant Secretary of Defense for Force Management and Personnel, 1987). It is important that this continued emphasis be encouraged. Fostering such a belief speaks well of the armed forces' system of education and increases society's gain when the service member returns to the civilian sector.

References

American Council on Education. *Guide to the Evaluation of Educational Credits in the Armed Services.* Washington, D.C.: American Council on Education, 1986.

Bailey, S. *Academic Quality Control: The Case of College Programs on Military Bases.* Washington, D.C.: American Association of Higher Education, 1979. (ED 213 271)

Castrovilli, M. (ed.). *Army Continuing Education.* New York: School Guide Publications, 1988.

Community College of the Air Force. *A New Degree of Success.* Washington, D.C.: U.S. Department of the Air Force, 1983.

Cross, K. P., and McCartan, A. *Adult Learning: State Policies and Institutional Practices.* ASHE/ERIC Higher Education Research Report no. 1. Washington, D.C.: Association for the Study of Higher Education, 1984.

Defense Activity for Nontraditional Education Support. *Mission and Activities.* Pensacola, Fla.: Defense Activity for Nontraditional Education Support, 1985.

Easterling, H. W., Jr. "Non-Military Education in the United States Air Force with Emphasis on the Period 1945-1979." Unpublished doctoral dissertation, Division of Applied Sciences, Indiana University, 1980.

Faux, G. "Demand for On-Base Higher Education Programs Surges with Well-Educated, All-Volunteer American Military Service Personnel." *NUCEA News,* 1988, *4* (2), 4-5.

Harbert, D., and Kowhler, R. "Education Services to Military Personnel." *Community Services Catalyst,* 1982, *13* (4), 7-10.

Horgan, J. J., and Parker, B. S. "Saint Leo College." *Educational Record,* 1985, *66,* 55-59.

Huff, S. M., Karasik, B. L., and Pratt, A. L. "SOCAD—An Innovative Associate Degree System." *Journal of Studies in Technical Careers,* 1981, *3* (4), 355-364.

Marienau, C. "Effective Liaison Within the Institution." In T. M. Rocco and L. R. Murphy (eds.), *Institutional and Staff Structures for Nontraditional Programs,* no. 2. Metuchen, N.J.: Scarecrow Press, 1985.

Massey, T. B. "The Administrator's Role in Insuring Quality in Off-Campus Programs." In J. L. Kramer (ed.), *Issues in Higher Education,* no. 3. Manhattan: Kansas State University, 1980.

NewMyer, R. A. "Maintaining Off-Campus Program Quality: On-Site Faculty Program Coordinators for Military Base Baccalaureate Programs." In J. L. Kramer (ed.), *Issues in Higher Education,* no. 5. Manhattan: Kansas State University, 1981.

Servicemembers Opportunity College. *Servicemembers Opportunity Colleges Guide.* Pensacola, Fla.: Defense Activity for Nontraditional Education Support, 1985.

Spikes, W. F. "Planning Programs for Members of the Armed Services: A Collaborative Endeavor." In C. E. Kasworm (ed.), *Educational Outreach to Select Adult Populations.* New Directions for Continuing Education, no. 20. San Francisco: Jossey-Bass, 1983.

U.S. Air Force Education Office. *Education Levels of Air Force Military Personnel.* Offutt Air Force Base, Nebr.: Air Force Education Office, 1983.

U.S. Department of Defense. *Voluntary Education Programs for Military Personnel.* Directive no. 1322.8. Washington, D.C.: U.S. Department of Defense, 1987.

U.S. Department of Defense, Office of the Assistant Secretary of Defense for Force Management and Personnel. *Education Programs in the Department of Defense*. Pensacola, Fla.: Defense Activity for Nontraditional Education Support, 1987.

U.S. Department of the Navy. *DANTES Guide to Educational Delivery Systems*. Pensacola, Fla.: Defense Activity for Nontraditional Education Support, 1987.

Winston, R. B., Jr., Miller, T. K., Ender, S. C., Grites, T. J., and Associates. *Developmental Academic Advising*. San Francisco: Jossey-Bass, 1984.

27

Correctional Facilities

Bruce I. Wolford

Education and corrections have been linked since the opening in Philadelphia, around 1790, of the Walnut Street Jail, when the word *penitentiary* was used for the first time. Corrections and related education programs have grown significantly since the early Sabbath Schools—with their programs for both literary and moral education—were operated by the Quakers in Pennsylvania. Currently, over 2.4 million United States citizens are under correctional supervision. Some adult and juvenile offenders are housed in prisons, jails, and detention facilities; others are supervised in community settings under conditions of probation, parole, and other aftercare services. By way of explanation, jails and prisons differ primarily based upon the residents' length of sentence. Jails in the United States primarily house preadjudicated individuals and convicted offenders with sentences of one year or less. Prisons are state or federally operated institutions designed primarily for convicted offenders with sentences in excess of one year.

Over 1.2 percent of adults over age eighteen and one in forty-five adult males are under some form of correctional supervision. The 700 U.S. prisons currently confine over 500,000 men and women. The nearly 3,500 jails in the nation have an average daily population of over 230,000 (U.S. Department of Justice, Bureau of Justice Statistics, 1983).

The predominantly male population incarcerated in the nation's long-term correctional institutions (prisons) includes a disproportionate number of unemployed, undereducated, and learning-handicapped individuals (Coffey, 1983). Over 80 percent of the prison population have not completed a high school education, fewer than 10 percent can pass a standardized achievement test at the 12.0 grade level, and 60 to 80 percent have been classified as functionally illiterate (Conrad, 1981). An analysis of adult correctional population figures indicates that nearly 300,000 illiterate adults are currently incarcerated (Rutherford, Nelson, and Wolford, 1984).

In many correctional institutions, educators provide one of the few positive change-oriented programs available to inmates. Approximately 7,000 educators work in the nation's long-term state and federal correctional institutions (Rutherford, Nelson, and Wolford, 1984), and many additional educators work in jail and other community-based correctional settings. Although correctional educators represent the largest noncustodial employee group in U.S. prisons (Horvath, 1982), the educators currently employed in correctional institutions are able to provide services to fewer than 12 percent of the total prison population. Only one in five jails provides any form of education for the incarcerated ("Correctional Education Policy Statement," 1984).

Overview

The Correctional Education Association has defined correctional education as follows: "Correctional education is an organized and individualized self-help strategy to interrupt nonsocial or antisocial behavior through vocational and academic learning activities that foster social attitudes and equip students in contact with the criminal justice system for lives as responsible community members" (Gehring, 1984, p. 138). This definition of correctional education includes programs for both adult and juvenile offenders. Depending upon one's concept of adult education, juvenile offenders (generally considered to be below age eighteen) may or may not be considered within this target population. Very few youthful offenders ever return to traditional public education (Haberman and Quinn, 1986). The programs that serve juveniles are highly individualized and frequently lead to a general equivalency diploma (GED) rather than a Carnegie-Unit-Based high school diploma. This author would argue that the majority of programs for the nearly 75,000 incarcerated juveniles in the United States (U.S. Department of Justice Bureau of Justice Statistics, 1983) should be considered within the realm of adult education.

History of Correctional Education. Although educational programs were operated in the first penitentiary, the early history of formal programming is limited. Most early programs focused on bible study and were directed by chaplains and religious volunteers. In 1847, New York became the first state to mandate that correctional education be available in all institutions. The reformatory movement, begun at Elmira, New York, about 1870, spread rapidly across the nation. This reform movement emphasized educational and vocational programming as key elements of the indeterminate prison sentence. Eventually, reformatories based upon the Elmira model were to be constructed in thirty states (Gehring, 1981).

The end of massive prison industry programs and the increasing population of institutions during the post-World War II era gave rise to expanded correctional education programming. It was the application of federally supported programs to correctional settings during the 1960s and 1970s that helped to make education an essential component of nearly all institutions. The Manpower Development Training Act (MDTA) of 1963, the 1966 Adult Education Act, and the Basic Education Opportunity Grant Program, initiated in 1972, although not designed with corrections in mind, all led to rapid expansion of educational programming in prisons. Other significant pieces of federal legislation that specifically included correctional institutions within their mandate are the Education Consolidation and Improvement Act Chapter I, Neglected or Delinquent Program, and Public Law 94–142, the Education for All Handicapped Children Act. The passage of the Carl Perkins Vocational Education Act of 1985 provided the first mandatory correctional education set-aside in a major piece of federal education legislation.

Although federal legislation provided the impetus for many expansions of education services within corrections, states also were supportive of new programs in these areas. In 1968, Texas established the Windham School District to serve Department of Corrections residents (Carona, 1977). Other early correctional school districts were established in Connecticut (1969) and Ohio (1974). School districts were established in only nine states (Coffey, 1986b), but the attention of corrections extended beyond the administrative restructuring of education.

Provisions of early release based on educational achievement were established in Texas and in other states. Mandatory educational programs that require participation in basic literacy programs for individuals achieving below predetermined levels, although first instituted by the Federal Bureau of Prisons, have been replicated in many state correctional systems (Farkas and Hambrick, 1987).

The Goals of Correctional Education. The increasingly punitive response of federal, state, and local governments to crime in the United States has resulted in an unprecedented expansion of the number of incarcerated offenders. While the incarcerated offender population has increased, the number and range of rehabilitative programs in adult correctional institutions often has decreased. Offenders, some prison administrators, and the public have looked to education to fill the void. Educators have been faced with the burden of addressing issues beyond the acquisition of basic literacy and vocational skills. Because educational programs often function as an institution within the larger institution of corrections, considerable ambiguity exists regarding the goals of correctional education. Six commonly accepted goals for correctional education programs are (1) to provide inmates with basic academic and vocational skills, (2) to provide inmates with an opportunity to change their personal behavior and values, (3) to reduce recidivism, (4) to provide passive control of inmate behavior, (5) to support the operational needs of the correctional institution, and (6) to provide institutional work assignments (Wolford, 1987). Educators report significant differences between their personal goals for educational programming and those perceived to exist within the correctional system. The conflict and confusion over the role of education in corrections are two of the major sources of stress and frustration for correctional educators.

Public Perceptions. Because correctional programs operate for the most part with only limited public attention or interaction, the public's attitudes toward correctional education are difficult to gauge. Few public opinion polls have addressed this issue, but one survey conducted in Kentucky indicated broad general support for most correctional education efforts (Faine and Bohlander, 1979). This study, commissioned by the Kentucky Corrections Cabinet, found that well over 80 percent of a randomly selected sample of the state's adult population were supportive of adult basic education, vocational, and life skills programs for inmates incarcerated in the state's correctional institutions. However, only 20 percent of the sample were supportive of higher education programs for the same population.

Despite some vocal complaints regarding the tendency to be soft on crime, it appears that the general public understands the need for, and is supportive of, correctional education programs that enhance the basic literacy and employment skills of offenders.

Program Administration. Correctional education programs are administered under a variety of different arrangements. In state correctional institutions, the traditional and currently most widely used approach (70 percent) is administration by the state department of corrections. Other arrangements include state department of education supervision, contract services with higher education and other entities, and the establishment of autonomous school authorities (Coffey, 1986b). Although nine states have established separate school districts for correctional programs, in most other states the responsibility for administering education is shared between central office and institutional personnel. The varied administrative structures and the lack of autonomy of many programs are reflective of the low priority assigned by correctional administrations to education in many systems. The absence of a strong autonomous education administration has resulted in a lack of coordination and, in some cases, under-funded and ineffective programs.

The provision of educational programs in other than state correctional settings is even more difficult to categorize. Locally operated jails and detention facilities frequently do not provide educational programs (Kerle and Ford, 1984). Those programs that do exist are usually found in the larger metropolitan facilities. The programs are often an extension of the community's adult education effort and may receive only limited administrative and financial support from correctional officials. There are, however, some excellent community-based education programs, most notably the PACE Institute, which operates within Chicago's Cook County Jail. PACE is supported primarily by private and corporate donations and provides academic and vocational training as well as employment assistance upon release.

The funding for educational programs also varies by jurisdiction. Most programs attempt to obtain available federal support; however, application of these funds to corrections is often at the discretion of state education officials. In some states, few federal dollars ever reach the correctional classroom, so the majority of funding for programs is derived from state or local general funds. These funds are not designated in a line-item budget for education, but rather fall under a broad category such as institutional operations. Without a specific line-item budget, many education units must compete for limited funds with a host of other program areas. All too frequently, educators are early victims of budget reductions, losing out to more essential basic services, such as food, medicine, laundry, and custody.

Professional Development. Most correctional educators pursue preparatory training in elementary or secondary areas (Gehring, 1981), and they enter the profession unfamiliar with both the principles of adult education and the operation of the criminal justice system. The emphasis in specific teacher preparation for corrections has been through in-service programs. The relatively limited number and geographic isolation of correctional educators have made it difficult to develop specialized teacher-training programs.

Efforts supported by the National Institute of Corrections and by the U.S. Department of Education have helped develop specialized in-service programs for correctional educators (Rutherford, Nelson, and Wolford, 1984). A number of the larger state correctional systems provide sophisticated training programs for educators; however, for the most part, in-service training for correctional educators is very limited.

Preservice teacher preparatory programs that focus on correctional education, although increasing throughout the 1980s, are still limited to fewer than fifteen. Many of the existing programs focus on special education and have been developed in part as a result of support from the U.S. Department of Education. Many correctional educators pursue interdisciplinary graduate programs that allow them to design a correctional education emphasis drawing upon disciplines such as adult education, criminal justice, and sociology. Preservice and in-service training opportunities for correctional educators are one of the most pressing needs in the profession.

Four organizations provide a sense of professional identification for correctional educators: the Correctional Education Association, the American Correctional Association Institution Libraries Committee, the Association of State and Federal Directors of Correctional Education, and the American Association for Adult and Continuing Education. The Correctional Education Association (CEA) is the largest and most active organization devoted exclusively to the interests and concerns of educators who work in adult and juvenile correctional settings. The CEA is an affiliate of the American Correctional Association, the nation's largest professional organization serving corrections. The CEA publishes the *Journal of Correctional Education,* a quarterly newsletter, and the annual *Yearbook of Correctional Education.*

The chief administrative correctional education officers in each state also are represented by the Association of State and Federal Directors of Correctional Education. The American Association for Adult and Continuing Education (AAACE) also has a division of corrections which includes members whose interests include adult correctional education. Additional information regarding correctional education can be obtained from the ERIC Clearinghouse in Adult, Career, and Vocational Education and from the National Institute of Corrections (NIC) Information Center. (The NIC Information Center is located at 1790 30th Street, Suite 130, Boulder, Colorado 80301.)

Correctional Education Programs and Services. Correctional education programs designed for adult offenders can be found in a variety of settings, but they are concentrated in long-term adult correctional institutions. Community-based programs (with the exception of jails) are limited and generally are not distinguishable from local adult basic education and literacy programs or from those programs provided through the employment service.

The majority of jails in the United States do not have formal education programs for offenders. Only a small percentage of jails have any educational programming: GED preparatory programs (29 percent); adult basic education (14 percent); job placement (16 percent); vocational training (8 percent); and life skills training (4 percent) (Kerle and Ford, 1984). Because of the relatively short period of incarceration (in most jails the average is less than seventy-two hours), small populations, and limited funding for programming, most jail education programs are concentrated in larger urban facilities. With the advent of new standards and increasing scrutiny from the judiciary, the number and scope of educational programs for the eight million individuals admitted to the nation's jails each year will certainly increase (U.S. Department of Justice, Bureau of Justice Statistics, 1984).

Nearly all state and federal long-term correctional institutions (those authorized to hold offenders for longer than one year) have some form of educational programming. The size, security level, location, and special nature of the inmate population can significantly affect the range and scope of educational programs available within a particular correctional institution.

Participation in educational programming by adult offenders remains largely voluntary; however, an increasing number of jurisdictions have instituted mandatory education programs for inmates functioning below preestablished academic achievement levels. In many work-oriented correctional institutions, education programs are primarily part-time, evening, or weekend activities in which inmates participate after completing their work assignments. There is tremendous variance in the level of participation in educational programs among correctional systems and among institutions within a jurisdiction. Although the national average level for incarcerated adult offender participation in educational programming is 30 percent, the reported level of involvement ranges from 3 to 58 percent (Rutherford, Nelson, and Wolford, 1985).

Over 80 percent of long-term correctional institutions provide adult basic education and GED preparatory classes (Norton and Simms, 1988).

Literacy initiatives have resulted in an expansion of one-on-one tutorial programs. These literacy efforts generally include a training program for the inmate community and the institutional employee volunteer tutors. Competency-based programming that emphasizes life skills has been adopted in a number of correctional systems. Both the Adult Performance Level (APL) Project and the Comprehensive Adult Student Assessment System (CASAS) were pilot tested and are used in correctional settings. Literacy programming, along with increased funding for traditional adult education programming in many jurisdictions, has helped to expand the participation in correctional education programs.

Although the major concentration of correctional education programming is directed at basic literacy skills, other programs do exist. Special education programs, for example, are available in an increasing number of correctional institutions. Services are generally provided only for the learning-handicapped population under twenty-one years of age, as mandated by federal law (Public Law 94-142). Vocational education programs are also provided in many correctional institutions. These programs, although available to only a small percentage of offenders (because of the limited number of slots and length of training), do provide an opportunity for some offenders to gain marketable job skills while incarcerated.

Moral or social education programs based upon the work of Kohlberg (1986) and others have been established in some correctional institutions. These programs are less concerned with the development of basic academic and vocational skills than they are with the development of moral and ethical reasoning skills. These programs have applied educational approaches to behavior change, and, although limited in number, moral-social education programs have generated a great deal of interest in the corrections profession.

Postsecondary education programs are offered in many adult correctional institutions. Recent surveys have indicated that, on average, 9 percent of the long-term incarcerated population are enrolled in postsecondary programs. The programs provided by over 350 colleges and universities that offer course work in correctional institutions are generally introductory or core in nature (Littlefield, 1986). Courses are offered within correctional institutions by full-time and adjunct college faculty as well as through correspondence study. This course work leads to certificate, associate, bachelor's and, in some cases, master's degrees for inmate students.

Correctional libraries are often included as an extension of educational services in many institutions. These centers not only provide support to educational programs, but they also serve as community libraries for the general inmate population. The federal court has mandated that adequate legal resources be provided to incarcerated felons; most systems meet this requirement in part through the operation of a law library. The library is an important component in the adult education program of a correctional institution. Even more important, the library provides one of the few quiet environments where an individual can "escape" the noise and confusion of the general inmate population to read, to relax, and to reflect on his or her life and circumstance.

Correctional Education in Canada

A different picture of corrections and correctional education can be found in Canada.* The rate of incarceration in Canada has remained relatively stable for the past three decades. The incarceration rate in Canada is 95 per 100,000 adults, while the U.S. rate is 200 per 100,000 (McKie, 1987). There are two prison jurisdictions in Canada: federal and provincial. Prisoners are assigned to one or the other jurisdiction solely on the basis of length of sentence. A sentence of two years less a day is served in a provincial institution and a sentence of two years or more is served in a federal institution.

Educational programs are provided in both provincial and federal institutions. Provincial institutions typically offer adult basic education, some vocational training, and GED-high school programs. The shorter length of stay and the limited size of provincial facilities have often placed constraints on the range of educational services provided, but federal institutions generally have the full range of education and training services, which may include on-site postsecondary programs. Programs include adult basic education, literacy, living skills, native studies, GED and secondary school programs, vocational training, as well as college- and university-level academic programs. Library services are generally included as an educational service in Canadian institutions.

Emerging Issues

Correctional educators must address a number of issues in the 1990s, including the following: mandatory participation; programming for learning-handicapped offenders; development of linkages among training, industries, and education programs; sex equity and the right to treatment; transitional services for released offenders; and program evaluation. Other emerging issues in Canadian correctional education are the following: federal initiatives to address the literacy issue through mandatory participation in adult basic education programs; the trend toward privatization of education through provisions for contracted services; and the merging of living skills and traditional academic programs, specifically addressing cognitive as well as affective issues. It should be noted that increased linkages have been developed between U.S. and Canadian correctional educators in recent years. The Correctional Education Association has attempted to facilitate this collaboration through expanded roles for Canadians in the association.

*This section of the chapter is based largely on the contributions of Dr. Stephen Duguid, Simon Frazier University, Burnham, British Columbia, obtained in a personal interview with the author, Feb. 1989.

Mandatory Participation. Increased public attention has been focused on the issue of mandatory inmate participation in correctional education. A number of jurisdictions (Virginia, Maryland, Ohio, and the Federal Bureau of Prisons) have adopted administrative regulations that make participation in correctional education programs mandatory for inmates who score below preestablished levels on standardized achievement tests.

In the case of the Federal Bureau of Prisons, which was the first major correctional system to initiate mandatory participation, the established minimum achievement level has been set at the grade level equivalent of 8.0. Inmates testing below this level must enroll in an educational program for a minimum of ninety days. Upon completion of the mandatory enrollment period, the inmate has the option to withdraw from the education program or to remain enrolled on a voluntary basis. Although no comprehensive reports have been published regarding mandatory education program outcomes, discussions with correctional officials in a number of jurisdictions indicate that a high percentage of offenders remain in educational programs beyond the required period of participation. Many critics of mandatory participation feared that the positive, self-directed atmosphere that existed in many correctional education programs would be disrupted by forced enrollment. Early indications are that the mandatory enrollees have not created any significant behavior or attitude problems. It appears that making participation mandatory in correctional institutions helps to remove the excuses based on antieducation machismo that many inmates used to rationalize their decisions not to enroll. In the prison environment, individuals are reluctant (with good reason) to show any sign of weakness or vulnerability. Consequently, inmates have not wanted to admit needing additional education. By making education mandatory, those inmates who, under a voluntary system, would have remained out of school are forced by the system to enroll, thus preventing the feelings associated with a personal admission of weakness. Mandatory education also brings in the inmate who would not have enrolled under a voluntary system because of negative experiences as a student in traditional public education systems.

The initiation of mandatory education programs has resulted in increased enrollment, expanded programs, and the entry into correctional education classes of a previously underrepresented group—the learning-handicapped offender.

Learning-Handicapped Offender. Numerous studies of both juvenile and adult correctional populations indicate significant levels of learning handicap among offenders (Brown and Courtless, 1971; Morgan, 1979; Rutherford, Nelson, and Wolford, 1985; Murphy, 1986). The range of reported learning-handicapped offenders goes from 0 to 80 percent of the incarcerated population (Nelson, Rutherford, and Wolford, 1987). The movement in correctional education to provide special programs for learning-handicapped inmates has come as a result of Public Law 94-142, which requires that free and appropriate educational services be made available to all individuals through age twenty-one. Although at least minimum compliance with the law has been obtained in most juvenile correctional systems, very few adult correctional systems have initiated comprehensive special education programs. In those adult institutions where special education programs do exist, services are generally not provided for individuals over the age of twenty-one. Clearly, one of the most pressing issues facing correctional education is addressing the special needs of learning-handicapped offenders regardless of age.

Establishing a TIE. The various programs and services provided in the correctional setting often function as autonomous units with little or no communication or cooperation. Efforts by correctional officials in a number of jurisdictions (Ohio, Illinois, the Federal Bureau of Prisons) have led to the development of linkages among training, industries, and education programs (TIE). The TIE concept, as it has become known, calls for a coordination of services and resources to provide the offender with an improved opportunity to develop marketable employment skills and to provide the correctional system with a more productive work force. TIE programs often require completion of, or participation in, education as a precondition for obtaining a correctional industries job assignment. The TIE concept supports the development of vocational training programs that both complement existing correctional industries and develop job skills that are marketable outside the correctional setting. TIE programs often include systematic on-the-job training (OJT) components to assure not only that the correctional institution will operate efficiently, but also that it will provide the inmate with an opportunity to learn new employment-related skills. The goal of TIE programs is to provide the education, skills, and work experience required to enable inmates to find and keep employment upon parole or release (Coffey, 1986a).

Equity and the Right to Programs. Litigation and corrections have been companions since the so-called "hands off" doctrine—under which the courts distanced themselves from the legal complaints of prisoners—was dropped in the 1960s. Only recently, however, has correctional education been the focus of major court interventions into corrections. Two major areas of litigation that have affected education are (1) the right to participate in programs and (2) gender discrimination. There does not appear to be a constitutional right, per se, to treatment in the form of education (Moke, 1986). However, many conditions-of-confinement cases have resulted in significant improvements in the area of educational services in correctional facilities. In most jurisdictions, there are adequate administrative regulations and state and federal statutes that can be applied to assure that educational programming is provided.

In the area of gender discrimination, the courts have applied the Fourteenth Amendment equal protection clause to correctional settings to assure that programs for female offenders are brought into parity with those for males (Moke, 1986). Arguments by correctional officials that the limited number of female offenders in many systems makes the equalization of programs impractical have not been accepted by the courts.

Transitional Services. Perhaps the weakest link in the provision of educational services to offenders has been in providing assistance and support for their transition to the community. Very few correctional education programs have established any effective linkages with community-based adult education programs. Offenders who are released to community-based programs such as halfway houses are sometimes provided with assistance in continuing their education. Volunteer organizations such as the Salvation Army and the Offender Aid and Restoration Program (OAR) support educational programming for released offenders. All too often, however, offenders end their adult education participation upon parole or release from a correctional institution. Involvement in community-based adult education programs could provide an important support for offenders in their attempts to reenter the world of freedom.

Evaluation. Correctional education, like all aspects of correctional programming, is judged by the rate of recidivism as the ultimate measure of program success. Although the use of recidivism as a measure of education programming success is understandable from a political sense, its use is difficult to comprehend when one appreciates the reality of both the offenders' correctional and life experiences. The causes of criminal behavior go far beyond the absence of an adequate education. The case histories of offenders do reflect woefully limited academic and vocational educational accomplishments, but a myriad of other social and personal problems also have faced most offenders. In all too many correctional institutions, education is the only viable change-oriented program that exists to assist offenders. Education alone has not proven adequate to reduce significantly the rate of recidivism among offenders.

Correctional populations have proved difficult to follow after release from parole, and very few studies of correctional education outcomes have been undertaken. The limited number of follow-up studies of correctional education graduates is attributable in part to the reluctance of educators to accept recidivism as a realistic outcome measure. Until such time as adequate correctional programs are provided to remediate the other problems faced by offenders, or until a new measure of educational program success other than recidivism can be found, it appears unlikely that the much-needed program evaluation and follow-up efforts will be implemented.

Conclusion

As the nation presses forward with its policy of increased use of incarceration for criminal offenders, the demand for correctional education programming will continue to increase. Calls for mandatory educational participation of illiterate offenders and the application of federal and state statutes requiring services for learning-handicapped and female offenders will certainly result in expanded correctional education programs. The question facing correctional educators in the 1990s is not, Will correctional education programs continue to grow? The more important question is, Will correctional education programs improve?

The growth of correctional education seems assured based on the projected incarceration rates of the 1990s. But the improvement of correctional education services is more than a growth issue. Significant improvement in correctional programming will require adequate funding, research and follow-up on existing programs, and the identification of a clear set of goals for education in corrections. Improvement can also result from an increasing educational focus on the transformation of values and attitudes in the classroom.

References

Brown, B. S., and Courtless, T. F. *The Mentally Retarded Offender.* Washington, D.C.: U.S. Government Printing Office, 1971.

Carona, P. B. "The Windham School District and Regional Accreditation." *Journal of Correctional Education,* 1977, *28* (4), 3–4.

Coffey, O. D. *Lobbying for Correctional Education.* College Park, Md.: Correctional Education Association, 1983.

Coffey, O. D. "T.I.E.: Integrating Training, Industry and Education." *Journal of Correctional Education,* 1986a, *37* (3), 104–107.

Coffey, O. D. "Trends in the Administration of Correctional Education." In B. I. Wolford (ed.), *Correctional Education: Perspectives on Programs for Adult Offenders.* Columbus, Ohio: Clearinghouse on Adult, Career, and Vocational Education, 1986b.

Conrad, J. P., and Cavros, J. *Adult Offender Education Programs.* Sacramento, Calif.: American Justice Institute, 1981.

"Correctional Education Policy Statement." *Federal Register,* 1984, *49* (85), 1967–1968.

Faine, J., and Bohlander, E. *Public Response to Correctional Programs in Kentucky.* Kentucky Criminal Justice Research Series, no. 6. Bowling Green: Western Kentucky University, 1979.

Farkas, G. M., and Hambrick, M. "New Partnership." *Corrections Today,* 1987, *49* (1), 52–54.

Gehring, T. "The Correctional Education Professional Identity Issue." In *Proceedings of the Thirty-Sixth Annual Correctional Education Association Conference.* College Park, Md.: Correctional Education Association, 1981.

Gehring, T. "CEA Executive Board Approves Resolutions, Begins Implementation." *Journal of Correctional Education,* 1984, *35,* 138.

Haberman, M., and Quinn, L. M. "The High School Re-Entry Myth: A Follow-Up Study of Juveniles Released from Two Correctional High Schools in Wisconsin." *Journal of Correctional Education,* 1986, *37* (3), 114–117.

Horvath, G. J. "Issues in Correctional Education: A Conundrum of Conflict." *Journal of Correctional Education,* 1982, *33* (3) 8–15.

Kerle, K. E., and Ford, F. R. *The State of Our Nation's Jails.* Washington, D.C.: National Sheriffs Association, 1984.

Kohlberg, L. "The Just Community Approach to Corrections." *Journal of Correctional Education,* 1986, *37* (2) 54–58.

Littlefield, J. F. "Postsecondary Correctional Education." In B. I. Wolford (ed.), *Correctional Education: Perspectives on Programs for Adult Offenders.* Columbus, Ohio: Clearinghouse on Adult, Career, and Vocational Education, 1986.

McKie, C. "Canada's Prison Population." *Canadian Social Trends,* Summer 1987, *28,* 268–279.

Moke, P. "Equity and Legal Issues in Correctional Education." In B. I. Wolford (ed.), *Correctional Education: Perspectives on Programs for Adult Offenders.* Columbus, Ohio: Clearinghouse on Adult, Career, and Vocational Education, 1986.

Morgan, D. J. "Prevalence and Types of Handicapping Conditions Found in Juvenile Correctional Institutions: A National Survey." *Remedial and Special Education,* 1979, *13,* 283–295.

Murphy, D. M. "The Prevalence of Handicapping Conditions Among Juvenile Delinquents." *Remedial and Special Education,* 1986, *7,* 7–17.

Nelson, C. M., Rutherford, R. B., and Wolford, B. I. *Special Education in the Criminal Justice System.* Westerville, Ohio: Merrill, 1987.

Norton, L., and Simms, B. *The Status of Correctional Education in the United States.* Columbus, Ohio: National Center for Research in Vocational Education, 1988.

Rutherford, R. B., Nelson, C. M., and Wolford, B. I. *Correctional/Special Education Training Technical Report #1.* Tempe: Arizona State University, 1984.

Rutherford, R. B., Nelson, C. M., and Wolford, B. I. "Special Education in the Most Restrictive Environment." *Journal of Special Education,* 1985, *19* (1), 59–71.

U.S. Department of Justice, Bureau of Justice Statistics. *Report to the Nation on Crime and Justice: The Data.* Washington, D.C.: U.S. Government Printing Office, 1983.

U.S. Department of Justice, Bureau of Justice Statistics. *Jail Inmates, 1984.* Washington, D.C.: U.S. Government Printing Office, 1986.

28

Public Libraries and Museums

Mary C. Chobot

Commenting on the mission of the museum, Nelson Goodman observed that it most parallels the mission of the public library. Both, he observed, collect and preserve works and make them available to the public; both are fundamentally educational rather than recreational organizations (Goodman, 1985). Libraries and museums share additional characteristics: client visits are irregular and often for a brief period of time, and the decision to visit is voluntary on the part of the client. The essence of the two institutions traditionally has been the collections they have selected, acquired, organized, and preserved. More recently, libraries and museums have placed greater emphasis on interpreting their collections to their publics.

The emphasis during the last decade on lifelong learning and the call for a learning society to meet the needs of the information age have created greater demands on these institutions to provide learning opportunities for their users throughout their lifespans. The objective of this chapter is to review the role and accomplishments of libraries and museums as providers of adult and continuing education during the 1980s.

Libraries and museums are discussed separately within the chapter. Within each section, a brief overview of relevant issues is followed by a description of selected adult and continuing education programs and activities. These examples were selected because they portray the variety and breadth of such services available through these institutions.

Libraries

As of 1986, the year for which the most recent statistics are available, there were a total of 115,065 libraries in the United States (Lynch, 1987, p. 9). This total includes all types of libraries: 3,398 college and university libraries; 10,263 special libraries in government, medical, legal, religious, industrial, and other organizations; 92,539 school library media centers in public and private schools; and 8,865 public libraries or systems. If the additional 6,350 branch libraries are counted, the total number of public library buildings in the United States is 15,215 (Lynch, 1987, p. 9; *Bowker Annual*, 1987, pp. 353–354).

All libraries, at one time or another, may engage in continuing education activities for adults. However, since most of the programs and activities with which we are concerned are planned and delivered by public libraries, this chapter will concentrate on the adult education services offered by these public institutions.

Adult Services in Public Libraries: A Context. Over thirty years ago, Lester Asheim, as quoted by Houle (1979, p. 115), saw clearly that the public library had an important role to play as a provider of adult education:

> For what purposes does the American public library exist? They are many and varied, and they differ in different communities. But in one essential all libraries subscribe to a similar goal: to provide equal opportunities for access to ideas to everyone in the community who wishes it. For some library users this means the opportunity to read the latest word on topics currently being talked about. For others, it means the opportunity to learn what the great minds of the past have had to say on the great questions of continuing importance. For still others, it means the opportunity to fill in gaps in formal schooling; or to increase his own knowledge of a particular technique or skill; or to enlarge appreciation of the arts and skills of others; or to meet more effectively the demands made upon one by renewing the mind through constructive relaxation or sharpening it through intellectual discipline. All of these purposes are educational in one sense or another, and the library, by making these opportunities available, can properly be called an agency of adult education.

The fifties saw the public library become increasingly supportive of extant community services. A benchmark study conducted by Helen Lyman Smith in 1952 and 1953 provided data on the activities of public libraries in adult education (Smith, 1954). Having sent surveys to 4,096 public libraries, and having received usable responses from 1,692, Smith showed conclusive evidence that U.S. public libraries were providing adult education services to outside agencies and groups.

The sixties and seventies witnessed the development and growth of library outreach services. Libraries became increasingly concerned with reaching out to previously unserved groups such as minorities, the illiterate, and other adults who traditionally had not been library users. Public libraries also became more involved in cooperative programming with other community groups and agencies.

Events Shaping Adult Education Services. During the last decade, a number of events have occurred that strengthened the ability of public libraries to provide adult and continuing education services in their communities. One important event, the White House Conference on Library and Information Services (WHCLIS), held in November 1979, was devoted to policy issues on five themes. One of these was lifelong learning. The conference set forth a basic philosophy of service: "that all learners, regardless of age, residence (including institutions), race, disability, ethnic or cultural background, should have continuing access to the information and material necessary to cope with the increasing complexity of our changing social, economic, and technological environment" (White House Conference on Library and Information Services, 1980, p. 44).

Of the sixty-four resolutions passed by delegates to the conference, several specifically addressed the library's role in lifelong learning. These resolutions included a strong recommendation to establish information and referral centers as well as to provide information and referral services "at centers for independent learning, bringing such services to those not now served" (p. 44). The resolutions also called for an aggressive public awareness effort, and a "comprehensive, nationwide campaign coordinated at the federal level" (p. 46) to promote the use of libraries and centers for information and referral.

In 1980, the first edition of *A Planning Process for Public Libraries* (Palmour, Bellassi, and DeWath, 1980) was published. This document, revised and expanded in 1987, has had a significant impact on the provision of adult education services in public libraries. Emphasis shifted from the previous quantitative input standards, which had been used for comparison with other libraries, to a process for assessing community needs as a basis for tailoring local services and programs in a given community. This orientation provides a higher probability that public library programs will be responsive to local needs, including the need for adult and continuing education programs.

The Public Library Association's (PLA) New Standards Task Force, established in 1983, more recently has created the Public Library Development Program (PLDP). The PLDP has as its purpose the provision of information, documentation, and training that will help library managers to define the mission, goals, and objectives of the library, and to plan and to evaluate results. The second editions of both *A Planning and Role Setting Manual for Public Libraries* (McClure and others, 1987) and *Output Measures for Public Libraries* (Van House and others, 1987) were published in 1987. In addition, the PLDP is developing and field-testing a computerized data base service that will enable local public libraries to compare their output measures and other variables with those of other libraries of similar size and demographics.

In 1982, the Public Library Association's board of directors adopted "The Public Library: Democracy's Resource. A Statement of Principles." This document delineated the multiple and varied roles of public libraries, including the provision of resources and the "opportunity and encouragement for children, young adults and adults to educate themselves continuously" (Public Library Association, 1982, p. 92).

In 1984, the library community responded to the publication of *A Nation at Risk* (National Commission on Excellence in Education, 1983) with the U.S. Department of Education's report *Alliance for Excellence: Librarians Respond to A Nation at Risk* (U.S. Department of Education, Office of Educational Research and Improvement, Center for Libraries and Education Improvement, 1984). This report was the product of a project known as Libraries and a Learning Society. An advisory board of leaders in the library and information science community was established, and issue papers were prepared to set forth a series of recommendations to encourage discussion and debate.

One of these issue papers, prepared by Douglas Zweizig (1984), was "Public Libraries and Excellence: The Public Library Response to *A Nation at Risk*." While recognizing the constraints under which public libraries were operating during the early eighties, this report stressed the importance of participating fully in the learning society and made several recommendations as to how this might be achieved.

A series of five seminars was held to examine how the library community could best respond to *A Nation at Risk*. The fifth seminar dealt with the ways in which libraries might "link their resources to help create a Learning Society" (U.S. Department of Education, Office of Educational Research and Improvement, Center for Libraries and Education Improvement, 1984, p. v). The advisory board reviewed the deliberations and recommendations emanating from the five seminars and produced a report containing thirteen recommendations intended to make "the library and its staff stronger allies of American education" (p. v). Throughout this document, library services to adults were singled out as critical to the establishment of an enduring learning society. Libraries were urged to develop resources and services to support lifelong learning and education, and literacy efforts were singled out as a principal service focus.

Libraries and Literacy. In 1981, the American Library Association initiated the formation of the Coalition for Literacy. Initially, the coalition comprised eleven national agencies and volunteer organizations. The goals of the coalition were (1) to conduct a campaign to inform the nation of the illiteracy problem and solutions and (2) to establish an information and referral service through which information about literacy resources could be readily obtained. The first objective was accomplished very successfully as the National Advertising Council, Inc. joined with the Coalition for Literacy in a three-year awareness campaign. This media campaign used the theme, Volunteer Against Illiteracy—with the slogan, ''The only degree you need is a degree of caring''—to recruit leaders and tutors and to encourage support for the effort to eradicate illiteracy. The coalition accomplished its second objective by establishing a toll-free telephone number (1-800-228-8813) at the Contact Literacy Center in Lincoln, Nebraska. The Center continues to serve as a national information and referral agency, maintaining a computerized data base of literacy resources and service agencies to respond to inquiries and requests. Library-sponsored literacy programs are included for referrals along with over 7,000 literacy resources nationwide and over 6,000 service agencies. Having accomplished its initial objectives, the Coalition for Literacy has entered a second phase. New members have been added, and the coalition is serving a coordinating function, providing for the exchange of information among literacy providers.

Literacy education programs have provided a means for libraries to reach out to those adults who traditionally are nonusers of library services. Although some of the larger public libraries have had literacy programs for some time, it often has been difficult for public libraries in smaller communities to fund such programs. In 1984, the Library Services and Construction Act amendments authorized expenditures for literacy programs in libraries. Many library literacy programs have been initiated or expanded as a result. In 1986, a total of 218 grants were awarded to local public libraries to acquire literacy materials, to recruit and train volunteers to be tutors, and to promote their literacy projects designed to reach the illiterate population in their communities. Twenty-two grants were awarded to state library agencies to establish and to coordinate statewide literacy programs and to provide assistance to local public library literacy projects. A fiscal year 1986 appropriation of $4,785,000 made possible these grants and the resulting projects. (U.S. Department of Education, Office of Planning, Budget and Evaluation, 1987). A few examples of the kinds of projects that have been made possible are a regional literacy hotline, the production of a local literacy directory, tutor training workshops on television, sensitivity training for librarians to help them deal with new adult readers, and development of locally oriented literacy materials for use in the library literacy program.

The Adult Services in the Eighties (ASE) Project is sponsored by the Services to Adults Committee of the Reference and Adult Services Division of the American Library Association and is funded in part by the 1982 Bailey K. Howard World Book Encyclopedia Goal Award. The project is an ambitious undertaking to collect data and to provide a state-of-the-art description of the extent to which adult services are provided in public libraries serving populations of 25,000 or more. Directed by Kathleen Heim at the School of Library and Information Science at Louisiana State University, the project was begun in 1983. From 1983 through 1986, a selected bibliography of over 2,000 items was developed to provide the base for theory development in the area of adult services. Data collection began with the mailing of the survey instrument in May 1986. Questionnaires were sent to all U.S. public libraries serving communities of 25,000 or more—that is, 1,758 library systems, representing more than 8,000 single unit libraries, central libraries, and branches. Responses were received from 4,215 individual libraries representing 1,114 systems—a response rate of 63 percent (Wallace, forthcoming). At this writing, the analysis of the data has just been completed, and the final report is in press (Heim and Wallace, forthcoming).

Four questions on the instrument dealt with literacy education in public libraries. Of the public libraries responding, 15.4 percent indicated they provide literacy education to groups. However, 24.6 percent indicated they provide this service to individuals. Over half of the libraries responding, 52.5 percent, answered yes to the question, Does your library provide facilities for literacy education? The largest number of libraries, 80.2 percent, indicated they provide referrals to another agency for literacy education. The final report of this study will provide further data on the current range of adult services in public libraries and on the extent to which they are being provided (Heim, 1986; Van Fleet, 1987; Wallace, forthcoming).

The U.S. Department of Education, Office of Libraries, also funded a research project, Libraries and Literacy Education, conducted at the School of Library and Information Studies, University of Wisconsin, Madison. The purposes of this study, begun in 1986, are to update an earlier study on the role of libraries in literacy education, to project an expanded role for libraries in this area, to identify some exemplary literacy programs conducted by libraries, and to assess the effectiveness of new technology in such literacy activities (Zweizig, Robbins, and Johnson, 1988). At this writing, the final report for this study is being prepared.

Public libraries continue to work cooperatively with local school-based adult education programs and other community service organizations by providing space for tutoring programs and collections of materials suitable for new adult readers, by supporting GED programs, by administering CLEP exams, and by tailoring their services to meet local community needs. Those interested in literacy and libraries may wish to read the Fall 1986 issue of *Library Trends* (Weingand, 1986), which was devoted to this topic. Further information on literacy will be found in Chapter Thirty-Five, "Adult Basic Education," and Chapter Thirty-Six, "Adult Secondary Education."

Other Examples of Public Library Programs. One-third of our citizens in the United States live in rural areas. Because of the long distances involved and the lack of adequate resources, the information and continuing education needs of these rural citizens have been poorly served. The Intermountain Community Learning and Information Centers (ICLIC) project seeks to address this problem by developing a model program designed to meet these needs. ICLIC uses new methods and technology to provide educational and informational services to rural Americans through Community Learning and Information Centers located in local public libraries. The W. K. Kellogg Foundation has provided major funding to implement the project in the intermountain states of Colorado, Montana, Utah, and Wyoming. The goal is "to develop a national model for bringing distance learning and informational resources to rural libraries'' (Chobot, 1987, p. 1).

Among the services offered are publicly accessible computers and software programs that provide access to a wide range of self-help and instructional programs for the improvement of educational opportunities. Technologies such as video projection systems, videotape, videodisc, and two-way audio allow rural learners to take advantage of a number of educational services ranging from self-directed learning approaches to formal college courses. The centers also provide adult-learning and referral services, as well as career and guidance counseling, to support self-assessment of desired educational and training goals. As new technologies become available, the ICLIC network standards will allow for the addition of systems and procedures to provide additional services to rural residents. (See Wilde, 1984, and Chobot, 1987.)

The North York Public Library in North York, Ontario, Canada, the second-largest library system in Canada, has had an extensive continuing education program for adults for several years. The library has offered programs in immigrant orientation, English as a second language classes, a large literacy program supervised by a literacy expert, a training program for volunteer tutors to work one-to-one with adult learners, and, in cooperation with the North York Board of Education, a program for adults who need to complete eighth grade (Goldman and Fulford, 1983).

The American Library Association's (1981–1987) yearbooks chronicle a range of adult and continuing education activities offered in public libraries during the eighties. A few of these are presented here to show the diversity of programming and the creativity of public librarians in designing programs to meet local needs.

There are many cooperative projects. The Saint Louis Public Library and Saint Louis County Library worked with the Museum Educators Round Table of Metropolitan Saint Louis, linking the Saint Louis Art Museum with the public libraries, which supported the curriculum of classes offered by several institutions within the Round Table.

The Nassau Library System (New York) established an Independent Scholars' Round Table to encourage and to assist adults engaged in serious independent learning and research. The group met monthly, chaired by a local university professor, to discuss the needs and problems that these independent adult learners face and to consider ways in which the public library could facilitate their learning.

In the state with the lowest adult literacy rate, hundreds of Louisiana citizens participated in a statewide reading and discussion program, Reading in Literature and Culture (RELIC). Supported by a grant from the Louisiana Endowment for the Humanities and the Louisiana Library Association, the program provided an opportunity for out-of-school adults to meet with local professors to discuss major American, southern, or women's literature.

The Brooklyn Public Library (New York) developed a model program to serve the special needs of older adults. The SAGE Program (Service to the Aging) developed a comprehensive plan of service with special programs for traditional library users, the homebound, and the impaired—for both readers and nonreaders alike.

In summary, frontline librarians continue to develop creative and responsive adult and continuing education services. Given adequate funding, these programs and services will continue to expand.

Museums

The past decade has witnessed increased discussion within the museum community of the role of museum education, particularly as it relates to adults. In this section of the chapter, we will briefly summarize the principal issues in this debate and provide examples of both traditional and innovative museum education practices.

A museum is a repository of artifacts of the past, preserved and interpreted for present and future generations. The 1979 Museum Universe Survey counted nearly 5,000 museums in the United States (Commission on Museums for a New Century, 1984, p. 28). These range from venerable institutions like New York's Metropolitan Museum of Art to specialized local collections such as the Canal Museum in Syracuse, New York. Museums range in size from the large and encyclopedic institutions, like the Smithsonian, to small, specialized collections like the Hall of Fame of the Trotter, in Goshen, New York. The family of museums ranges by type "from art galleries, to botanical gardens, to historic sites, to science-technology centers, to zoos" (Commission on Museums for a New Century, 1984, p. 17).

Osborne (1985) divides museums into two broad categories: (1) historical and (2) scientific or aesthetic. The former are primarily purveyors of knowledge to their visitors. People visit the latter mainly to gain an appreciation of the works exhibited.

Museums and Education. Museums for a New Century (Commission on Museums for a New Century, 1984, p. 55), a report of the American Association of Museums (AAM), states that "Since the early part of this century educators and scholars have written about the educational responsibilities of museums." The popularity of museums as a provider of both recreational and serious adult education cannot be questioned. The exhibit remains a powerful medium by which a museum can communicate with and educate its patrons. One had only to stand in line for the King Tut exhibit or the Treasure Houses of England exhibit to be reminded of the drawing power of the first-class exhibit. Other traditional educational tools of the museum include gallery labels, brochures and exhibit catalogs, talks by docents, special tours, and, more recently, computerized interpretation of displays.

Technological advances in computer and data-storage technologies continue to have a significant impact on museum education practices. For example, during the past five years, the National Portrait Gallery and a number of other museums have developed videodiscs containing significant portions of their collections. In addition to use in exhibits, the high visual fidelity and durability of this medium makes it increasingly possible to export the collection to interested learners. The rapidly emerging compact disc (CD) technology, which allows for the storage and retrieval of large masses of text and visual data in digital form on five-inch discs, has a number of potential applications in museum education, including computer accessible catalogs and increased access to information contained on fragile print holdings. The Museum Computer Network (MCN), headquartered at Syracuse University, is providing and facilitating the application of new information and educational technology in museums. The MCN provides various educational and support services to its members and publishers. *Spectra* is a quarterly devoted to museum automation.

   Needed: A Philosophical Basis for Museum Education. *Museums for a New Century* (Commission on Museums for a New Century, 1984, p. 57) states that, "Although museums are plainly institutions of object-centered learning, and there is an interest among [museum] educators and administrators alike in formulating learning theory more clearly, there is no accepted philosophical framework [for such theory]." Four seminars, sponsored by the American Association of Museums in 1979 and 1980, with support from the National Endowment for the Humanities, represented one attempt to provide a philosophical framework for museum education for adults. The seminars on the topic of Lifelong Learning in the Humanities brought together recognized experts on the humanities, on the adult learner, and on museum programming for adults. One of their goals was to develop a view of the museum as a resource for lifelong learning.

   Lifelong learning has been defined as the process of learning that continues throughout one's lifetime based on individual needs, circumstances, interests, and learning skills. Collins (1981, p. xv) observes that, "Applying adult learning concepts to the museum context . . . may require a change in perspective for museum professionals from . . . 'what do we have in the collections?' to . . . 'what are the needs and interests of the adult audience we want to attract?'"

   Carr (1986, p. 56) presents a somewhat different perspective on this issue. Reacting to a comment, similar to that presented above, he writes, "Certainly we must talk with our visitors, and, indeed, with those who have not visited the museum, to find out what works for them in visiting a museum, but as educators . . . if we simply ask them what they want and give it to them, we are abdicating our responsibility."

   The responsibility to which Carr (p. 56) refers, is "to determine what the [museum] curriculum should be . . . [and to] use every bit of wit and creativity to make it as interesting, exciting, even entertaining as it can be, all with the objective of helping them to absorb our information."

   A somewhat controversial 1986 study, *The Uncertain Profession: Observations on the State of Museum Education in Twenty American Art Museums* (Eisner and Dobbs, 1986) added fuel to this debate. Among the thirty-eight art museum directors and heads of museum education interviewed for the study, there appeared to be little consensus on what art museum education programs were designed to accomplish. The comments reported also suggested a high degree of ambiguity in the role of museum educator.

It has been mentioned in a number of recent studies that museums currently lack a sufficient base of research and evaluation data from which to determine what type of programming works most effectively with the adult learner.

A Model for Museum Education. In seeking to use resources most efficiently for adult education in the museum, a number of models have emerged. Based on an informal study of patterns of adult involvement, the Toledo Museum of Art developed the matrix chart, shown in Table 28.1, as a guide for program planning (Mandle, 1981).

The chart's utility lies in its differentiation of learning activities for three levels of visitors. It also suggests the range of possible learning activities and opportunities that museums might afford the adult learner at each of these levels.

Volunteers. Volunteers have been a mainstay in museums since the establishment of docent interpretation programs early in the twentieth century. Volunteer training is a significant adult education activity of many museums. It meets the multiple objectives of providing for personal development needs of volunteers, providing specific training on museum collection interpretation and maintenance, expanding the availability of museum resources, and broadening the museum's base of community support. For a more complete discussion on volunteers, the reader is referred to Chapter Eight, "The Voluntary Sector and Adult Education."

Examples of Museum-Based Learning for Adults. A variety of examples illustrate the current state of adult and continuing education in museums. Collins (1981) includes several case studies that showcase a variety of museum-based adult education activities; among them are the following six examples:

The National Endowment for the Humanities (NEH) Learning Museum Programs provided topical and thematic courses at six museums. The evaluation results of these courses indicated that relatively sophisticated courses at the adult level are both economically and programmatically viable.

The Philadelphia Museum of Art designed a seven-month program called Art as a Reflection of Human Concerns. The program was built around seven basic themes felt to be of interest to the public. Selected objects from the museum's collection were presented in the context of family, humor, religion, aging, death, birth, and love. A combination of activities that included speakers, gallery talks, films, and performances was used to portray each theme.

The Science Museum of Minnesota used theater techniques in an anthropology interpretation. That theater provided a context for the presentation of artifacts that, when detached from their settings and displayed, lacked meaning for most typical museum visitors.

The Boston Children's Museum describes itself as a hands-on, participatory, interactive museum. They report that approximately 45 percent of their visitors are adults. Because of the museum's orientation to children, adults appear to be willing to "learn content . . . that they might otherwise

Table 28.1. Matrix Chart for Museum and Departmental
Planning Used by the Toledo Museum of Art.

Level of Public Sophistication and Interest in Art	Intensity of Contact with Art, Staff, and Resources			
	A. Self-directed	B. More sustained	C. High involvement	D. Intense sustained
Level I Totally uninitiated general visitor	Floor map of museum Installations, general labels, maps, lighting, ambiance Introductory AV Temporary exhibitions of general and didactic nature Picture books Calendar of museum activities Films on seeing Video tape information	Guided tour (general) Gallery presentations: drama, music, poetry Speakers' bureau Television and radio programs	Short, general classes Adult education H.S. Studio classes	Curatorial expertise
Level II Visitor with some interest and knowledge	All of above plus: Guide books to collections Temporary exhibitions of specific and didactic nature Specific AV presentations "Open shelf" book study areas in gallery Films on art	All of above plus: Guided tour (specific) Auditorium lecture (general topic) Library	All of above plus: Luncheon lectures Corporate lectures (short classes) Survey classes	Curatorial expertise Teacher curriculum training College survey courses (undergraduate) Exhibitions by H.S. students Exhibitions by special adult classes AV/video production on special subjects
Level III Interested and knowledgeable visitor	All of above plus: Scholarly catalogues on collections Temporary exhibitions on specific subjects	All of above plus: Guided tour (scholarly) Registrar files Curatorial records (minus confidential data) Auditorium lecture (scholarly topic)	All of above plus: Seminars Teaching courses Collecting and connoisseurship courses	Expertise, collectors, advising Internships Graduate seminars Exhibitions by college students AV/video production on special topics

Source: Roger Mandle. "Adult Programming Approaches." In Zipporah W. Collins (ed.), *Museums, Adults and the Humanities.* Washington, D.C.: American Association of Museums, 1981, pp. 182–183.

find threatening'' (Gurian, 1981, p. 279). Recognizing this fact, the museum structured space and designed activities to facilitate this learning process.

Old Sturbridge Village is a living museum of regional New England history. Its Teacher Education Program is designed to foster linkages between the schools and the museum as an extension of the classroom. Two ten-day summer workshop sessions allow teachers the opportunity to experience the history portrayed at Old Sturbridge Village. A 1979 evaluation of the program indicated not only that the program had an impact on the participants' classroom activities but that 75 percent of respondents continued their involvement with museums and field-based learning several years after their summer workshop session.

The Ringling Museums, in Sarasota, Florida, were faced with the problem of bringing an excellent collection of Renaissance and baroque objects to life. A Medieval and Renaissance Fair was organized to meet this need. The fair has stimulated interest in costume, language, speech, architectural styles, crafts, games, food, art, literature, and competitions of the period.

The Royal Ontario Museum in Toronto, Ontario, Canada provides a coordinated museumwide program of learning activities for adults. In 1986 and 1987, the museum offered a variety of continuing education experiences to over 8,000 Canadians. These included lectures, courses, field trips, and workshops, all offered at the introductory level. Their continuing education program makes extensive use of videos and slides to depict the objects and to illustrate the concepts being discussed. Whenever feasible, the museum presents the artifacts and specimens for viewing and, sometimes, for handling. The museum's continuing education staff feels that the presence of the real thing is an important feature of its continuing education programs and that it leads to increased satisfaction for participants.

Some museums provide adult continuing education in highly specialized areas. For example, the Peace Museum in Chicago, which focuses on issues of war and peace, human rights, social change, social justice, peacemakers, and peacemaking provides an organized educational program for adults that includes peace education. The Anacostia Museum, in Washington, D.C., a community-based museum that is part of the Smithsonian, focuses on Afro-American history and culture. Throughout the year, the museum offers lectures and workshops generally related to the theme of the current exhibit (for example, the Black Church). And each December, the museum holds a Kwanzaa workshop—an Afro-American celebration based on the traditional African festival celebrating the harvest of the first crops.

Several ethnic museums are located in Chicago. Among these are the Polish Museum of America, the Swedish-American Museum Association of Chicago, the Mexican Fine Arts Center Museum, and the Balzekas Museum of Lithuanian Culture. These museums offer various continuing education activities including hobby workshops, participatory exhibits, and organized educational programs for adults.

An exemplary program of comprehensive museum adult education activities is found at Mystic Seaport (Carr, 1986). Mystic Seaport is a living history museum complex in Connecticut that provides, as part of an extensive adult education program, offshore sailing training for adults on a museum-owned schooner-yacht, courses in maritime skills such as celestial navigation, a concentrated small-boat-building course, courses and experience in period topics such as weaving and fireplace cooking, videotapes and videodiscs that preserve and provide increased access to various aspects of the museum's collection and programming, and live interpretations within formal exhibits of a variety of period crafts, trades, and lifestyles.

Since their inception, museums have recognized their responsibility to educate. Within the last decade, they have become increasingly active and creative in identifying the needs of adult learners and in attempting to meet them. In performing this work, museums, like public libraries, are seeking to develop a theory base upon which to structure their adult education offerings. To date, they have looked to the literature on adult education for guidance. However, as the role of the museum educator evolves, both institutionally and within formal preparation programs, a museum-specific basis upon which adult programming can be built will surely develop.

Summary

Three basic issues emerge from this consideration of adult and continuing education in public libraries and museums: (1) redefinition of roles; (2) responsiveness to user needs, especially extraordinary and focused needs; and (3) utilization of new technologies.

Both libraries and museums have become major resources for lifelong learning. Since they provide access to a wide range of materials and collections, they serve as valuable and readily accessible resources for adults engaged in learning at various stages of their lives. However, within both institutions, the manner in which this educational function is best served continues to be debated.

Libraries and museums are reaching out to potential users, with emphasis on special populations. The eighties have seen growth in library outreach and increased accessibility for social and economic groups who previously had been underserved. One area in which this active position on the part of libraries is especially evident is literacy. During the last decade, museums also have undertaken to assess and to meet the challenge of making their resources available to a wider public through creative programming.

Technology has played a significant role during the 1980s in fostering increased access to and utilization of the resources of libraries and museums. Public television has brought many of the world's treasures into the home; this could not have occurred without active institutional cooperation. Computers are powerful tools for cataloging collections, and for organizing, retrieving, and disseminating information in museums and libraries—as well as being tools of instruction for adult learners. Optical and digital media, such as videodisc and compact disc, permit the storage, integration, and viewing of large text and image data bases, adding a new dimension to library and museum programming. The issue for library and museum professionals is the way in which these new technologies can best be utilized.

The manner in which these issues are being addressed by both institutions suggests a bright future for libraries and museums as important resources for the adult learner during the decade of the nineties and beyond.

References

American Library Association. *ALA Yearbook of Library and Information Service.* Chicago: American Library Association, 1981–1987.

Bowker Annual. New York: Bowker, 1987.

Carr, J. R. "Education Everywhere for Everyone at Mystic Seaport." In *The American Museum Experience: In Search of Excellence.* Edinburgh: Scottish Museums Council, 1986.

Chobot, M. C. "ICLIS Project Serves Rural America." *Partnership Exchange,* 1987, *4* (2), 1.

Collins, Z. W. (ed.). *Museums, Adults and the Humanities: A Guide to Educational Programming.* Washington, D.C.: American Association of Museums, 1981.

Commission on Museums for a New Century. *Museums for a New Century.* Washington, D.C.: American Association of Museums, 1984.

Eisner, E. W., and Dobbs, S. M. *The Uncertain Profession: Observations on the State of Museum Education in Twenty American Art Museums.* Los Angeles: J. Paul Getty Center for Education in the Arts, 1986.

Goldman, P., and Fulford, J. "North York Library-Based Adult Learner Services: An Evaluative Case Study." *Library Trends,* 1983, *31* (4) 621–637.

Goodman, N. "The End of the Museum?" *Journal of Aesthetic Education,* 1985, *19* (2), 53–62.

Gurian, E. "Adult Learning at Children's Museum of Boston." In Z. W. Collins (ed.), *Museums, Adults and the Humanities: A Guide to Educational Programming.* Washington, D.C.: American Association of Museums, 1981.

Heim, K. "Adult Services as Reflective of the Changing Role of the Public Library," *RQ,* 1986, *26* (2), 180–187.

Heim, K., and Wallace, D. P. (eds.). *Adult Services: An Enduring Focus for the Public Library.* Chicago: American Library Association, forthcoming.

Houle, C. O. "Seven Adult Educational Roles of the Public Library." In J. M. Lee and B. A. Hamilton (eds.), *As Much to Learn as to Teach: Essays in Honor of Lester Asheim.* Hamden, Conn.: Linnet Books, 1979.

Lynch, M. J. *Libraries in an Information Society: A Statistical Summary.* Chicago: American Library Association, 1987.

McClure, C. R., and others. *Planning and Role Setting Manual for Public Libraries.* Chicago: American Library Association, 1987.

Mandle, R. "Adult Programming Approaches." In Z. W. Collins (ed.), *Museums, Adults and the Humanities: A Guide to Educational Programming.* Washington, D.C.: American Association of Museums, 1981.

National Commission on Excellence in Education. *A Nation at Risk: The Full Account.* Cambridge, Mass.: U.S.A. Research, 1983.

Osborne, H. "Museums and Their Functions." *Journal of Aesthetic Education,* 1985, *19* (2), 41–51.

Palmour, V. E., Bellassi, M. C., and DeWath, N. V. *A Planning Process for Public Libraries.* Chicago: American Library Association, 1980.

Public Library Association. "The Public Library: Democracy's Resource. A Statement of Principles." *Public Libraries,* 1982, *21,* 92.

Smith, H. L. *Adult Education Activities in Public Libraries: A Report of the ALA Survey of Adult Education Activities in Public Libraries and State Library Extension Agencies of the United States.* Chicago: American Library Association, 1954.

U.S. Department of Education, Office of Educational Research and Improvement, Center for Libraries and Education Improvement. *Alliance For Excellence: Librarians Respond to* A Nation at Risk: *Recommendations and Strategies from Libraries and the Learning Society.* Washington, D.C.: U.S. Government Printing Office, 1984.

U.S. Department of Education, Office of Planning, Budget and Evaluation. *Annual Evaluation Report, Fiscal Year 1986.* Washington, D.C.: U.S. Government Printing Office, 1987.

Van Fleet, C. "Special Report: The Adult Services in the Eighties Project." In *ALA Yearbook of Library and Information Services 1987.* Chicago: American Library Association, 1987.

Van House, N.A., and others. *Output Measures for Public Libraries: A Manual of Standardized Procedures.* (2nd ed.) Chicago: American Library Association, 1987.

Wallace, D. P. "The Character of Adult Services in the Eighties: Overview and Analysis of the ASE Questionnaire Data." In K. Heim and D. P. Wallace (eds.), *Adult Services: An Enduring Focus for the Public Library.* Chicago: American Library Association, forthcoming.

Weingand, D. E. (ed.). "Adult Education, Literacy and Libraries." *Library Trends,* 1986, *35* (2) (entire issue).

White House Conference on Library and Information Services. *Summary Report.* Washington, D.C.: U.S. Government Printing Office, 1980.

Wilde, G. R. *Intermountain Community Learning and Information Centers Concept, Processes and Results.* Paper presented at the annual meeting of the Rural Sociological Society, College Station, Tex., Aug. 1984. (ED 247 077)

Zweizig, D. "Public Libraries and Excellence: The Public Library Response to *A Nation at Risk.*" Washington, D.C.: U.S. Department of Education, Office of Educational Research and Improvement, Center for Libraries and Education Improvement, 1984. (ED 243 887)

Zweizig, D. L., Robbins, J., and Johnson, P. W. *Libraries and Literacy Education: Comprehensive Survey Report.* Washington, D.C.: U.S. Department of Education, Office of Educational Research and Improvement, Library Programs, 1988.

29

Federal and Provincial Adult Education Agencies in the United States and Canada

Michael Collins
Huey B. Long

Adult education is the most rapidly expanding area of education in North America (Cross, 1984; Long, 1987). It is an extremely complex and diverse enterprise that challenges conceptualization, description, and inventorying. Providers are as diverse as the program goals (Long, 1987), and financing ranges from individual responsibility to corporate funding to government funding.

This short chapter on federal and provincial agencies in both the United States and Canada cannot draw a completely detailed picture of the situation in either country. It will, however, attempt to give an accurate overall sense of the part played by federal and provincial (or state) agencies in shaping the provision of adult education on both sides of the border. Despite apparent similarities, the distinctions are important—more so from the perspective of Canadian adult educators than from that of their U.S. colleagues. The somewhat different orientations of the following sections on the United States and Canada, therefore, serve to highlight the significance of these distinctions while accounting for similarities.

Both the United States and Canada have legally placed the responsibility for education, including adult education, at the state or provincial level. The de jure federal role, however, often has been conveniently set aside on numerous occasions in both nations. De facto involvement of the federal government in education including the provision of funds, establishment of regulations, and so forth exists in Canada as well as the United States.

Not surprisingly, the current (and possibly the future) outlines of educational provision for adults emerge from the historical conditions in both countries. The unique history of each country contributes to idiosyncratic responses to educational needs, but it is difficult to ignore the influence of history in either nation.

There are also some common identifiable trends. The most obvious is the long-term growth of federal budgetary support for special groups, situations, and purposes. Despite occasional aberrations in funding patterns and political rhetoric, the trend toward greater rather than less involvement by federal agencies in the education of adults continues in both nations.

Adult Education Agencies in the United States

Historically, the United States has emerged as a world leader of the western technological enterprise. The cultural development of the nation has been successively enriched and challenged by differing waves of immigration. Originally, most of what is now the United States was dominated by British colonists. In the nineteenth century, larger numbers of African, Irish, German, and Nordic settlers arrived. These new immigrants were later joined by Italians and Chinese. Most recently, individuals of Asian and Hispanic origins have contributed to America's cultural, ethnic, and racial composition. By the time most of these newer immigrants arrived, the larger educational framework was already structured or in the process of developing. The common school and financial provision for the support of public education were realities of the nineteenth century. Yet, the change from an agricultural to an industrial nation and the continuing arrival of new Americans stimulated the development of a variety of mechanisms to meet the educational needs of adults. Evening high schools in urban areas met some of these needs. Americanization classes sponsored by businesses and industries also emerged in the northern population centers, while moonlight schools and other efforts to eradicate illiteracy were established in rural states.

In the last quarter of the nineteenth century, America began to emerge as a significant industrial nation that competed with Germany and Great Britain for world markets. As a consequence, the federal government began to take a more active role in supporting educational activities for both children and adults. It would be erroneous to imply that a federal role in education did not exist prior to this time. Federal involvement in American education actually existed prior to the adoption of the U.S. Constitution. The Northwest Ordinance of 1783 interjected the federal government into education. Later, the Morrill Land-Grant Act of 1862 increased the extent of federal involvement.

By the beginning of the twentieth century, effective lobbies for federal support of vocational and agricultural educational activities were developing. These two lobbies often competed and occasionally joined forces. Significant legislation supporting both vocational and agricultural education occurred between 1910 and 1919—the Smith-Lever Act of 1914 and the Smith-Hughes Act of 1917.

During that same decade, the U.S. Office of Education began to emphasize literacy and citizenship education for new immigrants. Even though little money was available and the federal effort was primarily limited to recommending and developing curriculum materials, the emphasis on literacy and citizenship was an important beginning. Thus, by the end of the first quarter of the twentieth century, federal support for adult education existed. Another pattern that continues to exist was also developing; funds for education of adults were provided to a number of agencies rather than solely to the Office of Education.

The Great Depression of the 1930s and welfare projects initiated during that period also provided opportunities for the federal government to work through a variety of programs and agencies. The exact extent of adult education in the various welfare and works projects of the 1930s has not been sufficiently studied.

World War II diverted the nation's attention, but the 1950s and 1960s witnessed an explosion of federal programs. Some of the more interesting programs included literacy, scientific education, the arts, the humanities, vocational-technical education, and job training activities. The volume and diversity of these activities are beyond our ability to discuss in detail here. The federal role in education in the late 1970s and 1980s could be described as erratic but generally moving toward a limited increase of support in areas such as literacy education. Perhaps the greatest disappointment of the 1970s was the Lifelong Learning Act of 1978, which amended the Higher Education Act of 1965. Failure of Congress to fund adequately the Lifelong Learning Act of 1978 indicated a reduction of federal interest in community improvement programs previously supported by higher education institutions.

The states have de jure responsibility for education in the United States. Nevertheless, the historical role of the federal government in education for both children and adults has been an expanding one since 1783. At least since about 1900, the rationale for a de facto active federal role has been fairly consistent and some interesting and provocative justifications have been written in federal law for the support of postcompulsory education.

The introductory chapter of each piece of federal legislation usually contains three similar observations. First, it is common for the purpose of the bill to include a statement to the effect that primary responsibility for education is at the state and local levels. Second, the legislation often implies that the federal government is addressing an emergency or critical situation. Third, the legislation is offered as a means to redress some problem of equity or accessibility or some other issue of national importance.

Thus, federal policy for postcompulsory education and training attempts to maintain the position that the responsibility for education is a state and local one. Simultaneously, the language of legislation justifies federal government intervention on the basis of national interest, acute situations or urgent needs, and issues of educational equity or accessibility that are unlikely to be met without federal assistance.

Accordingly, the purposes or goals of federal legislation are variously defined. Some of the more explicit objectives identified in selected legislation are (1) to provide educational opportunities for all, (2) to provide needed human resources in critical social and industrial occupations, (3) to provide basic, generalized, occupational competence, (4) to socialize and Americanize the population, and (5) to meet national defense needs.

The federal government has chosen to address the above and related objectives by dispersing funds for adult education among a number of agencies. This practice has a long history. In 1968, Liveright conducted a comprehensive study identifying thirteen federal agencies that received funds for adult education activities. A 1969 publication (Adult Education Association of the U.S.A., 1969) required 176 pages to list federally funded adult education programs. A 1977 report (House Committee on Education and Labor and Senate Committee on Human Resources, 1977) identified approximately eighty laws current in 1977. Many of these pertained to adult education in some way.

More recently, Irwin (1987) identified seventy-nine literacy programs in fourteen federal agencies with a total federal expenditure of $347 million for literacy in fiscal year 1985. Later, a staff report of the House Committee on Education and Labor (Irwin, 1987) offered a different view. According to the staff analysis, only ten of the seventy-nine programs definitely conduct literacy programs, and only $126.5 million of the $347 million was actually spent on adult literacy programs. If the federal government does not know the extent of its support for literacy education alone, it is clear the problems of accurately assessing and describing the extent and scope of involvement in other federal departments and agencies (such as the Departments of Commerce, Defense, Labor and others) are difficult indeed.

The Adult Education Act is the major federal program for basic education and literacy skills for adults. The fiscal year 1987 appropriation was $106 million and the fiscal year 1988 budget request was for $130 million. But, as noted, a variety of other acts address diverse objectives associated with other federal departments. For example, legislation introduced in 1987 included the Trade and Export Enhancement Act, School Improvement Act, Fair Work Opportunity Act, Urgent Relief for the Homeless Act, English Proficiency Act, Family Welfare Reform Act, Education Achievement Incentive Act, Opportunities for Employment Preparation Act, Education for Competitive America Act, Targeted Educational Assistance Act, Literacy Training Act, Readfare Act, and Adult Education Act Amendments.

In addition to the programs based in the Department of Education, a publication of the department (U.S. Department of Education, Division of Adult Education, 1986) lists programs in the Federal Bureau of Prisons, Department of Defense, Veterans Administration, U.S. Coast Guard, Department of the Interior, Department of Health and Human Services, Department of Labor, General Services Administration, Department of Agriculture,

National Endowment for the Humanities, Department of Energy, National Gallery of Art, and VISTA.

While it is extremely difficult to quantify trends in federal appropriations for support of all adult education programs, it is possible to examine a specific program. Thus, the Adult Education Act provides a useful item for analysis. The federal provision for literacy education is usually traced to the Economic Opportunity Act of 1964. From that origin, the Adult Education Act has progressed through several legislative identities including the Elementary and Secondary Act of 1965. The funds provided by the various amendments made during the evolution of the act generally have been in an upward direction. However, the fiscal year 1989 request at $140 million was even less than the $150 million recommended for fiscal year 1971 by the National Advisory Committee on Adult Basic Education (Cortwright and Brice, 1970). Nevertheless, the upward trend is important when one considers the negative attitudes of President Jimmy Carter and President Ronald Reagan toward federal support of education.

In real dollars, adjusted for inflation, the upward trend in appropriations was more apparent than real during Carter's and Reagan's presidential terms. Much of the limited increase in dollar amounts has been eroded by losses in purchasing power. Nevertheless, given the disappointing political atmosphere and the antipathy and opposition of two consecutive U.S. presidents, the apparent trend is symbolic.

At the time this chapter was written, initiatives were underway to broaden the support of the private sector for literacy education, and more pressure was being exerted on states to do more, while federal support was continuing to inch forward.

Speculation about broader trends are in the same vein. The dollar amount of appropriations for a variety of adult education programs likely will continue to grow. Yet, the growth in dollars is likely to be small, and actual improvements in the financial health of most adult education programs that are wholly dependent upon federal appropriations will be weak.

This section on federal government agencies in the United States included subsections on historical context, rationale, purposes, structures and agencies, and trends. The historical context suggests that early American society and ideas about education were in part derived from the British character of the colonists. The common school and ad valorem support for education were associated with state responsibilities for education. Succeeding waves of immigrants from other European nations, Asia, and Hispanic countries, as well as the results of slavery, contributed to a variety of continuing adjustments in educational provisions for adults. Despite the constitutional identification of education as a state and local responsibility, the federal government's role has increased steadily.

It was noted that the federal government's approach to funding education for adults has been to spread the purposes and funds among a wide range of governmental departments and agencies. As a result, an accurate, comprehensive analysis of all federal governmental expenditures on adult education is not available. Governmental departments cannot agree on some of the basic facts of the situation, and because of the absence of comprehensive and accurate information, trends are based on speculation. The trend of appropriated dollar amounts is perceived to be upward, but in terms of purchasing power, the upward trend is more apparent than real.

Adult Education Agencies in Canada

A great number of Canadians participate in adult education programs that are provided or supported by federal and provincial agencies. According to Statistics Canada (1985, p. 1), if adult education is defined for our purposes here as "all organized educational activities—everything from job-related training to hobby classes—taken outside of a full-time program," then "one in every five Canadians 17 and over took at least one adult education course during 1983." Most of them (90 percent) are part-time students. Following the trend highlighted in the opening sentence of this chapter, Canadian participation rates in organized adult education are on the increase.

In Canada, the assignment of education as a provincial responsibility seems fairly clear-cut. According to the British North America (B.N.A.) Act of 1867, education falls under provincial jurisdiction (Dawson, 1957). Although, as in the United States, federal government departments do manage to influence the shape of educational policy and practice in the regions through the allocation of conditional funding, provinces have tended to be protective of the arrangements for education as enshrined in the B.N.A. Act. As a result, the government in Ottawa does not have an equivalent of the U.S. Office of Education.

On the whole, providers of adult education in Canada cover the same wide range of learner interests, address similar program goals, and draw on the same kind of governmental funding sources as counterparts in the United States. Most adult education is offered in designated educational institutions. Statistics Canada (1985, p. 35) reported that together with private and commercial schools, the traditional educational institutions such as universities, colleges, and public schools accounted for 53 percent of all adult education courses in 1983. The remainder took place in nonschool settings such as the workplace, churches, YMCA, YWCA, Red Cross, and community centers.

A thorough treatment of the topic for the purpose of comparison would require an extensive analysis of relevant cultural, socioeconomic, political, and demographic factor. This is not feasible here. However, in setting the scene for an account of Canadian adult education agencies, it is useful to remind ourselves that Canada is the largest country in the Western Hemisphere and the second largest in the world. A land mass of 3,851,809 square miles is shared by ten provinces (British Columbia, Alberta, Saskatchewan, Manitoba, Ontario, Quebec, New Brunswick, Nova Scotia, Prince Edward

Island, and Newfoundland) and two territories (the Yukon Territory and the Northwest Territory). This large country encompasses a wide variety of topographic, climatic, and cultural conditions. At the time of the 1986 census, Statistics Canada (1987) reported that the population was 25,354,064— a million less than that of California. Despite the vastness of their country, most Canadians live within 100 miles of the U.S. border. Their institutions (including adult education agencies) are molded, to a far greater extent than many Canadians would like, by influences from the more densely populated and powerful political economy to the south.

Yet these influences from the United States are not quite so overwhelming as the casual observer might suppose. Any systematic overview, however brief, must take into account the discernible influences from Britain (which are even more apparent in Canada than they are in the United States) and the distinctive contributions of Quebec as the predominant cultural and political location of French-speaking Canada. In addition, reference should be made to some of the internationally recognized Canadian adult education programs and initiatives that have been sustained through public funding.

The British North America Act passed by the British Parliament in 1867 placed public education under the control of each province. This act confirmed differences in educational agencies of the various regions—differences that already had begun to appear at that time. However, although it had no constitutional role in education, the federal government, as was the case in the United States, soon began enacting statutes to assist in the financing of agriculture and vocational instruction. This trend increased immediately after World War II, but it was the Technical and Vocational Training Act of 1960 that signaled a remarkable expansion in the federal government's role. Next came the Canada Student Loan Act in 1964 followed by the Adult Occupational Training Act in 1967. As a result of the Fiscal Arrangements Act of 1967, federal funding to the provinces increased from $100 million in 1966 to $422 million in 1967 (Canadian Association for Adult Education and L'institute Canadien d'éducation des adultes, 1982, p. 23). The provinces were required to match the federal contributions dollar for dollar.

According to a joint report of the Canadian Association for Adult Education and L'institut Canadien d'éducation des adultes (1982, p. 23), "By 1981, federal educational expenditure had reached a level of $5.7 billion, of which more than $5 billion went toward the education of persons beyond the compulsory school leaving age in each of the Canadian jurisdictions." Along with the National Training Act of 1982, these federal interventions have had a significant bearing on the nature of adult education programming in provincial agencies. The National Training Act permitted the federal government, with provincial agreement, to assist private and nonprofit training organizations as well as postsecondary education institutions. In addition, the act allowed for subsidies to be granted toward the cost of training by employers.

British influence on adult education institutions is very much in evidence, especially in eastern Canada (including the largely francophone province of Quebec). According to E. A. Corbett (1952, p. 5), first director of the Canadian Association for Adult Education (CAAE), "Adult education in Canada had its beginning when the Mechanics' Institute Movement, already well developed in Great Britain, spread to this country early in the nineteenth century." Corbett indicated that this British adult education movement provided the pattern for early development in Canada's oldest universities, especially with regard to their extension (extramural) activities. Canadian public libraries, Corbett noted, were developed as part of the mechanics' institute movement.

If British influence on the development of institutionalized adult education is apparent in eastern Canada, it is also clearly discernible in the far western province of British Columbia where mechanics' institutes became relatively prevalent. And the now-prestigious University of British Columbia emerged as an extension of Quebec's McGill University, which itself carries the historical hallmark of a British institution (although it would be misleading to claim that McGill still remains a bastion of British culture).

American influence within institutionalized adult education is identifiable in all regions of Canada. However, it is probably most prevalent in the prairie provinces (Manitoba, Saskatchewan, Alberta) where the major universities, their extension divisions, and agricultural extension agencies have followed along lines similar to counterparts in the U.S. Midwest. E. A. Corbett (1952, p. 30) suggested almost forty years ago that Canadian adult education agencies are "likely to gain from the [U.S.] research in group development, from developing concepts of 'liberal adult education' and also from the more traditional agricultural extension." Adult educators in Canada share with other intellectuals and professionals a growing concern about U.S. influence on public agencies that are looked to for the sustenance of a distinctive Canadian culture.

English-speaking Canadian adult educators, on the whole, still tend to overlook the significant contribution of francophone initiatives to the texture of formal adult education in Canada. Like E. A. Corbett, Kidd (1953, p. 29) recognized the important influence of the British mechanics' institutes, but he also pointed out that the first Canadian adult education program grew out of an association (*l'ordre de Bon Temps*) formed by Champlain and his associates in the winter of 1604. Even so, the French-Canadian, or Québécois, dimension of formal adult education in Canada is insufficiently appreciated by many Canadian anglophone adult educators, though Hayden Roberts (1982) provides some relevant insight into the distinctions between approaches to adult education in English-speaking Canada and francophone Quebec. Roberts undertakes a thoughtful comparative study of policies, structures, and processes of adult education in Quebec and Alberta (widely regarded as the most Americanized of Canadian provinces), making a good case for his hypothesis that adult education is more socially oriented, more radical, in the French-speaking province. Differences in political philosophy do have consequences, he argues, and they even penetrate public (federally supported) agencies that the two provinces have in common.

Canada's nearest equivalent to the U.S. Office of Education is probably the Canada Employment and Immigration Commission (CEIC). Its policies and funding allocations have a considerable impact on the nature of basic adult education and on the agencies that deliver it. Emphasis is on job preparation and vocational training, and this kind of intervention by the federal government, with its sharp focus on occupational training, stands in the way of adult basic education's becoming a clearly defined field of practice as it is in the United States (Brooke, 1972). Since the passage of the National Training Act in 1982, a decision has been made to concentrate federal funds even more tightly in the areas of so-called critical skill shortage, reducing emphasis on training in other areas including basic education for illiterate adults. Like jurisdictions in other western political economies, Canadian provincial and federal authorities have adopted the notion that a heavy emphasis on specific skill development is causally linked to job creation.

The federal government's particular interest in job preparation led to a considerable amount of curriculum development and program planning under the rubric of Basic Training and Skill Development (BTSD). Since the BTSD orientation has been associated with government funding from the outset, it has had an important influence on adult education agencies across the country and on the ethos of adult education practice within these settings. In many respects, curriculum and program development associated with BTSD (Canada Manpower and Immigration, 1974) anticipated the competency-based adult education initiatives that emerged in many U.S. adult education agencies.

A significant federally supported program that allowed for flexibility and room for local embellishment was Canada Newstart, launched in the summer of 1967. Funded entirely by the federal government through Canada Manpower and Immigration, nonprofit organizations were set up in each of the provinces selected to operate a Newstart program. The purpose of Newstart corporations, according to Sloan (1974, p. 243), was "to seek out the disadvantaged themselves; and to seek through innovation and experimentation practical solutions to those problems." In provinces where Newstart initiatives thrived for a time, they left their mark on community-based adult education as well as on practice within the curriculum of adult education institutions. The program lends itself to further research and analysis if only to juxtapose it against more current conceptions of program delivery characterized by BTSD and Competency Based Adult Education (CBAE) formats. Literature and program materials on Newstart are still readily accessible.

During the past decade, a two-volume report commissioned by the Minister of Employment and Immigration, *Learning a Living in Canada* (Skill Development Leave Task Force, 1983) confirmed that the predominant emphasis for government-supported adult education agencies in Canada is on skill development for jobs in a dynamic labor market, which has yet to emerge. The narrow focus on skill development to meet perceived needs of the economy differs quite radically from the approaches of distinctive Canadian adult education agencies such as Frontier College, the Antigonish Movement, Farm Forum, the Women's Institutes, and the Wheat Pool—even though they were all very much concerned with practical problems of the world of work and with the development of individual competence. These Canadian adult education institutions, which received public funding directly or through other agencies such as universities, have earned international reputations and provide models for adult education programming in other countries.

Frontier College, the brainchild of a missionary from Nova Scotia, was established before the turn of the century to provide adult education for illiterate and semiliterate immigrant workers. The teachers were required to live and work in logging and railroad construction sites alongside prospective students. The strategies and teaching locations have changed considerably over the years, but Frontier College still strives for relevance by delivering practical adult literacy programs with the support of federal government grants.

Like Frontier, the Antigonish Movement thrived in a community-based setting. Its main source of inspiration was Moses Coady, who set out to coordinate meaningful adult education from the extension division of Saint Francis Xavier University on behalf of poverty stricken farmers, fishermen, and miners of Nova Scotia. According to Conger (1974, p. 10), as a result of this initiative, the first cooperative was organized in 1930, and "within 20 years, the Antigonish Movement in the Maritime provinces included 100,000 participants, 451 credit unions, 210 cooperative stores, 27 cooperative housing units, and also cooperative hospitals, insurance plans, and medical care." Locally organized study clubs and discussion groups provided the organized pedagogical settings of the movement.

Following a great deal of educational activity from 1930 through 1949, the Women's Institute movement, founded by Adelaide Hoodless in 1897, is now in a state of decline. Though falling membership has been accompanied by an inability to attract younger women, it would be a mistake to underrate the effects of educational programming delivered by Womens' Institutes in rural and urban settings throughout the world. Despite a marked reluctance to become engaged in political issues vital to the interests of women, the institutes have included within their ranks women who assumed prominent political roles in the affairs of their communities. Like Frontier College and the Antigonish movement, Women's Institutes have received some measure of support from public funding and from the resources of established institutions such as the universities.

The Canadian Association for Adult Education, with E. A. Corbett as its director, planned the Farm Radio Forum during the 1930s in conjunction with the Canadian Broadcasting Corporation (CBC). This large-scale adult education venture, which incorporated weekly broadcast reports by various Provincial Farm Forum secretaries and neighborhoood discussion groups, must count as one of CAAE's most outstanding achievements. The adult education process, which still provides a model for government-supported adult education programming in other parts of the world, entailed two-way communication. The Farm Forum national office was responsible for the radio broadcasts and for the provision of written study material. Local forums responded with reports on discussions informed by radio broadcasts and the readings. Through Farm Forum, then, a nationwide, public, government-funded broadcasting agency became engaged in a learning process that included critical discourse as well as the dissemination of useful information.

With the development of provincial adult education associations in recent years, CAAE has played a diminishing role in local initiatives. Its profile among practitioners is not as high as that of its U.S. counterpart, the American Association of Adult and Continuing Education (AAACE), or its predecessor, the Adult Education Association (AEA). However, an indication that this state of affairs may be changing came with the decision to organize a national CAAE Conference at Lennoxville, Quebec, in 1988.

In addition to occasional, though purposeful, educational programming by the CBC, the National Film Board (NFB) produces and makes available to the public first-rate documentaries in both English and French. The NFB is a leading agency for adult education in Canada—an agency for which there is no real counterpart in the United States. However, with the increasing trend toward privatization and the preeminence of commercial criteria in an assessment of what is worthwhile (even in the spheres of culture and education) NFB's current level and quality of government-funded programming could be seriously eroded. These trends also affect the prospects for offering once again, through government-subsidized broadcasting, the kind of adult education programming exemplified by Farm Forum. Even so, there are some creative distance education program initiatives throughout Canada that are characterized by a desire to establish outstanding innovative learning systems and that foster diversity of program content, style, and method of delivery (Mugridge and Kaufman, 1986). In British Columbia, for example, the provincial universities and the Open Learning Institute collaborate to provide accessible distance education programs through the Knowledge Network, while a postsecondary consortium in the neighboring province of Alberta has developed a unique approach to meeting the distance education needs of specific communities.

Long before isolated communities began to benefit from innovative distance education programs, the Wheat Pool, a marketing cooperative for farmers that is now coordinated at the federal level through the Canadian Wheat Board, had a marked influence on the quality of everyday rural life in the prairie provinces. In its formative stages, the Wheat Pool incorporated effective entrepreneurial and organizational strategies from the U.S. experience, subsequently adding adult education as a core dimension of its community commitment. Though its members are drawn from supporters of all three main political parties, the Wheat Pool's developmental activities have been closely aligned with the emergence of democratic socialism as a viable prospect in the political life of Canada. Certainly, the concept of the Wheat Pool in Canada is evocative of cooperative education activities and cooperative ventures. The Wheat Pool is yet another Canadian institution that many fear is at risk in an era of growing privatization and in the wake of a bilateral trade agreement with the United States.

These examples of outstanding Canadian initiatives in adult education lead in to our concluding remarks. Expectations that the federal government should take a major responsibility for the establishment and maintenance of key institutions to sustain a distinctive Canadian cultural identity are clearly identifiable in the nation's history. Despite continuing government support, however, these institutions have enjoyed a relatively high level of autonomy and their bureaucratic effects are tempered by a somewhat high-minded vision of Canada as a multicultural mosaic that fosters the ethnic diversity of its immigrant groups and Native Canadians. This vision contrasts sharply with the melting pot image that is thought to have inspired many public adult education initiatives (especially the Americanization and socialization programs) in the United States.

Conclusion

An interested observer, unacquainted with either context, would be inclined, based on an initial cursory examination, to emphasize similarities between Canadian and U.S. adult education agencies. However, as we have endeavored to show in this short chapter, relevant differences merit the attention and respect of adult educators on both sides of the border. Even the way adult educators in the two countries think, talk, and write about the agencies that influence their practice are indicative of two somewhat different orientations. Though metaphorical allusions to a melting pot and a cultural mosaic might not portray precisely the nature and aims of publicly funded adult education in either country, they do symbolize two quite distinctive frames of reference influencing policy implementation and practice.

References

Adult Education Association of the U.S.A., *Federal Support for Adult Education: Directory of Programs and Services* (Revised Edition) Washington D.C.: The Adult Education Association of the U.S.A. and Macmillan Company, 1969.

Brooke, M. *Adult Basic Education: A Resource Book of Readings.* Toronto: New Press, 1972.

Canada Manpower and Immigration. *Handbook of Adult Curriculum Development.* Saskatoon, Sask.: Modern Press, 1974.

Canadian Association for Adult Education and L'institute Canadien d'éducation des adultes. *From the Adult's Point of View.* Toronto and Montreal:

Canadian Association for Adult Education and L'institute Canadien d'éducation des adultes, 1982.

Conger, S. D. *Canadian Open Adult Learning Systems.* Prince Albert, Sask.: Department of Manpower and Immigration, 1974.

Corbett, E. A. *University Extension in Canada.* Learning for Living Series, Canadian Association for the Study of Adult Education. Toronto: Le Droit Press, 1952.

Cortwright, R., and Brice, E. W. "Adult Basic Education." In R. M. Smith, G. F. Aker, and J. R. Kidd (eds.), *Handbook of Adult Education.* New York: Macmillan, 1970.

Cross, K. P. "Adult Learning: State Policies and Institutional Practices." Higher Education Research Reports: Executive Summary no. 1. Washington, D.C.: Association for the Study of Higher Education and ERIC Clearinghouse on Higher Education, 1984.

Dawson, R. M. *The Government of Canada.* London: Oxford University Press, 1957.

House Committee on Education and Labor and Senate Committee on Human Resources. *A Compilation of Federal Education Laws.* Washington, D.C.: U.S. Government Printing Office, 1977.

Irwin, P. M. *Adult Literacy Issues, Programs and Options.* Issue Brief no. IB85167. Washington, D.C.: Education and Public Welfare Division, Congressional Research Service, 1987.

Kidd, J. R. *People Learning from Each Other.* Learning for Living Series, Canadian Association for the Study of Adult Education. Toronto: Le Droit Press, 1953.

Liveright, A. A. *A Study of Adult Education in the United States.* Boston: Center for the Study of Liberal Education for Adults, 1968.

Long, H. B. *New Perspectives on the Education of Adults in the United States.* London: Croom-Helm, 1987.

Mugridge, I., and Kaufman, D. (eds.). *Distance Education in Canada.* London: Croom-Helm, 1986.

Roberts, H. *Culture and Adult Education: A Study of Alberta and Quebec.* Edmonton: University of Alberta Press, 1982.

Skill Development Leave Task Force. *Learning a Living in Canada.* Vols. 1 and 2. Ottawa: Minister of Supply and Services Canada, 1983.

Sloan, E. P. "The Canada Newstart Program: An Overview." In J. Kidd and G. Selman (eds.), *Coming of Age: Canadian Adult Education in the 1960's.* Toronto: Canadian Association for Adult Education, 1974.

Statistics Canada. *One in Every Five: A Survey of Adult Education in Canada.* Ottawa: Department of the Secretary of State, 1985.

Statistics Canada. *1986 Census Summary Report.* Ottawa: Department of the Secretary of State, 1987.

U.S. Department of Education, Division of Adult Education. *Federal Directory: Adult Basic Education: Adult Education-Related Programs in the Federal Government.* Washington, D.C.: U.S. Department of Education, Division of Adult Education, 1986.

30

Religious Institutions

Paulette T. Beatty
Matthew J. Hayes

Diversity is one of the most characteristic hallmarks of adult religious education as a field of practice. Diversity exists in the institutions involved, purposes espoused, programs delivered, methodologies employed, learners attracted, and leadership provided. Yet, even in the presence of this diversity, one finds an array of similar concerns and challenges that confront the professionals as they approach their singular task of facilitating learning among adults. Five vignettes help capture a glimpse of this world.

Fifteen low- to middle-class Hispanic and Anglo men and women from area churches are gathered for an interdenominational meeting. It is being held in a church in a community on the United States–Mexican border. The evening meeting is being led by a woman who has been trained in organizing groups for social change. The agenda focuses on the development of strategies to influence an upcoming local school board election. Newsprint captures the strategies mapped out by the participants.

A minister's wife in a rural community has laid the groundwork for the establishment of a literacy mission for the local Methodist congregation. Three volunteers from the church are meeting with their students in the church hall on a Saturday afternoon. One tutor is reviewing a menu from a local cafe with an aspiring waitress. Another tutor is helping a young man study a driver's license manual that has been rewritten to a fourth-grade readability level. A third tutor is working with an elderly couple as they read aloud from the Bible.

Six middle-aged couples from a conservative urban synagogue in a major metropolitan center are gathered with their rabbi in the home of one of the couples. They are in the midst of an intermediate course in Hebrew. Their goal is to assume responsibility for teaching Hebrew to the youth in the synagogue school. Their text is the Torah. One couple is presenting the lesson they prepared on the Ten Commandments. The rabbi and the other couples will critique the lesson and offer suggestions for improvement.

Forty-five single adults from a Baptist congregation have gathered in the community center of a condominium complex for one of their monthly potluck dinner-and-dialogue evenings. This Saturday evening they are informally gathered around a large-screen television and have just put on a videotape by a nationally recognized psychologist. The agenda for the evening includes a viewing of the videotape "Alone But Not Lonely," a discussion moderated by the executive committee of the singles group, a two-way teleconference for discussion with the psychologist, distribution of the suggested reading list, and a generation of programming suggestions for future meetings.

Forty men and women who are preparing to assume new lay leadership roles within a Catholic diocese are in the midst of a weekend retreat at a regional retreat and renewal center. The focus of the retreat is on prayer and service. The weekend is being directed by staff from the diocesan office of religious education, seminary faculty, and several priests and lay leaders from throughout the diocese. Participants have studied their leadership manuals prior to the retreat and are therefore familiar with the major teachings from both Scripture and church documents. Using these basic teachings, the retreatants will attend lectures, engage in discussions, spend time in personal prayer, and participate in liturgical services.

Within this chapter, we will explore the purpose and functions, the content and programs, the programming and instructional approaches, the volunteer learners, the leadership dimensions, and the interfaith initiatives of adult religious education within the United States and Canada. Our exploration is facilitated by reflections of denominational leaders, a review of denominational publications, and literature found in the Religion Index and in the Educational Resources Information Center (ERIC). In addition, we have consulted United States and Canadian members of both the Religious Education Unit of the American Association for Adult and Continuing Education (AAACE) and the Religious Education Association (REA). Our approaches employed in gathering information for this chapter have resulted in certain limitations which should be made explicit. The chapter bypasses adult religious education as it is taking place in nonmainline churches in North America; it bypasses activities that are taking place in Central American and South American churches; and it bypasses the self-directed learning that is happening apart from denominational sponsorship. The perspective of this chapter is comparable to the view one has of the landscape from the window of an airplane at 36,000 feet. Broad contours and colors will be seen without texture or specificity; occasional clouds obscure vision; and the scene changes rapidly.

The Purposes

But what are the purposes and what is the scope of adult religious education? What functions does it serve for those who participate?

As one views current practice, one sees that programs most frequently focus first on the explicit religious content that is important within a given faith community; then they focus on the application of this content in the society at large. This pattern emerges whether one reads publications of denominational positions, whether one listens to reflections of denominational leaders, or whether one observes practice on the local level.

A sampling of perspectives from various denominations can help to capture the flavor of the purposes that adult religious education serves at the present time. Victor Constein (1980, pp. 20–21) from the national staff of the Lutheran Church, Missouri Synod, describes five specific goals for adult religious education: to enable members to "read intelligently, interpret faithfully, and integrate practically" the Bible, to improve understanding and explanation of the confessional doctrines, to "identify and then develop the skills" to improve human relations, to translate "personal convictions into decisions and actions that serve Christ in the church, at home, in leisure moments, and on the job," and to confront local, national, and international issues from a theological perspective.

The official position statements of the Union of American Hebrew Congregations and of the United States and Canadian Catholic Churches are illustrative of the purposes served by adult religious education as a whole. Ten educational goals have been identified by the Jewish Reform tradition— goals toward which adults should strive over the years. These educational goals pertain to Jewish identity, the law and the commandments, the state of Israel, Hebrew language, prayer, social justice, the Jewish holidays and festival observances, respect for self and others, kinship with Jews worldwide, and synagogue support and participation (Union of American Hebrew Congregations, 1988). Similar goals are reflected in Conservative and Orthodox Judaism. The goals for adult religious education within the Roman Catholic tradition are found in two national position papers. In the United States, three goals are mentioned: to help individuals and communities understand and live the Gospel to the fullest extent possible, to prepare believers to exercise a prophetic voice by focusing the light of the gospel on contemporary issues, and to enable adults to share their faith with the next generation (United States Catholic Conference, 1986). In Canada, the purposes to be served by adult religious education were identified as follows: to nurture a better-informed adult population, to build up the community of faith, to help adults discover their potential, to support adult decision making in responding to the challenges of faith in contemporary society, to provide updating, and to foster spiritual growth and ongoing conversion (Canadian Conference of Catholic Bishops, 1986).

A number of religious leaders, reflecting upon the goals and functions of adult religious education within their denominations, have identified the following major purposes: to bring the heritage of one's particular religious faith, history, observances, and literature to its members; to enter into a vital and loving relationship with God; to gain a true spiritual life; to increase understanding and desire to do the will of God, and to grow in spiritual fellowship; to nurture adults for mission and ministry in the church and in the world; to advocate justice, peace, and the integrity of creation; to further knowledge of the Bible and its application to life, growth in faith, and understanding of one's heritage and doctrine; to respond to human need; and to train for church leadership.

The Programs and Content

But what programs are offered for adults? Further, what is the content of these programs?

As one reviews the literature of the 1980s, peruses denominational publications, and captures the reflections of leaders, one observes that programs and content logically flow from clearly articulated denominational purposes espoused for adult religious education. Programs are congruent with purposes. First, one finds programs focused on that which forms the heart of the denominational heritage; then one finds programs that radiate out in a series of mandates for living out a religious commitment—programs offered either for the membership at large or for a specific segment of the community. Much less frequently does one find allusion to programs without an explicit religious agenda. Rather, what are found are scriptural, doctrinal, or theologically focused programs; programs of instruction about prayer, worship, liturgy, the sacraments, or festival observances; programs of outreach in evangelism, mission, discipleship, social justice, and peace; programs for new members or inquiring adults; initiatives of pastoral care, nurturing, or counseling of individual adults or entire families; programs focused on significant issues of polity, organization, history, and traditions of a denomination; programs in leadership development to serve the needs of the religious community and the community at large; and programs focused for specific segments of the membership in response to identified needs. In support of these programs, commercial publishing houses and virtually all denominations provide an array of curriculum materials.

The Processes

But what processes are employed in adult religious education? Where are programs conducted? And what methods, techniques, and devices would one most likely encounter in adult religious education?

Virtually every approach espoused in the field of adult education can be found within the adult education programs in religious institutions as they work to facilitate lifestyle development from both personal and social perspectives. Creativity on the local level appears as a major trend in all traditions. One example of local creativity is found in a publication of the Lutheran Church in America (1986) entitled *Adult Education in Twelve Congregations*. The publication highlights a variety of subjects, times, and people involved in the educational programs within these congregations.

Historically, churches, synagogues, and temples have been the sites for educational programming. But today, programming has broken out of its reliance upon institutionally housed activities. Hospitals, homes, schools, stadiums, television and radio stations, retreat centers, family camps, restaurants, and other community and civic facilities have accommodated adult educational programs sponsored by religious institutions.

The methods most frequently employed in adult religious education are evening classes, Sunday schools, courses for credit, prayer breakfasts, study circles, home study groups, revivals, retreats, summer institutes, weekend workshops, and even tours or pilgrimages. One of the most striking developments in methodology during the 1980s has been the emergence of television ministries. Today, virtually every household has access to religious broadcasting.

All of the above methods facilitate the faith development of adults in small or large group settings. Independent study tends to be less emphasized in current programming efforts; however, efforts such as the church study course and the diploma program of the Sunday School Board of the Southern Baptist Convention and the independent study courses available through Brigham Young University serve as examples of independent and self-directed approaches. A particular methodology of shared Christian praxis, based on Paulo Freire's literacy training, has deeply influenced approaches to adult religious education (Groome, 1980).

Techniques and devices employed are equally diverse, with increasing reliance on approaches other than the lecture. Leaders have identified extensive use of discussion groups, brainstorming, debates, role plays, panels, audiotapes, videotapes, films, filmstrips, newsletters, books, pamphlets, curriculum materials, and study guides.

The Learners

Who are the learners in adult religious education? And how many adults are participating in these programs?

All indications are that those adults who participate in religious education programs sponsored by churches or synagogues come from the ranks of the committed. Estimates of the number of adults participating are difficult to ascertain, and participation studies reported in the past are filled with contradictions (Stokes, 1970). Virtually every local religious institution offers some form of adult education programming. Consequently, accessibility to opportunities is high. However, since most adult religious education is produced and consumed on the local level, and since much of it is nonformal, accurate records are not to be found. But the clientele for Catholic, Jewish, and Protestant programs is estimated to be from about 10 percent to 50 percent of adult church membership.

Programs are beginning to be offered for most segments of the church membership. Programs for young adult, families, singles, interested inquirers, divorced, widowed, single parents, engaged, handicapped, imprisoned, and the elderly are becoming more common, although they certainly are not yet commonplace. Hispanics and blacks, the largest of the ethnic groups in the United States, have been and continue to be active participants in the worship, social, and educational lives of their churches.

The Leadership

How is adult religious education funded? How is it organized? Who are its leaders? And how are those who are to lead others to a full spiritual development to become models who compel, as much by their example as by their teaching?

Adult religious education is typically financed from local institutional funds and is provided at little or no cost to participants. Participants involved in independent study normally absorb any costs associated with the undertaking. Local congregations usually pay for workshops or retreats conducted for lay ministers. Organizational units beyond the congregational level provide funding for the research, development, and training undertakings required to support a comprehensive and viable system of locally based programs.

Within Protestantism, leadership at the church level is overwhelmingly lay. A similar pattern exists within the Catholic church, although to a lesser extent, and it varies depending on the role being performed. Within Judaism, synagogue-based adult learning depends on rabbis, on other synagogue staff, and on some lay leadership.

For all traditions, leadership development is an ever-present challenge. In this regard, there are signs of the movement toward the professionalization of adult religious education. Gradually increasing numbers of the full-time leaders in the field are receiving advanced degrees, not only in theology and ministry, but also in adult and adult religious education. The leaders are also conducting research directly related to the issues in the field today. The works of Hauk (1982), Lindsay (1983), Schmenk (1982), and Tebbe (1986) illustrate this trend.

Those leaders not pursuing advanced degrees are being supported by an increasingly pervasive system of staff development opportunities. Other support comes from resources designed for the local paid directors of adult religious education and for the extensive cadre of volunteer leaders. The works of Elias (1982), Foltz (1986), McKenzie (1982), Peterson (1984), and Vogel (1984) provide those in the field with excellent guidelines for designing adult religious education programs. These works offer perspectives on the philosophy of adult religious education to assist leaders in understanding the adults as learners, and they offer guidelines for both designing programs and facilitating learning. Further, a rich source of "how-to" curriculum literature has appeared, the results of successful practice as well as research. In addition, much literature is routinely available within the various denominations (Dale, 1986; Lutheran Church in America, 1986; Hughes, 1981; Monette, 1986; Nored, 1986; Parent, 1985; Parker, 1986). One example of the movement in this direction is the excellent five-volume series *Christian Adulthood* (Parent, 1982–1987) and the more recent volume under a different title (Parent, 1989), published for those involved in adult religious education. In these volumes, theology, adult development, and educational theory are merged with practical tools and suggestions for implementing adult religious education within the Roman Catholic perspective. Another example is a Canadian series entitled *Insight: A Journal for Adult Religious Educators* (Chafe, 1987, 1988).

The Interfaith Efforts

Interfaith activities and educational programs occur continually on the local level with the endorsement of leadership within the various denominations. However, during the 1980s, national and regional interdenominational initiatives of major import began to take place. Currently, leaders report significant activities in the ranks of the top leadership within the denominations. Such activities include engaging in trilateral dialogues, participating in adult forums, participating in joint international leadership development conferences, engaging in summer institutes, and affiliating with a number of interfaith associations. A few of these activities of the recent past will be highlighted here because of the magnitude of their impact.

Certainly one of the major and most exciting developments in interfaith dialogue is the research undertaking known as Faith Development in the Adult Life Cycle (FDALC). This undertaking is a response to increased interest in the religious developmental tasks of adults. This research, under the sponsorship of the Religious Education Association and twenty-two other religious denominations and organizations, was completed in 1987 (Stokes, 1987). As part of this undertaking, hypotheses regarding faith development during the adult life cycle were generated from the literature and refined as a result of an interdenominational international workshop (Stokes, 1983). Over 1,000 adults were then surveyed, and another small sample of forty-one persons were interviewed in depth in an effort to explore the experience of faith development. Pastoral leaders reviewed and refined the results of these surveys in a series of regional conferences. The FDALC data continue to be studied by Adult Faith Resources, established in 1988 to carry on the continued interpretation and presentation by means of a bimonthly newsletter.

Another interdenominational effort has been the trilateral conversations among Lutheran, Episcopal, and Roman Catholic leaders regarding adult Christian ministries. As part of this consultation, thirty-seven adult education leaders from national and diocesan levels gathered for reflection and sharing on three topics: "Themes of the Adult Christian Life; Adult Learning—Responding to the Diversity of Faith Development; and Adult Ministries—Aiding the Identification of Ministries" ("Adult Ministries Consultation," 1985). Subsequent to this consultation, over 100 congregations were surveyed regarding the nature of locally conducted ecumenical activities (Anderson, 1986). A final gathering of leaders resulted in recommendations for promoting the development of adult lay ministries.

A third interdenominational effort to exert great impact relates to curriculum initiatives. For example, the Bethel Series is a long-range program of Bible study that has been used in more than 10,000 churches in forty denominations. It attempts to build a strong base of biblical knowledge within the congregational membership by training a core of congregational leaders over a two-year period. These newly trained leaders, in turn, lead year-long Bible study in the local congregations. In addition, there is ongoing cooperation within the Protestant community to develop a denominationally specific adult curriculum that builds upon a common source. Examples include the International Sunday School Lessons, the Aldersgate Curriculum Consortium, and the Joint Educational Development Project.

A fourth area of interdenominational adult religious education consists of the many theological schools and retreat centers that focus upon growth and training experiences for clergy and laity.

A final area of interdenominational activity has been the networking that has developed among national denominational adult education staff through the biennial Adult Forums sponsored by the Division of Education and Ministry of the National Council of Churches.

The Challenges for the Future

As adult religious education leaders reflect upon their primary programmatic thrusts for the 1990s, they must consider the issues of purpose, content, processes, learners, and leadership. For all traditions, increased efforts will foster the development of spiritually mature adults whose life-styles reflect a fidelity to their heritage. Programs will continue to focus on spiritual growth while at the same time embracing a more comprehensive perspective of social mission. Programs increasingly will be tailored to the unique needs of all segments of the community and thus will be more learner centered than in the past. Greater diversity, sophistication, and integration into the life of the congregation will be the hallmarks of approaches and methodologies employed in adult religious education programming. And lastly, leadership development of clerics, religious educators, and lay volunteers will become a major thrust in virtually every tradition.

From the perspective of the authors, a number of challenges remain to be addressed. It is interesting to note that several of these challenges are similar to recommendations for adult learning in church and synagogue made by Kathan (1977) over a decade ago. These challenges call for careful attention by those in the field.

First, regarding purposes, church and synagogue should become, through their educational programs for adults, environments in which members can begin to address significant issues that face their society and their culture. Educational programs should engage adult learners, on a consistent basis, in reflection and action about the social context—particularly as it is influenced by insights and values of the denomination. As we continue into the future, religious educators can assist in bridging the gap between the growing complexity of our society and our capacity to cope with it. The blurring of distinctions between the sacred and the profane poses a major challenge for those charged with the religious education of adults. Leaders must work on the local level to articulate their own philosophies of adult religious education and to make explicit statements of the mission and scope of their religious education programs. Bold initiatives already have been undertaken, and they should continue. One such initiative is the work that the Interdenominational Theological Center in Atlanta has done with the National Issues Forum of the Domestic Policy Association in developing a specialized leadership handbook for ministers and churches (Nored, 1986).

Second, regarding programs, adult religious education programs should not only address doctrinal issues but also enable church members to view their religious traditions as immediately relevant to everyday life. The development of programs that more fully address the roles members of the congregation typically perform, particularly in the area of work, should ensure the infusion of religious principles learned into the fabric of the members' daily lives. Initiatives that have begun to assist adults in linking faith and the workplace should continue (Reber, 1984; Reber, 1986; Whitten and Everist, 1984).

Third, regarding methodology, adult religious educators should identify approaches whereby adult education efforts could become more fully integrated into the congregation's experience of worship, community, and mission. Educators need to become more conscious of the life and worship of the congregation itself as a vehicle for learning and spiritual growth. Educators who focus on this challenge could become catalysts for a more holistic approach to adult religious education—one that involves the hands and heart as well as the head. They could, in so doing, facilitate the movement of adult religious education from a marginal ministry to a fully central but distinct ministry within the church. Further, educational leaders should continually explore the relationship of adult religious education to its root disciplines, for one can skillfully and appropriately apply methodologies on a regular basis only when one has an understanding of the adult learner, a clear vision of the magnitude of the goals to be attained, and a grasp of educational principles.

Fourth, regarding learners, those involved in providing adult religious education on the local level must become increasingly sensitive and responsive to the needs of diverse segments of the congregation. Unless programming more consistently speaks to these needs, the numbers of those participating can be expected to decrease; and certainly, as a consequence, the increased potential of adult religious education will not be realized. One of the first approaches to be taken in meeting this challenge is to begin to maintain records on the local level, not only in terms of the total number of adults participating, but also in terms of the groups of individuals participating. Such records could serve as baseline data against which local directors of adult religious education could measure progress in reaching all segments of their diverse constituencies in significant numbers. The field of adult religious education would then have a base for measuring the growth of adult religious education in the future.

Fifth, regarding leadership, those in leadership positions in the field of adult religious education should take as one of their greatest challenges the facilitating, among their lay leaders, of greater awareness of and greater skills in program planning. Without such knowledge and skills, adult religious education will remain largely institution driven rather than participant driven. A learner-centered, systematic approach to the design, implementation, and evaluation of adult religious education programs should not only enhance motivation and participation but should also impact more positively the lives of the members and the entire congregation. Consequently, adult religious leaders should do the following: build programs *with* adults rather than *for* adults; ascertain learner needs and interests; articulate goals, content, and methodologies, the heart of the curriculum; put into place a structure and a climate in which amenities and personal needs are provided for; emphasize recruitment and promotion; identify and train staff for each program; develop a financial base to support the ongoing program; and develop an evaluation system to enable value judgments to be made concerning the worth of a program.

Sixth, regarding interfaith dialogue, leaders within adult religious education should increase their efforts at networking and communication between and among denominations. This effort should not be limited to dialogue within national boundaries. It should extend, at the very least, to collegial exchanges within the Americas, North, Central, and South. The value of such networking increases as leadership positions shift within the various denominations. And, as the adult religious education enterprises in different cultures strive to meet and address challenges posed by contemporary societal developments, a dialogue of mutual exchange between cultures becomes imperative. Perhaps professional associations such as the Religious Education Association and the American Association for Adult and Continuing Education should take the initiative in facilitating such exchanges. Specifically, religious educators at the local level need to be reminded of the benefits to be derived—collegial support and networking—through affiliation with the Religious Education Unit of AAACE.

Postscript

In the 1960 *Handbook of Adult Education,* Edward Miller (1960, p. 364) wrote, "If adult educators can continue for another twenty-five years in the direction taken in the last quarter century, not only will adult religious education become a most dynamic force in American life, but the religious institutions themselves will become more vital and dynamic."

While others have served the function of keeping us abreast of adult religious education since the 1960 handbook (Cohen, 1977; Kathan, 1977; Schaefer, 1977; Stokes, 1970, 1977), we have explored the diversity and the unity of adult religious education as a field of practice during the 1980s. Adult religious education may well be a dynamic and vital force within American life. However, the work of adult religious education in North America is far from complete; its potential as a force for shaping the lives of individuals and entire cultures has yet to be realized.

Those charged with the education of adults in religious institutions will continue to face the challenges of a secular, pluralistic, multicultural, technologically driven, mobile, impersonal, and aging society. Adults in all segments of society will continue to face critical demands to which religious institutions will have to become increasingly responsive. In sum, adult religious educators are in a pivotal position to assist adults as they face the challenges with which they will be confronted in the final decade of the twentieth century.

References

"Adult Ministries Consultation." *Origins,* 1985, *14* (36), 587–593.

Anderson, A. *A Report of a Survey on Local Ecumenical Activities.* Philadelphia: Lutheran Church in America, 1986.

Canadian Conference of Catholic Bishops. *Adult Faith, Adult Church.* Ottawa: Canadian Conference of Catholic Bishops, 1986.

Chafe, J. M. (ed.). *Insight: A Journal for Adult Religious Educators, 1987.* Ottawa: Canadian Conference of Catholic Bishops, 1987.

Chafe, J. M. (ed.). *Insight: A Journal for Adult Religious Educators, 1988.* Ottawa: Canadian Conference of Catholic Bishops, 1988.

Cohen, S. "Adult Jewish Education." *Religious Education,* 1977, *72* (2), 143–155.

Constein, V. *Adults Who Learn and Like It: A Guide for Workers in the Sunday School.* St. Louis, Mo.: Concordias, 1980.

Dale, D. *Teacher Growth Manual.* Nyack, N.Y.: The Christian and Missionary Alliance, 1986.

Elias, J. L. *The Foundations and Practice of Adult Religious Education.* Malabar, Fla.: Krieger, 1982.

Foltz, N. T. (ed.). *Handbook of Adult Religious Education.* Birmingham, Ala.: Religious Education Press, 1986.

Groome, T. *Christian Religious Education: Sharing our Story and Vision.* New York: Harper & Row, 1980.

Hauk, G. H. "Training Leaders Who Work with Older Persons in the Parish." Unpublished doctoral dissertation, Graduate Seminary, Phillips University, 1982.

Hughes, J. W. (ed.). *Ministering to Adult Learners: A Skills Workbook for Christian Educational Leaders.* Washington, D.C.: United States Catholic Conference, 1981.

Kathan, B. "Adult Learning in Church and Synagogue." *Religious Education,* 1977, *72* (2), 115–120.

Lindsay, L. R. "It's About Love: Teaching Agape in the Church." Unpublished doctoral dissertation, Louisville Presbyterian Theological Seminary, 1983.

Lutheran Church in America. *Adult Education in Twelve Congregations.* Philadelphia: Lutheran Church in America, 1986a.

Lutheran Church in America. *Guides for Adult Education.* Philadelphia: Lutheran Church in America, 1986b.

McKenzie, L. *The Religious Education of Adults.* Birmingham, Ala.: Religious Education Press, 1982.

Miller, E. K. "Adult Education in Religious Institutions." In M. Knowles (ed.), *Handbook of Adult Education.* Washington, D.C.: Adult Education Association of the U.S.A., 1960.

Monette, M. *Work and Faith in Society: A Handbook for Dioceses and Parishes.* Washington, D.C.: United States Catholic Conference, 1986.

Nored, R. *Leadership Handbook for Ministers and Churches, 1986–1987.* Dayton, Ohio: Domestic Policy Association, 1986.

Parent, N. (ed.). *Christian Adulthood: A Catechetical Resource.* Vols. 1–5. Washington, D.C.: United States Catholic Conference, 1982–1987.

Parent, N. (ed.). *Adult Learning and the Parish.* Dubuque, Iowa: William C. Brown, 1985.

Parent, N. (ed.). *Agenda for the 90s: Forging the Future of Adult Religious Education.* Washington, D.C.: United States Catholic Conference, 1989.

Parker, M. *Planning Committee Manual.* Nyack, N.Y.: The Christian and Missionary Alliance, 1986.

Peterson, G. A. (ed.). *The Christian Education of Adults.* Chicago: Moody Press, 1984.

Reber, R. *Final Report: Project on Linking Faith and the Workplace.* St. Louis, Mo.: Thompson Center, 1984.

Reber, R. "Vocation and Vision: A New Look at the Vocation of the Laity." *Auburn News,* Fall 1986, pp. 1–8.

Schaefer, J. "Roman Catholics." *Religious Education,* 1977, *72* (2), 133–143.

Schmenk, C. S. "The Development and Testing of a Teacher Manual and a Student Handbook Which Will Enable Lay People to Equip Themselves for Ministerial Roles in the Local Church." Unpublished doctoral dissertation, United Theological Seminary, 1982.

Stokes, K. "Protestantism." *Religious Education,* 1977, *72* (2), 121–132.

Stokes, K. (ed.). *Faith Development in the Adult Life Cycle.* New York: William H. Sadlier, 1983.

Stokes, K. "Religious Institutions." In R. M. Smith, G. Aker, and J. R. Kidd (eds.), *Handbook of Adult Education.* Washington, D.C.: Adult Education Association of the U.S.A., 1970.

Stokes, K. (ed.). *Report of the Faith Development in the Adult Life Cycle Project.* Minneapolis, Minn.: Faith Development in the Adult Life Cycle Project, 1987.

Tebbe, F. S. "Mentoring as an Image: The Supervision of Adult Religious Educators." Unpublished doctoral dissertation, Department of Church and Ministry, Andover Newton Theological School, 1986.

Union of American Hebrew Congregations. *To See the World Through Jewish Eyes: Guidelines for Adult Jewish Studies.* New York: Union of American Hebrew Congregations, 1988.

United States Catholic Conference. *Serving Life and Faith: Adult Religious Education and the American Catholic Community.* Washington, D.C.: United States Catholic Conference, 1986.

Vogel, L. J. *The Religious Education of Older Adults.* Birmingham, Ala.: Religious Education Press, 1984.

Whitten, M. H., and Everist, N. J. *All in a Day's Work: Ministry on the Job.* Philadelphia: Fortress Press, 1984.

31

Proprietary Schools

Don F. Seaman
Patricia McDivitt

The term *proprietary* connotes a venture undertaken for profit, and the proprietary school is just that. It may be a single-owner enterprise, a partnership, or a corporation. In any case, the schools are independently financed, and the operators assume the risks of free enterprise (Atwood, 1970).

The above description, from the 1970 *Handbook of Adult Education,* still adequately describes proprietary schools. They often have been viewed with suspicion and disdain by the public education sector, mostly due to the for-profit motive that undergirds their existence. However, that motive may also be the very strength of their existence and growth. As Atwood (1970, p. 388) points out, "To prosper, in fact even to survive, they must be flexible and extremely sensitive to the needs of adults and the demands for a variety of training opportunities."

Proprietary schools, in general, can be classified into four main divisions: (1) business schools, (2) trade and technical schools, (3) cosmetology schools, and (4) home study schools. To illustrate these classifications, of the 108 privately operated vocational schools in Alberta, Canada, in 1986, twenty-two were barber or beautician schools, twenty-seven were business schools, twenty-five were trade-oriented schools, eight were correspondence schools, and twenty-four were other programs licensed under the Private Vocational Schools Act (Office of the Minister of Advanced Education, 1987).

Although they are all grouped under the heading, *proprietary,* each division has its own national association and its own unique goals and programs. In addition, a small but growing percentage of these schools have become nonprofit in corporate structure. This, in turn, has caused some of the accrediting agencies to use the term *private career schools* instead of *proprietary schools* (J. W. Miller, letter to authors, Dec. 1987).

Scope and Functions of Proprietary Schools

The content of this chapter is divided into two major sections: Scope and Functions of Proprietary Schools, and Contemporary Issues and Concerns. Within the first section, subtopics include growth and development, purposes and objectives, programs and curriculum, and job placement. In the second section, the issues discussed include recognition, competition, program quality, funding, and acceptance by adult educators.

Growth and Development (1976–1986). The growth of proprietary schools in the United States has virtually tripled in the past 10 years. Although various reports give slightly different numbers, enrollment in 1976 was 655,000, whereas by 1986, it had increased to almost 2,000,000 students (National Association of Trade and Technical Schools, 1987; J. Murphy, telephone conversation with authors, July 1987). According to the National Association of Trade and Technical Schools (NATTS), enrollment in private, postsecondary occupational schools increased 18 percent during 1985 and 1986, and by 1986, women accounted for 42 percent of all students enrolled in those programs.

Wilms (1984) indicates that proprietary vocational schools actually conduct most of the postsecondary vocational training within the United States. He cites data from the National Center for Education Statistics that indicate, "In 1980, the proprietary vocational sector comprised 6,076 schools, accounting for almost two-thirds (64 percent) of all post-secondary vocational schools and close to three-fourths (72 percent) of all post-secondary vocational enrollments" (Wilms, 1984, p. 1).

Supporting the previous data is a report by the Association of Independent Colleges and Schools (AICS) (1986) which indicates that enrollment in private colleges and schools increased at the rate of almost 25 percent per year from 1980 to 1985. This increase includes higher percentages of students from lower economic backgrounds and increasingly greater numbers of minority students. During this same period, data from the National Association of Accredited Cosmetology Schools indicate that enrollments in cosmetology schools also increased substantially, and that enrollment has included a higher percentage of older students. Murphy (telephone conversation with authors, July 1987) feels that more displaced homemakers and adults seeking a midcareer change are reflected in the increasing average age of cosmetology school enrollees.

Purposes and Objectives of Proprietary Schools. The main purpose of proprietary schools, according to several annual reports (National Association of Trade and Technical Schools, 1987; Wilms, 1984; Fowler, 1986) is to prepare people to be successful in finding employment. In general, this purpose involves a meeting of the needs of three entities. The schools function to meet the needs of business and industry, of the community, and, most important, the needs of adults, ages sixteen and over, who wish to further their educations and to learn the skills necessary to enter into a particular career. The underlying philosophy of proprietary school education, therefore, is somewhat similar to the philosophy of adult basic education programs. The goal is to meet the educational, social, and economic needs of adults; meeting these needs, in turn, benefits not only business and industry, but the community as well.

Proprietary schools are often located in large urban areas, and they work closely with business and industry in the training of students to fill specific, vocational job vacancies. Proprietary schools try to stay on the so-called cutting edge of the rapidly changing job market, and they are able to respond quickly to new issues and ideas because they are not burdened with many of the bureaucratic barriers found in public education. Among those methods for remaining on the cutting edge are the following:

1. Maintaining close professional relationships with business and industry. These contacts enable proprietary schools to become market oriented and to remain sensitive to changes in the needs of employers. The schools stay well informed of the changes in business and industry, and they often quickly add or drop courses based upon these changes or upon employer requests. Proprietary schools attempt to prepare students adequately for specialized jobs available in the community, so it is not uncommon for a proprietary school to work closely with an industry on the design of programs to train students to meet that industry's specific job needs.
2. Recruiting teachers directly from industry who have many years of career experience. Along with an associate degree or bachelor's degree, most proprietary schools require instructors to have three or more years of work experience in their fields of expertise. These instructors emphasize the practical aspects of knowledge and stress hands-on applications of learning.
3. Enabling students to earn while they learn. Since many adults cannot afford to give up their earnings, part-time study and home study have great appeal and fit the needs of many students.

As an added result of helping to meet the needs of business and industry, the community also benefits. Graduates fill job vacancies, businesses create new jobs, and personal income as well as private sector sales increases. According to Moore (1986), New York proprietary schools contributed substantially to their communities as well as to the state's economy. In 1983 and 1984, within the schools themselves, 7,700 adults were employed, thus providing jobs within the state. In addition, school employees generated almost $1 billion of private sector sales in New York State and $341 million of personal income.

Proprietary schools also help to meet the needs of many adults by providing an alternative to the "widespread dissatisfaction with the public sector's apparent unresponsiveness to changing labor market needs" (Wilms, 1984, p. 1). Adults contemplating a midcareer change, or simply desiring to update and to improve their job skills, find the varied flexible schedules of proprietary schools, and the programs they offer, very appealing. The schools offer a variety of skill-training programs in a number of career areas. Therefore, by being among the major providers of postsecondary vocational education, proprietary schools try to meet the needs of adults who wish to further their educations but do not wish to attend public four-year colleges or community colleges.

Proprietary schools also provide education for a large number of adults from disadvantaged backgrounds. While a higher percentage of students from lower economic backgrounds and an increasing number of minority students are enrolling in public colleges and schools, enrollment of these groups is also increasing in proprietary schools.

Proprietary schools also provide education for those individuals who do not have a high school education. In New York, for example, in 1985, 25 percent of those adults enrolled in New York proprietary schools did not have a high school diploma (Moore, 1986). In lieu of the high school diploma, most proprietary schools administer a basic skills screening test. The results of the test are often used to determine whether the applicant should be admitted to a particular program offered by the school.

In most cases, proprietary schools carefully interview and counsel applicants. The initial interviewing process is important not only for the school, but also for the applicants. The process helps to place those applicants, with or without a high school diploma, into programs in which they can experience the greatest amount of success in appropriate educational environments that will challenge them to apply themselves.

Programs and Curriculum. Many proprietary schools offer both diploma programs and associate of applied science degree programs. Diplomas, for example, can be earned in career-training programs such as air-conditioning and refrigeration, welding, cosmetology, truck driving, and related areas. These vocational-technical programs are often short in duration, and, in many cases, a diploma can be earned in less than two years.

The programs are usually skills competency based, and the curriculum is detailed and defined, focusing upon the essentials needed to master a particular vocation. Therefore, instead of being required to complete an entire course that may include many weeks in a publicly supported school, students can select programs that include instruction for developing specific skills. In addition, since proprietary schools are not burdened by public regulatory agencies, the curriculum, scheduling, and even fee structures can be altered to meet the sudden changes in students' needs. The goal of the various programs, therefore, is to train students in a short amount of time and to enable them to be immediately employable upon graduation.

A medical assistant diploma program is one example of a skills-competency-based program offered by many proprietary schools. In some schools, the skills-training program is designed to enable students to earn a medical assistant diploma within six months. The curriculum for the program is quite detailed and focuses upon providing the students with basic knowledge and skills, not only in the areas of anatomy and physiology, but also in medical terminology, medical law and ethics, communications, administrative procedures, record keeping, and insurance. In addition, the program often requires an externship in a physician's office. Externships enhance the students' mastery of the basic skills required, and once the externship and course work have been successfully completed, and the diploma granted, students are immediately employable and have skills that can increase their wage-earning potential and standard of living.

Much like the adult students pursuing skills training offered in a medical assistant program, adults seeking training in business may also receive the necessary preparation in proprietary schools. Proprietary schools are currently offering diplomas that prepare adults to work in fields such as computer programming, computerized accounting, business administration, and general office science. The curriculum for such courses is skills competency based, and the students experience hands-on use of computers, word processors, and other types of equipment typically used in business offices.

In addition to offering diplomas in a variety of vocational-technical and other career fields, many proprietary schools also offer associate of applied science degree programs in areas such as business management, computer science, aviation, and electronics. In most cases, the associate of applied science degree can be earned in less than two years; and the programs, similar to the diploma programs, are designed to allow students the opportunity to attain a high standard of skill competency. For example, an associate of applied science degree in aviation technology requires students to take skills training in courses such as aviation sciences, aircraft welding, applied math, interpretation of drawings and descriptive geometry, English and technical writing, and related courses. The curriculum in each course is based upon a developmental system that clearly focuses upon the skills needed. Evaluation and testing are often computerized, allowing for an accurate measure of students' knowledge and performance. Upon receiving this degree, students will have acquired the necessary knowledge and will have obtained a high level of skill competency enabling them to enter the aviation industry as technicians.

Competency-based training and curriculum also rely heavily upon appropriate equipment and supplies. In general, proprietary schools provide for each program the necessary machines, props, laboratories, and, in some cases, tools to be used in training the students for a particular vocation. Students in their courses of study benefit not only from traditional lectures when appropriate, but also from the hands-on training and practical experience in the use of all types of equipment used in a given career field. In some cases, students are also given the opportunity to practice their skills with clients or consumers.

In addition to helping adults meet their educational needs, proprietary schools focus upon helping adults to meet their social needs. As part of the skills training, many schools focus on teaching students how to obtain jobs successfully upon graduation. In addition to the basic curriculum for a given program, instruction is often given in the areas of job-search skills including applications, resume writing, cover letters, and interviewing. Students are also encouraged, throughout their courses of study, to think about their futures and to evaluate their strengths and weaknesses in light of the job market.

In many cases, proprietary schools also require appropriate dress. Those training to become dental assistants, for example, are usually required to wear dental assistant uniforms to school. The environment of many proprietary schools is designed to imitate, if at all possible, the world of work. And throughout their courses of study, students are encouraged to become responsible members of society and to prepare for their future employment. Attendance is mandatory and carefully monitored. Counselors often contact students if they have not attended class, and they put much effort into helping students complete their programs.

Job Placement. Proprietary schools also help to meet the future economic needs of students by offering job placement services. In many cases, placement officers for the schools normally work full-time locating jobs for graduates. They contact local businesses, check daily newspapers, and keep informed of the job openings in the community and throughout the country. Placement officers also carefully screen the qualifications of each graduate and seek to match the individual with the best job. They advise the graduates on how to interview for positions and how to dress, and they make follow-up calls to potential employers. Often, proprietary schools offer a lifetime placement service for graduates. Occasionally, in addition to placing graduates in jobs throughout the community, they hire their own graduates and, in some cases, provide them with excellent opportunities for advancement.

As a result of the established job placement services offered by proprietary schools, many graduates are successful in obtaining jobs. For example, in New York, in 1983 and 1984, of the 43,677 students who completed programs in licensed trade schools, "Sixty-four percent were placed in jobs. Of these, fifty-six percent found jobs directly related to their training, four percent found jobs slightly related, and four percent found jobs unrelated to their training. Fifteen percent of the trade school completers were unemployed, and the status of the remaining 21 percent was unknown" (Moore, 1986, p. 7). However, Moore cautions that when judging the success of various programs in placing their graduates, one should keep in mind the numbers involved. For example, "Technical education programs in New York would appear to be highly successful in placing graduates since 81 percent of their students found field-related jobs. In contrast, only 54 percent of those students completing business and office education programs obtained field-related jobs. However, in New York alone, this amounted to 7,211 graduates'' (p. 8).

Contemporary Issues and Concerns

The issues faced by proprietary schools are many and varied. Since the number and scope of the schools have increased in recent years, the importance of the issues has also grown. Those issues that seem most important include recognition, quality, competition, funding, and acceptance by adult educators.

Recognition. According to Wilms (1984), although many U.S. postsecondary education commissions (or councils) include representation from the proprietary school sector, little credence is given to the private, for-profit schools in policy decisions. As he further states, "This pattern of neglect is curious not only because the proprietary sector is the largest single purveyor of school-based vocational training on the national scene but also because, given the current atmosphere of fiscal conservatism, one would expect policymakers to be aware of and hospitable toward any mechanism that supplements the public training sector which has suffered substantial budget cuts in the overall drive to reduce social service costs'' (p. 1). Growth of the proprietary school sector has resulted in a measure of recognition (or tolerance) from public educators, but recognition in the form of approval will not be easily acquired, as indicated by the following discussions of the remaining issues facing these private schools.

Program Quality. The quality of programs in proprietary schools is under constant attack by the public sector. Reports of students receiving low-quality education and training are not uncommon in publications representing public education. Individual cases are sometimes featured in articles when the quality of private training is being questioned (Wilson, 1987). This is especially true when the student was financed by public support, which more and more proprietary school participants are receiving. Critics also charge that schools admit students who are not academically prepared simply to get federal aid and that they often inflate student graduation rates.

For example, in January 1988, the *Chicago Sun-Times* published a series of articles that were critical of several schools (some of which had recently declared bankruptcy) in the Chicago area (Flaherty and Pitt, 1988a, 1988b). Among the criticisms were, (1) paying dropouts a fee to return and endorse loan checks, (2) offering training programs in fields for which no jobs existed, (3) enrolling functional illiterates, (4) deceiving applicants about the cost of their programs of study, and (5) falsifying admission test scores. In addition, the content of the articles indicated that poor supervision by state and by U.S. Education Department investigators contributed to the problems that students were having with proprietary schools in the Chicago area. In addition, several articles have appeared in the *Chronicle of Higher Educa-*

tion citing various concerns at for-profit schools, including questionable admissions procedures, financial abuses, insufficient enforcement of quality control, and failure to provide adequate information about their accreditation status (Wilson, 1987, 1988).

In Alberta, Canada, articles in various newspapers have indicated that when some private vocational schools fail (or lose their licenses), various people, mostly students, get hurt (Lord and Farquharson, 1988; Keyser, 1981). Not only do some students lose their fee money, but other private schools suffer from the adverse publicity even though their records and operations are quite open and professional. Because of such incidents, and because of the policies of some schools to not refund the fees of dropouts, private schools are usually viewed as putting profit above education (Lord and Farquharson, 1988).

However, proprietary school administrators respond by emphasizing that they meet the standards of the accrediting agencies that review their programs. In the United States, these agencies include the Association of Independent Colleges and Universities, the National Association of Accredited Cosmetology Schools, and the National Home Study Council. In Canada, each private vocational school must be registered and must provide information regarding length and cost of courses, qualifications of instructors, content, method of instruction, tuition and fees, and entrance requirements. They must also provide sales circulars and other advertising, and evidence of financial responsibility. Executive directors of the major proprietary school associations indicate that the small number of institutions that do not provide quality are soon denied accreditation, but those few are the schools that receive most of the publicity (Wilson, 1987). These executives distribute reports featuring testimonies and statistics that support their position to state and federal agencies, employers, schools, and other related entities (Valore and Diehl, 1987, Association of Independent Colleges and Schools, 1985).

Proprietary school staff also emphasize not only that they are accountable to national accrediting commissions and state licensing boards, but that their ultimate accountability is to their clientele, who are enrolling in their schools in ever-increasing numbers. That enrollment, they maintain, should be the ultimate gauge by which all schools in higher education are measured. Administrators also feel that the criticisms from the U.S. Department of Education are based upon interviews with state agency and loan agency officials instead of being based, as they should be, upon on-site visits to the schools themselves. "They just kind of swept the floor for anything they could find over the last several years, and the weight of the packages is supposed to convince somebody about the scope of the problem." (Wilson, 1988, p. A21).

Competition: Programs. Because of the recent growth of proprietary schools, they have become extremely competitive with the public community and junior colleges throughout the country. Because they offer similar programs, both entities compete for enrollments from the same pool of students—young adults who want to acquire job skills for immediate employment. Although fees at public institutions are much lower than those at private schools, public colleges are often at a disadvantage in other ways. A public college often must seek and obtain approval from within its own system, from the local community, from other colleges in its geographical region, and from the state higher education governing body before it can initiate and offer new training programs. The college must collect data supporting the need for the program; it must procure equipment through a somewhat cumbersome system of bids and slow deliveries; and it must employ staff. This process can take several weeks or even months.

In the meantime, the proprietary or private career school, not restrained by bureaucratic requirements in the public sector, already has initiated the same or similar training programs within a few weeks and may already have graduated students before the public college can get started. If students need the training soon, they are more likely to pay the higher fees and enroll as soon as possible instead of waiting for the public school's lower tuition.

One of the authors was involved in this kind of competition a few years ago. Community colleges and proprietary schools were competing in offering a thirty-hour certification course in real estate. Because the public colleges were charging lower fees, their enrollment was increasing. However, to attract students who did not want to give up many of their working hours to attend classes, proprietary schools began offering the course in three ten-hour days—Friday, Saturday, and Sunday. Although their enrollments increased, private school administrators became concerned about the quality of instruction (mostly lecture) and about the amount of learning being acquired. Ratings of the courses by students and by some employers were also low.

The author and a colleague were asked in a consulting role to develop and conduct a workshop to improve the quality of instruction for the three-day, thirty-hour course of study. After visiting several realtors to ascertain their problems and needs, the consultants developed a series of action learning activities including critical incidents, minicase studies, simulations, and demonstration experiences to achieve greater involvement and interaction among the students. Administrators and teachers who attended rated the workshop high in quality, but whether any of the teaching strategies utilized and demonstrated were even adopted is not known, since no opportunity for follow-up was provided. However, within a few months, the consultants learned that some community colleges were beginning to offer the real estate course on weekends.

Competition: Funding. Until recently, funding was not such a big issue. The student, or sometimes an employer, paid the tuition, and public schools were not concerned. However, recent trends have the public sector angry and complaining loudly. For example, in 1986, more Pell Grant money went to students at proprietary schools than to students at independent colleges and universities. In addition, "Between 1980 and 1986, Pell Grants to proprietary school students nearly tripled in value, while grant money to students at public four-year colleges increased by 36 percent, and money to students at private colleges increased by only 14 percent'' (Wilson, 1987, p. 18). As a result, college and university officials have expressed concern that the money may be wasted because many students drop out as a result of poor quality training.

To substantiate their concern, public officials cite specific cases of students having been deceived about their abilities to succeed or about the quality of their work—students who dropped out a few weeks after enrolling (Wilson, 1987). In other articles, statistics of high dropout rates—as high as 82.9 percent—are offered by various investigators (Flaherty and Pitt, 1988a). In most cases cited, those students who leave the program have paid their fees through Pell Grants, Perkins Loans, Guaranteed Student Loans, or Supplemental Educational Opportunity Grants.

Proprietary school administrators state that their dropout rates and tuitions compare favorably with most other schools. ''Two-thirds of the occupational students in this country attend private career schools, and most complete their course work'' (National Association of Trade and Technical Schools, 1987). As for tuition, most proprietary school reports indicate that it is not very different from other schools' tuitions. However, they indicate that a close correlation exists between the tuition charged and the earnings expected by the graduates. In addition, proprietary schools point out that they contribute substantially to the general economy. ''By providing training that would otherwise probably have to be provided at public expense, and by generating jobs and revenue on which substantial personal and corporate taxes are paid, the proprietary sector not only helps . . . to conserve tax revenues but at the same time adds to those revenues'' (Wilms, p. 10).

Acceptance by Adult Educators. There is some concern that the philosophy and objectives of proprietary schools are quite different from those held by many adult educators, as indicated by differences in sensitivity to adult needs, trends toward volunteerism, a learning atmosphere of caring and support, and so on. Indeed, the authors themselves were initially uneasy about the kinds of data they would find, because, as mentioned previously, some private schools do not deliver what is promised.

However, the generally negative perceptions held by many public educators about proprietary schools are not always supported by facts. True, in the United States, the private sector does have a lobby effort in Washington, D.C. and in most state legislatures, but so does public higher education. True, the private sector is now making strong inroads into the funding arena where public institutions once ruled, but is that practice unethical or illegal? True, the costs for attending proprietary schools seem high to public educators, but their job placement record appears good, and there are no data to indicate that cost efficiency or student return is any better in one arena or the other. Great effort is now being made by public colleges to develop closer ties with business and industry, but proprietary schools have had close working relationships with these groups for many years. As for a caring atmosphere, proprietary schools cite their extensive counseling and placement services and their staff development programs conducted by teachers who, themselves, were once students in the classes they are now teaching.

Summary

The issues between public institutions and proprietary schools will not go away in the near future. As competition for funding intensifies, the arguments will become more heated. Enrollments in private schools will undoubtedly continue to increase as long as public colleges and schools respond more slowly than does the private sector to adults' educational and training needs. Proprietary schools know that flexibility and ability to respond quickly are their strengths, and they will continue to capitalize upon those strengths. They are a part of the educational complex in the United States and Canada and are likely to remain so for many years. However, the scope of their involvement will depend upon how some of the aforementioned issues are addressed by legislators, by accrediting associations, and by the potential adult students themselves.

References

Association of Independent Colleges and Schools. *Private Career Education—A National Resource in an Ever-Changing Society.* Washington, D.C.: Association of Independent Colleges and Schools, 1986.

Atwood, M. A. "Some Other Institutions." In R. M. Smith, G. F. Aker, and J. R. Kidd (eds.), *Handbook of Adult Education.* New York: Macmillan, 1970.

Flaherty, R., and Pitt, L. "Bitter Lessons." *Chicago Sun-Times,* Jan. 3, 1988a, p. C1.

Flaherty, R., and Pitt, L. "How Schools Sell a Dream." *Chicago Sun-Times,* Jan. 4, 1988b, p. C1.

Fowler, W. A. *You and Home Study.* Washington, D.C.: National Home Study Council, 1986.

Keyser, T. "Pregate Fallout Hits Other Schools, Officials." *Calgary Herald,* Nov. 10, 1981, p. B2.

Lord, C., and Farquharson, D. "Computer Institute to Close." *Edmonton Journal,* Feb. 12, 1988, p. B1.

Moore, R. W. *Private Training and Public Goals: A Study of New York Proprietary Schools.* Santa Monica, Calif.: Training Research Corporation, 1986.

National Association of Trade and Technical Schools. *Annual Report.* Washington, D.C.: National Association of Trade and Technical Schools, 1987.

Office of the Minister of Advanced Education. *Annual Report of Alberta Advanced Education.* Edmonton, Alb.: Office of the Minister of Advanced Education, 1987.

Valore, L., and Diehl, G. E. *Effectiveness and Acceptance of Home Study.* Washington, D.C.: National Home Study Council, 1987.

Wilms, W. W. *Private Training and the Public Interest: A Study of California's Proprietary Vocational Schools.* Santa Monica, Calif.: Training Research Corporation, 1984.

Wilson, R. "Proprietary Schools' Growing Share of Pell Grant Money Means Less for College Students, Campus Officials Warn." *Chronicle of Higher Education,* July 22, 1987, p. 18.

Wilson, R. "For-Profit Trade Schools Defraud Students and Waste Federal Student-Aid Money, Bennett Charges in Scathing Report." *Chronicle of Higher Education,* Sept. 9, 1988, p. A21.

32

Business and Industry

Karen E. Watkins

Adult education in business and industry is the fastest growing area of practice in the field of adult education in the United States. It is as old as the need for people to learn work-related skills. Yet, as a field of inquiry, adult education in business and industry is relatively young. Like adult education generally, it is a field in search of a definition. This chapter will report the size and scope of human resource development (also referred to here as training) in business and industry. A review of some of the definitional problems that currently concern human resource developers will illustrate the need for a broadened definition of the field. Other issues or trends that significantly impact the field will be discussed; these include professionalization, retraining, externalization of the work force, and an increased demand for human resource developers to enhance informal learning in the workplace. Finally, the discussion will turn to the impact these trends have on the role of human resource developer.

The Nature of Human Resource Development

The Lakewood Research Group contends that the budgets of training departments are among the best indicators of the nature of training in industry. According to the annual industry status report conducted by this group for *Training* magazine (Gordon, 1986b), the average salary of trainers in 1986 was $39,729, with men averaging $43,574 and women averaging $34,110. Twenty-nine billion dollars was projected for training in 1986. This amount was divided among training staff salaries, which account for 72 percent of the total, facilities and overhead (7 percent), seminars and conferences (7 percent), hardware (4 percent), outside services (4 percent), custom materials (3 percent), and off-the-shelf materials (3 percent) (Feuer, 1986). About 30.5 million individuals were projected to receive formal employer-sponsored training in 1986, and they were projected to receive 1.3 billion hours of training.

Professionals are much more likely than nonprofessional employees to receive training. Approximately 69 percent of the organizations studied offered training for middle managers, and only 25 percent offered training for production workers. Nevertheless, production workers are the single largest group to receive training in terms of the total hours of training delivered. Organizations with fifty or more employees were projected to provide formal training to about 36.5 million people in 1986, or roughly 31 percent of the total civilian labor force. The types of training offered by the organization ranged from management skills development and technical skills to health promotion and remedial basic education (Gordon, 1986a).

Another way to reflect on the role of training in organizational life is to assess the percentage of the total budget in terms of the organization's sales and assets that are allocated to training. From a group of twenty-eight organizations, researchers were able to determine that twelve spent 1 percent or less on training; eleven organizations allocated from 1 to 5 percent; and five organizations allocated more than 5 percent (Lee, 1986b). The average across forty organizations was 1 percent of sales or 3.3 percent of the total payroll. Still another way to look at the distribution of training resources is in terms of time. Again using their in-depth profiles of forty organizations, researchers determined that the forty spent an average of 25.6 hours per employee and averaged 638 employees to one trainer (Lee, 1986b).

Just as important as the funding for training is the source of that funding. Organizationally sponsored training has been discussed, but individuals also sponsor their own continuing education. In Germany, for example, employees and employers underwrite equal amounts toward a fund from which either unemployment benefits or retraining for the unemployed may be financed. In some countries (Norway and Australia, for example), the government bears all or a large part of the costs. In the United Kingdom, the cost of training is financed by business and by government. In the United States, massive amounts of federal money have gone toward retraining of the unemployed, literacy development, and occupational training for special populations through the Job Training Partnership Act. This act also created Private Industry Councils to involve representatives from business and industry in an advisory and oversight capacity. In Canada, vocational training responsibility is shared by the provinces and the federal government, though Canadians have had little success in involving employers (Organization for Economic Cooperation and Development, 1983).

One of the critical issues for human resource development is the trainer's lack of prior training in the field—a characteristic of the majority of human resource developers. Only 8 percent of human resource developers report having human resource development degrees. Almost 18 percent hold bachelor's degrees in education, and 31.6 percent hold graduate degrees in education. Further, 16 percent of the bachelor's degrees in the sample were in business or management; psychology represented 10 percent of the bachelor's degrees. Communication, another core discipline, represented 4.4 percent of bachelor's degrees. Over 17 percent of the individuals surveyed were either school teachers or college instructors before they became trainers (Lee, 1985). The human resource developers' need for education in adult learning, psychology, organizational behavior, and communication is reflected by the diverse representation of these college majors among practitioners. A significant problem in human resource development is making this interdisciplinary education available to trainers. Findings by Watkins and Wiswell (1987) from a study of the learning practices of forty-seven human resource developers suggested that they were often too busy training others to seek training for themselves. Given the large numbers involved (about 50,000 members of the American Society for Training and Development (ASTD)— between national and local membership lists), the training of trainers is itself a massive educational undertaking (American Society for Training and Development, n.d.).

Overall, what do these figures tell us about the field of human resource development? On the one hand, one can clearly make the claim that this is a burgeoning area of adult learning. On the other hand is a disturbing trend toward reliance on outside sources to provide that education and on employees to obtain skills on their own. Human resource developers are becoming concerned about their ability to do professional work because of their lack of training and the escalating demands placed on them. One sign that this may be so is their growing interest in certification.

Trends Shaping the Future of Human Resource Development

The issue of professionalization is of concern to many fields at present, as can be seen in Chapters Ten and Thirty-Nine, and human resource development is no exception. Galbraith and Gilley (1986) note that the question of certification was an issue as early as 1972, when the membership of ASTD voted against it. ASTD asked the professional standards committee instead to concentrate its efforts on a means for acquiring basic competencies. The effort to identify basic competencies for human resource development has included a number of studies through the *Models of Excellence* study by McLagan (1983) for ASTD. ASTD, through its professional standards task force, called for the education of practitioners regarding standards and ethics for the field (Galbraith and Gilley, 1986). In a survey conducted by *Training* magazine with a random sample of 7,500 of their subscribers, 58.9 percent were in favor of having training and human resource development practitioners formally certified (Lee, 1986a). Seventy-seven percent of those surveyed also felt that human resource development practitioners should be required to demonstrate mastery of a body of knowledge. Another 81 percent said that practitioners should be required to demonstrate mastery of a set of skills.

Nadler (1984) recognizes three categories of human resource developers. Category one consists of those individuals who are professionally identified with the field of human resource development. Lee (1985) reported that only 24.6 percent of the trainers surveyed listed training and development as their long-term career objective. Category two consists of those who are organizationally identified. These are people who see their careers as working for a particular organization, though at the present time they may be assigned to human resource development. Their long-term employment prospects are with the organization and not necessarily with the field of human resource development. Category three consists of those individuals for whom human resource development constitutes a collateral duty. Clearly, credentialing would be most appropriate for those in category one. And yet all of these individuals are doing human resource development. So, what standards of practice should be expected of those in categories two and three?

One approach that may help resolve this dilemma is to rely less on certification and much more on an attitude or ethic of professionalism. The idea that professionalization is an appropriate response to the increasingly nonroutine and complex nature of work in modern organizations is offered by Benveniste (1987). Professionalization involves substituting rules and regulations with controls that rely instead on professional discretion, self-restraint, and self-regulation. Moreover, professionals have access to a specialized knowledge and an ability to bring that specialized knowledge to a wide variety of problems. Increased autonomy for human resource developers and the flexible application of professional expertise are needed if human resource development practitioners are to help organizations solve complex problems. Perhaps by adopting a code of ethics that calls for continual learning, rigorous standards for training programs, and constant peer review, more human resource developers will acquire the professional expertise needed to respond to the changing workplace.

Definitional Controversy. There is widespread agreement that the emerging field of human resource development needs definition if it is to emerge as a profession. Although many have stressed the need for a common definition of the field, divergent views remain. Nadler (1983, p. 1) defined human resource development as "organized learning experiences in a given period of time to bring about the possibility of performance change or general growth for the individual within an organization." Nadler's definition emphasizes organized learning experiences but excludes informal learning and more open-ended individual development projects that lack a definite time constraint. It is more a definition of training than of human resource development.

Jones (1981, p. 188) defines human resource development as "an approach to the systematic expansion of people's work-related abilities, focused on the attainment of both organizational and personal goals." Jones's definition offers greater clarity in naming the domain of activity—the work-related abilities of individuals, the systematic nature of the work, and the desired outcome of both individuals and organizations meeting their goals; but it fails to include group and organizational development activities.

In 1983, the American Society for Training and Development completed its study of the human resource development field. McLagan and Associates surveyed practitioners and identified nine areas of practice in human resource development: training and development, organization development, organization and job design, human resource planning, selection and staffing, personnel research and information systems, compensation and benefits, employee assistance, and union-labor relations. Nadler (1983, p. 1) quoted their definition as follows: "identifying, assessing, and through planned learning, helping develop the key competencies which enable individuals to perform current or future jobs." Under the category of training and development, McLagan and Associates identified fifteen unique training and development roles ranging from instructional writer to task analyst, group facilitator, and marketer. These roles then led to the identification of thirty-one specific role competencies. The American Society for Training and Development competency study was initiated because of the desire of practitioners to have a way of certifying themselves as competent against a known standard for the field; yet, because the standard was developed by describing current practice, it was inevitable that the wide range of activities and divergent viewpoints now characteristic of training practice would be reflected in the final product. Furthermore, emerging or desirable new roles were not identified. A new study, again conducted by McLagan, is using forecasting and trend projections to define future human resource development roles. The problem of certification is the decision whether to certify within each of the nine areas of human resource practice, since each has its own technology and disciplinary information base, or whether to evolve competencies that are generic to the nine areas and to certify those. A related question is whether to evolve a series of specializations rather than a field of practice labeled human resource development.

If the field elects further specialization, what impact might this have on the ability of practitioners to acquire the full range of information they need to be effective? For example, if cost accounting and hiring decisions are the province of human resource management, and planning educational programs and career development strategies are the province of human resource development, it could be argued that neither approach would yield as rich or as informed a decision as one that combined both types of information. Moreover, the organizational context Nadler labels human resource environment is equally important. An individual who is making a hiring decision needs to know the availability of trained individuals in the work force, the type of individual that will fit with the culture and demands of the organization, and the impact of hiring decisions on the organizational mission.

What is needed is a definition that encompasses the range of demands on the human resource developer while offering a vision or a focus for those activities. Over time, the term *training* gave way to *training and development* and, finally, to *human resource development* to reflect the movement from an activity or process (training) to a function that is the development of human beings in such a way that they will be enhanced resources for the organization (human resource development). The following definition includes not only a function but also a vision for the field: *Human resource development is the field of study and practice responsible for the fostering of a long-term, work-related learning capacity at the individual, group, and organizational level of organizations.* As such, it includes—but is not limited to—training, career development, and organizational development. This means that human resource developers are involved in facilitating or monitoring all types of learning in the workplace, including formal and informal learning. While the learner will vary from the individual level to a department to the organization, the mission of instilling an enhanced learning or learning-how-to-learn capacity will not. Viewed from this perspective, the range of activity in which human resource developers might engage is vast.

Informal Learning. One new area that may pressure human resource development to continue the move to a more broadly framed role is the growing interest in informal learning, fueled in part by Carnevale's 1984 report, *Jobs for the Nation: Challenges for a Society Based on Work.* Carnevale reported that workplace learning and formal education accounted for more growth in economic output than did improved employee health, the composition of the work force, population size, resource adaptation, or capital (Carnevale, 1986). Workplace learning accounted for 85 percent of the variation in lifetime earnings, while formal education accounted for only 15 percent of this variance. This finding was corroborated by a 1986 Rand study, which also added that this effect had persisted for over thirteen years (Lillard and Tan, 1986). Of the workers who need training, 79 percent get it in the workplace, and 70 percent of the training or retraining for professional, executive, and technical workers is provided by the employer. According to Carnevale, training and development is a $210 billion business, as compared to $238 billion per year for formal education—elementary, high school and postsecondary education combined. Since formal training in organizations accounts for only $30 billion of that $210 billion, a full $180 billion of the training Carnevale reports occurring in business and industry is in the form of informal training. If these figures are accurate, employee training by employers is the largest single delivery system for adult education. Carnevale used an econometric model in which he factored the estimated costs of instruction, wages lost by students and instructors, and other relevant elements to determine the amount spent on informal learning. Carnevale describes informal training as supervision, observation of fellow workers, learning from one's mistakes, reading, self-study, and other unstructured ways of acquiring work skills in the course of doing one's job—in short, on-the-job training. Carnevale's results are limited by the uncertain accuracy of these estimates and by the inflated costs that make up the model—costs that are not considered in the other figures he uses for comparison. For example, formal training costs should not include lost wages or student time, nor should these be computed in determining the costs of formal education—even though they are real costs. Their use here skews the comparison. But it should be noted that, as early as 1958, Jacob Minzer estimated that American males invested $13.5 billion in on-the-job training by accepting wages lower than the true value of their services in order to learn a new skill that offered more long-term promise of higher wages (Parnes, 1986). This kind of calculation is yet another way to think about on-the-job training, and it illustrates how difficult it is to capture, through econometric modeling, the total investment of individuals and organizations in informal training.

In a study of on-the-job training conducted at Ohio State University, a structured on-the-job training system developed by Ron Jacobs enabled an organization to reduce training time from twelve weeks to less than two weeks (*Training Director's Forum*, 1987b). The Ohio State program included manuals for technicians and supervisors, a supervisory coaching program, and performance rating checklists for feedback and certification. If one goal of the human resource development practitioner is to increase the productivity of the organization, then it may be desirable to view the $180 billion figure for on-the-job training from the Carnevale report not as spending on training, but as a cost that training departments can help reduce.

Strategies that trainers might use to increase their effectiveness in reducing the cost of on-the-job training, as identified by Kerrigan and Luke (1987), are manager shadowing, mentoring, coaching, guided delegation, counterpart training, and job rotation. Conditions for effective on-the-job training include the need for the individual who conducts such training, whether a manager or a peer or a trainer, to have skill in reinforcing learning and in sequencing learning experiences from less difficult to more difficult tasks. This means that the individual needs to have diagnostic skills, on-line observation capability, and the ability to give effective, precise behavioral feedback. Action training (also called action learning, action science, and action research) is another informal learning strategy. Action training consists of cycles: changes in project conditions lead to new training needs that require new training interventions which, in turn, change project conditions. The use of participants' actual work projects and problems to stimulate the design of training and the use of reflection on practice as a major training method are the two features that distinguish action training from other forms of informal learning. Marsick (1987) draws on the work of Schön (1983) and defines informal learning as reflection-in-action. She concentrates on three modes of informal learning: job assignments, relationships, and self-directed learning. Research has indicated that managers learn much of what they need for their work from job experiences (Honeywell Corporation, 1986) and from particularly challenging experiences (Lombardo, 1985). When asked to rank the factors that contributed to their career development, trainers also rated on-the-job experience first. Next came formal education, formal job-related training, mentors, and networking (Lee, 1985). This emphasis on informal learning mechanisms is of particular interest to the field of adult education. If adult educators are to influence learners in the workplace, they will need to develop a technology for enabling learners to use job experiences more effectively for learning. Critical reflection is one promising approach.

A recent report from the Work in America Institute (1985) makes a similar case but suggests an alternative model. The report emphasizes the need for a shift in emphasis from training to learning, echoing Nadler (1984) and Marsick (1987), pointing out that training focuses on what someone does to employees while learning involves employees as active participants in expanding their own skills. The report contends that learning must be continuous because changes facing members of an organization are continuous. The continuous learning model borrows much of its substance from the Japanese ideas of quality circles and the continuous manufacturing process model. The model consists of four themes: (1) Since learning is an everyday part of every job, the line between job performance and learning disappears. (2) Employees are required to learn the skills of others in their work unit and to understand the relationship between their work unit and the operation and goals of the organization as a whole. (3) Active, free-form interaction among employees, teams, trainers, and managers is encouraged and institutionalized. (4) Employees are required to transmit their job knowledge to, as well as to learn from, co-workers (Work in America Institute, 1985).

Common to each of these descriptions of on-the-job training or informal learning is the assumption that the rapidity of change and the need for constant upgrading of employee skills will require a continuous, lifelong commitment to ongoing training.

Retraining. Considerable federal attention has been paid to the issue of retraining the American work force. A fact sheet on retraining from the American Society for Training and Development (1987a) asserts that foreign competition, new technologies, and changing consumer demand have reshaped the job market in such a way that Americans may expect, on average, to change jobs three or four times in their careers. By the year 2000, 75 percent of all workers currently employed will need retraining because of changes in the nature of existing jobs or because of the creation of new jobs that will require new and higher levels of skills. Since 75 percent of those who will be in the work force in the next decade are already working, retraining programs may be business's only option to develop a skilled work force as the needs change.

Arguing that the cost of dislocating workers without providing retraining is a human capital cost that this country cannot afford, Perelman (1984, p. xvi) states that, "Economic security in the post-industrial economy depends less on expertise and more on *flexpertise*—the ability to continually adapt individual knowledge and skill. Unless we in America greatly increase the flexibility of our human capital, the economic transition threatens turbulent, even violent, social upheaval as the economic ambitions of a major portion of the working population become increasingly frustrated.''

A Department of Labor survey quoted by Parnes disclosed that, in the four-year period from 1979 to 1983, 5.1 million workers with at least three years of service had lost their jobs because of plant closings or lay-offs, and, of these, 1.3 million remained unemployed as of January 1984. This finding is similar to findings of another five-year study by the Bureau of Labor Statistics that showed only 60 percent of workers displaced during that period were reemployed, and only 45 percent of those reemployed were earning as much or more in their new jobs (American Society for Training and Development, 1987a).

Perelman (1984, pp. xvi–xvii) presents a dramatic case for retraining: ''Virtually the entire adult population needs retraining and new learning to be economically productive. A fifth of the present adult population is functionally illiterate. Most of the rest—including skilled workers, managers, and professionals—have knowledge and skills that technological change is rendering obsolete. . . . The emergence of a knowledge-based economy requires a new synthesis of the functions of training, education, and other forms of communication and learning under the single umbrella of the learning enterprise.''

Federal initiatives to retrain workers have proven inadequate. Parnes (1986) found that programs established as a result of the federal Job Training Partnership Act (JTPA) have had mixed reviews. The inability to demonstrate the efficacy or the return on investment of workplace learning and of other retraining programs led to the awarding of a two-year, $750,000 grant by the Department of Labor to the American Society for Training and Development. With this grant money, ASTD examined workplace training practices and their transferability through public and private employment systems (American Society for Training and Development, 1987b). Perhaps as a result of this study, human resource development activities in business and industry will serve as a model for federal programs for the unemployed.

Trainers are faced with different challenges in retraining. Retraining involves unlearning old behaviors or skills. Employees are often involved in retraining programs as a result of traumatic circumstances such as being told that their skills are obsolete or inadequate or that their functions or job areas are being eliminated. Often, individuals entering retraining must first work through this challenge to their self-esteem. Even when individuals seek out retraining in order to upgrade their skills, they may still be concerned about investing so much of themselves and their disposable income in training for a career or a job that may not be there when they complete the training. Finally, adults in retraining increasingly are older adults with unique developmental and physiological concerns. Effective retraining not only should be appropriate to a particular job content, but also should be sensitive to the emotional issues related to unlearning, dealing with crisis, and building a capacity and willingness to continue learning.

Externalization of the Work Force. One approach to the problem of rapidly adapting a work force to contractions and expansions into new areas is to externalize the work force. Pfeffer and Beron (forthcoming) suggest that a diminished attachment or increased externalization of the work force is occurring along three dimensions: (1) externalization of place through work-at-home arrangements, (2) externalization by reducing the duration of employment through temporary and part-time work, and (3) externalization of administrative control over responsibility for the employee through employee leasing and home work. It is interesting to note that the temporary-help industry outgrew the gross national product by almost two to one in the period from 1970 to 1984. Approximately 33 percent of that growth occurred in just one year (1983 to 1984).

Externalization of the work force means that the organization carries less risk, pays fewer (or no) benefits, and can terminate an employee's services at will. Temporary help and employee leasing agencies become the employing organizations, although individuals report to and work for managers in different companies. The training of these individuals is done both by the temporary help and leasing organizations and by the hiring organizations. Research substantiates that reliance on temporaries reduces the costs of unemployment insurance, other benefits, and legal expenses resulting from wrongful termination suits. However, increased costs in terms of training and decreased productivity due to less motivation and loyalty from temporary employees may be experienced (Pfeffer and Beron, forthcoming).

What is the impact on human resource development of this trend toward externalization? In the *Training* magazine survey of 1986, the movement to externalize the training function can be seen. Comparing the 1985 budgets to the 1986 budgets, the *Training* survey found an 11.7 percent real increase in outside expenditures. To determine whether organizations were doing less of the training themselves, the survey asked which of three options were chosen by the responding organizations: (1) training developed and delivered by internal training staff; (2) training developed by an external source but delivered by an internal training staff; or (3) training done entirely by a vendor. Training using the first option decreased by almost 12 percent from 1983 to 1986. Training using the second option was down by 1.2 percent and training using the third option was up by almost 6 percent for public seminars and workshops. Self-instruction under the first option, however, was up by almost 6 percent indicating that internal trainers may be turning to computer-assisted and self-directed learning as alternatives to classroom instruction (Gordon, 1986a).

Another form of externalization in training can be seen in the use of community colleges, technical institutes, and universities to provide professional development in the workplace. Moser and Seaman (1987) surveyed 522 individuals who functioned as training managers in the southwest region of the United States. The results of the survey indicated that the companies had budgeted 2.5 percent of their budget for training from community colleges, 0.89 percent for training from technical institutes, and 10.12 percent for training from universities. Nell Eurich (1985) identified the growing trend of corporations creating their own colleges and offering their own degrees, predominately in technical areas such as electrical engineering and computer science. This approach is typically used only when existing academic programs do not fit the immediate needs of these very large corporations. A much more common approach is to develop a relationship with a postsecondary institution. This approach enables the organization to identify training outcomes while the college provides the needed training. (See also Chapters Twenty-Three and Twenty-Four.) Moser and Seaman's data suggest that when these college-sponsored programs are included in the figures, only 57.5 percent of the training budget goes to in-house training efforts. Expanding organization-sponsored learning to include tuition reimbursement, attendance at conferences, membership in professional organizations, and other subscriptions would increase even further the percentage of learning in the workplace already being delivered through external agencies.

New Roles for Facilitating Workplace Learning

One implication of professionalization, retraining, on-the-job training, and externalization is that there will be a number of new roles for human resource developers in facilitating workplace learning. The facilitator of action learning is one such role. Competencies for this new role will require an individual who is skilled at problem framing, able to communicate perceptions using directly observable data while inquiring into others' views of the world, and able to question actively his or her own and others' previous assumptions and perceptions. Knowles (1985) encourages human resource developers to think of the organization as a learning system and to take an active stance in promoting learning throughout all aspects of the organization. This might include identifying individuals with special expertise and making them available for peer learning, developing a library of print and nonprint media resources, and promoting the use of learning contracts throughout the organization.

Externalization of the work force may lead to the formation by independent human resource consultants of a temporary-help agency consisting of human resource developers with a variety of different types of expertise. Recently, for example, a large hospital chain released its entire corporate training staff and made the decision to use external training firms to provide the technical training needed by its hospitals. Staffing and training such an agency or serving as a broker to locate training specialists might be a new career possibility for individuals in human resource development. Another implication of an externalized work force is that trainers will increasingly find themselves to be the internal marketers working to instill the organizational culture in a dispersed group of employees.

Another new role for human resource developers will be that of auditor. This role is a direct outgrowth of the increasing demand that human resource developers be fiscally accountable. The Training and Development Research Center of Saint Paul, Minnesota, has developed a training audit that collects data in five basic areas: compliance, process, operations and finance, trainees, and business results (Training Director's Forum, 1987a). Such an audit of the training function offers management the opportunity to compare the outcomes of their training efforts to their training expenditures. Accordingly, trainers may need to take a more active role in connecting the results of performance appraisals to the training available in the organization. From a trainer's perspective, performance appraisals help justify training expenses and also reinforce training efforts while motivating individuals to seek continued learning through an individual education plan (Training Director's Forum, 1987a).

A primary task of human resource developers in the 1990s will be to ensure educational accountability as rigorous as their financial accountability. The auditing function, if focused on learning outcomes, can show evidence of the effectiveness of human resource development efforts. However, as in education at other levels, the most significant impact of training will be seen over the long term. It is hoped that evaluation models that take into account retraining, informal learning, on-the-job experience and nonformal or peer learning, and that take into account the overall impact of these activities on employee productivity and on long-term career effectiveness, will serve to develop employee contributions to the organization.

In each of these new roles, it is clear that an expanded conception of human resource development, from predominantly classroom training to the promotion of learning throughout the organization, is needed. The changing workplace is bringing with it a new vision of learning with a much greater emphasis on interpersonal helping skills. Human resource developers must actively strive to shape that new vision.

References

American Society for Training and Development. *Facts About Training and the American Society for Training and Development.* Alexandria, Va.: American Society for Training and Development, n.d.

American Society for Training and Development. *Facts About Retraining America's Workforce.* Alexandria, Va.: American Society for Training and Development, 1987a.

American Society for Training and Development. "Training and Development Grabs National Attention." *Dialog,* March 1987b, p. 1.

Benveniste, G. *Professionalizing the Organization: Reducing Bureaucracy to Enhance Effectiveness.* San Francisco: Jossey-Bass, 1987.

Carnevale, A. *Jobs for the Nation: Challenges for a Society Based on Work.* Alexandria, Va.: American Society for Training and Development, 1984.

Carnevale, A. "The Learning Enterprise." *Training and Development Journal,* 1986, *40* (1), 18–26.

Eurich, N. *Corporate Classrooms: The Learning Business.* Princeton, N.J.: Carnegie Foundation for the Advancement of Teaching, 1985.

Feuer, D. "Training Budgets." *Training,* 1986, *23* (10), 32–48.

Galbraith, M., and Gilley, J. *Professional Certification: Implications for Adult Education and HRD.* Information Series, no. 307. Columbus, Ohio: ERIC Clearinghouse on Adult, Career, and Vocational Education, 1986.

Gordon, J. "Where the Training Goes." *Training,* 1986a, *23* (10), 49–66.

Gordon, J. "*Training's* 1986 Salary Survey." *Training,* 1986b, *23* (11), 35–51.

Honeywell Corporation. *The Job Experience and Relationship Study: Final Report.* Minneapolis, Minn.: Honeywell Corporation, 1986.

Jones, J. "Human Resource Development: What It Is and How to Become Involved." In J. Pfeiffer and J. Jones (eds.), *1981 Annual Handbook for Group Facilitators.* San Diego, Calif.: University Associates, 1981.

Kerrigan, J., and Luke, J. *Management Training Strategies for Developing Countries.* Boulder, Colo.: Lynne Rienner, 1987.

Knowles, M. "Shifting to an HRD Systems Approach." *Training and Development Journal,* 1985, *39* (5), 24–25.

Lee, C. "Trainers' Careers." *Training,* 1985, *22* (10), 75–80.

Lee, C. "Certification for Trainers: Thumbs Up." *Training,* 1986a, *23* (11), 56–66.

Lee, C. "*Training* Profiles: The View from Ground Level." *Training,* 1986b, *23* (10), 67–84.

Lillard, L., and Tan, H. *Private Sector Training: Who Gets It and What Are Its Effects?* Santa Monica, Calif.: Rand Corporation, 1986.

Lombardo, M. "Five Challenging Assignments." *Issues and Observations,* 1985, *5* (2), 1–8.

McLagan, P. *Models for Excellence: The Conclusions and Recommendations of the ASTD Training and Development Competency Study.* Alexandria, Va.: American Society for Training and Development, 1983.

Marsick, V. "New Paradigms for Learning in the Workplace." In V. Marsick (ed.), *Learning in the Workplace.* London: Croom-Helm, 1987.

Moser, S., and Seaman, D. "Implications for Potential Linkages Between Business-Industry and Higher Education." *Adult Education Quarterly,* 1987, *37* (4), 223–229.

Nadler, L. *Human Resource Development: The Perspective of Business and Industry.* Information Series, no. 259. Columbus, Ohio: ERIC Clearinghouse on Adult, Career, and Vocational Education, 1983.

Nadler, L. "Human Resource Development." In L. Nadler (ed.), *The Handbook of Human Resource Development.* New York: Wiley, 1984.

Organization for Economic Cooperation and Development. *The Future of Vocational Education and Training.* Paris: Organization for Economic Cooperation and Development, 1983.

Parnes, H. *Developing Human Capital.* Columbus, Ohio: National Center for Research and Vocational Education, 1986.

Perelman, L. *The Learning Enterprise: Adult Learning, Human Capital, and Economic Development.* Washington, D.C.: Council of State Planning Agencies, 1984.

Pfeffer, J., and Beron, J. "Taking the Workers Back Out: Recent Trends in the Structuring of Employment." In B. Staw and L. Cummings (eds.), *Research in Organizational Behavior.* Vol. 10. Greenwich, Conn.: JAI Press, forthcoming.

Schön, D. *The Reflective Practitioner.* New York: Basic Books, 1983.

Training Director's Forum. "Companies Benefit When Appraisals Reflect Training Needs." *Training Director's Forum Newsletter,* 1987a, *3* (2), 1–4.

Training Director's Forum. "On-The-Job Training." *Training Director's Forum Newsletter,* 1987b, *3* (5), 8.

Watkins, K., and Wiswell, B. "Incidental Learning in the Workplace." In H. Copur (ed.), *Proceedings of the Human Resources Management and Organizational Behavior Western Regional Conference.* Virginia Beach, Va.: Association of Human Resources Management and Organizational Behavior, 1987.

Work in America Institute. *Training for New Technology.* Part 2: *Toward Continuous Learning.* Scarsdale, N.Y.: Work in America Institute, 1985.

Part 4

Adult Education Program Areas and Special Clienteles

As can be seen from reviewing the previous section of this handbook, many institutions, agencies, and organizations deliver educational programs to adults. Many adult educators define themselves in terms of the institutions in which they work, and they often join professional groups that are institutionally based. This behavior has led, in part, to a fragmented identity of adult education. That is, many adult educators see themselves first as, for example, hospital staff, library personnel, or university administrators. Or, as will become evident in this section, adult educators identify with a specific content area such as literacy, health, or civic education, or with a specific clientele such as women, older adults, or minority groups. A long list of programs could be developed based on content area or type of participant. But rather than attempt to cover all possibilities, the chapters in Part Four will focus on those areas in which significant changes have taken place in the last decade.

Content areas in adult education cut across institutional lines. Many organizations offer adult secondary education and health information, for example. But regardless of the particular delivery system, several common issues run through the various program areas in adult education. Of interest to most programs are who else is offering similar programs, and who is most likely to participate. For program areas such as adult basic education, this information is of paramount concern, since funding is often a function of participation and demonstrated need. Other issues have to do with access and opportunity, power and control, means and ends. These and other issues are discussed in individual chapters as appropriate.

Part Four begins with chapters on community-based education and public affairs education. Due to a growing awareness of the cost to society of a federally sponsored literacy initiative, illiteracy has become a special issue within the last decade. Programs that deal directly with adults' literacy needs include adult basic education, adult secondary education, English as a second language, and some community-based programs. There is a chapter on each of these program areas. Finally, two other content areas in adult education have grown dramatically in the last decade—health education and continuing professional education. Changes in content and delivery, increasing awareness of the need for programs in health and continuing professional education, and issues of access and control are discussed in the chapters on these content areas.

The adult education "pie" can also be sliced according to the type of participant. Five chapters are devoted to adult education's efforts to serve older adults, rural adults, women, black and minority groups, and developmentally disabled learners. Each of these clienteles has unique needs and interests. Adult education has responded creatively in both program content and mode of delivery. Elderhostel, an enormously successful cultural enrichment program held on college campuses for older persons, is but one example of creative programming. Programs broadcast via satellite to rural areas are examples of innovative delivery. Adult educators are also grappling with some of the philosophical issues related to serving particular groups of adults. Other topics discussed in the following chapters are the clientele, participation patterns, barriers to participation, programming, delivery systems, and philosophical and political issues related to serving adults.

33

Community-Based Adult Education

Edwin Hamilton
Phyllis M. Cunningham

Community-based education programs in North America cover a wide variety of learning activities conducted in neighborhood locations by a broad range of independent sponsoring institutions, agencies, and organizations. Many of these sponsors regard adult education as their primary function, while others consider it to be a secondary function. The aims and purposes of community-based adult education usually are directly related to specific community issues such as career training, consumerism, environmental concerns, basic education, ethnic history and culture, governmental policies, and civic and political education. The common organizational elements that characterize most of these are local initiative, control, maintenance, evaluation, and program development. Funds for program operations are derived from both internal and external sources.

Community-based education operates on the assumption that a given community, whether urban or rural, has the potential to solve many of its own problems by relying on its own resources and by mobilizing community action for problem resolution. Two important adult education strategies appear to be most appropriate in analyzing and discussing this ambitious proposition: community development and popular education. This chapter examines the relationship between community development and popular education as they relate to community-based education.

Overview of Community Development and Popular Education

A review of the vast literature dealing with community development reveals a great deal of confusion regarding its definition, aims, and approaches.

Many writers discuss community development from a formalized, institutional perspective—an approach that erroneously implies it is somehow not conducive to community control. However, a careful analysis of the essential properties of community development leads to the conclusion that it is indeed conducive to community control, but that its implementation depends on the intent and design of a particular community development initiative. Popular education shares many of the philosophical assumptions of highly participatory community development models and can therefore be viewed as a compatible strategy for enhancing the effectiveness of community-based education. So, on the one hand, community development and popular education can be seen as compatible. However, on the other hand, subtle but important distinctions can be made indicating that these two approaches are contradictory. Both arguments will be examined in this chapter.

Community Development Defined and Described. The term *community development* refers to "a social process by which human beings can become more competent to live with and gain some control over local aspects of a frustrating and changing world" (Biddle and Biddle, 1965, p. 78). This statement provides a philosophical basis for defining the term. Mezirow (1961, p. 16) stresses the educational significance of community development by stating, "The community development process is, in essence, a planned and organized effort to assist individuals to acquire the attitudes, skills and concepts required for their democratic participation in the effective solutions of as wide a range of community improvement problems as possible in an order of priority determined by their increasing levels of competence." Many writers emphasize the necessity of learning new skills and knowledge about existing social problems (McClusky, 1960; Roberts, 1979; Kerensky, 1981). In their view, learning is a dominant factor and becomes the driving force that propels community development toward definite educational outcomes. To highlight explicitly the educational aspect of community development, Compton and McClusky (1980) use the term *community education for development.* They define it as "a process whereby community members come together to identify their problems and needs, seek solutions among themselves, mobilize the necessary resources, and execute a plan of action or learning or both. This educative approach is one in which community is seen as both agent and objective, education is the process, and leaders are the facilitators, in inducing change for the better" (p. 229).

Historically, community development is derived from a broad-based framework that consists of four major areas of concentration: agricultural development, industrial development, economic development, and social development. An interrelationship and an interdependency exist among these groupings because they all aim to improve the human condition. However, community development from the perspective of the adult educator primarily flows out of the social development concern.

Sanders (1970, p. 19) describes four distinct configurations of community development, "as a *process,* a *method,* a *program,* or a *movement*" (emphasis added). A brief description of these four ways of viewing community development follows.

Process. The principal focus of the process view is on the social (horizontal) relationships that develop as a result of interactions. These interactions usually start with two or more community residents and progressively expand to include many others. Individuals are drawn together because of common concerns and desires to participate in learning and decision making. In the process, residents learn more about the issues and make maximum use of local resources to solve problems, and they identify and control external sources of assistance. The primary emphasis of community development as a process is the psychological effect it has on the community residents as they expand social relationships for learning.

Method. The method view is a goal-oriented perspective designed to realize the attainment of specific objectives by means of community development. It often reflects a set of procedures that are followed to attain a concrete benefit. Generally, professionals, who may be external to the community, are involved in formulating the methods and procedures. The principal objectives are the use and replication of research findings related to methods that appear to be useful in attacking specific community problems.

Program. The program view of community development involves organized activity, replete with procedures and objectives, that is recognized as ongoing and self-contained. The activity may be short term or long range depending on the specific objectives. The focus is on program maintenance and on adherence to policy and procedures. When a program is highly specialized, it requires the assistance of subject-matter professionals who are usually employed by governmental units of health, education, sanitation, social services, or other relevant specialties. The emphasis on activities can sometimes overshadow participation of community residents in the decision-making process.

Movement. The movement view is perhaps the most idealistic view of community development, which is seen, from this perspective, as a crusade driven by emotional issues and charismatic leadership. It is often an ideology seeking to become institutionalized through a regional or national movement for some cause of social betterment. The movement reflects a philosophy that serves as a source of stimulation but not necessarily as a source of domination. This type of community development requires a large cadre of professionals who are skilled in public relations and in specialty areas related to the movement's goals.

Regardless of the particular view or typology of community development, all seem to stress the importance of the participation of community residents in the activity. This emphasis, in addition to learning, should be considered a basic principle of community development. Lee Cary (1970, p. 145) points out that the active participation of citizens should be as inclusive as possible, and that there are some specific conditions of participation that must be present if meaningful participation is to take place: "(1)

freedom to participate; (2) ability to participate; and (3) willingness to participate.''

Popular participation is a key element in the basic needs determination strategy elaborated in recent years. According to Dore and Mars (1981), four different streams of thinking characterize participation in community development:

1. A project that seeks to fill a need of which citizens are aware elicits more cooperation than does a project that fills no perceived need.
2. Irrespective of whether the project reflects long-standing needs or newly discovered needs, the extent to which citizens share in the decision making will determine their commitment to undertaking action and follow-through.
3. Most bureaucrats and professionals (doctors, engineers, and so on) engaged in a project often have different motivations and alliances and therefore need to be under the firm control of community authority.
4. Community self-determination and values of independence and autonomy require a general refusal to accept institutional authority blindly. Universal values dictate that people must seize the opportunity to control their own destinies as much as possible.

The first two streams of thinking are typical of early discussions of community development. The last two are more reflective of contemporary and future directions of community development. Effective participation requires knowledge, skills, and understandings that can be learned. Hence, a major component of community development is the education of adult citizens—the key to effective community development. In practical terms, adults acting collectively are the most able agents for community problem solving and change. They are the parents, workers, consumers, civic activists, taxpayers, and performers of many other adult social roles. They are the ones whose services and participation are of critical importance in the planning and execution of community development. They cannot carry out the roles of formulating, implementing, and evaluating plans unless they are sufficiently well informed to be able to choose among the many options open to them (Hamilton, 1984).

"Community development is an educational process. It is this, first, last and all the time. All else is secondary to it and must take its place as a reflection, not as the end result" (Biddle and Biddle, 1965, p. 243). McClusky (1960, p. 416) pinpointed the significance of education as an end result of community development by stating, "The ultimate test of community development, both as object (what) and process (how), is what it does to the people who make up the membership of the community being developed." Adult education is a vital prerequisite and an ongoing component of any community development effort that has popular support and that has social change as its ultimate object (Long, 1973).

Popular Education: Philosophy, Definition, and Strategy. The popular education of adults is a movement that originated in Latin America. Its philosophical basis is defined as "a social behavior which situates itself within a framework broader than that dealing exclusively with education and which aims at the popular sectors, so that persons in these sectors will become self-aware political subjects" (Hernandez, 1985).

There is no one definition of popular education, although there are characterizations such as participatory, democratic, involving, and consensual. The word *popular* does not mean "in vogue," as often used in the English language; it is more aligned with the word *populist*—for and by the people. Popular education is characterized by, and therefore partly defined by, (1) horizontal relationships between facilitators and participants, (2) response to a need expressed by an organized group, (3) group involvement in planning the training and political action, and (4) acknowledgement that the community is the source of knowledge.

In the last twenty years, a close relationship has existed between popular education and political movements. "Popular education aims at providing social skills useful to people's struggles. It is an alternative idea of development with people at the center; it generates a sense of life; learning to action; and encourages analytical skills to analyze the world. It has many currents and no one truth; there is interest in supporting the truth of diversity. It is too young to be systematized" (Osorio, 1986).

Conceptually, popular education is linked to resistance theory (Giroux, 1983) and to cultural and social hegemony analyses (Bourdieu and Passeron, 1977; Gramsci, 1985). Accordingly, to promote social change through education, the strategy is to strengthen popular hegemony as a counterforce to the imposed silent oppression by the dominant culture. Popular adult education plays an important role in helping spontaneous resistance evolve into conscious social movements and in consolidating the organizational structure thus formed. The control is always in the hands of the people; the ends are to serve the people.

Popular education is not formal education, nor is it usually nonformal education, informal education, or community development. These forms of education or activities usually transmit the dominant forms of knowledge and culture and have as their goal the maintenance or reform of the society. By definition, popular education must establish and specify relationships between knowledge and power. Its goal is to transform social reality into a more democratic state by confronting dominant and dominating institutions through the creation of opposing knowledges—through the celebration of many indigenous cultures and the writing of many histories of and by the people.

The education that helps people to create their own knowledge, to celebrate their own culture, and to study their own history must not be an education *for* the people but an education *with* the people. Education *for* people is a social activity that is not controlled by the people. Education *with* the people is an activity that is in the interests of the people and that builds popular power.

In summary, popular education rests on the analysis that social control is exercised not only by economic and productive relationships but also by the establishment of a cultural and social hegemony (see Chapter Five). This hegemony is perceived as common sense, and the dominant culture, its values, its explanations, its knowledge, and its interpretation of history are accepted uncritically by those very people it oppresses. To the end that one group in society not be able so silently to establish power to oppress other groups, there is a need to develop counterhegemonic forces that critically confront this so-called common sense in order to transform the society.

A Formulation for Popular Education. Felix Cadena (1984, pp. 33–34) has given us a conceptual scheme used throughout Latin America for the development of popular education: "This type of education is often initiated from outside [the community] and requires an external agent such as an animateur, popular educator, social mediator. . . . Programs begin with an attempt to identify the problems, expectations, and daily needs of [the community] and have commitment to help them. . . . The main goal of the popular educator should be to help the people reclaim their collective history so that they can bring about the structural changes that ensure the fulfilling of their needs and wishes, both in their daily lives and on a broader cultural level. This is the building up of popular power."

Popular power must be accomplished by popular participation. Thus, popular education seeks in its daily activities to implement the social relationships envisioned in the alternative society. The goal is to expand the numbers of people and organizations committed to the alternative society into a critical mass to challenge oppressive practices. Popular participation is not a horizontal activity in which there is simply participatory decision making based on the status quo. Rather, popular participation has as its goals so-called critical conscientization (Freire, 1978), the development of a capacity to transform reality, and the strengthening of the organizational structure to challenge existing power arrangements.

Through the processes to accomplish the above three goals, the results should be an increasing ability of people (1) consciously to appropriate their own reality, (2) to influence and to control the processes in their daily lives, including equalization of distribution of goals and services, (3) to defend their own interests and to define the type of society that would serve them best, and (4) to make the society less hegemonic and more responsive to them (Cadena, 1984).

Historically, four characteristics describe popular education: it challenges schools and distances itself from such traditional models; it reproduces an economic and social countermovement to formal education; it requires active participation of the popular sectors; and it provides a critical analysis of traditional adult education and community development activities (Osorio, 1986).

Popular education finds its conceptual home in the sociology of knowledge. One view is that critical knowing and knowledge production by dominant groups in a society are linked directly with the exercise of power, but that providing categories for official and unofficial knowledge exposes hegemonic domination. Two assumptions of popular education are that knowledge resides in a community and that using such unofficial knowledge is much more appropriate than consulting an outside expert for so-called official knowledge to solve community problems. A state-run university housing governmental intellectuals is only one form of expert with one kind of knowledge which, by definition, should be suspect. Community intellectuals are ordinary citizens who are better prepared to identify, research, and solve their own problems; clearly they are more committed to the community interests (see "Participatory Research" in Chapter Twelve).

Popular education has been adopted by North Americans as community-based education (CBE), complete with a national Association of Community Based Education. These CBE groups define themselves in much the same way as popular educators, and many are Freireian in their philosophy. The Highlander Folk School is an example of a long-standing North American form of popular or community-based education.

What Do Community Development and Popular Education Have in Common?

At the Buenos Aires Third World Congress of the International Council for Adult Education, the commonalities and the distinctions between the two concepts of community development and popular education were hotly debated in the civic education group. Two views emerged: popular education is not new but has existed in slightly different forms in community development and civic education (see Chapter Thirty-Four), both in Europe and in the United States; popular education is a new form of social activity with the goal of transforming (not reforming) society. It is distinct from community development. Both views will be examined.

Interfacing Community Development with Popular Education

The reality of community development and the ideology of popular education in mobilizing grass-roots participation offer a potent force for community-based learning that leads to critical consciousness and social action. Although the practice of popular education has advanced, its theoretical formulation is limited. This lack of theory development is the result of failure to link popular education with contemporary analyses and debates on community development and social movements (Parajuli, 1986). An effective interface of community development and popular education requires some modifications of each in a quest for accommodation. In general, community development procedures must be more humanized, less rigid, and more flexible to facilitate popular participation and management. On the other side, popular education strategies appear to be somewhat unfocused and loosely organized. The ultimate object of both concepts is social change, but in a different context. Community development traditionally has sought social change in an evolutionary manner, as compared with a revolutionary agenda for popular education. The 1960s witnessed a radical shift of community development approaches in the United States with regard to civil rights and political enfranchisement initiatives. Conflict and confrontational approaches were used by American ethnic and minority communities to bring about a more revolutionary social change. This shift in the 1960s clearly demonstrated the potential for community development to accommodate the goals and objectives of popular education and, at the same time, to provide a more organized and systematic approach. Four community development approaches can be adapted to popular education: self-help, civic education, conflict models of change, and the contingency approach.

Self-Help. Self-help is an approach that emphasizes process over task. Its purpose is to strengthen horizontal ties in the community. Local residents share in decision making by deciding what is to be done and then actually doing it. Self-help requires an expressive leader who is concerned about group emotions and who is able to minimize tensions within the group. The self-help approach works best in socioeconomically homogeneous communities and is easiest to implement in isolated areas. The constant problem faced by this approach is the tendency of task to supplant process. Nevertheless, this relatively pragmatic approach appears to be compatible with popular education.

Popular Civic Education. Five principles undergird the theory and practice of popular education; they are the guiding principles for implementing the central functions and design of adult education. Oliver (1987, pp. 48–49) provides a sketch of these girding principles in the context of popular education and adult civic education:

1. *Link with popular movements:* Adult civic education should be integrated with relevant existing social movements such as civil rights groups, trade unions, and political forums.
2. *Capacity building:* Adult civic education should enable citizens to develop the ability to participate effectively in all social, political, and economic institutions.
3. *Neutrality of adult educator:* The adult educator should be personally neutral so as to enable citizens to develop their own positions on the issues and to develop ability to analyze.
4. *National cultural distinctions:* Given the sociopolitical, cultural, and economic differences in approaches to adult civic education, programs must relate to citizens on the basis of their most immediate needs in becoming fully informed and participating citizens.

5. *Teaching and practice:* Adult civic education's role is to assure that teaching is directly related to the skills needed for democratic participation and self-government.

Conflict Models of Community Development. Saul Alinsky (1971) provides a set of principles that form the rationale for mass organizing that focuses on an appeal to the self-interest of residents. Alinsky's ideas of the essential factors of effective community organization are summarized by Stephen Rose (1964, p. 145) as follows: "(1) The organization must recognize self-interest as its raison d'être, but to be effective it must aim at a multiplicity of goals. It should attract and involve most of the groups in the community. (2) In order to create self-respect through success, the program must be specific, immediate and feasible. (3) The organization must choose its means on the basis of what means are available and likely to be most effective. And (4) it must recognize and accept the fact that controversy has always been the 'seed of creation' and that it is inevitable that resentment will focus on the prevailing dominant interest of the status quo." It appears that certain aspects of this approach may be highly compatible with popular education.

The Contingency Approach. The reliance on a single approach to community development in support of popular education is rarely sufficient to maximize program impact in the context of multidimensional sociopolitical factors found in most communities. This is particularly the case in North America where there are long-established traditions of local political autonomy. Extreme caution must be exercised in the choice of an approach in Third World countries where the concept of community development may have a completely different meaning (Lyon, 1987).

Generally, three factors must be considered in the choice of the community development approach—values of the indigenous leaders, the nature of the local problem, and the characteristics of the community. In making this choice, the important skill is the ability to make a situational diagnosis and analysis that will reveal the approach most appropriate to the problem (Gurin, 1966). This action requires skills found in few adult educators and in only a limited number of popular educators (Buttedahl, 1985). Since the three basic approaches are not mutually exclusive, it seems logical to employ a contingency approach that incorporates all approaches into one strategy. Rothman (1979, p. 43) calls for a "mixing and phasing" of self-help, technical assistance, and conflict-based models, since many "problems require blending, and organizational structure may permit adaptations." The contingency approach not only relates to overall strategy but should be employed in the delivery of adult education. Goodnow (1982) provides a conceptual framework for determining the appropriateness of various methodologies along the pedagogy and andragogy continuum. She emphasizes that "the effectiveness of a methodology is contingent upon environmental characteristics" (p. 350).

An Opposing View: Popular Education as Distinct from Community Development

Persons from marginal communities or societies are extremely suspicious of community development models—even of those more recent models that insist on full participation of the community. One fundamental criticism is that community development seeks reformation, not transformation. The issue is not evolution or revolution but rather transformation. Popular education has a clear conceptual base, as shown by Cadena's four points cited earlier: Transformation begins with conscious appropriation of one's own reality. Those who are oppressed must recognize their oppression, initiate equitable resource allocation, develop the ability to define and defend the type of society that serves them best, and struggle to counter the hegemony of oppressive power relationships.

Self-help programs concentrate on pragmatic solutions to problems; they require neither transformation of the problem situation nor analysis of ways to reconstruct the power relationships. Civic educators, in most cases, do not start with a clear conceptual base, such as a theory of knowledge or of social conflict. Popular educators recognize that they cannot be neutral, a position important to civic education, according to Oliver (1987). And clearly Alinsky's (1971, p. 116) "rubbing raw the resentments of the people of the community" in order to counter citizen apathy is hardly a conceptual trumpet for transformation. In fact, action was central to Alinsky's model, and there was no call for education or for producing community knowledge to counter hegemony.

Wright (1988) observed a tenant management group in two public housing complexes in Chicago. One complex utilized a highly participatory, technical-assistance, community-development model; the other utilized participatory research and the popular education approach associated with it. Wright concluded that, while the technical-assistance model brought about change in the direction of tenant management, it was highly dependent on the university and settlement house that organized the effort. On the other hand, the participatory research model stimulated the tenant group to develop community-based education programs with conrol truly in the hands of the people. Although Wright did not espouse one form as being best, he clearly saw them as distinct from one another.

DeArruda (forthcoming) divides community education groups into voluntary agencies (such as Literacy Volunteers of America), community organizations (such as libraries or YMCAs offering educational programs) and grass-roots groups (community-based education controlled by participants). Fingeret (1983) recognized that literacy groups can be *in* or *with* the community. Many observers note distinctions among educational programs that spring from community development and those that have the emphasis on a popular movement to transform society.

Conclusion

In this chapter, community development and popular education have been described. Based on these descriptions, two different views were developed: community development and popular education are similar and should be interfaced to strengthen both; popular education is distinct from and in opposition to most community development models.

References

Alinsky, S. D. *Rules for Radicals.* New York: Random House, 1971.

Biddle, W. W., and Biddle, L. J. *The Community Development Process: The Rediscovery of Local Initiative.* New York: Holt, Rinehart & Winston, 1965.

Bourdieu, P., and Passeron, J. C. *Reproduction in Education, Society and Culture.* Beverly Hills, Calif.: Sage, 1977.

Buttedahl, P. "Training of Adult and Popular Educators in Latin America." *Convergence,* 1985, *18* (3-4), 94-102.

Cadena, F. "Popular Education and Peasant Movements for Change." *Convergence,* 1984, *27* (3), 31-36.

Cary, L. J. (ed.). *Community Development as a Process.* Columbia: University of Missouri Press, 1970.

Compton, J. L., and McClusky, H. J. "Community Education for Community Development." In E. J. Boone, R. W. Shearon, E. E. White, and Associates (eds.), *Serving Personal and Community Needs Through Adult Education.* San Francisco: Jossey-Bass, 1980.

DeArruda, E. "Patterns of Conflict in Community-Based Organizations of Inner City Chicago." Unpublished doctoral dissertation, Department of Leadership and Educational Policy Studies, Northern Illinois University, forthcoming.

Dore, R., and Mars, Z. (eds.). *Community Development.* London: Croom-Helm, 1981.

Fingeret, A. "Social Network: A New Perspective on Independence and Illiterate Adults." *Adult Education Quarterly,* 1983, *33* (3), 133-146.

Freire, P. *Pedagogy of the Oppressed.* New York: Seabury Press, 1978.

Giroux, H. A. "Theories of Reproduction and Resistance in the New Sociology of Education: A Critical Analysis." *Harvard Educational Review,* 1983, *53* (3), 257-292.

Goodnow, W. E. "The Contingency Theory of Education." *International Journal of Lifelong Education,* 1982, *1* (4), 341-352.

Gramsci, A. *Selections from the Prison Notebook.* New York: International Publishers, 1985.

Gurin, A. *Current Issues in Community Organization Practice and Education.* Brandeis University Reprint Series, no. 21. Waltham, Mass.: Florence Heller Graduate School for Advanced Studies in Social Welfare, 1966.

Hamilton, E. "Adult Education and Community Development in Nigeria." *Graduate Studies Journal,* 1984, *2,* 63–75.

Hernandez, I., and others. *Theoretical Contribution: Popular Education.* Buenos Aires: Third World Assembly of Adult Education, 1985.

Kerensky, V. M. "Ten Educational Myths: A Community Educator's Perspective." *Community Education Journal,* 1981, *8* (2), 9–13.

Long, H. B. (ed.). *Approaches to Community Development.* Iowa City, Iowa: American City Testing Program and National American University Extension Association, 1973.

Lyon, L. *The Community in Urban Society.* Philadelphia: Temple University Press, 1987.

McClusky, H. Y. "Community Development." In M. S. Knowles (ed.), *Handbook of Adult Education in the United States.* Washington, D.C.: Adult Education Association of the U.S.A., 1960.

Mezirow, J. D. "Community Development as an Educational Process." In *Community Development.* Selected Reading Series, no. 4. Washington, D.C.: National Training Laboratories, 1961.

Oliver, L. P. "Popular Education and Adult Civic Education: The Third World Is a Different Place." *Convergence,* 1987, *20,* 40–50.

Osorio, J. "Participatory Formation of Adult Educators Conference." Unpublished notes, Nairobi, Kenya, Sept. 1986.

Parajuli, P. "Grassroots Movements, Development Discourse and Popular Education." *Convergence,* 1986, *19* (2), 29–40.

Roberts, H. *Community Development: Learning and Action.* Toronto: University of Toronto, 1979.

Rose, S. C. "Saul Alinsky and His Critics." *Christianity and Crisis,* July 20, 1964, p. 145.

Rothman, J. "Three Models of Community Organization Practice, Their Mixing and Phasing." In F. M. Cox (ed.), *Strategies of Community Organization.* Itasca, Ill.: F. E. Peacock, 1979.

Sanders, I. T. "The Concept of Community Development." In L. J. Cary (ed.), *Community Development as a Process.* Columbia: University of Missouri Press, 1970.

Wright, L. "Participatory Research: A Study of Empowerment in Public Housing Through Resident Management." Unpublished doctoral dissertation, Department of Leadership and Educational Policy Studies, Northern Illinois University, 1988.

34

Public Affairs Education

Ronald M. Jimmerson
Laird W. Hastay
James S. Long

This chapter outlines the historical basis of adult public affairs education and features programs in the United States and Canada that provide information for adults who participate in making public decisions. The goal of the chapter is to enable adult educators to grasp three dimensions of public affairs education, to identify a range of choices, and to consider their professional role within public affairs education.

Roots of Public Affairs Education

In what is now the United States, the roots of adult education for civic participation in public policy-making go back to the New England town meeting—a little more than a decade after the Pilgrims' arrival in 1620. (See Chapter Three.) These town meetings were living laboratories where the American experiment in self-government began (Mathews, 1987). Offspring of the New Englanders' town meetings were the so-called committees of correspondence during the revolutionary war. The committees helped unite the disparate interests of the colonists by extending the practice of formulating and resolving public issues through careful citizen investigations and mutual decision making. (Mathews, 1987; Cooke, 1975; Oliver, 1983).

These colonial experiences began a pattern of adult education for civic purposes—a praxis combining (1) public consideration of current issues, (2) programs to increase citizens' ability to act collectively on issues, and (3) efforts to create institutional frameworks to perpetuate this acquired ability.

Each succeeding generation has witnessed an elaboration of this enduring praxis. The lyceum movement of the early nineteenth century, for instance, contained elements of general education for participation in public life. The last decades of the nineteenth century were the golden era of the Chautauqua movement, a revival of the ideal of a community-based, national network with an explicit goal of adult education for participation in issues of public life (Knowles, 1960; Oliver, 1983; Mathews, 1987). During the same era, the settlement house movement, as exemplified by Jane Addams's Hull House, set a standard for working with citizens of poor neighborhoods (Stubblefield, 1981).

Following the example of the University of Wisconsin's innovative program of statewide extension programs, the U.S. Congress passed the Smith-Lever Act in 1914 to authorize federal support for creating the Cooperative Extension Service to promote rural citizenship. The Progressive movement of the early 1900s extended suffrage to women and provided the initiative and referendum provisions in state constitutions—institutional changes that entailed a great deal of education before they enjoyed enough popular support to win approval.

Education to promote progressive attitudes outlasted the heyday of the progressive movement itself. One of the more enduring programs has been the efforts of the League of Women Voters. From local discussion groups to nationally televised debates with presidential candidates, the League has worked to broaden and to inform public participation in the business of running the republic.

Some other groups attract specific clientele who have not been active in traditional adult education programs or in public life or in either—groups such as the National Organization for Women, the La Raza movement, Citizen Action, some churches, labor unions, professional societies, environmental groups, and peace education lobbying organizations (Koek, Martin, and Novallo, 1988).

Modern Era Programs

Each program discussed in this section reflects elements of the philosophy of John Dewey. He held that experiential education for citizenship was necessary to ensure democracy's well-being and that all citizens, with appropriate opportunities, could learn to contribute to the American experiment in self-government. He believed that it is education's role to help universalize democratic habits of public deliberation and action. Dewey held that participation in self-government presupposes social and economic conditions that make such participation a practical possibility (Kazemek, 1984).

Adopting that orientation, Myles Horton, founder of Highlander Folk School, committed himself to working with the poor of Appalachia, whose poverty excluded them from full participation in civic life (Adams, 1975). Horton's career as an educator began during the latter part of John Dewey's professional life, and it extended well into an era when many reform-minded educators embraced the perspective of Brazilian adult educator and author Paulo Freire, whose work and thought likewise reflect Dewey's ideas. Horton's trust in people's ability to understand and to take charge of their lives reflected Dewey's influence, and his work at Highlander Folk School exemplified Freire's core idea that the experience of adult education should itself liberate learners whose lives have been characterized by civic passivity and impotence in the face of systematic oppression (Freire, 1970; 1973; Shor and Freire, 1987).

Highlander has liberated members of its learning community, often in subtle and unexpected ways. For instance, Horton discussed Highlander's early problem with whites who excluded blacks from their definition of community. The school was located in Tennessee, at that time a staunchly segregationist state. When black farmers showed up at Highlander for a gathering of farmers, several white farmers asked Myles what the blacks were doing there. He responded that perhaps the blacks were mixed up and had come to the wrong conference; he suggested that the white farmers "Go ask those guys if they are farmers or not." After confirming that they indeed were farmers, Myles told the slightly confused whites, "Oh good. I'm glad they're farmers; I sure wouldn't want to turn farmers away" (Horton, 1981). Such episodes that enlarge participants' views of community illustrate Horton's and Freire's commitment to education as a liberating experience.

Freire's immense reputation as an adult educator derives largely from his work as an adult literacy teacher and theorist. It is interesting, therefore, that Highlander's most famous educational program also began as an adult literacy campaign. It began in response to a request in the early 1950s from local leaders to help black residents of John's Island, South Carolina, learn to read and to write well enough to pass that state's stringent voter registration test. This effort eventually burgeoned into a network of Citizenship Schools throughout the Deep South; those schools had a major impact on the civil rights movement of the 1950s and 1960s (C. Tjerandsen, 1980).

By bringing local leaders from similar situations to Highlander, Horton was able to develop and to perfect a group learning process uniquely suited to the specific needs of the school's clientele. In line with John Dewey's theories and with Jane Addams' work, the school adopted a problem-oriented approach, relying on the learners' needs to determine the curriculum and on the learners' own experiences to create potential solutions. Teachers and learners educated each other in a learning community. As Horton said, "Education mushrooms when the students in one area become teachers in another" (E. Tjerandsen, 1983).

Highlander's Citizenship Schools identified community leaders, brought them together, and helped them teach each other how to be more effective adult educators and organizers when they returned home. From another perspective, Saul Alinsky and his Industrial Areas Foundation were less concerned with developing leaders' capabilities and more concerned with helping people gain citizenship skills through participation in community organizations (Alinsky, 1972; C. Tjerandsen, 1980). Just as Horton regarded leaders from the poor as his community of learners, Alinsky was committed to helping the have-nots of America learn skills to obtain their share of rights as citizens. Alinsky believed that people learn these skills when they are empowered—a result of being well enough organized to achieve victory in a conflict with the haves. His role was to help people identify issues they could win, so that by winning, they would understand their power to achieve change in their lives (Alinsky, 1972).

As organizers and teachers, Alinsky and his disciples emphasized tight and exhaustive communication within a community of learners. Immediate evaluations of each day's efforts to help a particular group or community organize effectively characterized the Alinsky curriculum. Achieving that would teach group members how to participate in a social and political system that otherwise would exclude them (Alinsky, 1972; C. Tjerandsen, 1980).

Alinsky had many notable successes before his untimely death in 1972. He organized the Back of the Yards community in Chicago during the depression, Hispanic communities in California during the 1950s, and the Woodlawn community near the University of Chicago during the sixties. However, he acknowledged that he was less successful at teaching other organizers his methods than he was at doing organizing work himself (C. Tjerandsen, 1980; Alinsky, 1972.)

Nevertheless, the Alinsky legacy lives on. His disciples and emulators continue to organize the downtrodden to confront a power elite that seems as determined as ever to retain its political and economic domination. The Industrial Areas Foundation, founded by Alinsky, is still actively teaching Alinsky's method. The Midwest Academy, in Chicago, has trained a new generation of activist educators committed to teaching communities of learners how to empower themselves through organized confrontations with the power structure. The Midwest Academy is the training arm of the national group Citizen Action, whose purpose is to build a national constituency for redistribution of political and economic power (Ohanian, 1988).

Horton accepted and Alinsky encouraged intergroup conflict and confrontation; but they both sought harmonious intragroup dynamics within their communities of learners. In contrast, other groups, such as the Foreign Policy Association and the Domestic Policy Association, have created programs in which all persons, including potential antagonists, can discuss issues in an atmosphere that encourages communication to preclude polarization.

The Great Decisions Program of the Foreign Policy Association and the National Issues forums of the Domestic Policy Association are somewhat reminiscent of Alexander Meiklejohn's San Francisco School of Social Studies, which he founded in 1933. This was a noncredit school for adults, whose curriculum and methods were derived from Meiklejohn's earlier Experimental College at the University of Wisconsin. Students studied a series of seminal works related to a theme being explored in one of the school's twenty or so classes. Students then compared the readings in small group discussions. Finally, students were expected to carry their new learning into the community and to engage in social or political work to practice what they had learned. The school was an early casualty of World War II, but Meiklejohn's emphasis on individual study, rigorous group analysis, and action has had its echoes in the postwar era (Powell, 1942).

Great Decisions and the National Issues forums reflect a confidence in the efficacy of civic public discourse to facilitate understanding of complex issues and resolution of otherwise seemingly intractable dilemmas. The programs exemplify Dewey's confidence in all citizens' ability to learn to contribute to democratic self-government. They also reflect his belief that small, open forums of citizens using rigorous group analysis to confront their common problems together are appropriate instruments for teaching democratic decision making (Jimmerson, 1977; Kazamek, 1984; Mathews, 1987; Oliver, 1983).

Along these lines, some people call for explicitly participatory democracy to complement representative democracy. A principal advocate, Benjamin Barber (1984, p. 117), called for a "strong democracy . . . a distinctively modern form of participatory democracy that rests on the idea of a self-governing community of citizens who are united less by homogeneous interests than by civic education and who are made capable of common purpose and mutual action by virtue of their civic attitudes and participatory institutions rather than their altruism or their good nature."

Both the Great Decisions and the National Issues Forums programs are clearly consistent with the goal of creating national institutions for participatory democracy. They differ from the more activist educational efforts of Alinsky, for instance, in the avoidance of confrontational methods of learning in favor of systematic but freewheeling dialogue within an inclusive community of learners. These two programs are similar to activist efforts in that they engage participants in some of the most contentious issues of our time. In this orientation, both programs adhere to Ziegler's (1976, p. 283) position that the "avoidance of public controversy—the reluctance to stand up and say your piece in public—is [a] withdrawal or . . . [an] adaptive strategy. We avoid public controversy when we no longer trust our fellow citizens, when we no longer believe they will learn to choose with us the right courses of action."

The Great Decisions Program began in 1955 and was profiled in the *1960 Handbook of Adult Education.* Designed to be a nationwide network of so-called living room forums, Great Decisions has helped a generation of concerned Americans become informed about international issues. In a seminar format, participants typically read a briefing article about the designated issue, then attend a public program in which they interact with experts and discuss the issue in small groups. Participants then may register their opinions by completing and mailing ballots to a public opinion consultant who, in turn, presents a summary to federal officials and to the national media (Oliver, 1983).

Begun in 1982, the National Issues Forums have treated a wide diversity of topics—retirement and social security, inflation, productivity, education, deficit spending, nuclear weaponry, health care costs, taxes, and relationships with the Soviet Union. The topics for 1986 were immigration, the farm crisis, and crime; for 1987, they were freedom of speech, the superpowers, and the trade gap, and for 1988 they were health care for the elderly, coping with AIDS, and the public debt—breaking the habit of deficit spending. Its yearly format includes reading nonpartisan issue books that present balanced overviews of opposing opinions on the chosen issues, viewing starter videotapes, and discussing policy issues in public forums and study circles led by local moderators. Representatives then communicate the outcomes of the programs to local, state, and national policymakers through an annual conference of citizen-policymakers at one of the presidential libraries. And during Washington Week, National Issues Forums participants go to Washington, D.C. to discuss their forums and study circles with congressional representatives and administration officials. The essence of National Issues forums is to work through an issue together on the local level, to examine the choices inherent in public issues, and to move from first opinions to more reflective second opinions that are then communicated to policymakers.

Family Community Leadership (FCL) represents a further elaboration of the concept of peer education. FCL was initiated in 1981 by the Western Region Extension Homemakers and the Cooperative Extension Services of several states. Together they received a grant from the W. K. Kellogg Foundation to develop educational programs that increase homemakers' ability to participate in public decisions that influence families.

The FCL board used a train-the-trainer approach; both trainers and trainees were homemakers, other community volunteers, and extension faculty. Training content included leadership skills, group process, public policy analysis and resolution strategies, volunteerism, and adult teaching techniques. State and regional institutes enabled local teams of trainers to replicate the training in local communities. Results represented several outcomes—personal development, personal activism, group formation, issue resolution, community building, and continuing institutional development. In 1987, FCL became a nationwide program cosponsored by the U.S. Department of Agriculture, state extension services, and the National Extension Homemakers Council.

Thus, FCL has become a nationwide laboratory for working through public issues important to families; it has become an exemplar of public affairs education that engages both professionals and volunteers as partners in learning and teaching; it has become an institution that captures the result of earlier trials and forges new public affairs education opportunities for others and for the future (Young, 1985).

Another illustration of new partnerships for public affairs education is the Washington Agriculture and Forestry Leadership Program (WAFLP). It follows a long tradition of public affairs leadership development (Howell,

1977). The WAFLP Foundation was established in 1977, and, since 1978, has sponsored a two-year program for thirty new participants each year.

Participants are selected from young adult men and women in the agricultural and forestry industries who have demonstrated leadership skills or potential. The first year includes a series of residential seminars and a national traveling seminar that focuses on policy-making processes within rural and urban communities and interest groups. The second year includes another seminar series and an international study tour in selected countries to foster understanding of public affairs issues as they relate to the United States. A distinct feature of WAFLP is that it involves both emerging and incumbent leaders from the public arenas of agriculture and forestry and it draws upon the resources of educational institutions and governments— all key actors of the arenas in which the substantive public issues themselves are considered.

Another distinct kind of public affairs education is Ziegler's so-called futures-invention within civic literacy programs. The emphasis is not so much on current issues or on applying earlier ideals in today's society; instead, the emphasis is on collectively projecting a desired future and inventing it (Ziegler, Healy, and Ellsworth, 1976). An example of such a program is the Alternatives for Washington program of the 1970s whereby a governor's office contracted with an outside consulting firm to facilitate citizen involvement in developing recommendations for community and state action (Cook and Wardwell, 1978; Wardwell and Dellman, 1975).

The Role of Media

Information-age technologies can help build communities among learners who do not live in close physical proximity. This ability presents new challenges to public affairs educators. But again, earlier experiments offer alternatives and guidance. The Courses by Newspaper program in the 1970s, underwritten by the National Endowment for the Humanities, focused readers on public issues such as food policies. Broadcast radio has been used for decades in Canada as a technique for public affairs education. An example is Canada's National Farm Radio Forum (Faris, 1975). And Canada's National Film Board has supported the use of television for community policy development. The Challenge for Change program offered assistance to local communities to videotape interviews with residents about their aspirations for their communities; the recordings were consolidated and shown for communitywide forums. The forums, in turn, defined a consensus from which new public initiatives for development emerged (Henaut, 1971; McGechaen, 1971).

An early example of the use of interactive cable television comes from an experiment in 1973 dubbed the electronic town hall. The Multiple Input Network for Evaluating Reactions, Votes, and Attitudes—MINERVA— utilized cable television to provide information and perspectives to residents of a housing project, for example. Feedback from residents was facilitated through a variety of means such as on-site video cameras, telephone conferences, and "telepollers" (Castleman and Doty, 1973).

More recently, interactive television has been used successfully in pilot projects on both coasts, according to Barber (1984), who believes that the potential of this new technology justifies using it nationally despite its inherent risks. Many social and economic problems are national in scope and their solutions require national constituencies. The need to store high-level nuclear wastes safely for the next several thousand years is a modern problem that requires a national commitment to its resolution. Considering Yucca Flats, Utah; Hanford, Washington; and Deaf Smith County, Texas, for this dubious honor generated nationwide interest—mainly in the form of largely uncoordinated local activity. Resolving this issue democratically may require a series of national town meetings—an idea that may now be possible.

Interactive radio and television "space bridges" are bringing together Russians and Americans who have become a new, international public for peaceful resolution of issues between the two superpowers (Demac, 1986). One relatively new citizens' group, Beyond War, uses space bridges to help break the mass assumption that war is rational or inevitable (Faludi, 1987).

Computer networks have spawned electronic bulletin boards through which persons involved in public policy activities seek out and obtain information. For instance, lobbyists request detailed, technical information from such networks without having to know whom to ask. Similarly, lobbyists inform organizations about legislative and bureaucratic developments (Horvitz, 1986).

Potential problems abound with electronic telecommunications as a teaching device in civic participation education. Barber (1984) noted that the advantages of face-to-face encounters between potential antagonists may be muted by electronic mediation. Electronic forums are expensive and technically complex, a situation that suggests the danger of elite dominance of this medium. Nevertheless, Barber believes that the use of electronic telecommunications to broaden public participation is attractive and that educators should prepare to deal with potential problems in order to realize the benefits of media in education.

Adult Educators' Choices

For adult educators in public affairs education, the programs described above illustrate important choices related to the three major elements of public affairs education as defined here: directly engaging citizens in current public issues, developing programs to increase citizens' ability to act collectively on issues, and creating institutions to perpetuate this acquired capacity. This section highlights some of these choices, their relationships, and a range of options.

Issue Choices

Public affairs education involves a choice of public issues. The sample programs illustrate three types of options.

Philosophy and Goal. A wide range of philosophies and goals influence the choice of public issues around which an adult educator may develop a program. For instance, some adult educators—revolutionary adult educators—assume a need for major change in the structure of society to overcome an imbalance between the haves and have-nots. Others, who may be called functionalists, assume that structures of society are basically sound but that citizens need training to use the system better.

Alinsky and Horton leaned toward the revolutionary orientation. Their goal was to help the poor and disenfranchised gain more power to overcome a system that forced them into poverty and powerlessness. On the other hand, Meiklejohn's school, the Foreign Policy Association's Great Decisions Program, the Washington Agriculture and Forestry Leadership Program, and the Family Community Leadership program tend to focus on helping people gain skills so they can better use the system for their own purposes. While these two orientations are not mutually exclusive, adult educators need to be clear about their decisions. Are educators attempting to help people gain skills to use the system better? Are they helping people to develop new institutions or to change existing structures in society? Or are they pursuing more than one goal? Conclusions about these questions influence the choice of issues for public affairs education.

Clientele. Closely related to the philosophical choice is the decision about the clientele of public affairs education. Horton and Alinsky saw a world in which some people have great resources and others have little. They aligned themselves with the have-nots. Other educators work primarily with mainstream groups.

Another way to view clientele focus is to note that Highlander and the Washington Agriculture and Forestry Leadership Program work with community leaders while other programs attempt to reach ordinary citizens directly. Other distinctions relate to whether programs view specific groups or a generalized community as their clientele. Some deal with homogeneous groups such as the rural poor; others (the Great Decisions Program is an example) serve a heterogeneous mix. Decisions about the program clientele influence the issue focus because the substantive issue itself is defined by the parties interested in that issue.

Time Orientation. A third dimension that illustrates differences in the issue focus relates to the emphasis on past knowledge and wisdom of society, current societal issues, or a view of a desired future society. For example, Meiklejohn's school was in the so-called classical movement within U.S. academic circles. Its basic premise was that all citizens should learn from the classics and should put these ideas to work in dealing with current issues.

This approach is quite different from Highlander's where the issues chosen grew out of the experience of peoples' lives. National Issues Forums and Ziegler's futures-invention represent yet a third perspective; the issue is determined more by citizen's views of a desired future toward which public affairs programs work.

Again, these perspectives are not mutually exclusive, but a clear preference for one approach is seen in each of the sample programs; each identifies an approach to defining the public affairs issue.

Action Choices

A second major choice in public affairs education relates to adult educators helping learners take group action related to public issues. Three dimensions relate to the action dimension.

Use of Conflict. Because public affairs inherently involves disagreements, conflict is a given in these educational programs. Horton, for example, did not advocate conflict per se, but he recognized that his clients' actions might well lead to conflict with power groups they challenge. Alinsky, on the other hand, saw successful confrontations with the power structure by the have-nots as an essential method to learn skills for empowerment. The Foreign Policy Association and the Domestic Policy Association promote discussion of potentially divisive issues in an inclusive atmosphere that encourages communication to demarcate areas of consensus. Each approach represents an alternative view on the use of conflict.

Experiential Learning. While all public affairs education as defined here involves learning by taking action on issues, the relative emphasis and the timing of the experiential learning vary. Meiklejohn's approach placed emphasis on rigorous academic study first, followed by experiential learning through pragmatic application. Family Community Leadership provides short lessons through workshops where participants practice the skills before returning to their community to work with others. Great Decisions and National Issues Forums are experiential in that participants discuss with peers and experts, then register their opinions with public opinion consultants or decision makers. Alinsky and Horton used experiential learning a great deal because they relied on the learners' experiences for their curricula.

Peer Education. Public affairs education involves helping citizens—professionals and volunteers alike—learn from each other. The scope and intensity of peer education vary, and these differences pose choices for adult educators. Should peer education be built in as a part of planning to learn basic concepts, as in Family Community Leadership? Should volunteers learn skills so they can return to their communities to teach others? Is peer education used only to the extent of having peers discuss issues and work out compromises?

Institutional Framework Choices

The third element of the praxis of public affairs education is institutionalizing learning opportunities for citizens who deal with public concerns. This quote attributed to Thomas Paine catches this element: ''In the progress of politics as in the common occurrences of life, we are not only apt to forget the ground we have traveled over, but frequently neglect to gather up experience as we go.'' Public affairs educators can help gather up experiences in several ways: (1) by strengthening the capacity of existing institutions, for example, citizenship schools, churches, and university extension, (2) by combining institutions in new ways, as was done in creating Family Community Leadership, and (3) by creating new institutions out of educational programs—neighborhood associations or consumer organizations, for example.

These institutional choices for public affairs educators and for their clientele relate to their responses to questions such as the following: Are current institutions meeting the public affairs educational needs in an ongoing way? Can those institutions that are not meeting learners' needs be changed to do better? Can and should new institutions be invented as the image of the community changes?

These three types of choices—issue, action, and institutional building—imply a variety of roles that public affairs educators can play. An educator might become an expert on a substantive issue, an advocate for a client group, a historian or a futurist, a facilitator of individuals and groups strengthening their analytic skills, or an institution builder to assure continuity and continued support of citizen efforts. Any of these roles may help citizens identify important public issues, promote citizen capacity to deal collectively with those issues, and enhance institutions that perpetuate a people's capacity to inform their discretion.

Continued Learning for Adult
Educators in Public Affairs Education

This chapter highlights some of the complex, intricate sets of choices in public affairs education. The chapter also illustrates earlier successes that might bolster the confidence of other venturesome adult educators.

Another bit of assurance comes from recognizing the ongoing opportunities for adult educators to continue their own learning in this area—reading the growing literature (as sampled in the reference section of this chapter) or studying the orientation materials and participating in workshops for professional programmers and volunteer facilitators.

Philanthropic foundations provide continuing support for adult educators. For example, the Farm Foundation (1988), since 1970, has helped sponsor an annual national public policy education conference and has produced its proceedings—*Increasing Understanding of Public Problems and Policies*.

With support from foundations, institutions such as Cooperative Extension offer yet other opportunities. New training materials, entitled "Working with Our Publics, Inservice Education for Cooperative Extension," were introduced nationally in 1988. The project, supported by the W. K. Kellogg Foundation, was directed by Edgar J. Boone, professor of adult education, North Carolina State University. One segment, authored by Verne House of Montana and Ardis Armstrong Young from Washington State, focused on "Education for Public Decisions."

Adult educators, themselves, are coming together to sponsor their own continuing education. One example is the 1988 conference of the International League for Social Commitment in Adult Education near Toronto, Canada. Another encouraging trend is the emerging university-based preservice education programs. An example of this trend is the Agriculture and Liberal Arts Programs and their courses on policy analysis at the University of Florida, Washington State University, and elsewhere.

Finally, to define further the dimensions of public affairs education, adult educators in North America can look to their colleagues' experiments in other disciplines, such as developmental anthropology (James, 1988) and in other countries (Miller, 1985). One internationally acclaimed example of citizenship education occurred in Nicaragua in 1980. Fulfilling a promise made in the closing days of the national insurrection against the Somoza dictatorship, Nicaragua's revolutionary leaders launched a massive adult literacy campaign during their first year in power. By mobilizing some 100,000 teachers, students, and other volunteers, the campaign was able to reach virtually every village in the country. In a five-month campaign, the nation's illiteracy rate dropped from 40 to 13 percent. Furthermore, the campaign introduced the people of urban and rural Nicaragua to each other, a secondary effect that did as much as the literacy campaign to help create a new Nicaraguan national citizenry (Miller, 1985).

In short, adult educators face complex choices when developing public affairs curricula, but they enjoy a rich heritage of experience; they have companions; they can access an increasingly sophisticated literature; they can participate in preservice and in-service education opportunities worldwide.

And for adult educators who personally believe in experiential learning as an integral part of public affairs education, Barber (1984, p. 152) offers this perspective: "Community grows out of participation and at the same time makes participation possible; civic activity educates individuals how to think publicly as citizens even as citizenship informs civic activity with the required sense of publicness and justice. Politics becomes its own university, citizenship its own training ground, and participation its own tutor. Freedom is what comes out of this process, not what goes into it."

References

Adams, F. *Unearthing Seeds of Fire: The Idea of Highlander.* Winston-Salem, N.C.: John F. Blair, 1975.

Alinsky, S. *Rules for Radicals: A Practical Primer for Realistic Radicals.* New York: Random House, 1972.

Barber, B. R. *Strong Democracy: Participatory Politics for a New Age.* Berkeley: University of California Press, 1984.

Barrows, R. *Public Policy Education, Key Concepts and Methods.* North Central Regional Extension Publication, no. 203. Ames: Cooperative Extension Service, Iowa State University, 1982.

Castleman, N., and Doty, P. *Center for Policy Research—The First Five Years 1968-73.* New York: Center for Policy Research, 1973.

Cook, A. K., and Wardwell, J. M. "Population Policies and Public Opinion." *Social Science Quarterly,* 1978, *58* (4), 683-691.

Cooke, A. *America.* New York: Knopf, 1975.

Demac, D. A. "On Global TV." *Whole Earth Review,* March 10, 1986, pp. 26-29.

Faludi, S. "Inner Peaceniks." *Mother Jones,* April 1987, pp. 20-26, 51-53.

Faris, R. *The Passionate Educators: Voluntary Associations and the Struggle for Control of Adult Educational Broadcasting in Canada 1919-1952.* Richmond Hill, Ont.: Irwin, 1975.

Farm Foundation. *Increasing Understanding of Public Problems and Policies—1987.* Oak Brook, Ill.: Farm Foundation, 1988.

Freire, P. *Pedagogy of the Oppressed.* New York: Seabury Press, 1970.

Freire, P. *Education for Critical Consciousness.* New York: Seabury Press, 1973.

Henaut, D. T. "The Media: Powerful Catalyst for Community Change." In J. Niemi (ed.), *Mars Media and Adult Education.* Englewood Cliffs, N.J.: Educational Technology Publications, 1971.

Horton, M. "Bill Moyers Journal: The Adventures of a Radical Hillbilly, Part Two." Interview by B. Moyers. New York: WNET/Thirteen, Educational Broadcasting Corporation, 1981.

Horvitz, R. "The Public Matter of Electronic Privacy." *Whole Earth Review,* Dec. 2, 1986, pp. 99-105.

House, V. M. *Shaping Public Policy: The Educators' Role.* Bozeman, Mont.: Westridge, 1981.

House, V. W., and Young, A. A. *Education for Public Decisions.* Working with Our Publics, Inservice Education for Cooperative Extension, Module 6. Raleigh, N.C.: North Carolina Agricultural Extension Service, 1988.

Howell, R. E. "Four Kellogg Foundation-Assisted Leadership Development Programs—An Assessment." In R. J. Hildreth (ed.), *Increasing Understanding of Public Problems and Policies—1979.* Oak Brook, Ill.: Farm Foundation, 1977.

James, C. "People and Projects in Development Anthropology: A Literacy Project in Madhya Pradesh, India." Unpublished doctoral dissertation, Department of Anthropology, Washington State University, 1988.

Jimmerson, R. M. "The Relationship Between the Adult Educator's Self-Actualization and Growth in Community Problem Solving Groups." Unpublished doctoral dissertation, Continuing and Vocational Education Department, University of Wisconsin, Madison, 1977.

Kazemek, F. E. "Adult Literacy Education and Ethical Endeavor." Washington, D.C.: Educational Resources Information Clearinghouse, 1984. (EO 239 043)

Knowles, M. "Historical Development of the Adult Education Movement." In M. Knowles (ed.), *1960 Handbook of Adult Education.* Washington, D.C.: Adult Education Association of the U.S.A., 1960.

Koek, K. E., Martin, S. B., and Novallo, A. (eds.). *Encyclopedia of Associations.* (22nd ed.) Detroit, Mich.: Gale Research, 1988.

McGechaen, A. "The Role of the National Film Board in the Development of Adult Education Programs in the Province of British Columbia: 1942 to 1960." Unpublished master's thesis, Administrative, Adult and Higher Education Department, University of British Columbia, 1971.

Mathews, D. *Democracy: Principles and Practices—A Source Book for Use with the National Issues Forums.* Dayton, Ohio: Kettering Foundation, 1987.

Miller, V. *Between Struggle and Hope: The Nicaraguan Literacy Crusade.* Boulder, Colo.: Westview Press, 1985.

Ohanian, B. "Troublemakers in Training." *Mother Jones,* Jan. 1988, pp. 39–46.

Oliver, L. P. *The Art of Citizenship: Public Issue Forums.* Dayton, Ohio: Kettering Foundation, 1983.

Powell, J. W. *School for Americans.* New York: American Association for Adult Education, 1942.

Shor, I., and Freire, P. *Pedagogy for Liberation.* Granby, Mass.: Bergin & Garvey, 1987.

Stubblefield, H. W. "Continuing Education for Community Problem Solving: A Historical Perspective." In H. W. Stubblefield (ed.), *Continuing Education for Community Leadership.* San Francisco: Jossey-Bass, 1981.

Tjerandsen, C. *Education for Citizenship: A Foundation's Experience.* Santa Cruz, Calif.: Emil Schwartzhaupt Foundation, 1980.

Tjerandsen, E. "The Highlander Heritage: Education for Social Change." *Convergence: An International Journal of Adult Education,* 1983, *16* (2), 10–21.

Wardwell, J., and Dellman, D. *Alternatives for Washington.* Vol. 6: *Public Communication and Survey Phase Results.* Olympia, Wash.: Office of Program Planning and Fiscal Management, 1979.

Young, A. A. "Value Change of Adult Learners in the Washington Family-Community-Leadership Program." Unpublished doctoral dissertation, Department of Educational Administration and Supervision, Washington State University, 1985.

Ziegler, W. L. "The Life of the Public and the Life of Learning." *Adult Leadership,* April 1976, *24* (8), pp. 254–256, 281–284.

Ziegler, W. L., Healy, G. M., and Ellsworth, J. H. "Futures-Invention: An Approach to Civic Literacy." In C. Klevins (ed.), *Materials and Methods in Continuing Education.* New York: Klevens Publications, 1976.

35

Adult Basic Education

Maurice C. Taylor

In North America, *adult basic education* is a generic term used to denote the building blocks of the lifelong learning structure. Basic education refers to the fundamental areas of reading, writing, listening, speaking, and mathematics. These basic areas of communication and computation are the foundation that gives individuals the power and freedom to control their own lives and to meet the demands of an ever-changing society. With the provision of these skills, the building of a basic education is possible.

In the United States and Canada, the rubric *adult literacy and basic education* connotes a field of practice that includes programs of adult basic education (ABE) and, in some communities, English as a second language (ESL). ABE usually aims not only at developing competence with printed English, but also at computational and other coping skills. As described in Chapter Thirty-Seven, the main emphasis in ESL is on teaching conversational skills and, more recently, on teaching reading.

Delker (1984) conducted a study to determine the status of adult literacy programs funded by the state-administered programs of the Adult Education Act (Public Law 91-230). He concluded that the act supported three distinct programs: (1) ABE, (2) adult secondary education (ASE) or high school completion, and (3) ESL. In Canada, under the British North American Act of 1867, education became a provincial responsibility. Therefore, adult literacy and basic education in Canada is the exclusive responsibility of the ten provinces and two territories. Each has a slightly different mechanism for the delivery of specific instruction, but, generally, basic education refers to courses and programs designed to develop the knowledge and skills necessary for an adult to function in modern society. These programs include adult basic literacy and numeracy, high school equivalency, citizenship training, instruction in English as a second language and, in some provinces, French as a second language. In both the United States and Canada, ESL literacy is becoming a linking component between separately administered ABE and ESL programs. In Canada, ASE or high school equivalency, which provides the credentials for job entry or further training, is usually delivered under the auspices of an adult basic education or adult retraining department in a community college, or in an adult day school in a board of education, or through a correspondence course offered by a ministry of education.

Toward an Operational Definition of Literacy

Over the past decade, researchers and practitioners in North America have been involved in a rigorous debate over the key term of *adult literacy* and over related terms such as *literacy, general literacy, functional literacy,* and *functional competency*. As Harman (1987, p. 3) suggests, "The attempt to define literacy is like a walk to the horizon: as one walks towards it, it continuously recedes. Similarly, as groups of people achieve the skills formerly defined as literacy, altered circumstances often render definitions obsolete. New definitions replace the old ones as new goals are set. People considered literate by a previous yardstick are now regarded as illiterate. The term functional literacy, invented to distinguish advanced concepts of literacy has itself become a variable lending itself to constant redefinition." Aker and Aker (1987) explain that, as with many complex concepts, literacy is not something one arrives at or becomes perfect in; rather, it is a goal that one must continuously move toward. In a similar manner, Lytle, Marmor, and Penner (1986) explain that the best definition, at least in terms of accurately reflecting the social and cultural nature of literacy, would be those that emanate from individually defined goals and purposes and those that view literacy as a process rather than a product. As Fingeret (1984, p. 9) points out, "to establish a national set of standards for a concept that is relative in relation to time and culture, will to some extent, undermine efforts to develop literacy programs that are appropriate to the varying needs of adults in their social contexts."

Although there is no commonly accepted definition of adult literacy, according to Cervero (1985), one can detect an increasingly common element in many definitions proposed in the last fifteen years. Most current definitions have broadened the scope of literacy beyond reading and writing skills and describe it in terms of an adult's ability to function within a social context. Viewed in this light, literacy is not something that can be measured in an absolute sense, but it can be measured in a relative sense. Adding to this relativistic definition, Draper (1986, p. 22) claims that "For literacy education to become truly functional, one would have to identify the skills and knowledge an individual would need to have in order to effectively function in one's society. To this extent, functional literacy is individualized and is defined and characterized by a social, economic and cultural context. It includes, as well, the expectations that one has of self and society." In a recent Canadian literacy study, Nesbitt (1987) also suggests that the determination of a required literacy level can be from a societal perspective or from the individual's perspective whereby the ultimate criterion would be individual self-actualization. In a similar vein, Valentine (1986) maintains that if functional literacy is to be more than a decoration, it must be distinguishable from general literacy. Supporting the notion of contextual or environmental literacy demands, he argues that general literacy can be expressed in terms of an adult's reading and writing ability without considering the broader context, while functional literacy "must be expressed as an individual's ability in relation to the reading and writing tasks by, or existing in, the environment in which that individual resides and seeks to function (p. 109).

Because of the pluralism of North American values, a common operational definition may not be feasible, but, as Thomas (1989) points out, there appears to be more or less general agreement on some of the underlying principles of adult literacy. First, grade level completion measures are inadequate for definitional purposes. Second, there is a literacy continuum ranging from the mechanisms of learning how to decode and encode to the mature utilization of literacy skills and processes for informed action and aesthetic appreciation. Third, with a few exceptions, there is general agreement with the principle that literacy should be defined as the ability of individuals to function within a specific social, economic, or cultural context. Fourth, in an increasingly technological and changing North American society, literacy thresholds are likely to be in a continuing state of flux.

Mikulecky (1987, p. 213) explains that, "Since literacy appears to be more in the nature of changing relationships than measurable quantities, it is unlikely that anyone will arrive at an acceptable level or criterion allowing one to accurately and usefully state the number of illiterates. It may be more useful to define functional literacy for individuals and specific communities at a particular time." Despite the current weaknesses in inadequate research, data, and definitions, it is enough to know that the major research efforts that have been made tend to verify each other in the finding that the problem is staggering. One recent event in the United States that focused national attention on the topic of adult illiteracy was the announcement of the Adult Literacy Initiative in 1983. This initiative, carried out by the U.S. Department of Education, emphasized the importance of the role of volunteers in adult literacy education. The initiative was designed to promote collaboration between the public and private sectors in order to offer literacy training more effectively and economically to those who seek and need it. Vines (1983) reports that two specific programs encouraged the use of volunteers: college work-study programs and the establishment of the Federal Employee Literacy Training Program. The initiative also attempted to increase cooperation among Federal agencies and to promote greater efforts among states and localities to address problems of adult literacy. Two major criticisms of the initiative were that such activities are superficial responses to a severe problem and that funding is needed for operating programs rather than for supporting advertising campaigns. In Canada, several national organizations have been working toward the eradication of illiteracy. One such networking and advocacy organization is the Movement for Canadian Literacy (MCL). It is unique in Canada among adult education and literacy organizations in that its sole focus is literacy and its membership includes people from all other organizations of literacy practitioners in Canada. A central objective of the organization is to promote, to support, and to encourage the development of local bases for developing literacy education that meets the self-determined needs of learners. Major work has been accomplished by the MCL in four central areas: a literacy information and resource network, learner conferences, public awareness, and a forum for policy discussions.

The Source of Learners

The continuous need to provide basic skills education to adults in North America comes primarily from two sources. First, like most developed nations, both the United States and Canada continue to receive immigrants and refugees who have little or no understanding of English (Mocker, 1986). According to Huyck and Bouvier (1983), over two-thirds of the refugees who have immigrated to the United States legally since 1975 have come from Southeast Asia. For the most part, the first wave of these refugees consisted of individuals who had been educated in their first language and who had previously worked for Western firms. Because most of these immigrants were highly motivated by the need to survive in a foreign land, this population was not difficult to recruit and to teach in formal and traditional educational programs. But the more recent arrivals who have entered since 1980 generally have had little or no schooling, are semiliterate or nonliterate in any language, and never have held positions in a Western setting (Longfield, 1984). As Penfield (1986) maintains, there is growing evidence that this latter group of new refugees is encountering very serious adjustment problems in resettlement, in the acquisition of English oral and writing skills, and in obtaining employment. The 1987 Southam Literacy Survey, which defined functional literacy as the ability to read, write, and use numbers well enough to meet the demands of today's society, reported that large-scale immigration accounts for about 1.0 million of Canada's 4.5 million adult functional illiterates. The literacy survey also confirmed high illiteracy among older immigrants. Nearly half of the immigrants who came to Canada at thirty years of age or older are functionally illiterate—double the rate among those who arrived at age nineteen or younger.

Native-born Americans and Canadians are the second source of learners for adult literacy and basic education. Native-born adults who are classified as adult basic education students can be divided into two categories. According to Mocker (1986), the first category is made up of those who have developed some proficiency in the basic skills and want to earn a high school equivalent degree. This group of learners have developed operative basic skills and now seek out expansion, specialization, and refinement. These are individuals who are ready to enter a General Educational Development (GED) program to pursue grade twelve equivalency. The second category of native-born ABE students can be classified as functionally illiterate (Mocker, 1986). These are individuals who have marginal skills in reading, writing, and mathematics. They are adults who have difficulty coping with everyday tasks. In Canada, until a few years ago, the term ABE covered the grades normally associated with elementary schooling—grades one through eight. More recently, the term has been expanded to cover the grade spectrum from one through twelve. Within this ABE range, the lower grade levels are designated for adult literacy training (Thomas, 1983).

In the United States, several national surveys on adult literacy have been conducted. The Bureau of Census in 1986 conducted a test consisting of twenty-six reading tasks considered by the researchers to be essential for adults living in the United States (Harman, 1987, p. 30). The bureau claimed that the functionally illiterate adult population numbers between seventeen million and twenty-one million. Using different criteria, another study, by the University of Texas, identified sixty-five objectives considered necessary for adult life and produced batteries of exercises to examine proficiency in accomplishing them. Results placed the number of functionally illiterate between twenty-three million and fifty-seven million, depending on the reading tasks thought necessary. This difference between the two studies reflects the search for clarity around the issue of fundamental requirements of adult roles and functions and the need for a benchmark for functional literacy.

The 1987 Southam Literacy Survey (Nesbitt, 1987) indicated that 4.5 million Canadians are so confounded by printed and written information that they have difficulty coping. The research found 8 percent of the adult population to be basically illiterate and 16 percent to be functionally illiterate. In 1985, the National Assessment of Educational Progress (NAEP) administered fifty-nine literacy questions to 3,538 Americans, ages twenty-one to twenty-five. In the 1987 Southam Literacy Survey, the same tasks were adapted slightly for 334 Canadians in the same age range in the national survey of 2,398 adults. Both in terms of general reading proficiency and in the use of everyday documents such as bus schedules and the telephone book yellow pages, young Americans scored higher than young Canadians (Calamai, 1987). The two groups were roughly equal in understanding prose, while Canadians tested slightly higher when working with numbers. Overall, the U.S. youth scored 78 percent correct, compared with 74 percent for Canadians. Calamai also states that another difference between the two groups was the high school dropout rate. Roughly 25 percent of the young Canadians did not finish high school—nearly double the U.S. average. Youth on both sides of the border performed reasonably well on school-type reading but had trouble with real-life written materials that required more complicated information processing, for example, finding headings in the telephone book yellow pages or summarizing general themes.

Although some researchers claim that it is virtually impossible to attach a responsible figure to the phenomenon, some definite trends can be noted. According to Harman (1987), illiteracy is highest among those with less than a complete high school education, among members of ethnic minority groups, in regions of the country with high unemployment, and among the economically disadvantaged. In each of these populations, illiteracy is but one defining characteristic interacting with other manifestations of disadvantage. When analyzing such trends, caution should be used in order not to jump to a conclusion that all minority members or all of those not completing high school or all unemployed or all incarcerated are illiterate. It is interesting to note that in the recent Southam Literacy Survey, it was found that students no longer drop out of school because their parents need them to help at home or on the farm. Half of those ages eighteen to thirty-four mentioned boredom, lack of interest in education, or wanting to work as their reasons for dropping out. Another 20 percent blamed the school system.

English as a Second Language Literacy Programs. In both Canada and the United States, there has been an increasing awareness that a number of English as a second language (ESL) learners have specific needs relating to literacy in English. Penfield (1986) reports that there are various approaches to ESL literacy instruction in adult education. Some basic skills education programs delay ESL literacy training until a degree of oral proficiency has been achieved, while others integrate the teaching of all three skills of speaking, reading, and writing concurrently (Ranard, 1984). Although there is no available research on the strengths or limitations of the different approaches, experience suggests better achievement results when courses separate learners by literacy levels. In classes of students with various language proficiency levels, the demands are greater upon the nonliterate ESL learners. Anxiety is heightened because nonliterate individuals are placed at such a great disadvantage in comparison with other students.

Penfield (1986) maintains that some research evidence suggests that nonliterate, unschooled, limited-English-proficient adults encounter difficulty acquiring both a second language and initial literacy in a classroom setting. In a study of refugees in Canada, D'Anglejan (1984) compared the successful and unsuccessful adult learners. The investigation revealed that low levels of schooling, marginal literacy or illiteracy, and high levels of anxiety characterized the unsuccessful adult learner. She also found that unsuccessful learners tend to be from rural backgrounds and consequently have difficulty adjusting to urban conditions. Those who failed to acquire the second language generally had experienced little contact with native speakers of that language; their primary contact with the language was in the classroom where it had been treated as an academic subject rather than as a meaningful tool for students to accomplish tasks in their own lives. D'Anglejan (1984, p. 22) reported that, ''Those with little or no schooling, may be accustomed to acquiring important skills and knowledge in settings very different from classrooms where active participation in tasks and tacit observation of the performance of others are the privileged modes of learning.'' As Penfield (1986) suggests, based on such evidence, language learning for such a population may result in higher success rates if it were to take place in nonacademic, nonformal settings based more precisely on refugees' needs. One approach may be to relate employment and ESL literacy acquisition (See Chapter Thirty-Seven.)

Adult Literacy and Basic Education Programs. In the United States, a great many literacy programs in numerous settings use a multitude of curricula and varied instructional approaches and cater to diverse groups. Thomas (1983) reported that the ABE professionals in Canada are inclined to use an eclectic approach based on adaptations and modifications of methods from various sources. She concluded that no single highly specialized method secured superior results in teaching illiterates. More recently, research at the Calgary Reading and Language Centre came to the same conclusion after directly comparing the Laubach phonetic approach with the whole language approach, which avoids phonics as much as possible (Calamai, 1987). Collectively, these experiences provide proof of only one point— there is no one correct way, no best way, to teach basic skills. As people and the communities they live in change, so too must the educational programs designed to meet their requirements.

As previously mentioned, native-born adults who can be classified as ABE students are divided into two categories: those with marginal skills and those who have developed some proficiency in the basic skills. Both categories participate in various forms of ABE classes. Classes at the lower levels of ability are composed largely of minority-group adults, many of whom are school dropouts. Their participation in ABE is an attempt to break the cycle of poverty and disadvantage in which they find themselves, but the attempt is often frustrating. They are constantly subjected to pressures that conflict with regular participation, and family and friends are not always actively supportive of their participation. Since the groups are usually heterogenous, they are limited in their ability to provide meaningful support (Harman, 1987, pp. 81–82).

Classes of ABE learners who have developed some proficiency in basic skills exhibit greater durability. This group is made up of people with higher ability and prior formal schooling. They are motivated to attend a program as a precondition to taking courses that lead to a high school equivalency certificate (GED), or grade twelve equivalency in Canada. Students view this certificate as important because it has some labor market value or because it provides entrance into further skill training.

Some programs for both types of ABE learners have been more effective than others. An appropriate educational program is one that caters to a specific group of participants, deriving its content and methods from individual needs such as the adult competency-based education approach. Crandall, Lerche, and Marchilonis (1984) reported that characteristics of a successful program include clarity about overall goals and philosophy of instruction, explicitness about intended learning outcomes including standards for judging success in achieving these outcomes, careful diagnosis of educational needs of individual learners, provision of frequent feedback to learners on their progress toward learning objectives, and frequent evaluation of program effectiveness in meeting goals. A study conducted by Philips and Ballorado (1985), which analyzed data from various ABE programs (including programs focused on the military, prisons, job skill centers, and libraries, as well as ESL and community-based programs) concluded that the teacher's attitude of respect for the learners' backgrounds and experiences also was crucial to program effectiveness.

It is a fact that some ABE programs are able to sustain participation and generate learning, while others experience high dropout rates. The literature on participation in adult education is abundant and provides many useful insights for the program planner (Duke, 1985; Scalan, 1986; Charner and Fraser, 1986). A particular study by Bova (1985) analyzed the reasons for adult participation in ABE programs using the Education Participation Scale. Students involved in the study attended classes in reading, developmental mathematics, language art skills, and English for non-English speakers. Based on factor patterns and trends in relationship to Levinson's life stages (the Early Adult Transition, the First Adult Life Structure, the Age Thirty Transition, Settling Down, the Mid-Life Transition, Entering Middle Adulthood, the Age Fifty Transition, and Culmination of Middle Adulthood) Bova recommended that ABE instructors make more use of small group instruction, mentoring programs, field trips, and community awareness programs. He suggested that a knowledge of the reasons adults attend ABE classes should provide the focus for program development for this clientele.

In an attempt to predict dropout in ABE using interaction effects among school and nonschool variables, Garrison (1985) found that many ABE learners appear to set unrealistic occupational goals considering their scholastic and socioeconomic status. Subjects in the study were adult learners in tenth grade English and mathematics courses of a Canadian high school completion program. Implications of the study are that practitioners should counsel prospective adult learners as to the expectations of the program and should help provide realistic goals congruent with learners' abilities and with the time they may have to reach such goals.

Individually Based and Community-Based Programs. Much debate has taken place between two seemingly disparate approaches to adult literacy within North America—the individually based and community-based approaches. The individually based program seeks to equip the individual to function in the existing social system while maintaining a stance of political neutrality; the community-based program, through direct political action, seeks to empower groups of individuals to confront and to change the status quo (see Chapter Thirty-Three). In this type of program, the social context in which learners reside becomes the central focus of instruction. Literacy in these programs refers not to mere reading and writing skills, but to the host of strategies that enable people to control their lives through collective action. Although the two approaches are often placed at opposite ends of an ideological continuum, as Snow (1986) explains, they do overlap to some extent. For example, "both serve to acculturate adults within a society; both include a pedagogy of skill development; both address an inequality of communicative competencies; both are concerned with issues of social mobility and social integration and both are partially or wholly committed to the goal of bettering individual situations within an ever-changing world" (p. 344).

Latin American Approaches. Meritorious efforts have been made in the struggle against illiteracy throughout Latin America and the Caribbean. In 1980, Nicaragua launched a mass literacy campaign and, at the same time, organized post-literacy programs in order to consolidate and to build upon the achievements of the initial campaigns. More than 500,000 persons, including 375,000 women, were taught to read and write in a very short period as a result of effective, decentralized organizational measures coordinated by teams operating at different levels. The necessary financial resources were obtained through contributions from national and international bodies, as well as from individual donations. In the Caribbean, the Jamaica Movement for the Advancement of Literacy attracted attention for its use of original approaches ranging from the advanced technology of the mass media to the traditions of folk music. The movement was also noted for its work in establishing an infrastructure that enabled the country to make an important methodological contribution to personnel training, research, and evaluation. And, in Cuba, a vast program known as the Battle of the Sixth Grade was undertaken by the Technical Workers Collective for workers and peasants with a view to postliteracy instruction regarded as an essential factor in social change (United Nations Educational, Scientific, and Cultural Organization, 1983).

Resource Guides. In terms of handbooks and training guides for ABE and ESL programs, Tucker (1987) provides a good summary of references for practitioners to assist in planning, developing, and implementing programs. Through the Educational Resources Information Clearinghouse (ERIC) data base, and under the categories of recruitment and retention, staff development, tutor volunteer training, curricular guides, special needs, and high risk students, Tucker outlines numerous practical resources for both new and established ABE and ESL programs. Bowes (1985) provides a good listing of articles and publications that either deal directly with the state-administered adult education program funded under the Adult Education Act or provide support to adult basic education activities.

Occupational Literacy

Occupational literacy development is a vital aspect of prevocational, vocational, and on-the-job education. Rush, Moe, and Storlie (1986) define occupational literacy as the ability to competently read required work-related materials. Kirsch and Guthrie (1977–1978) proposed that functional literacy be defined according to the demands of specific situations in terms of competency in reading alone. But more recent research into occupational literacy has included listening, speaking, and writing as literacy-related competencies. As Spikes and Cornell (1987, p. 181) point out, "Beyond reading competence and with reference to the wide variety of occupations, occupational literacy is a term that should be perceived as 'fluid' in terms of individual competencies related to situations."

By definition, functional literacy varies according to individual demands of divergent roles, settings, and materials. Occupational literacy competencies constitute a subset of functional literacy. Rush, Moe, and Storlie (1986) explain that required competencies vary from occupation to occupation and from job to job within occupations. Efforts to gather information relevant to defining occupational literacy have been either general job analyses or efforts designed specifically to provide information on functional job literacy.

Research on occupational literacy, sponsored largely by the United States armed forces, has provided insight about the extent to which reading is used in work and training settings and about the nature of reading tasks in those settings (Rush, Moe, and Storlie, 1986). Within the military environment, research has been conducted to distinguish between two dominant uses of reading in occupational settings: reading to do tasks and reading to learn tasks (Sticht and others, 1971; Sticht, 1975, 1978). The two uses differ in that the former is used to accomplish work while the latter involves retention of information for later use. Although research is less plentiful on civilian occupations, Diehl and Mikulecky (1980) indicate that requirements of civilian occupations are similar to those of military occupations and that daily reading is almost universally required across a broad section of occupations. Mikulecky (1987) reported that most jobs require about two hours of reading per day, ranging between a grade ten and grade twelve level. Even blue collar workers were reading forms, directions, order forms, and printouts. A retail or clerical worker was found to read about three hours daily. Most categories of workers, in fact, read more than most students. Only 2 percent of occupations examined required no reading or writing. These findings concur with the research of Rush, Moe, and Storlie (1986) and with findings in other civilian and military settings. Having a wealth of background knowledge on a topic can effectively lower reading difficulty levels; but the most heavy job-related reading is performed by new workers least likely to have the wealth of background experience.

The uses to which literacy is put on the job appear to be more complex than are the typical uses of literacy in schools. The vast majority of school-related reading is reading to learn factual materials, while a comparable majority of job-related reading is for problem-solving and making applications. In addition, the literacy strategies associated with high job performance ratings are primarily higher level metacognitive strategies involving monitoring, focusing, and managing information (Mikulecky and Ehlinger, 1986). Researchers are now pointing out that formal settings in educational institutions may not serve the hard-to-reach adults. More and more companies, unions, and industries are beginning to offer remedial literacy training. As Hull and Sechler (1987) suggest, industry-based education programs increasingly may become the setting for adults to begin or to continue the development of basic literacy skills.

Current Issues and Implications. Recently a number of events have occurred that have increased awareness of adult literacy and basic education in Canada and in the United States. Along with this awareness, certain issues have been brought to center stage. In North America there is a growing understanding of two types of adults who lack basic literacy skills—those who can barely read and write and those who cannot read and write well enough to meet the increasing demands of our society. Each type requires a different teaching method, and providers are recognizing that effective basic literacy training needs to be integrated with functional uses of literacy.

A second concern is that the decision by individuals to participate in a basic education program is a matter of personal choice and that individuals most in need of such programs may not recognize the advantages of participation; or, recognizing the advantages, they may be too embarrassed to admit their inability because of the stigma of illiteracy. Therefore the provision of widespread publicity and information on adult illiteracy must continue in order to further increase public awareness and understanding of the problem.

A third issue is the need for expanding training facilities for literacy personnel. As literacy partnerships among business, industry, and governments continue to grow in order to meet the basic skill needs of entry-level and dislocated workers, different types of teaching methodologies and curricula are required. Clearly, the ability to connect basic skills and literacy development to job training will be an important teaching skill in the future.

References

Aker, G., and Aker, J. "Illiteracy in America." In C. Klevins (ed.), *Materials and Methods in Adult and Continuing Education.* Los Angeles: Klevens Publications, 1987.

Bova, B. M. "Participation Patterns of ABE Students." *Adult Literacy and Basic Education,* 1985, *9,* (2), 95–105.

Bowes, S. "Adult Basic Education: 310 Projects." *Adult Literacy and Basic Education,* 1985, *9* (3), 163–170.

Calamai, P. *Broken Words.* Toronto: Southam, 1987.

Cervero, R. M. "Is a Common Definition of Adult Literacy Possible?" *Adult Education Quarterly,* 1985, *36* (1), 50–54.

Charner, I., and Fraser, B. *Different Strokes for Different Folks.* Washington, D.C.: National Institute for Work and Learning, 1986. (ED 268 367)

Crandall, D., Lerche, R., and Marchilonis, B. *Guidebook for Effective Literacy Practice 1983–1984.* San Francisco: National Adult Literacy Project, 1984. (ED 253 776)

D'Anglejan, A. "Learning the Language." *Language and Society,* 1984, *13,* 21–24.

Delker, P. "State of the Art in Adult Basic Education." Paper presented at the National Adult Literacy Conference, Washington, D.C., June 1984. (ED 241 698)

Diehl, W. A. "Functional Literacy as a Variable Construct." Unpublished doctoral dissertation, College of Education, Indiana University, 1980.

Diehl, W. A., and Mikulecky, L. "The Nature of Reading at Work." *Journal of Reading,* 1980, *24,* 221–227.

Draper, J. A. *Re-thinking Adult Literacy.* Toronto: World Literacy of Canada, 1986.

Duke, C. "Participation Research." In C. Duke (ed.), *Participation Research.* Canberra: Australian National University, Centre for Continuing Education, 1985.

Fingeret, A. *Adult Literacy Education: Current and Future Directions.* Columbus, Ohio: ERIC Clearinghouse on Adult, Career, and Vocational Education, 1984.

Garrison, D. R. "Predicting Dropout in Adult Basic Education Using Interaction Effects Among School and Nonschool Variables." *Adult Education Quarterly,* 1985, *36* (1), 25–38.

Harman, D. *Illiteracy: A National Dilemma.* New York: Cambridge Book, 1987.

Horne, G. P. *Functional Job Literacy Implications for Instruction.* Wellesley, Mass.: Commonwealth Center for High Technology/Education, 1979.

Hull, W., and Sechler, J. *Adult Literacy: Skills for the American Workforce.* Columbus, Ohio: National Center for Research in Vocational Education, 1987.

Huyck, E., and Bouvier, L. "Demography of Refugees." *The Annals of the American Academy of Social Sciences,* 1983, *467,* 39–61.

Kirsch, I., and Guthrie, J. "The Concept and Measurement of Functional Literacy." *Reading Research Quarterly,* 1977–1978, *13,* 485–507.

Longfield, D. "Teaching English as a Language to Adults." Paper presented at the National Conference on Adult Literacy, Washington, D.C., June 1984.

Lytle, S., Marmor, T., and Penner, F. *Literacy Theory in Practice.* Philadelphia: Graduate School of Education, University of Pennsylvania, 1986.

Mikulecky, L. "The Status of Literacy in Our Society." In J. Readance and S. Baldwin (eds.), *Research in Literacy: Merging Perspectives.* Chicago: National Reading Conference, 1987.

Mikulecky, L., and Ehlinger, J. "The Influence of Metacognitive Aspects of Literacy on Job Performance of Electronic Technicians." *Journal of Reading Behavior,* 1986, *18,* 41–62.

Mocker, D. W. "Adult Basic Education in the United States." Paper presented at the 6th International Seminar on the Education of Adults, Guildford, Eng., University of Surrey, 1986.

Nesbitt, P. *Literacy in Canada: Southam Literacy Study.* Toronto: Creative Research Group, 1987.

Penfield, J. "ESL Literacy and the New Refugees." *Adult Literacy and Basic Education,* 1986, *10* (1), 47–57.

Philips, K., and Ballorado, D. *Affective Aspects of Adult Literacy Programs.* San Francisco: National Adult Literacy Project, 1985. (ED 253 776)

Ranard, D. "ESL Literacy: Questions and Issues." *TESOL Newsletter,* 1984, *18* (2), 20.

Rush, R. T., Moe, A. J., and Storlie, R. *Occupational Literacy Education.* Newark, Del.: International Reading Association, 1986.

Scalan, C. L. *Deterrents to Participation: An Adult Education Dilemma.* Information Series, no. 308. Columbus, Ohio: ERIC Clearinghouse on Adult, Career, and Vocational Education, 1986.

Snow, B. "The Ends and Means of Adult Literacy." In T. Valentine (ed.), *Proceedings from the 1986 Adult Education Research Conference.* Syracuse, N.Y.: Syracuse University, 1986.

Spikes, F., and Cornell, T. "Occupational Literacy in the Classroom." In C. Klevins (ed.), *Materials and Methods in Adult Continuing Education.* Los Angeles: Klevens Publications, 1987.

Sticht, T. G. (ed.). *Reading for Working: A Functional Literacy Anthology.* Alexandria, Va.: Human Resources Research Organization, 1975.

Sticht, T. G. *Literacy and Vocational Competence.* Occasional Paper, no. 39. Columbus, Ohio: National Center for Research in Vocational Education, 1978.

Sticht, T. G., and others. *Determination of Literacy Skill Requirements in Four Military Occupational Specialties.* Technical Report, no. 71–23. Alexandria, Va.: Human Resources Research Organization, 1971.

Thomas, A. *Adult Illiteracy in Canada.* Occasional Paper, no. 42. Ottawa: Canadian Commission for UNESCO, 1983.

Thomas, A. "Definitions and Evolution of the Concepts." In J. A. Draper and M. C. Taylor (eds.), *Adult Basic Education: Bridging Theory and Practice.* Toronto: Culture Concepts, 1989.

Tucker, B. "ABE and ESL Guides and Handbooks." *Adult Literacy and Basic Education,* 1987, *11* (1), 55–62.

United Nations Educational, Scientific, and Cultural Organization (UNESCO). *The Struggle Against Illiteracy Throughout the World.* Paris: UNESCO, 1983.

Valentine, T. "Adult Functional Literacy as a Goal of Instruction." *Adult Education Quarterly,* 1986, *36* (2), 108–113.

Vines, D. "Secretary's Initiative on Adult Literacy." Paper presented at the National Adult Education Conference, Philadelphia, Apr. 1983.

36

Adult Secondary Education

Larry G. Martin
James C. Fisher

Adult secondary education (ASE) is intended to serve the needs of about 25.6 million adults who have completed at least nine years but fewer than twelve years of school (Pugsley, 1987). These programs seek to enhance learners' reading, writing, computing, and thinking skills so they can obtain a high school diploma or its equivalent; however, these programs occupy an ambiguous and often obscure place in the presentation of educational services to adult high school noncompleters. Less well known than their adult basic education (ABE) and English as a second language (ESL) counterparts (see Chapters Thirty-Five and Thirty-Seven), ASE programs provide the credentials most in demand for entering employment or for furthering educational opportunities. Basic skills and ESL training are supported largely by state and federal funds, but ASE programs are funded more by state and local taxes—and requirements for high school diplomas are established by state and local standards.

This chapter discusses the varying roles that secondary education has assumed in response to societal expectations and in response to the increasing value of the high school diploma as an educational credential. Characteristics of the adult high school noncompleter obtained in both longitudinal and cross-sectional studies are examined. Approaches to adult secondary education (ASE), such as the traditional day and evening school, alternative high school programs, competency-based education (CBE) programs, and the General Education Development (GED) test program, are described, together with methods, materials, staffing, and funding sources. The chapter concludes with an examination of issues relating to the role of adult secondary education as it changes in response to the current educational expectations of American society.

The Role of Schools in American Society

Throughout the recent history of North America, schooling has played a series of roles designed to respond to the expectations and values of society. In the United States, at the time of the founding of the republic, schools were viewed as a means to transmit the knowledge and skills necessary to develop an informed electorate considered necessary to the survival of the infant nation. Later this function was expanded to include the transmission of both a prescribed body of scientifically accepted knowledge and the information deemed relevant to the career goals of students.

Schools also have been viewed as the institutions responsible for socializing students. According to Carlson (1987, p. 2), social conformity by students gave evidence of a "person's commitment to the more vaguely defined U.S. ideology." Schools prepared students for work by creating good habits such as punctuality and respect for authority. With the arrival of new immigrants from diverse ethnic, racial, religious, and economic backgrounds, education was used to create a homogeneous America, based on the principles of democracy and the Judeo-Christian heritage, to unify the multicultural and heterogeneous melting pot.

The nation's schools also have been the focus of efforts to redress various economic and international problems. For example, during times when skilled professionals have been in short supply or when graduates have had difficulty securing employment, schools have been encouraged to focus more directly on vocational training. Similarly, when Sputnik was launched by the Soviet Union, or when an unfavorable balance of trade has occurred with other nations, the American schools were considered instrumental to the solutions of these problems.

During recent decades, schools have been the setting for efforts to establish equity of opportunity for economic advancement in the American society. Courts and legislatures have joined in prescribing particular standards of conduct and organization in the schools in order to ensure equal levels of educational opportunity for all citizens, despite differences of gender, socioeconomic status, race, ethnic group, or language.

Although the American society has had an agenda for its schools, the size of this agenda, coupled with factors such as restricted budgets, state regulations, and union contracts, has inhibited the schools from responding as effectively as they might to many social problems, such as the high school noncompletion rate (Wehlage and Rutter, 1986).

High School Completion

The high school as a distinctly North American secondary educational institution emerged from the roots of the Latin grammar school tradition during the middle third of the nineteenth century. Since that time, high school completion has become an important indicator of attainment in the American education system. In both the United States and Canada, the high school diploma has come to symbolize that its holder possesses the social values and attitudes espoused by the larger society and the knowledge and skills necessary for employment in the secondary labor market (that is, in occupations requiring minimal skills) or for pursuit of further education.

In the early years, a small proportion of eligible youths attended high school, and of those who attended, few completed. For example, in 1900, about 10 percent of the male youth in the United States received high school diplomas. Not until the 1950s did the rate of completion rise about 50 percent. By 1968, the completion rate reached its highest point of 76.7 percent and began to decrease incrementally until 1983, when it rose by 1.0 percent to 73.9 percent (Cibulka, 1986). The rate of noncompletion experienced in the 1980s (between 25 and 30 percent) translates into nearly one million youth who leave school annually without receiving a high school diploma (Weber, 1986). In 1986, 51.8 million persons in the United States, sixteen years of age and older, had not completed high school. Of these, 26.2 million had failed to complete eighth grade, and 25.6 million had failed to complete twelfth grade (Pugsley, 1987). In Canada, during the 1979–1980 school year, 21 percent of students enrolled in the twelfth grade did not graduate (Statistics Canada, 1982).

Trends Toward Increasing Skill and Credential Requirements

The elimination of jobs as a result of technological change or international trade, the higher skill level required for many new positions, the population increases represented by persons born from 1946 to 1964 and their children, and the increased proportion of females in the population who work outside the home contribute to an intense competition for jobs. In such an environment, the high school diploma has emerged as a critically important credential. Students who fail to complete the ideal minimum numbers of years of schooling, in addition to being potentially unemployable, are perceived by the wider society as social deviants and are assumed to suffer from some form of defect (Martin, 1986).

Several major trends are projected to influence negatively the economic well-being of both school noncompleters and the society at large. First, those who lack basic literacy skills, career skills, and the social skills to be successful in the workplace will face deteriorating employment prospects in the future (Weidman and Friedmann, 1984). Second, if current employment conditions, school noncompletion rates, and wage rates continue, noncompleters will earn $237 billion less over their lifetimes than will high school graduates (Cox, Holley, Kite, and Durham, 1985). Thus, state and local governments will collect $71 billion less in taxes.

Third, the aging of the baby-boom generation and the absence of a subsequent generation of equal size have resulted in an aging society, which is becoming economically dependent on a smaller, younger cohort. As our society ages, it is becoming economically more dependent on a smaller and increasingly undereducated and disadvantaged minority youth population (Institute for Educational Leadership, 1986).

These factors suggest that it is a social and economic imperative to reduce significantly the pool of adults who have not completed high school. Although most arguments supporting ASE, including federal legislation, depend on what Darkenwald and Valentine (1984) described as narrowly utilitarian socioeconomic goals (such as training and employment), other arguments focus on larger outcomes such as social change, personal empowerment, development of critical-thinking skills, and human dignity. Thus, the success of most ASE programs depends on the extent to which they can achieve a balance between the utilitarian goals established by funding sources and the broader outcomes sought by participants.

Characteristics of School Noncompleters

Two approaches to the identification of noncompleter characteristics have been used—longitudinal studies of high school students and studies of the general adult population. The former attempt to isolate noncompleters from their counterparts in high school; the latter attempt to differentiate noncompleters' characteristics from those of the general adult population. However, Fingeret (1984) argues that much of the research on school noncompleters focuses on middle-class culture as the criterion against which other cultures are judged. Such research projects a deficit perspective that emphasizes the need for treatment to rehabilitate malfunctioning adults into normal society. Therefore, the results of such research should be interpreted with caution.

Longitudinal Studies. Much of the longitudinal research on school noncompletion has been motivated by a desire to find the causes, correlates, or motives underlying the actions of those who do not complete school. Both social and personal attributes are analyzed to identify those that separate noncompleters from completers. The most recent longitudinal research suggests that noncompleters possess several characteristics that distinguish them from college-bound students and others who complete school. Noncompleters were significantly more likely (1) to have low academic achievement or ability as demonstrated by low expected school attainment, low test scores, low socioeconomic status, and low grades (Wehlage and Rutter, 1986); (2) to experience significant difficulty functioning in the social context of schooling as demonstrated by high levels of truancy and tardiness, discipline problems, and working to generate income (Wehlage and Rutter, 1986); (3) to come from academically less stimulating home and family environments (Ekstrom, Goertz, Pollack, and Rock, 1986); and (4) to make poor course selections and to take fewer credits while in school (Weber, 1986).

Several studies have found that noncompleters were more likely to be members of a minority group (Alexander, Natriello, and Pallas, 1985;

Weidman and Friedmann, 1984). However, Wehlage and Rutter (1986) found that when family background (such as income and education) was statistically controlled, race was not predictive of failure to complete school.

Cross-Sectional Studies. In 1985 and 1986, state-operated ASE programs enrolled 900,000 of the 25.6 million adults eligible to attend the programs—a participation rate of 3.5 percent. During this same year, 186,090 (13.0 percent) of those enrolled received GEDs, and 43,492 (3.0 percent) received high school diplomas; the rate of completion for those eligible was 0.9 percent (Pugsley, 1987). In addition to low levels of participation and completion, the programs have been plagued with rates of absenteeism and attrition that average from 40 percent to 60 percent (Cain and Walen, 1979). Therefore, cross-sectional studies of noncompleters in the general population have focused mainly on the life-style, demographic, and psychographic characteristics associated with participation and persistence in adult literacy programs (Fisher and Martin, 1987). Most research on participation has been directed toward sociodemographic analysis; participation has been explained as a function of race, sex, age, income, education, place of residence, and so on. However, these variables account for only 10 percent of the variance associated with adult participation in organized learning activities (Cross, 1981). In addition, several psychographic variables were found to be associated with the demographic profiles of nonparticipants; they tended to be past oriented, emotional, limited in the sense of personal freedom and choice, less willing to take risks, concrete in thought, reliant on family and friends, and action oriented (Shipp and McKenzie, 1981).

Martin (1987) produced a typology that statistically differentiated six life-style categories of noncompleters: entrepreneurs (owners of private businesses), superiors (managers of businesses or organizations), regulars (employed skilled and semiskilled workers), suppliants (recipients of an indirect means of financial support), marginals (recipients of public assistance) and underclass (consistently engaged in antisocial acts, for example, crime and illicit drug use).

Martin observed that a majority of individuals possessing the ability to pursue education (for example, regulars, superiors, and entrepreneurs) appeared to be unwilling to attend school; conversely, those who appeared to be willing (for example, suppliants and marginals) were, for various reasons, unable to attend. These findings suggest that adult literacy programs should develop their programming efforts and marketing strategies around the needs of specific segments of learners rather than viewing all noncompleters as members of a single homogeneous population.

Program Approaches in Adult Secondary Education

The service delivery system of ASE programs consists of a network of different types of programs that are defined largely by the prerogative of individual states. The great majority of students are enrolled in adult secondary education (ASE) programs sponsored by public schools, by two-year community colleges, or by correctional institutions. The U.S. military, several large employers, and government employment and training programs also sponsor ASE programs for individuals seeking to develop further their academic skills and to receive high school diplomas. Although situated in different settings, there are essentially two major alternatives for adults to complete high school: acquire a high school diploma or pass an examination.

High School Diploma Programs. The adult high school provides traditional high school and evening classes for out-of-school youth and adults who desire to take a high school refresher course or who wish to obtain a high school diploma. The particular requirements vary with the requirements of the state in which the school is located. Students are able to combine general education courses with vocational and business courses as well as elective courses of particular interest. Student services are provided, although there are usually no compulsory physical education classes, study halls, or homeroom periods. Typical requirements to earn a high school diploma include eight units of English, six units of social studies, four units of mathematics, four units of science, one unit of computer education, and four units of health and physical education.

Alternative High School Diploma Programs. Programs described as alternative tend to combine somewhat traditional graduation requirements with credit for informal learning experiences and flexible structures that allow choices in content and scheduling. One program used in several New Jersey school districts (Nickse, 1980) requires eighty credits including ten credits of American history plus a minimal performance for graduation (10.5 grade level in reading, mathematics, and English on the Test of Adult Basic Education). Graduation requirements are met through previously completed courses, credit for nonschool experience, credit received for courses taken as part of the program, and credit received for learning gained in informal classes, learning contracts, home study, and self-developed projects. Instruction for these learning strategies is self-paced, rather than time based, and is individualized with no required classroom attendance. The individual learning is evaluated on the basis of previously written objectives.

Competency-Based Education Programs. Developed as a means to counteract the perceived negative characteristics and effects of traditional approaches to education, proponents of competency-based education (CBE) have argued that it emphasizes acquired knowledge instead of the learning process, life coping skills instead of disciplinary content, learner-centered knowledge rather than socially or institutionally centered knowledge, learner-relevant goals instead of abstract goals, and curriculum flexibility in response to changing environmental conditions rather than curriculum rigidity (Collins, 1987).

The CBE movement in the area of adult literacy education received a significant boost with the funding of the Adult Performance Level (APL) Project and the subsequent development of curriculum materials and competency tests during the latter half of the 1970s. By 1980, twenty-three states reported CBE high school projects and programs in development or in operation at ninety different sites that provided competency-based alternative credentialing programs for adults (Nickse, 1980). Competency-based educational programming was introduced to Canadian adult literacy education with the implementation of the Alberta ABE Project during the early and middle 1980s (Collins, 1987).

Those CBE programs that currently provide certification for high school completion differ from each other in their approaches to program development, implementation, operational parameters and requirements, and assessment procedures. For example, Nickse (1980) identified nine areas in which three focal programs differed: the number and types of skills required for certification, the types of instructional processes utilized, the types of assessment procedures used to document the knowledge and skills obtained, the extent to which credit was awarded for prior learning, the amount of time and attendance required of participants, the range of ages accepted into the programs, the instructional sites used by the programs, the individuals assigned to review students' portfolios, and the content of students' transcripts.

Examination Programs. The most popular alternative among adults for completing their high school education is to pass the General Educational Development (GED) test. These tests were developed by the Educational Testing Service and are administered jointly by the American Council on Education and sixty-nine state, province, and territory departments and ministries in the United States and Canada (Whitney, 1983). Cervero (1983) estimates that, in 1980, over 800,000 people were tested at almost 2,800 testing sites. Approximately 500,000 high school equivalency certificates were issued based on GED test scores. A GED certificate has the legal status of a high school diploma in most states and may be used as such for job applications or community and state college entrance requirements. Many choose the GED approach because it requires a smaller investment of time. Although class attendance is not required to take the test, 80 percent of candidates use some form of preparation, and about 50 percent use classroom instruction (Cervero, 1983).

Normed on a national sample of high school seniors (beginning in 1988), the GED test program provides a certificate of equivalency to high school graduation for individuals who are able to pass a test in each of five subject areas. The writing skills test assesses both the knowledge of the conventions of written English and the ability to write an essay. The social studies test measures knowledge of history, economics, political science, geography, and behavioral science. The science test measures knowledge of the life sciences and the physical sciences. The interpreting literature and the arts test measures knowledge of popular literature, classical literature, and the ability to write commentary about literature and the arts. The mathematics test assesses skills in arithmetic, algebra, and geometry (Whitney and others, 1985).

Methods and Materials

The types of learning materials used in ASE programs are largely a function of the goals of the programs. For example, in programs that prepare students to take the GED test, the primary criterion for the selection of materials is the ability to facilitate the passing of the test. In the adult high school, materials selected closely parallel those used in the traditional high school. The materials that provide the instructional content vary from published workbooks, texts, and other assigned readings to audiovisual and video sources.

In developing an effective system of instruction, ASE programs often endeavor to accommodate the instructional needs of the students in their service areas by controlling the allocation and use of staff time and instructional materials. Lerche (1985) conducted an extensive survey of successful ABE and ASE programs in the United States. She found that the most consistently successful programs were those that structured and systematized their instructional designs; materials, methods, and the assessment of student progress were based on clearly identified instructional objectives. Further, these programs individualized instructional plans to reflect learner strengths and to address learner deficiencies. In order to monitor learner progress and to provide frequent feedback to learners on their progress, the programs also included an instructional management and documentation system.

However, Lerche also noted that teachers and tutors may not have either the time or sufficient expertise in adult education to implement the type of analysis, preparation, and monitoring required of a truly individualized educational program. Staffing patterns, educational philosophy, or the assessment of resources may lead program designers to structure their systems for large or small group instruction (with lecture and small group discussion) as opposed to individualized, one-on-one tutorial sessions or instruction via computer. Programs may also choose to adopt a packaged model for individualizing instruction—a model in which instructional objectives are linked to diagnostic instruments, to given sets of materials, and to assessment strategies.

Staffing

The credential requirements of ASE staff vary in accordance with the sponsorship of the programs. For example, when programs are under the jurisdiction of the public school system, the administrative, instructional, and counseling staff are subject to the credentialing requirements of that system. In this case, the staff persons in ASE programs are usually required to possess appropriate credentials in secondary education. If the programs are sponsored by community or technical colleges, additional credentials, often relating to the teaching of adults, may be imposed. However, entry level requirements of staff in adult high school programs generally consist of elementary or secondary education certification.

Staff in ASE programs sponsored by a local elementary and secondary school district may be full-time or part-time members of the local district's high school staff. Similarly, in ASE programs sponsored by community or technical colleges, staff may be full-time or part-time members of the college faculty or administrative staff.

Adult secondary education programs disproportionately employ part-time staff, that is, those who work in the programs fewer than twenty hours per week. In 1985 and 1986, the total personnel—teachers (72 percent), administrators (6.5 percent), paraprofessionals (18.3 percent), and counselors (2.9 percent)—employed in state-operated literacy programs (ABE, ESL, and ASE) numbered 113,552. Of these personnel, 57 percent were part time, 11 percent were full time, and 33 percent were volunteers. Teachers and paraprofessionals made up over 90.0 percent of the adult literacy work force, and 25.0 percent of all instruction was conducted by 20,284 volunteers (Pugsley, 1987). Although advantages of administrative flexibility (that is, the ability to contract on an as-needed basis) and low costs can be achieved with part-time staff, there are several disadvantages for staff—difficulty in achieving a sense of professional identity (James and Kellar, 1980), minimal job security and lack of career aspirations in adult education (Lopez and Smith, 1977), and low salaries without fringe benefits.

State-operated programs that receive federal funds are required by federal regulations to appropriate a minimum of 10 percent of their annual budgets for both staff development and special projects. Staff development training is offered through a variety of formal learning activities, such as graduate education courses, workshops, conferences, and so on, designed to upgrade the ability of staff to perform assigned tasks. Although the quantity and quality of staff development training efforts vary greatly, the content focus of the programs often includes instructional materials, methods, human relations, counseling, diagnosis of student needs, student recruitment and retention, and coping skills.

Funding and Sponsorship of ASE Progams

In the United States, the primary federally funded effort to support and to encourage the development of ASE programs began in 1966 when ABE funding became Title III of the Elementary and Secondary Education Act and subsequently became the Adult Education Act. The responsibility for financing and administering programs funded under the act was delegated to the states; federal funds were then allocated to each state on the basis of a state plan describing the procedures to be employed in implementing a comprehensive program of educational services to adults in need of literacy education. The federal share was set at 90 percent of the cost of implementing each state's plan. AEA funds were initially targeted toward adults with fewer than eight years of schooling, with top priority given to adults with four or fewer years of schooling; in practice, however, ABE funds were being expended for ASE. Subsequently, new federal guidelines were developed allowing the states to expend up to 20 percent of their ABE funds for ASE programs, provided the ABE need was being met. During the eight-year period from 1979 through 1986, the total expenditure for state-operated adult literacy programs increased from $153.8 million (41 percent of which were state and local funds) to $405.1 million (76.4 percent of which were state and local funds). As the result, state and local governments now have become the dominant sources of funding for adult literacy programs (Pugsley, 1987).

Testing programs such as the GED tend to be administered differently from high school diploma programs, which usually are administered by the public school system (Rockhill, 1978). Most states' policies favor either taking courses or the testing alternative. As the GED test has grown in popularity, many states have earmarked categorical funds to provide GED preparation; in these states, the program of ASE is dominated by GED preparation (Rockhill, 1978). Rockhill also found that, in addition to earning a state certificate, passing the GED also can count as credit toward the awarding of a high school diploma at the local district level; hence diploma programs frequently provide opportunities for GED preparation.

Future Issues and Research Concerns

Although many current issues and trends will likely determine the focus and direction of ASE programming in the 1990s, several require immediate attention.

Participation in ASE. The low rates of participation and completion in ASE programs are intolerable. After two decades, the assumption that underfunded, independently operated, decentralized programs staffed by part-time and volunteer personnel can effectively address the learning and empowerment needs of noncompleters has proven to be woefully mistaken. The development of a systematic delivery system of ASE programs will require intensive and harmonious efforts among policymakers, funders, practitioners, and researchers. Meanwhile, the small proportion of the larger population currently being reached utilizes all available resources, causing crowded sites and waiting lists in many areas (Lerche, 1985).

Competition for Funds. While total funding for adult literacy programs has increased exponentially since 1978, the level of participation in ASE programs increased by 47 percent compared to increases of 219 percent and 14 percent for ESL and ABE, respectively (Pugsley, 1987). These discrepancies and the absence of clear policy initiatives for allocating resources could lead to reduced cooperation and increased competition among these programs.

Effectiveness of the GED. Research findings conflict with regard to whether holders of the GED perform on a level equal to holders of a traditional high school diploma in both employment and postsecondary education.

The extent to which the GED reflects a substantive and meaningful difference between the holder of a GED and others is largely undetermined.

Development of Empowerment Programs. The movement toward competency-based adult literacy programs represents a significant shift toward prescribed curricula. This shift mitigates against the development of programs designed to assist learners to reflect critically on their natural and social environments. Learners' ability to gain personal empowerment and to bring about societal change is thereby impaired. In a larger sense, the extent to which present policies for financing ASE programs and for credentialing their graduates inhibit the development of personal empowerment will require further research.

References

Alexander, K. L., Natriello, G., and Pallas, A. M. "For Whom the School Bell Tolls: The Impact of Dropping Out on Cognitive Performance." *American Sociological Review,* 1985, *50* (3), 409–420.

Cain, S. H., and Walen, B. A. *Adult Basic and Secondary Education Statistics: Fiscal Year 1976.* Washington, D.C.: National Center for Educational Statistics, 1979. (ED 178 765)

Carlson, R. A. *The Americanization Syndrome: A Quest for Conformity.* London: Croom-Helm, 1987.

Cervero, R. M. "A National Survey of GED Test Candidates: Preparation, Performance, and 18-Month Outcomes." *Adult Literacy and Basic Education,* 1983, *7* (1), 13–29.

Cibulka, J. C. "State-Level Policy Options for Dropout Prevention." *Metropolitan Education,* 1986, *2* (3), 13–29.

Collins, M. *Competence in Adult Education: A New Perspective.* Lanham, Md.: University Press of America, 1987.

Cox, J. L., Holley, J. N., Kite, R. H., and Durham, W. Y. *Study of High School Dropouts in Appalachia.* Research Triangle Park, N.C.: Center for Educational Studies, 1985. (ED 264 992)

Cross, K. P. *Adults as Learners: Increasing Participation and Facilitating Learning.* San Francisco: Jossey-Bass, 1981.

Darkenwald, G., and Valentine, T. *Outcomes and Impact of Adult Basic Education.* Research Monograph No. 6. New Brunswick, N.J.: Center for Adult Development, Rutgers University, 1984.

Ekstrom, R. B., Goertz, M. E., Pollack, J. M., and Rock, D. A. "Who Drops Out of High School and Why? Findings from a National Study." *Teachers College Record,* 1986, *87* (3), 356–373.

Fingeret, A. *Adult Literacy Education: Current and Future Directions.* Columbus, Ohio: National Center for Research in Vocational Education, 1984.

Fisher, J. C., and Martin, L. G. "A Decade of Research Contributions to the Adult Basic Education Literature." In *Proceedings of the Midwest Research to Practice Conference in Adult and Continuing Education.* East Lansing: Michigan State University, 1987.

Institute for Educational Leadership, Inc. *School Dropouts: Everybody's Problem*. Washington, D.C.: Institute for Educational Leadership, 1986.

James, W., and Kellar, M. "Using Modules for Improving Staff Development." *Lifelong Learning: The Adult Years*, 1980, *3* (5), 12–13, 25, 27.

Lerche, R. S. *Effective Adult Literacy Programs: A Practitioner's Guide*. New York: Cambridge Book, 1985.

Lopez, N., and Smith, R. M. "Adult Basic Education in Illinois." *Lifelong Learning: The Adult Years*, 1977, *1* (2), 24–27, 31.

Martin, L. G. "Antecedent Stigmatizing Experiences: Associations to the Life-Style Classifications of Adult High School Noncompleters." In K. Landers (ed.), *Exchanging at the Crossroads: Research and Practice*. Program and proceedings for the annual Adult Education Research Conference, Syracuse University, May 1986. (ED 269 571)

Martin, L. G. "Life-Style Classifications of Adult High School Noncompleters." *Adult Education Quarterly*, 1987, *38* (1), 32–45.

Nickse, R. S. *Assessing Life-Skills: The New York State External High School Diploma Program*. Belmont, Calif.: Fearon Education, 1980.

Pugsley, R. *National Data Update—Annual Conference: State Directors of Adult Education*. Washington, D.C.: Division of Adult Education, U.S. Department of Education, 1987.

Rockhill, K. *From Diplomas to Alternatives: Education and Learning Among Adults with Less Than 12 Years of Schooling*. Washington, D.C.: Division of Adult Education, U.S. Department of Education, 1978.

Shipp, T., and McKenzie, L. R. "Adult Learners and Non-Learners: Demographic Characteristics as an Indicator of Psychographic Characteristics." *Adult Education*, 1981, *31* (4), 187–198.

Statistics Canada. *Education in Canada: A Statistical Review for 1980–81*. Ottawa: Statistics Canada, 1982.

Weber, J. M. *The Role of Vocational Educational in Decreasing the Dropout Rate*. Columbus, Ohio: National Center for Research in Vocational Education, 1986. (ED 264 444)

Wehlage, G. G., and Rutter, R. A. "Dropping Out: How Much Do Schools Contribute to the Problem?" *Teachers College Record*, 1986, *87* (3), 374–392.

Weidman, J. C., and Friedmann, R. R. "The School-to-Work Transition for High School Dropouts." *Urban Review*, 1984, *16* (1), 25–42.

Whitney, D. R. "Summary Phase of the GED Testing Service Five-Year Review Process." Paper presented at the National Adult Education Conference, Philadelphia, Nov. 29–Dec. 4, 1983. (ED 239-090)

Whitney, D. R., and others. *The 1988 Tests of General Educational Development: A Preview*. Washington, D.C.: American Council on Education, 1985.

37

English as a Second Language

Richard A. Orem

The teaching of English as a second language (ESL) in the United States and Canada is an important theme running throughout the history of adult education in North America. It is important because the populations of these two nations are composed largely of immigrants from all other continents of the globe. Coupled with this immigrant population is a rich history of second language teaching, the roots of which can be traced back to the ancient world (Kelly, 1969). Yet, only in the twentieth century has the teaching of English as a second language been recognized as a discipline—as evidenced by the growth of teacher preparation programs in colleges and universities throughout North America (Blatchford, 1982).

In this chapter we will take a brief look at the development of language teaching programs for adults in the United States. We will discuss current methods and materials for teaching English as a second language to adult learners, and we will look at the current trends in communicative language teaching. We will also discuss the influence of advances in language program development in Western Europe upon language programs in North America. (See also Chapter Thirty-Five.)

Because the future of adult second language teaching is largely determined by social and political forces beyond the control of the adult educator, we will look at several such forces that will likely have a great impact on the field of practice in the 1990s. These forces include the changing nature of public and private funding, immigration reform and the related issue of language rights, and the nature of professional development in the face of increasing efforts to rely on volunteers while the job market remains heavily dominated by part-time employment.

Finally, we will discuss some of the many resources available for adult educators engaged in the teaching of language to minority adults in the United States and Canada. We will provide names and addresses of key professional associations in the United States and Canada, and we will list information clearinghouses established for purposes of providing information and technical assistance to adult educators working with limited-English-proficient adults.

A Historical Perspective

The development of programs for the teaching of English as a second language in the United States has grown directly out of the American experience of growth due to the immigration of peoples from other lands and other cultures. And the nature of such programs has been largely influenced by political decisions stemming from our tolerance of language-minority peoples. For example, in the half century preceding World War I, major immigration to North America originated in Northern Europe and in the British Isles. Whether immigrants settled in cities or in rural villages, they often maintained their native languages and perpetuated their native cultures by educating their youth in their first language, without government intervention.

World War I abruptly changed this pattern of laissez-faire pluralism. Hostilities in Europe were manifested in the United States by antagonism toward Germans and by growing concerns about the political movements of communism and socialism. For the first time, laws that sharply restricted immigration into the United States were enacted. The National Origins Act of 1924 established quotas for each country outside the Western Hemisphere, and those affected most were the immigrants from Southern and Eastern Europe. Political repression and anarchy in Europe forced many to seek refuge in the United States. Reaction of the American political and educational establishments was expressed in programs designed to Americanize these immigrants. Children were forbidden from using their first language at school, and parents often discouraged first language use in the home. The metaphor of America as a melting pot was used to describe attempts to erase immigrants' native languages and cultures, to be replaced by a homogeneous blend of English and so-called American culture.

Adult education played a prominent role in the Americanization programs of the 1920s and 1930s (Lewis, 1934). A quasifictitious account of these programs can by found in *The Education of Hyman Kaplan* (Rosten, 1937), the story of a young Polish adult in New York City and his sometimes futile, and often humorous, attempts to work through the maze of English composition and conversation.

After World War II, both Canada and the United States began to experience immigration from a different source—from the Pacific and Asia. In 1948, the United States began to admit war refugees, followed by victims of the Korean conflict. In 1952, the McCarran-Walter Act allowed a small number of Asians to immigrate.

The Immigration Act of 1965, signed by President Lyndon Johnson, modified the system that had favored Europeans and opened up large-scale immigration from the Third World. In the three decades beginning in 1960, Hispanics in the United States have dominated the changing demographic patterns in urban America. As recently as 1950, the census counted fewer than four million residents on the U.S. mainland who would today fall under the category Hispanic, the majority being of Mexican descent. By 1985, there were an estimated 17.6 million Hispanics, with roughly 60 percent tracing their ancestry to Mexico. The remaining 40 percent were from Puerto Rico, Cuba, El Salvador, the Dominican Republic, Colombia, Venezuela, and about two dozen other countries of Central and South America.

Beginning in 1975, with the first exodus of Vietnamese refugees and continuing with Laotian and Cambodian refugees, the United States and Canada were inundated with wave after wave of Southeast Asians. The 1960s and 1970s marked the beginning of the shift from largely European sources of immigrants to largely Asian and Latin American sources.

In the 1980s, immigration patterns could still be seen as a function of civil and political unrest throughout the world. Major sources of immigrants and refugees into North America included Afghanistan, Cuba, Iran, Ethiopia, Haiti, Vietnam, Laos, Kampuchea (Cambodia), El Salvador, Nicaragua, Guatemala, and various countries of Eastern Europe, as well as the Soviet Union. As long as civil wars, regional conflicts, and economic and ecological disasters continue to displace large groups of people, the United States and Canada will continue to receive immigrants and refugees. Inevitably, the demand for refuge is coupled with the demand for education, including language education for children and adults. English, along with its many varieties, is now the most widely studied foreign language in the world. It is estimated that as many as one billion people, or one-fourth of the entire world's population, may speak English as a first or additional language.

Methods and Materials

Many fine accounts of language teaching methodology are available to the adult educator (Brown, 1980; Diller, 1978; Kelly, 1969; Richards and Rodgers, 1986). Such accounts reveal that language teaching methodology reflects the fluctuations in education in general. Different methodologies reflect the changing goals of language learners, whether they be to gain literacy skills, oral skills, job skills, or academic skills.

Grammar-Translation Method. The grammar-translation method is based on a classical view of language teaching. Essential to grammar-translation is the study of grammar of the target language and the practice of translating written discourse from target to native language. Higher education foreign language teaching still reflects this classical tradition of second or foreign language teaching, which can trace its roots to ancient Rome (McArthur, 1983).

Audio-Lingual Method. During World War II, the United States realized a need for rapid training of military and diplomatic personnel in a variety of foreign languages. This demand occurred at a time when anthropologists and linguists were advocating a structural view of language coupled with principles of behavioral psychology resulting in a methodology that is prominent throughout the world even today—the audio-lingual method.

Although the audio-lingual method of foreign language teaching has been largely discredited by the second language teaching community, evidence of it can be found in many of the materials currently produced for adult learners and in the techniques used in English as a second language classrooms. One reason for this residual activity is that many of today's ESL teachers learned a second language in the fifties and sixties in a strictly audio-lingual context. The U.S. Peace Corps also trained thousands of English teachers in the sixties and seventies in this approach, spreading it beyond the cities to rural villages and hamlets of scores of developing nations.

Cognitive-Code Methodologies. The principles of audio-lingual methodology were effectively replaced in the seventies by the emphasis on meaningful situational language learning that looks at the role of motivation and context in language learning. Dissatisfaction with audio-lingualism and an emphasis on motivation led to the development of a number of new approaches, some rooted in more cognitive notions of language learning, some rooted in humanistic notions of learning. Whereas audio-lingualism stresses repetition, pattern practice, and strict avoidance of the learner's native language, cognitive-code methodologies stress understanding, meaningful language use, situational dialogues, and acceptance of the person's native language as a tool for analysis of the target language.

Comprehension Approaches. Beginning in the mid-1970s, a revolution (Bodman, 1979) swept through the language teaching community spearheaded not by linguists, but by clinical psychologists, among others. Criticism of audio-lingualism's emphasis on mechanical production led in the 1970s to an emphasis on receptive skills (listening comprehension). So-called comprehension approaches (Winitz, 1981; Asher, 1982) offered new insights into adult second language learning and began to change radically the approaches to materials and program development. This change, coupled with advances in a relatively new branch of linguistics called sociolinguistics, led in the 1970s to the development of communicative approaches to language teaching.

Communicative Approaches. Communicative approaches place less emphasis on language form (syntax) and more emphasis on language use (semantics). The appearance of Asher's Total Physical Response Approach (Asher, 1982), Community Language Learning (Curran, 1976), and The Silent Way (Gattegno, 1976) began to attract the attention of adult educators in the 1970s. At the same time, advances in the research of adult second language acquisition began to supply the field with valuable new insights into how adults obtain competence in a second language.

Krashen's Monitor Model (1977) and acquisition-learning distinction (1981) led to advocacy of so-called natural language learning (Krashen and Terrell, 1983). Adult educators' receptiveness to these new approaches may be attributed, at least in part, to many adult educators' learning on-the-job, without the benefit of formal training in linguistics. In the 1970s, money from the Federal Adult Education Act was being channeled into special projects that in turn began to encourage others to look more creatively at the teaching-learning process in ESL programs for adults.

Workplace English. Concurrently, across the Atlantic, the Western European community was facing challenges from increasing numbers of so-called guest workers flooding England, France, Germany, and Italy from Turkey, Yugoslavia, Greece, and North Africa. These guest workers presented their employers with the problems of illiteracy and foreign languages in the workplace which, if not resolved, would (and did) lead to decreased productivity and inefficiency. Europe's open-door policy encouraged workers to bring families, thereby creating pressures on the schooling systems of these countries. The European community, in an effort to work collaboratively to solve these educational and social problems, began to study how best to teach this new labor force in the many languages represented on the continent. Results of these efforts were soon realized in the form of so-called threshold levels (Ek, 1975), unit-credit systems (Trim, 1978), and emphasis on English in the workplace (Jupp and Hodlin, 1975). Threshold levels refer to those minimum skills required to comprehend and be comprehended. The unit-credit system referred to in the literature is basically a system of language learning objectives that are learner oriented, highly explicit, flexible, and comparable for different groups of learners.

English language teaching in the United States and Canada also saw a movement toward vocational skills training, bilingual vocational programs, and special purpose English (Center for Applied Linguistics, 1983). English for special purposes (ESP) often has been seen in the form of vocational ESL with an emphasis on job-seeking and job-keeping skills. This emphasis, in turn, on vocational skills and competency-based approaches to program development has influenced materials in the adult ESL market. Publishers in the 1980s quickly saw the benefit of developing special readers, workbooks, and graded programs designed to teach job-related skills to adult learners. At the same time in Canada, attention was being paid to programs to assist adult immigrants in their search for meaningful employment (Pratt, 1982).

Issues Confronting Adult Educators in the 1990s

The United States and Canada witnessed a revival of conservative ideology in the 1980s—in education as well as in politics. In the United States the Reagan administration sought unsuccessfully to abolish the Department of Education. Suddenly, education became a political platform plank of both major political parties in the United States as a result of a series of influential task force reports that began in 1983 with *A Nation at Risk* (National Commission on Excellence in Education, 1983) from the Department of Education itself.

Expanding Funding Sources. The single greatest obstacle to increasing effectiveness of adult education programs for the limited-English-proficient adult will likely continue to be inadequate funding. Adult education in the United States reaped a peculiar windfall of attention in the 1980s as a result of reports focusing on illiteracy in the schools and in the workplace. Not even the Adult Performance Level Study of the 1970s was able to arouse as much attention as did later reports in the eighties. Kozol's (1985) *Illiterate America* became required reading in several state offices of education. The private sector entered the arena with the formation of the Business Council for Effective Literacy, the brainchild of Howard McGraw of McGraw-Hill Publishers. The Gannett Corporation, publishers of *U.S.A. Today,* and several national book retailers have joined in these efforts by offering financial support to local programs. Yet, with all of the attention paid to the problems of literacy, funding is inadequate.

The Illiterate Second Language Learner. The 1990s should continue to see efforts to decrease illiteracy rates. Second language learners present a special problem in this area. In many cases, limited-English-proficient adults are literate in their first language, but may be illiterate in English. Others may even have immigrated from preliterate societies. Such is the case with many Laotian Hmong, for example, whose native language has been in written form only in the twentieth century. These preliterate peoples present a special problem in that even traditional approaches to literacy instruction, which are often successful with those who are at least aware of a written form of their language, have no impact on those for whom a written form of language is meaningless. Holistic language approaches, such as language experience, have been relatively successful with these illiterates. The language experience approach uses the student's own vocabulary, language patterns, and experiences to create the reading text and make reading a meaningful process. It is holistic in that it combines oral and written language in the process of developing meaningful learning activities and materials.

Immigration Reform and Language Rights. The 1980s also saw fresh attempts at reforming the immigration laws of the United States—attempts sparked by Alan Simpson, senator from Wyoming, and by Romano Mazzoli, representative from Kentucky. The resulting law, the Immigration Reform and Control Act of 1986, will have a great impact on the nature of the immigrant population in the United States in the 1990s. One immediate effect of this legislation has already been to increase demand for adult ESL programs throughout the country, due particularly to the provision for amnesty in the law.

Related to the growing concern with immigration reform is a movement in the United States to designate English as the official language by constitutional amendment—a movement led by former U.S. senator from

California and noted linguist S. I. Hayakawa. Proponents of English-only laws argue that such legislation is needed to ensure that English is preserved as the country's common bond. They contend that the nation's heritage is threatened by language conflicts and ethnic separatism, and they say they want to avoid problems similar to those in Canada, with its large French-speaking population.

Opponents counter that English is already the official language and doesn't have to be mandated by law. They contend that most immigrants want to learn English anyway, since it is the key to getting ahead. To these opponents, the English-only movement is fueled in part by the xenophobia that also has accompanied calls for immigration reform (Judd, 1987).

Ironically, California, the state with the highest percentage of non-native English-speaking immigrants, passed a proposition in 1986 (Proposition 63) that would decree English as the official language of the state. Already the legislatures of Nebraska, Georgia, Virginia, Illinois, Kentucky, and Indiana have declared English as the official language in their states. At least a dozen other states, including several with large Hispanic populations such as Texas and New York, are considering similar laws through resolutions, legislation, or constitutional amendments.

So far, mainly Hispanic groups in these states have opposed such legislation. Arturo Vargas, senior educational policy fellow of the National Council of La Raza, a national Hispanic organization formed in 1965 to help Hispanic immigrants adjust to life in the United States, says, "On paper Proposition 63 is innocuous. Its effect is much deeper. It would eliminate all public use of any non-English language. The end result would be a community divided along ethnic lines" (Overbea, 1986, p. 5).

The major target of the English-only movement at this time appears to be the bilingual education laws of the United States. Bilingual education has been highly controversial since its inception, and political opponents have tried to weaken it through a variety of means. Critics say that, not only do children in bilingual programs fail to learn English, they also fail to learn their native languages well, so many drop out of school. And even many of those who graduate find they need remedial help when they try to enroll in postsecondary programs. On the other hand, proponents of bilingual education cite a litany of successes and lay blame for large-scale failure on the lack of national commitment to the concept of equal opportunity for language-minority populations.

Several major professional associations have come out in opposition to English-only legislation. The National Council of Teachers of English (NCTE) pledged "to oppose actively action intended to mandate or declare English as an official language or to 'preserve,' 'purify,' or 'enhance,' the language (Overbea, 1986, p. 6). At a 1987 convention, Teachers of English to Speakers of Other Languages (TESOL) passed a resolution that "oppose[s] all measures declaring English the official language of the United States of America or of any legally constituted part thereof" ("TESOL Resolution on Language Rights," 1987, p. 3).

Barriers to Professional Development. A fourth major issue that will continue to plague adult educators who work with limited-English-proficient adults is the issue of part-time employment. Although part-time employment is an issue that has affected all of education as well as the economy in general, the adult educator working with limited-English-proficient learners may be in the position least likely to experience positive change in the 1990s. This situation may be due in part to adult educators' continuing to work in a marginal field of education; although several states currently certify adult educators, most states continue to rely on uncertified part-time teachers to fill their classes.

One effect of this part-time employment is a growing attrition of adult educators and a growing dissatisfaction among those who stay (Heresz, 1985). In Illinois, over 90 percent of those teaching adult ESL are doing so on a part-time basis. Most of these part-time teachers are women who entered the field in the 1970s at a time when demand for part-time employment was great. Entering the 1990s, many of those part-time teachers have become "hopeful full-timers" (Tuckman, Caldwell, and Vogler, 1978, p. 189)— those who have not been able to find full-time academic positions. Many academic institutions that conduct ESL programs for adult learners now rely heavily on part-time employees for their teaching staffs. They argue that since funding for these programs is "soft," and since their needs will vary from term to term, they cannot offer tenure-track positions (Gappa, 1984).

Despite what appears to be steady growth in the numbers of adult ESL learners, especially in urban metropolitan areas, and despite a rich pool of highly trained and motivated teachers, full-time employment will continue to be an evasive goal in the 1990s. Part-time employment has become a hallmark of our economy in the 1980s. Flexibility, economy, and accountability have become the criteria for decision making in public higher education, just as they have become in the private sector. Even reports of high-level task forces have had little influence on changing this mentality.

What are the implications of these trends for the professional development of the field? One possible outcome of the continuing dependence on part-time teachers is that we will eventually experience a vacuum of leadership in the classroom and in the field at large. Part-time teachers, who are paid only for the time spent teaching in the classroom, are usually unavailable for student consultations or for the work of important committees within the institution. Increasingly the work load in these areas will fall on an overburdened full-time staff or on administrators. Faculty-controlled processes will be increasingly controlled by administrators.

Graduate education may suffer as a result of an increasingly dissatisfied teaching force. Many part-time teachers are already realizing the futility of obtaining that next degree if it will offer no assurance of eventual full-time employment. Many of the current cohort of experienced teachers in the field will become increasingly impatient with institutions of education that continue to adopt management models from business and to treat students and learning as commodities that can be packaged and marketed in a society increasingly impressed with slick brochures and quick results.

The issues identified in this section are, of course, all interrelated. Immigration reform and the English-only movement are sure to impact the professional field of adult ESL. Already, programs that were having to put students on waiting lists are experiencing even more pressures as public awareness of the literacy problem in the United States increases.

Yet, at the same time that such programs must turn students away, and in the face of inadequate funding, state and national programs have focused on the use of volunteers to teach. Widespread use of volunteers will not work in the United States as they may have worked in Cuba or Nicaragua. The United States is much more ethnically diverse; its programs are more geographically scattered; and employment requires a higher level of literacy than might normally be required in a more agrarian society.

Resources for Adult Educators

As bleak as the picture may be for adult educators who wish to make a career in the field, there is hope. For just as there may be limits on the opportunities apparent in more traditional educational outlets, there are increasing opportunities for those who are mobile and motivated by the opportunities to work in cross-cultural settings. To support that work, several important agencies and organizations have been established in whole or in part to service the needs of adult ESL teachers.

Professional Associations. Several professional associations continue to work for the benefit of those who wish to pursue careers in the field of adult ESL. Among them in the United States are the following:

The American Association for Adult and Continuing Education
1201 16th St. N.W., Suite 230
Washington, D.C. 20036
U.S.A.

Teachers of English to Speakers of Other Languages
1118 22nd St. N.W., Suite 205
Washington, D.C. 20037
U.S.A.

Both of these American organizations have units whose specific purpose is to work for the interests of ESL teachers in adult education. In Canada, the following organization is the contact:

TESL Canada
136 Grenbeck Dr.
Scarborough, Ontario M1V 2H6
Canada

Information. In addition, clearinghouses can provide information for adult educators working with limited-English-proficient learners. Primary among these clearinghouses are the following:

Clearinghouse on Adult Education
U.S. Department of Education
400 Maryland Avenue S.W.
Room 522, Reporters Building
Washington, D.C. 20202
U.S.A.

ERIC Clearinghouse on Languages and Linguistics
The Center for Applied Linguistics
1118 22nd St. N.W.
Washington, D.C. 20037
U.S.A.

National Clearinghouse for Bilingual Education
11501 Georgia Avenue
Wheaton, Maryland 20901
U.S.A.

Emerging Trends

For adult educators working with limited-English-proficient learners, the 1990s will likely see the continuation of some dominant trends from the 1980s:

1. The numbers of limited-English-proficient adults served in adult education programs will continue to increase.
2. Workplace English will displace general "survival" English.
3. There will be a shortage of qualified trained ESL teachers and an increased use of volunteers.
4. There will be a greater focus on teacher training, especially in-service training, because of high numbers of inexperienced teachers entering the field.
5. Technology, including computer assisted instruction, should continue to occupy a more prominent position in classroom instruction.

Summary

In spite of a general uncertainty over employment conditions in the United States and Canada, well-trained adult educators will be in great demand to meet the needs of public and private institutions and agencies that provide services to limited-English-proficient adults in the local community. Immigrants and displaced persons from all over the world will continue to look to North America as a final destination. Many more will seek the services of trained language specialists on a more temporary basis as they work and study in North America in preparation for their return to their home countries. Opportunities for research and for creative programming will contribute to the excitement that waits for all of us as we approach the twenty-first century.

References

Asher, J. J. *Learning Another Language Through Actions: The Complete Teacher's Guidebook.* (2nd ed.) Los Gatos, Calif.: Sky Oaks Productions, 1982.

Blatchford, C. H. (ed.). *Directory of Teacher Preparation Programs in TESOL and Bilingual Education 1981–1984.* Washington, D.C.: Teachers of English to Speakers of Other Languages, 1982.

Bodman, J. "Student-Centering Education: The Gentle Revolution in ESL Teaching." In D. E. Bartley (ed.), *The Adult Basic Education TESOL Handbook.* New York: Collier Macmillan International, 1979.

Brown, H. D. *Principles of Language Learning and Teaching.* Englewood Cliffs, N.J.: Prentice-Hall, 1980.

Center for Applied Linguistics. *From the Classroom to the Workplace: Teaching ESL to Adults.* Washington, D.C.: Center for Applied Linguistics/ERIC, 1983.

Curran, C. *Counseling-Learning in Second Languages.* Apple River, Ill.: Apple River Press, 1976.

Diller, K. C. *The Language Teaching Controversy.* Rowley, Mass.: Newbury House, 1978.

Ek, J.A.V. *The Threshold Level in a European Unit/Credit System for Modern Language Learning by Adults.* Strasbourg, France: Council of Europe, 1975.

Gappa, J. M. *Part-Time Faculty: Higher Education at a Crossroads.* Washington, D.C.: Association for the Study of Higher Education, 1984.

Gattegno, C. *The Common Sense of Teaching Foreign Languages.* New York: Educational Solutions, 1976.

Heresz, A. J. "Factors Leading to Job Satisfaction and Job Dissatisfaction Among Adult Basic Education Teachers in Northern Illinois." Unpublished master's thesis, Department of Leadership and Educational Policy Studies, Northern Illinois University, 1985.

Judd, E. L. "The English Language Amendment: A Case Study on Language and Politics." *TESOL Quarterly,* 1987, *21* (1), 113–135.

Jupp, T. C., and Hodlin, S. *Industrial English: An Example of Theory and Practice in Functional Language Teaching.* London: Heinemann Educational Books, 1975.

Kelly, L. G. *25 Centuries of Language Teaching.* Rowley, Mass.: Newbury House, 1969.

Kozol, J. *Illiterate America.* New York: Doubleday, 1985.

Krashen, S. D. "Some Issues Relating to the Monitor Model." In H. D.

Brown, C. Yorio, and R. Crymes (eds.), *On TESOL '77: Teaching and Learning English as a Second Language: Trends in Research and Practice.* Washington, D.C.: Teachers of English to Speakers of Other Languages, 1977.

Krashen, S. D. *Second Language Acquisition and Second Language Learning.* Elmsford, N.Y.: Pergamon Press, 1981.

Krashen, S. D., and Terrell, T. *The Natural Approach: Language Acquisition in the Classroom.* Oxford, Eng.: Pergamon Press, 1983.

Lewis, R. "Adult Education and the Foreign Born." In D. Rowden (ed.), *Handbook of Adult Education in the United States 1934.* New York: American Association for Adult Education, 1934.

McArthur, T. *A Foundation Course for Language Teachers.* Cambridge, Eng.: Cambridge University Press, 1983.

National Commission on Excellence in Education. *A Nation at Risk: The Imperative for Educational Reform.* Washington, D.C.: U.S. Department of Education, 1983.

Overbea, L. "California Vote Speeds U.S. Drive to Make English 'Official.'" *Christian Science Monitor,* Dec. 17, 1986, pp. 5–6.

Pratt, S. (ed.). *English in the Workplace (TESL Talk).* Toronto: Ministry of Citizenship and Culture, 1982.

Richards, J. C., and Rodgers, T. S. *Approaches and Methods in Language Teaching: A Description and Analysis.* Cambridge, Eng.: Cambridge University Press, 1986.

Rosten, L. Q. *The Education of Hyman Kaplan.* San Diego, Calif.: Harcourt Brace Jovanovich, 1937.

"TESOL Resolution on Language Rights." *TESOL Newsletter,* 1987, *21* (3), 3.

Trim, J.L.M. *Developing a Unit/Credit Scheme of Adult Language Learning.* Elmsford, N.Y.: Pergamon Press, 1978.

Tuckman, H. P., Caldwell, J., and Vogler, W. D. "Part-Timers and the Academic Labor Market of the Eighties." *The American Sociologist,* 1978, *13,* 184–195.

Winitz, H. (ed.). *The Comprehension Approach to Foreign Language Instruction.* Rowley, Mass.: Newbury House, 1981.

38

Health Education

Victoria J. Marsick
Robert R. Smedley

Health education is being transformed by sweeping changes in society, by the way in which both professionals and consumers understand health and access services, and by the fields of medicine and education themselves. The authors suggest that a shift in fundamental beliefs underlies this transformation. This chapter reviews some of these changes, and explores implications for the meaning and practice of health education.

The Social Side of Health Education

Epp (1986, p. 2), minister of national health and welfare in Canada, describes "health as a part of everyday living, an essential dimension of the quality of our lives." Epp links health with citizen and community choices "to gain satisfaction from living," a very broad definition and a radical departure from "merely . . . treating and curing illness and injuries." Epp puts into words an increasing expectation of many North Americans that good health be a natural part of their lifelong development (Aldrich, 1987).

Epp breaks with what is frequently referred to as the traditional medical model. In this model, people who are defined as ill look to Western medicine and to the physicians who practice it for a cure. However, Epp recognizes that people must be helped to take more control over their health habits. Mortality and disease have been greatly reduced, but a concomitant increase in chronic illness, disability, and stress has slowed progress toward the goal of health for all—a goal called for by the World Health Organization. The most serious health problems that plague North Americans are related to environmental pressures and life-style—diseases such as stroke, cancer, mental illness, diabetes, arthritis, high blood pressure, heart disease, and other chronic illnesses. Health status is thus greatly affected by social habits that are not easily changed by physicians.

A major challenge is the reduction of inequities in access to the health care delivery system. Despite the many successes of the existing system, the United States has failed miserably to provide equal access to proper medical care for the poor. This situation represents a failure in public policy as well as a failure on the part of health care providers (Thier, 1987).

Human behavior plays a pivotal role in health status. Brundage (1980) notes that human behavior is organized around three tendencies: to master, to be mastered, and to belong. The tendency to master is central to emerging new concepts of health prevention and promotion, discussed later in this chapter, because it is concerned with autonomy, independence, and personal control over conditions in one's life. The tendency to be mastered is reflected in a traditional dependence on the medical model. And the tendency to belong relates to a growing recognition of social interdependence in managing many of today's health problems. Changing human behavior requires more than the golden key, the missing link, the magic bullet, or the serendipitous breakthrough of the traditional medical model. Critics of the health establishment suggest the key might not be available because the answers do not reside solely in technology and because physicians often have the crippling hold on changes in health delivery and a vested interest in the maintenance of their power.

The medical profession has been the beneficiary of a centuries-old social contract that says it will receive autonomy and respect as long as its members behave in a professional, responsible manner. But society can and will take away that respect and autonomy. That social contract is at risk with government, insurance companies, and large corporations asking, How can it be that a profession generates and uses more and more medications, more and more laboratory tests, and more and more devices but does not really know when they are indicated or what their effectiveness is in practice and yet expects to be reimbursed at a continuously increasing rate? Failure to answer this question has placed the traditional medical model in a defensive stance since the early 1980s. The president of the Institute of Medicine of the American Academy of Sciences has indicated that medicine as a profession is not held in high esteem in Washington, D.C. or by members of many segments of society. It is viewed as self-serving and as more interested in its own prerogatives than in its patients (Thier, 1987).

Given the complexity of the challenge, it is clear that physicians cannot alone respond to emerging health needs. A partnership of professionals, paraprofessionals, and consumers is emerging to address life-style and environmental changes needed for health, even though the roles and power relationships among these partners are still being worked out. Education assumes a key role in this partnership, in part to provide information to individuals and in part to address societal changes. Since doctors are not always considered good educators, this education role is increasingly being claimed by other health professionals, including health educators, and by many consumers.

Laws and public policies regarding health education have responded to societal changes and have helped shape some of these forces. Green (1981, p. 13) identified four influential eras of federal investment in U.S. health. The first era (1940s and 1950s) emphasized expertise and infrastructure. Thier (1987) notes that in this era, clinical and public health expertise developed separately, thus building a wall between the two that has never been bridged. In the 1960s, resources were redistributed as policy dealt with access to services and as laws were passed requiring citizen participation in the planning of neighborhood health centers. Cost containment in the third era, the 1970s, led to less expensive patient consumer health education. And this change broke ground for a fourth era of health promotion and disease prevention in the 1980s.

In the next section, we describe changes in health care management—changes by both providers and consumers that clarify the emerging role played by health promotion in this era.

Changes in Health Care Management

Societal changes have had a significant impact upon medical practice and the medical profession (Mawby, 1986). Bureaucracy and institutionalization have encroached upon collegiality and entrepreneurship. At the same time, professional review organizations, third-party payers, and payment guidelines (for example, reimbursement based on diagnostic related groups) have moved decisions out of the hands of physicians into those of hospital administrators, quality assurance experts, organizational accountants, and oversight bodies at institutional, state, and federal levels. Hospitals and health care institutions are no longer nonprofit agencies, and they vie with one another for both inpatient care and outpatient educational wellness programs (Califano, 1986).

Rapid change has left the medical profession confused about defining standards of professional competence. In the meantime, the health care industry has stepped in by default and has imposed standards for allowable medical interventions. For some, this climate represents the sad but ongoing drama of the demise of professional autonomy and dominance. For others, it represents a reality whose time has finally come. For still others, it is a challenge to make operational a more holistic ethic of medicine—a movement away from the dualism and mind-body split of Western Cartesian medicine, an emphasis on natural remedies over chemical solutions, and a movement away from childlike dependence on the authority of the doctor.

An issue of concern to all health providers and regulatory bodies is the quality and cost of care—the efficacy of certain common medical practices, the harmful side effects of widely prescribed drugs, the necessity of frequently performed surgical procedures, and the widely differing medical management of patients with the same condition. This concern is reflected in the growth of self-help groups, in the rising numbers of malpractice suits, in the increase of illness caused by medical treatment, and in the proliferation of federal programs to monitor and to assess the efficacy and safety of new medical technologies and drugs (Caporael-Katz and Levin, 1987).

Quality assurance problems facing the health educator and the health practitioner are similar since difficulties of noncompliance and multiple health problems result as much from socioeconomic and life-style conditions as from disease. The health educator and provider both need to know how to evaluate their work to be assured that they understand the true nature of the problem and that they have taken appropriate action.

For allied health professionals, these realities reaffirm and institutionalize an existing holistic practice that has been built up since the early sixties. Nurses, physical therapists, mental health workers, and other paraprofessionals have joined the health educators to work as a multidisciplinary team in integrated health care, prevention, and promotion. Joining them are myriad health-related volunteer agencies such as the American Cancer Society, whose primary function is education of the public.

The public also has changed its attitude toward health care. Many have become disenchanted with the mystique of medicine and have turned instead to an elaborate system of self-care. Canadian policy on health promotion is built on self-care, mutual aid, and healthful environments (Epp, 1986, p. 7). Women have played a key role in this shift from passive to active involvement (Clement, 1987). Caporael-Katz and Levin (1987) point out that, historically, self-care has always competed with professional care, that self-care is frequently preferred, and that this mode has gained ascendancy for some of the reasons described earlier in this chapter. Self-care can be highly idiosyncratic to the individual, but many programs in which education plays a central role have been developed to assist the consumer. Examples include consumer resource centers, lectures and home demonstrations, courses in alternative therapies, self-help groups, and health collectives.

Not all subscribe to self-care philosophies; yet even those who place their faith in traditional medicine have become informed consumers. Trends discussed above show that people are becoming more educated and active at the same time that the health system has been forced to become more entrepreneurial. The result is an expanded marketplace for health education. School health now includes colleges, community colleges, and universities. According to a 1986 survey, 44 percent of private employers with more than fifty employees sponsored workplace health promotion programs (U.S. Department of Health and Human Services, 1987). Health education is available over the telephone, on television, and in nutrition and exercise centers. For example, Burch-Minakan (1987) maps a burgeoning field of mainframe and microcomputer interactive software aimed at health risk appraisal, at education on various health and nutrition topics, and at combined exercise and nutrition programs. And finally, individuals unite in social action when group consciousness is raised through crises such as nuclear accidents or toxic waste dump emergencies.

Paradigm Shifts

From the above discussion it is clear that radical changes have affected the entire health care system. Green (1981) suggests that a number of paradigm shifts are going on today in the health care field—shifts that have major implications for the way education is provided. Less emphasis is now placed on activities than is placed on health impact, less on diagnosis than on prognosis, less on the biomedical model than on a biosocial model, less on acute conditions than on chronic conditions, less on cure than on prevention or control, and less on the expert role than on the consumer. Green's analysis implies a shift in educational perspective from providing "shots" of information as supplements for doctors' prescriptions to empowering people to educate themselves on an ongoing basis as they change life-styles to maintain their health. Epp (1986) confirms this analysis.

Schön (1983) examines a paradigm in the professional world shifting away from what he calls technical rationality—an exclusive reliance on scientific objectivity that characterizes mainstream Western medicine. Advocates of technical rationality solve problems that conform to a scientific method and thus avoid the complex situations that most health educators face. Health education often reinforces the technical rationality of traditional medicine in that people are thought to be best educated by diagnosing the problem and giving them the right information to solve it. This model does not sufficiently consider the context in which people make decisions—the personal viewpoints of both clients and staff, the organization and community in which people interact, and the physical setting. It also does not account for the empowerment that occurs when people take more control over their own health decisions.

Adult educators advocate putting control of learning into the hands of clients—an approach more in consonance with their active role. Andragogy, popularized by Knowles (1980) and often used in the health professions, emphasizes learner choice more than expert control, although Knowles is often criticized as not helping learners to become more critically reflective and autonomous. Freire (1970) goes even further by putting control directly into the hands of the clients, with a facilitator acting as catalyst for critical reflection and analysis. Freire, however, is often perceived as too radical for many government-sponsored programs since his strategy speaks directly to social and political change based on heightened awareness of oppressive social structures.

Paradigm shifts in the educational world parallel shifts taking place in the health world, and they both have implications for the models that health educators choose (Marsick, 1987). These paradigm shifts signal changes in the meaning of health education to different populations. Health education not only has moved from a primary focus on giving information to a focus on helping people change life-styles, but it also has evolved "from focusing on individual behavior change to a concern for organizational, economic and environmental factors which are conducive to healthy lifestyles, self-reliance and political action for health promotion" (World Health Organization, 1983, p. 10). As Labonte (1987) points out, this shift in focus often involves movement from a politically neutral position to an advocate or social activist role. The next section examines implications for an expanded concept of health education.

Expanded Concept of Health Education

Many still interpret health education primarily in terms of communication of health information, although the definition most widely accepted in the United States is that of Green and others (1980, p. 7)—"any combination of learning experiences designed to facilitate voluntary adaptations of behavior conducive to health." Education is thus one small part of the equation, as it is in health promotion. The stance one takes toward education and how it is carried out depends greatly on one's interpretation of the terms *education* and *promotion*.

In the United States, health promotion is focused primarily on individual life-style changes and is separated from environmental health protection and preventive health services (U.S. Department of Health and Human Services, 1980). Canada (Epp, 1986), by contrast, subscribes to the World Health Organization's (1983, p. 6) more integrated definition of health promotion: "the process of enabling people to increase control over, and to improve, their health." Canada's solutions are oriented more to public participation, community health, and policy support (pp. 9–11). Allegrante (1984), contends that health educators in the United States may pay too much attention to changing individuals and not enough to larger political, economic, and social forces. He draws on a story about a dilemma of modern medicine in which a doctor finds himself so busy pulling drowning people to shore than he can never investigate who upstream is pushing them in. Allegrante (p. 372) concludes that health promotion should empower the disadvantaged and should foster "critical political analysis of those environmental and organizational conditions in society that lead to the manufacture of disease and illness."

Allegrante's call is closer to the notion of empowerment embraced by some adult educators such as Freire. On the other hand, not all interpret education and promotion primarily as empowerment with social action overtones. For example, competency-based education sets out to achieve clearly defined, criterion-referenced, behavioral objectives specific to health practices. Competency-based education is considered critical to the accuracy of technical procedures on which lives depend. Its advocates argue that health educators translate technical information for laypersons, and that empowerment rests in people's understanding of what is good for them and in their understanding of their ability to practice it. Health promotion from this perspective has less to do with critical reflection on external social norms that might be oppressive and more to do with changes in life-styles, whether the motivation for change be the result of internal conviction or of external incentives.

Shifts toward an expanded definition of health education have implications for the role of the health educator. Caporael-Katz and Levin (1987) describe two of these new roles. First, the health educator must help consumers evaluate medical practices and assess health care options. The health educator must thus become more knowledgeable to ensure that consumers understand the consequences of health decisions. A second related role is advocacy for informed consent. Since health educators bridge the gap between health information and health practices, they have an ethical obligation to determine benefits and risks and then to advise the consumer.

Finally, a communications problem caused by a mix of highly trained specialists with different professional subspecialties, each with its own special language, must be addressed. Technical jargon, different ways of thinking, and different professional approaches may make an integrated view of broad, complex problems difficult. Health educators face the double responsibility of bridging a communication gap between and among professionals, while interpreting for the consumer the combined professional schools of thought.

International Context

As noted in Chapter Seven, nowhere are contrasts in interpretation of health greater than in developing countries, in part because Western medicine has been layered on top of indigenous health systems with different explanations of disease and health. Values of scientific objectivity that undergird all development efforts clash with local values, and health reform is intricately intertwined with issues of social justice between the haves and the have-nots.

Empowerment is at the heart of international health education because of a commitment made to primary health care (PHC) at an international conference at Alma-Ata, USSR in 1978. Based on concepts such as equity, community self-reliance, and the integration of social and economic development, PHC demands a total restructuring and decentralization of health service. PHC starts with people in underserved communities defining their own health needs and developing basic self-help systems to meet them. The health infrastructure is then reoriented to serve these basic needs.

Interpretations of health education or promotion in the international context vary with the points of view of the programs, many of which are run by governments with some assistance from international agencies. Health education programs were often information oriented, but they have moved more recently toward behavioral-change strategies that emphasize adoption of often-unfamiliar Western concepts of health service. As PHC becomes accepted, education is also aimed, ideally, at individual and social empowerment. However, there is an inherent contradiction between a philosophy of empowerment and the reality of government persuasion to adopt a recommended practice, even though basic health interventions do ensure a better chance of survival and development.

Adult educators active in PHC sit in both the persuasion and empowerment camps, as perhaps do health educators in the United States who combine aspects of transformation and competency basing. Adult educators inform people about problems and solutions, mobilize them for action, empower them, integrate health with other sectors, consolidate gains, and ensure ongoing support (Cervinskas, 1984). One key difference is that the developing world typically has less education, less affluence, and less access to information and resources. Health education is thus often focused on survival and on health promotion and empowerment involving resource distribution and community action.

Educational Strategies

This last section takes a closer look at educational strategies used for the different purposes of health education. Favin and others (1986) note the absence of neat categories for health education activities due to the immense variety of target populations, the numerous communications channels, the need for integration with other development activities, the management by government or private agencies, and the vast degree of comprehensiveness. They cite two basic approaches to health education that cut across this variety—the community development or nonformal education approach and the social marketing approach.

This dichotomy is, to some extent, a more advanced stage of the early disagreement among health educators as to whether face-to-face methods were more effective or whether one should rely primarily on mass media. The first approach, as a pure type, emphasizes face-to-face methods while the second approach, as a pure type, emphasizes the mass media. The dichotomy can also be seen as a continuum that reflects both consumer and provider themes. Nonformal education and face-to-face interaction are often seen as consumer oriented, while social marketing and mass media can be viewed as expert oriented.

These two different strategies also reflect historical development of societies. In the early days of health education, emphasis was placed on developing audiovisual aids and on using different methods. As low-cost technology and public acceptance of media advanced, so too did the strategies used for education. Not only can the mass media provide information to a larger group of people, but they can also shape public opinion and motivate action. In the United States, the trend is toward video and computer education, even though pamphlets and other written material still form the backbone of many programs.

A distinction made by Mezirow (1985) is helpful in understanding the appropriateness of different educational strategies for health programs. He differentiates among three domains of learning: instrumental, dialogic, and self-reflective, each of which is served by a different educational strategy. Instrumental learning refers to task-oriented problem solving; dialogic refers to the way in which people come to understand consensual norms; and self-reflective refers to the way in which people understand themselves.

Most health education programs are primarily instrumental in nature, particularly when their role is to communicate information to a motivated public, as for example, when discussing AIDS with highly aware, at-risk populations. When programs move toward health promotion, interpreted as empowerment, they involve the critical examination of social, cultural, and organizational norms—sometimes followed by social action to change those norms. For example, AIDS has spurred public debate and policy proposals regarding quarantine, mandatory testing, and workplace exclusionary laws that require review of highly valued social norms such as privacy and equality of opportunity. Self-reflective learning may be triggered voluntarily or through a crisis and typically involves a deep examination of one's personal perspectives. The nature of AIDS, has, for example, spurred personal reevaluations of sexual habits and social interaction.

Educational strategies for instrumental learning have been better documented in the health education field than have those for dialogic and self-reflective learning. For example, various sourcebooks in health and adult education outline the advantages and disadvantages of different media for instrumental learning by audience, by message, and by focus (Green and others, 1980; Knowles, 1980; Favin and others, 1986). The media do not differ for dialogic or self-reflective learning, but the purposes and approaches do. Dialogic learning relies upon free and informed discussion. It is problem posing in the Freire tradition more than it is problem solving in nature, and hence it emphasizes client analysis of dilemmas, open-ended problem dramas, critical incidents, projective stories, and other means of stimulating awareness. Self-reflective learning depends primarily on the critical examination of personal experience, often in support groups with others facing the same problem, and draws on the psychoanalytic tradition.

Conclusion

The decade of the 1980s may well be viewed as a pivotal era in health education. Throughout this chapter, we have identified significant developments that call for expanded concepts and broader definitions of health education. And we have described the need for new educational strategies in the provision of health education. Societal changes, legal and public policy issues, changes in the health care system, changes in the attitudes of providers and consumers of health care, and the growing recognition that human behavior plays a major role in health status have all contributed to an expanded marketplace for health education. Traditional models of health education are being critically examined and new models are being carefully evaluated and modified to incorporate the sweeping changes and the impact of society upon health status. The growing body of knowledge of health education and its application to health problems is a formidable challenge to the health educator in the final decade of the twentieth century.

References

Aldrich, R. "The Social Context of Change." In L. D. Duhl and N. Cummings (eds.), *The Future of Mental Health Services—Coping with Crisis.* New York: Springer, 1987.

Allegrante, J. P. "Potential Uses and Misuses of Education in Health Promotion and Disease Prevention." *Teachers College Record,* 1984, *86,* (2), 359–373.

Brundage, B. *Adult Learning Principles and Their Application to Program Planning.* Toronto: Ministry of Education, 1980.

Burch-Minakan, L. "The Use of Computers in Health Education." In P.M. Lazes, L. H. Kaplan, and K. A. Gordon (eds.), *The Handbook of Health Education.* (2nd ed.) Rockville, Md.: Aspen Publications, 1987.

Califano, J. *America's Health Care Revolution: Who Lives? Who Dies? Who Pays?* New York: Random House, 1986.

Caporael-Katz, B., and Levin, L. S. "Self-Care Education." In P. M. Lazes, L. H. Kaplan, and K. A. Gordon (eds.), *The Handbook of Health Education.* (2nd ed.) Rockville, Md.: Aspen Publications, 1987.

Cervinskas, J. *Organizing for Health.* Toronto: International Council for Adult Education, 1984.

Clement, C. "Women and Health: From Passive to Active." *Health Promotion,* 1987, *25* (4), 5–8.

Epp, J. "Achieving Health for All: A Framework for Health Promotion." Special insert. *Health Promotion,* 1986, *25* (1–2), 1–13.

Favin, M., and others. *Health Education.* Information for Action issue paper, World Federation of Public Health Associations for the United Nations Children's Fund (UNICEF) and the Aga Khan Foundation. Washington, D.C.: American Public Health Association, 1986.

Freire, P. *Pedagogy of the Oppressed.* (M. Bergman, trans.) San Francisco: Seabury Press, 1970.

Green, L. W. *Emerging Federal Perspectives on Health Promotion.* Health Promotion Monographs, no. 1. New York: Teachers College Press, 1981.

Green, L. W., and others. *Health Education Planning: A Diagnostic Approach.* Palo Alto, Calif.: Mayfield, 1980.

Knowles, M. S. *The Modern Practice of Adult Education.* (Rev. ed.) Chicago: Association Press/Follett, 1980.

Labonte, R. "Community Health Promotion Strategies." *Health Promotion,* 1987, *26* (1), 5–10, 32.

Marsick, V. J. "Designing Health Education Programs." In P. M. Lazes, L. H. Kaplan, and K. A. Gordon (eds.), *The Handbook of Health Education.* (2nd ed.) Rockville, Md.: Aspen Publications, 1987.

Mawby, R. "Lifelong Learning and the Professional." *MOBIUS,* 1986, *6* (2), 35–39.

Mezirow, J. D. "A Critical Theory of Self-Directed Learning." In S. Brookfield (ed.), *Self-Directed Learning: From Theory to Practice.* New Directions for Continuing Education, no. 25. San Francisco: Jossey-Bass, 1985.

Schön, D. *The Reflective Practitioner.* New York: Basic Books, 1983.

Thier, S. "The Future of American Medicine: The Social Contract at Risk." Speech delivered at Temple University Hospital Grand Rounds, Philadelphia, Dec. 1987.

U.S. Department of Health and Human Services. *Promoting Health and Preventing Disease: Objectives for the Nation.* Washington, D.C.: Office of the Assistant Secretary for Health, Public Health Service, 1980.

U.S. Department of Health and Human Services. *National Survey of Worksite Health Promotion Activities.* Washington, D.C.: Office of Disease Prevention and Health Promotion, 1987.

World Health Organization. *New Policies for Health Education in Primary Health Care.* Background document for technical discussions, 36th World Health Assembly, Geneva, Switzerland, Feb. 1983.

39

Continuing Education for the Professions

Ronald M. Cervero

There can be little argument that the professions are central to the functioning of society. They teach our children, manage and account for our money, settle our disputes, diagnose our mental and physical ills, guide our businesses, help many of us mediate our relationship to God, and fight our wars. Their members represent upwards of a quarter of the work force and are the primary decision makers for the major institutions of society. The work of professionals is important not only because of their technical skill, but also because they define, to a great extent, the problems on which they work. As a result, they have the power to define our needs. For example, educators decide what our children will learn as well as how they will learn it. Physicians decide who is healthy and who is not. The special place of the professions in society results as much from their symbolic leadership as from the application of their technical knowledge and skills.

From the beginning of the move to organize professional groups, both their leaders and the public have assumed that practitioners would engage in learning throughout their working lives. They were correct about this: professionals have learned through books, discussions with colleagues, formal and informal educational programs, and the rigors of their everyday practice. The provision of one of these forms of learning, formal continuing education programs, has increased dramatically in the past quarter century. Although no precise data are available, most knowledgeable observers estimate that billions of dollars are spent annually to provide and attend such programs (Eurich, 1985). As a result, organized and comprehensive continuing education programs exist today in management, architecture, engineering, law, medicine, pharmacy, veterinary medicine, social work, nursing home administration, the military, nursing, public school education, and many other professions.

There is a great deal of evidence to indicate that most professions now embrace the seriousness of lifelong professional education. Medicine, perhaps more than most professions, has recognized this for many years (Meyer, 1975). The president of the Association of American Law Schools recently chided those who seek a solution to the problem of lawyer proficiency by focusing solely on law schools. He said these people fail to appreciate that, "Legal education is a lifelong process that requires a joint effort by the law schools, the bench and the bar, and individual lawyers" (Vernon, 1983, pp. 559–560). A prominent member of the library profession said that even fifteen years ago the discussion of the term *continuing education* was thought to be unimportant by the leaders of the field. Yet, in 1985, at the first World Conference on Continuing Education for Librarians, she observed that, "Continuing library education was advocated as an essential element of a librarian's lifetime education" (Stone, 1986, p. 489).

These visions reflect the increasing amount of attention being paid to continuing education in the professions. Many professions have a system of accreditation for providers of continuing education (Kenny, 1985). All fifty states use participation in continuing education as a basis for relicensing members of professions. Phillips (1987) lists sixteen professions that are regulated in this way. The future of continuing professional education appears to be headed for rapid growth, possibly culminating in the development of systems of continuing education that rival the preprofessional preparation programs currently in existence.

What Is Continuing Professional Education?

An area of educational practice devoted to continuing education for the professions has sprung into existence within the past two decades. This field is becoming increasingly differentiated from the educational practices of preprofessional education. For example, many practitioners think of themselves, and are considered by others, to be continuing medical educators or continuing engineering educators. In fact, many of these individuals may not have had any experience in the preprofessional education of the groups with whom they work. The evidence for this movement toward a distinct field of practice is unmistakable. For example, several journals in North America are devoted exclusively to the theory and research of continuing education for a specific profession. These include the *Journal of Continuing Education in the Health Professions,* the *Journal of Continuing Social Work Education,* *The Journal of Continuing Education in Nursing,* and the *Journal of Nursing Staff Development.* In addition, there is a trend for continuing educators in specific occupations to form interest groups within their national professional organizations, such as the American Nurses' Association. Other educators choose to form their own associations that are organized on a national level, such as the National Association of State Judicial Educators, or at a North American level, such as the Society of Medical School Directors of Continuing Medical Education and the Society for the Advancement of Continuing Education in Ministry.

In building their continuing education systems, most professions have relied for guidance and models on the distinctive knowledge base and structures of their own professions. In fact, this is the dominant frame of reference used to conceptualize the continuing education processes of a particular professional group. For example, many physicians, accountants, and lawyers would claim that the guiding motivation of their continuing education is to keep them up-to-date. Without knowledge of the other professional educational systems, the leaders of many professions assume that their continuing education processes are unique to their own profession. This frame of reference assumes that the continuing education systems of various professions have little in common.

Consistent with this viewpoint, the leaders of most professions believe that the continuing education function must be directed by its own members. However, a competing viewpoint is emerging based on the premise that individuals trained in the field of continuing education have the most appropriate background for this function. While there is an increasing movement toward this emerging view, its adherents are still in a significant minority. One estimate (Griffith, 1985) is that of all people performing continuing education functions within the professions, 95 percent have been trained only in the content of their own professions. The remaining 5 percent either have their formal training only in education (4.5 percent) or have been trained both in their profession and in education (0.5 percent).

As the intellectual base for the emerging view, many people have noted the similarities in the continuing education efforts of individual professions in terms of goals, processes, and issues (Cervero, 1988; Cervero and Scanlan, 1985; Houle, 1980; LeBreton and others, 1979; Nowlen, 1988; Stern, 1983). The early advocates for this comparative approach were adult and continuing educators who were struck by the similarities in the educational processes used by the different professions with which they worked. The concept of continuing professional education began to be used in the late 1960s to describe this identifiable field of study and practice.

The most important person in the development of this concept is Cyril O. Houle, who began writing about the comparative approach to continuing education for the professions in the late 1960s, culminating in his seminal book, *Continuing Learning in the Professions* (1980). His comparative study of seventeen professions convinced him that, "Certain dominant conceptions guide all of them as they turn to the task of educating their members and that they tend to use essentially the same kinds of facilities, techniques, and thought processes" (Houle, 1980, p. 15). The most important rationale for this movement is that the study of similarities across the professions can yield a fresh exchange of ideas, practices, and solutions to common problems.

The comparative approach to continuing education for the professions has an identity both in a literature base as well as in the social organization of educators. Several books (Cervero, 1988; Cervero and Scanlan, 1985; Green, Grosswald, Suter, and Walthall, 1984; Houle, 1980; Nowlen, 1988; Stern, 1983), numerous articles (Pennington and Green, 1976; *Canadian Journal of University Continuing Education*, 1983), and many conference reports from Canada (Baskett and Taylor, 1980) and from the United States (Haag, 1987) have been published on the topic of continuing professional education. The way in which professional associations organize themselves reflects an increasing awareness of continuing professional education. For example, two major associations of adult and continuing educators in North America (the National University Continuing Education Association and the American Association for Adult and Continuing Education) have specialized divisions devoted to continuing professional education. Finally, many North American graduate programs in adult and continuing education have a course or sequence of courses devoted to the special knowledge, skills, and issues necessary for effective practice in continuing professional education.

Although continuing professional education is a recognizable area of educational practice, its conceptual base is a product of several other fields of study. The emerging view of educational practice applies the concepts, theories, and research from several frames of reference to the practice of continuing professional education. In this view, members of a specific profession are like *all* other adults in that they share basic human processes such as motivation, cognition, and emotions; like *some* other adults in that they belong to a profession; and like *no* other adults in that they belong to a particular profession. Each of these frames of reference implies important dimensions that need to be taken into account in the practice of continuing professional education. This view recognizes the importance of the structure, issues, and content of preservice preparation programs and the context of professional practice. However, a significant shift in emphasis from the dominant view holds that this is not the only perspective needed, and that it must be blended with what we know from other areas of education, such as continuing education and human resource development (see Chapter Thirty-Two), in order to offer the strongest conceptual base for practice.

The Audience for Continuing Professional Education

In order to talk intelligently about continuing professional education as a field of practice, we need to examine the differences between professions and other occupations. If this distinction were not made, we may as well talk about adult occupational education (as was done in the 1960 handbook) or about adult and continuing education, because the audience would be undifferentiated from adult learners in general. The problem of defining professions has a long and controversial history, which has been comprehensively analyzed by Friedson (1986). As anyone who has examined the literature on the professions will readily attest, there is no commonly agreed upon answer to the question of what a profession is. Rather, there are schools of thought with different approaches yielding different answers.

The oldest approach was pioneered by Flexner who believed that certain objective criteria distinguish professions from other occupations (Flexner, 1915). Since the 1960s, this approach has received considerable criticism such that almost no one who seriously studies the professions uses it. The major problem with this approach is the persistent lack of consensus about the criteria that should be used to define professions. In contrast to this either-or way of classifying occupations, a second approach considers all occupations existing on a continuum of professionalization. Thus, there is no clear-cut boundary between professions and other occupations. This approach forms the basis of Houle's book, with the educational implication that "all occupations seeking the ideals of professionalization are worthy of sympathetic study" (Houle, 1980, p. 27). While this focus on process appears to avoid the need for a definition of profession, it does not. To discuss the process of professionalization requires one to define the direction of the process—to define the ideal for which occupations are striving. The same critique can be made of this list of ideals as can be made of any of the other lists of defining characteristics of a profession—there is a persistent lack of consensus about what these criteria should be.

The most defensible approach (Friedson, 1986) assumes there is no such thing as an ideal profession and no set of criteria for professional status. There are only those occupations that are commonly regarded as professions and those that are not. Thus, the term *profession* is defined by determining which occupations have achieved the title and privileges of professions. The most common way to determine which occupations are accepted as professions in the United States has been to use the categories of the federal government's Bureau of the Census. Although there is some disagreement about how to use the census categories, the debate has been framed in such a way as to produce a least restrictive and a most restrictive approach to defining professional occupations. In the more restrictive definition, some amount of higher education must be a prerequisite to employment in particular positions. For example, most types of management positions, airline pilots, and legal assistants fail to meet this criterion. In contrast, the least restrictive definition uses all of the occupations included in the Census Bureau's category of professional workers, such as business executives, teachers, nurses, and lawyers. Applying the least restrictive definition to the 1986 census figures, Cervero (1988) concludes that there are nearly 30 million professionals in the United States. This collectivity of occupations made up 27 percent of the work force in 1986. The application of the more restrictive definition produces an estimate of 16 million professionals in the United States, representing about 15 percent of the work force. A similar analysis can be made for the professions in Canada by using its census data (Statistics Canada, 1988). Without a doubt, professions are an important social reality in society. While there is no agreement on which occupations constitute that reality, we know its parameters. Somewhere between 16 million and 30 million people in the United States are given the label of professional by the general public.

Purposes of Continuing Professional Education

Professions have a relatively high degree of control over and influence on the lives of other people in society. This is manifested in the central roles that professionals have in educational, cultural, and health institutions, in businesses, and in the public policy arenas of federal and state governments. Accordingly, it is important to consider the functions and roles that professions have in the larger society and how continuing education should relate to this broader picture. The various viewpoints about the relationship between the professions and society may be distilled into three fundamentally different conceptions. The *functionalist* viewpoint has deep roots in American social theory and practice and has the greatest number of adherents in continuing professional education today. This viewpoint is generally positive about the place of professions in society in contrast to the *conflict* viewpoint, which is essentially negative. The adherents of the *critical* viewpoint wish to restructure the professions in order to minimize their problems. These viewpoints provide the context for thinking about the purposes of continuing professional education.

The Functionalist Viewpoint. The functionalist approach posits that the professions are service- or community-oriented occupations applying a systematic body of knowledge to problems that are highly relevant to the central values of society. This approach stresses the functional value of professional activity for the maintenance of an orderly society. The key concept in this viewpoint is *expertise*. As described by Schön (1983, p. 21), "Professional activity consists in instrumental problem solving made rigorous by the application of scientific theory and technique." The two key assumptions are that practice problems are well formed and unambiguous and that these problems are solved by the application of scientific knowledge. With the ends of professional practice being fixed and unambiguous, the purpose of continuing professional education is to help professionals provide higher quality service to clients by improving their knowledge, competence, or performance. In this viewpoint, there is consensus about what constitutes good practice in a given profession. The educator simply needs to help professionals keep up-to-date with the newest information in their fields and to correct existing deficiencies in their practices.

The Conflict Viewpoint. The conflict approach asserts that professions are in conflict with other groups in society for power, status, and money. The professions use knowledge, skills, and an altruistic orientation as a form of ideology in their quest for these social rewards (Larson, 1977). The key concept in the conflict viewpoint is *power*. Professionals' importance in society comes not from their expertise but rather from their power to prescribe what people need. By being able to define their clients' problems and to prescribe solutions, professionals can create needs for their services (McKnight, 1977). All occupations aspire to have this power because its lack makes a worker a mere technician carrying out someone else's directives. According to the conflict viewpoint, the competence of professionals is not the problem to which educational solutions must be addressed. Rather, the problem lies in the oppressive system of which professionals are a part. The purpose of continuing professional education in this viewpoint is to reduce the power of professions so as to create a more equal relationship between clients and professionals. In this view, continuing educators work with professions in the same way that Ralph Nader worked with the auto industry, that is, in an adversarial role.

The Critical Viewpoint. In the past decade, a third viewpoint has crystallized in reaction to the functionalist and conflict viewpoints. Where functionalism sees well-defined problems, this new viewpoint assumes that professionals construct the problem from the situation. While proponents of the conflict viewpoint believe each profession possesses a monolithic value orientation so as to secure the largest market share, advocates of this new viewpoint provide evidence for conflicting value orientations among members of a profession in terms of societal ends. Because professionals are always making choices about which problems to solve and how to solve them, this approach stresses the need for professionals to be critically aware of these choices and their implications (Schön, 1987). The key concept in the critical viewpoint is *dialectic*. Practitioners are always in a dialectical relationship with situations that are characterized by uniqueness, uncertainty, or value conflict. Thus, problem setting rather than problem solving is the key to professional practice.

The critical viewpoint argues for the abandonment of the idea that there is consensus regarding professional quality. If there were consensus about professional quality (as there is presumed to be in the functionalist viewpoint), educators would simply be involved in a technical process of determining the best means (knowledge, skills, attitudes) to achieve those ends. Because there is a lack of consensus in most situations, the purpose of continuing professional education is to help professionals understand the ethical and political, as well as the technical, dimensions of their work. Educational efforts based on this viewpoint seek to help professionals critically analyze the technical and ethical choices they make in their practice. For example, in planning an in-service education program for science teachers, the principles of evolutionism and creationism might both be taught.

Institutional Providers of Continuing Professional Education

The four major providers of continuing professional education are universities and professional schools, professional associations, employing agencies, and independent providers. It is impossible to estimate which of these types of providers is most or least prominent in terms of number of offerings or participants. Arnstein (1983, p. 238) notes that while there are reasonably well-established rules for counting participants in continuing higher education, "These rules do not extend to continuing education when offered by business and professional societies." Thus, there is no common metric nor a national collection agency for data on continuing professional education. Also, the relative importance of each type of provider varies with the individual profession. Whereas universities are major providers in medicine and engineering, they are second to professional associations in the field of certified public accountancy, and they provide virtually no continuing education in the field of real estate (Stern, 1983).

The provision of continuing education by universities and professional schools is characterized by a great diversity (Knox, 1982; Nowlen, 1988) in annual numbers of participants (from a few hundred to forty thousand), size of budget (from $30,000 to $17,000,000), and staff (from one person to more than fifty). The programs may be sponsored by professional schools, colleges, or departments, or by a universitywide continuing education unit. A recent development is the sponsorship of professional schools by corporations such as the Rand Corporation. Eurich (1985) has identified eighteen such corporate colleges. In this handbook, Chapter Twenty-Three offers a more complete description of colleges and universities as providers of continuing professional education.

Nowlen (1988) estimates there are at least 3,000 national professional associations and many more state and local associations. These associations deliver continuing education in considerably different ways depending on the number of members, on the scope of purpose, and on the size and structure of staff. In many cases, however, the educational program would be defined as having to do with the "accreditation of professional schools or other training programs, the issuance of publications, the sponsorships of conventions and conferences, and the operation of special training programs, such as courses, conferences, workshops, and other activities clearly defined as instructional" (Houle, 1980, p. 172).

Employers such as hospitals, social agencies, business firms, and governments offer a tremendous amount of continuing education to their professional employees (see Chapters Twenty-Nine and Thirty-Two for an overview). For example, half of continuing education in health care is provided by employers, in contrast with other providers, and most management education is done by employers (Shelton and Craig, 1983). The central task of educators in employment settings is to improve participants' performance with respect to the mission of the agency.

The independent providers represent a wide range of institutions and constitute a growing segment of the field. Research organizations and consulting firms such as Arthur D. Little, accounting firms, and manufacturers-suppliers such as IBM often use seminars and conferences to increase exposure to client groups and customers. Publishers are also moving into continuing professional education as another way to serve well-defined audiences to whom they currently provide print materials. There are also the so-called privates (Suleiman, 1983)—institutions organized on a free-standing basis that treat continuing professional education as a business.

Future Prospects

The growth and development of continuing education for the professions is certain to be sustained over the coming decades. By way of analogy, we can say that continuing education is in the same state of organization as preprofessional education was in at the beginning of this century. At that time, systems of professional education were in their infancy, in contrast to the highly elaborated forms that exist today. Medical education serves as a useful example on this point. The Flexner report (1910), which revolutionized preservice medical education in the early part of this century, strongly argued that physicians must have at least a high school diploma before being allowed to practice. It is clear that no one at that time would have predicted the structure of medical education today. Likewise, systems of continuing education in the professions are likely to grow in size and in stature until they are considered to be as important as the preservice stage of professional education.

In addition to the growth in importance of continuing education for the professions, we are likely to see the emerging concept of continuing professional education gain a stronger foothold in the professions. Evidence for this movement will be a greater proportion of continuing education positions in the professions held not by individuals who are members of those professions but rather by people trained in adult and continuing education. As a result, continuing professional education will become a more prominent subfield of practice in adult and continuing education.

The dynamic quality of the field of continuing professional education is likely to bring different concerns and issues forward at different points in its expansion. For example, a prominent issue of the 1970s and early 1980s was mandatory continuing education. On one side was the argument that the public was being protected by laws requiring professionals to participate in thirty to fifty hours of formal continuing education programs every year in order to renew their licenses. Opponents of mandatory continuing education argued that participation in continuing education could not possibly guarantee that professionals would learn anything, much less ensure that the public would be protected against incompetent practitioners. There has been very little overall growth since 1980 in the number of states implementing mandatory continuing education for the professions; some states have rescinded existing requirements, while a few others have implemented them for the first time (Phillips, 1987). The passions around this issue have begun to subside over the past several years. A major reason for this subsiding is experience and research that have demonstrated when mandatory continuing education goes into effect for a profession, approximately 75 percent of its members are found already to be participating in continuing education at levels exceeding the minimum requirements (Phillips, 1987). Because of this, it appears that mandatory continuing education will not be a controversial dimension of future systems of continuing professional education.

Current issues likely to be debated more intensely in the next decade include the aims of continuing professional education and the proper relationships among its institutional providers. As the stakes become greater in terms of numbers of participants and amount of revenue, the issue of the form interorganizational relationships should take will be debated more intensely. Should providers compete with one another, or is collaboration a more desirable approach? Which type of relationship leads to a higher quality education—according to what criteria? Most important, who will decide these questions? This author supports the view that collaborative relationships do not necessarily produce the best programs. The formation of relationships is simply a means to an end. Once the ends are defined and the effectiveness of these types of relationships is established, we will know whether collaboration is worth promoting as a general strategy.

The most important issue in the future will continue to be the choice of purposes that should guide the field of continuing professional education. What is the continuing educator's vision of the ends of professional practice and of the role of the professions in society? There are at least three competing viewpoints on the appropriate vision and purpose of continuing professional education. The educational efforts based on these different viewpoints lead to very different outcomes in terms of professional practice and in terms of the relationship of professions to the larger society. Continuing professional educators will need to examine critically this issue on a continual basis in order to understand better their role and to communicate it effectively to the professionals with whom they work and, ultimately, to society at large.

References

Arnstein, G. E. "The Federal Interest." In M. R. Stern (ed.), *Power and Conflict in Continuing Professional Education.* Belmont, Calif.: Wadsworth, 1983.

Baskett, M. K., and Taylor, W. H. (eds.). *Continuing Professional Education: Moving into the 1980's.* Calgary, Alb.: University of Calgary, 1980.

Canadian Journal of University Continuing Education, 1983, *9* (2).

Cervero, R. M. *Effective Practice in Continuing Professional Education.* San Francisco: Jossey-Bass, 1988.

Cervero, R. M., and Scanlan, C. L. (eds.). *Problems and Prospects in Continuing Professional Education.* New Directions for Continuing Education, no. 27. San Francisco: Jossey-Bass, 1985.

Eurich, N. P. *Corporate Classrooms: The Learning Business.* Princeton, N.J.: The Carnegie Foundation for the Advancement of Teaching, 1985.

Flexner, A. *Medical Education in the United States and Canada.* Boston: Merrymount Press, 1910.

Flexner, A. "Is Social Work a Profession?" *School and Society,* 1915, *1,* 901–911.

Friedson, E. *Professional Powers.* Chicago: University of Chicago Press, 1986.

Green, J. S., Grosswald, S. J., Suter, E., and Walthall, D. B. (eds.). *Continuing Education for the Health Professions.* San Francisco: Jossey-Bass, 1984.

Griffith, W. S. "Persistent Problems and Promising Prospects in Continuing Professional Education." In R. M. Cervero and C. L. Scanlan (eds.), *Problems and Prospects in Continuing Professional Education.* New Directions for Continuing Education, no. 27. San Francisco: Jossey-Bass, 1985.

Haag, W. B. *A Call to Action: A Report of the National Conference on Continuing Professional Education.* University Park: Pennsylvania State University Press, 1987.

Houle, C. O. *Continuing Learning in the Professions.* San Francisco: Jossey-Bass, 1980.

Kenny, W. R. "Program Planning and Accreditation." In R. M. Cervero and C. L. Scanlan (eds.), *Problems and Prospects in Continuing Professional Education.* New Directions for Continuing Education, no. 27. San Francisco: Jossey-Bass, 1985.

Knox, A. B. "Organizational Dynamics in Continuing Professional Education." *Adult Education,* 1982, *32,* 117–129.

Larson, M. S. *The Rise of Professionalism.* Berkeley: University of California Press, 1977.

LeBreton, P. P., and others (eds.). *The Evaluation of Continuing Education for Professionals: A Systems View.* Seattle: University of Washington Press, 1979.

McKnight, J. "The Professional Service Business." *Social Policy,* 1977, *8,* 110–116.

Meyer, T. C. "Toward a Continuum in Medical Education." *Bulletin of the New York Academy of Medicine,* 1975, *51,* 719–726.

Nowlen, P. M. *A New Approach to Continuing Education for Business and the Professions: The Performance Model.* New York: Macmillan, 1988.

Pennington, F. C., and Green, J. "Comparative Analysis of Program Development Processes in Six Professions." *Adult Education,* 1976, *27,* 13–23.

Phillips, L. E. "Is Mandatory Continuing Education Working?" *MOBIUS,* 1987, *7,* 57–64.

Schön, D. A. *The Reflective Practitioner.* New York: Basic Books, 1983.

Schön, D. A. *Educating the Reflective Practitioner.* San Francisco: Jossey-Bass, 1987.

Shelton, H. R., and Craig, R. L. "Continuing Professional Development: The Employer's Perspective." In M. R. Stern (ed.), *Power and Conflict in Continuing Professional Education.* Belmont, Calif.: Wadsworth, 1983.

Statistics Canada. Household Survey Division. *The Labour Force, December 1987.* Ottawa: Canadian Government Publishing Centre, 1988.

Stern, M. S. (ed.). *Power and Conflict in Continuing Professional Education.* Belmont, Calif.: Wadsworth, 1983.

Stone, E. W. "The Growth of Continuing Education." *Library Trends,* 1986, *34,* 489–513.

Suleiman, A. "Private Enterprise: The Independent Provider." In M. R. Stern (ed.), *Power and Conflict in Continuing Professional Education.* Belmont, Calif.: Wadsworth, 1983.

Vernon, D. H. "Education for Proficiency: The Continuum." *Journal of Legal Education,* 1983, *33,* 559–569.

40

Education for Older Adults

Bradley C. Courtenay

Two factors suggest the importance of education for older adults. First, the proportion of adults aged sixty-five and over in the United States and Canada continues to rise faster than other age groups. According to the American Association of Retired Persons (AARP) (1987, p. 1), "The number of older Americans increased by 3.6 million or 14% since 1980, compared to an increase of 5% for the under-65 population." The upward trend is expected to continue into the twenty-first century, so that in the year 2000, older Americans will represent 13 percent of the population; in the year 2030, the population of older Americans is expected to increase to 21.2 percent.

A similar trend is evident for the population growth of older adults in Canada. Although the proportional increases are not as high as in the United States, Canada's older population has increased from 8 percent in 1976 to 11 percent in 1986 (Statistics Canada, 1988). By the year 2000, the population of older adults in Canada will be at 12 percent (Pitman, 1984).

The second factor indicating the importance of the older adult for adult education providers is the diminishing gap in educational level between older and younger learners. In 1940, the median number of years of school completed by persons sixty-five and over was 8.1 years (U.S. Senate Special Committee on Aging, 1984). That number had increased to only 8.7 years by 1970, compared to 12.2 years completed for the entire population. By 1986, for persons sixty-five and over, the median number of years of school completed was 11.8 (AARP, 1987). It has been projected that by 2014, approximately three-fourths of the older adult population will have graduated from high school (Ventura and Worthy, 1982). The rise in educational level is significant because of its usefulness in predicting participation in educational opportunities. Because "succeeding cohorts of older people will have more years of formal schooling" and "because amount of formal education is a significant predictor of participation in adult education, future generations of older persons will be more likely to engage in educational activities" (Ventura and Worthy, 1982, p. iv).

Concurrent with the rise in the number and educational level of older adults is the emergence of the field of educational gerontology. While educational gerontology may have other geneses, it is reported to have been used first in the United States in a doctoral program initiated at the University of Michigan in 1970 by Howard McClusky, who is often referred to as the father of educational gerontology. The first national use of the term *educational gerontology* was in the journal *Educational Gerontology* in 1976 (Peterson, 1980). The concept is defined by Peterson (1980, p. 67) as, "the study and practice of instructional endeavors for and about the aged and aging." The study of instruction of older adults involves the examination of circumstances that affect learning in older adults. The practical aspect of educational gerontology includes adult education opportunities for the elderly to enhance their knowledge and skills in order that they might have a more enjoyable life and meet the challenges of contemporary society. Education for older adults and with older adults are the focal points for this chapter.

The first major section of this chapter is on participation characteristics of older adults, including enrollment data, motivating factors, subject matter preferences, barriers to participation, locations of educational opportunities, and informal education for older adults. The second part of the chapter identifies the broad range of program offerings for older students and describes a few exemplary programs. The chapter concludes with a look at the critical issues emerging from education and the older adult.

Participation Characteristics of the Older Student

Participation characteristics of older students in the United States and Canada are derived from formal educational activities and do not include the various educational opportunities for older adults outside the traditional classroom. In their review of national attendance data gathered by the National Center for Education Statistics (NCES), Ventura and Worthy (1982) found that 5 percent of the elderly population took traditional courses in 1981. That figure reflects a significant increase from 2 percent in 1974. The Center for Education Statistics' *Digest of Education Statistics, 1987* indicates that the participation level of older adults has risen to 6 percent. In Canada, while the percentage of older adult participation has not risen significantly, the number of older student enrollees has almost doubled (Statistics Canada, 1980, 1987). Thus, the participation data reflect an upward trend in the number of older adults involved in educational opportunities. However, as noted above, these data reflect only those older adults who engaged in traditional educational experiences. Larger rates of participation would be evident were it possible to quantify participation in nonformal educational experiences.

Given that older adults are participating in adult education, what motivates them to enroll and what are they interested in learning? Ventura and Worthy (1982, p. 28) conclude that, "There is no question that the predominant motivation for older adults enrolling in education programs is to learn." Dellman-Jenkins, Fruit, and Lambert (1984) would agree. Their analysis of eight studies on intergenerational programs indicated that older participants were motivated to participate by an intrinsic need for intellectual growth.

Subject matter of interest to older adults is difficult to generalize about because of the variety of interests of the older students. The one possible exception to this assertion would be the older college enrollees' interest in liberal arts courses. Covey (1982) and Graney and Hays (1976) found liberal arts to be the primary topic of interest to older adults enrolled in higher education classes.

Ventura and Worthy (1982) indicate that older students take courses that provide a sense of meaning—courses such as philosophy, religion, and language arts. However, they also indicate that 34 percent (compared to 39 percent for liberal arts) of participants in the 1981 NCES data took courses that provided a sense of control or the ability to cope—courses such as physical education, health care, sciences, business, and home economics. Similar data appear in the Center for Education Statistics' *Digest of Education Statistics, 1987.* More liberal arts courses (41 percent) than any other course were taken by both men and women. However, the data also indicate that older adults were enrolled in a variety of course topics from business to physical education, from home economics to engineering, and from health care to interdisciplinary studies.

Perhaps one explanation for the significant interest in liberal arts courses is the need to rediscover personal and social identity, especially after retirement. In a needs assessment study of Golden Age Club members in Canada, Leclerc (1985) asked the respondents to match their perceptions of the advantages and disadvantages of aging to their educational needs. Leclerc (p. 141) found that the older adults' first five needs were to learn "how to make new friends, how to age physically, intellectually and morally, how to live in harmony with oneself, how to develop a good philosophy and psychology on aging, and how to cope with changes in society."

Studies conducted with undereducated older adults indicate a somewhat diferent range of interests among this group. McClusky (n.d.) listed the need for basic skills education first in his five major categories of educational opportunities for older adults. However, when Courtenay, Suhart, McConatha, and Stevenson (1983) asked a sample of 500 older, undereducated adults what subjects they would prefer to learn about, topics relating to personal health ranked first—topics such as checking vital signs and consumer information relating to drugs. Learning to read and to write fell into the bottom one-third of preferred study topics among the undereducated.

There are several studies that have explored barriers to participation (Courtenay, Suhart, McConatha, and Stevenson, 1983; Sheppard, 1983; Kingston and Drotter, 1983; Fishtein and Feier, 1982; Kingston, 1982; Price and Lyon, 1982; Ventura and Worthy, 1982; Marcus, 1978; Graney and Hays, 1976; Goodrow, 1975). As a result of their comprehensive literature review, Ventura and Worthy (1982) conclude that lack of interest is the major barrier to participation by the older student. Graney and Hays (1976), Hiemstra (1976), March, Hooper, and Baum (1977), and Wasserman (1976) all confirm lack of interest as the major barrier.

Being too old, having poor health, lack of time, and costs also have been cited as major barriers to participation. Sheppard (1983) and Courtenay, Suhart, McConatha, and Stevenson (1983) found fear of being out at night, lack of transportation, and being tired of school to be major barriers. Price and Lyon (1982) expand the list to include the absence of a companion and lack of information about the activity. Kingston (1982) discovered that, for college-enrolled older students, parking was the major problem.

On the other hand, Fishtein and Feier (1982) uncovered psychological barriers in their Union College study of potential, older participants. Respondents cited fear of competition with younger students, fear of exposure of their inadequate backgrounds, and fear of the unknown as reasons for little or no participation.

Finally, Marcus (1978) suggests that socioeconomic condition is a major barrier affecting participation of older adults. His study of the effects of age, sex, and status relative to educational participation found that older adults with lower income and status were least likely to participate in educational programs and were particularly unlikely to participate for the purpose of meeting pressing needs. On the other hand, according to Marcus, older adults who have high income and status are more likely to participate in education—not to meet pressing needs, but to continue personal growth and enjoyment.

A final, major participation variable related to older adults is the location of the educational opportunity. Ventura (1982) has developed a catalog of program profiles that identifies the several kinds of places offering educational programs for older adults. Although not considered an exhaustive list, the content is reflective of the current educational providers and includes educational institutions and organizations such as community and technical colleges, four-year colleges and universities, and nonprofit, independent education organizations (for example, Elderhostel). The list also includes community-based educational programs for older adults, such as community or senior centers, area agencies for the aging, and public libraries, as well as other miscellaneous organizations, such as national voluntary organizations (for example, the National Council on the Aging Senior Center Humanities Program), state departments of education, and unions.

Ventura and Worthy (1982) indicate a college or university as the place of greatest enrollment (27 percent) in courses. Community or senior centers (24 percent), businesses (18 percent), high schools (7 percent) and others including libraries, churches, and museums (24 percent) follow.

Price and Lyon (1982) provide one explanation for the diversity of locations chosen by older adults—older persons attend institutions that are close and familiar. Peterson (1987) lends support to this conclusion, summarizing that the setting preferred by older students is one that is accessible and familiar. Fisher (1986) discovered that awareness of sites where education is available is the best predictor of participation.

Although there is no single collection of participation data for older adults in nonformal settings, the elderly are engaged in a number of learning activities outside the traditional mode. First, older adults engage in activities in informal settings such as senior centers, churches, labor unions, clubs, public libraries, regional groups of national associations, and area agencies on aging. Second, the elderly participate in self-directed learning, never having to attend a class. However, Fisher (1986, p. 205) found a significant statistical relationship between participation at senior centers and "propensity to engage in self-directed learning activities," suggesting, perhaps, that those individuals who are involved in directing their own learning also engage in structured activities. Third, older adults engage in informal education through electronic means such as television (Straka, 1987) and computers (Kearsley and Furlong, 1984).

Older adults also participate in education through intergenerational learning activities. Usually, such activities involve older adults and children or adolescents. Occasionally, traditional college-age students and older adults take courses together. Intergenerational learning activities may be formal or informal, and several studies have indicated the benefits of both kinds of activities for both generations (Firman, Gelford, and Ventura, 1983; Long, 1983a; Dellman-Jenkins, Fruit, and Lambert, 1984; Peacock and Talley, 1984; Spalding and Rogers, 1985; Miko, 1986; Allen, 1987; Tierce and Seelbach, 1987; Corbin, Kagan, and Metal-Corbin, 1987). Temple University recognized the importance of multiple generation interaction by establishing the Center for Intergenerational Learning to promote the development and networking of intergenerational programs.

Generally, programs in which two different generations learn together result in each generation learning more about the other and exiting the experience with positive attitudes about each other. For example, Corbin, Kagan, and Metal-Corbin (1987) found sixth graders to become progressively more interactive with older participants over seven days of singing, dance, and discussion with elderly participants. Peacock and Talley (1984) identify several successful intergenerational programs in Canada including Schools and Community Service Programs for the Elderly (SCOPE) in Toronto and the Caring Center at the Jewish Family Services Organization in Montreal.

Programs for Older Adults

A wide variety of agencies and institutions offer programs for older adults (Ventura, 1982; Peterson, 1983; Lumsden, 1985; Peterson, 1987). Public institutions, including secondary schools, universities, colleges, and community colleges, have been especially active in addressing the learning needs of older adults.

Tuition waiver provisions have made it possible for older adults to attend college and university programs. However, as reported in studies of tuition waiver programs (free or reduced college and university tuition for older adults), the provisions for participation of older students are more restrictive than supportive (Long and Rossing, 1979; Long, 1980; Romaniuk, 1982a, 1982b, 1983, 1984). Long and Rossing (1979) note the rigorous entrance requirements (student achievement test scores and minimum high school grade point averages) adopted by some states. In a later study, Romaniuk (1983) observes that participation in these programs remains low, due in large part to little or no marketing effort by the institution. Peterson (1987, p. 47) concludes that, "Tuition waiver policies, though common, do not appear to be widely used by older persons."

There are some excellent university-affiliated programs for older adults throughout the United States and Canada. Those frequently cited are the Herbert L. Donovan Scholar's Program at the University of Kentucky, Academy of Lifelong Learning at the University of Delaware, Institute of Lifelong Learning at Duke University, Elderhostel (Long, 1983b), and Toward an Active Retirement at the Collège Marie-Victorin in Montreal (Peacock and Talley, 1985).

Successful programs also have emerged outside of university settings. The Life Enrichment Center in Atlanta, Georgia, managed almost exclusively by older volunteers, has an impressive continuing education program enrolling up to 700 individuals in fall, winter, and spring quarters. In Chula Vista, California, older adults are taught how to produce videotape cable television programs through project PACE (Public Access Cabletelevision by and for Elders). Older retirees of New York City's largest municipal unions participate in the American Federation of State, County, and Municipal Employees District Council 37 Retirees Educational Program. The educational program includes courses in literature, history, symphony, opera, art, and health issues, as well as self-help groups.

Critical Issues in Education and Aging

The development and growth of education for older adults has raised several issues of importance to the design and implementation of educational programs for older individuals. Thornton (1987, p. 88) provides a framework for examining these issues: "The question is not whether we can or cannot teach or retrain an older adult. Rather, the questions are 'To what end?

And why?' The questions are fundamentally *social* and *philosophical.* If we fail to support learning and educative opportunity throughout the lifespan, then the question becomes 'What will be the cost in general social well-being, depleted human resources, and dignity for people of all ages, and for our own futures as an aging society?''

As implied in Thornton's quote, the first issue—a philosophical issue— is whether society views learning as ending at the traditional high school or college age. If the majority of society believes in the so-called terminal system, then there will be less emphasis given to provisions for learning in the later years; this is the current prevailing perspective in both the United States and Canada (Long, 1987; Peterson, 1987; Pitman, 1984). To maintain the terminal perspective of learning is to maintain distribution of resources for education to the younger learners. The terminal perspective of learning implicitly doubts the capability of older adults and defines the older students' learning interests as primarily of a recreational nature. Thus, Thornton would advocate that society adopt a life-span perspective of education in order to reverse the focus of learning on the young. This broader view of learning perceives older adults as capable of and interested in learning beyond recreational and leisure activities.

Assuming that life-span education became the norm in the United States and Canada, the question of purpose of education for older learners emerges as a second issue. McClusky (n.d.) identified five major areas of need of older adults: the need to have basic skills, the need to be expressive, the need to make a contribution, the need to be influential, and the need for transcendence. Should the ultimate purpose of education for older adults be directed toward advocacy—enabling older persons to improve their situations? Or should the ultimate purpose of educational opportunities for the elderly be to enable them to be influential and contributing members of society? On the other hand, should educational experiences for older persons address the need to learn for the sake of learning or to learn for the experience of transcending the mundane activities of reality? The implication of this issue for program development is that there is no single, generic ultimate purpose of education for older adults.

Within the issue of ultimate purpose is the third issue of appropriate content for older persons. Should subject matter be expressive, instrumental, or both? Are older adults more interested in learning subjects that empower or simply in learning? The foregoing pages of this chapter suggest that there is no easy answer to these questions because of the variety of the programs now available for older learners.

A fourth issue reflects the question of who should be served. Should resources be directed to older individuals who have acknowledged an interest in learning or who are already participating in learning activities? Or should programs be provided mostly for the underserved and isolated older adult? As noted in a preceding section of this chapter, both groups have genuine needs for learning, although the underserved older adults are a distinct minority as participants. To what extent is the gap between the haves and the have-nots made larger by perpetuating activity for the better educated and interested older adults?

Classroom environment, including instructional methods, is a fifth issue in education and aging. Do older adults learn better and are they more satisfied in age-integrated or age-segregated classrooms? A previous section of this chapter indicates the benefits to both older and younger learners when the two groups learn together. At the same time, some of the most successful educational programs for the elderly are managed by and limited to older persons. Of equal importance is the question of instructional methods. Do older persons learn best in a lecture or in group discussion or both? To what extent can computer assisted instruction improve learning opportunities for older adults? There is no norm or average answer to these questions, just as there is no typical classroom environment or instructional method for younger learners. Whether a group should be age segregated or age integrated and whether a class should use a lecture or case study are questions that have to be answered for each learning experience and in the context of purpose, content, and clientele.

The question of who should pay for education for older adults is a sixth issue. Long (1987), Peterson (1987), and Thornton (1987) clearly indicate that public funds are directed primarily toward education for the young. Consequently, the largest revenue sources for educational programs for the elderly are from fees and voluntary donations. Thornton and others (Havighurst, 1976; Midwinter, 1984) advocate increased public support, arguing that older adults already have made an investment in the economy and deserve some repayment. A question emerging from this issue and still in need of analysis is, to what extent is funding a barrier to participation of older persons? Do the underserved, isolated elderly not participate in educational opportunities because of scarce financial resources? One answer to these questions, given the importance of educational level in predicting participation of older persons, is that increasing public funds might not have the desired effect of increased participation.

A seventh and final issue regarding education and aging has to do with one's view of the nature of the older population. This issue is probably the most important of the seven because the preceding six are affected by it. If one accepts the proposition that there is diversity among individuals in later life, then a variety of educational experiences should be planned. On the other hand, if older adults are viewed as relatively homogenous, then more generic educational programs are in order. Most educational gerontology literature indicates a heterogenous older population. Consequently, more than one ultimate purpose and more than one clientele should be considered in designing educational experiences for older people. Similarly, a diverse content and a variety of classroom environments and instructional methods should be developed during the planning of educational experiences for older learners.

Summary

Older adults represent a significant clientele for adult educators over the next several decades. Current participation data, though limited to institutionalized learning, reflect the variety of interests among individual older learners and serve to rebut the myth that older adults cannot learn or are not interested in learning.

This chapter reflects the theme that educational researchers and programmers must redirect their perspective on education and the older student to include the variety of backgrounds extant in the older population. While improvements are needed in formal educational experiences, ways must also be explored for enhancing nonformal learning opportunities. There will be new developments in educational gerontology, such as the emergence of lifelong education as a conceptual and operational mode for all of education, but education for older adults is no longer a future event.

References

Allen, K. R. "Promoting Family Awareness and Intergenerational Exchange: An Informal Life-History Program." *Educational Gerontology,* 1987, *13,* 43–52.

American Association of Retired Persons. *A Profile of Older Americans, 1987.* Washington, D.C.: Program Resources Department, American Association for Retired Persons, 1987.

Center for Education Statistics. *Digest of Education Statistics, 1987.* Washington, D.C.: Office of Educational Research and Improvement, U.S. Department of Education, 1987.

Corbin, D. E., Kagan, D. M., and Metal-Corbin, J. "Content Analysis of an Intergenerational Unit on Aging in a Sixth-Grade Classroom." *Educational Gerontology,* 1987, *13,* 403–410.

Courtenay, B., Suhart, M., McConatha, D., and Stevenson, R. "Assessing the Educational Needs of Undereducated Older Adults: A Case for the Service Provider." *Educational Gerontology,* 1983, *9,* 205–216.

Covey, H. "Preliminary Findings on Designing Higher Education Programs for Older People." *Educational Gerontology,* 1982, *8,* 463–471.

Dellman-Jenkins, M., Fruit, D., and Lambert, D. "Exploring Age Integration in the University Classroom: Middle Age and Younger Students' Educational Motives and Instructional Preferences." *Educational Gerontology,* 1984, *10,* 429–440.

Firman, G., Gelford, D. E., and Ventura, C., "Intergenerational Service-Learning: Contributions to Curricula." *Educational Gerontology,* 1983, *9,* 405–415.

Fisher, J. C. "Participation in Educational Activities by Active Older Adults." *Adult Education Quarterly,* 1986, *4,* 202–210.

Fishtein, O., and Feier, C. "Education for Older Adults: Out of the College and into the Community." *Educational Gerontology,* 1982, *8,* 243–249.

Goodrow, B. A. "Limiting Factors in Reducing Participation in Older Adult Learning Opportunities." *The Gerontologist*, 1975, *15*, 418–422.

Graney, M., and Hays, W. "Seminar Students: Higher Education After Age 62." *Educational Gerontology*, 1976, *1*, 343–359.

Havighurst, R. "Education Through the Adult Life Span." *Educational Gerontology*, 1976, *1*, 41–51.

Hiemstra, R. "The Older Adult's Learning Projects." *Educational Gerontology*, 1976, *1*, 331–341.

Kearsley, G., and Furlong, M. *Computers for Kids Over Sixty: Keeping Up with the Computer Generation*. Reading, Mass.: Addison-Wesley, 1984.

Kingston, A. "Attitudes and Problems of Elderly Students in the University System of Georgia." *Educational Gerontology*, 1982, *8*, 87–92.

Kingston, A., and Drotter, M. "A Comparison of Elderly College Students in Two Geographically Different Areas." *Educational Gerontology*, 1983, *9*, 399–403.

Leclerc, G. J. "Understanding the Educational Needs of Older Adults: A New Approach." *Educational Gerontology*, 1985, *11*, 137–144.

Long, H. B. "Characteristics of Senior Citizens' Educational Tuitional Waivers in Twenty-One States: A Follow-Up Study." *Educational Gerontology*, 1980, *5*, 139–149.

Long, H. B. "Academic Performance, Attitudes, and Social Relations in Intergenerational College Classes." *Educational Gerontology*, 1983a, *9*, 471–481.

Long, H. B. *Adult and Continuing Education: Responding to Change*. New York: Teachers College Press, 1983b.

Long, H. B. "A Brief History of Education in the United States." In D. Peterson, J. Thornton, and J. Birren (eds.), *Education and Aging*. Englewood Cliffs, N.J.: Prentice-Hall, 1987.

Long, H. B., and Rossing, B. "Tuition Waiver Plans for Older Americans in Postsecondary Public Education Institutions." *Educational Gerontology*, 1979, *4*, 161–174.

Lumsden, D. B. (ed.). *The Older Adult as Learner: Aspects of Educational Gerontology*. Washington, D.C.: Hemisphere, 1985.

McClusky, H. Y. "Education for Aging: The Scope of the Field and Perspectives for the Future." In S. Grabowski and W. D. Mason (eds.), *Learning for Aging*. Washington, D.C.: Adult Education Association of the U.S.A., n.d.

March, G., Hooper, J., and Baum, J. "Life Span Education and the Older Adult: Living Is Learning." *Educational Gerontology*, 1977, *2*, 163–172.

Marcus, E. "Effects of Age, Sex, and Status on Perception of the Utility of Educational Participation." *Educational Gerontology*, 1978, *3*, 295–319.

Midwinter, E. "The Social Determinants of Educational Policy in the United Kingdom and Their Likely Effects on the Provision of Educational Opportunies for the Elderly." *Educational Gerontology*, 1984, *10*, 197–206.

Miko, P. S. "College Students and Institutionalized Elderly: Attitudinal

Effects of Interactive Contact." *Gerontology and Geriatrics Education,* 1986, *6,* 37–42.

Peacock, E. W., and Talley, W. M. "Intergenerational Contact: A Way to Counteract Ageism." *Educational Gerontology,* 1984, *10,* 13–24.

Peacock, E. W., and Talley, W. M. "Developing Leisure Competence: A Goal for Late Adulthood." *Educational Gerontology,* 1985, *11,* 261–276.

Peterson, D. A. "Who Are the Educational Gerontologists?" *Educational Gerontology,* 1980, *5,* 65–77.

Peterson, D. A. *Facilitating Education for Older Learners.* San Francisco: Jossey-Bass, 1983.

Peterson, D. A. "Aging and Higher Education." In D. Peterson, J. Thornton, and J. Birren (eds.), *Education and Aging.* Englewood Cliffs, N.J.: Prentice-Hall, 1987.

Pitman, W. "Education for a Maturing Population in Canada: Reactions and Speculation." *Educational Gerontology,* 1984, *10,* 207–217.

Price, W., and Lyon, L. "Educational Orientation of the Aged: An Attitudinal Inquiry." *Educational Gerontology,* 1982, *8,* 478–484.

Romaniuk, J. *The Older Adult Learner in Higher Education: An Analysis of State Public Policy.* Washington, D.C.: National Council on the Aging, 1982a.

Romaniuk, J. *Tuition-Waiver Policies for Older Adults: Impact on States and Institutions of Higher Education.* Washington, D.C.: National Council on the Aging, 1982b.

Romaniuk, J. "Educational Tuition-Waiver Policies: A Secondary Analysis of Institutional Impact in Virginia." *Educational Gerontology,* 1983, *9,* 279–292.

Romaniuk, J. "Tuition-Waiver Policies for Older Adults: What Are the Assumptions?" *Educational Gerontology,* 1984, *10,* 119–133.

Sheppard, N. A. "Vocational Education Needs Assessment of Older Americans: Methodology and Some Findings." *Educational Gerontology,* 1983, *9,* 359–376.

Spalding, J. W., and Rogers, J. C. "Intergenerational Intervention: A Reciprocal Service Delivery System for Preschoolers, Adolescents, and Older Persons." *Educational Gerontology,* 1985, *11,* 41–55.

Statistics Canada. *Universities: Enrolment and Degrees, 1978.* Ottawa: Statistics Canada, 1980.

Statistics Canada. *Universities: Enrolment and Degrees, 1985.* Ottawa: Statistics Canada, 1987.

Statistics Canada. *Canada Yearbook, 1988.* Ottawa: Statistics Canada, 1988.

Straka, G. A. "Television and the Elderly." In D. Peterson, J. Thornton, and J. Birren (eds.), *Education and Aging.* Englewood Cliffs, N.J.: Prentice-Hall, 1987.

Thornton, J. E. "Life Span Learning and Education." In D. Peterson, J. Thornton, and J. Birren (eds.), *Education and Aging.* Englewood Cliffs, N.J.: Prentice-Hall, 1987.

Tierce, J. W., and Seelbach, W. C. "Elders as School Volunteers: An Untapped Resource." *Educational Gerontology,* 1987, *13,* 33–41.

U.S. Senate Special Committee on Aging. *Developments in Aging: 1983.* Vol. 1. Report of the Special Committee on Aging. Washington, D.C.: U.S. Government Printing Office, 1984.

Ventura, C. *Education for Older Adults: A Catalogue of Program Profiles.* Washington, D.C.: National Council on the Aging, 1982.

Ventura, C., and Worthy, E., Jr. *Education for Older Adults: A Synthesis of Significant Data.* Washington, D.C.: National Council on the Aging, 1982.

Wasserman, F. M. "The Educational Interests of the Elderly: A Case Study." *Educational Gerontology,* 1976, *1,* 323–330.

41

Education for Rural Adults

Emmalou Van Tilburg
Allen B. Moore

What comes to mind when you hear the word *rural*—An Appalachian coal mining town, a small fishing village on the Atlantic coast, a lonely road in the Alaskan tundra, a high mountain village in the Canadian Rockies, a steamy hot and humid red-earth clay road winding across the Mississippi Valley?

Rural areas are all of these images and none of these images. A description that rings true for one rural area can grossly misrepresent another. Helge (1984a, p. 296), addressing needs of handicapped children in rural school districts, suggested that, "Even rural communities with the same population numbers, densities, etc., vary tremendously because of the variety of community subcultures they contain."

Willits, Bealer, and Crider (1982) addressed the heterogeneity of rural society citing three major factors that vary greatly within that grouping of communities called rural: the degree of ecological or occupational rurality (farmland and farmers differ), personal characteristics of the population (age, income, education, sex, race, ethnicity), and the variety of geographic regions that make up rural North America (topography and related occupations).

Notwithstanding the difficulty in identifying rural people as a unique subgroup within the North American society, the authors agree with Willits, Bealer, and Crider (1982, p. 69) that, "Important distinctions between rural and urban sectors of the United States [and all of North America] continue to exist." Thus, the focus of this chapter and the charge of the authors will be to describe clearly rural adults as a unique subculture and to identify those issues that appear to be most related to the delivery of education to that subculture.

Why This Chapter Devoted to Educating Rural Adults?

"The majority of the world's population lives in rural areas, the great bulk of the world's land is used for rural activities, and most settlement units are rural" (Bunce, 1982, p. 13). In the United States, one-fourth of the population is classified as rural—those who "live on farms, in the open countryside, or in non-metropolitan areas with populations of less than ten thousand people" (Miller, n.d.). Using a broad statistical definition of rural settlements—those with fewer than 2,000 people—there are more than 14 million such settlements in the world (Bunce, 1982). But even with the abundance of land, communities, and individuals associated with rurality, scholars readily admit that there has been a strong urban bias to most educational research (Darnell and Simpson, 1981; Nash, 1980; Sher, 1981). The trend is beginning to turn around, however, and the increased interest in rural education is due in part to the slowing and, in some cases, reversal of the out-migration from farms and small towns (DeYoung, 1987). Even though some rural areas are dying because of the loss of the economic base caused by the farm financial crisis (Avery, 1985), many other rural areas are experiencing tremendous growth. Despite the increased interest, much of the rural education literature has focused on special populations such as Appalachians, migrants, Native Americans, Eskimos, and blacks (DeYoung, 1987), and has not addressed the rural subculture as a unified group sharing common characteristics, attitudes, values, and motivations.

The very fact that this chapter exists as a separate unit in this handbook is evidence that there is a distinctiveness of the rural individual and community and that a unique subculture called rural does exist. Now, let us work toward a clear description of rural in North America as it relates to individuals and communities.

Toward an Understanding of Rural

Do not expect to discover within this chapter an all-inclusive definition for the word *rural*. Educators, administrators, politicians, sociologists, and other users of the word have attempted for years to capture those elusive qualities of the rural individual and community and to organize them into an all-encompassing definition. Because of the inseparability of the urban-rural concept from cultural, historical, political, administrative, ecological, and occupational issues, several approaches are presented here to describing what rural is and is not. Be aware, however, that to employ one definitional approach precludes the use of another, and that each carries with it a myriad of assumptions.

The U.S. Office of Special Education Programs employs the following statistical definition for use in classifying school districts: "A district is considered rural when the number of inhabitants is fewer than 150 per square mile or when located in counties with 60% or more of the population living in communities no larger than 5,000 inhabitants. Districts with more than 10,000 students and those within a Standard Metropolitan Statistical Area (SMSA), as determined by the U.S. Census Bureau, are not considered rural'' (Helge, 1984a, p. 296).

A criticism of statistical definitions is that they do not allow for a separation of urban and rural characteristics, demographically defined, that include cultural, historical, political, and administrative considerations. With regard to this criticism, Bunce (1982) cited four main criteria that can be employed to distinguish urban areas from rural: demographic, political, economic, and sociocultural. Of these four, the sociocultural criteria appear to be the most definitive for identifying and understanding the term *rural*. According to Bunce (1982, p. 16), ''In its most behavioral form, this approach attempts to tap the psychology and sociology of the rural inhabitant in an attempt to identify differences in behavior and attitudes between urban and rural society.''

In line with Bunce is Heimlich and Van Tilburg's (1987) suggestion of the concept of rural as a unique subculture. A subculture represents a group of people who share a unique life experience or unique qualities within the larger society.

Adult educators who desire to approach rural adult education as part of a rural subculture can benefit from five pieces of advice offered by Heimlich and Van Tilburg (1987, pp. 11–13):

1. Learn the beliefs of the subculture, appreciate that those beliefs may be different, learn to live with those beliefs, not necessarily accepting behavior spawned by those beliefs.
2. Understand rural values—gain respect and trust by respecting those values and by incorporating them into the educational approaches.
3. Know how the subculture learns—who and what will members accept? Tradition has a great influence on learning styles of groups.
4. Every subculture has beliefs about the major culture to which the educator belongs. Learn the history of the interaction between the two groups to help facilitate trust and cooperation.
5. Understand the past history of the subculture with the topics of the educational programs. Attitudes have already been formed through past experiences which may serve as barriers or encouragers.

Through the process of defining rural adults as a subculture, remember that learning about roles within a culture is different from acquiring habits or skills, and that it may require a different level of cognitive operation (Hallowell, 1953). Educators can approach rural adult education by drawing on the cultural traits that bind all rural adults together.

Still another approach is represented in the dialectic (Mirkovic, 1980) discussion of rural-urban comparisons by Tehranian (1986). Tehranian's point and contrast approach may be best illustrated in an adaptation of the classic work by Sorokin and Zimmerman (1929) in which they focused on the contrasts between rural and urban characteristics such as occupations, environment, community size, population density, social differentiation and stratification, mobility, and systems of interaction (see Table 41.1).

Table 41.1. Modification of the Sorokin and Zimmerman Contrasts of Rural and Urban.

Characteristic	Rural	Urban
Occupation	Agrarian, agribusiness, and extractive activities	Manufacturing, trade, commerce, and governing activities
Environment	Association with nature, more natural environments than man-made	Isolation from nature, more man-made environments than natural
Community size	Small communities, villages, countryside	Larger collections of people, neighborhoods within cities
Population density	Lower density—fewer than 150 people per square mile, or 60 percent of the people in a county living in communities of 5,000 or fewer	Greater density—more people per square mile, people living in cities or towns of 5,000 or more
Population characteristics	Tendency toward more homogeneous groups	Tendency toward more heterogeneous groups
Social differentiation and stratification	Tendency toward less differentiation and stratification	Tendency toward more differentiation and stratification
Mobility	Tendency in sixties to move to cities, in seventies to move back to rural areas, in eighties to move back toward or near cities	Move away from cities in seventies, back toward or near cities (suburbs) in eighties
System of interaction	Tendency toward individual, personal, and face-to-face	Tendency toward mass and less personal; focus at neighborhood can be individual and personal

Dillman and Hobbs (1982, p. 70) helped to characterize the information displayed in Table 41.1: "Characteristics of physical areas and/or attributes of people are often used in making rural/urban distinctions. Similarly, ecological, occupational, and sociocultural criteria are used either separately or in combination in making distinctions. Ecologically, rural areas have low population density, settlements of small absolute size, and communities that are relatively isolated from other segments of society. Occupationally, rural areas involve extractive-types of industries. Agriculture is the most widespread such industry in rural America, although mining, forestry, and fishing are also included. Socioculturally, rural areas are characterized by a predominance of personal, face-to-face social relationships among similar people and a comparative slowness in altering traditional cultural heritage.''

Characteristics of the Rural Individual and Community

A major criticism of studies comparing rural and nonrural characteristics is the ignoring of diversity of rural adults—again, highlighting the problem of definition. The problems with the rural-urban distinction are that it implies rural America collectively consists of all our society's nonmetropolitan areas, and that it does not provide any measure of how truly rural or isolated one's residence in a nonmetropolitan area really is (Barker, 1985a).

There is an equally difficult task of defining who is so-called nonrural. Goodenough (1971) makes reference to the diversity of urban groups, to mixed ethnic and linguistic backgrounds, to different social classes, to various religious cults or sects, and, of course, to the infinite variety of specialized and differentiated occupations. This diversity is found to a great degree in nonurban areas as well. Therefore, whether rural or nonrural, identification of those values, beliefs, traditions, and unique life experiences that bind members of a subculture together can provide educators with the information they need to proceed and can help educators circumvent the issues involved in superficial characteristic differences.

Barker (1985b) identified certain characteristics of rural communities that may represent values, beliefs, and traditions. He suggested that rural areas have sparse populations and are isolated, that communities are loose knit, are long distances from services, and are more likely to have higher percentages of poverty, poor housing standards, and less opportunity for adequate medical care. And he pointed out that rural areas have few cultural attractions, limited public services, and generally have been deprived of America's wealth. Conversely, positive values, beliefs, and traditions are represented by a slower pace, a wealth of natural resources, diverse rural activities, friendliness, and lower crime rates. Whether these positive and restrictive values of rural life are real or myth is not in contention. Rather, those are the values and beliefs that form the rural image.

Are the characteristics of rural America representing the traditions, beliefs, and values of that group of people, or are they representing the oppression of that group? In simpler terms, are rural adults isolated and far away from services because they choose to be, or are they truly without power due to certain problematic characteristics? Preliminary results of a study done by Van Tilburg (1988), using adult participants of Ohio Cooperative Extension Service educational programs, suggested that values and attitudes of independence and self-reliance do prevail in rural populations. Study participants were asked to rate factors related to their participation in educational programs as to whether the factors were either barriers or motivators to participation. Of the factors that acted as barriers, most were directly related to interaction with other people. Barriers named included anticipating or having interaction with others at the program, sharing information with others, and sharing interests of others at the program. Another trend in the data suggested that having to interrupt a personal schedule and having to invest personal time were also barriers to rural participation. One interpretation of these findings in Ohio might be that rural adults pay particular attention to personal matters and do not especially want to interact with others—suggesting that isolation is a choice for some rural adults.

Another recent study (Archer, 1988), addressing educational needs of individuals, employed a random mail survey technique. Response from a sample of 5,000 citizens in Ohio indicated a difference between urban and rural individuals in the information sources they most use and respect. Rural respondents identified libraries, banks, churches, and local institutions such as the Soil Conservation Service and the Cooperative Extension Service as important sources of educational information. In contrast, urban adults listed professionals and universities as most important.

A question for educators to ponder is, again, that of choice versus chance. Do rural residents choose these sources of information because they have no other convenient sources (such as universities or formal programs), or are their choices spawned by firm beliefs in these trusted sources of information?

McCannon, in a 1981 study that compared rural and nonrural adult education programs in Minnesota, reported differences in course content. When attempting to use information such as McCannon's, educators must consider not only the differences themselves, but also the reasons the differences exist.

Efforts to Provide Education for Adults in Rural Areas

From the one-room schoolhouse for grades one through six to the addition of local or consolidated schools, youth education has been a component of rural communities throughout North America. As educational systems and networks evolved, adults were gradually provided opportunities for lifelong learning (Gelpi, 1985). Grange, Farm Bureau, and other organizations were designed to give adult members information valuable to their livelihood. The Cooperative Extension Service (see Chapter Twenty-Five) was a pioneer in extending faculty availability from universities to local rural residents. Other agencies that have a tradition of rural adult education include hospitals, libraries (see Chapter Eight), vocational-technical schools, colleges and universities, and local, state, and national commissions (Hone, 1984; Treadway, 1984). As the information society expands, so do opportunities and challenges in providing continuing education to the diverse rural adult population.

Reports by Spears and Maes (1985) and Hone (1984) indicated that no single provider was best suited for the diverse rural scene. In fact, Hone listed fifty-four separate programs that have provided rural education. Characteristics of organizations that successfully have provided education for rural adults have been suggested by Spears and Maes (1985). According to these authors, a successful agency responds to a specific community need, responds to the adult learner's expectations, engages in extensive cooperation with other community agencies, and offers concise and jargon-free decriptive materials about programs and services.

The University for Man (UFM) is one agency that has demonstrated these characteristics identified by Spears and Maes. A UFM publication by Maes (1981) reported on the experience of four community agencies that delivered adult education programs for adults in rural areas. The agencies included libraries, a private college consortium, a state cooperative extension service, and a state office of rural affairs. According to Maes, most of these agencies were successful in delivering education to rural adults because they knew the audience and their needs and because they cooperated with other local agencies and marketed their services in an efficient manner.

Community colleges are very involved with the delivery of educational programming in rural areas (Sullins and Atwell, 1986). Uniquely American in philosophy, the community college was originally designed to provide the linking and coordinating educational role in the community.

Other unique approaches to rural education have included the Alaskan model, which utilizes a distance education network with telecommunications (Alaska State Commission on Postsecondary Education, 1985), and the Kansis City Initiative, reported by Margolis (1981), which specified a bill of rights and action agendas as guides for promoting education for adults in rural areas.

The Fund for the Improvement of Postsecondary Education (FIPSE) has been instrumental in identifying problems, in conceptualizing the needs for rural postsecondary and adult education, and in supporting research and development of tools (action agendas, identification of existing programs, evaluation of delivery system models) to facilitate serving the educational needs of rural adults. The Action Agenda Project (1986) provided a framework and a network for designing and delivering educational services to adults in rural areas.

Borrowing from European educators the concept of the folk high school, some American adult educators have attempted to introduce rural education centers into the United States. Highlander Folk School in New Market, Tennessee is an original American rural education center that emphasizes empowerment through self-discovery, increased self-confidence, and improved self-concept. Originally active in civil rights issues, Highlander has been and continues to be involved with many rural empowerment issues. The story of the Highlander Folk School lends support to an alternative interpretation of our educational tradition (Adams, 1972).

Challenges for Rural Adult Education

Agencies undertaking rural education are not without stumbling blocks to quality services (McDaniel, 1986). Social and professional isolation, long

distances from services, and geographic barriers plague educational organizations in the quest to obtain and to keep qualified professionals. Rural settings many times have less qualified staff, lower salary levels, less efficient
facilities, and fewer career opportunities. And they lack the voice of a constituency group that could lobby for improvements (Helge, 1984a).

However, being responsive to unique learning situations, becoming
aware of values and beliefs, learning to appreciate the important differences,
and developing approaches to incorporate these differences into educational
opportunities will provide the adult educator a good chance for success. The
following are some challenges for adult educators working with rural adults.

Problem Solving. A reader of Killacky's report (1984) may perceive
adults living in rural areas as being creative, resourceful, and having a high
energy level. Individual resourcefulness creates independence, which must
be dealt with in the methods and delivery systems employed by adult educators. Careful situational assessment can aid in the presentation of educational programming that will encourage individuals to work together without
displaying their needs as weaknesses. The so-called rural free university
(Maes, 1981) is one model that seems to meet the rural adult's need for learning and educational access.

Communication Networks. Communication within rural areas tends
to be better than that between rural and urban areas and, in some cases,
better than communication within urban areas. Therefore, local networks
can be an effective means of disseminating information. Further study of
previously mentioned models (Spears and Maes, 1985; Maes, 1981) could
provide the missing links for educational programming now in place and
could identify successful approaches for future ventures. Networks using local
leadership can function as structures for cooperative programs and services.

Involvement. Rural individuals are not separate, uninvolved entities,
apart from family, community, and environment. Coombs and Ahmed (1974)
offered suggestions to improve opportunities for rural adult involvement in
educational programs by incorporating specific adult interests such as the
following:

- General or basic education—literacy, numeracy, elementary understanding of environment
- Family improvement education—designed to provide knowledge, skills,
  and attitudes useful in improving the quality of family life related to
  health, homemaking, and child care
- Community improvement education—for strengthening local and national institutions and processes
- Occupational education—the development of knowledge and skills associated with job finding and job keeping

Programs aimed at more than one of these areas tend to be more successful with rural adults than are programs focused on one particular area.

Rural adults appear to have family, career, and community integrated more tightly than do others.

One rural adult education program that uses this holistic approach is Havercamp's (1988) study of farm families in Michigan, which encouraged decision-making control over agricultural problems and issues in rural areas. He found that families who worked together on specific agricultural problems were able to improve their likelihood for survival. This group of families built a communication network and learning process whereby they were able to inform and to educate themselves and to develop agriculture plans and practices not previously available. Specifically, they were able to reduce the level of synthetic chemicals used in producing livestock feed crops. Also, they were able to identify a new market in the city for adults who were now able to purchase more chemically clean food products. Working and learning together, these farm families became more self-reliant in their agriculture plans and practices.

These are but a few examples of the issues with which rural adult educators must struggle. Many of these issues are directly related to the determination of answers to the following three questions: (1) What is and should be the message? (2) Toward whom is it targeted? (3) What is the most appropriate medium for conveying the message?

Educators are faced with innumerable choices of possible answers to these questions. Whether working with adults as individuals, with individuals in groups, or with groups having a collective identity, the rural adult educator must be able to formulate choices, to assess these choices, and to select the most appropriate solutions for the specific situation. The number of challenges faced by the rural adult educator is not greater than those of other educators. However, the challenges may be unique in the breadth of creativity and depth of sensitivity to subculture issues they require of the educator.

Methodological Approaches, Technology, and Delivery Modes

There is a myriad of methodological approaches to working with rural adults. Instinctively, adult educators seem to migrate to group approaches. Many successful rural adult education organizations employ group methods such as Cooperative Extension Service and community health and fitness agencies. The group approach does, however, create a problem for educators when dealing directly with rural adults and their individualistic learning styles. Comments from the Van Tilburg (1988, Appendix D, p. 17) study included, "Just show me how to do it, or tell me how and then I'll get on with it," and "Don't bother me with groups, or socializing." These traditional sentiments seem to indicate that rural learners prefer an individual learning setting and that they separate their time for work and socializing. Education is work. When the work is done, it may be time for socializing.

Adult education programs can and must be targeted toward constituencies of rural populations. A variety of tools are available to assist adults in rural areas (see also Chapter Forty-Six). Examples include satellites, downlinks, cable TV, video cassette recorders (VCRs) and videotapes, computer programs and networks, interactive video, two-way radios, and telephones. One or more of these tools can be accessed in the home, office, community center, business, or industry. They also are accessible in public and private schools or colleges and in other community service agencies such as government offices or voluntary associations. The provision of educational opportunities for adults in rural areas depends upon the geographic region; the learners; the teacher, trainers, and facilitators; the content or subject matter; the cultural biases; and the availability of technology and tools to deliver programs. Helge (1984a, 1984b), Hofmeister (1984), and Dillman (1985) provide several examples of how technology can facilitate access to information and learning opportunities:

- Cable TV can be used to deliver programs that can be received directly or from satellite transmissions.
- For some occupations, such as auto mechanics and plumbers, videotapes can be used to teach skills.
- Mobile vans with computers and interactive video equipment can visit schools, businesses, industries, shopping areas, community stores, and villages.
- Telephone conference calls may be practical for some groups.
- Two-way radios (CBs and other more sophisticated equipment) can be used by pilots, oil rig operators, truckers, and others to pass on information.
- Regional libraries have radio and TV stations, books, magazines, and personnel to assist adults in a variety of learning activities.
- Networks of individuals in professional and technical occupations use computer bulletin boards to send and to receive messages, information, and knowledge about issues and concepts.

All of these tools and delivery modes assume a basic income or resource support level in order to travel or to gain access to software and hardware. Generally, no provision is made for the rural poor who (1) have to work long hours for low wages, (2) have limited resources for travel within or outside the region, (3) do not have the knowledge or skills to use these tools, and (4) do not have the financial resources to subscribe to, rent, or buy software or hardware. How will these adults be served? Hone (1985) and others indicate that some minimal level of support should be available for all adults who need it in a given area.

The Future of Rural Adult Education

Dillman (1985) raised several questions, which remain unanswered, for those who facilitate problem solving with adults in rural areas. First, how will technology change, advance, or eliminate the rural subculture? Will technology so radically change rural areas and rural people that there will no longer be a different place, different values, different needs, or different social interactions?

Second, who will live in the rural areas of the future? Will rural areas decline and become abandoned as did ghost towns of the Southwest, or will they prosper and grow?

Third, who will interact with whom, and what will be the consequences of these interactions? Because of telecommunications, will people be more or less dispersed? Will people identify with a local town, city, or county; or will they relate to a regional or national network of individuals?

Finally, what institutional structures (see also Chapters Twenty-One through Thirty-Two) will be left or newly formed to serve rural adults? Will institutions be located in the village or community or in some distant town, or will they be part of a telecommunications network in a distant location?

Viewing the rural adult as a member of a broad-based subculture can provide the educator a framework within which to operate while looking for those values and beliefs that give rise to behavioral characteristics and a world view that bind rural adults together.

Understanding the characteristics common to most rural adults and knowing the values and beliefs that underlie those characteristics can provide an integrated portrait of the rural adult. This understanding then can illustrate the differences between the rural and urban adult learners by helping paint a portrait that can graphically display otherwise hidden cultural traits. Traditions intricately woven into the past, present, and future of a culture can offer a deeper understanding of the reasons associated with providing educational services to rural adults.

References

Action Agenda Project. *Serving the Rural Adult.* Proceedings of the Action Agenda Project, University for Man (UFM), Kansas State University, Manhattan, May 1986. (ED 265 010)

Adams, F. "Highlander Folk School: Getting Information, Going Back and Teaching It." *Harvard Educational Review,* 1972, *42* (4), 497–520.

Alaska State Commission on Postsecondary Education. *Alaska Statewide Plan for Postsecondary Education 1986–1990; A Draft for Public Comment.* Juneau: Alaska State Commission on Postsecondary Education, 1985. (ED 258 646)

Archer, T. M. *Three Concurrent Perspectives on Ohioans' Educational Needs: Preliminary Report, Strategic/Long Range Planning Task Force.* Columbus: Ohio Cooperative Extension Service, 1988.

Avery, D. "U.S. Farm Dilemma: The Global Bad News Is Wrong." *Science,* 1985, *230* (4724), 408–412.

Barker, B. O. "Adult Education in Rural America: A Review of Recent Research and Identification of Future Research Needs." Paper presented at the annual meeting of the Texas Association for Community Service and Continuing Education, Lubbock, Nov. 20–22, 1985a.

Barker, B. O. "Understanding Rural Adult Learners: Characteristics and Challenges." *Lifelong Learning: The Adult Years*, 1985b, *9* (2), 4–7.

Bunce, M. *Rural Settlement in an Urban World*. New York: St. Martin's Press, 1982.

Coombs, P. H., and Ahmed, M. *Attacking Rural Poverty, How Nonformal Education Can Help*. Baltimore, Md.: Johns Hopkins University Press, 1974.

Darnell, F., and Simpson, P. *Rural Education: In Pursuit of Excellence*. Nedlands, Western Australia: National Center for Research on Rural Education, 1981.

DeYoung, A. J. "The Status of American Rural Education Research: An Integrated Review and Commentary." *Review of Educational Research*, 1987, *57* (2), 123–148.

Dillman, D. A. "The Social Impacts of Information Technologies in Rural North America." *Rural Sociology*, 1985, *50* (1), 1–26.

Dillman, D. A., and Hobbs, D. J. *Rural Society in the U.S.: Issues for the 1980's*. Boulder, Colo.: Westview, 1982.

Gelpi, E. *Lifelong Education and International Relations*. London: Croom-Helm, 1985.

Goodenough, W. "Culture, Language, and Society." In *Current Topics in Anthropology*. Vol. 2. Reading, Mass.: Addison-Wesley, 1971.

Hallowell, A. I. "Culture, Personality, and Society." In A. L. Kroeber (chair), *Anthropology Today: An Encyclopedic Inventory*. Chicago: University of Chicago Press, 1953.

Havercamp, M. J. "Learning and Involvement in the Research Discernment Process by Community Members." Paper presented at the Adult Education Research Conference, Leeds, England, July 10–14, 1988.

Heimlich, J. E., and Van Tilburg, E. "Subcultures and Educators—Concerns of Membership in Education." Paper presented at the American Association For Adult and Continuing Education, Washington, D.C., Oct. 1987.

Helge, D. "The State of the Art of Rural Special Education." *Exceptional Children*, 1984a, *50* (4), 294–305.

Helge, D. "Technologies as Rural Special Education Problem Solvers." *Exceptional Children*, 1984b, *50* (4), 351–359.

Hofmeister, A. M. "Technological Tools for Rural Special Education." *Exceptional Children*, 1984, *50* (4), 344–349.

Hone, K. A. *Serving the Rural Adult: Inventory of Model Programs in Rural Adult Postsecondary Education*. Manhattan: Kansas State University, 1984. (ED 256 527)

Killacky, J. *Furthering Nonformal Adult Education in Rural America: The Rural Free University and Three Traditional Providers*. Las Cruces, N. Mex.: ERIC Clearinghouse on Rural Education and Small Schools, 1984. (ED 242 470)

McCannon, R. S. "Comparative Patterns in Rural and Adult Education Programs: Participation, Focus and Barriers." Paper presented at the National Adult Education Conference, Anaheim, Calif., Oct. 1981. (ED 209 472)

McDaniel, R. H. (ed.). "Barriers to Rural Adult Education: A Survey of Seven Northwest States." A report of the Northwest Action Agenda Project. Washington, D.C.: Fund for the Improvement of Post Secondary Education, 1986. (ED 275 462)

Maes, S. C. "Rural Free Universities: Extending the UFM Model." Formal report. Manhattan: Kansas State University, 1981. (ED 247 062)

Margolis, R. J. *Rural Postsecondary Education.* Manhattan: Kansas State University, 1981. (ED 244 763)

Miller, J. *ERIC Overview—Fact Sheet No. 15.* Columbus, Ohio: Clearinghouse on Adult, Career, and Vocational Education, National Center for Research in Vocational Education, n.d.

Mirkovic, D. *Dialectic and Sociological Thought.* St. Catharines, Ont.: Deleton Publications, 1980.

Nash, R. *Schooling in Rural Societies.* London: Methuen, 1980.

Sher, J. (ed.), *Rural Education in Urbanized Nations: Issues and Innovations.* Boulder, Colo.: Westview, 1981.

Sorokin, P., and Zimmerman, C. C. *Principles of Rural-Urban Sociology.* New York: Holt, Rinehart & Winston, 1929.

Spears, J. D., and Maes, S. C. "Postsecondary and Adult Education in Rural Communities." Paper presented at the National Rural Education Forum, Kansas City, Mo., Aug. 12–14, 1985. (ED 258 790)

Sullins, W. R., and Atwell, C. A. "The Role of Small Rural Community Colleges in Providing Access." *Community College Review,* 1986, *13* (4), 45–51.

Tehranian, M. "The Dialectics of Education and Catastrophe: Communication, Democracy and World Development." In A. Thomas and E. W. Ploman (eds.), *Learning and Development: A Global Perspective.* Toronto Symposium Series, no. 15. Toronto: Ontario Institute for Studies in Education, 1986.

Treadway, D. M. *Higher Education in Rural America: Serving the Adult Learner.* New York: College Entrance Examination Board, 1984.

Van Tilburg, E. *A Study of Advantaged and Disadvantaged Adult Learners Using the Expectancy Valence Model of Human Motivation.* Project report—Ohio Agricultural Research and Development Center. Columbus: Ohio State University, 1988.

Willits, F. K., Bealer, R. C., and Crider, D. M. "Persistence of Rural/Urban Differences." In D. A. Dillman and D. J. Hobbs (eds.), *Rural Society in the U.S.: Issues for the 1980's.* Boulder, Colo.: Westview, 1982.

42

Continuing Education
For Women

Joy K. Rice
with Susan Meyer

Thirty years ago she was a rarity; today she graces every campus. The presence of returning or reentry women students in postsecondary education is now well established. Reentry women in higher education outnumber men in the same age groups. The number of women thirty-five and older enrolled in college has more than doubled since 1972 (U.S. Department of Education, Center for Educational Statistics, 1984), and the continuing decline in the population of college and university students aged eighteen to twenty-four years has been significantly offset by the increased participation of older women students (U.S. Department of Education, Center for Education Statistics, 1987). Unlike her predecessor, today's reentry woman is younger, in the work force, and juggling the demands of family, young children, and full-time or part-time employment. It is no surprise then that 95 percent of all the women participating in some form of adult or continuing education are part-time rather than full-time students (U.S. Department of Education, Center for Educational Statistics, 1984).

This chapter will review the last decade of research on continuing education for women (CEW), with special emphasis on the personal and familial needs and barriers that these women face. Recent attempts of CEW programmers to reach groups of disadvantaged women and the impact of decreased federal funding will also be discussed. The chapter ends with a critique of the philosophical assumptions underlying CEW policy and programming, with some recommendations for future change.

Needs and Barriers

While more women than men express personal or social reasons for taking courses in adult and continuing education, the most frequent reason given by women today is economic need (U.S. Department of Education, Center for Education Statistics, 1987; Clayton and Smith, 1987). This trend directly reflects the changing composition of American families and the roles within them. In 1970, 50 percent of families were married couples with children under eighteen; by 1984, that figure had fallen to 39 percent. Women heads of households with children under eighteen accounted for 10.2 percent of all families in 1970; in 1985 the figure had risen to 19.3 percent. As the main or cocontributor to their families' financial well-being, women between the ages of twenty and fifty-five increasingly have formed larger proportions of the civilian labor force—from 43.4 percent in 1970 to 54.5 percent in 1985, and a projected 59.0 percent in 1995 (U.S. Bureau of the Census, 1987). Longer life spans, better health, fewer children, and a longer delay of marriage and birth of first child also have acted to keep women as active participants in the labor force and to motivate them to seek more education for job upgrading or training.

While reentry women are choosing more job-related courses in business and in health-related fields than they are in the liberal arts and sciences (U.S. Department of Education, Center for Education Statistics, 1984), many reentry women still end up working in lower-paying, traditionally female fields (Martin and others, 1980; Hildreth and others, 1983). Age and socialization may be factors here; McCrea (1979) found that, while older reentry women were more likely to choose careers as teachers, nurses, and social workers, younger reentry women were more likely to aim for new careers as doctors, accountants, and business managers. And although many reentry women find employment in lower, entry-level positions after their schooling, studies have found that they express general satisfaction with their training (Mishler, 1983) and with their jobs (Hendel, 1983; Erdwins and Mellinger, 1986).

In response to the visible presence of millions of older women students on college campuses, a large literature has developed in the past two decades that repeatedly has addressed the special problems of reentry women and of adult students in general. The institutional barriers these students face are well known and well documented and will not be repeated here (see Tittle and Denker, 1977, and Scott, 1980 for reviews of the literature). The series of policy papers published in 1980 by the Project on the Status and Education of Women cogently outlined the special problems of reentry women. Perhaps the most valuable part of this outstanding series are the hundreds of practical suggestions for institutional change that can help women returning to school. These suggestions vary from innovative recruitment strategies and materials that highlight the mature woman to removing restrictions on financial aid and housing for part-time students and developing short-term, drop-in day care for their children.

Until recently, little attention was given in the writing on continuing education for women to psychological and familial barriers related to a successful return to school. Reentry women have problems different from those of younger students and male reentry students. Problems of reentry women typically are more related to aspects of feminine sex role socialization. Because women are socialized to bear primary responsibility for family responsibilities and child rearing, a return to school often creates significant role strain and feelings of guilt, inadequacy, and self-blame over difficulties in handling multiple roles (Patterson and Blank, 1985). Reentry women with lower incomes report more difficulties in meeting child-care and family responsibilities (Smallwood, 1980) and more symptoms of stress, including depression, anxiety, and compulsivity (Sands and Richardson, 1984). Nonetheless, while reentry women report more role strain than do comparable groups of housewives, they also experience significantly greater role gratification, that is, feelings of self-respect, respect from others, and a more diversified and meaningful life (Gerson, 1985). From a developmental perspective, the woman who returns to school may be exercising what could be termed the androgyny of later life, that is, a greater societal permissiveness to act out nontraditional roles and behaviors associated with the opposite sex (Datan and Hughes, 1985). In support of this conceptualization, samples of reentry women were more androgynous in their sex role identification and were more likely to question their sex role identity than were traditional homemakers (Amstey and Whitbourne, 1981). In another study, reentry women also expressed less fear of professional success than did college-age women (Freilino and Hummel, 1985).

The degree to which a woman experiences a successful return to school is often closely related to the support she receives from significant others, particularly from her spouse and family (Rice, 1979b, 1982). Support from one's family seems to act as a buffer for the role stress and attendant feelings of depression and conflict a woman may experience in returning to school (Roehl and Okun, 1984). A follow-up of women who had received continuing education counseling revealed that those who had made changes in their lives, such as returning to school, were more likely to be attuned to their family's attitudes toward change and to ensure they had support before they undertook change (Hooper and Rice, 1978). When asked to make a global judgment, a majority of reentry women report positive support from their families for a return to school (Astin, 1976; Rice, 1979b; Hendel, 1983; Hildreth, 1983; Spreadbury, 1983). While emotional support may be present, however, actual behavioral support from husbands and children and changes in their role behavior are less likely to occur. The majority of reentry women continue to perform dual roles and to take care of the bulk of domestic chores and child care, a fact that may explain why reentry women generally report their families are not negatively affected by their role change (Spreadbury, 1983) and why these women end up feeling significant role strain (Gerson, 1985). A life change such as a return to school is likely to have positive as well as negative impact. In one study, for example, there was less cohesiveness and more conflict between family members of returnees; but there was also more independence, less rigidity, and a greater concern for social, political, cultural, and intellectual pursuits (Ballmer and Cozby, 1981).

Studies on the personal and familial barriers faced by reentry women are consistent with a model of behavioral change that predicts growth will develop out of conflict. Thus, reentry women and their families are likely to experience more stress, but also more satisfaction and meaning in their lives, than are those who opt for less stressful change. These conclusions also mirror the results of studies from dual career families (Lein and others, 1974; Rapoport and Rapoport, 1976).

In summary, internal and external pressures combine to produce formidable barriers to reentry for the woman desiring to update her skills, to reenter the labor market, to retrain, or to revitalize. Institutions still lag in providing the special supportive services and milieu that enable a woman to fulfill the multiple and often conflicting demands of family, work, and student roles. And women themselves feel the internal constraints of role strain, guilt, and lack of self-confidence that make it difficult for them to succeed. As Tittle and Denker (1980, p. 47) note, "Many of these barriers rest upon a fundamental social fact: the power relationships between men and women. Women have less power than men in marriage, divorce, the job market and in major institutions of social and economic life in this country. Both the policies and programs of institutions of higher education can do much in assisting women in overcoming these barriers to returning to higher education." The following section explores what current institutions and programs are doing to help reentry women.

The Institutional Response

Continuing education for women (CEW) programs began in the early sixties and became institutionalized at the college level by the formation of hundreds of programs, centers, and courses on campuses across the nation. From around 100 in 1966, they grew to nearly 500 by the seventies (Wells, 1974), and there are probably double that number today. Historically, the early pioneers of the CEW movement initiated, piloted, and field-tested nearly all of the so-called innovations in flexible programming and stop-out education (Rice, 1983). Preadmission counseling, advising and orientation, individual vocational educational assessment and counseling, daytime noncredit seminars, small group discussion and advising groups, workshops on building self-esteem and self-awareness, and employment information are still key features of many of these programs (Franck, 1985; Karr-Kidwell,

1984; Roy, 1986; Trevor and Locas, 1986). Within the past decade, CEW programs have increasingly expanded their horizons by offering special courses in career development for employed women seeking advancement to managerial positions and by establishing linkages with undergraduate women, community groups, women's studies programs, resource centers, and caucuses (Wells, 1974; McGraw, 1982). Research is also becoming a part of the larger, better-known programs; for example, the University of Michigan's CEW Center sponsors CEW fellows and a large program of research on issues related to women and education.

The reentry woman who was well served by these CEW programs in the sixties and seventies was generally white, married, fairly affluent with a professional husband, and middle-class—a composite of demographics confirmed earlier by Doty (1966) and later by Scott (1976) and Astin (1976). Today CEW is beginning to move beyond the original mission of helping women of means obtain higher education for enrichment and professional training to empowering groups of disadvantaged women. This shift means providing opportunities at all levels of education in a multitude of settings, many of them nonacademic. A good example of a nonacademic setting is the Lutheran Settlement House Women's Program in Philadelphia, which offers adult basic education classes, self-development workshops, a community-based, degree-oriented college program, a bilingual crisis hotline for abused women and children, employment counseling and job readiness training, personal counseling, and free child care for participants (Luttrell, 1982). Such a program reflects an increasingly diversified population of reentry women that includes significant numbers of single mothers, divorced women, displaced homemakers, and minority and disadvantaged reentry students (Rice, 1978; Rice and Rice, 1986; McCrea, 1979; Hall and Gleaves, 1981).

Divorced Women and Single Mothers. The process of divorce is frequently accompanied by a personal identity crisis, and the divorced woman returning to school is also coming to terms with who she is, her aloneness, her self-esteem, and her reliance on others for support (Mezirow and Marsick, 1978; Rice and Rice, 1986). The mix of having a lower income and sole responsibility for children, the need to work, the assaults on confidence and self-esteem, and the time requirements and constraints of the institution creates a special complex of problems for these reentry students (Hooper and March, 1980). In addition, single mothers and divorced women face social disapproval and isolation, and they enjoy few institutionalized sources of personal or familial support. Many cannot get loans because they are poor risks, or they cannot get scholarships because they are part-time and because, no matter what their academic ability, they cannot find enough time to study (Hooper and March, 1980).

Smallwood (1980) found that more than one-third of the potential problems of adult women students were significantly related to low income, and that divorced women consistently reported the highest degree of concern for the largest number of problems related to reentry; separated women were a close second. Child-care assistance, financial aid for educational and vocational skills, and job readiness programs are frequently recommended for low-income women struggling to support their families; however, while such help may enable them to complete training programs, it does not necessarily ensure their long-term employment (Knox, 1983). Reentry single mothers must also be encouraged to enter nontraditional occupations that offer higher wages and better benefits. A follow-up study of a reentry program for disadvantaged women in a community college, for example, revealed that 82 percent of the women were working, but that over half were employed in clerical occupations, traditionally a low-paying work ghetto for women (Forrest, 1981).

Community colleges have provided innovative leadership in establishing successful programs that enable disadvantaged women to enter nontraditional employment. Brevard Community College used an innovative Job Club, designed with an educational self-help approach and a peer counseling format (Van der Lust, 1984). Daytona Beach Community College instituted a successful mentor system and a recruitment and placement program that increased female enrollment in nontraditional vocational-technical education by 22 percent; nearly 88 percent of the women who graduated in nontraditional vocations found jobs (Sparks, 1984).

Displaced Homemakers. There is substantial overlap in the programs designed for low-income women who are single parents and heads of households and the programs recently initiated for displaced homemakers. Since 1975, when the first program began in Baltimore, the term *displaced homemakers* has been used to describe women who were forced through the death, disability, or absence of the spouse to give up the homemaker role and to reenter the work force. Estimates of the number of displaced homemakers range from four million, using Department of Labor Federal Assistance statistics (Friedrichs, 1982) to twelve million, using figures from the National Displaced Homemaker Network (Morgan, 1987).

In 1986, there were 750 displaced homemaker programs nationally (Morgan, 1987). These programs are found in a variety of settings, including vocational-technical high schools, colleges, and community agencies. Some focus on displaced homemakers within special groups. Thus, the displaced homemaker program at Miami-Dade Community College, in Florida, offers bilingual group counseling to serve better a population of Hispanic women; and Blackfeet Community College in Browning, Montana, provides services for displaced homemakers with a counseling center for Native American women (Hall and Gleaves, 1981). Funding for these programs has come from a variety of sources, including private funds, the Comprehensive Employment and Training Act (CETA), (now replaced by the Job Training Partnership Act [JTPA]), the U.S. Department of Labor, and the U.S. Department of Education.

Displaced homemakers generally have limited financial resources. Having spent many years in the home caring for family members, their educations may be limited, their time out of the labor market substantial, and their marketable skills few. These women often have a negative self-concept, and they fear entering the labor market. They may also face complex legal and familial problems when they attempt to do so (Shields, 1981). Some of these women are older, impoverished adults who are likely to face age discrimination in both education and employment. Because they must cope with the impact of inflation on fixed incomes, many older women seek more education to prepare for employment, but they find themselves limited to poorly paying jobs as clerks, salespersons, or domestic workers (Weinstock, 1978; Miller, 1977).

Displaced homemaker programs assist these women through counseling, educational or technical training, career planning, and job search assistance. Morgan (1987) suggests that programs must address both intrapsychic and pragmatic issues in order to help women recover from the loss of their former status, rebuild self-confidence, and develop specific skills. Peer support, faculty role models and mentors, individual validation, and taking personal responsibility are key program elements (Morgan, 1987; Delworth and Seeman, 1984).

Minority Women. Minority reentry women share many of the economic problems and needs for educational support services that displaced homemakers and single parent mothers do (see Chapter Forty-four). Programs for minority women tend to be based on the common concerns of disadvantaged women in general, including underemployment, poverty, negative self-concepts, poor academic and career counseling, and inadequate educational preparation for careers. Minority women must also deal with multiple barriers and discrimination related to age, race, gender, marital status, and economic status. They may face a lack of familial and community support, they may fear being isolated and alone in school, and they may find that programs are not geared to their employment, community, and cultural needs. The lack of affordable child care and safe, inexpensive transportation are other formidable barriers to their participation in further training and education (Hall and Gleaves, 1981).

Some minority women may also perceive reentry CEW programs as created for bored, affluent, white housewives. Fewer than 9 percent of Mexican-American women on campuses sampled said that they had taken advantage of women's centers or reentry programs, even though they also indicated their need for the services provided (Chacon and others, 1982). Because of cultural patterns and pressures to fulfill traditional family roles, black and Chicana women may also experience a lack of support for pursuing higher education. Education may even cost these women friends and spouses (Meyer, 1986; Chacon and others, 1982).

Asian-American women encounter a form of reverse discrimination. Labeled a model minority, their needs are often overlooked, yet they, as are black women, are overrepresented in low-paying, low-status jobs. Large numbers of Asian-American women, for example, are employed as undocumented workers in the garment industry and in other small businesses (Hall and Gleaves, 1981).

Programs of continuing education for women have attempted to serve minority reentry women in a variety of ways and in many settings. Such programs include special reentry programs affiliated with traditional degree programs, nontraditional vocational-technical programs, programs offered by proprietary schools open to both men and women, government programs associated with the receipt of public assistance, and programs at community-based colleges serving specific minority populations. Examples of this last type of program include Native American Educational Services College serving Native Americans, Sojourner-Douglass College and Malcolm-King College serving blacks, and Boricua College serving Hispanics. These colleges offer an extensive array of remediation courses and strong faculty and peer support. They emphasize the acquiring of basic skills and competency-based, career-oriented learning (Gittell, 1985). Other college-based programs, such as ACCESS for Women at New York City Technical College, offer minority women basic math and science courses before teaching them the skills needed for entry into male-dominated trades such as air conditioning and refrigeration, apartment superintendency, and computer technology.

For some women, reentry includes acculturation to the workplace. The National Puerto Rican Forum tries to facilitate this process by providing business skills and job placement services to Hispanic women. This organization also assists bilingual women in developing an English business vocabulary through BOLT (Basic Occupational Language Training) classes. The National Congress of Neighborhood Women assists women from primarily black, Hispanic, and white ethnic areas of Brooklyn, New York, through adult basic education (ABE) and general educational development (GED) preparation and through associate degree programs offered by Empire State College. Many graduates of these programs have gone on to provide community organizing, counseling, and legal services to their neighborhoods.

Reentry programs for minority women need to balance their emphasis on technical expertise with the critical-thinking and analytical skills that will allow these women to advance in their careers. However, minority women need more than mere training in technical or analytic skills; they must learn to operate in a male-dominated environment with a different language and mores (Persico, 1987). Thus, reentry programs must also help minority women find ways to cope with cultural adaptations (Davis and Watson, 1982), with perceptions of racism (Hale, 1980), and with their lack of power in society.

Funding for Educational Equity. Overall, federal policy in the eighties has had an increasingly negative impact on women in continuing education and has intensified the feminization of poverty. Two significant gains for women in the seventies were the inclusion of funding programs for displaced homemakers as part of CETA monies in 1976 and the reauthorization of the Women's Educational Equity Act (WEEA) under Title IX in 1978

(Simonson and Menzer, 1984). In 1980, the Women in Science program, designed to give women greater access to scientific and technological fields, was incorporated into the Education Act, and in 1985, as part of the Carl Perkins Vocational Education Act, a significant increase was provided in funding for displaced homemaker programs. Since then, there has been a definite retreat in the federal funding for educational equity. Tetreault and Schmuck (1985), in their analysis of educational reform reports, noted the omission of the needs of women, an observation that may characterize the current federal direction. Although, in 1985, the WEEA was again reauthorized with appropriations approved from $10 million in 1985 to $20 million in 1987, actual funding was $6 million for 1985 and $3.5 million in 1986. The program was deemed to have outlived its usefulness and was eliminated from the 1987 federal budget (U.S. Office of Management and Budget, 1987).

Appropriating financial aid for college students has become increasingly complex. Doyle and Hartle (1985) argue that current policies fail to focus on the neediest students. This argument is supported by an analysis of shifts within the budget. Although College Work Study appropriations have increased, direct grant portions of the financial aid package have decreased. Thus, the same total dollar amount per student is simply reallocated (U.S. Congress, House Budget Committee, 1983). For reentry women who are heads of households, juggling multiple roles and obtaining public assistance, the result may be a significant decrease in accessible aid.

Vocational educational funds for women also have been eroded and redistributed. Analysis of patterns in funding reveal a shift away from training for those on public assistance (many of whom are female heads of households) to short-term employment for youth (increases in Job Corps and Summer Youth requests) and to substantial funding for dislocated workers—primarily men displaced by increased technology (U.S. Congress, House Budget Committee, 1983). Even when services for retraining disadvantaged women are specified in legislation, they may not receive high priority in the implementation. Title II of the Job Training Partnership Act is funded at about $1.8 billion annually and is the major federal intervention aimed at providing employment and training services for the economically disadvantaged. Special programming targeted for low-income women, however, was limited to a very small percentage of training dollars (Solow and Walker, 1986).

Poverty in America falls heavily on women, particularly on single heads of households and on older women. For the single mother, complex ties to public assistance may exacerbate more than alleviate the situation. In the past, welfare recipients have been severely restricted in terms of work and educational activities. Today, women with Aid to Families with Dependent Children (AFDC) grants receive work incentives allowing them to maintain partial grants and to continue Medicaid eligibility for one year. Current policy on educational participation while on welfare varies by state. As of July 1987, New York City women receiving AFDC grants may participate in both associate and baccalaureate degree programs without being deemed ineligible. Minnesota legislation on AFDC does not include educational grants or loans in its definition of income. In Wisconsin, however, 22 percent to 46 percent of women students with financially dependent children on welfare had their AFDC benefits cut when they received loans, grants, or scholarships, and 60 percent had benefits cut when they worked outside the home (Trani, 1987). Federal policy requires recipients of AFDC funds to participate in some form of so-called workfare. These programs have been criticized severely for providing neither adequate work experience nor training for the participants. The NETwork program, in the 1987 federal budget, represents an attempt to address these concerns by adding ABE and GED components to work experience and by providing funded job training (U.S. Office of Management and Budget, 1987).

A broadening of populations served under the portions of the Vocational Education Act that address the needs of displaced homemakers and other women may help. Including such groups as workers with limited English and all single heads of households may allow states to shift monies to programs that will preserve the jobs of individuals already in the workforce and may reduce public assistance rolls (Worthington, 1985).

Nongovernmental programs designed to assist women in breaking out of the cycle of poverty are also falling victim to federal cutbacks. For example, access to higher education through the National Congress of Neighborhood Women was initially provided through a Fund for the Improvement of Postsecondary Education grant in the 1970s. In 1987, this funding was no longer available, and such programs are barely maintained by piecing together funds from other sources. Other programs have reduced services drastically or simply have ceased to exist. *Creativity* will be the buzzword for the funding of educational equity in the next decades.

Reflections on the Future

CEW programs have been very successful in offering reentry women more choices leading to the integration rather than to the separation of work and family roles. Moreover, they have attempted to raise institutions' awareness of family needs in educational policy and planning. This aim is laudable. However, the continuing assumption of a permanent disparity between the lives of men and the lives of women and the notion of separate spheres of life based on gender role may not be helpful.

The viability of continuing education programs for women is predicated on four basic assumptions: (1) Women are expected to have a discontinuous rather than a continuous education and employment pattern (primarily because of marital and child-rearing commitments). (2) Women also are expected to accommodate the needs of others and to adjust their own career plans accordingly. (3) Separate and special programming for women is needed to help them cope with the discontinuity and need for accommodation in their lives. (4) Solutions to these problems are achieved through a remedial approach rather than through a preventative approach (Rice, 1976). As long as men do not participate equally in family life and child rearing, women must adjust to the demands of a discontinuous educational and employment pattern, accommodating their needs for personal fulfillment and vocational development to the needs of family and significant others. Under these circumstances there will be a continuing need for separate, remedial programming to help women in these positions.

Widespread social change is very slow. Nonetheless, the latter half of this century has witnessed some remarkable changes in gender roles, and both men and women are participating in areas of family and public life that would have been unthinkable a few decades ago. Giele (1987) has studied patterns of changes in men's and women's lives and roles and has concluded that the changes in the life patterns of educated women are a template for a new, more general pattern of modern adulthood. The new pattern is related to a higher degree of education, to longer lives, to the replacement of a rural family economy by an industrial one, and to a rise in concurrent or multiple roles. These shifts cross cultures as well as genders; men's roles are slowly changing in a similar fashion, and a pattern comparable to that in the United States is developing in Western Europe (Giele, 1987). More years to live, more years in school, and new multiple work and family roles for both men and women mean that continuing education will have to develop creative, flexible solutions to helping adults deal with the new patterns of modern adulthood. With a view to the future viability of CEW programs, we offer the following six sections of observations and recommendations.

Redefining the Field and Mission. Continuing education for women as a movement needs to expand its original premises, the populations it has targeted, and the settings in which it traditionally has served its clients. In this chapter, continuing education for women has been very broadly defined. At the national level, however, the CEW movement still needs to articulate clearly its formal embracing of all types of basic and continuing education for women—education that occurs far beyond the confines of settings of higher education and that reaches out to new populations of disadvantaged women in their homes, workplaces, churches, neighborhoods, nursing homes, prisons, women's centers, community vocational-technical and proprietary schools, or wherever they are found. This outreach effort will mean an important shift in the thinking that has characterized the mission and priorities of the professional organizations concerned with continuing education for women—organizations such as the American Association for Adult and Continuing Education and the National Association of Women Deans, Administrators and Counselors, the two professional organizations that have had large voices in addressing the needs of reentry women and in representing the programs that serve them.

In both policy and research, there must be a rethinking and a broader redefinition of the term *reentry women.* If the major thrust becomes advocacy and service for the new poor, including single mothers, minority women, older women, and low-income displaced homemakers, then educators will have to press and lobby for funding at state and federal levels to increase substantially the appropriations to these most needy of groups.

Learning from Others. Continuing education programs for women need to strengthen their linkages with women's studies programs and centers. The research, resources, and personnel of these programs have much to offer CEW programs in keeping them abreast of feminist scholarship at the cutting edge of changes in sex roles and gender patterns. Along these lines, Christian and Wilson (1985) have developed a career counseling model for reentry women based on the tenets of feminist theory and practice, and Mason and Chew (1983) have applied strategies of feminist pedagogy to traditional courses for reentry women. Innovative techniques borrowed from women's studies courses have included interdisciplinary content, peer teaching, and affective as well as cognitive approaches to learning.

Networking needs to occur at all levels between CEW programs in educational institutions and programs for women in the community, such as abortion and pregnancy counseling services, centers for battered women and victims of rape, and programs for displaced homemakers. Formal and informal linkages can also be profitably developed with educators working in sex equity areas in the elementary and secondary schools, as well as at the college level—an approach related to the objective of developing a more preventive approach to the efforts of CEW programmers.

Preventing the Problems. Thus far, CEW has concentrated on helping women who currently are in the throes of coping with multiple roles of student, worker, and wife or mother. A more preventive approach involves reaching young women and girls at a far earlier stage and educating them about the realities of the shared and multiple roles they will play throughout their lives and about how to prepare for those realities. We are beginning to see this kind of thinking integrated into program practice. An example is the program at Santa Fe Community College in Gainesville, Florida, which, for the first time, has included workshops and presentations on sex-role stereotyping and nontraditional career options to elementary and middle school children (Bromley and others, 1984). Boys, as well as girls, must not be neglected. Parents and educators are beginning to socialize boys to expect to achieve a degree of integration, rather than separation, in their future family roles.

A Key Priority. Along these lines, CEW educators and programmers will need to press their institutions, communities, businesses, and industries to attend to the needs of men and women in multiple roles. Low-cost, quality child care, made available in all work and educational settings, is still the key priority. The number of preschool-aged children is expected to increase by 36 percent, from a low of 17.1 million in 1977 to a high of 23.3 million in 1990. The strong relationship between the need for campus child care among women students and equal educational opportunity has not been clearly recognized or addressed. A survey of women students at Portland

State University found that one-third would have increased their course loads if their child-care problems had been resolved; another one-third had to withdraw from school due to these problems. In other surveys, nearly half of the reentry women at Northwestern University stated that having young children had prevented them from returning to school earlier, and 80 percent of 200 student families enrolled in the University of California, Berkeley reported that they would be forced to withdraw if campus centers were to close (Creange, 1980).

Although the number of child-care facilities at both two- and four-year colleges has increased, it still remains relatively low. Infant care, drop-in centers, and before- and after-school day care are especially needed for parents returning to school and work. Continuing education personnel also need to work with business and industry to develop more alternative work patterns and choices such as flextime, part-time, and shared job models, which are found in a few progressive work settings today. If these workplace options are not made widely available to men as well as to women, we will continue to see educational policy and planning that emphasizes flexibility and accommodation for women, but not for men.

Empowering Women. It has been documented that, while women are returning to school in unprecedented numbers, many of them still end up in traditional, female-dominated vocations that tend to have lower status, lower pay, and less opportunity for advancement. The work of some pioneering community colleges and vocational-technical schools in helping to train women for nontraditional careers is very important and needs to be expanded. Women have been primary victims of the impact of high technology as unskilled manual, clerical, and domestic work is made obsolete by computerization and mechanization. Cooperative education opportunities for women must be broadened, and special programs must be developed to help them break through the discriminatory barriers they face in obtaining apprenticeships, training, and union membership in the skilled trades. Again, the job for educators includes not only helping women train for and obtain these better-paying jobs, but also educating boys and men to accept them readily in these traditionally highly sex-segregated occupations.

At the managerial and professional level, we can point to the great progress women have made in entering medicine, law, and business; however, the number of women in highly technical fields, engineering, and the sciences remains small. Inadequate, minimal, or no training in higher mathematics eliminates a large number of careers for women who are anxious about taking more math and who consciously or unconsciously view it as a male domain (Sells, 1980; Eccles and Jacobs, 1987). Adult educators can help women and girls become aware of these barriers and can assist them in overcoming them. Despite all the progress women have made in the workplace, our occupational structure largely remains sex segregated. Helping to undo this inequitable situation is a formidable but extremely important task that faces educators working in consort with business, industry, and government personnel.

Beyond Service and Advocacy. University-based reentry programs for women are generally inadequately financed, understaffed, and peripheral to the university (Mulligan, 1973; Mattfield, 1971; Leland, 1976). Rarely do the staff hold faculty appointments, even when credit or noncredit courses are offered and taught to students. The lack of a direct administrative line, in addition to having little academic clout, forces many of these programs continually to justify their existence and to protect their miniscule budgets and precarious positions (Rice, 1979a). One way to justify existence and to protect budgets is to do systematic follow-up and collection of data and client statistics that document the program's use and effectiveness. In the only study investigating this practice, a mere 4 percent of 356 CEW programs surveyed reported that they had tried to keep data on past or present reentry women (Mattfield, 1971). Demonstrating program use and effectiveness through systematic evaluation and follow-up is a crucial step in achieving the program accountability, security, and growth that CEW personnel desire, and it requires that assessment, evaluation, and research be seen as integral to the CEW program's mission of service and advocacy. The larger university-based CEW Centers that have established strong research and service missions (for example, University of California, Berkeley, Northwestern University, and University of Michigan) have published occasional papers and have sponsored symposia and dissertations on a wide variety of variables related to reentry women. We hope this kind of research will be broadened and encouraged to the point where gender is recognized as a valid variable of study and insights from gender-based research become widely disseminated and integrated into the knowledge base of adult and continuing education.

References

Amstey, F. H., and Whitbourne, S. K. "Continuing Education, Identity, Sex Role, and Psychosocial Development in Adult Women." *Sex Roles: A Journal of Research,* 1981, *1* (1), 49–58.

Astin, H. *Some Action of Her Own: The Adult Woman and Higher Education.* Lexington, Mass.: Lexington Books, 1976.

Ballmer, H., and Cozby, P. C. "Family Environments of Women Who Return to College." *Sex Roles: A Journal of Research,* 1981, *7*(10), 1019–1026.

Bromley, A., and others. "A Model Program for Sex Equity in Vocation Education." Gainesville, Fla.: Santa Fe Community College, 1984. (ED 250 535)

Chacon, M., and others. *Chicanas in Postsecondary Education: Executive Summary.* Stanford, Calif.: Center for Research on Women, 1982.

Christian, C., and Wilson, J. "Reentry Women and Feminist Therapy: A Career Counseling Model." *Journal of College Student Personnel,* 1985, *26* (6), 496–500.

Clayton, D. E., and Smith, M. M. "Motivational Typology of Reentry Women." *Adult Education Quarterly,* 1987, *37* (2), 90–104.

Creange, R. *Campus Child Care: A Challenge for the 80's.* Washington, D.C.: Project on the Status and Education of Women, Association of American Colleges, 1980.

Datan, N., and Hughes, F. "Burning Books and Briefcases: Agency, Communion, and the Social Context of Learning in Adulthood." *Academic Psychology Bulletin,* 1985, *7* (2), 175–186.

Davis, G., and Watson, G. *Black Life in Corporate America: Swimming in the Mainstream.* New York: Anchor Books, 1982.

Delworth, U., and Seeman, D. "The Ethics of Care: Implications of Gilligan for the Student Services Professions." *Journal of College Student Personnel,* 1984, *25* (4), 489–492.

Doty, B. A. "Why Do Mature Women Return to College?" *Journal of the National Association of Women Deans, Administrators, and Counselors,* 1966, *29,* 171–174.

Doyle, D., and Hartle, T. "Facing the Fiscal Chopping Block." *Change,* 1985, *17* (4), 8–10, 54–56.

Eccles, J. S., and Jacobs, J. E. "Social Forces Shape Math Attitudes and Performance." In M. R. Walsh (ed.), *The Psychology of Women, Ongoing Debates.* New Haven, Conn.: Yale University Press, 1987.

Erdwins, C. J., and Mellinger, J. C. "Reentry Women After Graduation." *Journal of Genetic Psychology,* 1986, *147* (4), 437–446.

Forrest, J. D. "An Assessment of a Community College Reentry Program for Women." Unpublished master's thesis, Department of Education, Stetson University, 1981. (ED 214 557)

Franck, S. A. "Cognitive Restructuring: A Program for Reentry Women." *Journal of College Student Personnel,* 1985, *26* (6), 554–556.

Freilino, M. K., and Hummel, R. "Achievement and Identity in College-Age Versus Adult Women Students." *Journal of Youth and Adolescence,* 1985, *14* (1), 1–10.

Friedrichs, K. M. *Displaced Homemakers.* Ann Arbor: School of Education, University of Michigan, 1982.

Gerson, J. M. "Women Returning to School: The Consequences of Multiple Roles." *Sex Roles, A Journal of Research,* 1985, *13* (1–2), 77–92.

Giele, J. *Charting Women's Major Life Events.* Ann Arbor: Center for Continuing Education of Women, University of Michigan, 1987.

Gittell, M. "Reaching the Hard to Reach." *Change,* Sept.–Oct. 1985, *17,* 51–60.

Hale, J. "The Black Woman and Child Rearing." In L. Rodgers-Ross (ed.), *The Black Woman.* Beverly Hills, Calif.: Sage, 1980.

Hall, R. M., and Gleaves, F. D. "Reentry Women: Special Programs for Special Populations." Washington, D.C.: Project on the Status and Education of Women, Association of American Colleges, 1981.

Hendel, D. D. "Adult Women's Perceptions of Continuing Education for Women." *Journal of the National Association of Women Deans, Administrators, and Counselors,* 1983, *46* (4), 38–42.

Hildreth, G. J., and others. "Family and Social Life of Women over Age Fifty Who Are in College." *Educational Gerontology*, 1983, *9* (4), 339–350.

Hooper, J. O., and March, G. B. "The Female Single Parent in the University." *Journal of College Student Personnel*, 1980, *21* (2), 141–146.

Hooper, J. O., and Rice, J. K. "Locus of Control and Outcomes Following the Counseling of Returning Adults." *Journal of College Student Personnel*, 1978, *19* (1), 42–47.

Karr-Kidwell, P. J. "Reentry Women Students in Higher Education: A Model for Non-Traditional Support Programs in Counseling and Career Advisement." Paper presented at the Women and Work Symposium, Arlington, Tex., May 4, 1984. (ED 251 595)

Knox, J. J. *A Study to Conduct an Analysis of Fall-Out Among Low-Income Head of Household Women Seeking Employment*. San Antonio, Tex.: San Antonio College, 1983. (ED 234 201)

Lein, L., and others. *Final Report: Work and Family Life*. National Institute of Education project, no. 3-3094. Cambridge, Mass.: Center for the Study of Public Policy, 1974.

Leland, C. "The Case-Study Programs: Academic Misfits Which Lasted." In H. S. Astin (ed.), *Some Action of Her Own: The Adult Woman and Higher Education*. Lexington, Mass.: Lexington Books, 1976.

Luttrell, W. *Building Multi-Cultural Awareness, A Teaching Approach for Learner Centered Education*. Philadelphia: Lutheran Settlement House, 1982. (ED 222 638)

McCrea, J. M. "The New Student Body: Women Returning to College." *Journal of the National Association of Women Deans, Administrators, and Counselors*, 1979, *43* (1), 13–16.

McGraw, L. K. "A Selective Review of Programs and Counseling Interventions for the Reentry Woman." *The Personnel and Guidance Journal*, 1982, *60* (8), 469–472.

Martin, M., and others. *Statewide Assessment of Career Aspiration and Job Attainment Among Women Returning to College in Maryland*. Annapolis: Maryland State Board for Higher Education, 1980. (ED 194 786)

Mason, M., and Chew, M. *Two Studies: A Feminist Approach to Teaching Non-Traditional Students*. Wellesley, Mass.: Center for Research on Women, Wellesley College, 1983.

Mattfield, J. A. "A Decade of Continuing Education: Dead or Open Door." Unpublished study, Brown University, 1971.

Meyer, S. "An Investigation of Self-Concept Change in Black Reentry Women." Unpublished doctoral dissertation, Teachers College, Columbia University, 1986.

Mezirow, J., and Marsick, V. *Education for Perspective Transformation: Women's Reentry Programs in Community Colleges*. New York: Teachers College, Columbia University Center for Adult Education, 1978.

Miller, H. *Double Jeopardy*. Washington, D.C.: National Retired Teachers Association, 1977.

Mishler, C. "From Adult Learner to Wage Earner: What Happens to Homemakers After College Graduation." *Journal of the National Association of Women Deans, Administrators, and Counselors,* 1983, *46* (4), 15–21.

Morgan, J. "The Nature and Dynamics of the Transition from Homemaker to Independent Person for Displaced Homemakers and the Role of Displaced Homemaker Programs in Facilitating Transition." Unpublished doctoral dissertation, Teachers College, Columbia University, 1987.

Mulligan, K. L. *A Question of Opportunity: Women and Continuing Education.* Washington, D.C.: National Advisory Council on Extension and Continuing Education, 1973. (ED 981 323)

Patterson, C. D., and Blank, T. O. "Doubt, Struggle, and Growth: A Profile of the Mature Woman in the Student Role." Paper presented at the annual meeting of the Eastern Psychological Association, Boston, March 1985.

Persico, C. "Non-Traditional Technical Programs for Women: Barriers and Facilitators." Unpublished doctoral dissertation, Teachers College, Columbia University, 1987.

Project on the Status and Education of Women. *Field Evaluation Reports on Reentry Women.* Washington, D.C.: Women's Reentry Project, Association of American Colleges, 1980.

Rapoport, R., and Rapoport, R. N. *Dual-Career Families Re-examined: New Integrations of Work and Family.* New York: Harper & Row, 1976.

Rice, J. K. "Continuing Education for Women, 1960–75: A Critical Appraisal." *Educational Record,* 1976, *56,* 240–249.

Rice, J. K. "Divorce and a Return to School." *Journal of Divorce,* 1978, *1,* 247–257.

Rice, J. K. "Continuing Education for Women: A Clarion." *Lifelong Learning,* 1979a, *3,* 16–19, 25.

Rice, J. K. "Self Esteem, Sex-Role Orientation, and Perceived Spouse Support for a Return to School." *Adult Education Quarterly,* 1979b, *29* (4), 215–233.

Rice, J. K. "Spouse Support: Couples in Educational Transition." *Lifelong Learning,* 1982, *6,* 4–6.

Rice, J. K. "Operation Second Chance." *Journal of the National Association of Women Deans, Administrators, and Counselors,* 1983, *46* (4), 3–10.

Rice, J. K., and Rice, D. G. *Living Through Divorce: A Developmental Approach to Divorce Therapy.* New York: Guilford, 1986.

Roehl, J. E., and Okun, M. A. "Depressive Symptoms Among Women Reentering College: The Role of Negative Life Events and Family Social Support." *Journal of College Student Personnel,* 1984, *25* (3), 251–254.

Roy, S. W. "Programming for Returning Women Students." *Journal of College Student Personnel,* 1986, *27* (1), 75–76.

Sands, R. G., and Richardson, V. "Educational and Mental Health Factors Associated with the Return of Mid-Life Women to School." *Educational Gerontology,* 1984, *10* (1–2), 155–170.

Scott, N. A. "The Effects of Returning to College and Assertiveness Training on Self Concept and Personality Variables of Mature Women." Unpublished doctoral dissertation, School of Education, University of Colorado, 1976.

Scott, N. A. *Returning Women Students: A Review of Research and Descriptive Studies.* Washington, D.C.: National Association of Women Deans, Administrators, and Counselors, 1980.

Sells, L. W. "The Mathematical Filter and the Education of Women and Minorities." In L. H. Fox, L. Brody, and D. Tobin (eds.), *Women and the Mathematical Mystique.* Baltimore, Md.: Johns Hopkins University Press, 1980.

Shields, L. *Displaced Homemakers: Organizing for a New Life.* New York: McGraw-Hill, 1981.

Simonson, J. R., and Menzer, J. A. "Catching Up: A Review of the Women's Educational Equity Act Program." Washington, D.C.: National Coalition for Women and Girls in Education, 1984. (ED 247 849)

Smallwood, K. B. "What Do Adult Women College Students Really Need?" *Journal of College Student Personnel,* 1980, *21* (1), 65–73.

Solow, K., and Walker, G. *The Job Training Partnership Act: Service to Women.* New York: Grinker Associates, 1986.

Sparks, L. J. *Career Advancement Training: A Project to Provide Career Information and Services to Women Interested in Training for Non-Traditional Vocational/ Technical Occupations.* Daytona Beach, Fla.: Daytona Beach Community College, 1984. (ED 250 534)

Spreadbury, C. "Family Adjustment When Adult Women Return to School." *Journal of the National Association of Women Deans, Administrators, and Counselors,* 1983, *46* (4), 26–31.

Tetreault, M., and Schmuck, P. "Equity, Educational Reform, and Gender." *Issues in Education,* 1985, *3* (1), 45–67.

Tittle, C. K., and Denker, E. R. "Reentry Women: A Selective Review of the Educational Process, Career Choice, and Interest Measurement." *Review of Educational Research,* 1977, *47* (4), 531–584.

Tittle, C. K., and Denker, E. R. *Returning Women Students in Higher Education: Defining Policy Issues.* New York: Praeger, 1980.

Trani, E. *University of Wisconsin System Students with Dependent Children: Finances and Their Educational Impact.* Madison: University of Wisconsin System, 1987.

Trevor, R., and Locas, J. A. *Profile and Evaluation of Women's Program (1983) and Impact of Project Turning Point (Displaced Homemakers Program, 1979–1981).* Vol. 14, no. 5. Palatine, Ill.: Office of Planning and Research, William Rainey Harper College, 1986.

U.S. Bureau of the Census. *Statistical Abstract of the United States, 1987.* (107th ed.) Washington, D.C.: U.S. Bureau of the Census, 1987.

U.S. Congress, House Budget Committee. *President Reagan's Fiscal Year 1984 Budget.* Washington, D.C.: U.S. Government Printing Office, 1983.

U.S. Department of Education, Center for Education Statistics. *Survey of Adult Education.* Current population survey, May 1984. Washington, D.C.: U.S. Department of Education, Center for Education Statistics, 1984.

U.S. Department of Education, Center for Education Statistics. *Digest of Educational Statistics.* Washington, D.C.: U.S. Department of Education, Center for Education Statistics, 1987.

U.S. Office of Management and Budget. *Budget of the United States Government.* Washington, D.C.: Executive Office of the President and Office of Management and Budget, 1987.

Van der Lust, M. J. *Transition, Retraining, and Change for Entry.* Cocoa, Fla.: Brevard Community College, 1984.

Weinstock, R. *The Greying of the Campus.* New York: Educational Facilities Laboratories, 1978.

Wells, J. A. *Continuing Education Programs and Services for Women.* U.S. Department of Labor pamphlet, no. 10. Washington, D.C.: Women's Bureau, U.S. Department of Labor, 1974.

Worthington, R. M. *Vocational Education for Displaced Homemakers and Single Heads of Households.* Washington, D.C.: Office of Vocational and Adult Education, 1985.

43

Workers' Education

Mickey R. Hellyer
Beth Schulman

Previous handbooks have emphasized education of working people as union members. Too little attention has been given to the education of nonunion workers and to education occurring outside national and local formal organizations—education that has received little support or sanction, at least publicly, from the leadership of national unions. The challenge to examine and to evaluate this entire tradition in a single, brief chapter has proved to be an insurmountable task. Instead, we have chosen to concentrate on three areas we believe most important.

First, we will attempt to explain what we mean by working-class education. We hope that such an explanation will help clarify further discussions of this topic. Second, we use some historical background to demonstrate how the changing consciousness and activity of the working class has been a major and progressive force in the American experience. Third, we provide a few specific examples of working-class education in its contemporary American context.

Workers as a Class: New Perspectives for Adult Education

Traditionally, a major difficulty in discussions of education for, of, or by workers revolves around a consensual definition of the term *worker*. The terms *workers' education, labor education,* and *labor studies* have been used interchangeably (Schied, 1982; Linton, 1966), viewed as mere semantic differences (Gray, 1966), or treated as specific and definable stages in a developmental, historical process (Rogin and Rachlin, 1968; Gray, 1966;

Dwyer, 1977). Although each approach has its merits, in this chapter, workers' education, labor education, and labor studies will all be considered working-class education. This is a designation that places working peoples' educational experiences into their wider culture—an approach that has been previously absent in most American adult education literature.

Many who are students of the labor movement simply define *class* as an "objective function" in which the worker (as a member of a class) does not "possess society's means of production and distribution and therefore must work for others who do" (Brecher, 1972, p. 283). Although we agree in principle with this approach, we argue that it is too limited, since it does not incorporate the dynamic and contact conflict that continues to exist between wage earners and those who pay their wages as both groups evolve. For us, the working class is defined by its dialectical relationship to the owners' class—that is, one class cannot exist without the other in a capitalist society. (The term *ownership* should not be confused with those enterprises, such as cooperatives and other production and service industries, in which the workers, after deducting operating costs, democratically divide the profits in some proportion among their membership.) We agree with the perspective of internationally known historian E. P. Thompson (1971, p. 9), who writes that "class is not a category . . . but rather a historical relationship between one group of people and another."

Thus, workers will be treated as a historical and modern force as they relate to and continually oppose the ownership class in the workplace as well as in other areas of their social milieu. We hope this approach will be a beginning for providing a broader and richer understanding of working people as they relate to the totality of the culture. Also, we hope to dispel a widespread underlying assumption, and a conventional view among many adult educators, that working people should be viewed somehow merely as economic and occupational groups, positioned by their rank in a static social hierarchy. Instead, we seek to create a new interest among adult educators to undertake further research in working-class education.

In the past, as today, workers as a class or historical force have been profoundly divided by differences such as income, gender, trade, nationality, race, religion, politics, formal education, and an assortment of ideologies and cultures. We also find the widespread practice of dividing workers into homogeneous groups, such as white-collar and blue-collar, to be quite arbitrary. The majority of male blue-collar workers has remained essentially stable for some time, with the increase in white-collar workers being closely related to the influx of women workers into the labor force (*Government Statistics,* 1987, pp. 188–89). Moreover, the distinction between blue-collar and white-collar is progressively becoming less meaningful. There is little fundamental difference in interest and outlook between a postal clerk (white-collar) and a letter carrier (blue-collar) or between a business machine operator and a computer specialist in an office. But as the majority of white-collar workers lose their privileges and become acclimatized to the conditions of blue-collar workers, both groups become increasingly defined by their relation to ownership. In short, they simply become members of the working class.

Throughout the world, workers represent a homogeneous group only in the sense that they share a subordination to the control of owners and managers who have the power to make decisions that shape their daily lives. However, workers always have responded by educating and enlightening themselves and by taking control of their own decision making. Workers create co-ops, communes, unions, political parties, pressure groups, boycotts, study groups, socialism, and communism (in various forms), anarchism, and syndicalism. Workers have consistently challenged authority. They have promoted mass strikes, spread solidarity, and entered into other adventures to control their own activities and to produce social change. For example, workers have been directly and indirectly responsible for legislation leading to social security and to subsidies and programs for the elderly, the disabled, and the disadvantaged. Workers are largely responsible for federal and state aid to education and for a variety of social legislation for millions of Americans who have sought redress for their grievances. Due to their continual and often unpublicized active participation, both within the workplace and in society at large, we today take for granted conditions such as shorter work weeks, paid holidays and extended vacations, the end of the brutality of child labor, on-the-job safety standards, pensions, profit sharing, and automatic cost-of-living hikes. At the turn of the twentieth century, these examples of social change and progress were considered by many to be simply the dreams of utopian cranks who were considered un-American. Today, these programs are considered a matter of common sense. The list of workers' educational, social, and political creations is endless.

A habit of many adult educators, particularly historians in the field, seems to be the viewing of past educational efforts made by our grandparents, to promote social change, as propaganda. This conjecture is based on the noticeable absence of accounts of these educational activities in our literature. Only occasionally are institutions for adult education, such as Highlander, the Rand School of the Social Sciences, the Workers' Education Bureau, and the Bryn Mawr Summer School for Women Workers in Industry mentioned in passing, and even then with little analysis.

In fact, during the early part of this century, over 300 workers' schools were created (Tobin, 1981). Many lasted only a few years, but some continued and prospered well into the 1930s and 1940s. A few even survive today (Adams, 1980; Horton, 1971; Altenbaugh, 1980). Altenbaugh, in a study of three of the more important labor colleges, argues that workers who were dissatisfied with the existing social structure and social institutions (particularly with the public schools, unaffordable private colleges, and the policies of the American Federation of Labor [AFL]) fashioned these sometimes radical labor colleges and schools (Altenbaugh, 1980).

The Kochs (1972), in a study of Commonwealth College in Arkansas, focus on the radical workers who founded the college and who promoted a cooperative, communal atmosphere. The college offered a variety of courses—everything from painting, dancing, and Shakespeare to nontraditional American and world history and critical economics.

At Brookwood Labor College, a residential college located in upper New York state, students all had the same course options, and they spent a portion of time off campus organizing and supporting unions and strikes. But while on campus, everyone worked (Altenbaugh and Paulston, 1972).

Another labor school that has been examined in detail is the residential Work Peoples' College in Duluth, Minnesota. Founded by Finnish Socialists, the college sought to provide basic academic skills, to teach English, to train labor advocates, and to educate radical teachers in its attempts to build a national labor movement (Altenbaugh, 1977).

Altenbaugh (1977), Paulston (1980), Tobin (1981), and the Kochs (1972) broadly agree on the roots of this movement. Influenced and supported by the Socialist Party of America, by the International Workers of the World, and by liberal social theorists and activists, the founders and supporters of the labor college movement argued that working-class education in a structured labor college or labor school better prepared individuals for service in the labor movement. Until recently, many adult educators either have excluded or glossed over these aspects of education for the working class. These investigators echo the position of Owen D. Evans (1926), who authored a book sponsored by the Carnegie Corporation entitled *Educational Opportunities for Young Workers*. "Workers' education," he wrote, "is a continuing process for an army of young people who have dropped out of school or graduated," adding that there was a need "for *specific* vocational training designed to make them more effective producers" (p. v; emphasis added). Evans's analysis is more consistent with a specialized area within the professional realm of adult education—human resource development (HRD)—than it is with worker-centered education. HRD is based in part on human capital theory and focuses on employer and production needs—limiting education for the working class to personal development and job skills (Karabel and Halsey, 1977). HRD is not, in our view, the major thrust of working-class education. Clearly, Evans's concept of employee personal development and education for workers was limited by a position that underestimated the extent to which workers and their allies could unite by using education to bring about change in the workplace and in the wider social context.

The contents of working-class educational programs may differ radically, and thus the objectives of these programs must be critically examined. For example, programs created for workers by people outside the labor movement, as well as by workers themselves, may be based on a deep commitment to major social change but with little official support by national unions. Some programs may be directed to improving the level of the educationally disadvantaged while others are designed to build class consciousness, organizational loyalty, and participation. Still others may foster preparation for union leadership. But all working-class educational programs contain, at least in some form, elements of each. The common thread running throughout all these educational approaches is a need by workers to enjoy a better quality of life.

Background

The American worker, as he or she is conceived in the popular consciousness, is a relatively recent phenomenon. From the late colonial period to the middle of the nineteenth century, mass production did not exist except in a few scattered enterprises located in cities along the northeastern Atlantic seaboard. These early ventures into mass production were staffed mainly by women and children, whom employers used as a cheap source of labor power. Even the Mechanics' Institutes and the lyceum movement, so long identified by adult educators as essential elements in the history of workers' education, were generally attended by aspiring entrepreneurs and independent producers rather than by workers (Keane, 1982).

Following the Civil War, as America was transforming from a preindustrial and agrarian country into a mass-production factory society, working people began to emerge as a viable social and political force. As a nascent social class, they differed from previous working people in that they constituted a growing group of wage earners. To survive, they were forced to sell their physical and mental powers to others. Unlike working people of previous decades, such as artisans and independent farmers, they no longer controlled their own labor time, their tools, or the finished product. This shared lack of control began to unite workers as a homogeneous group. Moreover, they collectively and increasingly became entwined in a system that had as its primary objective production for exchange rather than for use. At the same time, the rationalization of the workplace imposed new disciplines. This scientific organization of the workers tied them closer to the clock (rather than the natural cycles of day, night, and the seasons), and made them feel like extensions of the machine—insignificant members of a rigid and routine bureaucracy, over which they had virtually no control. In addition, their job security (their only means of survival) depended on the often unexpected decisions of those who had hired them—and could indiscriminately fire them. More significant, perhaps, they were constantly at the mercy of a capricious and erratic business cycle, which, as today, posed the perpetual threat of unemployment. It seems ironic that today over 90 percent of the labor force—those who earn wages by selling their mental and physical proficiencies—are workers in the sense that they are also actors in the scenario presented above, although many do not see themselves as "workers."

Clearly, an ambiguous area exists in the managerial and supervisory occupations. Although these groups are also wage earners and dependent on ownership for their survival, they represent those who control and own the production and service industries. They act as intermediaries between owners and other workers. Their educational concerns, at least as they relate to the workplace, tend to focus on evaluating workers in order to increase their job skills and productivity. However, their positions are more tenuous than the positions of those under their direction and control, since they lack the organizational power and the sympathetic group support—collective bargaining—to challenge the control of private ownership.

Thus, workers as a separate class must be discussed in terms of their power relationship to the ownership class and its various auxiliary representatives. Each class cannot exist without the other, but the classes are almost constantly involved in conflicts with one another. Educational matters for both revolve around control at the work site—educational issues related not only to wages, length of work week, and other job benefits, but also to matters of working-class decision making and workplace control. The last two factors in particular have been given little attention in our literature, which stresses working-class education as a set of courses and programs offered to union officials so they may become more proficient in advocacy and collective bargaining skills (Mire, 1970; Rogin and Rachlin, 1968). The image conveyed in the literature is that of a harmonious and consensual relationship between labor and management as the only common-sense means for labor's survival in a world controlled to a large extent by corporate planning.

Adult educators seemed to accept this image of consensus as objective truth. On the basis of such so-called truth, workers appeared to be concerned only with bread and butter issues. Presumably, such workers accepted the business unionism education and strategies whose roots can be traced to the so-called pragmatic philosophy of the essentially conservative AFL. Yet until the late 1930s, only a small minority of the labor force, as defined by the federal government, belonged to unions. The percentage of unionized workers markedly increased in the twenty-five years following World War II, reaching about 23 percent of the workers in the 1970s. But late in the same decade, this number slowly decreased, until today, by some estimates, about 16 percent of the work force belong to unions. These unions are usually found in larger corporations, where the costs of wage increases and other workers' benefits can be passed along in higher prices to the consumer. Many unionists argue that it is because industries are organized that they pay higher wages and therefore are prosperous. The reverse, however, is true. Where and when corporations are not prosperous and cannot pass on their costs, they resist unionism vigorously. Farm workers' organizations have been particularly vulnerable to this phenomenon (McDermott, 1980).

Should the study of working-class education be reduced to terms like *workers' education, labor education,* or *labor studies*—terms that usually denote the development of proficiencies for collective bargaining? We think not. As this section illustrates, the educational activities of workers, when defined by their interests, go beyond the acquiring of job skills or managing a union. Educational activities must be an integral part of social action. While acknowledging the limitations we face, both in the field and in this piece, we choose to stress the educational activities that occur in the realm of the greatest urgency for workers—activities that impact workers' own efforts to influence their day-to-day circumstances as well as their future options. To these ends, we will now discuss some aspects of the modern educational activities of workers as members of a class.

Contemporary Working-Class Education

As we look at some contemporary examples of working-class education, we begin with the premise that such education, whether incidental or intentional, occurs as an aspect of working peoples' struggle to achieve power over their own economic survival and to achieve goals that may or may not coincide with those of their employers or potential employers. In the past decade, as well as historically, some of the most compelling struggles by workers for their economic survival have been shaped by the experiences of unemployment and homelessness, prominent experiences for a group many in the 1980s identified as the underclass. Another group of workers driven by economic survival needs to often-creative educational strategies are the embattled factory workers of the Northeast and upper Midwest—the so-called rust belt. These groups of workers, and the hundreds of labor union locals, community-based organizations, and church groups who support them, generally have been too busy with survival strategies to document their own efforts.

In this contemporary context, then, working-class education is designed by, with, and for workers to satisfy their own goals for daily survival, long-term security, and, if possible, empowerment. The exigencies of late twentieth-century capitalism have combined with the aspirations of workers, both individually and collectively, to create some workers' educational initiatives that would have been familiar to their counterparts 100 years ago. In the past two decades, much of the energy in workers' educational experiences has gone into intensified attempts to support workers' efforts to salvage old jobs, to train for new ones, and to create alternative business structures in which to work. A focus on self-determination has also shaped some innovative approaches to formalized educational enterprises such as vocational education and on-the-job training. In the balance of this section, we will attempt to describe the theory and practice of a few of these educational efforts for worker control and self-determination.

Worker Ownership and Worker Control:
Educational Implications

Since the mid-1970s, the American industrial worker has been buffeted by waves of plant closings, relocations (both domestic and foreign), intensified foreign competition, and corporate mergers that often leave in their wake unemployment, reduced wage-and-benefit packages, and decimated company towns.

One increasingly popular response to these events, especially in the midwestern rust belt and in the Northeast, is the worker buy out. In most states, there are two legal forms through which the workers can assume ownership of a business enterprise—a workers' cooperative or an employee stock ownership plan (ESOP), whereby company shares are placed in a trust on behalf of the employees (Midwest Center for Labor Research, 1985). The business structure chosen is significant for our purposes because the learning demands of each are usually (but not uniformly) different. In a true workers' cooperative, authority and responsibility for the business reside with the worker members based upon their investment of labor, not capital. ESOPs are not so clear-cut. Although the workers hold a majority of corporate shares in most ESOPs, their control of the business is dependent upon the arrangement they have with the trustees of their capital. The workers often have little real authority over management of the business, as the trustees often vote on the basis of their shares according to their judgment without consulting with the workers (Midwest Center for Labor Research, 1985).

In the workers' cooperative, or in the occasional ESOP in which workers do control the business, the educational needs become significant. According to Coker and Vanderslice (1987, p. 15), the educator's task is "to develop a cooperative culture within each organization."

PACE of Philadelphia, Inc., is one of the dozens of consulting groups, law firms, and university technical assistance entities that have emerged to foster workplace democracy in recent years. PACE has designed a workplace democracy curriculum through their work helping to convert five struggling food stores into successful worker-owned and operated supermarkets (O&O) in the Philadelphia area. They divide their program into two distinct phases: informal and formal. The informal education begins in the interview conducted with would-be worker members of a new cooperative. The first sessions "give potential workers realistic expectations about the worker member role . . . by answering questions such as: What is an O&O supermarket? What do you gain by being a member? . . . What are the responsibilities and risks?" (Vanderslice and Leventhal, 1987, p. 35). A subsequent interview acquaints workers with the ownership structure. This second interview also begins to convey to the workers the value placed upon them as decision makers when interviewers ask them to supply references for other members being considered. Workers are introduced to the store's committee structures and are urged to begin assessing and evaluating the needs of the store so that it can be prepared for opening day.

The formal educational program has two basic components. The first component comprises general information sessions, and all workers and managers are required to attend. Topics include legal, business, and financial areas. The often-overwhelming technical details of operating a large business are important to the enterprises's success and the sooner the members master these conceptually, the sooner they will develop the competence and confidence essential for successful participation as cooperators. Strategies presented in information sessions cover the following topics: "team building, communication skills, cooperative value development, group decision making and problem solving, and running effective meetings (Vanderslice and Leventhal, 1987, p. 35). After the information sessions, the educators attend committee and work-group meetings, helping members exercise new skills and evaluate their own progress. PACE argues that all phases of this educational program are critically important to the success of a cooperative venture among a group of workers accustomed to viewing their participation as insignificant to the success or failure of the business for which they work. It takes a concerted effort to overcome the lack of skills, confidence, and experience they bring to their status as worker owners.

Groups providing educational support to worker-run businesses have a variety of different emphases. The Chicago-based Midwest Center for Labor Research (MCLR) works closely with labor locals and communities whose plants are threatened by shutdowns. Although MCLR's most powerful expertise is in research-based feasibility analyses, it is also one of several organizations throughout the country that trains workers and community members to watch for and act on the early-warning signs of plant closings or relocations. Other groups that focus primarily on education and technical assistance for conversion of conventional businesses to worker ownership include the Michigan Employee Ownership Center, the Center for Economic Organizing in Washington, D.C., and several state-funded task forces such as those in California and Wisconsin (Midwest Center for Labor Research, 1985).

Worker-owner enterprises do not always result from conversions of conventional businesses to some form of worker ownership, however. For example, the cooperative form, as a remedy to poverty and powerlessness for chronically unemployed and underemployed workers, has been supported by many national church organizations through their philanthropies. They have provided start-up capital and consulting fees for cooperative businesses starting from scratch, with significant participation by low-income people. (See, for example, *Pastoral Letter . . . ,* 1985.) Several groups have emerged to meet the peculiar educational challenges presented by these start-up co-ops. The Community Service Society of New York City has helped found an innovative cooperative home health care agency in the Bronx (Congress for a Working America, 1985). Weatherization and Retrofit Maintenance of Detroit first provides training in home repair or janitorial services and then helps successful trainees found cooperatives (Congress for a Working America, 1987). The Industrial Cooperative Association (ICA), based in Somerville, Massachusetts, is one of the most successful and flexible of these providers. Its successes range from 200-member factory conversions to rural start-ups of as few as five members (Turner, 1986).

Chuck Turner, a long-time worker and community educator who has worked with ICA, has developed what he calls "Principles of Creative Process," which he has found appropriate for all democratic workplaces. These principles are especially relevant for workers who feel they have been locked out of the primary job market and who have spent their lives in casual, temporary, and part-time jobs (Gordon, Edwards, and Reich, 1982). Turner's program can be reduced to five elements: clear goals, careful plans, hard work, frequent and explicit evaluation, and patience. In addition, he maintains that a group's creative power can best be fostered by teaching them how to use three specific relational tools: dialogue, appreciation, and equality. Dialogue is important, according to Turner, because it is the only effective vehicle for resolving problems and conflicts that occur throughout the workday. Appreciation is Turner's corrective to "the process of psychological devaluation which has been practiced among people of color, women and the poor of this country" (Turner, 1986, p. 8). Equality refers to the need to enforce absolute fairness in distribution of both rewards and sacrifices. Turner argues that, like appreciation, equality is a new experience for many of the oppressed in start-up cooperatives. They have, he argues, been accustomed to exploitation, which they continue to expect unless it is scrupulously and overtly avoided.

As Turner's principles suggest, many practitioners view education for workplace democracy as a tool with the potential to transform not just the workplace status, but also the self-concept and sense of collective power of the workers involved. Interviews with individual cooperators corroborate his belief (Schulman, 1986). But we should avoid unfounded optimism about the potential impact of this movement. After a full decade of intense activity on the part of dozens of groups, and despite the over 5,000 democratic workplaces in the United States (Guilford College, Department of Management, Democratic Management Program, staff interview with author, Apr. 1988), the holders of capital, not labor, are firmly in control of the American economy. The vast majority of the American working class are not involved in any significant way in learning to control their workplaces.

Education for Job-Seeking Workers: Training and Empowerment. In his recent manual for Freirean-style job training, Ira Shor (1988, p. 1) argues that "training courses themselves limit student interest in critical thinking." To recreate workers and future workers as critical thinkers, we must, he maintains, challenge workers to do critical analysis of their social and economic conditions while they learn the skills for a particular job. Shor offers an agenda of nine values that must inform job-training education: participation, critical inquiry, pedagogy situated in the student's context, dialogue, desocialization of student passivity, desocialization of classroom behaviors, democracy, interdisciplinary approaches, and activism. Students in this role of critical analyst perform investigations of their communities and future workplaces. They explore the experiences of workers already in industry through personal interviews, research, and observation, and they uncover the extent to which the labor force they wish to join is unionized. They learn more than the technical skills required to perform a task; they unpack the culture of the particular vocation and its position in the economy.

Although Shor does not detail the sites in which his particular approach is being pursued, a recently founded employment agency in Milwaukee has evolved a kindred approach. The Milwaukee Careers Co-op is a church- and foundation-funded organization that uses its status as a temporary employment agency to help unemployed workers acquire the experience they need to secure permanent jobs. The agency then works through its employer network to find such permanent placement. At weekly training meetings, workers compare and reflect upon experiences and often have the oppor- tunity to interview representatives from a local company's personnel office. Through these sessions, workers become sophisticated about the local job market and, over time, about the local economy (Congress for a Working America, 1988).

Labor Union Programs: Beyond Collective Bargaining. The AFL-CIO and its member unions also develop programs that increase workers' oppor- tunities for self-determination. The United Auto Workers (UAW), for ex- ample, has recently included a workers' education fund in all of its national collective bargaining agreements. Each UAW employer has agreed to place a few cents per hour worked by every employee into the fund. The workers at every site then decide how they want the money to be used (although some offerings are determined through the national contracts). Workers have chosen a wide range of options from basic skills through specific technical training to communications workshops. The money can also be used to retrain workers facing dislocation because of pending layoffs (United Auto Workers Chrysler National Training Center, staff interview with author, May 1988).

Unions often make educational programs available through arrange- ments with university labor studies programs. At Indiana University, for example, the labor studies faculty works on a contract basis with individual labor organizations, designing any course the membership requests. Topics range from the conventional study of collective bargaining skills to worker self-management and the use of so-called quality of work life circles (Univer- sity of Indiana, Division of Labor Studies, staff interview with author, May 1988). In the early 1980s, unions, especially the United Auto Workers, also collaborated with college faculties throughout the country in an ambitious effort to attract union members to college-degree programs. The prototype of these efforts was developed at Wayne State University in Detroit. These colleges for working adults were to be based in workers' communities offer- ing interdisciplinary courses on topics such as work and society. They were to be offered in contexts, and with scheduling arrangements, hoped to be more conducive than conventional campus settings to worker participation.

Unfortunately, this community-based approach was feasible, accord- ing to Larry Olds of the Minneapolis Community College for Working Adults, only as long as it was underwritten by concentrated foundation fund- ing. Since that funding diminished in the mid-1980s, the union member- ship in the programs has declined until it is now roughly equal to union membership in the population as a whole. The non-campus-based Colleges for Working Adults resemble other higher education programs for adults more than they do the labor colleges of the 1920s and 1930s, which originally inspired them. Olds suggests that this resemblance to conventional higher education reflects the fact that education designed to develop a labor community, or any community, is contradictory to the individualistic quest for accreditation that fuels most higher education institutions (Minneapolis Community College for Working Adults, staff interviews with author, May, July 1988).

One recent innovation in union education involves an experiment by the Bricklayers and Allied Craftsmen Union using the Swedish study circle model to engage its members in an analysis of the results of an eighteen-month study by its Year 2000 Committee. ''Offered free to members and their families, each study circle would have a minimum of five members and a maximum of twenty and would meet weekly for five weeks in 2 and 1/2 hours sessions for a total of 12 and 1/2 hours'' (Oliver, 1987, p. 122). The program resulted in 210 members participating in twenty-seven study groups. Virtually all groups reported a substantially heightened interest and understanding of the union, its plans, and its context. The union plans to enlarge the experiment to include an even broader representation of its membership in the next study circle effort (Oliver, 1987).

Summary

This brief survey is designed to raise more questions than it answers. Our discussion—indeed our knowledge—of working-class educational alternatives designed to challenge conventional workplace power arrangements is limited and idiosyncratic. As long as we do not make serious efforts to explore working-class culture and the educational hybrids that culture nurtures, we can expect little more.

Many adult educators have rejected workers' so-called radical past and their involvement with liberation elements that have sought and still seek social change—elements that cling to the dream of a more egalitarian society. Adult educators have overemphasized their focus on education programs of national union organizations, and, concomitantly, they have neglected investigation of local movements. Often they have treated counterhegemonic educational planning and action as a pathology, and, as a result, they have justified the leadership policies and corporate ideologies of conservative unions' education. They have assumed the American labor movement functioned as little more than a junior partner in a giant corporate society that was responsible for what many consider reactionary foreign policies, racism, sexism, and avoidance of social issues. Some adult educators have reconsidered their positions on American labor, and they now concentrate their investigations to show that working-class education has been more than the story of the rise and fall of organizations. An examination of the role of the working class and their sympathizers will certainly reveal that some of the most significant educational movements have focused on the American working class.

References

Adams, F. "Highlander Folk School: Social Movements and Social Change in the American South." In R. Paulston (ed.), *Other Dreams, Other Schools: Folk Colleges in Social and Ethnic Movements*. Pittsburgh, Pa.: Pittsburgh University Press, 1980.

Altenbaugh, R. *Work Peoples' College: A Finnish Folk High School in the American Labor College Movement*. Pittsburgh, Pa.: International Development Education Program, University of Pittsburgh, 1977. (ED 153 888)

Altenbaugh, R. "Forming the Structure of a New Society Within the Shell of the Old: A Study of Three Labor Colleges and Their Contributions to the American Labor Movement." Unpublished doctoral dissertation, Department of Education, University of Pittsburgh, 1980.

Altenbaugh, R., and Paulston, R. "The Work Peoples' College and the American Labor College Movement." In R. Paulston (ed.), *Other Dreams, Other Schools: Folk Colleges in Social and Ethnic Movements*. Pittsburgh, Pa.: Pittsburgh University Press, 1980.

Brecher, J. *Strike! The True History of Mass Insurance in America from 1877 to the Present*. San Francisco: Straight Arrow, 1972.

Coker, C., and Vanderslice, V. "The PACE Worker-Education Program." *Worker Co-ops*, 1987, *7*, 15–16.

Congress for a Working America. *Notes for a Working America*. Milwaukee, Wis.: Congress for a Working America, 1985.

Congress for a Working America. *Notes for a Working America*. Milwaukee, Wis.: Congress for a Working America, 1987.

Congress for a Working America. *Notes for a Working America*. Milwaukee, Wis.: Congress for a Working America, 1988.

Dwyer, R. *Labor Education in the United States*. Metuchen, N.J.: Scarecrow Press, 1977.

Evans, O. *Educational Opportunities for Young Workers*. New York: Macmillan, 1926.

Gordon, D., Edwards, R., and Reich, M. *Segmented Work/Divided Workers*. Cambridge, Eng.: Cambridge University Press, 1982.

Government Statistics. Washington, D.C.: U.S. Government Printing Office, 1987.

Gray, L. "American Way in Labor Education." *Industrial Relations*, 1966, *15*, 53–66.

Horton, A. "The Highlander Folk School." Unpublished doctoral dissertation, Department of Education, University of Chicago, 1971.

Karabel, J., and Halsey, A. *Power and Ideology in Education*. New York: Oxford University Press, 1977.

Keane, P. "Avenues of Historical Inquiry: The Mechanics' Institutes of the U.S.A." Paper presented at the Adult Education Research Conference, University of Nebraska, Lincoln, April 1982.

Koch, R., and Koch, C. *Educational Commune: The Story of Commonwealth College*. New York: Schoken Books, 1972.

Linton, T. "Reality and Distortion in the Articles on Labor Education." *Adult Leadership,* 1966, *15,* 45–49.

McDermott, J. *The Crisis in the Working Class.* Boston: South End Press, 1980.

Midwest Center for Labor Research. "Workers as Owners." *Labor Research Review,* 1985, *6.*

Mire, P. "Labor Education." In R. M. Smith, G. Aker, and R. Kidd (eds.), *Adult Education Handbook.* New York: American Association of Adult Education, 1970.

Oliver, L. *Study Circles: Coming Together for Personal Growth and Social Change.* Washington, D.C.: Seven Locks Press, 1987.

Pastoral Letter on Catholic Social Teaching and the U.S. Economy. Baltimore, Md.: U.S. Catholic Conference of Bishops, 1985.

Paulston, R. (ed.). *Other Dreams, Other Schools: Folk Colleges in Social and Ethnic Movements.* Pittsburgh, Pa.: Pittsburgh University Press, 1980.

Rogin, L., and Rachlin, M. *Survey of Adult Education Opportunities for Labor: Labor Education in the United States.* Washington, D.C.: National Institute of Labor Education at American University, 1968. (ED 023 061)

Schied, F. "From the Education of Workers to Working Class Education: A Critical Review of the Significant Literature." Seminar paper, Northern Illinois University, De Kalb, Ill., June 1982.

Schulman, B. "Workers' Cooperatives: Freirean Opportunity in the Workplace." *Proceedings of the Twenty-Seventh Annual Adult Education Research Conference.* Syracuse, N.Y.: Adult Education Research Conference, 1986.

Shor, I. *Working Hands and Critical Minds: A Paulo Freire Model for Job-Training.* Chicago: Alternative Schools Network, 1988.

Thompson, E. P. *The Making of the English Working Class.* Oxford, Eng.: Oxford University Press, 1971.

Tobin, E. "Academics and Insurgents: Brookwood Labor College, 1921–1933." Paper presented at the annual meeting of the Organization of American Historians, Detroit, Mich.: April 1981.

Turner, C. "Education for Ownership/Developing the Creative Power of Worker Owners." Unpublished manuscript, Boston, 1986.

Vanderslice, V., and Leventhal, B. "Employee Participation: A Game Plan for the Real World." *Training and Development Journal,* 1987, *41* (2), 34–35.

44

Racial and Ethnic Minorities and Adult Education

Diane Buck Briscoe
Jovita Martin Ross

There is an obvious gap in the knowledge and research base relative to minority participation in adult education in the United States. An attempt to review the literature, to identify crucial issues, and to challenge the field to action is needed, given demographic trends. Development of effective strategies to serve minority adults better will require critical reflection on current practice and innovative models of action.

In this chapter, we will review population data and participation patterns of underserved minority groups in both formal and nonformal settings of adult education; we will examine variables that may be affecting participation; and we will describe adult education activities that occur in nonformal settings. The minority populations selected for primary emphasis here are blacks, Native Americans, and Hispanics. These groups are included for several reasons: (1) Demographic patterns indicate blacks and Hispanics to be the largest minority populations in the United States. (2) All three groups have a long-standing presence in North America, although historical racial discrimination, economic disadvantage, de jure and de facto segregation, linguistic differences, and cultural pride have limited the degree of assimilation of these groups into American society, despite the willingness of some group members to be acculturated into North American values and life-styles. (3) All three groups (Carlson, 1987; Deloria, 1981) have experienced inequality in educational opportunity and participation, largely because of the factors cited in (2) above.

The lack of statistical data on participation patterns of these groups, the lack of published information appearing in mainstream adult education sources, the limitations of space and time, and the limited expertise of the authors in locating more obscure data on particular minority groups have constrained the amount of information we could include in this chapter. Improved data collection methods and increased research in this area is essential if a more complete account of the adult education participation patterns of racial and ethnic minorities is to be included in the next handbook. At the end of the chapter, three future scenarios will outline glimpses of what life might be like for minority adults assuming (1) marginal action, (2) inaction, or (3) positive action by the adult education field. Several general recommendations will also be made for improving professional assistance to minority adult learners.

Participation in Formal Settings

We often hear educators discussing the so-called graying of America. This phrase refers to the increasing average age of the American population; however, not only is America graying, the skin color of America is also changing and in a way that cannot continue to be ignored. The gap between the educational achievements of the majority populations and those of most minorities is widening at an alarming rate. Projected growth trends indicate that the disparities will continue to increase at unprecedented rates. With information and an understanding of the needs of these groups, more responsive program and policy decisions can be implemented.

A study of demographic trends shows that, within a decade, Hispanics are projected to be the largest minority group in America, with blacks becoming the second largest (Coulter, 1985; Samuels, 1985; Valverde, 1987; Warren, 1985). The average age of the minority population is decreasing, while the majority population is growing older. Minorities tend to cluster in metropolitan areas, and, in the future, fifty-three major U.S. cities will have minority populations that outnumber the present majority population. Additionally, at only one other time in history have more immigrants become a part of the U.S. society—those immigrants from European countries (McNett, 1983). By 1990, minorities of all ages will constitute as much as 25 percent of the total population and 30 percent among youth cohorts.

Data regarding minority participation in formal institutions of adult education are scarce. Information must be gleaned from a variety of sources. But variation in data collection methods, inconsistent criteria for inclusion of minority groups, and differing definitions of the term *adult* all contribute to the difficulty of collecting and analyzing reliable data. Some trends do emerge, however. The high school noncompletion rate for Hispanics ranges from 33 percent to as high as 88 percent of a cohort (National Center for Education Statistics, 1982; Orum, 1984; Valverde, 1987). Blacks are underrepresented among participants in adult education; the proportion of black adults participating in adult education has declined; and blacks are falling farther behind their white counterparts in adult education participation (Boaz,

1978; Charner, 1980; Cross, 1981; Long, 1983; Momeni, 1980). Unemployed adults, adults with low income levels, and high school noncompleters are far less likely to participate (Cross, 1981; Reder, 1985). To the extent that minority adults are disproportionately represented among these groups, we can expect their participation in adult education activities to continue to be low.

Many minorities are included in the ranks of the illiterate, but Fingeret (1983) noted that many illiterates are contributing and well-respected members of their communities. Far from being unable to cope, many have coped quite well in their environments and are reluctant to trade their locally recognized status, relative security, and system of common-sense knowledge for the environment, knowledge, and values of the so-called educated, an exchange they feel many adult education programs require them to make.

Connectedness Between Early Schooling and Adult Education. Some of the literature on high school noncompletion, minority student achievement, and later adult participation in education suggests the necessity for early intervention. Apps (1986, p. 5) stated that, "In our zeal for adult education, we magnify our uniqueness, and thus we see no connection between what we do as educators of adults and what first grade teachers do." Attitudes toward learning in formal institutions may be formed early in development, and there may very well be some direct connection between these early experiences and nonparticipation in adult years.

The literature provides documentation to support the notion that Mexican-Americans, blacks, and Native Americans do not benefit from public education at a rate equal to the majority population (Burciaga, 1983). Fine (1985) suggests that societal inequities as well as institutional barriers contribute to the so-called purging of students from schools, whether by coercion or by choice.

Educational sociologists subscribing to a social reproduction theory of education would explain this phenomenon in terms of economic, cultural, or hegemonic reproduction, focusing respectively on the function of the school in reproducing labor stratification, on legitimizing selected knowledge, values, and language, or on preserving ideological imperatives of the state (Giroux, 1983). In this theoretical tradition, schools are said to function as a part of state apparatus, protecting the hegemony of the dominant class. Teachers and students are portrayed as often-unwitting actors teaching and learning a hidden curriculum (Apple, 1979). Resistance theory may offer a plausible alternative interpretation to reproduction theory, since resistance theory gives more credit to the agency of teachers and learners. According to resistance theory, learners or teachers may passively or aggressively resist the perceived inequities of society as transmitted through school culture.

Although some adult educators would argue that application of these theories to adult education contexts is inappropriate, since they were developed to explain schooling processes, Keddie (1980) maintains that adult education is more similar than dissimilar to the rest of education in its forms of cultural reproduction. She notes that the concept of disadvantage in adult education reflects a concern with helping the supposedly different adult but neglects to challenge the modes by which education controls differential access to knowledge and power. Chapter Five of this handbook examines in greater depth the sociological perspectives of adult education.

The growing minority populations represent a national human resource, and the consequences to North American society of leaving this resource undeveloped are great. It is likely that young people who leave school early will never participate fully in society or in the decision-making processes of government, and that they will neither enjoy the benefits of good health nor experience the upward mobility needed as adults to make them full contributors and partners in shaping and participating in the larger society. One cause of the problem is educational institutions not responding quickly enough to change, even though educators are aware of the impact they can have on societal systems. Strategies designed to address these issues are not being developed consistently, collaboratively, or on a national scale; and the need for solutions to promote full participation by minorities is urgent.

Possible Barriers to Minority Participation. An examination of the factors that appear to have contributed to minority nonparticipation and disengagement usually reveals barriers most often categorized as institutional, situational, or dispositional. Many of these identified barriers to participation apply to both minority and majority nonparticipants who share similar economic or educational levels. However, other factors, unique to certain minority groups in the United States, may affect participation, and some of these factors have been observed early in the educational process. The practice of so-called second generation discrimination, manifested in part through policies such as tracking or grouping, is one such factor. This type of discrimination, more subtle than that of earlier years, is marked, in part, by placing students in class sections that are not representative of their abilities. The research of Fraga, Meier, and England (1986) revealed that black and Hispanic students were disproportionately placed in lower-ability groups, often resulting in low educational attainment.

According to Darling-Hammond (1985), black students were exposed less to challenging educational programs than were white students, thus greatly reducing their opportunity to expand or to modify course options in later grades. She further observed that, with the emphasis being placed on minimum competency testing, those who started out behind received the least exposure to real books, to writing, to exploration of ideas, and to critical thinking. Ability grouping and tracking were found to have a particularly deleterious effect on minority students because the grouping generally proceeded along racial or ethnic lines, inhibiting contact and interaction with those who were different; and the low status attached to the classes in which minorities were generally tracked reduced self-esteem, produced resentment among minority group members, contributed to discipline problems, increased high school noncompletion, and resulted in inferior education due to low teacher expectations (McConahay, 1981; Rosenbaum, 1976; U.S. Commission on Civil Rights, 1976). When individuals are denied a quality education, they are also denied access to political and economic literacy, to social integration into the mainstream, to employment opportunities, and, thus, to upward mobility.

There is also sufficient evidence to suggest that insensitivity to cultural differences can create barriers in areas such as counseling and education. The need to recognize and to accept cultural differences, without attaching labels to groups based on their differences, are goals yet to be realized in North American society. Ignorance of students' backgrounds and inability to penetrate language barriers are two of the greatest hindrances in the counselor-student relationship. Counselors from dissimilar cultural environments are deprived of an understanding of basic assumptions, perceptions, motivation, nonverbal language, feelings, defenses, basic needs, conflicts, cultural norms, and patterns of behavior common to the cultures of the minority students. Inability to understand the language renders the counselor ineffective because communication oftentimes occurs in abstractions and words that convey motivation and that transmit, modify, and refine feelings (Clarke, 1973; Vontress, 1969).

Mezirow, Darkenwald, and Knox (1975) observed that many adult basic education programs reflect middle-class values, and that adults having different values or life-styles rarely participate in them. Educationally disadvantaged adults have different goals and different definitions of success (Reder, 1985). All adults define who they are based on their accumulation of unique sets of experiences. Because adults define themselves in this way, they have a deep investment in the value of those experiences. When those experiences and their worth are minimized, as they often are for minority adults, not only are the experiences rejected, but the adult also feels rejected as a person (Knowles, 1970). Adult educators are responsible for facilitating learning and for providing avenues for self-actualization, and they must accomplish this within the framework of existing cultural differences. Any attempt to ignore or to suppress these differences is inappropriate and ineffective.

Samuels (1985) concludes that there is a direct connection between the extent and quality of minority student learning and the presence of minority staff. Teacher-facilitators, because of their direct contact with students, are in excellent positions to exercise the equitable application of policies, to influence the quality of the educational experience, and to serve as role models. The minority teacher is also needed to serve as an advocate for minority students (Fraga, Meier, and England, 1986; Massey, Scott, and Dornbusch, 1975; Meier and Nigro, 1976; Saltzstein, 1979).

Valverde (1987), Charner (1980), and others have sought to identify and to examine factors that may affect the participation of minorities in formal educational settings. A cause-effect relationship has been difficult to pinpoint because of possible response bias, because of the disengagement of affected participants from the institution, or because of the failure of participants to respond to barrier questions.

Momeni (1980) predicts that the rising costs of education will have a depressing effect on adult participation rates, and that continued high unemployment and the expansion of industry-sponsored training will also negatively impact participation in the future. Underemployment and cuts in federal aid to education since 1980 also have been cited as contributing to reduced participation. If economic barriers affect adult participation to the extent that researchers indicate, participation rates will be slow to change, since future projections show little economic relief for the nation's minorities.

Participation in Nonformal Education

While the picture painted from an analysis of minority participation in formal programs of adult education historically has been bleak, rich descriptions of a long tradition of lifelong learning in nonformal settings can be found. The diversity of early educational programs conducted for black adults through sources such as churches, civil rights organizations, community and parent-teacher organizations, tenant associations, and women's organizations has been reported extensively in the *Journal of Negro Education* (Gandy, 1945; Heningburg, 1945; Horne and Robinson, 1945; Neverdon-Morton, 1982). For example, Williams (1985) described the role of organizations such as black literacy societies, the YMCA, black churches, the NAACP, the National Urban League, and the Universal Negro Improvement Association in the thriving educational life of the Boston black community between 1900 and 1930.

Recently, accounts of nonformal adult education in minority communities have become more prevalent in the proceedings and journals directly associated with adult education (DeVaughan, 1986; McGee, 1984; Rachal, 1986; Spaights, Dixon, and Bridges, 1985). For instance, Morgan (1981) contrasts the well-attended adult education activities offered by church lyceums, by service and voluntary agencies, and by the public library in New York's Harlem area during the peak of the Harlem black renaissance with the modestly attended evening school programs for blacks under the auspices of the board of education. The success of such endeavors suggests that the design of programs that address the social, economic, and cultural values of minority communities can indeed increase levels of participation. Whaples and Booth (1982) have spoken of the high level of interest in learning shown by at least one sample of black public housing residents, but the authors suggest that we must be prepared to develop program designs that take learning to the home and the street—preferred learning environments for some adults.

Published research, however, both on the history of adult education activities in other minority communities and on contemporary adult education in the black community, appears to be more scarce than historical studies of adult education of blacks. Despite the inadequacies of the research base, what follows is an attempt to provide a sampling of adult education programs for minorities in a variety of nonformal settings. The educational needs of older minority adults will be considered briefly as well. This educationally deprived segment of the United States is certain to grow larger as we enter the twenty-first century.

Community-Based Extension and Public Service Programs. Community-based adult education programs sponsored by educational organizations represent a link between formal education and minority communities. While Chapter Thirty-Three in this book, authored by Phyllis Cunningham and Edwin Hamilton, deals much more extensively with community-based education programs, some mention is warranted here. Efforts by university continuing education units, such as those mentioned by Miller (1967) at New York University, Starr and Medlin (1977) at Michigan State University, and Upton (1984) at Ohio State University, suggest that there has been recognition of the need to tailor continuing education programs to the needs of nearby minority communities. Yet, as Willie (1977) illustrates in describing Syracuse University's experiences with a unique leadership program, universities are not free from public censure when involvement with community action groups is seen as training agitators rather than empowering adult learners. Similarly, literacy programs remaining close to traditional adult basic education models are more likely to be accepted by the educational and general community than are the more radical community-based programs seeking to build on existing helping networks as suggested by Reder (1985). Those educational organizations wishing to launch successful adult education programs within minority communities will have to be prepared to give full partnership to community members as well as to face possible opposition from more conservative educators and members of the larger community.

Some minority-controlled postsecondary institutions have shown a particular commitment to serving the interests of minority adults through community-based programs. Hamilton (1977) discussed the critical role historically black institutions have played in providing leadership in the black community, and he identified nontraditional programs for adults at Howard University. Winchell, Safforn, and Porter (1980) have discussed the unique capabilities of community colleges, a number of which are under tribal control, for meeting the management training needs of Native American communities. Roberts (1982) also has discussed the role of the community college in offering educational programs on the cultural traditions of native peoples. Cohnstaedt (1973) has described the process by which the Meadow Lake Vocational School in Saskatchewan was redesigned to address the community needs by preparing native Metis people as paraprofessionals to teach in their own communities.

Voluntary Organizations. Voluntary community organizations represent perhaps the primary nonformal setting for adult education in minority communities and provide a valuable resource for adult educators interested in increasing links with adult learners in such communities. Florin, Jones, and Wandersman (1987) have reviewed numerous studies dating back to the 1960s indicating that blacks participate in such organizations at a higher rate than any other racial or ethnic group (Babchuk and Thompson, 1962; Klobus-Edwards, Edwards, and Klemnack, 1978; Olsen, 1970), and that Mexican-Americans participate at a rate lower than whites (Antunes and Gaitz, 1975; Cohen and Kapsis, 1978). Florin, Jones, and Wandersman traced sociologists' attempts to explain the high level of black participation in such organizations from Babchuk and Thompson's 1962 hypothesis of participation as pathological to Olsen's 1970 theory of the ethnic community. Building on Mischel's (1973) cognitive social learning theory of personality, Florin, Jones, and Wandersman have identified a specific set of cognitive social learning variables (including perceived confidence as a group leader, sense of community, expectancies of political efficacy, and higher sense of citizen duty) that predict social participation among blacks at least as well as do traditional demographic variables (related to rootedness, social status, and psychological confidence).

One example of community voluntary associations involved in adult education was the Boston Literary and Historical Association, an organization that saw the need to collect and to preserve Afro-American history and to correct long-standing misconceptions about Afro-Americans (DeVaughan, 1986b). Similarly, Native organizations, such as the Indian Association in Alberta, have sought to promote cultural adult education by supporting research in and practice of Native traditions (Roberts, 1982). Fraternal organizations, such as Prince Hall Freemasonry, also have served as vehicles for education in values, business administration, and community leadership (Muraskan, 1976). Baba and Abonyi's (1979) description of the development of Detroit's Mexican-American *Colonia* reveals the role of community-based organizations, such as the Mexican Mutual Aid Circle, the League of Mexican Peasants and Workers, and the Cultural Center, in fostering adult education and community development. The National Council of La Raza (Perrilla and Orum, 1984) has assembled a guide to Hispanic community-based educational resources and programs, including both nonprofit organizations and voluntary agencies nationwide. Women's organizations, such as the National Council of Negro Women and the Hispanic Women's Council, have also provided education for and about minority women. These and many other women's organizations are cataloged in a document titled, *In Recognition of Culture: A Resource Guide for Adult Educators About Women of Color* (Hoffman, 1983). This guide includes adult education concerns as interpreted by Asian, American, black, Hispanic, Native American, and Haitian women; it also lists numerous organizational and literary resources focusing on minority women.

Education in the Workplace. The workplace represents another important setting for learning by minority adults. Medoff (1975) observed that only 4.6 percent of the total number of participants in apprenticeship trade programs in 1970 were black, and he provided data to challenge the apprenticeship establishment's arguments that lack of black entry is due to lack of qualifications or lack of desire to enter. His arguments focused on the bias of entry tests and on the ability of unions to ration entry subjectively. Hills (1981) used a sample from the National Longitudinal Surveys to demonstrate that blacks practicing in skill trades were less likely to have acquired their skills through apprenticeships or job-sponsored training and more likely to have learned through informal training or high school vocational programs.

Nonformal education is also important for minority adults hoping to establish businesses. Noting the stagnating growth of black-owned business relative to white, Hispanic, and Asian businesses, Mescon (1987) described the Entrepreneurial Institute, which was developed in Dade County, Florida, to provide skill training, technical assistance, access to bidding and procurement, and to facilitate loan packaging for minority business persons. This award-winning program represents an unusual partnership between government (through the Dade County Office of Economic Planning), the private sector (cooperating businesses), and higher education (a consortium of five two-year and four-year institutions). With increasing attention in the 1990s to business-school partnerships, cooperative efforts such as this one may provide the field of adult education new opportunities for reaching minority adults.

Church-Related Adult Education. Young (1985) also suggested that partnerships between adult educators and religious educators offer a promising avenue for increasing programming related to minority adults. Lloyd (1976), in his examination of the black church from 1950 through 1974, credits church leaders with providing much of the leadership of the civil rights age. It was the black church, he points out, that gave birth to organizations such as the Southern Christian Leadership Conference and the Congress of Racial Equality in the 1960s. Lloyd maintains that Christian religion and social change have always gone hand in hand in the black church, and he includes, as an example, Leon Sullivan's founding of the Opportunities Industrialization Center (OIC) in Philadelphia. Leadership in the Native American community also has been supported by the efforts of church-related groups such as Church Women United (Chatham and Redbird-Selam, 1973). A relationship between the Catholic church and adult education in community organizations has long existed in Hispanic-American communities (Baba and Abonyi, 1979). Deck (1986) describes the three separate schools of thought among those involved in the Catholic ministry to Hispanics today: traditionalist, reformist, and transformationist. Both reformist and transformationist traditions have been concerned with conscientization, although the transformationists are more clearly concerned with radical sociopolitical and economic change. Protestant traditions also exist historically in the Hispanic community (Baba and Abonyi, 1979), with increasing inroads by fundamentalist sects that offer a blend of traditional religious conservatism with Americanization and secularization (Deck, 1985).

Education of Older Minority Adults. The environment for adult education activities chosen by older minority adults is the church. Ehrlich (1975) refers to the aged black as "The Forgotten Person" and notes that little has been offered to these individuals through continuing or formal education programs. He suggests that alliances between churches and educational institutions would be an appropriate way to expand the educationally related activities of older blacks in churches, residential organizations, or centers. Heisel's (1985) work also indicates that, despite the low educational attainment typical of this population, many are actively engaged in learning. Opportunities for programming relevant to the needs of this population are myriad, although, as Talmer (1977) noted, the educational needs of older minority adults may differ significantly from those of older whites. Often minority adults have experienced a lifetime of low autonomy and little power exacerbated by poverty, limited physical resources, and discrimination.

Studying blacks, Latinos, and Anglos over fifty-five years of age in Denver and San Diego, McFadden (1981) found older minority adults disadvantaged relative to whites in terms of educational attainments, income levels, health, and satisfaction with retirement. Blacks were at the greatest disadvantage with regard to health and income level, and most minorities interviewed expected to retire involuntarily for health reasons. Conventional retirement education programs are likely to have little relevance to these older adults. Therefore, adult educators will need to develop specific programs to meet the unique needs of minorities in this age group.

Future Scenarios

Chapter Forty-Seven of this handbook offers "Alternative Images of the Future in Adult Education." Several alternative pictures of the future of adult education for minorities might be predicted as we enter the twenty-first century. These are by no means intended to be exhaustive of the possibilities since, as always, the multitude of responses possible in individual and group interaction makes it difficult to predict future occurrences.

The first scenario is one that assumes little change from the status quo—minority participation in officially cited adult education programs will hover below the 10 percent level, and community voluntary associations, churches, and informal networks will continue to serve a viable role in the educational life of minority adults. Disillusioned with the promise of upward mobility, only inconsistently provided by education, minority adults will continue to view education apart from learning. Adult educators will continue to write books about the hard-to-serve minorities while offering programs designed to meet the rising demands of a largely well-educated white middle-class population.

A second scenario reveals a worsening picture as the gap between the haves and have-nots grows, even within minority communities themselves. Minorities in the middle- and upper-income brackets will spend more time and more energy attempting to hold on to mainstream lifestyles, and they will spend less time devoting themselves to community voluntary associations dedicated to social change. Their evenings will be devoted to mandatory continuing education required to keep pace in their professional and managerial positions, leaving little room for community service. Adult educators will have given up hope of reaching the so-called hard-to-reach when their participation models lead them back to dispositional barriers and social contexts that negate the value of formal education. It becomes increasingly clear that major changes are needed in the economic and social patterns that trap most minority children into lives as poor adults; but initiating such changes is, after all, not seen as within the role of adult educators.

A final and more hopeful scenario can be envisioned. Increasing partnerships between adult education professionals and leaders in minority communities will create a broader array of options for lifelong learning. New research efforts will tell us more than we have ever known about adult learning and development across cultures, and community-based programs that address minority learning needs and styles will be developed in increasing numbers, with financial support from governmental and private sources for those unable to pay the costs of such programs. Minority and nonminority adults will come to know more about the contributions of all ethnic groups to American life through new programs supported by the National Endowment for the Humanities. Minority adults will engage in an increasing array of programs at their own convenience, as a major philanthropic organization decides to subsidize home computers to bring distance education to communities that had been as shut out from distance learning as they are from face-to-face learning. Adult educators will create community-based learning centers in urban and rural areas to support networks of minority adult learners who find trips to the university or school setting remote, expensive, or threatening, and minority adults will be involved in the design and evaluation of programs to be offered at these centers.

Conclusions and Recommendations

Data regarding the participation of minority adults in adult education, in both formal and informal settings, have been presented in this chapter. The possible roots of adult nonparticipation, beginning with early experiences with formal education, have been discussed along with other barriers particularly salient to minority adults. A less discouraging picture has been portrayed of minority participation in nonformal settings, although data are admittedly scarce regarding the actual extent of minority participation in these settings.

Several scenarios have been offered to depict possible future directions. If the most hopeful picture is to be realized, at least four identifiable changes in the field of adult education will be necessary. First, research must determine more specifically the conditions under which minority adults do and do not participate in adult education. Centralized data bases at the state and national levels would facilitate collection and analysis of data on the participation patterns of minorities served through adult education. Research also needs to examine adult development, motivation patterns, and the learning preferences and styles of minority adults. Second, adult education graduate students must (as suggested by Apps, 1986) be provided opportunities in their graduate programs to study the demographic, economic, and social trends in society, to pursue research on the effects of these trends in relation to minority participation patterns, to examine ethics and morality in decision making relative to minority participants, and to acquire skills in critical thought so as to be able to evaluate generally held assumptions. Third, collaboration with educators of young people must be developed to enable us to address the educational needs of minorities before they are turned off to formal learning. Finally, partnerships must be formed with the appropriate community leaders and organizations to enable adult educators to reach and to serve minority adults better.

The challenge to the field of adult education is immediate and urgent. Development of effective strategies to serve minority adults better must become a priority for all adult educators if the society of the future is to be viable. We must narrow the gap. Quality education must become more than a goal, and full participation must become a reality for all.

References

Antunes, G., and Gaitz, C. "Ethnicity and Participation: A Study of Mexican Americans, Blacks and Whites." *American Journal of Sociology,* 1975, *80,* 1192–1211.

Apple, M. *Ideology and Curriculum.* Boston: Routledge & Kegan Paul, 1979.

Apps, J. "Prospects for and Challenges to the Professionalization of Adult and Continuing Education Toward the Year 2000." Paper presented at the Commission of Professors of Adult Education Conference, Hollywood, Fla., Oct. 1986.

Baba, M. L., and Abonyi, M. H. *Mexicans of Detroit.* People of Michigan Series. Detroit, Mich.: Wayne State University, Center for Urban Studies, 1979. (ED 224 650)

Babchuk, N., and Thompson, R. "The Voluntary Associations of Negros." *American Sociological Review,* 1962, *27,* 647–655.

Boaz, R. L. *Participation in Adult Education: Final Report, 1975.* Washington, D.C.: U.S. Government Printing Office, 1978.

Burciaga, J. A. "45 Percent of Latinos Don't Complete School." In S. Farkas (ed.), *Changes and Challenges: City Schools in America.* Washington, D.C.: Institution for Educational Leadership Publications, 1983.

Carlson, R. A. *The Americanization Syndrome: A Quest for Conformity.* London: Croom-Helm, 1987.

Charner, I. *Patterns of Adult Participation in Learning Activities.* Worker Education and Training Policies Project. Washington, D.C.: National Institute for Work and Learning, 1980.

Chatham, R. L., and Redbird-Selam, H. M. (eds.). *Indian Adult Education and the Voluntary Sector.* Proceedings of conference sponsored by Church Women United, Monmouth, Oregon College of Education, Oct. 1972. (ED 072 333)

Clarke, C. H. "Personal Counseling Across Cultural Boundaries." Paper presented at the International Communication Association Conference, Montreal, Apr. 1973.

Cohen, S., and Kapsis, R. "Participation of Blacks, Puerto Ricans, and Whites in Voluntary Associations: A Test of Current Theories." *Social Forces,* 1978, *56,* 1053–1071.

Cohnstaedt, M. L. *Northern Opportunities and Economic Development Through Community-Centered Education: Report on Meadow Lake Vocational Center.* Regina: Saskatchewan Department of Education, 1973. (ED 170 080)

Coulter, B. "Hispanics Gaining in Number, but Losing in Education System." *Houston Post,* July 21, 1985, p. 4.

Cross, K. P. *Adults as Learners.* San Francisco: Jossey-Bass, 1981.

Darling-Hammond, L. *Equality and Excellence: The Educational Status of Black Americans.* New York: College Board Publications, 1985.

Deck, A. F. "Fundamentalism and the Hispanic Catholic." *America,* 1985, *152* (2), 64–66.

Deck, A. F. "Hispanic Ministry Comes of Age." *America,* 1986, *154* (18), 400–402.

Deloria, V. "Identity and Culture." *Daedalus,* 1981, *110* (2), 13–28.

DeVaughan, B. T. "The Boston Literary Society and Historical Association: An Early 20th Century Example of Adult Education as Conducted by a Black Voluntary Association." *Lifelong Learning,* 1986, *9* (4), 11–12, 16.

Ehrlich, I. F. "The Aged Black in America: The Forgotten Person." *Journal of Negro Education,* 1975, *44* (1), 12–23.

Fine, M. "Dropping Out of High School: An Inside Look." *Social Policy,* 1985, *16* (2), pp. 43–50.

Fingeret, A. "Social Network: A New Perspective on Independence and Illiterate Adults." *Adult Education Quarterly,* 1983, *33* (3), 133–146.

Florin, P., Jones, E., and Wandersman, A. "Black Participation in Voluntary Associations." *Journal of Voluntary Action Research,* 1987, *15* (1), 65–86.

Fraga, L., Meier, K., and England, R. "Hispanic Americans and Educational Policy: Limits to Equal Access." *Journal of Politics,* 1986, *48,* 851–876.

Gandy, S. L. "The Negro Church and the Adult Education Phase of Its Program." *Journal of Negro Education,* 1945, *14,* 381–382.

Giroux, H. "Theories of Reproduction: Resistance in the New Sociology of Education: A Critical Analysis." *Harvard Educational Review,* 1983, *53* (3), 257–293.

Hamilton, E. "Black Colleges: Opportunity for Non-Traditional Study." *Journal of Negro Education*. 1977, 46 (3), 254–263.

Heisel, M. A. "Assessment of Learning Activity in a Group of Black Aged." *Adult Education Quarterly,* 1985, *36,* 1–14.

Heningburg, A. "Adult Education and the National Urban League." *Journal of Negro Education,* 1945, *14,* 396–402.

Hills, S. M. "How Craftsmen Learn Their Skills: A Longitudinal Analysis." Columbus: Center for Human Resource Research, Ohio State University, 1981. (ED 222 696)

Hoffman, S. *In Recognition of Culture: A Resource Guide for Adult Educators About Women of Color.* Tallahassee: Florida State Department of Education, 1983. (ED 236 419)

Horne, F. S., and Robinson, C. K. "Adult Educational Programs in Housing Projects with Negro Tenants." *Journal of Negro Education,* 1945, *14,* 353–362.

Keddie, N. "Adult Education: An Ideology of Individualism." In J. Thompson (ed.), *Adult Education for a Change.* London: Hutchison, 1980.

Klobus-Edwards, P., Edwards, J., and Klemnack, D. "Differences in Social Participation of Blacks and Whites." *Social Forces,* 1978, *56,* 1035–1051.

Knowles, M. S. *The Modern Practice of Adult Education.* New York: Association Press, 1970.

Lloyd, G. "A Quarter Century of the Black Experience with the Church, 1950–1974." *Negro Educational Review,* 1976, *27* (1), 34–45.

Long, H. B. *Adult Learning: Research and Practice.* New York: Cambridge Book, 1983.

McConahay, J. B. "Reducing Racial Prejudice in Segregated Schools." In E. G. Epps (ed.), *Effective School Desegregation: Equity, Quality, and Feasibility.* Beverly Hills, Calif.: Sage, 1981.

McFadden, M., and others. "Dimensions of Retirement Among Minority Elderly." Paper presented at joint annual meeting of the Scientific Gerontological Society and Educational Canadian Association of Gerontology, Toronto, Nov. 1981.

McGee, L. "Booker T. Washington and G. W. Carver: A Tandem of Adult Educators at Tuskegee." *Lifelong Learning,* 1984, *8* (2), 16–18.

McNett, I. *Demographic Imperatives: Implications for Educational Policy.* Washington, D.C.: American Council on Education, 1983.

Massey, G., Scott, M., and Dornbusch, S. "Institutional Racism in Urban Schools." *Black Scholar,* 1975, *7* (3), 10–19.

Medoff, M. H. "Discrimination, Blacks and the Apprenticeship Trade Programs." *Negro Educational Review,* 1975, *26* (4), 147–154.

Meier, K. J., and Nigro, L. G. "Representative Bureaucracy and Policy Preferences." *Public Administration Review,* 1976, *36,* 458–470.

Mescon, T. S. "The Entrepreneurial Institute: Education and Training for Minority Small Business Owners." *Journal of Small Business Management,* 1987, *25,* 61–66.

Mezirow, D., Darkenwald, G., and Knox, A. *Last Gamble on Education: Dynamics of Adult Basic Education.* Washington, D.C.: Adult Education Association of the U.S.A., 1975.

Miller, H. *New York University's Harlem Seminar.* New York: New York University School of Continuing Education, 1967. (ED 014 652)

Mischel, W. "Toward a Cognitive Social Learning Reconceptualization of Personality." *Psychological Review,* 1973, *80,* 252–283.

Momeni, J. *Adult Participation in Education: Past Trends and Some Projections for the 1990s.* Walker Education and Training Policies Report. Washington, D.C.: National Institute of Education, 1980. (ED 200 735)

Morgan, C. "Racial Interests in the Education of Black Adults, Manhattan, 1880–1930." Paper presented at the 6th Lifelong Learning Research Conference, College Park, Md., Feb. 1981.

Muraskan, W. "The Hidden Role of Fraternal Organizations in the Education of Black Adults: Prince Hall Freemasonry as a Case Study." *Adult Education,* 1976, *26* (4), 235–252.

National Center for Education Statistics. Digest of Education Statistics, 1982. Washington, D.C.: U.S. Department of Education, 1982.

Neverdon-Morton, C. "Self-Help Programs as Educative Activity of Black Women in the South, 1895–1925: Focus on Four Key Areas." *Journal of Negro Education,* 1982, *51* (3), 207–220.

Olsen, M. "Social and Political Participation of Blacks." *American Sociological Review,* 1970, *35,* 682–692.

Orum, L. S. *Hispanic Dropouts: Community Responses.* Washington, D.C.: Office of Research, Advocacy and Legislation and National Council of La Raza, 1984.

Perrilla, A., and Orum, L. *Working Together: A Guide to Community-Based Educational Resources and Programs.* (2nd ed.) Washington, D.C.: National Council of La Raza, 1984. (ED 253 606)

Rachal, J. "Freedom's Crucible: William T. Richardson and the Schooling of the Freedmen." *Adult Education Quarterly,* 1986, *37,* 14–22.

Reder, S. *Giving Literacy Away: Alternative Strategies for Increasing Adult Literacy Development.* Washington, D.C.: National Institute of Education, 1985. (ED 253 775)

Roberts, H. *Culture and Adult Education: A Study of Alberta and Quebec.* Edmonton: University of Alberta Press, 1982.

Rosenbaum, J. E. *Making Inequality: The Hidden Curriculum of High School Training.* New York: Wiley, 1976.

Saltzstein, G. H. "Representative Bureaucracy and Bureaucratic Responsibility." *Administration and Society,* 1979, *10,* 465–475.

Samuels, F. "Closing the Door: The Future of Minorities in Two-Year Institutions." Paper presented at the National Adult Education Conference of the American Association for Adult and Continuing Education, Milwaukee, Wis., Nov. 1985.

Spaights, E., Dixon, H. E., and Bridges, E. "Leon Howard Sullivan: A Man of Vision." *Lifelong Learning,* 1985, *9* (2), 8–11.

Starr, G., and Medlin, K. "Analysis of Continuing Education for Planning Community Development." *Journal of Negro Education,* 1977, *46,* 264–277.

Talmer, M. "Some Factors in the Education of Older Members of Minority Groups." *Journal of Geriatric Psychiatry,* 1977, *10* (1) 89–98.

U.S. Commission on Civil Rights. *Fulfilling the Letter and Spirit of the Law: Desegregation of the Nation's Schools.* Washington, D.C.: U.S. Government Printing Office, 1976.

Upton, J. N. "Applied Black Studies: Adult Education in the Black Community—A Case Study." *Journal of Negro Education,* 1984, *54,* 322–333.

Valverde, S. A. "A Comparative Study of Hispanic High School Dropouts and Graduates." *Education and Urban Society,* 1987, *19* (3), 320–329.

Vontress, C. E. "Cultural Barriers in the Counseling Relationship." *Personnel and Guidance Journal,* 1969, *48,* 11–17.

Warren, S. *Minorities in Teacher Education.* Bloomington: Coalition of Teacher Education Programs, Indiana University, 1985.

Whaples, G., and Booth, N. "Alternative Learning Environments Providing for the Urban Low-Income Black Adult." *Lifelong Learning,* 1982, *6* (1) 12–14, 27.

Williams, L. S. "Community Educational Activities and the Liberation of Black Buffalo, 1900–1930." *Journal of Negro Education,* 1985, *54,* 174–188.

Willie, C. V. "Educating the Urban Student for the Urban Way of Life." In T. Cummings (ed.), *Notes and Essays on Education for Adults,* no. 53. Syracuse, N.Y.: Center for the Study of Liberal Education for Adults, Syracuse University, 1977.

Winchell, D. G., Safforn, S., and Porter, R. N. "Indian Self-Determination and the Community College." *Journal of American Indian Education,* 1980, *19* (3), 17–23.

Young, G. J. "Black Adult Learners: Demographics as an Indicator of Psychographic Profiles." Unpublished doctoral dissertation, School of Education, Indiana University, 1985.

45

Developmentally Disabled Adult Learners

Phyllis B. Klugerman

This chapter focuses on the visually impaired, the hearing impaired, individuals with mobility constraints, and those for whom an IQ test would indicate a learning capacity less than normal.

It is obvious that all learners are not created equal, and our educational system for many years has relegated handicapped individuals to a back seat. As a consequence of this neglect, a large number of adults have been treated as second-class citizens with regard to schooling. Developmentally disabled adults can learn, but they have considerable catching up to do (Klugerman, 1981). As a result of the enactment of Public Law 94–142 in 1975, so-called special children are now being educated in our public schools. Many adults, however, have not benefited from this law, and educators are now faced with the dilemma of how best to deliver these services to afford the possibility of independence to all of our citizens.

The beginning pages of this chapter present background statistics and definitions. The reader, however, must be cautioned that the statistical data presented are approximate, since accurate, current data do not exist. Moreover, terminology used in publications to refer to the handicapped population is not universal and is often contradictory. It differs depending upon the time, the place, and the author. For purposes of this chapter, the terms *handicapped, developmentally disabled,* and *special* are used interchangeably. I have learned in my years of experience that dated statistics and often ambiguous terminology used to define this population are irrelevant when it comes to justifying the current need and possibility for the creation of meaningful programming goals to address the learning needs and abilities of adults who are disabled.

There is a disabled population out there that for too long has been educationally ignored; it is large and diverse and underserved. Some government money is now available for the education of disabled children—funding initiated in the early to middle 1970s—and programs have begun to focus on handicapped children's specific learning needs. However, for the disabled learner over twenty-one years old, continuing adult education is (with the exception of higher education) still minimal. This important issue is the major focus of this chapter.

Background

A multitude of adults who are disabled and over the age of twenty-one reside in the United States today. Estimates of this population vary significantly from one source to another. The best estimate is that between 20 million and 50 million individuals have at least one disability.

For the purposes of this chapter, the following statistics are a benchmark from which to proceed. In 1979, the President's Committee on Mental Retardation indicated that approximately 606 million individuals with mental retardation lived in the United States. Of these, approximately 4.0 million were adults over the age of twenty-one; this number has since grown, but an accurate statistic is unavailable.

Approximately 21.0 million individuals with hearing impairments live in the United States. Of these, approximately 20.0 million are over the age of eighteen, with approximately 9.0 million over the age of sixty-four (Hotchkiss, 1987, p. 1). Of the approximately 6.4 million visually impaired individuals in the United States, approximately 1.7 million are severely visually impaired (Thomas and Thomas, 1980, p. 234).

These statistics illustrate that the numbers of individuals in these categories are large. But the numbers are only approximations. Clearly, a well-defined census needs to be administered. Conducting a survey to obtain accurate statistics is one of the major recommendations made by the First National Congress on Adults with Special Learning Needs, held at Gallaudet University, Washington, D.C., in October 1987.

Terminology

A group of professionals from various parts of the United States interested in furthering the educational possibilities of adult handicapped learners was given the responsibility of defining disability at the First National Congress on Adults with Special Learning Needs. The definition arrived at by this subcommittee is: "a performance deficit requiring some accommodation in learning, daily living, and employment." The intent of this definition, although not the exact wording, can be found in the program published by the First National Congress on Adults with Special Learning Needs (1988). Although there are many categories of disability, this chapter will concern itself only with mental, physical, visual, and auditory disabilities.

Mentally Disabled (Retarded). It is important to differentiate between mental retardation and mental illness. This distinction will eliminate a whole category of persons often confused with individuals who are retarded. Mainord and Love (1973, pp. 25–26) define mental illness as, "a disorder of the emotions; the mind, so to speak, is sick. The mentally ill person may be of normal or high intelligence. Mental retardation on the other hand, is not an illness or disease but a condition. The mentally retarded individual is one who has difficulty learning and has less than normal intellectual ability."

The definition of mental retardation as published by the American Association on Mental Deficiency (AAMD) in 1973 reads, "Mental retardation refers to significantly sub-average general intellectual functioning existing concurrently with deficits in adaptive behavior, and manifested during the developmental period" (Grossman, 1973, p. 5).

Physically Disabled. A physical disability is one requiring a supportive or mechanical device to compensate for a physical deficiency or immobility. Physical disabilities range from minor impairment to major disablement; they may be present at birth or may be a consequence of illness or accident during a lifetime.

Visually Impaired. In practice, terminology supposedly describing the various classifications of visual impairment reflects the divergent roles of the professionals associated with persons who are blind or visually impaired more often than it describes a consistent typology of impairment. Currently, the term *visual handicap* describes the population of children having impairments in the structure or functioning of the eye, regardless of the nature or extent of the impairment. However, definitions used for adults, dealing with legal, vocational, and medical factors, might be quite different.

Between the two extreme classifications of *blind* (indicating the need for learning through braille and related media without the use of vision, although the perception of light may be present) and *visual perception* (indicating the ability to interpret what is seen and to understand and to interpret meaningfully all information received through the visual sense), lie many other intermediary classifications denoting limitations in distance perception, discrimination of fine or small objects, or peripheral vision. Students who are visually impaired can compensate for their disabilities through the use of optical aids and special materials (Barragna, 1976).

Auditory Impairment. There are two major categories of individuals with hearing impairment: those who hear with difficulty what is said in normal conversation, and those who are unable to hear what is said in normal conversation (Hotchkiss, 1987). Those who experience difficulty in hearing may employ the use of mechanical or other supportive devices. Those unable to hear may be able to communicate via sign language or lip reading.

The Law in the United States

Concrete information on disabled individuals' educational involvement and growth prior to 1975 is extremely vague. With the passage of Public

Laws 93-112 and 94-142 in 1975, things began to change. Public Law 93-112, the Vocational Rehabilitation Act Amendments of 1973, Section 504, applies to all handicapped persons ages three through twenty-one and reads: "No otherwise qualified handicapped individual in the United States, . . . shall solely by reason of his handicap, be excluded from the participation in, be denied the benefits of, or be subjected to discrimination under any program or activity receiving Federal financial assistance" (U.S. Department of Health, Education, and Welfare, 1978).

Public Law 94-142, Section 1412(A), applies to all handicapped persons, ages three through twenty-one, who require special and related services. It states, "There is established (i) a goal providing full educational opportunity to all children, (ii) a detailed timetable for accomplishing such a goal, and (iii) a description of the kind and number of facilities, personnel, and services necessary throughout the State to meet such a goal" (Data Research, 1986, p. 218). For the first time, in 1975, Public Law 94-142 guaranteed the availability of special education programming to all handicapped children and youth who required it.

In Section 1401(19) of this law, use of the phrase "specially designed instruction" (U.S. Code Service, 1982, p. 676) that would meet the unique needs of the child's handicap is extremely significant. Prior to this date, handicapped children were either not identified or were grouped homogeneously in a special type of classroom which, through the years, had been given a number of different labels. They received poor and inadequate instruction because of a number of factors, including lack of teacher training to deal with a child's specific learning problems. A school's usual procedure was to segregate these children from the so-called normal children and to "baby-sit" them. Moreover, many of these children simply did not attend public school.

With the advent of Public Law 94-142, not only was there a commitment to teach the disabled learner in the public schools, but there was also government money backing this commitment. Teacher training in colleges throughout the country followed suit, and within a few years, children were being identified and classified. They were placed in classrooms in which they would receive the most appropriate instruction based on their unique individual needs, either in their own or a neighboring school district.

What does it mean for the adult disabled learner? Basically, until the last few years, government-supported instruction ended at age twenty-one. Currently, some programs are available through the Department of Health and Human Services to deal with the over-twenty-one population. Those fortunate enough to have benefited from Public Law 94-142 can seek to continue their education where programs are available. However, those individuals who attained age twenty-one prior to 1980, when implementation of this law for ages eighteen through twenty-one was finalized, have not received the benefit of Public Law 94-142 and are still a major part of our disabled population who require training, education, and support toward independence—and who have little or no foundation to build upon. These two groups of learners—those who attained age twenty-one prior to 1975 (or 1980) and those reaching that age since that date—are the ones who can and should be served by the adult education programs throughout the country.

The situation in Canada is somewhat different. Under the provisions of the British North America Act and the constitution approved in 1982, education, including special education, has become the responsibility of each of the ten provinces and two territories rather than being the responsibility of the national government. This shift in responsibility has resulted in a variety of programming efforts based primarily on individual provincial populations, demographic patterns, financial resources, and language (Canada has two national languages, French and English). For example, Ontario, through its Association for Children with Learning Disabilities, has a program for handicapped individuals past the age of twenty-one. It is organized in two or three rural settings on remodeled farms and has been designed mainly for individuals who did not benefit from special education while in school. Its effort is to fill the gap in their learning. Information on these programs is available from the Ontario Ministry of Education, Special Education and Professional Schools branch (Reynolds and Mann, 1987).

Learning as a Route to Independence

When setting goals for the populations discussed in this chapter, one must consider the variety of their educational backgrounds and the different social experiences they have had. A person who is different in looks or behavior often experiences inappropriate reactions, such as avoidance, mocking, or oversolicitousness. Accordingly, those who set goals must remember that creating an atmosphere in which comfortable interaction can take place is as important an educational goal as any other.

Individuals who are disabled need to learn to accept themselves as they are and to deal with the reactions of others. Harold Russell, former chairman of the President's Committee on Employment of the Handicapped (n.d., p. 1) and a man who had both of his arms amputated and was fitted with prosthetic devices, said, "Handicapped people have to learn to accept themselves fully if they want the rest of the world to accept them."

Inclusion of disabled learners as part of a regular adult school program can afford both the disabled and unimpaired populations the possibility of interaction on a more comfortable and honest basis. However, community reaction needs to be dealt with in advance in order to promote successful integration of any kind.

The overall goal of adult and continuing education is to provide learning opportunities that will enhance an adult's academic, social, avocational, and vocational skills and abilities. This goal also applies to the learners who are disabled, although additional attention must be given to their special needs including facility access, suitable instructional equipment and devices, and provisions for individual curriculum modifications.

Although the goal is clear, opportunities for continued learning for adults over the age of twenty-one and with learning disabilities have been and still are minimal. In order to expand these opportunities and to provide possibilities for greater success, a better understanding of the population is necessary. For example, handicapped individuals should not be treated as one homogeneous group solely because they are handicapped. Attempts at homogeneously grouping mentally handicapped adults in an instructional setting have met only with frustration and failure for both the instructor and the student (Klugerman, 1981). The backgrounds and abilities of these individuals are very diverse, and skill and ability grouping based upon family history and life experience is essential for successful learning to take place.

In addition, the results obtained from skill and ability assessments should be used as a guide for setting learning goals. An adult who is mentally retarded should not necessarily choose or eliminate from his or her choices a career as a mechanic. Mechanical skill ability must be assessed prior to making that decision. An individual's self-esteem must also be considered. Poor self-esteem, particularly for individuals who are disabled, greatly impacts their potential for success.

Often, lack of success with disabled populations is attributed to their inability to learn or to their lack of perseverance. This conclusion is often erroneous. If the individual situation were examined, one might discover that inappropriate assessment, grouping, or method of instruction was the cause of failure, rather than the student's lack of ability (Larson, 1982).

Issues

The first major issue we are faced with is how to define *handicap*. There is no clear and universal definition. As defined by Larson (1982, pp. 2–3), "A handicapping condition arises from the interaction of the disabled individual with his or her social environment. Generally, it results in a loss of independence or self-fulfillment." Ross (1987, p. 4) also refers to the difficulty in finding a universal definition and suggests, "A clear definition is important to assure that we are identifying a specific population. All too often the term has been used generically to denote learning problems due to a wide variety of causes."

The Education for All Handicapped Children Act of 1975 defines the handicapping conditions that are eligible for services and that are reimbursable by the federal government. This law defines a handicapped person "as being mentally retarded, hard-of-hearing, deaf, speech impaired, physically handicapped, seriously emotionally disturbed, orthopedically impaired, other health impaired, deaf-blind, multi-handicapped or as having specific learning disabilities, who because of those impairments need special education and related services" (Reynolds and Mann, Vol. 2, 1987, p. 754).

These definitions merely touch on the numerous definitions emanating from various sources. One of the major issues discussed at the First National Congress for Adults With Special Learning Needs was the need for a concrete and universally accepted definition of handicapping conditions that will enable educators to identify, to categorize, and to set learning goals and guidelines.

Assessment. Handicapped individuals come from as many diverse backgrounds and experiences as do the rest of the population. Therefore, there is a great need for development of instruments that can be universally administered to handicapped individuals and that are capable of producing clear educational, environmental, medical, and vocational data, along with accurate information pertaining to agency involvement and social ability.

Since most tests rely on reading and verbal ability, virtually no reliable assessment instruments are available to determine the learning capacity of retarded adults. Further, Larson (1982, p. 15) points out that, "Tests of learning capacity rely heavily on verbal ability, [and] they are largely invalid for measuring the intelligence of the deaf."

In addition to the need for adequate instruments to measure the intelligence or learning capacity of the handicapped is the need for an instrument that can accurately measure an individual's self-esteem. Although Coopersmith's (1967) study was conducted some time ago, the results are still relevant in education today. His studies were conducted with normal children. The findings suggested that individuals with high self-esteem set significantly higher goals for themselves than do persons with medium or low self-esteem. He further suggested that, "Social expectations of individuals with low self-esteem are marked by a lack of faith, expectations of failure, and anticipation of rejections" (p. 251). The implication of these studies is that, if normal individuals are affected in their social abilities by their self-esteem, it might also be that handicapped individuals are similarly affected.

In 1980, with the support of the New Jersey Department of Human Services, Division of Developmental Disabilities, a study was conducted questioning (1) whether self-esteem affects learning, (2) whether success in learning affects an individual's self-esteem, and (3) whether counseling specifically for self-esteem growth would enhance an individual's self-esteem (Klugerman, 1981). Fifty mentally retarded subjects between the ages of eighteen and fifty-five, with an IQ range of 10 to 85, and who participated in the East Brunswick Board of Education's Adult and Continuing Education Program, were randomly assigned to experimental and control groups to ascertain the effects of a counseling intervention on both self-esteem and basic skills growth. The experimental group received both counseling that focused specifically on the clients' self-esteem and skill training. The control group received only skill training. Although results indicated that one-to-one counseling did not affect either self-esteem or skill ability growth, supplementary analysis revealed that significant self-esteem gains and learning gains in skill ability occurred in both experimental and control group subjects. Thus, it appeared that involvement and success in skill training may be important factors in self-esteem growth.

A follow-up study with twenty-four subjects from the original population, who had continued to participate in a variety of adult education classes, was conducted in February 1987. The study compared the results of the self-esteem inventory given in 1980 with the results of the test given in 1987. The statistical analysis indicated highly significant gains in self-esteem for the total population with all subjects realizing gains (Klugerman, 1987).

Delivery Systems and Funding. The only higher educational institutions in the United States dedicated to a specific handicapped population are Gallaudet University and the National Technical Institute for the Deaf. Gallaudet University is a multipurpose educational institution and resource center that serves the hearing impaired through a full range of academic research and public service programs. The main campus is located in Washington, D.C., with regional branches in California, Florida, Hawaii, Kansas, Texas, Massachusetts, and Puerto Rico. The National Technical Institute for the Deaf offers training in various aspects of technology. This institute and the National Center on Employment of the Deaf are parts of Rochester Institute of Technology located in Rochester, New York. All other handicaps are serviced by a large number of colleges and universities throughout the country. Some services are offered as an integrated part of regular classes with modifications to the traditional learning environment. Others are offered within the college confines in specially assigned areas.

The most comprehensive sources for identifying community colleges, four-year colleges, and universities that can best accommodate a student's specific handicap, educational goals, national location, and financial status are the four individual guides to colleges for learning disabled students, for visually impaired students, for hearing impaired students, and for mobility impaired students (Liscio, 1984).

Another major resource in higher education is the American Council on Education's Higher Education and the Handicapped Resource Center (HEATH).

Funding has become available for school-age children over the last few years since the passage of Public Law 94-142. Funding for adults, however, still remains insufficient. Attention needs to be given to legislation that can provide funds for program development, facility access, adaptive materials and devices, and transportation. Some monies are available for public school adult education programs through state agencies and their divisions of adult and continuing education. For example, adult basic education (ABE) funds, which are federal funds filtered through the states, can be used for adult handicapped instruction. Also, vocational education funds are becoming more available for handicapped adults; however the amount of available funding is limited and cannot accommodate the large population requiring services.

The number of community colleges and four-year colleges that have provisions for handicapped adults is increasing constantly. Many of the colleges offer scholarships or some form of student assistance based on need.

Data Collection and Dissemination. Obtaining information about available programs and services for the handicapped is difficult because, although there are many small programs in the United States and Canada that are successfully serving adult handicapped individuals, information on them is limited to their local areas. A central clearinghouse to compile and to categorize this information is needed.

What currently does exist as a resource for general information is the three-volume *Encyclopedia of Special Education* (Reynolds and Mann, 1987). The only national data bank for adult education is the Educational Resources Information Center (ERIC), and its documents dealing with the handicapped are limited. A number of major journals also offer a variety of pertinent data:

American Annals of the Deaf
American Journal on Mental Retardation
American Journal of Occupational Therapy
Annals of Dyslexia
Journal of the American Association for the Severely Handicapped
Journal of Autism and Developmental Disorders
Journal of Communication Disorders
Journal of Learning Disabilities
Journal of Mental Deficiency Research
Journal of Special Education
Journal of Speech and Hearing Disorders
Journal of Visual Impairment and Blindness
Learning Disabilities Quarterly
Lifelong Learning: An Omnibus of Practice and Research
Special Education Across Canada

Implications for Adult Education Programming

Even with the implementation of Public Law 94-142, most public schools remain institutions serving only children. Individuals twenty-one years and older must seek other means of continuing their educations. For some, formal higher education in community colleges, four-year colleges, and universities is appropriate. For others, particularly the mentally retarded, options for continued learning include adult activity centers that focus on daily living skills and sheltered workshops that provide preemployment training. However, these activities are conducted in restricted environments during daytime hours and often have waiting lists. A prime alternative is adult education programming conducted in an integrated community setting and offering a full complement of training and instructional components from self-care through vocational training and job placement. Functioning in a community environment offers the best opportunity for influencing community attitudes and increases the developmentally disabled learners' chances for independent living.

Some public school adult education programs have begun to offer classes for the handicapped. Adult education has expanded over recent years to include not only social and avocational programs, which are important and necessary in themselves, but also adult basic education, high school equivalency, English as a second language, as well as vocational training and career counseling. The growth and refinement in most adult education programs, and the fact that they deal mainly with adults, make them a perfect vehicle for embracing the learning needs of adults who are disabled. However, this transition from public school to adult school cannot happen effectively without the understanding by program directors and staff of the special requirements for facilities, equipment, materials, and curriculum modifications necessary to provide successful programming for handicapped learners.

Conclusion

A concrete, universal set of definitions needs to be developed to describe the various handicapped populations. The notion that all disabled adults can be grouped and discussed as though they were one entity is very misleading. This and other issues discussed in this chapter began to be addressed in October 1987, when concerned individuals nationwide attended the First National Congress for Adults with Special Learning Needs, jointly sponsored by Gallaudet University and the Adult Learners with Disabilities unit of the American Association for Adult and Continuing Education in Washington, D.C. The theme of the congress was "Empowering the Adult with Special Learning Needs: A National Challenge." Its basic charge was to determine exactly what the educational issues are and how to proceed.* One of the major outcomes of these meetings was the knowledge that the unique characteristics and needs of each individual disability must be attended to and that setting program goals and guidelines is essential to meet these very specific needs.

Providing appropriate services for the adult handicapped learner cannot be accomplished without reliable and valid assessment instruments. Legislation is also needed to obtain funds necessary to maintain programs and services for the over-twenty-one population. The creation of a national clearinghouse to receive, to organize, and to disseminate information regarding programs for all types of handicaps is necessary to maximize the sharing of existing data and to minimize duplication of efforts. It is hoped that this chapter will be a beginning in an attempt to meet these needs.

References

Barragna, N. *Visual Handicaps and Learning: A Developmental Approach.* Belmont, Calif.: Wadsworth, 1976.

Coopersmith, S. *The Antecedents of Self-Esteem.* New York: W. H. Freeman, 1967.

---

*In August 1988, a second conference was held; its theme was: "Building a Consensus of Understanding: Lifelong Learning for Adults with Special Learning Needs."

Data Research. *Handicapped Students and Special Education.* (3rd ed.) Rose-
mount, Minn.: Data Research, 1986.

First National Congress on Adults with Special Learning Needs. *Program
Booklet: Programs in Adult and Continuing Education.* Washington, D.C.:
Gallaudet University, 1988.

Grossman, H. J. *Manual on Terminology and Classification in Mental Retardation.* (Rev. ed.) Special Publication, no. 2. Washington, D.C.: American
Association on Mental Deficiency, 1973.

Hotchkiss, D. *Demographic Aspects of Hearing Impairment: Questions and Answers.*
Washington, D.C.: Center for Assessment and Demographic Studies,
Gallaudet University, 1987.

Klugerman, P. B. "The Effect of Self-Esteem Counseling on the Growth
of Skill Ability and Self-Esteem in Adult Mentally Handicapped
Learners." Unpublished doctoral dissertation, Graduate School of Education, Rutgers—The State University, 1981.

Klugerman, P. B. "The Effects of Continued Program Participation and
Vocational Training on Self-Esteem Among Adult Mentally Handicapped Learners." *Journal of Lifelong Learning Research,* 1987, *1* (1), 11–29.

Larson, G. A. *Adult Education for the Handicapped.* Columbus, Ohio: ERIC
Clearinghouse on Adult, Career, and Vocational Education, National
Center for Research in Vocational Education, 1982.

Liscio, M. A. *A Guide to Colleges for Learning Disabled Students.* Orlando, Fla.:
Academic Press, 1984.

Mainord, J. C., and Love, H. D. *Teaching Educable Mentally Retarded Children.*
Springfield, Ill.: Charles C. Thomas, 1973.

President's Committee on Employment of the Handicapped. *How to Communicate to and About People Who Happen to Be Handicapped.* Washington,
D.C.: School of Business Administration, American University, n.d.

President's Committee on Mental Retardation. *Summary Sheet: Selected Data.*
Washington, D.C.: U.S. Government Printing Office, 1979.

Reynolds, C. R., and Mann, L. *Encyclopedia of Special Education.* vols. 1–3.
New York: Wiley-Interscience, 1987.

Ross, J. M. "Learning Disabled Adults: Who Are They and What Do We
Do with Them?" *Lifelong Learning,* 1987, *11* (3), 4–7.

Thomas, C. H., and Thomas, J. L. *Meeting the Needs of the Handicapped: A
Resource for Teachers and Librarians.* Phoenix, Ariz.: Oryx Press, 1980.

U.S. Code Service. *Education.* Vol. 20. Rochester, N.Y.: Lawyer's Cooperative, 1982.

U.S. Department of Health, Education, and Welfare. *Handicapped Persons
Rights Under Federal Law.* Fact sheet. Washington, D.C.: U.S. Government Printing Office, 1978.

Part 5

Adult Education in the Future

The futurist section presents the key trends in adult education's future and the ways we have of looking at that future. Accordingly, these three chapters provide three types of future scenarios for your consideration.

This section opens with a chapter on new educational technologies and the future. Technology has a way of determining our future regardless of what we do. The microchip, for example, as a single event, has revolutionized all of our futures by altering the basis for trend extrapolation and by imposing itself on our alternative images of the future.

Some futurists rely on emerging images, often those that confront present reality, as a method of identifying what the future may bring. Such imaging allows humans to create their futures through intervention rather than viewing the future as determined by the past and the present. The author uses this approach in his chapter on alternative images of the future.

Finally, the handbook's capstone chapter uses a trend extrapolation approach to forecasting the future. By using a process that projects the future from the past, the authors have examined data and have identified four trends and the implications of those trends for adult education practice in the 1990s.

46

New Educational Technologies for the Future

Linda H. Lewis

The difficulty in writing a chapter about the new technologies is that, at the same time descriptions are committed to paper, newer advances are rendering earlier technologies obsolete. In fact, the technological avalanche is opening such wide-ranging options that an enumeration of the array can be overwhelming. Microcomputers, electronic mail, interactive video, laser discs, satellites, and teleconferencing are but a few examples of technologies that have combined to make the communications revolution and information age a challenging era for adult educators.

The purpose of this chapter is to move the reader from the here and now into the not-too-distant future by describing varied applications of the new technologies in adult education and by exploring possible implications of their use. In providing such an overview, several questions emerge. What devices and systems belong to the new information technologies, and how does each contribute to enhancing adult learning? What are the advantages and disadvantages of the technologies that are currently available to adult educators? What are the attitudes of adult education professionals toward the new technologies? What is the impact of various technological aids on the teaching-learning process? In addressing these questions and related issues, it is useful to begin with a description of some of the more familiar and more widely used technologies in adult education before exploring what lies ahead.

The arrival on the market of a steady stream of new technologies has the promise of profoundly influencing the nature of adult education. Computers, audio, video, and telecommunications all have individual attributes that provide multiple opportunities for enhancing the learning process. Although adult education is involved with a number of technological improvements, the reality is that several decades may pass before the full range of abilities of the information technologies is realized and before educators gain mastery in their application.

Computers

The computer is the most significant of all the new products of the technological revolution. With the nearly universal adoption of the personal computer, a fair amount of drudgery and routine is being eliminated as the computer becomes a workhorse for management and informational support. Many adult educators are making more effective use of their time by employing personal computers as teaching machines to help individuals learn new material, as learning tools to promote the formation of new ideas, and as learning resources to access information (Heermann, 1986).

Highly sophisticated software is currently available to support computer usage and to assist students and teachers with everything from writing, graphing, idea generation, word processing, and managerial applications to problem solving and research. Applications programs, combined with the increased use of the computer for accessing data and for communication, make information readily available and increase the efficiency of adults in learning, controlling, and organizing information. According to Gerver (1984), these may be the greatest roles microcomputers play, since they alleviate tedious activities such as memorization and spending time hunting for information.

Computers possess attributes that are valued by adult educators. They are portable; they provide immediate feedback to the learner's input; and they can be programmed to be interactive with additional technologies to facilitate intertechnological communication. Above all, computers are personal. They provide spontaneous access on an individualized basis to meet the needs of an increasingly diverse adult population. Learners can proceed at their own pace, skip ahead, or review. Particularly advantageous for undereducated, nontraditional, or reentry students, computers allow individuals to work in a risk-free environment where they can avoid embarrassment, track their own progress, and engage in drill and practice until they achieve competence. As adults work to master ambiguous situations, computers allow individuals to express their curiosity and to demonstrate their creativity.

While many are familiar with computer-assisted instruction (CAI), touted over twenty years ago as a teaching machine for enhancing learning, today the microcomputer has expanded the notion of CAI with the advent of newer modeling, record-keeping, testing, and assessment programs. Today's personal computer, rather than simply posing questions, accepting answers, and providing appropriate feedback messages, allows for a variety of responses through interactive input or branching. Animation, graphics, and audio, as well as increased speed and memory capacity, are additional enhancements that make constant interaction possible.

Although there are numerous issues related to the future use of microcomputers in the adult education instructional process, the key to their acceptance or rejection is the attitude of adult and continuing educators toward the technology. Some continue to emphasize the dehumanizing nature of the technology and to suggest a lack of fit between computers and the aims of adult learning. Loss of ability for self-expression, increased social isolation, learner passivity, and the valuing of machines over people are just a few additional arguments that are advanced to encourage mistrust of the technology (Heermann, 1988). "The electronic machine, the argument goes, is a threat to the best teaching, which takes place through human interaction and discovery" (Gueulette, 1982, p. 176).

To date, there have been no studies to assess adult educators' willingness to incorporate computers into the curriculum. Additionally, only spotty information is available to indicate the variety of ways in which computers are actually being used in classes and programs nationwide. Data have not been systematically collected. Because there is no central communications network in the field, anecdotal accounts at meetings and at adult education conferences serve as the means of determining what is really going on; however, it does appear that traditional and limited utlization patterns are the norm. Kasworm and Anderson (1982), researching the attitudes of adult basic education (ABE) administrators, in a variety of educational settings, toward computer instruction, found those surveyed ranked basic math and computational skills, basic reading skills, and general educational development (GED) preparation among the top three areas of adult education they perceived as benefiting from microcomputer instruction. "Among volunteer literacy councils and services the use of computers is virtually nonexistent, although some current efforts are being made to utilize computers as a resource for training volunteers. Among state adult basic education programs (ABE), correctional facilities, and job-training programs, computers are being used to a limited extent" (Luttrell, 1986, p. 5).

In addition, issues of utilization, attitudes toward computers, and the benefits of the technology itself remain in dispute. Research on the use of computers for education shows no significant differences from traditional modes of instruction, and there is still little proof that new devices yield lasting improvements in learning (Clark, 1983). While many studies purport to find gains, these advances can be explained on the grounds that students using computers were temporarily motivated by the novelty of the machines. Learning improvements reported in early investigations of CAI instruction "shrank to virtually nothing when the same teacher taught both the experimental and the conventional classes with comparable amounts of preparation" (Bok, 1985, p. 31).

High tech companies are spending large sums of money to prove otherwise. IBM, for example, has undertaken a year-long project in cooperation with twenty providers of adult literacy education around the country. The objective is to develop software designed specifically for low-literate adults and to assess the impact of computers and course software on teachers and students (Lewis, 1987a). While recent research examining the effects of computer-assisted instruction indicates more positive attitudes about learning, increased motivation, and improved self-esteem among learners (Luttrell, 1986; Lewis, 1987a), the fact remains that adult learning theory is still being defined, and further evaluation is needed before the increased efficacy of computers can be touted.

Despite the lack of consensus regarding the merits of the new technology, computers are proving to be a major stimulus for initiating studies and for formulating new ideas about teaching methods and the processes that facilitate adult learning. At this time, there is no reason to conclude that computers necessarily diminish contacts between students and teachers. In reality, technology may free adult educators from routine tasks so that they can dedicate more time to the less formal kinds of teaching and counseling. There is also no reason to believe that computers will isolate students or dehumanize the learning process. Through the facilitation of appropriate instructional strategies, the new technologies can help to bring learners together to work cooperatively with peers and teachers. Used as enhancements to traditional instruction, not as replacements or substitutes for student-teacher interaction, the technology holds great promise.

High Tech Peripherals

The greatest contribution of the microcomputer may be realized when it is harnessed with other technologies. Specialized peripherals—electronic devices that attach to computers—open a whole new world of source materials that can dramatically expand the computer's use. Adult educators who work with blind, handicapped, or learning disabled adults can speak to the dramatic results that have been achieved through the use of specialized peripheral devices designed to circumvent the keyboard. The light pen, the joystick, the paddle, and the mouse are devices that provide users options for registering decisions on the screen and enable physically challenged adults to participate actively in the learning process.

Another advance, and one that has the potential of changing the nature of classroom-based instruction, is the LAN—local area network. Through the physical linking of computers, software from a host computer is shared electronically with other computers in the same network, making it possible to link computers in separate classes and to send bulletin board messages to everyone in the system. The main advantages of a LAN are its ability to maintain records of student progress, to chart time-on-task, and to facilitate administrative reporting information. For situations in which the size of the typical monitor screen is too small for whole-class instruction, large-screen video projection makes it possible to produce computer displays, visible to hundreds, on a screen or wall. Enhanced projection can be an especially powerful tool in a dynamic or interactive environment. Take the case of a simulation program for training anesthesiologists that monitors vital signs such as temperature, brain waves, and fluid levels. The continuously changing readouts can be charted and displayed on a nine-foot screen as new models are generated by the computer, thus allowing for discussion in a group context.

Video

The videodisc, a prerecorded eight- or twelve-inch recordlike platter that operates on a laser-read videodisc player, is a compelling tool when joined with a computer to allow random access to particular scenes or segments appropriate to a topic being studied. The videodisc produces full color pictures and a dual sound track on a television monitor, combining the advantages of text, graphics, photos, slides, and film into a single medium. Each videodisc holds some 54,000 separate frames of information, which translates to about 900 carousels of color slides; theoretically, this is equivalent to a year's worth of instructional audiovisual materials on a single platter. As of this writing, a mixed-mode disc is being pressed that is capable of holding a whole hour of full motion on video by virtue of signal compression technique. Such an advance effectively cuts production costs by half, making videodiscs affordable—particularly for public adult education programs that have traditionally been unable to purchase the technology.

At the present time, an even less costly alternative is the purchase of commercially produced videotapes to train, to remediate, and to supplement regular programming. Not only does this portable medium allow educators to capture the expertise of notables in the field, but it means that a substantial portion of instructional and professional resources can be brought directly to students who, working at home or in classrooms, can stop, interrupt, or review the tape as they see fit. Additional advances are now being made in the area of interactive video, a technique that allows a viewer to participate in a simulated conversation on the screen. Although interactive video is still beyond the reach of conventional public adult education programs, it is within the grasp of some colleges. Current applications include the use of interactive programs for decision making in career planning and placement centers where, through software and hardware consortia, institutions are sharing resources (Andrade, 1982).

Optical Data Storage

Optical data storage devices make it possible to house huge amounts of data at a relatively low cost. "On a CD you've got a cheap little parking space for 250,000 pages of text, the equivalent of 500 books—a truckload—instantly searchable and publishable at one-fiftieth the cost of printing on page" (Brand, 1987, p. 22). One of the first popular CD-ROM publications was Grolier's *Academic American Encyclopedia,* whose twenty volumes and index cost $200 and took up only 20 percent of a disc. Currently, copyright laws are holding back the proliferation of optical media; however, when issues of authors' permissions and royalties are resolved, this dense media will bring the information age into maturity and cure many publishers' problems, such as inventory excess, high distribution costs, and lack of shelf space (Brand, 1987).

In the scope of a single chapter, it is impossible to enumerate all of the multiple options that peripheral technologies offer. High-resolution printing and professional graphic design capabilities, previously available only through expensive typesetting, are now possible through so-called desktop publishing. Digital video interactive (DVI), a technology that combines the best attributes of video and CD-ROM into one medium, and three-dimensional (3-D) holography (Brand, 1987) will further advance our present capabilities. And while the list is impressive and ever changing, one thing is evident. The new technologies are converging at such a rapid rate that it is no longer clear which component is really peripheral to the other.

Telecommunication and Telecomputing

Telecommunication—the transmission and reception of messages over long distance—is pervasive throughout the developed world. Because telecommunication allows for the transfer of both the spoken and written word to anyone, anywhere, at any time, it has the potential of changing the very nature of our field. With the advent of fiber-optic technology, cost-effective enough to fit the educational pocketbook, current transmission capabilities are a billion bits of information per second. This is equivalent to sending the Encyclopedia Britannica across the Atlantic Ocean some six times a minute. By the end of the century, it is projected that laser and satellite communication capabilities will be as high as 100 billion bits of information per second (Pelton, 1982).

Teleconferencing is one of the most important examples of how telecommunication is being adapted within the learning environment. Designed as a substitute for face-to-face meetings and travel, teleconferencing has the ability to transmit voices, and sometimes images, and allows for instruction at off-campus locations. Not only does it extend programs to rural and outlying areas, but it greatly enhances the potential of adult education to deliver informational and professional services everywhere—from a student's back door, to the board room, to a corporate classroom.

Televised instruction for distance learning is another option that is afforded through the development of telecommunication networks. The only viewer equipment required is a television set. The British Open University (O.U.), which enrolls over 100,000 students in televised courses, is the best-known example of broadcast instruction in the world; however, the O.U. relies heavily on printed material as well as on the use of mailed assignments and self-administered tests to assess student progress. Televised instruction is not employed as a stand-alone medium. Local tutorial centers housing reference materials offer a human, interactive option to give additional structure and support to adult learners.

Telecomputing, whereby a classroom computer can be used to search through data base information sources and to retrieve topic information, is one of the exciting next steps in instructional computing. Systems such as videotext and viewdata facilitate the flow of two-way messages by using a video display, local processing, and a remote data base that is accessed through the telephone network. Telecomputing makes possible the sending and receiving of electronic mail almost anywhere in the world and permits participation in both public and private conferences on a specific topic. BITNET, a network commonly used by teachers and students to leave questions and to make comments, requires frequent review of incoming messages; this kind of electronic mail can intensify interaction in numerous ways. In 1986, for example, the Computer Task Force of the Commission of Professors of Adult Education developed a Directory of Computer Users containing the BITNET numbers of professors on the system along with additional information to facilitate independent long-distance computing. The directory has become an excellent resource for extending instructional and scholarly activities by facilitating networking among adult educators throughout North America. In 1986, the editors of the journal *Lifelong Learning* put another long-distance computing option in place by allowing authors to submit manuscripts through a computer bulletin board. This technological enhancement enables authors to uplink manuscripts to the board and to leave messages inquiring as to the status of their submissions. As the field continues to incorporate similar options to facilitate long-distance communication, we move closer to making the concept of the so-called global village a reality.

Social, Political, and Economic Implications of the New Technologies

The impact of the new technologies can be likened to the array of concentric circles that radiate from the center of a pool of water when a pebble breaks the surface. Each pebble has a slightly different impact, and each ripple contributes to the pattern in a decidedly unique way. Like the pebble, the microchip has initiated a reaction, and its impact is radically changing the nature and configuration of adult education.

With the ever-increasing volume of available data, the diversity of data pools is allowing both teachers and students to exercise more control in selecting information and programming. Educators are no longer the primary source of factual information. And, as the acquisition of factual information becomes less relevant, changes are occurring in the methods and content of instruction, both supplementing and changing the relationship between the teacher and the learner.

Several years ago at the opening session of the annual conference of the Commission of Professors of Adult Education, a Socratic symposium was held to discuss issues arising from the microchip revolution. Professors asked then, and are still asking the following questions: Will the technology increase the gap between the literate and nonliterate poor? What are some of the potential value conflicts and ethical issues that are likely to occur as a result of the new technologies? What are the political implications of the widespread availability of data and information, not only here, but in poorer, underdeveloped nations? Will increasing world interdependence and spontaneous communication systems broaden our concepts of basic or liberal education and lead to new definitions of literacy? These questions continue to be key agenda items for adult educators.

In the distribution of information, as with any resource, those groups whose values, status, and behavior patterns are already conducive to using a particular resource will be able to access and acquire it at a faster rate than others. Furthermore, information, like other social resources, is distributed and controlled in ways that direct it to those who can most easily use it. It is clear that the relatively large expenditures required to purchase some of the more advanced communication technologies may well have the potential of broadening the gap between haves and have-nots, both in our society and throughout the world.

Economic and employment projections suggest that there will be an increasing gap between those who work with computers and those who do not, a greater schism between skilled and unskilled workers, and a radical redistribution of wealth and the bases of wealth (Strange, 1981). In addition, unless something is done to encourage greater participation by women and minorities in the new technologies, the current underrepresentation of women, both as computer users and computer professionals, will mean further gender divisions in the labor force (Lewis, 1987b). A loss of jobs and bitter social battles between younger, better-equipped individuals and older, less computer-literate adults represent the less attractive implications of the new technologies.

Clearly, the new technologies have freed many individuals to enjoy their leisure and to work at home in a distraction-free environment. As a result, a whole new cottage industry—those engaged in home work—has emerged. While this is a benefit for many, some fear that this trend will result in the emergence of an underpaid, exploited group of women workers who, originally forced out of the labor market due to lack of day care or transportation, or because of job redundancy, will turn to home work as a last resort (Gerver, 1984). Thus, economic disparities, along with social and educational issues, appear to be emerging as additional considerations related to technology's use. While the new technologies bring the promise of unimagined capabilities, there will undoubtedly be unanticipated problems, litigations, glitches, disputes, and issues of privacy, ethics, and legality to be resolved. Access, sabotage, governmental regulation, and the exploitation of user fees are just a few examples of the potential dilemmas that will arise. Adult educators should not only be forewarned, but they should be challenged to participate in adjudicating such issues as they work to formulate policies related to the control of the new technologies.

New Technologies and the Future

It is hard to believe that when Toffler wrote *Future Shock* in 1970, the microprocessor did not exist, and that he was criticized as being a sensationalist for suggesting the world was moving into an era of change that would stretch existing institutions to their limits. Although prognostication is not the purpose of this chapter, Knowles's prophetic vision of the future, while neither sensational nor alarming, provides a reasonable picture of what lies ahead. "By the end of this century most educational services will be delivered electronically by teleconferencing, cable and satellite television, computer networks and other means yet to be discovered—provided educators learn how to use the media in congruence with principles of adult learning" (Knowles, 1986, p. 4).

According to Naisbitt (1982, p. 41), the interplay of technology and our reactions to it does not proceed in a direct course: "It weaves and bobs and lurches and sputters." However, one thing about the progression is certain. The degree to which desirable and undesirable effects of the new technologies will be felt is dependent upon our ability to accept the challenges of their integration into the continuing educational process. In the future, improvements can be expected in the design of technology-based educational resources and technological capabilities. Computers will become dramatically smaller, and reductions in size will be matched by reductions in cost. Computer-assisted instruction will deliver audio messages as well as the traditional visual information. "First-class speech recognition and intimate dialogue between student and computer tutor will be standard methods of CAI" (Suppes, 1979, p. 9).

As increases in memory capacity and reliability occur, the availability of communication services to all people around the world, particularly in developing countries, will expand dramatically. The widespread availability of inexpensive communication channels will increase demands for distance education. Thus, through satellite transmission and teleconferencing, widely scattered groups will be easily able to access peers, experts, and information. In turn, increased independence in learning will be fostered. Individuals will develop sophisticated skills as educational consumers who will be able to identify their own learning styles and needs and to determine selectively what to use from the array of educational resources distributed by an ever-increasing number of educational institutions and private suppliers. Additionally, the distinctions between formal and informal education will blur as learning at home and in other nonclassroom settings increases.

In the future, adult educators will need to encourage greater independence in learning as they guide learners to appropriate learning resources. The technology will demand that facilitators of adult learning be involved in preparing and evaluating technology-based materials and that they incorporate administrative, instructional, and information features of the new technologies into the learning environment. Strange (1981) predicts that, in the future, formal instruction in adult education will no longer be the result of a course prepared exclusively by an individual and delivered by a program or institution to a group of students. Rather, courses will be developed by teams and delivered in a variety of ways to individual consumers.

In the coming years, computer conferencing will not be limited in scope to accomplishing a short-term objective as past practice suggests. Instead, the possibility of an electronic community, in which anyone can participate, will become a reality. One will be able to join numerous communities voluntarily, as needs or interests change, and permanent transcripts of all communications will be kept on file in a central computer so as to preserve the history of communities and to provide resource information for interested parties (Lynton and Elman, 1987). Library systems also will be altered as new methods for storing, retrieving, and disseminating information are put into place. Traditional connotations of libraries are already changing as their identification with books expands to include the recognition of alternative forms of information such as films, records, and video. The new technologies will render libraries fertile places for technological innovation for adult learners, who, in the coming years, will be able not only to access books in local libraries, but to obtain volumes from participating libraries across the country. Syracuse University's Kellogg Project, a four-year research effort to provide broad access to the University's unparalleled collection of adult education materials, is a promising example of how technology is promoting information exchange among adult educators. Ultimately, AEDNET (Adult Education Network), a mediated network currently in place, will enable adult educators to communicate with each other and to access information about the Syracuse collection.

Along the continuum of technological advances, the concept of the Educational Utility, a service product of the National Information Utility Corporation, holds promise for adult education. Although still in the development stages, its features would include a repository for software, data bases, and other instructional material stored in a computer center; a distribution system or network to send materials to sites upon demand; a computer at a given location where materials are temporarily stored for use by administrators, students, and teachers; and computers and other equipment in the learning environment that can access materials directly from an on-site computer (Middletown, 1986).

Using the utility's electronic mail system, adult educators would be able to communicate with each other, with homebound or remote learners, or with other countries. The resources stored in the repository might include diagnostic tests, software, journals, curriculum guides, and course syllabi (Gooler, 1987). Users of the utility would pay a fee, similar to that paid for gas or electricity, which would accrue when the utility was being used. In turn, as individuals develop new programs that are picked up by the utility, there would be a dollar value placed on the material, and a payback would be credited accordingly.

If the utility becomes a reality, it would mean not only significant reductions in the current cost of using the new technologies to promote adult learning, but it would solve memory and compatibility problems, make rich resources available through financially accessible data bases, and ensure copy protection. Constant feedback from users would also ensure the continual updating and modification of programs needed to individualize instruction. In turn, concerns about potential obsolescence, a common fear among those who have already purchased software and systems, would be eliminated.

Finally, any discussion of future technological applications in adult education must include mention of artificial intelligence (AI). Computer programs written by investigators of AI have demonstrated conclusively that, in certain activities, including those that most people would say require intelligence, the computer can outperform human reasoning.

All intelligent training systems fall on a continuum between two extremes—tutors and learning environments (Skrmetti, 1987). With tutors, students are guided by the system through a series of learning experiences. Decisions about when, what, and how to teach are made by the system. A student's progress in mastering a given domain can be evaluated and appropriate strategies can be formulated to meet individual needs. Progress is measured against well-defined criteria, and the amount of new information is controlled by the tutor to facilitate the integration of new knowledge with the student's present store. In the learning environment approach, AI makes it possible for students to enter a world in which they can interact with objects, control the tutoring session, and perform experiments as their curiosity directs. There are no set tutoring strategies, for it is the individual who actively explores the domain and interacts with the system. Students control the rate of exposure to new information and discover facts and relationships for themselves. The mental models that one develops through this approach are described as robust and have a high motivational appeal (Skrmetti, 1987). However, learning environments can also be less efficient than a structured tutor, because students can spend nonproductive time investigating, and because individual mastery is difficult to ascertain.

It is exciting to think about the possibility of having available learning opportunities that include all the features adult educators tout as being optimal for a learning environment. For example, as the future capabilities of intelligent tutoring expand, systems will not only include sophisticated models that incorporate the mastery of content, but will also include models that assess the student's background knowledge, preferred or most efficient style of learning, and learning rate (Davis and Skrmetti, 1986). The availability of different teaching approaches, such as structured, guided, open ended, and discovery learning, would enable systems to optimize presentations for different types of content and for different levels of learners. Such systems could also be expanded to include mechanisms for identifying or inferring a student's plans or goals in order to maximize individualized instruction. Future intelligent tutoring systems could also have links to other basic tutors so that a learner having problems due to a lack of foundational skills could be shifted within the system into the proper tutor to remediate specific skills. Successful implementation of this technology will permit the development of systems that are capable of learning from encounters with students, thereby altering tutoring strategies, changing knowledge bases, making new inferences, and understanding new or unspecified relationships in order ultimately to develop a customized and successful remediation strategy (Davis and Skrmetti, 1986). According to Papert (1980), this kind of contact with the computer can open access to knowledge, not instrumentally by providing people with processed information but by challenging the constraining assumptions that they have about themselves. Expert programs, although prohibitively expensive now, may someday provide adults access to experienced mentors and may allow learners to probe in a manner not afforded in real life.

As work continues in the area of AI, further advantages will be reaped by adult educators interested in an interdisciplinary approach to adult learning. Because AI research requires the collaboration of professionals from various disciplines, there will be numerous opportunities to link with mathematicians, cognitive psychologists, computer scientists, and the like in further refining and maximizing scientific inquiry (Gerver, 1984).

It is clear from the previous discussion that the phantom electron is leading the way to unprecedented changes in the nature of technology. Even the nature of change is changing. Digitization, robotics, and microengineering all herald the need for training, continuing education, and retraining. However, in order to ensure the successful integration of these new technologies to promote adult learning, adult education must take an active role.

First, adult educators must attend to the value questions that surround this new technological revolution. While it is impossible completely and accurately to predict the nature of the changes that will occur, the political, economic, and social implications of the new technologies must be monitored and steps must be taken to preempt inequities in access and utilization (Gerver and Lewis, 1984). Organizations such as the American Association for Adult and Continuing Education (AAACE), the International League for Social Commitment in Adult Education, and the Commission of Professors of Adult Education have an opportunity to become leaders in the development of and access to appropriate technologies and their application in the field.

Second, linkages need to be established with business and industry in order to maximize the potential of the new technologies. Because limited adult education budgets preclude the kind of capital allocations necessary to develop technology fully for educational purposes, the creation of cooperative alliances with neighboring programs, agencies, and institutions can mean opportunities for research and application of the new technologies where none would otherwise exist.

Adult educators also need to serve as critical evaluators of the new technologies. Before decisions to purchase hardware, software, or sophisticated peripherals are made, individuals must undertake to learn as much as they can about these new media. A substantive issue in the field is finding time and money to support the professional development efforts of part-time and full-time teachers to acquire skills in assessing, using, and evaluating the new technologies. Sales promotions and sophisticated marketing campaigns have led many districts, programs, and institutions to purchase both systems and software that do not meet the needs of adult learners; yet, without options, adult educators must use what is already in place. In many cases, purchased software was designed originally for children, and the old nemesis of having to use materials that are inappropriate for adults resurfaces. Therefore, adult educators must ensure not only that they are part of the decision-making process, but that they have a working knowledge of the technical aspects of the technologies in order to provide relevant input as to the merits or disadvantages of each. Heretofore, misuse and lack of understanding of the technology have contributed to putting these new media in a bad light. Education is the vehicle for rectifying the situation, but, until research and evaluations are conducted, caution should be exercised when purchasing that which is being marketed as the newest and best.

Beyond decisions related to software and hardware selection is the additional issue of information retrieval. With the variety of data bases that are available, individuals need opportunities to understand not only how to access information but how to sift through what is there. Support in the form of information exchanges, networking among adult educators, professional development seminars, in-service training, participation in adult education conferences, and membership on task forces are all key to developing the keen evaluative skills necessary for selecting and using information retrieval systems and data bases.

Evaluation must not end with the development of good assessment and evaluative skills, however. It must expand to include responsibility for determining efficacy of new technologies. Assertions as to the value of computers still rest on unproven hypotheses. There is so much more to learn, such as how the new technologies contribute to motivation, which programs are most effective, and whether, in fact, individuals learn more quickly and thoroughly with the new technologies. These new media open the way for limitless research by adult educators and by doctoral students inspired to investigate the learning process. Each combination of new technologies presents exciting possibilities for creating and testing various learning theories. This theoretical work means moving beyond mere extension of behaviorist models of CAI and on to exploration of cognitive and humanistic learning theory as the bases for creating new designs that use our full technological capacities.

Last, care must be taken to ensure the careful integration and application of the new technologies into the learning environment. ''It seems appropriate for those interested in teaching and learning, including those whose interest is primarily in the teaching and learning that occurs outside the classroom, to grasp opportunities to influence the design of new technology systems to work for learners, rather than to require learners to adapt to the requirements of technology" (Gooler, 1987, p. 72). Thus, despite technological advances, meeting the needs of individuals while simultaneously seeing to it that learners are central to the process will remain a major tenet of adult and continuing education.

References

Andrade, S. C. "Interactive Video: Television with a Teaching Touch." *Journal of College Placement,* 1982, *42* (4), 15–16.

Bok, D. "President's Report to the Harvard Board of Overseers, 1983–84." *Harvard Magazine,* May–June 1985, pp. 29–38.

Brand, S. *The Media Lab: Inventing the Future at MIT.* New York: Viking Penguin, 1987.

Clark, C. A. "Reconsidering Research on Learning from Media." *Review of Educational Research,* 1983, *53,* 450–455.

Davis, C. A., and Skrmetti, T. J. "The Application of Artificial Intelligence and CD/ROM Technologies to Individualized Training." In J. Fox (ed.), *Proceedings of the Second Learning Technology Institute Conference on Applications of AI and CD/ROM in Education and Training.* Warington, Va.: Learning Technology Institute, 1986.

Gerver, E. *Computers and Adult Learning.* Milton Keynes, Eng.: Open University Press, 1984.

Gerver, E., and Lewis, L. "Women, Computers and Adult Education." *Convergence: International Journal of Adult Education,* 1984, *17* (4), 5–15.

Gooler, D. D. "Using Integrated Information Technologies for Out-of-Classroom Learning." In J. A. Niemi and D. D. Gooler (eds.), *Technologies for Learning Outside the Classroom.* New Directions for Continuing Education, no. 34. San Francisco: Jossey-Bass, 1987.

Gueulette, D. (ed.). *Microcomputers for Adult Learning: Potentials and Perils.* Chicago: Follett, 1982.

Heermann, B. "Strategies for Adult Learning." In B. Heermann (ed.), *Personal Computers and the Adult Learner.* New Directions for Continuing Education, no. 29. San Francisco: Jossey-Bass, 1986.

Heermann, B. *Teaching and Learning with Computers.* San Francisco: Jossey-Bass, 1988.

Kasworm, C. E., and Anderson, C. A. "Perceptions of Decision Makers Concerning Microcomputers for Adult Learning." In D. G. Gueulette (ed.), *Microcomputers for Adult Learning: Potentials and Perils.* Chicago: Follett, 1982.

Knowles, M. "How the Media Can Make It or Bust in Education." In D. G. Gueulette (ed.), *Using Technology in Adult Education.* Washington, D.C.: American Association for Adult and Continuing Education, 1986.

Lewis, L. H. "IBM Joint Literacy Project." Paper presented at the Connecticut Association of Adult and Continuing Education Conference, Meriden, Conn., Oct. 1987a.

Lewis, L. H. "Women and Computers: Fostering Involvement." In B. Wright (ed.), *Women, Work and Technology: Transformations.* Ann Arbor: University of Michigan Press, 1987b.

Luttrell, W. "Contemplating PLATO: Potentials and Provisions of Computer-Assisted Instruction in Adult Basic Education." Paper presented at the Adult Literacy and Technology Conference, Pennsylvania State University, June 1986.

Lynton, E. A., and Elman, S. E. *New Priorities for the University: Meeting Society's Needs for Applied Knowledge and Competent Individuals.* San Francisco: Jossey-Bass, 1987.

Middletown, T. "The Educational Utility." *American Educator,* 1986, *10* (4), 18-15.

Naisbitt, J. *Megatrends.* New York: Warner Communications, 1982.

Papert, S. *Mind-Storms: Children, Computers, and Powerful Ideas.* New York: Basic Books, 1980.

Pelton, J. N. "Global Talk and the World of Telecomputerenergetics." In H. Didsbury, Jr. (ed.), *Communications and the Future.* Bethesda, Md.: World Futures Society, 1982.

Skrmetti, T. J. "The Use of Intelligent Graphics Models in Intelligent Training Systems." In J. Fox (ed.), *Proceedings of the Third Learning Technology Institute Conference on Applications of AI and CD/ROM in Education and Training.* Warington, Va.: Learning Technology Institute, 1987.

Strange, J. H. "Adapting to the Computer Revolution." *Current Issues in Higher Education,* 1981, pp. 14-18.

Suppes, P. "Future of Computers in Education." *Journal of Computer-Based Instruction,* 1987, *6* (1), 5-10.

Toffler, A. *Future Shock.* New York: Bantam Books, 1970.

47

Alternative Images
of the Future
in Adult Education

John Ohliger

"Images are not arguments, rarely even lead to proof, but the mind craves them, and, of late more than ever, the keenest experimenters find twenty images better than one, especially if contradictory." These words, written by Henry Adams over eighty years ago (1906, p. 1167), appeared in a true adult education classic—the engrossing story of a personal lifelong search for education and its meaning. Adams is America's greatest man of letters (Zinsser, 1986), as well as the great-grandson of President John Adams and grandson of President John Quincy Adams. Henry Adams's words may be even truer today than they were when he put them down at the opening of the twentieth century. While the twenty-first century looms only a decade away, the mind's craving for images must now deal with the contradictory stimulus overload from the constant bombardment of mass media symbols and from the inundation of computer-molded facts from the so-called information revolution.

Combine the awareness of that bombardment with the recognition that this is a time of fundamental social crisis, a period of "perilous condition for humanity" (Marien and Ziegler, 1972, p. 124). Then it should come as no surprise that images, unadorned or carefully programmed, quietly hidden or boldly displayed, shaping present, value-laden action or nurturing future goal-directed thought, flood the literature of adult education. And beyond the printed literature, as Adams notes, our minds are filled with them—not just images as visualized pictures in the head, but ones including sound, touch, smell, taste, (E. Boulding, 1983) and other senses beyond words to describe them.

Since this chapter deals with those images labeled *alternative,* that term will be traced historically and defined first. It will then be distinguished from its opposite—the mainstream, the dominant society, the establishment, the standard view of the world. To focus on a few of the myriad specific alternative images, six paths to them or to their fulfillment will be surveyed: (1) wordless communitarian visions, (2) the dystopian, (3) fiction as wisdom, (4) entrepreneurial creations, (5) eclectic conferencing, and (6) focused imaging. To conclude, there will be brief critical speculation on possible futures for alternative images, on the crucial problem of the time dimensions (past, present, and future) as the twenty-first century approaches, and finally on the concepts of *image* and *alternative* themselves.

Alternative, in the sense of an alternative society, school, or newspaper, is a child of the sixties, specifically the late 1960s and the early 1970s (Barnhart, Steinmetz, and Barnhart, 1973; Flexner, 1987). The concept flourished as a workable umbrella for the burgeoning radical groups and for the many reformist activists of the period who were trying to find common ground with each other in order to build a powerful social movement. As one self-identified radical adult educator put it, "The term is shorthand for those of us who want to work toward a better world through fundamental social and political change, but don't want to suffer the isolation of proclaimed ideological radicalism and aren't all that dogmatically sure of how to get from here to there anyway" (Ohliger, 1979, p. 8). It was a new sense of the word, not seen before the late sixties. Alternative means not merely something that can be substituted easily (alternate), but "something that is completely opposite" (Quinn, 1980, p. 72). For most, it is preferable to the word *underground,* which had been "co-opted by the establishment" (Danky and Shore, 1982, p. 13). But the word *alternative* has nuances of meaning which vary so greatly from one source to another that no single definition of it is acceptable to everyone (Danky and Shore, 1982, p. 13).

Bearing in mind the problems of definition, in the context of images of the future in adult education, alternatives can be distinguished from dominant mainstream images in at least two ways: (1) by their association with a view of prediction or forecasting, and (2) by their meshing with an attitude toward high technology. A few futurists and forecasters place themselves in the alternative camp, and mainstream prognosticators usually hedge their predictions and forecasts by developing scenarios. But the typical alternative view is more in line with "the Japanese proverb that when one forecasts the future the devil laughs" (Whitelock, 1974, p. 315). While a few who hold alternative positions still cling to the technological utopianism, optimism, and determinism of an earlier radical period, most distinguish themselves from the current establishment by a more critical view. They "ask how technological progress, once hailed by millions as the panacea for virtually all of humanity's problems—and not merely its material problems—not only failed to solve a number of material and nonmaterial problems but became a principal problem in itself" (Segal, 1985, p. 134). The words *Chernobyl* and *Challenger* come quickly to mind.

Thus, mainstream adult educators generally stick to the straight-and-narrow path. They frequently confidently predict what they think will happen. Worthwhile alternative or off-center educators are more tentative and eschew bliss about the future for the steady stare at the present. Mainstream protagonists foster the enhancement and extrapolation of present dominant technological trends, for instance, the so-called knowledge explosion, the information revolution, or the specter of human obsolescence. In adult education, the alternative view grows from the tradition encapsulated by the late, esteemed Coolie Verner in the following sentence: "Adult education cannot become a viable alternative to a decadent educational system when those in it see it only as an extension of that system, rather than as a unique opportunity to create a new learning alternative" (Ohliger, 1975, p. 38).

When Leon McKenzie's (1978) book *Adult Education and the Burden of the Future* was published, Sharan Merriam (1978, p. 58) concluded that the book "represents one of the few serious attempts by an adult educator to question the meaning and direction of the field of adult education." To put it succinctly, alternative images of the future of adult education partake of McKenzie's (1978, p. 94) conclusion: "The gospel of the possibility of a new age must be the leitmotif of adult education or there will be no real hope."

However, the dividing line between alternative and mainstream adult education is not always clear-cut. For example, University of Wisconsin Extension, the center of the so-called Wisconsin Idea, has in the past exemplified institutions that fit into both categories. Its vast programs range from conservative agricultural extension to liberal, even radical, programs supporting social criticism and action. It may be that there is a trend these days to separate this combination. Extension has recently undergone such drastic, massive cuts (generally unreported) that the further existence of the Wisconsin Idea as a path to combining alternative and mainstream approaches is in fundamental doubt (Lehman, 1984; Ohliger and Fewster, 1975).

Those supporting alternative images generally proclaim their great social value. But an alternative image also can encompass activities of negative worth. Adolph Hitler is generally depicted as the epitome of evil in the world. Recent historical research by Mickey Hellyer and others ("Adolph Hitler . . . ," 1988) has shown that, according to Hitler (1943, pp. 209–210) himself, he "found the way to one of the most essential premises of a new party," the Nazi party, in a mandatory continuing education course he was ordered to take right after World War I. In addition, Hitler's first postwar job was as an adult educator for the German government (Davidson, 1977). Hitler was certainly engaged in evil alternative adult education activities from a worldwide perspective. This example and that of the Wisconsin Idea illustrate that alternative images are not always easily identifiable, nor are they necessarily ones of great virtue. Attention needs to be paid to the context, the content, the process, and the people involved.

Six Paths to Alternative Images

Looked at in the large view, there are at least six different paths by which alternative images of the future in adult education can be traced to their origins and followed to their destinations. There are a great many alternative images, but there is only space to sample a few representative ones. (For the full range, see Ohliger, 1985; Boshier, 1981; "Implications . . . ," 1975; and Roberts, 1988.)

Wordless Communitarian Visions. Historically (and beyond history to the metaphor of the timeless golden age), the wordless images appear first, possibly unconsciously, as adults cooperate convivially with each other in the day-to-day life of organic communities. In those cultures, images of adult education are, by their nature, alternative to present mainstream images and are so organically integrated with the broad intentional visions of the community that they are inseparable and unidentifiable. Reva Crawford (1981, p. 3), the founder of the National Indian Adult Education Association, points out that in those societies, including Native American ones, "You are of a culture in which the idea of going to a special building with separate people called 'educators' to learn is itself a foreign concept." These wordless communitarian visions also play an important part in the philosophical work of seminal world figures such as Lao Tzu (Ohliger, 1987b), Gustav Landauer (Lunn, 1973), and Ivan Illich (1971).

The Dystopian. Adult educational images of alternative futures are not necessarily all positive or utopian. An image can just as well be one that should be avoided in the future as one to be worked toward. Mainstream images of the adult education future generally leave out negative possibilities, since their bottom-line assumption is that the world will muddle through. The anti-utopian specters of Ivan Illich and those of his mentor on educational issues, Everett Reimer, stand out among the work of the alternative education proponents. The strangling image of schooling from womb to tomb and beyond intrudes its skull-like grimace throughout the Illich and Reimer writings on education. Reimer (1971) actually wanted his book *School Is Dead* to be called *School Is Death* (Everett Reimer, conversation with the author, Oct. 1981). And Illich, who in *Deschooling Society* (1971, p. 21) advocated "the disestablishment of schools, in the sense in which the Church in the U.S. has been disestablished" began to conjure up an even more baleful vision, "that the disestablishment of the educational church could lead to a fanatic revival of many forms of degraded education" (1987, p. 11). Other adult educators picked up these dystopian warnings to create negative images of the future (Ohliger, 1971; Gueulette, 1972; Lister, 1975; Williams, 1974; Heyting, 1987) including the trend toward forcing all adults—now over half of the American adult population—to go back to school (Ohliger, 1983).

In work by Illich and others (Illich, 1987; Ohliger, 1971; Purcell, 1974), the Orwellian year of 1984 loomed large as a hideous image (Orwell, 1949). For many adult educators and others concerned with the threat of nuclear war, as the year 1984 passed, the vision of a scorched earth suffering from a so-called nuclear winter replaced the Orwell chronology.

The positive and practical philosophical vision of the four learning networks or webs, outlined in the work of Illich and Reimer in the early 1970s, provided much meat for adult educators as they worked toward an alternative to the rigid educational system of schools and colleges. Also, Mike Rossman's (1979) experience growing out of the political climate of the sixties presented some cogent visions for younger adult educators.

Fiction as Wisdom. Fiction, by its very nature as imaginative work, has offered much to possible conceptions of alternative futures, especially in its implied criticism of present practices. Fiction has another strength. It is always indirect—that is, it is impossible to tell exactly what point the authors have in mind, since everything is presented through the minds of the characters. Even the authors themselves cannot say for sure, because they are producing the results of their own fantasies and are building on the collective imagination of other authors and sources. In this sense, fiction and other works of the creative imagination are analogues of wisdom, which is always indirect and elusive and which cannot be attached to the inventiveness of a single person (Ohliger, 1988a). Hundreds of creative examples abound that focus on adult education themes. They go at least as far back as Shaw's ([1913], 1981) play *Pygmalion,* up through Rosten's (1937) *The Education of Hyman Kaplan,* and up to and beyond the recent play and film *Educating Rita* (Russell, 1986). Some examples are even more specific and provide concrete practical perspectives for critical imaging. (See the chapter titled "Gatherstretch," presenting a feminist adult education conference approach in Gearhart, 1979.) Science fiction novels and short stories also offer particularly fruitful examples of this path (Tremor, 1974). For instance, many science fiction works focus on adult education conferences (Ohliger, 1987c).

Entrepreneurial Creations. The work of adult educators such as Ron Gross (1982), Bill Draves (1980), and Bob Theobald (Bowman and Kierstead, 1985) illustrates the occasional overlap between alternative and mainstream images of the future. Such overlap could be helpful in bridging the gap between the two views. On the other hand, such overlap sometimes co-opts new directions to protect the old, outworn ones. Gross, Draves, and Theobald are currently involved in alternative routes, and each has a long history of such involvement. Gross returned his college degree to his alma mater and fostered the independent scholarship approach (Gross, 1982); Draves worked hard in the free university movement (Draves, 1980); and Theobald (1968) may well be responsible for the first use of the term *alternative* in book form. All three now espouse a kind of social entrepreneurship that combines fresh and original thinking with more traditional, sometimes crassly commercial, moralizing, establishment cliches. Only time will tell the value of this path. Theobald's (1987) most recent book includes a long roster of over sixty groups—many of them engaged in alternative adult education—that agree with his basic approach and support its direction. And despite his embrace of conventional wisdom about future shock, which he calls the rapids of change, Theobald (1987, p. 140) does recognize that "you can only teach people what they already know. The skilled helper of others, whether credentialed or not, enables people to surface what they already know but have not yet faced."

Eclectic Conferencing. Some adult education conferences are organized around an image that both alternative and mainstream groups find congenial—for instance, the 1987 National Adult Education Conference and the theme *empowerment.* In the mid-1970s, with a large grant from the U.S. Office of Education, a series of regional conferences and one national conference were held, focusing specifically on images of future adult education. These conferences embraced the widest possible eclectic range of political, social, and personal views. These so-called think tanks on the future of adult education were the brainchild of Gerry Hanberry at the University of Maryland. They created a great deal of excitement, were very well organized, attracted important figures as well as just plain workers in the field, and bid fair to become a base for a series of bold sorties into alternative futures. It is still not clear why the initiative died after the culminating national conference. One guess is that internal politics at the University of Maryland and the U.S. Office of Education quashed the follow-through. Whatever the sad ending to a powerful beginning, Hanberry and his cohorts introduced large numbers of adult educators to the energizing force of focused imaging.

Focused Imaging. The focused imaging approach to alternative images in adult education is best known through the work of Warren Ziegler in collaboration with Elise Boulding. This approach builds on the value of personal daydreaming, night dream exploration, and fantasizing to facilitate "focused imaging in the social dimension" (E. Boulding, 1983, p. 50). Not only has this approach been used to generate alternative adult education images, but it also finds application in even broader areas such as working toward a "world without weapons" (p. 51).

The Future of Alternative Images

Dogmatic pragmatics believe they have defeated visionaries when they ask them how to get from here to there and receive what they regard as vague answers or even a "We don't know." But the pragmatists have already ruled out the possibility that a cogent and authentic image is sometimes socially energizing in itself. And they do not realize that their narrow emphasis on practicality is itself impractical. Witness the current dire straits of a world locked in the rigid embrace of those who see little else but nuts-and-bolts practicality and the ideologies behind the construction and sale of nuts and bolts.

In the broadest sense, imaging is an aspect of prophecy. Prophecy is on the minds of many millions of Americans these days including futurists, feminists, fundamentalists, popular culture artists, technocratic developers, some leftists who find prophecy being fulfilled in Marxist countries, and some who are attracted to the language of prophecy in new age approaches (Ohliger, 1987a). As Hilton Power has written, "A function of adult education is to keep the prophets and their prophecies alive by constantly confronting each of us with the current and emerging ones. After all adult education and literacy campaigns have all had a strong impetus from peoples' wish to read and understand the Bible, or, to understand Marx, Freud, or I Ching" (Hilton Power, letter to the author, Apr. 1987).

The prophetic activities of some feminists point to one possible future for alternative adult education images—toward a world beyond brute power in which the imaging of the powerless would have a fundamental effect (French, 1986). The feminist holistic equation of the personal and the political portends a vastly different ethos than the one Henry Adams ([1906] 1983, p. 727) perceived when he concluded, "Politics, as a practice, whatever its professions, had always been the systematic organization of hatreds." The work of Sonia Johnson could be important here.

Sonia Johnson is the Mormon woman who was excommunicated from her church for supporting the Equal Rights Amendment. She went on to become the first third-party candidate for president in history to qualify for federal preprimary matching funds with the help of supporters such as Gloria Steinem, Mary Daly, and Barbara Deming. Recently, Johnson looked back on her years of feminist struggles and the use of focused future imaging techniques as an aid in those struggles. She and her colleagues in this retrospection concluded that the error they were making was to attempt to project the present into the future instead of seeing that the future already exists in the present. Johnson (1987) and her friends have developed a new present-oriented approach and some accompanying techniques for future imaging that are not dissimilar to the latest views of biblical scholarship depicting Jesus as a prophet who proclaimed the existence of the future in the present (Sheehan, 1986). Thus, seeing the future as already living in the present moment, instead of separating the two time perspectives, may not be the wave of the future, but it could be the splendor of the now.

Beyond Alternative Images of the Future?

However, the splendor of the now may not be enough. It leaves unanswered some of the questions raised by the massive accumulation of the past—the past recognized as the history of oppression. The splendor of now leaves unresolved the dilemma of a future that appears to remain stubbornly resistant to fundamental change.

It may be that, if we restrict our view of the future to the linear extrapolation of apparently dominant or emerging trends, our power to transform the present by living in the future at this very moment is greatly diminished. The predominant view of time has the effect on most people of a giant shell game. Under which shell—past, present, or future—is the pea of happiness, fulfillment, knowledge, understanding, or power?

What is needed is an approach whereby "humankind would consciously and responsibly build the future, putting an end to the feverish chase after an ever fugitive utopia. Past, present, and future would constitute a harmonious whole" (Heyting, 1987, p. 227). Such an approach would leave historians and futurists the custodians of their respective temporalities, while others work together in an atmosphere that would encompass, but not be a slave to, linear time perspectives. It would also bring adult education into line with modern science, as Albert Einstein says, "For us who are convinced physicists, the distinction between past, present, and future is only an illusion, even if a stubborn one" (Fagg, 1985, p. 149). The activities of Rifkin (1987), Fagg (1985), Krishnamurti and Bohm (1985), and other thoughtful writers on time in the alternative mode could be helpful here.

The image of the concept of *image* itself may need transcending. Though embedded in the language, mainly from mass media influence, image is coming under increasing criticism for its vacuity as an approach without an authentic holistic tradition to back it up (K. Boulding, 1956; Ellul, 1976, 1985).

All that is left is the term *alternative,* and that too may have lost its usefulness. Like the word *underground,* it may have been co-opted by the establishment. There are now alternative ski schools, alternative network television programs, and even alternative Miss World contests. It is significant that as *alternative* loses its distinctive sixties meaning, *underground* is recovering its place as a designator of the socially different and dissident (Gunderloy, 1987; Fleming and Wilson, 1987).

But no term really serves the purpose of characterizing the nonmainstream approaches in adult education. Grim and cheerless, but currently proposed, constructs such as *critical pegagogy* and *theories of resistance* offer little. The lesson of the sixties, out of which the current use of the word *alternative* developed, is that any term that gains mass media attention will be either distorted or co-opted. Perhaps no word at all is needed to characterize the groups and individuals engaged in the long stroll through, around, over, under, and against our massive institutions. Mutual identification and support could then come from specific activities around which dissidents gather— not from the mainstream institutional cocoons, such as universities, with which adult education as a field typically is identified.

Indeed, the twentieth century is almost over. As we enter its last decade, the year 2000 is a sharp and enticing focus shared by dissident and mainstream adult educators alike (Brockett, 1987; Petska, 1982). Over 600 books and 5,000 articles have been published recently with prophecies about the year 2000 (Ohliger, 1988b). As the year draws closer, dominant religious and political groups, government agencies, futurists, and planning technologists are zeroing in on it as the time of transition to a global millennium. They see the new millennium as the opportunity to introduce special interest reforms, including pushing more continuing education, or as the time to market the latest mass-produced miracle of the electronic, computerized, postindustrial information revolution (Ohliger, 1987d). Surely all this dynamic energy aimed at the one moment when the clock ticks past December 31, 1999 provides an opportunity for concerned adult educators to band together in a common positive movement to harmonize the past, the present, and the future.

A positive but dissident approach will be valuable for adult educators if it is clear that the hope it inspires cannot be planned, produced, or packaged in a continuing education course. It will flower—if explored in a friendly climate—spontaneously, serendipitously, and intuitively. It will grow if we are on the alert against the twin dangers of vagueness and sloppy sentimentality. A positive dissident approach may even be realistic in the best sense, although it may not embody all the tactics for its fruition. Narrow, cold, hard realists in the mainstream give reality a bad name. The powerful force of a positive but dissident approach could give reality the good name it deserves—if it is nurtured in the calmly strengthening and sharply energizing climate of human fellowship.

References

Adams, H. *The Education of Henry Adams.* In *Novels, Mont Saint Michel, The Education.* New York: Literary Classics of the United States, 1983. (Originally published 1906.)

"Adolph Hitler—An Adult Educator?" *Adult Education News,* 1988, *53* (1), 3.

Barnhart, C., Steinmetz, S., and Barnhart, K. (eds.). *The Barnhart Dictionary of New English Since 1963.* Bronxville, N.Y.: Barnhart/Harper & Row, 1973.

Boshier, R. "Adult Education: Issues of the Future." In B. Kreitlow and Associates, *Examining Controversies in Adult Education.* San Francisco: Jossey-Bass, 1981.

Boulding, E. "The Social Imagination and the Crisis of Human Futures: A North American Perspective." *Forum for Correspondence and Contact,* 1983, *13* (2), 43–60.

Boulding, K. *The Image: Knowledge in Life and Society.* Ann Arbor: University of Michigan Press, 1956.

Bowman, J., and Kierstead, F. "Robert Theobald: Futurist, Economist and Educational Theorist." *Vitae Scholasticae,* 1985, *4* (1–2), 183–189.

Brockett, R. (ed.). *Continuing Education in the Year 2000.* San Francisco: Jossey-Bass, 1987.

Crawford, R. "Inverted Parachutes." *Second Thoughts,* 1981, *4,* 1.

Danky, J., and Shore, E. (eds.). *Alternative Materials in Libraries.* Metuchen, N.J.: Scarecrow Press, 1982.

Davidson, E. *The Making of Adolph Hitler.* New York: Macmillan, 1977.

Draves, W. *The Free University: A Model for Lifelong Learning.* Chicago: Follett, 1980.

Ellul, J. "Search for an Image." In R. Bundy (ed.), *Images of the Future: The Twenty-First Century and Beyond.* Buffalo, N.Y.: Prometheus Books, 1976.

Ellul, J. *The Humiliation of the Word.* Grand Rapids, Mich.: William B. Eerdmans Publishing, 1985.

Fagg, L. *Two Faces of Time.* Wheaton, Ill.: Quest Books, 1985.

Fleming, J., and Wilson, P. (eds.). "Special Issue: The Dadblamed Sears 'n' Roebuck Catalog of th' American Underground." *Semiotext[e],* 1987, entire issue 13.

Flexner, S. (ed.). *The Random House Dictionary of the English Language.* (2nd ed.) New York: Random House, 1987.

French, M. *Beyond Power: Of Women, Men and Morals.* New York: Ballantine Books, 1986.

Gearhart, S. *The Wanderground: Stories of the Hill Women.* Watertown, Mass.: Persephone Press, 1979.

Gross, R. *The Independent Scholars' Handbook.* Reading, Mass.: Addison-Wesley, 1982.

Gueulette, D. "Is There School After Death?" *Adult Leadership,* 1972, *21* (3), p. 72.

Gunderloy, M. *Give a Damn: Interview with the Founding Editor of Factsheet Five.* Madison, Wis.: Basic Choices, 1987.

Heyting, E. *An International Fraud: How the Schools Cheat Your Children.* New York: Vantage Press, 1987.

Hitler, A. *Mein Kampf* [My Struggle]. (R. Mannheim, trans.) Boston: Houghton Mifflin, 1943.

Illich, I. *Deschooling Society.* New York: Harper & Row, 1971.

Illich, I. "A Plea for Research on Lay Literacy." *North American Review,* 1987, *272* (3), 10–17.

"Implications of Future Studies for Adult Education: Special Feature." *Convergence,* 1975, *8* (3), 17–90.

Johnson, S. *Going Out of Our Minds: The Metaphysics of Liberation.* Freedom, Calif.: Crossing Press, 1987.

Krishnamurti, J., and Bohm, D. *The Ending of Time.* New York: Harper & Row, 1985.

Lehman, K. "Death of 'The Wisconsin Idea'?" *Second Thoughts,* 1984, *6* (1), 2.

Lister, I. "The Threat of Recurrent Education and the Nightmare of Permanent Education." *Indian Journal of Adult Education,* 1975, *36* (12), 19.

Lunn, E. *Prophet of Community: The Romantic Socialism of Gustav Landauer.* Berkeley: University of California Press, 1973.

McKenzie, L. *Adult Education and the Burden of the Future.* Washington, D.C.: University Press of America, 1978.

Marien, M., and Ziegler, W. L. (eds.). *The Potential of Educational Futures.* Worthington, Ohio: Charles Jones, 1972.

Merriam, S. "Book Review." *Adult Education Quarterly,* 1978, *29* (1), 57–59.

Ohliger, J. "Adult Education: 1984." *Adult Leadership,* 1971, *19* (7), 223–224.

Ohliger, J. "Prospects for a Learning Society." *Adult Leadership,* 1975, *24* (1), 37–39.

Ohliger, J. "Alternative Media—Up to Your Ass in Alligators." *Media/Adult Learning,* 1979, *1* (50), 8–9.

Ohliger, J. "Reconciling Education with Liberty." *Prospects: UNESCO Quarterly Journal of Education,* 1983, *13,* 161–179.

Ohliger, J. *Basic Choices in Adult Education.* Madison, Wis.: Basic Choices, 1985.

Ohliger, J. *If Winter Comes: Life Affirming Prophecies, Moses, Shelley, and Lao Tzu.* Madison, Wis.: Basic Choices, 1987a.

Ohliger, J. *Lao Tzu: Learning How to Unlearn.* Madison, Wis.: Basic Choices, 1987b.

Ohliger, J. "Really Creative Conferences." *Media and Adult Learning,* 1987c, *9* (2), 3–18.

Ohliger, J. "The Millennium: Are You Ready For It?" *Adult and Continuing Education Today,* 1987d, *17* (25), 6.

Ohliger, J. *The Fictional Adult Educator.* Madison, Wis.: Basic Choices, 1988a.

Ohliger, J. *Millennia: The Past, The Present Issues, and the Future of Adult Education: A Quotational Bibliography.* Madison, Wis.: Basic Choices, 1988b.

Ohliger, J., and Fewster, L. *The Wisconsin Idea: Some Reflections on Historical Context and Issues.* Madison, Wis.: Social Policy Action Research Center, 1975. (ED 120 432)

Orwell, G. *1984.* New York: New American Library, 1949.

Petska, D. "Adult Education for the Year 2000." *Lifelong Learning,* 1982, *5* (5), 21–23.

Purcell, J. "Getting Ready for 1984." *Adult Leadership,* May 1974, pp. 21–22.

Quinn, J. *American Tongue in Cheek: A Populist Guide to Our Language.* New York: Penguin Books, 1980.

Reimer, E. *School Is Dead: Alternatives in Education.* New York: Doubleday, 1971.

Rifkin, J. *Time Wars: The Primary Conflict in Human History.* New York: Henry Holt, 1987.

Roberts, H. *Alternative Adult Education.* New York: Methuen, 1988.

Rossman, M. *New Age Blues: On the Politics of Consciousness.* New York: Dutton, 1979.

Rosten, L. *The Education of Hyman Kaplan.* San Diego, Calif.: Harcourt Brace Jovanovich, 1937.

Russell, W. *Educating Rita, Stags and Hens, and Blood Brothers: Two Plays and a Musical.* New York: Methuen, 1986.

Segal, H. *Technological Utopianism in American Culture.* Chicago: University of Chicago Press, 1985.

Shaw, B. *Pygmalion.* In *Bernard Shaw: Selected Plays.* New York: Dodd, Mead, 1981. (Originally published 1913.)

Sheehan, T. *The First Coming: How the Kingdom of God Became Christianity.* New York: Random House, 1986.

Theobald, R. *An Alternative Future for America: Essays and Speeches of Robert Theobald.* Chicago: Swallow Press, 1968.

Theobald, R. *The Rapids of Change: Social Entrepreneurship in Turbulent Times.* Indianapolis, Ind.: Knowledge Systems, 1987.

Tremor, M. "The Adult Educators' Guide to Future Fiction: An Inventory of Ideas in Science Fiction, Utopian and Related Literature Pertinent to Future Study and Educational Planning." Unpublished doctoral dissertation, College of Education, Florida State University, 1974.

Whitelock, D. *The Great Tradition: A History of Adult Education in Australia.* St. Lucia, Australia: University of Queensland Press, 1974.

Williams, D. "The Specter of Permanent Schooling." *Teachers College Record,* 1974, *76* (1), 47–62.

Zinsser, W. (ed.). *Extraordinary Lives: The Art and Craft of American Biography.* New York: American Heritage, 1986.

48

The Future
of Adult Education

George E. Spear
Donald W. Mocker

The delights of imagination are realized never more fully than when applied to prediction and prophecy. Although biblical tradition suggests that prophets are without honor in their own lands, contemporary seers find broad audiences, notoriety, and even wealth. Wisely calling themselves *futurists* instead of prophets, they pique their followers' fancies with visions of a world to come that is both exciting and unsettling. A recent publication from the World Future Society (1988) forecasts the advent of mind-reading computers, transplant surgery to enable the mentally retarded to achieve normal intelligence, individuals being cloned in order to have a set of spare parts, large numbers of people living beyond the age of 100 years, and much of the world's economy returning to the barter system. The current pace of scientific and technical development encourages imaginations to run wild, if not amok. Forecasting, although frequently error filled, is generally a low risk business, and seers are almost never held responsible for their mistakes.

Current interest and concern for the future has been amplified by rapid technological and social change and by an accompanying uncertainty about what is to come. Forecasting and planning today are outgrowths of systems devised by combatant nations in World War II in trying to anticipate their enemies' strategies. John Naisbitt (1982) attributes his forecasting methods to those wartime roots. At the war's end, people who had been a part of military forecasting and planning groups became members of the labor force absorbed by reviving businesses and industries. They brought with them a new expertise with potential for changing the foundations of managerial decision making. In the decades since World War II, forecasting and planning groups have become routinely a part of large business and production organizations.

Advances in technology in recent times have been so dazzling as to leave a widespread impression that these tools have lives and minds of their own. Remarkable as these tools are, the major determinants of the future still are people. What people know, think, and believe as they work with the technology and with one another become the critical factors that will shape the future. How adult educators contribute to adult thinking, knowing, and believing will determine the vitality and value of the field of adult education.

Selecting from a spate of prophecy in current futurist literature, we will necessarily neglect some trends that some readers may consider to be of central importance. Our selection has been guided, first, by assumptions about the current levels of training and expertise representative of adult educators. A second criterion has been the identity of those trends and changes that appear most amenable to impact through adult education. The selection of these trends carries the expectation that the field will continue to be enlarged by untrained practitioners and that those who are trained will continue to be a minority.

So it is the purpose here to suggest not what the future of adult education will be, but rather what it can or might be. Given some reasonable expectations regarding social and technological trends and constraints in the decade ahead, we offer suggestions for some specific actions adult educators might take to give direction and substance to the field.

Trend I: The Aging of the U.S. Population and a Shift From a Youth to a Maturity Orientation in the Society

In the mid-1980s, the United States population shifted quietly but decisively from youth into maturity and old age. This was most clearly illustrated by the fact that by 1987, more Americans were over age sixty-five than were under twenty-five years of age. The baby boom age cohort, which ushered in the youth dominance of the 1950s, 1960s, and 1970s, reached, or was at the steps of, middle age. The population of the United States was predominately adult and it was growing older. (The topic of older adults is addressed in depth in Chapter Forty.)

This coming of age of the baby boomers, combined with a large surviving population of older adults, heralds a unique era for a technological society. Historically, most societies have relied on the young and the strong for productivity and have distributed rewards accordingly. Life spans shortened by disease, poor nutrition, fatigue, and natural disaster have taken their tolls on adult populations in the past and have reduced the numbers of older adults to levels of minor social consequence.

This has changed. No modern society has had to accommodate and to take into account an advanced, mature population with such potential power and influence. Observers and planners for the future can only guess what the impact of such a population will be. There is little experience upon which to base expectations for the years ahead.

A few facts and trends do provide, perhaps, some hints of things to come. Older adults are healthier or have access to science and technology that contribute to longer life spans. Although the frail and dependent elderly have been the objects of society's emotional attention, fewer than 15 percent of the over-sixty-five age population fall within that category.

In addition to being healthier, the population as a whole is increasingly better educated and more affluent. When large numbers of older workers entered the labor force after World War II, pension plans, which supplemented federal society security, became the norm in business and in other public and private sector organizations. One result has been a lowering of the average age of retirement to sixty-two and an expectation that it will fall into the upper fifties.

With all this, a new age cohort that is healthy and vigorous, well educated, politically aware, adequately financed, and free of institutional constraints has been established. Its power derives from a combination of its numbers, its ability to influence political issues, its economic strength, and its freedom and willingness to devote the time necessary to pursue its hard-won best interests.

In the future, adult educators will become more committed to programs by and for older adults. It is axiomatic that education is addictive and that participation in adult learning activities increases with the educational level of the learner. Better educated older adults therefore may be expected to turn increasingly to organized learning programs. The seeds of such movement are already observable in the return of older adults to special admission programs in colleges and universities, in the Elderhostel movement, and in an international network of local weekly programs called Adventures in Learning. The hallmark of this trend is a body of learners who are free to pursue personal interests and whose diversity is greater than that of any other age cohort.

Certainly, many adult educators have viewed this growing population as a potential program bonanza. It has become popular practice to gain entry into nutrition sites and other natural gathering places for older adults in order to present packaged programs of the educators' choosing.

This is not unlike the so-called capture-and-teach approach common to public school education. Anecdotal reports to the contrary notwithstanding, this approach has limited success and even less impact on the lives of the learners (University of Missouri, Kansas City Project Staff, 1986).

One striking difference in programming for older adults lies in the program planner's lack of personal experience comparable to that of the learner. In traditional education, the school teacher was once an elementary school pupil, the college professor was once an undergraduate, and the trainer once a trainee. However, the typical adult educator has yet to experience the life and needs that go with being an older person in the society. These educators have impressions rather than knowledge of aging and older adulthood.

In the decade ahead, professional adult educators will come to recognize their imperfect understanding of older adulthood and will turn their attention and energies toward developing a cadre of adult educators who are themselves older adults. The pool of potential new candidates comprises people with knowledge and experience in every field of endeavor. Many have been teachers; others have been responsible for the training and development of people in their organizations; they have served as mentors, coaches, models, and counselors. This richness and diversity are currently present in the field of adult education.

The task at hand is to devise ways to identify these new adult educators, to provide them with knowledge that will assist them in making successful transitions to their new roles, and to introduce them into systems in which their expertise can be most useful and rewarding.

Some current evidence indicates that programs planned and administered by older adults for older adults generate enthusiastic support and tend to endure. (The prototype for the Adventures in Learning, noted above, has a nearly twenty-year history of being organized and administered by an entire staff of retired adults.) Such programs, however, depend essentially upon the common wisdom of their leadership—wisdom which, though often keenly insightful, could be enhanced by knowledge of adult education planning and instruction principles. Professional adult educators can be instrumental in adding science to the art of such efforts by encouraging and educating older adults to take leadership roles and responsibilities for their own continued learning and that of their peers.

Trend II: The Increasing Sophistication and Influence of Technology

If there is consensus among the futurists, it lies with the recognition that societies around the world are entering a new age brought about and dominated by the growth of technology. Called variously the postindustrial era, the information age, and info-sphere, the new era is characterized by information, communications, and pervasiveness. The transistor and the silicon chip which, in turn, spawned satellite communications and the miniaturization of the computer, ushered in an era that has changed or is changing the relationships among people, organizations, and nations the world over. (See "New Educational Technologies for the Future," Chapter Forty-Six.)

While the fleetingly current generation of in-use technology always stands at the brink of obsolescence, its impact invades every corner of every society. Copy for a newspaper typeset in one location on computers is transmitted to printing plants across the country and becomes available simultaneously in thousands of newsstands. Stock markets rise and fall on the trading of stocks by computers without prompting from human buyers or sellers. Medical experts diagnose and direct treatment of patients they have never seen. Colleagues who have never met communicate regularly, exchange ideas, and provide each other with extensive documentation without either person leaving his or her office or home. Citizens in developed countries have grown accustomed to their governments and other organizations knowing how much money they have made in recent years, what they have purchased and when they bought the items, their physical and medical histories, their credit ratings, debts and assets, and the publications they read. They take for granted and remember as history seeing a man's first step on the moon, a president shot, and a civilian assassinated in a war zone.

The field of education does not stand apart from this pervasive invasion of computer technology. Few elementary or secondary schools are without computer labs, and even preschools are expected to provide such access to students at least on a limited basis. In the fall of 1987, one midwestern university announced that every dormitory room would be equipped with a computer. It is obvious that the coming generation of adult educators will, as a group, be far more computer literate than were their immediate predecessors, and they will be better prepared to make the current technology even more significant to the field. Aronowitz and Giroux (1985, p. 14) put it this way: "The wondrous machine, once used exclusively for payrolls and as a tool for storing information, has now been elevated to a savior, the embodiment of technologically based culture, a way of life for millions of Americans." Earlier, Seymour Papert (1980) had sounded a word of caution, however, suggesting computers can become a form of domination and oppression or, alternatively, they can be used to solve educational problems.

In the future, during the 1990s, national and world conferences of adult educators will be convened regularly via computer and satellite technology. Sparsely staffed and generally underfunded, the field of adult education has suffered underdevelopment professionally because of a consequential isolation. Nationally and internationally, adult educators have been unable to meet regularly, since most were without the resources required to travel to distant conferences where the field gathered. This lack of interaction has slowed the dissemination of knowledge, has impeded the cross-fertilization of ideas that leads to the growth of research, and has inhibited the development of professional networks that support and enrich the individual members of the field. The constraints on interaction are multiple at the international level, largely because foreign travel has been precluded for all but the favored few. To a great extent, the global community that is frequently discussed and applauded does not, in fact, exist for most adult educators.

Toffler (1980) a decade ago suggested that society is moving into an era in which communication is replacing transportation. The computer and satellite transmission can now bring adult educators together from anyplace in the world. The opportunity is at hand for adult educators to meet on a regular basis, breaking the bonds of isolation. The computer age provides the means for adult educators to redefine their roles in terms of world problems. It will be possible to develop a critical mass of concern around the globe for universal problems such as ecology, world peace, hunger, and human rights.

Adult educators will first develop great personal sophistication and skill in technology applications. These in turn will lead to the organizing of a strong lobby to persuade government agencies to establish and to permit use of public satellite communications, giving adult educators access to their peers around the world.

Face-to-face conferences will still be held to satisfy the social or high-touch requirements (Naisbitt 1982) of individuals. Such conferences will be scheduled simultaneously in countries across the world. Discussion groups devoted to issues of mutual concern will meet at each site and then share their ideas and react to colleagues in the United States, Europe, Asia, Africa, and Australia. Other individuals unable to attend the group meetings will participate by personal computers from their homes and workplaces. This frequent and regular interaction among and between adult educators will contribute to the redefining of their collective role in helping to alleviate national and world problems.

Trend III: The Redefinition of Work, Productivity, and Participation in the Information Era

Traditionally, work and productivity have been defined by the labors and outputs of the likes of farmers, steelworkers, and carpenters—people who use the earth and material from the earth to provide the society's needs for sustenance and survival. Their work requires not only skill, but also labor; and their products are, for the most part, tangible.

With the coming of the information era, however, ideas become the principal and most prized products—articles to be bought and sold in an ever-growing commerce. Information and data are raw materials required for technological development and to feed systems that undergird changing economic, social, and political institutions. These systems often exchange information, conduct commercial transactions, and charge one another for services without benefit of human intervention.

Technical sophistication notwithstanding, the creators of ideas and those who assimilate and purvey information are the new production workers of the information era. Schools and colleges, research laboratories, and think tanks replace the farms, factories, and stores as the major seats of production and commerce. In such an age, educational institutions become economic rather than social service systems.

It follows that the character of the labor force in the information era will significantly differ from the current norm. In the industrial era, most jobs in the economy could be mastered with six weeks of on-the-job training, and employment was secured by lining up outside a plant that was hiring workers. In the United States, an alarm was sounded in a joint publication by the U.S. Departments of Education and Labor (1988) concerning the growing disparity between workers' literacy skills and changing job demands. Quoting a Hudson Institute (1987) report, the publication predicted that by the early twenty-first century, a majority of jobs will require at least some postsecondary education. Information era workers will necessarily bring technical expertise to the jobs as well as familiarity with appropriate information systems, access to those systems, and the ability to assimilate and to manipulate large bodies of information. They will need skills of differentiation, recognition, synthesis, and abstraction. Their labors will be essentially mental, and educational preparation will be the key to their participation in the information society.

In the future, the term literacy will be redefined, and adult educators will seek new colleagues and new solutions. The diversity of roles performed by adult educators does not lend itself to singular expectations for the future. Some educators will undoubtedly be the creators of new ideas and knowledge, and others will be part of the purveyor system meeting the ongoing training and retraining needs of workers in the information systems.

It has become a part of common wisdom to recognize that many, perhaps most, of the world's major economic powers have work forces educationally superior to that of the United States. Many U.S. workers are ill-prepared for the jobs at hand and are totally inadequate for the future. The need for upgrading the work force to compete internationally, and to meet the demands of new job requirements, will be a major challenge and opportunity for some adult educators. They will take leadership roles in bringing together business, labor, and government resources to meet the needs of workers and organizations. They will view their efforts less as education and more as part of the nation's labor capital. They will be less affiliated with schools and more associated with the workplace. At best, they will become the planners and leaders of new levels of worker literacy rather than merely suppliers to program contracts conceived by others.

On the other hand, those who are dedicated to assisting deprived and disenfranchised populations to gain entry into social and economic systems face the most difficult challenges. It was apparent by the late 1980s that the gap was widening between advantaged and disadvantaged populations. The problem was aggravated by the emergence of a new group of disadvantaged persons whose skills had become obsolete and who were dismissed from productive avenues. A sharp distinction exists between those prepared and those not prepared to function in the new era.

In the coming decade, the term *literacy* will be redefined by adult educators. The ability to read, to do simple calculations, and to function minimally in the society will be recognized as totally inadequate, and education programs directed to these simplistic ends will be eliminated. No longer will emphasis be on basic education or on putting clients in touch with social service agencies where their dependence is reinforced. Adult educators will form new collaborative relationships with psychologists and sociologists to gain greater insights into the problems their clients face. They will establish working relationships with private sector businesses and industry to provide resources and to help guide programs in keeping with rapidly changing needs and expectations of the marketplace.

Acting as both teacher and mentor, the adult educator will help clients establish resource networks that extend beyond the narrow limits of their usual circumstances. Personal networking will become the foundation for building avenues out of poverty and isolation.

The new definition of literacy will be the ability to establish a goal and to have the knowledge and connections to pursue it with a reasonable expectation for success.

Trend IV: The Growth of Dissensus, the Influence of Information Access, and the Struggle for Power by Special Interest Groups

For the blindly optimistic, the prospects for increased interaction among peoples of the world, for access to almost unlimited information, and for the crumbling of parochial barriers give a bright hue to the future. However, if the experience of the past few decades is an indication, the increase of information and communications has an often dramatically different effect. Greater awareness of alternatives has led to greater dissatisfactions with things as they are. The media's choices of news stories for public viewing tend to portray human beings as unlikely candidates for trust or compassion. Seeing the opportunities and benefits that many other people enjoy gives rise to the question, "Why not me?" (Note Chapter One, "The Social Context of Adult and Continuing Education.") And political parties no longer represent majority or even representative interests; they struggle internally with clashes between liberal and conservative branches, between corporate backers and worker issues, and between farmers and city dwellers.

The consequence of all this is *dissensus*—the resultant state of myriads of pieces of information being filtered through individual values and circumstances and then translated into the special interests of individuals. (The word *dissensus* was coined in the early 1960s when the traditional order of U.S. society began to experience clashes over values, beliefs, and interests of segments of the citizenry. The assumed societal consensus was replaced by dissensus.)

Short of a catastrophic unifying event that erases all other considerations, the information era is likely to produce greater diversity and a diminishing base for consensus in and among nations and societies. As contending interests and forces vie for attention and support, citizens can look with less and less confidence to the media and national leadership for guidance. Individuals will be increasingly inclined to represent themselves in matters of importance.

To function effectively on their own behalf, people must be prepared to think critically, taking into account information of importance while discarding the unimportant.

In the future, adult educators will take a leading role in fostering thinking as a major component of education. For all its protestations to the contrary, education traditionally has fixed its attention on information transfer with a blind belief that critical thinking is a natural and inevitable by-product. The two are, of course, unrelated, since critical thinking predates education by thousands of years and can be detected in the general population without regard to formal learning. It may also be assumed that critical-thinking ability is unevenly distributed among those in the field of adult education.

But it must be recognized that critical-thinking skills can be taught. The teaching of critical thinking begins with educators who are themselves critical thinkers. So it follows that the first stage of the movement must begin with the training of such teachers in programs that model critical thinking rather than formats designed to deposit information into the heads of learners. "Teach them how to think and they will teach themselves the facts" is the basic assumption behind the goal of developing critical thinkers. To achieve this goal, first for adult educators and ultimately for adult learners, instruction plans will be developed around the following principles:

1. For adults to improve their critical-thinking skills, they must be given continual opportunities to think critically. Learners must not only be given the opportunity to think, but they must also be given the opportunity to discuss their thought processes with other students and with their teachers. If adult educators want to improve the critical-thinking skills of learners, then self-paced and individualized instruction will need to be balanced with group instruction for which dialogue is the primary instructional technique.

2. Critical thinking is developed through the process of discovering the answer, but not from the answer itself (Renner, 1971). Depositing information into the heads of learners—what Freire refers to as banking education—will help learners do better on some standardized achievement tests, such as the GED test. However, such teaching does little to encourage or to improve the quality of critical thinking.

3. Fundamental to most learning, particularly in adult education, is motivation. At the core of motivation is using the learners' interests and experiences as the basis of instructional planning rather than using the interests and experiences of some textbook editor. Improving critical-thinking skills of adults cannot be achieved by a single teacher in a single class. It is a task for all the teachers who contribute to the adults' lifelong learning. It will take the commitment of many teachers who are themselves critical thinkers and who are willing to incorporate appropriate techniques into their plans of instruction.

Conclusion

The future of adult education will take very different turns if adult educators simply wait for it to happen instead of taking action to direct its course. Taking action is a matter of grasping ideas and visions of a better life and then working toward specific goals that are both promising and possible.

The field can wait during the next decade to see what happens and, perhaps, devote a chapter in the handbook for the year 2000 to what went wrong. A happier chapter would recount the goals that 1990 adult educators chose and then achieved in the final decade of the twentieth century.

References

Aronowitz, S., and Giroux, H. A. *Education Under Siege.* South Hadley, Mass.: Bergin and Garvey, 1985.

Hudson Institute. *Workforce 2000: Work and Workers for the 21st Century.* Indianapolis, Ind.: Hudson Institute, 1987.

Naisbitt, J. *Megatrends.* New York: Warner Book, 1982.

Papert, S. *Mindstorms.* New York: Basic Books, 1980.

Renner, J. W. "Educational Purpose, Curriculum and Methodology." *Journal of Thought,* 1971, *6,* 162–167.

Toffler, A. *The Third Wave.* New York: William Morrow, 1980.

U.S. Department of Education and U.S. Department of Labor. *The Bottom Line: Basic Skills in the Workplace.* Washington, D.C.: U.S. Department of Education and U.S. Department of Labor, 1988.

University of Missouri, Kansas City, Project Staff. *Report of a Three Year Impact Study of Cooperative Extension Programs for the Elderly in a 15 County Area.* Kansas City: Department of Sociology, University of Missouri, Kansas City, 1986.

World Future Society. *Outlook '88.* Bethesda, Md.: World Future Society, 1988.

Resource

Contents of
Past Handbooks

Handbook of Adult Education in the United States

Dorothy Rowden, *Editor*
American Association for Adult Education, 1934

Agricultural Extension, *Benson Y. Landis*
Alumni Education
American Association for Adult Education, *Ralph A. Beals*
The Arts in Adult Education, *Erwin O. Christensen*
Community and State Organizations of Adult Education Agencies
Private Correspondence Schools, *J. S. Noffsinger*
Courses in Adult Education
Adult Education and the Foreign Born, *Read Lewis*
Open Forums
Libraries and Adult Education, *Carl H. Milam*
Lyceums and Chautauquas
Men's and Women's Clubs
Museums and Adult Education, *Laurence Vail Coleman*
Music in Adult Education, *Augustus D. Zanzig*
Adult Education for Negroes
Parent Education, *Ralph P. Bridgman*
Political Education, *Charles Ascher*
The Education of Adult Prisoners, *Austin H. MacCormick*
Adult Education Under Public School Auspices, *L. R. Alderman*
Puppets in Adult Education, *Catherine F. Reighard*
The Radio in Adult Education, *Levering Tyson*
The Place of Recreation in Adult Education, *Weaver Pangborn*
Programs of Social Education Conducted by Religious Groups
Adult Education in Settlements, *Lillie M. Peck*
Special Schools and Institutes for Adults
The Little Theater
Training by Corporations
Training Leaders for Adult Groups
Educational Opportunities for the Unemployed, *Mary Frank*
University Extension, *W. S. Bittner*
Visual Education
Vocational Education for Adults, *Franklin J. Keller*
Vocational Guidance of Adults, *Robert Hoppock*
Vocational Rehabilitation of Physically Handicapped Adults,
    Edgar B. Porter
Workers' Education, *Spencer Miller, Jr.*
Schools for Women Workers in Industry, *Hilda W. Smith*
National Organizations with Adult Education Programs

Handbook of Adult Education in the United States

Dorothy Rowden, Editor
American Association for Adult Education, 1936

Preface

Adult Education in Action

Mary L. Ely, Editor
American Association for Adult Education, 1936

The General Staff
    Introduction
    The American Association for Adult Education,
       Morse Adams Cartwright
The Forces of Adult Education—Agencies
  PUBLIC LIBRARIES
    Readers' Advisory Service, *Jennie M. Flexner*
    Students' Information Service, *Annie P. Dingman*
    A Variety of Services, *Malcolm G. Wyer*
  THE UNITED STATES GOVERNMENT
    Education on the Farms, *Clyde William Warburton*
    Education in the C.C.C. Camps, *Frank Ernest Hill*
    Education in the National Parks, *Harold C. Bryant*
  THE EMERGENCY PROGRAMS IN THE PUBLIC SCHOOLS
    Federal Emergency Education, *Arthur E. Bestor*
    An Emergency School in Operation, *Benjamin Fine*
    Emergency Education for Industrial Workers, *Hilda W. Smith*
    Emergency Classes in Drama, *Eve Chappell*
    Hopes and Fears for Emergency Education, *Walter Dan Griffith*
  PUBLIC AND SEMI-PUBLIC PROJECTS
    The Denver Opportunity School, *Robert Tudor Hill*
    South Carolina's Opportunities for the Underprivileged,
       Edgar Wallace Knight
    Shorewood (Wisconsin) Opportunity School, *Harvey M. Genskow*
    High School Institutes, *Eve Chappell*
  UNIVERSITIES
    University Correspondence Courses, *Walton S. Bittner*
    Far-flung University Extension, *Harmon B. Stephens*
  MUSEUMS
    New Uses for Museum Exhibits, *Laurence Vail Coleman*
    Circulating Art through Branch Museums, *Philip N. Youtz*
    Classes in an Art Museum, *Roberta Murray Fansler*
  THEATERS
    Our Emerging Native Theater, *Edith J. R. Isaacs*
    A Thousand Little Theaters, *Kenneth Macgowan*
  CHURCHES
    The Church an Educational Asset, *F. Ernest Johnson*
    Education in a Metropolitan Church, *Elsie Gray Cambridge*
    Church Nights in a Suburban Church, *R. E. Wolseley*
    A Church That Has Always Been a School, *Louis Wolsey*
  RELIGIOUS ORGANIZATIONS
    The Y.M.C.A., *Ruth Kotinsky*
    The Y.W.C.A., *Sarah E. D. Sturges*
  INDUSTRY
    Training on the Job, *Nathaniel Peffer*

Handbook of Adult Education in the United States

Mary L. Ely, Editor
Institute of Adult Education, Teachers College,
Columbia University, 1948

Foreword, *Alain Locke*
Preface, *Morse A. Cartwright*

Handbook of Adult Education in the United States

Malcolm S. Knowles, Editor
Adult Education Association of the U.S.A., 1960

Handbook of Adult Education

Robert M. Smith, George F. Aker, and J. R. Kidd, Editors
Macmillan, 1970

Building an Effective Adult Education Enterprise

John M. Peters and Associates
Adult Education Association Handbook Series in Adult Education
Jossey-Bass, 1980

Foreword, *William S. Griffith, Howard Y. McClusky*
Preface
The Authors

Changing Approaches to Studying Adult Education
Huey B. Long, Roger Hiemstra, and Associates
Adult Education Association Handbook Series in Adult Education
Jossey-Bass, 1980

Developing, Administering, and Evaluating Adult Education

Alan B. Knox and Associates

Adult Education Association Handbook Series in Adult Education
Jossey-Bass, 1980

Redefining the Discipline of Adult Education

Robert D. Boyd, Jerold W. Apps, and Associates
Adult Education Association Handbook Series in Adult Education
Jossey-Bass, 1980

Serving Personal and Community Needs Through Adult Education

Edgar J. Boone, Ronald W. Shearon, Estelle E. White, and Associates
Adult Education Association Handbook Series in Adult Education
Jossey-Bass, 1980

Comparing Adult Education Worldwide

Alexander N. Charters and Associates
    Adult Education Association Handbook Series in Adult Education
    Jossey-Bass, 1981

Examining Controversies in Adult Education

Burton W. Kreitlow and Associates
> Adult Education Association Handbook Series in Adult Education
> Jossey-Bass, 1981

Preparing Educators of Adults

Stanley M. Grabowski and Associates
Adult Education Association Handbook Series in Adult Education
Jossey-Bass, 1981

Name Index

Subject Index

A

Accountability: for extension services, 341; in human resource development, 433

Accreditation: and armed forces programs, 346, 349–350; for continuing professional education, 514; of proprietary schools, 417

ACTION, 108

Action Agenda Project, 543, 547

Action research, purpose of, 152

Action training, for human resource development, 428, 432

Administration: of colleges and universities, 309–310; of correctional education programs, 359–360; and planning, 240–241

Administration on Aging, 3n, 13

Adult and continuing education: and alternative America, 30, 34–35; background on, 15–16; benefits of professional associations for, 113–114, 115–117; boundaries of, 59–61; and colonial culture, 27; concepts of, 24, 278, 389; conclusions on, 23–24, 36; defining, 15–25; early schooling connected with, 585–586; and economic development, 33–34; and education of adults, 18–19; evaluation for, 260–272; field of, 1–180; financing, 168–180; formal, 59, 63; functions and goals of, 22–23; future of, 611–649; and higher education, 281–282; historical concepts of, 16–17; history of, 26–36; image unclear for, 169–170; under independence and expansion, 28–30; informal, 60; in institutions, 17–18; in interdependent society, 30–31; international and comparative, 70–83; and international development, 84–98; literature and information sources for, 134–146; management of, 246–259; need for, 38; as new agency, 32; nonformal, 59–60; philosophy of, 44–48; process of, 181–272; as profession or discipline, 19–20; professional associations for, 112–123; programs and clienteles for, 437–609; and progressive reform, 30–31; providers of, 273–435; purposes of, 37–44; received tradition for, 26–30; recent history of, 33–36; in repression and depression, 31–33; research in, 147–167; roles of, 4, 624–626; beyond schooling, 35; social functions of, 61–65; and social movements, 20–22; social setting of, 3–14; sociology of, 51–69; structural-functional framework of, 52–53, 55; technological role of, 624–626; terminology for, 303–305; trends for, 640–649; typology of, 18; uniqueness of, 57, 59; and voluntarism, 99–111

Adult basic education (ABE): and adult secondary education, 478, 485, 486, 487; aspects of, 465–477; background on, 465–466; clientele for, 468–473; concept of, 465; and continuing education for women, 557, 559; in correctional education, 361, 363; and

X

Y

Z